W9-CDM-519

Contemporary Business Communication

THIRD EDITION

Contemporary Business Communication

SCOT OBER

Ball State University

HOUGHTON MIFFLIN COMPANY   Boston   New York

Editor-in-Chief: Bonnie Binkert
Associate Sponsoring Editor: Joanne Dauksewicz
Senior Project Editor: Chere Bemelmans
Senior Production/Design Coordinator: Sarah Ambrose
Senior Manufacturing Coordinator: Priscilla J. Bailey
Marketing Manager: Juli Bliss
Editorial Assistants: Daniel Bouchard and Joy Park

Cover design: Harold Burch, Harold Burch Design, New York City.
Cover image: Giraudon/Art Resource, NY.
Mondrian, Peit. New York City, 1940–41. Private Collection.

The model letters provided on authentic company stationery have been included by permission to provide realistic examples of company documents for educational purposes. They do not represent actual business documents created by these companies.

Screen shots reprinted with permission from Microsoft Corporation.

Netscape Communications Corporation has not authorized, sponsored, or endorsed or approved this publication and is not responsible for its content. Netscape and the Netscape Communications Corporate Logos are trademarks and trade names of Netscape Communications Corporation. All other product names and/or logos are trademarks of their respective owners.
(Acknowledgments continued on page 585.)

Copyright © 1998 by Houghton Mifflin Company. All rights reserved.

No part of this work may be reproduced or transmitted in any form or by any means, electronic or mechanical, including photocopying and recording, or by any information storage or retrieval system without the prior written permission of Houghton Mifflin Company unless such copying is expressly permitted by federal copyright law. Address inquiries to College Permissions, Houghton Mifflin Company, 222 Berkeley Street, Boston, MA 02116-3764.

Printed in the U.S.A.

Library of Congress Catalog Card Number: 97-72529

ISBN: 0-395-870844

Instructor's Annotated Edition ISBN: 0-395-870852

3456789-WOC-01 00 99 98

To my wife, Diana, with love.

Brief Contents

Contents

6 The Process of Writing   152

PART THREE
Basic Correspondence   183

7 Routine Messages   184

11   Collecting and Analyzing Data   326

12   Writing the Report   366

Preface

S tudents don't have to be convinced of the need for high-level communication skills. By the time they enter business communication classes, students know enough about the business environment to appreciate the critical role communication plays in the contemporary organization; they're also aware of the role communication will play in helping them to get a job and be successful on the job. To sustain this inherent interest, students need a textbook that is current, fast-paced, and interesting—just like business itself. Thus, a major objective of *Contemporary Business Communication (CBC)* is to present comprehensive coverage of real-world concepts in an interesting and lively manner.

On the basis of the helpful feedback received from current users around the country and, indeed, around the English-speaking world, changes in the discipline, and, especially, changes in the workplace itself, this edition of *CBC* has been extensively revised to provide students with the skills they need to communicate effectively in the complex and ever-changing contemporary business environment.

Features New to This Edition

Several features have been added to make this edition of *CBC* even more effective for the student and more convenient for the instructor.

Technology Centered

If, in the 1967 movie *The Graduate*, the buzzword was "plastics," today it is "technology." And with good reason. Every aspect of contemporary business communication—from determining what ideas to communicate to processing the ideas and sharing them—depends on technology.

What a difference a few years make. Five years ago, if students knew word processing, they were considered technologically literate. Not so, today. Among other skills, today's competent communicator must know how to:

- send and receive (and manage) e-mail;
- access the Internet and World Wide Web;
- format an electronic résumé and search online for a job; and
- give an electronic presentation, perhaps using PowerPoint software.

Students need many of these skills up front, that is, before they study other business communication topics. For example, students may need to log on to the

Internet to find an address (either postal or e-mail) before they write even the simplest letter. Thus, in some ways, technological skills can be considered prerequisite to the more traditional business communication skills of reading, writing, speaking, and listening.

New Technology Chapter   New to the third edition of *Contemporary Business Communication* is Chapter 3, "Using Technology to Access and Share Information." Here, students will learn such topics as how to browse and search the Internet using Yahoo! and Excite; how to evaluate the quality of the information they locate; and how to compose and format e-mail messages for readability. This new chapter concentrates on those skills students need right from the beginning of their study of business communication.

Technology Instruction Infused Throughout   However, technological communication skills are neither learned nor practiced in isolation. Integrated into every chapter in the third edition are discussions of the technologies (both their advantages and disadvantages) needed for specific communication skills. For example, students learn how to:

- interpret computerized readability formulas in Chapter 5;

- search online for business information in Chapter 10;

- prepare slides and transparencies using presentation software in Chapter 13;

- access job information and prepare electronic résumés in Chapter 14; and

- document online sources (in both APA and MLA styles) in the Reference Manual.

New Internet Home Pages   Complementing this infusion of technological skills in the text is the addition of two new home pages on the Internet—a *BusCom Online Learning Center* for students and a *BusCom Online Teaching Center* for instructors. As illustrated in the Appendix to Chapter 3 on pages 100–101, students can use this online resource to explore the Internet, locate business information, get help with writing, secure job information, and the like.

Instructors using this text can access their own site via a free password. Features in this site will enable instructors to enrich their lectures by discussing "hot-off-the-press" current events items that illustrate a particular chapter concept, preview the PowerPoint slides that illustrate each chapter (which are also available on computer disk), review detailed lecture and supplemental discussion notes for each chapter, and exchange ideas with the author, publisher, and other instructors around the country who are teaching this course.

Emphasis on Work-Team Communication

Fed by global competition (and global opportunities), contemporary organizations are making extensive use of project management, continuous process improvement, and work teams to encourage their employees to work and communicate collaboratively to solve workplace problems. Thus, competent communicators need to develop their interpersonal skills for working in small groups as well as their communication skills in writing and presenting collaboratively.

New Chapter on Work-Team Communication Work-team communication competence is another one of those "up-front" skills students need to benefit completely from the discussion of other business communication topics. Many instructors (in both this and other courses) assign group projects right from the beginning of the term. Unfortunately, the instructor often erroneously assumes students already know how to work together effectively.

In this edition of *CBC,* several topics previously scattered among different chapters have been reorganized, along with substantial new content, into a comprehensive discussion in Chapter 2, "Work-Team Communication." Included in this new chapter are the following major topics:

- the role of conflict, conformity, and consensus in work teams;

- proven methods for giving constructive feedback;

- diversity and ethical issues in team membership (especially the use of nonverbal messages communicated in different cultures);

- team-writing strategies;

- effective listening strategies;

- planning, conducting, and participating in business meetings; and

- using a professional demeanor and appropriate behavior to maintain effective working relationships, including a new section on dressing appropriately in the workplace (for example, what does "Casual Friday" really mean?).

Work-Team Communication Projects Throughout the text, many end-of-chapter exercises require students to work effectively in teams. Thus, throughout the course, students have an opportunity to practice and refine the team communication skills they learn in Chapter 2. Team projects include both written and oral projects—some of them also requiring the use of the Internet for gathering data needed to solve a problem.

New 5 × 3 Text Organization

The addition of two new chapters (one on technology and one on work-team communication) in the early part of the third edition provided the opportunity to streamline and reorganize the chapters into a 5 × 3 plan—five parts with three chapters each—for a total of fifteen chapters, as follows:

1. **Core Concepts in Business Communication**
   1. Understanding Business Communication
   2. Work-Team Communication
   3. Using Technology to Access and Share Information
2. **Developing Your Writing Skills**
   4. Writing with Style: Individual Elements
   5. Writing with Style: Overall Tone
   6. The Process of Writing
3. **Basic Correspondence**
   7. Routine Messages
   8. Persuasive Messages

Students learn to communicate by communicating—not by just *reading* about communicating. The fifteen chapters in this edition (down from seventeen in the previous edition) are succinct; yet they contain comprehensive coverage of contemporary business communication topics.

Students will find this organizational plan logical. They first learn the overall framework of business communication and the work-team and technological skills they will use in the remainder of the course (Part 1). They next concentrate on basic writing skills (Part 2) and then apply these skills first to composing shorter documents such as letters, memos, and e-mail (Part 3). Then they move on to composing longer documents—reports (Part 4). Because many oral presentations in the workplace stem from written reports, the chapter on oral presentations follows the report chapters; then, when students near the end of their course, they learn contemporary job-getting strategies (Part 5).

Instructors will also find this organizational plan flexible. Dividing the five major content areas into three-chapter units provides them with a flexible arrangement to mix and match. They can choose the chapters (and select from the many end-of-chapter exercises) that best fit the needs of their particular students.

Additional Features

Your students will benefit from the many new or expanded learning aids that have been incorporated into the third edition.

Developing Revision Skills   Because students learn as much (if not more) from rewriting as from drafting, a new feature added to Chapters 6 through 15 is "Help Wanted." This feature presents a sample student-written draft, marked up with typical instructor comments, which students then revise and resubmit as homework.

The purpose of these exercises is to provide students with *guided* editing practice. The content is a complete business document (instead of isolated sentences), and guidance is provided regarding the writing weaknesses to look for (instead of just providing a complete "bad" document and telling students to revise it). Both rhetorical and stylistic weaknesses are identified for students to correct.

Student-Interest Enhancements   Business communication textbooks should be interesting and contemporary. Any business communication instructor who has read the popular Dilbert cartoon strip has probably cut out one or more of the panels to use in class as an illustration of how *not* to communicate in business. Chapter 1 of the third edition opens with a communication profile of Scott Adams, creator of Dilbert; and Dilbert cartoons that reinforce text content appear throughout the text.

Users of previous editions frequently mentioned that students enjoy "Word-wise"—a "fun-with-words" feature that appears in each chapter in the text. All of the Wordwise boxes in this edition are completely new.

Coverage of Communication Ethics   A major section on communication ethics has now been added to Chapter 1, but ethics coverage does not stop there. The ethical dimension of communicating is revisited frequently throughout the text—sometimes in the chapter content itself and at other times in a special "Spotlight—On Law and Ethics" box. From learning how to behave ethically while online to making ethical decisions regarding the visual aids one uses, students are constantly reminded that nearly every communication decision a writer or speaker makes has ethical implications.

Retained from the Previous Edition

In addition to these features new to the third edition, many of the features introduced in earlier editions have been enhanced to make them even more effective.

The 3Ps Microwriting Activities

Microwriting activities—step-by-step analyses of typical communication tasks—proved to be one of the most popular features of previous editions. Beginning with the first writing chapter (Chapter 6), each chapter of the third edition contains a 3Ps microwriting activity, including a *Problem* (a situation that requires a communication task), *Process* (step-by-step guidance for accomplishing the communication task), and *Product* (a fully formatted finished document).

The 3Ps microwriting activities require students to focus their efforts on developing a strategy for any message (even e-mail messages) before beginning to compose it; and they serve as a step-by-step model for composing the end-of-chapter exercises.

The 3Ps microwriting activities within each chapter all contain the solutions to the process questions. The 3Ps microwriting exercises at the end of the chapter (plus additional ones in the *Instructor's Resource Manual*) pose process questions and then require the student to provide the solutions. This format more actively engages the student in the problem-solving process.

Urban Systems: An Ongoing Case Study

As in previous editions, every chapter in the new edition ends with a case study involving Urban Systems (US), a small entrepreneurial company whose primary product is Ultra Light, a new paper-thin light source that promises to revolutionize the illumination industry. A company profile (complete with a photograph of each major player) is contained in the Appendix to Chapter 1, and each chapter presents a communication problem faced by one of these managers. As students systematically solve these fifteen case studies, they face communication problems similar to those typically found in the workplace. The continuing nature of the case study provides these positive learning experiences:

- Students are able to use richer contextual clues to solve communication problems than are possible in the shorter end-of-chapter exercises.

- Students become intimately familiar with the managers and the company and must select what is relevant from a mass of data, thereby learning to handle information overload. (New to this edition are requirements for locating additional needed information on the Internet.)

- Because the same situations frequently carry over into subsequent chapters, students must face the consequences of their earlier decisions.

- Many cases require students to solve the same communication problem from two different perspectives—thereby enhancing the process of audience analysis.

These cases provide realistic opportunities for practicing work-team communication and critical-thinking skills.

Continuing Text Examples and End-of-Chapter Exercises

At the beginning of each chapter, profiles of actual business communicators provide "An Insider's Perspective" of the communication situations that arise in today's organizations. Students learn about the communication challenges facing employees in organizations as diverse as CNN/CNNfn, The Wilderness Society, 3M, Domino's Pizza, and Royal Caribbean International. In addition to end-of-chapter review and discussion questions based on these "Insider Perspectives," new to this edition are the 3Ps microwriting exercises relating to them. These exercises build students' critical-thinking skills in the early chapters and then give them an opportunity to practice their writing skills in later chapters.

Communication problems in the real world do not occur in a vacuum. Events have happened before the problem and will happen after the problem that affect its resolution. Thus, in this edition continuing examples are often used throughout the chapters (or even carried forward from one chapter to the next) in both the text and the end-of-chapter exercises. For example, in Chapter 7, students first assume the role of buyer and write a claim letter; then, in a later exercise, they assume the role of seller and respond to that claim letter by writing an adjustment letter.

These continuing examples and exercises are realistic because they give a sense of following a problem through to completion. They're interesting because they provide a continuing thread to the chapter. And they reinforce the concept of audience analysis because students must first assume the role of sender and later the role of receiver for the same communication task.

Annotated Models and Checklists

Full-page models of each major writing task appear in this edition, shown in complete, ready-to-send format so that students become familiar with the appropriate format for every major type of writing assignment. Each model provides marginal step-by-step composing notes as well as grammar and mechanics notes that point out specific illustrations of the grammar and mechanics rules presented in the Reference Manual. In addition, the eighteen checklists scattered throughout the text provide brief, step-by-step outlines for completing specific types of communication tasks.

Complete Package of Instructor Support Materials

Accompanying the third edition of this text is a full array of instructor-support materials.

Instructor's Annotated Edition

Complementing the "easy-to-learn" approach of the student text is the "easy-to-teach" approach of the *Instructor's Annotated Edition* of this text. *CBC* is the first major business communication text to offer this special resource, which provides specific teaching aids right at the point where you need them. Included in the margin of the *IAE* (but not in the student text) are numerous brief anecdotes and quotations gathered from contemporary business publications that you can use to enrich your lectures. Marginal notes also include teaching tips and references to supplementary instructional materials available in the teaching support package. In addition, miniature copies of the PowerPoint slides are shown in the margins of the *IAE* so that you can see immediately what presentation materials are available for each section of the text.

Instructor's Resource Manual

The *Instructor's Resource Manual* presents useful guidelines and additional teaching materials, including chapter overviews, supplemental lecture notes, answers to review and discussion questions, suggestions for and sample solutions to chapter exercises, fully formatted solutions to all letter-writing exercises, solutions to Urban Systems cases, sample reports, additional microwriting samples, and answers to all exercises in the Reference Manual. More than fifty transparency masters include solutions to selected in-text exercises.

PowerPoint Slides

Nearly 250 PowerPoint slides include summaries of key concepts, good/bad paired examples, and supplementary information, including answers to selected exercises. These slides are all new or updated for this edition and contain original material rather than duplicates of textbook examples.

Overhead Transparencies

Close to one hundred acetate transparencies are also available, including summaries of key concepts, writing examples, and text figures.

The BusCom Online Teaching Center

The *BusCom Online Teaching Center* (a Web site designed for instructors) can be accessed via a free password provided to instructors using this text. The site provides current event items that illustrate a particular chapter, the PowerPoint slides for previewing and downloading, detailed lecture and supplemental discussion notes for each chapter, and a forum for exchanging ideas with the author, publisher, and other instructors who are teaching this course.

Test Bank and Computerized Test Bank

The *Test Bank* and computerized testing program contain approximately 1,200 test items, including multiple-choice, short answer, true-false, revision exercises, and writing cases. The computerized test bank allows instructors to prepare examinations consisting of any quantity and combination of questions. Using the program, the instructor selects questions from the test bank and produces a test master—and alternate versions, if desired—for easy duplication.

Video Case Studies

Five video cases, relating to each part of the textbook, give students an opportunity to view interesting and well-known companies in action. These videos reinforce text concepts by directly relating particular business communication concepts to the footage being shown. In addition, for each video case, discussion questions and suggested writing assignments are provided.

Complete Package of Student Support Materials

The BusCom Online Learning Center

The *BusCom Online Learning Center* (a Web site designed for students) gives students an online resource and guide to the world of Internet business communication. Here they will be able to learn more about the Internet, find links to help them locate reliable business information, find links to online writing labs, complete exercises designed to help them learn more from the course, and learn more about available jobs and employers.

BusCom Writer

BusCom Writer provides a set of interactive computer modules that guide students through the development of ten basic business documents. Based on the textbook's 3Ps (Problem/Process/Product) microwriting model, each module presents students with a unique business situation; guides them step-by-step through the process of analyzing the situation, developing communication goals, and preparing the document; and then prompts them to proofread, revise, and print out the finished product.

Grammar II CD-ROM

The *Grammar II* CD-ROM (by ProOne Software, a division of Sofsource, Inc.) supplements the grammar and mechanics coverage in the text through interactive review and reinforcement exercises. More than 500 practice problems and samples with step-by-step explanations and individualized feedback are provided.

The Business Communicator's Guide to the Internet

This supplementary booklet, available for shrink-wrapping with the text, provides students with a detailed introduction to the Internet. It specifically covers the use of key Internet tools and features, Internet browsers, e-mail, discussion lists, newsgroups, and the like, by focusing on the specific needs of business communicators.

The Business Communicator's Guide to PowerPoint

This supplementary booklet, also available for shrink-wrapping with the text, provides students with a detailed introduction to this powerful presentation tool and emphasizes techniques for creating effective business presentations.

The American Heritage Dictionary

The American Heritage Dictionary is an invaluable resource for college and career success. The best-selling third edition is the most complete, up-to-date, and heavily illustrated dictionary available. Instructors may order the hardcover, thumb-indexed *American Heritage College Dictionary,* Third Edition, in a shrink-wrapped package with *Contemporary Business Communication.* Also available is a brief hardcover version, *The American Heritage Concise Dictionary,* Third Edition, which also may be shrink-wrapped with *Contemporary Business Communication.*

Acknowledgments

During the revision of this text, it has been my great pleasure to work with a dedicated and skillful team of professionals at Houghton Mifflin, and I gratefully salute the Houghton Mifflin editorial, design, production, and marketing staff for the major contributions they have made to the success of this text. Although it is always dangerous to name names, I would be remiss if I did not specifically acknowledge with deep gratitude the special assistance of Joanne Dauksewicz and Chere Bemelmans. What a genuine pleasure it has been to work with this talented and dynamic duo.

I also wish to express my sincere appreciation to Harriet M. Augustin of Southwest Texas State University who has for three editions prepared the *Instructor's Resource Manual;* to Keith Mulbery of Utah Valley State College who prepared the *Test Bank* for this text; and to Marian Woods, consultant and writer extraordinaire, for the many bits and pieces of work she created for this edition.

In addition, I wish to thank the following reviewers for their thoughtful contributions:

Carl Bridges, *Arthur Andersen Consulting*
Annette Briscoe, *Indiana University Southeast*
Mitchel T. Burchfield, *Southwest Texas Junior College*
Janice Burke, *South Suburban College*
Doris L. Cost, *Metropolitan State College of Denver*
L. Ben Crane, *Temple University*
Ava Cross, *Ryerson Polytechnic University*
Nancy J. Daugherty, *Indiana University-Purdue University, Indianapolis*

Rosemarie Dittmer, *Northeastern University*
Graham N. Drake, *State University of New York, Geneseo*
Kay Durden, *The University of Tennessee at Martin*
Phillip A. Holcomb, *Angelo State University*
Larry R. Honl, *University of Wisconsin, Eau Claire*
Anne Hutta Colvin, *Montgomery County Community College*
Alice Kinder, *Virginia Polytechnic Institute and State University*
Richard N. Kleeberg, *Solano Community College*
Lowell Lamberton, *Central Oregon Community College*
E. Jay Larson, *Lewis and Clark State College*
Michael Liberman, *East Stroudsburg University*
Marsha C. Markman, *California Lutheran University*
Diana McKowen, *Indiana University, Bloomington*
Maureen McLaughlin, *Highline Community College*
Wayne Moore, *Indiana University of Pennsylvania*
Gerald W. Morton, *Auburn University of Montgomery*
Rosemary Olds, *Des Moines Area Community College*
Karen Sterkel Powell, *Colorado State University*
Jeanette Ritzenthaler, *New Hampshire College*
Betty Robbins, *University of Oklahoma*
Joan C. Roderick, *Southwest Texas State University*
Sue Seymour, *Cameron University*
Sherry Sherrill, *Forsyth Technical Community College*
John R. Sinton, *Finger Lakes Community College*
Curtis J. Smith, *Finger Lakes Community College*
Ted O. Stoddard, *Brigham Young University*
Vincent C. Trofi, *Providence College*
Randall L. Waller, *Baylor University*
Maria W. Warren, *University of West Florida*
Michael R. Wunsch, *Northern Arizona University*
Annette Wyandotte, *Indiana University, Southeast*
Betty Rogers Youngkin, *University of Dayton*

PART ONE

Core Concepts in Business Communication

1

Understanding Business Communication

An Insider's Perspective

In the cubicled world of Dilbert, memos are filed in the wastebasket and meetings are excuses to eat doughnuts and trade insults. Admittedly, these antics are not a blueprint for effective business communication, but they're commonplace in the wildly popular "Dilbert" syndicated cartoon strip created by Scott Adams. With a keen eye and a sharp ear, Adams cleverly lampoons everyday life in the workplace by chronicling the trials and triumphs of Dilbert, Dogbert, Catbert, and his other characters.

After years of doodling his way through seemingly endless meetings, first at Crocker National Bank and later at Pacific Bell, Adams developed a nerdy cartoon character with a bumpy-crowned head and an unruly striped tie. Despite a series of rejections and intense competition from other would-be cartoonists, his determination paid off when United Features Syndicate launched the strip in 1989 in 50 U.S. newspapers. Now that "Dilbert" appears in more than 1,400 newspapers in 35 countries and has spawned several best-selling books about business, Adams has successfully made the transition from cubicle-based employee to home-based entrepreneur.

Adams strongly prefers electronic communication, using it for everything from cartoon transmission to magazine interviews to fan newsletters. "I'm really big on automation," he explains. "I'm optimized toward making everything as efficient as possible." His home office includes a top-of-the-line Macintosh computer, a scanner to digitize his hand-drawn cartoons, a modem for connecting to publishers and the Internet, and a fax machine for receiving documents.

Since he began including his e-mail address in the strip several years ago, Adams has received more than 300 e-mail messages every day, which he reads and answers late into the evening. Most of the messages echo the complaints of Dilbert and his colleagues, telling more stories of office absurdities that serve as fodder for "Dilbert" storylines. "I get a lot of mail from other countries, in particular, Sweden, Canada, Australia, New Zealand, Denmark, and England," he says. "They say, 'You must be

COMMUNICATION OBJECTIVES

After you have finished this chapter, you should be able to

■ Describe the components of communication.

■ Explain the directions that make up the formal communication network.

■ Describe the characteristics of the grapevine and provide guidelines for managing it.

■ Identify the major verbal and nonverbal barriers to communication.

■ Explain the legal and ethical dimensions of communicating.

working at my company; what is your real name?'" His electronic newsletter has more than 100,000 online subscribers, and his Dilbert Zone World Wide Web site (http://www.unitedmedia.com/comics/dilbert) draws 55,000 daily visitors. As much as Adams enjoys the convenience of electronic communication, he does communicate in other ways. He no longer has to write status reports and attend round after round of office meetings, but every day brings a new raft of invitations to make speeches. Even though the cartoonist refuses most requests, he has stepped up his schedule of public speaking. And, from time to time, he agrees to be interviewed for a newspaper, magazine, or radio feature. However, because the demands on his time have grown as the fame of "Dilbert" spreads, he is careful to manage his communication contacts so they don't interfere with his work. For example, noting that he usually draws "Dilbert" before noon, Adams warns, "I don't answer the phone in the morning." In fact, working alone in his home office has had an effect on his voice: "I spend so little of my day talking to people live that I've lost that feedback mechanism that tells you how loud you're talking," he says.

Tongue in cheek, Adams offers his opinion about how pointy-haired, clueless bosses should use business communication. In *The Dilbert Principle,* he writes: "The real objective of business communication is to advance your career. That objective is generally at odds with the notion of 'clear transfer of information.' The success-

ful manager knows that the best kind of communication is one that conveys the message 'I am worthy of promotion' without accidentally transferring any other information. Clear communication can only get you in trouble." Look for "Dilbert" cartoons throughout this text, with witty and wry observations on communication at work—and beyond.

Sources: Michelle Locke, "Dilbert's Irreverent Take Lands on Best-Seller Lists," *News-Times* (Danbury, CT), March 13, 1997, pp. C-1, C-3; George Gendron, "FYI: Dilbert Fired! Starts New Biz," *Inc.,* July 1996, pp. 9-11; Scott Adams, *The Dilbert Principle,* HarperBusiness, New York, 1996, pp. 35-36; Ralph Vader, "The Conference Room: A Conversation with Dilbert's Scott Adams," accessed on Disgruntled World Wide Web Site, April, 1997; Rhonda Abrams, "Life Without a Safety Net: Dilbert's Creator Gets the Ax," accessed on Idea Caf? World Wide Web Site, April, 1997.

Communicating in Organizations

Communication is necessary if an organization is to achieve its goals.

Walk through the halls of a contemporary organization, and what do you see? Managers and other employees reading reports, drafting electronic mail on their computers, attending meetings, conducting interviews, talking on the telephone, conferring with subordinates, holding business lunches, reading mail, dictating correspondence, and making presentations. In short, you see people *communicating*.

An organization is a group of people working together to achieve a common goal, and communication is a vital part of that process. Indeed, communication must have occurred before a common goal could even be established. And a group of people working together must interact; that is, they must *communicate* their needs, thoughts, plans, expertise, and so on. Communication is the means by which information is shared, activities are coordinated, and decision making is enhanced.

Understanding how communication works in business and how to communicate competently within an organization will help you participate more effectively in every aspect of business. Consider these recent research findings—all of which come from studies conducted in the 1990s:[1]

- A survey of 224 recent business graduates ranked communication as the most important area of knowledge both for securing employment after graduation and for advancement and promotion once on the job.

- A survey of 6,000 people conducted by *Young Executive* magazine found that the most annoying habit of American bosses was poor communication.

- A survey of 200 corporate vice presidents reported they spend the equivalent of nearly three months a year writing letters, memos, and reports.

As Goldman Sachs & Co.'s partner for information technology, Leslie Tortora installed document-sharing software so that Goldman professionals all over the world can call in to their internal Web site, collect their e-mail, and work collaboratively on a document.

- A survey of 1,000 white- and blue-collar workers found that the most frequent cause of workplace resentment and misunderstandings is poor communication.

- Eighty percent of the managers at 402 firms surveyed nationwide say most of their employees need to improve their writing skills, up from 65% the previous year. But only 21% of the firms offer training in writing skills.

Clearly, good communication skills are crucial to your success in the organization. Competent writing and speaking skills will help you get hired, perform well, and earn promotions. If you decide to go into business for yourself, writing and speaking skills will help you obtain venture capital, promote your product, and manage your employees. These same skills will also help you achieve your personal and social goals.

The Components of Communication

Because communication is such a vital part of the organizational structure, our study of communication begins with an analysis of its components. **Communication** is the process of sending and receiving messages—sometimes through spoken or written words and sometimes through such nonverbal means as facial expressions, gestures, and voice qualities. As illustrated in Figure 1.1, the communication model consists of five components: the stimulus, filter, message, medium, and destination. Ideally, the process ends with feedback to the sender, although feedback is not necessary in order for communication to have taken place.

Communication is the sending and receiving of verbal and nonverbal messages.

To illustrate the model, let us follow the case of Dave Kaplan, a chemical engineer at Industrial Chemical, Inc. (We'll become quite familiar with Dave and his company in the coming chapters.) In 1992, in the process of working on another project, Dave developed Ultra Light, a flat, electroluminescent sheet of material that serves as a light source. Dave could see the enormous business opportunity offered by a paper-thin light fixture such as Ultra Light, which was bendable and could be produced in a variety of shapes and sizes.

The market for lighting is vast, and Dave, even though at the time an engineer and not a businessman, felt the sting of inventing a device that had great potential

FIGURE 1.1   The Components of Communication

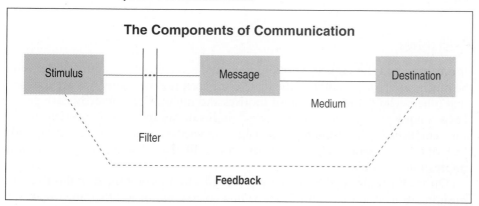

but that belonged to somebody else (Industrial Chemical, Inc.). He was disappointed in IC's eventual decision not to manufacture and market this product. As we learn what happened to Dave Kaplan after IC's decision, we'll examine the components of communication, one at a time.

Incident	*Communication Component*
Dave receives a memorandum from the head of R & D.	Dave receives a *stimulus*.
He interprets the memo to mean that IC has no interest in his invention.	He *filters* the stimulus.
He decides to relay this information to his brother.	He forms a *message*.
He telephones Marc.	He selects a *medium*.
His brother receives the call.	The message reaches its *destination*.
Marc listens and gives Dave his reaction.	Marc provides *feedback*.

The Stimulus

Step 1: *A stimulus creates a need to communicate.*

In order for communication to take place, there first must be a **stimulus,** an event that creates within an individual the need to communicate. This stimulus can be internal or external. An internal stimulus is simply an idea that forms within your mind. External stimuli come to you through your sensory organs—your eyes, ears, nose, mouth, and skin. A stimulus for communicating in business might be an e-mail message you just read, a presentation you heard at a staff meeting, a bit of gossip you heard over lunch, your perception that the general manager has been acting preoccupied lately, or even the hot air generated by an overworked heating system (or colleague!).

You respond to the stimulus by formulating a message, either a **verbal message** (written or spoken words), a **nonverbal message** (nonwritten and nonspoken signals), or some combination of the two. For Dave Kaplan, the stimulus for communication was a memorandum he received from the head of the research and development (R & D) department informing him that IC was not interested in developing Ultra Light but would, instead, sell the patent to some company that *was* interested.

The Filter

Step 2: *Our knowledge, experience, and viewpoints act as a filter to help us interpret (decode) the stimulus.*

If everyone had the same perception of events, your job of communicating would be much easier; you could assume that your perception of reality was accurate and that others would understand your motives and intent. Unfortunately, each person has a unique perception of reality, based on his or her individual experiences, culture, emotions at the moment, personality, knowledge, socioeconomic status, and a host of other variables. These variables act as a **filter** in shaping everyone's unique impressions of reality.

Once your brain receives a message, it begins to interpret the stimulus to derive meaning from it so that you will know how to respond or whether any response is even necessary. Stimuli that reinforce existing beliefs are likely to create a more lasting impression and to generate a stronger response than those that call into question your existing beliefs.

Likewise, stimuli are affected by your current emotional or physical frame of reference. An event that might normally cause you to react strongly might not even register if you're suffering from a bad cold or from lack of sleep. Or a remark made innocently might cause a strong negative reaction if you're angry or upset about some earlier event.

The memo Dave received from R & D simply reinforced what he had come to expect at his company, which had become successful by focusing on its own predetermined long-range objectives and which showed little interest in exploiting unexpected discoveries such as Ultra Light. Dave's long involvement in the research that had led to this product caused him to assume a protective, almost paternalistic, interest in its future. Besides, after so many years in the lab, Dave was ready for a new challenge. These factors, then, acted as a filter through which Dave interpreted the memo and formulated his response—a phone call to his brother in Chicago.

At the time of Dave's call, Marc Kaplan was sitting alone in his office at a Chicago advertising agency sampling four different brands of cheese pizza (see Figure 1.2). As a marketing manager in charge of a new pizza account, he was preoccupied with finding a competitive edge for his client's product, and his perception of Dave's message was filtered by his current situation.

FIGURE 1.2   An Example of Communication at Work

To hear his scientist brother, the MIT graduate who all his life had preferred to pursue solitary scholarly research, suddenly erupting over the phone with the idea of starting a business contradicted Marc's lifelong preconceptions about Dave and acted as a strong filter resisting Dave's urgent message. Furthermore, Marc's emotional and physical frame of reference—hunkered down as he was over several cheese pizzas—did not put him in a receptive mood for a grand scheme that would take tens of thousands of dollars and many years of hard work. But Marc's background—his economic status, his education, and his current job—added another point of view, in this case a highly favorable filter for taking in Dave's message.

If Dave is good enough at communicating his message, he might be able to persuade Marc to join him in buying the Ultra Light patent from IC and starting a business of their own.

The Message

Step 3: We formulate (encode) a verbal or nonverbal response to the stimulus.

Dave's message to Marc was, "Let's form our own company." The extent to which any communication effort achieves its desired goal depends very directly on how well you construct the **message** (the information to be communicated). Success at communicating depends not only on the purpose and content of the message but also, just as important, on how skillful you are at communicating, how well you know your **audience** (the person or persons with whom you're communicating), and how much you hold in common with your audience.

As a scientist, Dave Kaplan did not have an extensive business vocabulary. Nor did he have much practice at oral business presentations and the careful pacing and selective reinforcement required in such circumstances. In effect, Dave was attempting to make an oral business proposal, unfortunately without much technique or skill.

"You're crazy, Dave. You don't know what you're talking about." This initial response from Marc made it clear to Dave that his message wasn't getting through. But what Dave lacked in skill, he made up for in knowing his audience (his kid brother) backward and forward.

"You're chicken, Marc" had always gotten Marc's attention and interest in the past, and it worked again. Dave kept challenging Marc, something he knew Marc couldn't resist, and kept reminding him of their common ground: all the happy adventures they had shared as kids and adults.

The Medium

Step 4: We select the form of the message (medium).

Once the sender has encoded a message, the next step in the process is to transmit that message to the receiver. At this point, the sender must choose the form of message to send, or **medium.** Oral messages might be transmitted through a staff meeting, personal conference, telephone conversation, press conference, voice mail, or even such informal means as the company grapevine. Written messages might be transmitted through a memorandum, a report, a letter, a contract, a brochure, a bulletin-board notice, electronic mail, a company newsletter, a press release, or an addition to the policies and procedures manual. And nonverbal messages might be transmitted through facial expressions, gestures, or body movement.

Because Dave is in the process of talking with Marc over the phone, his medium is a telephone conversation.

The Destination

The message is transmitted and then enters the sensory environment of the receiver, at which point control passes from the sender to the receiver. Once the message reaches its destination, there is no guarantee that communication will actually occur. We are constantly bombarded with stimuli and our sensory organs pick up only part of them. Even assuming your receiver *does* perceive your message, you have no assurance that it will be interpreted (filtered) as you intended. Your transmitted message becomes the source, or stimulus, for the next communication episode, and the process begins anew.

After Dave's enthusiastic, one-hour phone call, Marc promised to consider the venture seriously. Marc's response provided **feedback** (reaction to a message) to Dave on how accurately his own message had been received. In time, it led to many more versions of the communication process, both written and oral, before the two brothers founded Urban Systems, a small "start-up" company whose primary product is Ultra Light and which employs 178 people at its corporate headquarters in Ann Arbor, Michigan, and at a completely automated manufacturing plant in Charlotte, North Carolina.

Step 5: The message reaches its destination and, if successful, is perceived accurately by the receiver.

The Dynamic Nature of Communication

From our look at the components of communication and the model presented in Figure 1.1, you might erroneously infer that communication is a linear, static process—flowing in an orderly fashion from one stage to the next—and that you can easily separate the communicators into senders and receivers. That is not the case.

Two or more people often send and receive messages simultaneously. While you are receiving one message, you may at the same time be sending another message. For example, the look on your face as you are receiving a message may be sending a new message to the sender that you either understand, agree with, or are baffled by the message being sent. And the feedback thus given may prompt the sender to modify his or her intended message.

Thus, artificially "freezing" the action in order to examine each step of the communication process separately causes us to lose some of the dynamic richness of that process in terms of both its verbal and nonverbal components.

Urban Systems: A Continuing Case Study

As we join Urban Systems (US), Dave and Marc's company has annual sales in the $30 million range, with a net profit last year of $1.4 million. It is considered a progressive company by the investment community, with skillful management and healthy earnings potential. The local community considers US to be a good corporate citizen; it is nonpolluting, and its officers are active in community affairs.

You will be seeing more of the Kaplan brothers and Urban Systems in the chapters ahead, as communication within the organization serves as an ongoing case study for each of the major areas of business communication—from this basic model of communication all the way through to the final chapter. You'll have the opportunity to get to know the people in the company and watch from the inside as they handle every type of business communication in concrete terms. Right now, you can learn more of the background of Urban Systems by reading the Appendix to Chapter 1(beginning on page 29), an overview of the company's history, products, financial data, and all-too-human personnel.

Verbal Communication

Verbal messages are composed of words—either written or spoken.

It is the ability to communicate by using words that separates human beings from the rest of the animal kingdom. Our verbal ability also enables us to learn from the past—to benefit from the experience of others.

Oral Communication

Oral communication is one of the most common functions in business. Consider, for example, how limiting it would be if a manager could not attend meetings, ask questions of colleagues, make presentations, appraise performance, handle customer complaints, or give instructions.

Oral communication is different from written communication in that it allows more ways to get a message across to others. You can clear up any questions immediately; use nonverbal clues; provide additional information; and use pauses, emphasis, and voice tone to stress certain points.

For oral communication to be effective, a second communication skill—listening—is also required. No matter how well crafted the content and delivery of an oral presentation, it cannot achieve its goal if the intended audience does not have effective listening skills. Some research has found that nearly 60% of all communication problems in business are caused by poor listening.[2]

Oral communication doesn't have to be human. Tony Lovell, shown here driving his "Cow Car," invented the Wildfire "electronic assistant," which acts as a voice-activated telephone secretary that can check for messages, return or place phone calls, conduct conference calls, or leave voice messages for specific people who might call in.

Written Communication

Writing is more difficult than speaking because you have to get your message correct the first time; you do not have the advantage of immediate feedback and nonverbal clues such as facial expressions to help you achieve your objective. Examples of typical written communication, in industry include the following:

- *Memorandums:* A **memorandum** is a written message sent to someone working in the same organization.

- *Letters:* A **letter** is a written message sent to someone outside the organization; it also can be sent by computer via commercial electronic mail networks, such as MCI or CompuServe.

- *E-mail (electronic mail):* **E-mail** (see Figure 1.3) is a message transmitted electronically over a computer network most often connected by cable, telephone lines, or satellites. The recipient's computer receives and stores the message almost instantaneously after it is sent. The recipient may read, respond to, file, or discard the message—all without the use of paper.

FIGURE 1.3   Example of E-mail (Screen shot reprinted with permission from Microsoft Corporation)

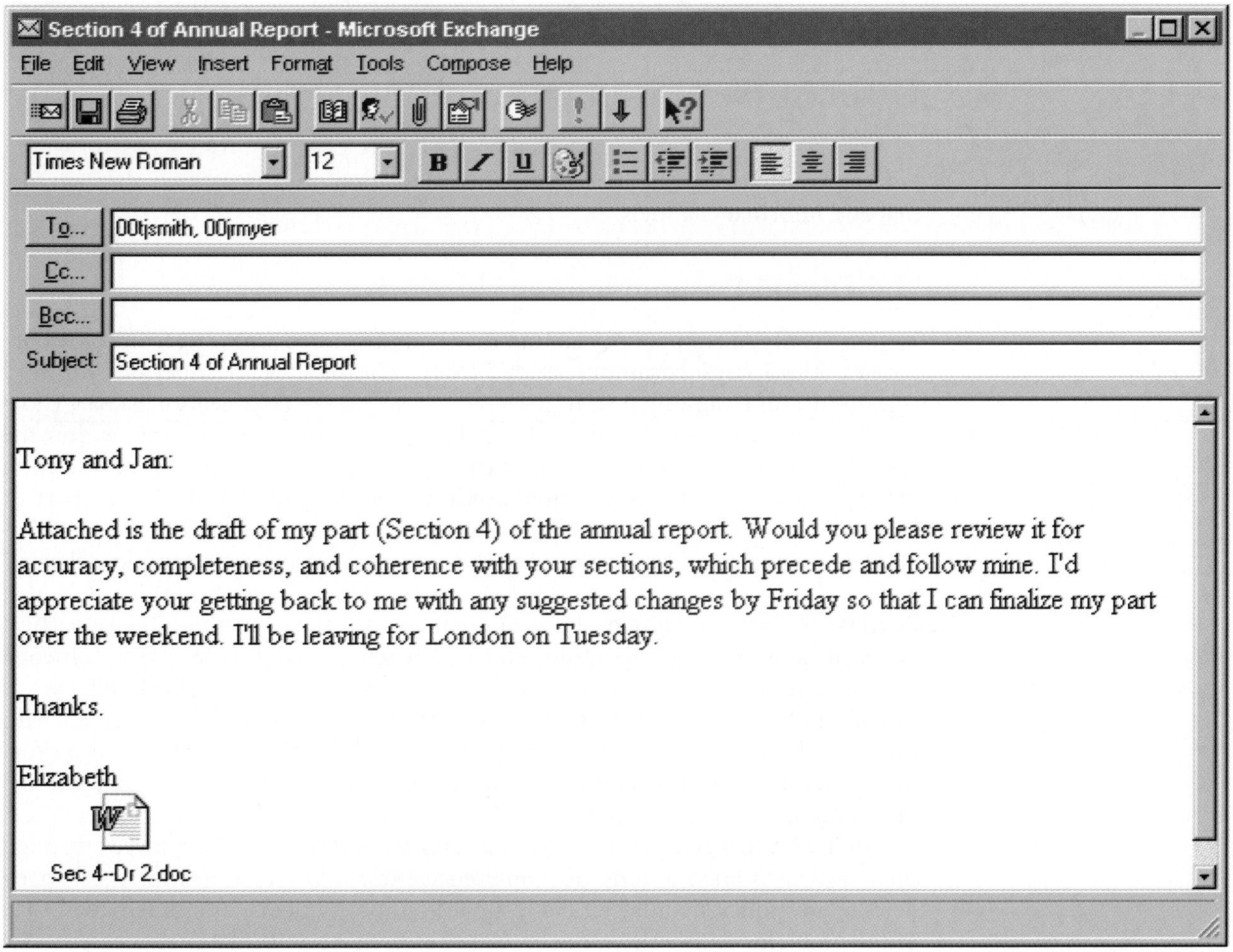

■ *Reports:* A **report** is an orderly and objective presentation of information that assists in decision making and problem solving. Examples of common business reports include policies and procedures, status reports, minutes of meetings, financial reports, personnel evaluations, press releases, and computer printouts.

■ *Miscellaneous:* Other examples of written communication include contracts, sales literature, newsletters, and bulletin-board notices.

Most oral communication is temporary; written communication is permanent.

Writing is crucial to the modern organization because it serves as the major source of documentation. A speech may make a striking impression, but a memorandum leaves a permanent record for others to refer to in the future in case memory fails or a dispute arises.

For written messages to achieve their goals, they must be read. The skill of efficient reading is becoming more important in today's technological society. The abundance of widespread computing and word processing capabilities, along with the proliferation of convenient and economical photocopying and faxing, has created *more* paperwork rather than less. Thus, information overload is one of the unfortunate by-products of our times (see Spotlight 1—On Technology, on page 14). These and other implications of technology on business communication are discussed throughout this text.

Directions of Communication

For an organization to be successful, communication must flow freely through formal and informal channels.

The Formal Communication Network

Within the organization, information may be transmitted from superiors to subordinates (downward communication), from subordinates to superiors (upward communication), among people at the same level on the organizational chart (horizontal communication), and among people in different departments within the organization (cross-channel communication). These four types of communication make up the organization's **formal communication network.** We'll use part of Urban Systems' organizational chart, shown in Figure 1.4, to illustrate the directions of communication. (See the Appendix to Chapter 1 for the complete chart.)

Downward Communication   In most organizations the largest number of vertical communications move downward—from someone of higher authority to someone of lower authority. For example, at Urban Systems (Figure 1.4), Dave Kaplan sends a memo to Neelima Shrikhande about a computer report; she, in turn, confers with Eric Fox. Through written and oral channels, information regarding job performance, policies and procedures, day-to-day operations, and other organizational information is communicated.

Higher-level management communicates with lower-level employees through such means as memorandums, conferences, telephone conversations, company newsletters, policy manuals, bulletin-board announcements, and videotapes. One of the problems with written downward communication is that management may

FIGURE 1.4   Part of the Formal Communication Network at Urban Systems

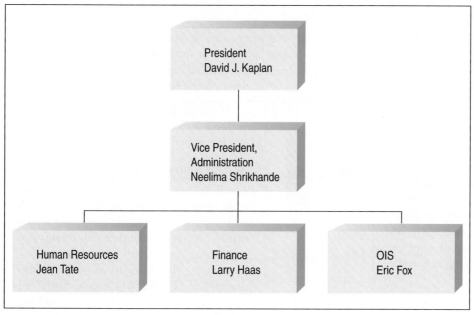

assume that what is sent downward is received and understood. Unfortunately, that is not always the case.

Upward Communication   Upward communication is the flow of information from lower-level employees to upper-level employees. In Figure 1.4, for example, Jean Tate sends a monthly status report to the president regarding human resources actions for the month, and Neelima responds to Dave's memo regarding the computer report. Upward communication can take the form of memorandums, conferences, reports, suggestion systems, employee surveys, or union publications, among others.

Upward communication is important because it provides higher management with the information needed for decision making. It also cultivates employee loyalty by giving employees an opportunity to be heard, to air their grievances, and to offer suggestions. Finally, upward communication provides the feedback necessary to let supervisors know whether subordinates received and understood messages that were sent downward.

The free flow of communication upward helps prevent management isolation.

Horizontal Communication   Horizontal communication is the flow of information among peers within the same work unit. For example, the administration division holds a weekly staff meeting at which the three managers (Jean, Larry, and Eric) exchange information about the status of their operations.

Horizontal communication is important to help coordinate work assignments, share information on plans and activities, negotiate differences, and develop interpersonal support, thereby creating a more cohesive work unit. The more that individuals or departments within an organization must interact with each other to accomplish their objectives, the more frequent and intense will be the horizontal communication.

The most common form of horizontal communication is the committee meeting, where most coordination, sharing of information, and problem solving take

Overcoming Information Anxiety

Executives, like nearly everyone else in this information-laden society, are being bombarded by more data than they can absorb. According to Richard Wurman, author of *Information Anxiety,* in order to function in business we are being forced to assimilate a body of knowledge that is expanding by the minute. For example, about 9,600 periodicals are published in the United States each year. Wurman believes it's a myth that the more choices you have, the more freedom you enjoy. More choices simply produce more anxiety. So as you decrease the number of choices, you decrease the fear of having made the wrong one.

SPOTLIGHT 1
ON TECHNOLOGY

The Black Hole

Trying to process all this information can induce "information anxiety"—apprehension about the ever-widening gap between what we understand and what we think we *should* understand. In other words, it is the black hole between data and knowledge. Here are some symptoms of information anxiety as Wurman describes them:

- Nodding your head knowingly when someone mentions a book, artist, or news story that you have actually never heard of.
- Feeling guilty about that ever-higher stack of periodicals waiting to be read.
- Blaming yourself for not being able to follow the instructions for putting a bike together.
- Feeling depressed because you don't know what all the buttons on your VCR do.

Wurman believes that "the System" is at fault—too many people are putting out too much data.

Nobody Knows It All

The first step in overcoming information anxiety is to accept that there is much you won't understand. Let your ignorance be an inspiration to learn, not something to conceal. Wurman recommends standing in front of a mirror and practicing, "Could you repeat that?" or "I'm not sure I understand what you're talking about" instead of pretending to understand what you do not.

Other suggestions include the following:

- Separate what you are really interested in from what you merely think you *should* be interested in.
- Moderate your use of technology.
- Minimize the time you spend reading or watching news that isn't relevant to your life.
- Reduce your pile of office reading.

Source: Richard Saul Wurman, *Information Anxiety*, Doubleday, Garden City, NY; 1989.

place. Intense competition for scarce resources, lack of trust among coworkers, or concerns about job security or promotions can sometimes create barriers to the free flow of horizontal information.

Cross-Channel Communication   Cross-channel communication is the exchange of information among employees in different work units who are neither subordinate nor superior to each other. For example, each year a payroll clerk in Jean Tate's department sends out a request to all company employees for updated information about the number of exemptions they claim on their tax forms.

Staff specialists use cross-channel communications frequently because their responsibilities typically involve many departments within the organization. Because they lack line authority to direct those with whom they communicate, they must often rely on their persuasive skills, as, for instance, when the human resources department encourages employees to complete a job-satisfaction questionnaire.

The Informal Communication Network

The **informal communication network** (or the *grapevine,* as it is called) is the transmission of information through nonofficial channels within the organization. Carpooling to work, waiting to use the photocopier, jogging at noon, in the cafeteria during lunch, or chatting at a local PTA meeting—wherever workers come together, they are likely to hear and pass on information about possible happenings in the organization. Employees often say that the grapevine is their most frequent source of information on company plans and performance. In one recent survey of 451 executives, 91% reported that employees typically use the grapevine for information on company "bad news" such as layoffs and takeovers. Office politics was cited as a grapevine topic by 73%, whereas only 41% said their employees turned to the grapevine for "good news."[3]

These are the common characteristics of the grapevine:[4]

The informal communication network (grapevine) transmits information through nonofficial channels within the organization.

- Most of the information passed along the grapevine (about 80%) is business related, and most of it (75% to 95%) is accurate.

- The grapevine is pervasive. It exists at all levels in the organization—from corporate boardroom to the assembly line.

- Information moves rapidly along the grapevine.

- The grapevine is most active when change is taking place and when one's need to know or level of fear is highest—during layoffs, plant closings, acquisitions, mergers, and the like.

- The grapevine is a normal, often vital, part of every organization.

Rather than trying to eliminate the grapevine (a futile effort), competent managers accept its existence and pay attention to it. They act promptly to counteract false rumors. Most of all, they use the formal communication network (including meetings, memos, newsletters, and bulletin boards) to ensure that all news—positive and negative—gets out to employees as quickly and as completely as possible. The free flow of information within the organization not only stops rumors; it's simply good business.

Barriers to Communication

Considering the complex nature of the communication process, your messages may not always be received exactly as you intended. As a matter of fact, sometimes your messages will not be received at all; at other times, they will be received incompletely or inaccurately. Some of the obstacles to effective and efficient communication are verbal; others are nonverbal. As illustrated in Figure 1.5, these barriers can create an impenetrable "brick wall" that makes effective communication impossible.

Verbal Barriers

Verbal barriers are related to what you write or say. They include inadequate knowledge or vocabulary, differences in interpretation, language differences, inappropriate use of expressions, overabstraction and ambiguity, and polarization.

Yahoo! cofounders Jerry Yang and David Filo help Internet users overcome information anxiety by locating and organizing the mass of data available on the Web.

Inadequate Knowledge or Vocabulary   Before you can even begin to think about how you will communicate an idea, you must, first of all, *have* the idea; that is, you must have sufficient knowledge about the topic to know what you want to say. Regardless of your level of technical expertise, this may not be as simple as it sounds. Assume, for example, that you are Larry Haas, manager of the finance department at Urban Systems. Dave Kaplan, president of the company, has asked you to evaluate an investment opportunity. You've completed all the necessary research and are now ready to write your report. Or are you?

You must know enough about both your topic and your audience to express yourself precisely and appropriately.

Have you analyzed your audience? Do you know how much the president knows about the investment so that you'll know how much background information to include? Do you know how familiar Dave is with investment terminology? Can you safely use abbreviations like *NPV* and *RRR,* or will you have to spell out and perhaps define *net present value* and *required rate of return?* Do you know whether the president would prefer to have your conclusions at the beginning of the report, followed by your analysis, or at the end? What tone should the report take? The answers to such questions will be important if you are to achieve your objective in writing the report.

Differences in Interpretation   Sometimes senders and receivers attribute different meanings to the same word or attribute the same meaning to different words. When this happens, miscommunication can occur.

Every word has both a denotative and a connotative meaning. **Denotation** refers to the literal, dictionary meaning of a word. **Connotation** refers to the subjective, emotional meaning that you attach to a word. For example, the denotative meaning of the word *plastic* is "a synthetic material that can be easily molded into different forms." For some people, the word also has a negative connotative meaning— "cheap or artificial substitute."

A word's denotation defines its meaning; its connotation indicates our associations with the word.

Most of the interpretation problems occur because of the personal reactions engendered by the connotative meaning of a word. Do you have a positive, neutral, or negative reaction to the terms *broad, bad, aggressive, hard-hitting, workaholic,*

FIGURE 1.5   **Verbal and Nonverbal Barriers to Communication**

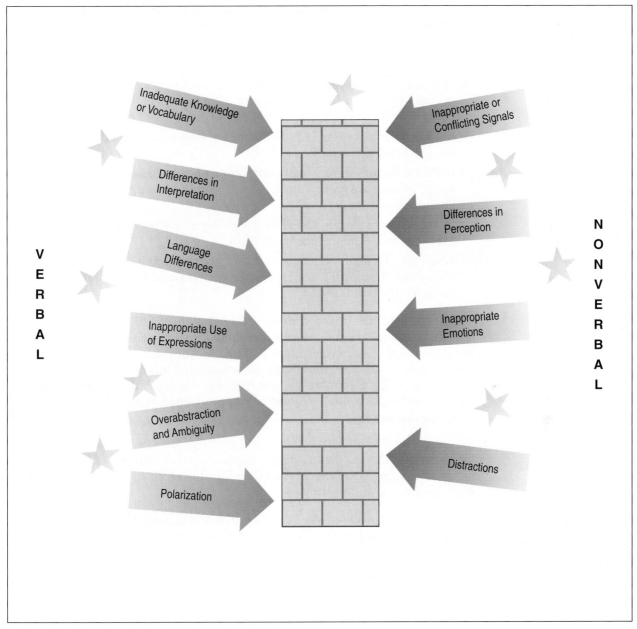

corporate raider, head-hunter, gay, golden parachute, or wasted? Are your reactions likely to be the same as everyone else's? The problem with some terms is not only that people assign different meanings to the term but also that the term itself might cause such an emotional reaction that the receiver is "turned off" to any further communication with the sender.

Language Differences   In an ideal world, all managers would know the language of each culture with which they deal. International businesspeople often say that you can buy in your native language anywhere in the world, but you can sell only in the language of the local community.

Most of the correspondence between American or Canadian firms and foreign firms is in English; in other cases, the services of a qualified interpreter (for oral communication) or translator (for written communication) may be available. But even with such services, problems can occur. Consider, for example, the following blunders:[5]

- In Brazil, where Portuguese is spoken, a U.S. airline advertised that its Boeing 747s had "rendezvous lounges," without realizing that *rendezvous* in Portuguese implies prostitution.
- In China, Kentucky Fried Chicken's slogan "Finger-lickin' good" was translated "So good you suck your fingers."
- In Puerto Rico, General Motors had difficulties advertising Chevrolet's Nova model because the name sounds like the Spanish phrase *No va,* which means "It doesn't go."
- In Thailand, the slogan "Come alive with Pepsi" was translated "Bring your ancestors back from the dead with Pepsi."
- When the CIA used a machine translation system to translate Russian, the Bible verse "The spirit is willing, but the flesh is weak" became "The vodka is good, but the beef is rotten."

To ensure that the intended meaning is not lost during translation, legal, technical, and all other important documents should first be translated into the second language and then retranslated into English. Be aware, however, that communication difficulties can arise even among native English speakers. For example, a British advertisement for Electrolux vacuum cleaners displayed the headline "Nothing Sucks Like An Electrolux." Copywriters in the United States and Canada would never use this wording!

Inappropriate Use of Expressions   Expressions are groups of words whose intended meanings are different from their literal interpretations. Examples include slang, jargon, and euphemisms.

The use of slang, jargon, and euphemisms is sometimes appropriate and sometimes inappropriate.

- **Slang** is an expression, often short-lived, that is identified with a specific group of people. Here, for example, are some slang terms (and their meanings) currently popular on college campuses:[6]

  Barbie—A painstakingly dressed and groomed female
  Brain burp—A random thought
  Circle of death—A lousy pizza
  Zoo a course—To fail
  Go for sushi—To kiss passionately
  McPaper—A quickly or poorly written paper
  Phat—Very cool
  Posse—Group of friends
  Rocks for jocks—Easy introductory geology course
  Velveeta—Something or someone cheesy

Teenagers, construction workers, immigrants, computer technology professionals, and just about every other subgroup you can imagine all have their own sets of slang. Using appropriate slang in everyday speech presents no problem; it conveys precise information and may indicate group membership. Problems arise, however, when the sender uses slang that the receiver doesn't understand. Slang that sends a negative nonverbal message about the sender can also be a source of problems.

■ **Jargon** is the technical terminology used within specialized groups; it has sometimes been called "the pros' prose." As with slang, the problem is not in using jargon—jargon provides a very precise and efficient way of communicating with those familiar with it. The problem comes in using jargon either with someone who doesn't understand it or in using jargon in an effort to impress others.

■ **Euphemisms** are inoffensive expressions used in place of words that may offend or suggest something unpleasant. Sensitive writers and speakers use euphemisms occasionally, especially to describe bodily functions. How many ways, for example, can you think of to say that someone has died?

Slang, jargon, and euphemisms all have important roles to play in business communication—as long as they're used with appropriate people and in appropriate contexts. They can, however, prove to be barriers to effective communication when used to impress, when used too often, or when used in inappropriate settings.

> **wordwise**
>
> **Anagrams**   An *anagram* is a word or phrase formed by reordering the letters of another word or phrase; for example:
>
> | | |
> |---|---|
> | ■ Conversation | *Voices rant on* |
> | ■ Listen | *Silent* |
> | ■ The Morse code | *Here come the dots* |
> | ■ The countryside | *No city dust here* |
> | ■ Clothespins | *So let's pinch* |
> | ■ Dormitory | *Dirty room* |

Overabstraction and Ambiguity   An **abstract word** identifies an idea or feeling instead of a concrete object. For example, *communication* is an abstract word, whereas *memorandum* is a **concrete word,** a word that identifies something that can be perceived by the senses. Abstract words are necessary in order to communicate about things you cannot see or touch. However, communication problems result when you use too many abstract words or when you use too high a level of abstraction. The higher the level of abstraction, the more difficult it is for the receiver to visualize exactly what the sender has in mind. For example, which sentence communicates more information: "I acquired an asset at the store" or "I purchased a laser printer at ComputerLand"?

The word transportation *is abstract; the word* automobile *is concrete.*

Similar communication problems result from the overuse of ambiguous terms such as *a few, some, several,* and *far away,* which have too broad a meaning for use in much business communication. For example, a report contained the following sentence: "The shipping department received a lot of complaints last month." Isn't it important to know exactly how many complaints they received?

Polarization   At times, some people act as though every situation is divided into two opposite and distinct poles, with no allowance for a middle ground. Of course, there are some true dichotomies. You are either male or female, and your company either will or will not make a profit this year. But most aspects of life involve more than two alternatives.

For example, you might assume that a speaker either is telling the truth or is lying. In fact, what the speaker actually says may be true, but by selectively omitting some important information, he or she may be giving an inaccurate impression. Is the speaker telling the truth or not? Most likely, the answer lies somewhere in between. Likewise, you are not necessarily either tall or short, rich or poor, smart or dumb. Competent communicators avoid inappropriate *either/or* logic and instead make the effort to search for middle-ground words when such language best describes a situation.

Thinking in terms of all or nothing limits our choices.

Nonverbal Barriers

Not all communication problems are related to what you write or say. Some are related to how you act. Nonverbal barriers to communication include inappropriate or conflicting signals, differences in perception, inappropriate emotions, and distractions.

Inappropriate or Conflicting Signals   Suppose a well-qualified applicant for a secretarial position submits a résumé with a typographical error or an accountant's personal office is in such disorder that she could not find the papers she needed for a meeting with the president. When verbal and nonverbal signals conflict, the receiver tends to put more faith in the nonverbal signals because nonverbal messages are more difficult to manipulate than verbal messages.

Many nonverbal signals vary from culture to culture. Remember also that the United States itself is a multicultural country: a banker from Boston, an art shop owner from San Francisco, and a farmer from North Dakota are likely to both use and interpret nonverbal signals in quite different ways. What is appropriate in one context might not be appropriate in another.

Communication competence requires that you communicate nonverbal messages that are consistent with your verbal messages and that are appropriate for the context.

Differences in Perception   Even when they hear the same speech or read the same document, people of different ages, socioeconomic backgrounds, cultures, and so forth often form very different perceptions. We discussed earlier the mental filter by which each communication source is interpreted. Because each person is unique, with unique experiences, knowledge, and viewpoints, each person forms a different opinion about what he or she reads and hears.

Some people tend automatically to believe certain people and to distrust other people. For example, when reading a memo from the company president, one employee may be so intimidated by the president that he or she accepts everything the president says, whereas another employee may have such negative feelings about the president that he or she believes nothing the president says.

It is generally more effective to depend on logic instead of emotions when communicating.

Inappropriate Emotions   In most cases, a moderate level of emotional involvement intensifies the communication and makes it more personal. However, too much emotional involvement can be an obstacle to communication. For example, excessive anger can create such an emotionally charged environment that reasonable discussion is not possible. Likewise, prejudice (automatically rejecting certain people or ideas), stereotyping (placing individuals into categories), and boredom all hinder effective communication. Such emotions tend to create a blocked mind that is closed to ideas, rejecting or ignoring information that is contrary to one's prevailing belief.

Distractions   Any environmental or competing element that restricts one's ability to concentrate on the communication task hinders effective communication. Such distractions are called **noise.** Examples of *environmental noise* are poor acoustics, extreme temperature, uncomfortable seating, body odor, poor telephone connections, and illegible photocopies. Examples of *competing noise* are other important business to attend to, too many meetings, and too many reports to read.

Competent communicators make the effort to write and speak clearly and consistently and try to avoid or minimize any verbal or nonverbal barriers that might cause misunderstandings.

Ethics and Communication

Each of us has a personal code of **ethics,** or rules of conduct, that might go beyond legal rules to tell us how to act when the law is silent. When composing a business proposal, drafting a sales letter, writing a personnel policy, or recruiting a candidate for a job, we make conscious decisions regarding what information to include and what information to exclude from our messages. For the information that *is* included, we make conscious decisions about how to phrase the language, how much to emphasize each point, and how to organize the message. Such decisions have legal and moral dimensions—both for you as the writer and for the organization.

Defamation

Any false and malicious statement that is communicated to others and that injures a person's good name or reputation may constitute **defamation.** Defamation in a temporary form such as in oral communication is called **slander;** defamation in a permanent form such as in writing or videotape is called **libel.** The three major conditions for defamation are that the statement be false, be communicated to others, and be harmful to a person's good name or reputation. Thus, telling Joe Smith to his face that he is a liar and a crook does not constitute defamation (slander) unless a third person hears the remarks. In addition, truth is generally an acceptable defense to a charge of defamation.

Competent communicators use objective language and verifiable information when communicating about others. For example, instead of saying, "Mr. Baker is a poor credit risk," they might say, "Mr. Baker was at least ten days late in making his payments to us four times during the past six months."

Invasion of Privacy

Any unreasonable intrusion into the private life of another person or denial of a person's right to be left alone may constitute an **invasion of privacy.** Thus, using someone's name or photograph in a sales promotion without that person's permission may be an invasion of privacy. Of particular concern today are the vast amounts of employee and customer information being maintained in corporate data banks. The proliferation of microcomputers, networks, and electronic mail makes it possible to access large amounts of data about employees and customers very freely.

Various state and federal laws protect the individual's right to privacy. The federal government defines *right to privacy* as "the right of individuals to participate in decisions regarding the collection, use, and disclosure of information personally identifiable to that individual."[7] Thus, someone's right to privacy may be violated if his or her records are read by someone not authorized to examine them.

Customers' perceptions of a company's ethical behavior can affect the bottom line. Consumers upset by the Valdez oil spill in Alaska's Prince William Sound returned 40,000 Exxon credit cards.

Oral defamation is slander. *Written defamation is* libel.

Competent communicators ensure that they do not misuse information about others in their communications and that their communications are available only to authorized people.

Fraud and Misrepresentation

A deliberate misrepresentation of the truth for the purpose of inducing someone to give up something of value is called **fraud.** Fraud can occur either when one party actually makes a deliberately false statement (called *active fraud*) or when one party deliberately conceals some information that he or she is required to reveal (*passive fraud*).

To be fraudulent, the statements must involve facts. Opinions and persuasive arguments or exaggerated claims about a product (called *sales puffery*) do not constitute fraud even if they turn out to be false. For example, "The Celeste is the only American-made car that comes with leather seats as standard equipment" is a statement of fact, which, if incorrect, might constitute fraud. However, "The Celeste is the most luxurious car in America" is an opinion; even if most car buyers did not agree with the statement, it would still not be considered fraud.

You should also recognize that a statement of opinion, even if it is not fraudulent, might still be unethical. For example, advertising that "The Celeste is the most luxurious car in America" might not be fraudulent; but it would be highly unethical if, in fact, you did not believe that to be the case.

Misrepresentation is a false statement that is made innocently with no intent to deceive the other party. If misrepresentation is proven, the contract or agreement may be rescinded. If fraud is proven, the contract or agreement may be rescinded, and the offended party may collect monetary compensation.

Competent communicators are aware of the relevant laws and ensure that their oral and written messages are accurate, in terms of what is communicated *and* what is left uncommunicated.

Other Ethical Considerations

A message can be true and still be unethical.

Sometimes being legally right is not sufficient justification for our actions (see Spotlight 2—On Law and Ethics on page 23). Many corporations have developed their own code of ethics to govern employee behavior. For the business communicator, the matter of ethics governs not only one's behavior but also one's communication of behavior. In other words, how we use language involves ethical choices.

When you have doubts about the ethical propriety of your writing, ask yourself these questions:

1. Is this message true?
2. Does it exaggerate?
3. Does it withhold or obscure information that should be communicated?
4. Does it promise something that cannot be delivered?
5. Does it betray a confidence?
6. Does it play unduly on the fears of the reader?
7. Does it reflect the wishes of the organization?

Competent communicators use their knowledge of communication to achieve their goals while acting in an ethical manner.

How Would You Respond?

How would you react to each of the following minicases on business ethics developed by Kirk Hanson, a senior lecturer at the Stanford University Graduate School of Business and corporate ethics consultant? Formulate your own responses before reading the suggested solutions.

SPOTLIGHT 2

ON LAW AND ETHICS

Situations

1. You are about to take a job with Almost Perfect, Inc. You like everything you have learned about the company except the reputation the firm has for long working hours. You have a young family and are committed to spending time with them. What role should the hours have in your decision?

2. You have been on the job for four days. Your boss hands you a report she hasn't had time to complete. "Just copy the numbers off last month's report," she says. "Nobody at headquarters ever really reads these." What do you do?

3. A new engineer who has just joined your group drops by your office and hands you a file stamped with the name of his former employer. "I thought you'd like to have a look at their list of key customers," he says. What do you do?

4. Despite a strongly worded company policy prohibiting gratuities from suppliers, you know your boss in the purchasing department is taking weeklong vacations paid for by a key vendor. What do you do?

Suggested Solutions

1. Turn down the job or negotiate openly for more reasonable hours. You will never be satisfied if you take a job that sets up a constant value conflict. Be willing to pay the price for a good family life.

2. Offer to collect the real data for the report. Everyone is tested in the first weeks by coworkers who favor shortcuts or small ethical compromises. Establish your values; insist on getting the real data if push comes to shove.

3. Give him back the folder unread and tell him, "We don't do things like that around here." Watch him carefully. If he wasn't faithful to his obligations to his former employer, he won't be faithful to you.

4. Report him to a higher authority in the company, but be sure you have some proof before you do. He has violated such a clear standard that it is unlikely he can be persuaded to stop. Ask the higher authority to protect you from retaliation.

Source: The Hanson Group, a corporate-ethics consultancy in Los Altos, California.

SUMMARY

The study of communication is important because communication is such a pervasive part of the organization and because it is so critical for achieving organizational goals. In fact, most managers spend the vast majority of their workday in some form of verbal communication.

The communication process begins with a stimulus. Based on your unique knowledge, experience, and viewpoints, you then filter, or interpret, the stimulus and formulate the message you wish to communicate. The next step is to select a medium of transmission for the message. Finally, the message reaches its destination. If it is successful, the receiver picks it up as a source for communication and provides appropriate feedback to you.

Verbal communication includes oral (speaking and listening) and written (writing and reading) communication. Common forms of written communication in business include memorandums, letters, e-mail messages, and reports.

The organization's formal communication network consists of downward communication from superiors to subordinates, upward communication from subordinates to superiors, horizontal communication among people at the same level, and cross-channel communication among people in different departments within the organization. The informal communication network (also called the grapevine) consists of information transmitted through nonofficial channels. Rather than try to eliminate it, managers should accept its existence and pay attention to it.

Sometimes barriers are present that interfere with effective communication. Examples of verbal barriers are inadequate knowledge or vocabulary, differences in interpretation, language differences, inappropriate use of expressions, overabstraction and ambiguity, and polarization. Examples of nonverbal barriers are inappropriate or conflicting signals, differences in perception, inappropriate emotions, and distractions.

Regardless of the size of the organization, every business writer faces ethical questions when communicating orally and in writing. Legal questions arise with regard to defamation, invasion of privacy, and fraud or misrepresentation. In choosing what information to convey, and by which words and sentences, we make ethical choices—moral decisions about what is right, even when no question of law is involved.

KEY TERMS

abstract word	invasion of privacy
audience	jargon
communication	letter
concrete word	libel
connotation	medium
defamation	memorandum
denotation	message
e-mail	misrepresentation
ethics	noise
euphemisms	nonverbal message
feedback	report
filter	slander
formal communication network	slang
fraud	stimulus
informal communication network	verbal message

REVIEW AND DISCUSSION

1. **Communication by Scott Adams Revisited**   Although Scott Adams lampoons business communication in his "Dilbert" cartoons, he is quite skilled at getting his points across in interviews, documents, and meetings.
   a.   When Adams participates in live interviews conducted via the Internet, he uses his PC to type in answers to questions posed by interviewers or people who have logged on to the event. What is the stimulus in this situation?

b. During an Internet interview, what is the destination of Adams's message?

c. Dilbert and his colleagues sometimes have to decipher memos from their pointy-haired boss. Are they receiving upward, downward, horizontal, or cross-channel communication?

2. What are the five components of the communication process?

3. What is meant by the statement "The stimulus is filtered through your brain"?

4. Give an example of a medium.

5. What are two forms of verbal communication? Give examples.

6. What four directions make up the formal communication network?

7. Why is it difficult to get objective information flowing upward in the organization?

8. What is the difference between horizontal and cross-channel communication?

9. What are the characteristics of the grapevine?

10. Give an example of the denotation and the connotation of a word.

11. What is the difference between slang and jargon? Give an example of each.

12. Compose a sentence containing an overabstraction. Then revise the sentence to make it more concrete.

13. Define *defamation* and describe the two types.

14. What is the difference between fraud and misrepresentation?

15. "Communicating is an ethical act." Discuss this statement.

EXERCISES

1. Communication Applications at the Office of Scott Adams   Now that his comic strip "Dilbert" has become a global sensation, Scott Adams is often called on to share his wit and wisdom through books, articles, interviews, and public speaking engagements. His corporate experience—and the anecdotes submitted by cubicle dwellers all over the world—have provided Adams with a wealth of information about the barriers to effective communication.

In this exercise, you are helping Scott Adams plan a speech about business communication, which he will deliver at a university commencement in Tokyo. He will be speaking in English to the graduating students, their professors, and the university's officials. As you help Adams, also think about how he can anticipate and plan to overcome the barriers to communication that sometimes lead to misunderstandings.

a. Why should Adams analyze his audience before planning the content of his speech?

b. What questions should he ask about his audience?

c. What is the medium that Adams will use for his message?

d. Which of the nonverbal barriers can Adams influence as he delivers his speech?

2. Getting to Know You   Write a two-page (typed, double-spaced) report introducing yourself to your instructor and to other members of the class. Include such information as the following:

■ *Background:* Your grade level, major, extracurricular activities, work experience, and the like.

■ *Career Objectives:* What type of position would you like immediately upon graduation? With what type of organization and in what part of the country would you like to work? Where do you expect to be in terms of your profession five years from now?

■ *Course Objectives:* Why are you taking this course? What specific skill or skills do you hope to master? What aspects of the course do you expect to find most challenging?

- *Small-Group Experiences:* What experience have you had in working on group projects? What are the advantages and disadvantages of such assignments? What type of group would you find most satisfying to work with?

Include any other information you think would be useful. Edit and proofread your draft and submit it.

3. **Communication Process**   Use an incident from a recent television program to illustrate each of the five components of the communication process. Identify any communication barriers that you observed.

4. **Work-Team Communication**   Approximately 1,500 words in this chapter were devoted to the discussion of the components of communication. Working in small groups, write a 250-word abstract (summary) of this discussion. Since this is an informational abstract, you may pick up the exact wording of the original discussion when appropriate. Ensure that all important points are covered, your narrative flows smoothly from one topic to another, and your writing is error-free.

5. **Communication Directions**   Think of an organization to which you belong or a business with which you are familiar. Provide a specific illustration of each of the four directions in the formal communication network. Then develop an organizational chart similar to the one in Figure 1.4.

6. **Grapevine**   Read a journal article about the company grapevine. Then write a one-page summary of the article. Proofread for content and language errors and revise as needed. Staple a photocopy of the article to your summary, and submit both to your instructor.

7. **Meanings Are in People**   Record your personal connotative meaning of each of the following terms: *tree hugger, profit, stress, conservative, alternative lifestyle, Japanese, affirmative action.*

8. **International**   "I'll never understand our people in Pakistan," Eileen said. "I wrote our local agent over there, who's supposedly a financial wizard, this note: 'If your firm wants to play ball with us, we'll need the straight scoop. What's your bottom-line price on the STX model with all the bells and whistles? Also, if you pull out all the stops, can we get delivery by Xmas?' And you know what he did? He wrote me back a long letter, inquiring about my health and my family, but never answering my questions! If they don't get on the ball, I'm going to recommend that we stop doing business with them." From a communication standpoint, what is happening here? What advice can you give Eileen? Rewrite her message to the Pakistani agent to make it more effective.

9. **Legal**   Sam was thinking of hiring Olivia Mason for an open sales territory. Knowing she had previously worked at Kentron, he called his friend there, Barry Kelley, to ask about her performance. "She's very smart, but I wouldn't hire her again, Sam," Barry said. "She's a little lazy. Sometimes she wouldn't begin making her calls until late morning or even after lunch. And she was also sloppy with her paperwork. I assume she's honest, but I never could get her to file receipts for all her expenses. Of course, she was going through a messy divorce then, so maybe that affected her job performance." Sam thanked his friend and notified Olivia that she was not being hired for the job. If Olivia learned of Kelley's com-

ments, would she have the basis for a legal suit? If so, what type and on what grounds? How could Kelley have reworded his comments to convey the information in a businesslike, ethical manner?

10. **Ethics**   After testing several new word processing programs, you wrote a memo to your supervisor requesting the purchase of 15 copies of WordPerfect for Windows® so that each member of your staff would have a copy. You just received your memo back from your supervisor with this handwritten note attached to it:

> I'm tired of purchasing software and then not have it do what it says it will do. Let's order one copy of the program first and make copies for all your staff. If in two months everyone is still happy with the program, I'll buy 14 more copies to make us legitimate.

How do you respond?

**CONTINUING
CASE 1**

Urban Systems Sees the Light

Marc Kaplan asked Dave to approve the following draft sales letter, which Marc wanted to mail out next month to the 4,200 members of the Office Furniture Dealers' Association (OFDA) as the kickoff campaign for Urban Systems' Ultra Light Strips. After reading the letter twice, Dave had still not approved it. Something about the tone of the letter bothered him.

Dear Manager:

Would you like us to come visit you in jail?

Now, it's true that you probably won't be put in jail for requiring your computer operators to sit in front of a monitor eight hours a day, but you just might get slapped with a lawsuit from a disgruntled employee who complains of back problems or failing eyesight. One pregnant employee even won damages by blaming her miscarriage on emotional stress caused by too many hours at her word processor! And two studies published this past year that warn of dangers from long periods of working at a computer don't help the situation any.

Before going to your lawyer, come to US—to Urban Systems—for the answer to your problems. We have recently patented a new strip lighting system for modular furniture that will throw precisely the right amount of soft light around the monitor. With Ultra Light Strips, your operators won't have to put up with glare from their monitors, they won't have to position themselves in a certain way just to read the monitor, and they won't have shadows falling on their copy holders.

And if wiring is in place, just about anyone can install Ultra Light Strips. Just order the lengths you need—from 1 foot to 20 feet long. They are completely flexible, so that you can easily bend them around your modular furniture. And because they attach with Velcro strips, you can move them around and reuse them as your needs change.

We're really the only game in town when it comes to flexible task lighting. For example, the Mod Light by GME produces 200 foot-candles—far too much light to provide the needed contrast between the screen and surrounding light; your operators will soon begin to make careless errors from visual fatigue. And the Light Mite from Tedesco has long had a reputation for poor reliability. In addition, both GME and Tedesco produce their light fixtures abroad, while Ultra Light Strips are 100% American-made! With Ultra Light Strips lighting the way, your operators will be more productive, easily paying the cost of these strips within the first six months of use. Get a jump on the competition. And avoid those costly legal battles. Call us toll-free at 1-800-555-2883 for a free on-site demonstration. We can also show you the many other uses of Ultra Light that will save your company money.

Sincerely,
Marc Kaplan
Vice President, Marketing

Critical Thinking

1. What is your reaction to this letter? Is it effective or not? Is it ethical? Explain.

2. If this letter represented your only knowledge of Urban Systems, what would be your opinion of the company? In other words, what kind of corporate image does the letter portray?

3. Without actually rewriting the letter, what revisions can you suggest for giving Marc's letter a more ethical tone?

APPENDIX TO CHAPTER 1

Urban Systems Inc.

The Company

Urban Systems, Inc. (US) is a small "start-up" company whose primary product is Ultra Light, a new, paper-thin light source that promises to revolutionize the illumination industry. The company employs 178 people at its corporate headquarters in Ann Arbor, Michigan, and in a completely automated manufacturing plant in Charlotte, North Carolina. It is incorporated under the laws of the state of Michigan, with all stock privately held by the founders and their families.

Urban Systems has annual sales in the $30 million range, with a net profit last year of $1.4 million. It is considered a progressive company by the investment community, with good management and good earnings potential. The local community considers US to be a good corporate citizen; it is a nonpolluting firm, and its officers are active in the local chamber of commerce and in community affairs.

The Product

Ultra Light is a flat, electroluminescent sheet of material that serves as a light source. It is capable of replacing most fluorescent, neon, and incandescent light fixtures. Physically, Ultra Light is a paper-thin sheet of chemically treated material laminated between thin layers of clear plastic. In effect, it is a credit-card–thin light fixture that is bendable and that can be produced in a variety of shapes and sizes. Operated either by battery or wall current, it generates a bright white or colored light.

Ultra Light is cost-competitive with other, more conventional lighting, and its life expectancy is measured in years. All of this, combined with the appeal of its very thin profile, battery operation ("use it anywhere"), the evenly distributed light it produces, and the way it can conform to a variety of physical shapes, makes Ultra Light a new product with a lot of potential.

Company History

US was founded in 1992 by two brothers, David and Marc Kaplan. David was a chemical engineer at Industrial Chemical, Inc., when he developed the basic concept of Ultra Light while working on another project.

Urban Systems headquarters in Ann Arbor, Michigan.

Because IC was not interested in pursuing the manufacturing and marketing of this product, David bought all rights to Ultra Light from IC and patented it in 1991. Then he and his younger brother Marc, formerly a marketing manager for an advertising agency in Chicago, started Urban Systems in an abandoned warehouse in Midland, Michigan.

The company received startup funds through personal investments of $50,000 by David Kaplan and $35,000 by Marc and a $68,500 five-year loan from the United States Small Business Administration. Because of Marc's advertising background, the company's five-year business plan focused on marketing Ultra Light initially for advertising purposes—to illuminate signs, point-of-purchase displays, and the like. Later, as the company became better established in the marketplace, plans were to expand into industrial, office, and consumer applications. Hence, a company name— Urban Systems—was selected that was broad enough to encompass a variety of products.

After a somewhat uneven start, US had become profitable by the end of its fourth year of operations and had outgrown its original building. The company recently built an 11,000-square-foot facility in an attractive office park in Ann Arbor, Michigan, to house its administrative, marketing, and R & D functions. The company also moved its manufacturing operations to Charlotte, North Carolina, in a leased facility. The manufacturing facility is completely automated, with state-of-the-art robotics, just-in-time inventory control, and a progressive union-management agreement. The latest three-year labor contract expires next year.

Personnel

The organization chart for Urban Systems is shown in Figure 1. Each corporate position and the person currently occupying that position are described below.

Board of Directors   The board is comprised of David J. Kaplan, chair; Marc Kaplan, vice-chair; Judith Klehr Kaplan (David Kaplan's wife), secretary/treasurer; Thomas V. Robertson, general counsel; and Eileen Jennings (vice president of U.S. National Bank of Michigan). As required by the articles of incorporation, the board meets quarterly at company headquarters.

FIGURE 1 Urban Systems Organizational Chart

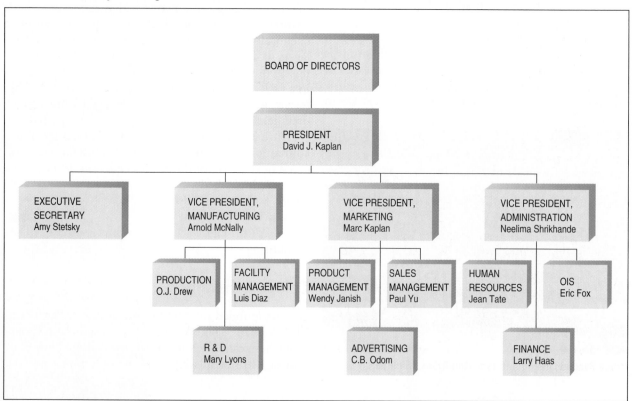

President
David J. Kaplan

Dave Kaplan, age 46, is a professional engineer-turned-manager. He graduated with honors from the Massachusetts Institute of Technology with a degree in chemical engineering. Upon graduation from MIT, he began working as a chemical engineer in the polymer division at Industrial Chemical, where he worked until 1992 when he started US. During his time at IC, he attended graduate school part-time at Central Michigan University, where he received his MBA degree in 1978. Although he was offered numerous management positions at IC, he elected to continue working as a chemical engineer. His work resulted in numerous profitable patents for IC, and he was considered a highly respected member of the scientific staff.

Dave has published numerous articles in scholarly journals, has presented papers in his area of specialty at several international conferences, and has served as president of the Michigan Society of Chemical Engineers.

Although he manages his new company effectively, Dave will tell you that some of his happiest times were working in the lab at IC—pursuing some esoteric research project alone and at his own pace. He will also tell you that the aspects of managing Urban Systems that he dislikes the most are the incessant meetings and having to manage and be responsible for the work of others. At US, Dave is considered a perfectionist and a workaholic. Although not an especially warm person, he is highly respected by his staff.

Dave married Judith Klehr immediately upon graduation from college. They have three children (Jonathan, 23, a newspaper reporter in Washington, DC; Michael, 22, a senior at Syracuse University; and Marla, 16, a sophomore in a private school in Ann Arbor). The family lives in Ann Arbor, where Judy is very active in community affairs.

Executive Secretary
Amy Stetsky

Amy Stetsky, or "Stetsky" as she is called by nearly everyone who knows her, was one of the first people hired by Dave Kaplan. She is 32 years old, has an associate's degree in office systems, and recently earned the Certified Professional Secretary (CPS®) designation as a result of passing an intensive two-day exam administered by a division of Professional Secretaries International. She is highly respected and well-liked by everyone in the organization.

Vice President, Manufacturing
Arnold McNally

Arnie McNally knows the production business from top to bottom. He is 57 years old and has been with the company from the beginning, having been hired away from a similar job at Steelcase Corporation. Although only a high school graduate, McNally has earned the respect of both Dave and his subordinates, including the engineers in the research and development unit.

Arnie gives his staff wide latitude in running their units. He supports them, even when they make mistakes. He does insist, however, on being kept informed at every step of the way. He is a very direct type of person—you always know where you stand with him. If any of his subordinates have some bad news to convey, they know he wants to know immediately and directly—with no beating around the bush.

Although he gets along well with both Dave and his subordinates, he and Marc Kaplan have had several run-ins during the past five years. Privately, he would tell you that he believes Marc is a "lightweight" who is not particularly effective in marketing the firm's products. Arnie is especially upset that Marc has shot down several new product ideas proposed by Arnie's R & D staff.

Vice President, Marketing
Marc Kaplan

People who know both Dave and Marc Kaplan cannot believe they are brothers. Marc, age 42, is the complete opposite of Dave. He is warm and outgoing, with a wide circle of friends both in and out of business. His extensive network of personal and professional contacts has resulted in numerous large and lucrative orders for the firm.

Marc depends heavily on his three managers, especially for inhouse operations. He spends a great deal of time away from the office—entertaining customers and prospective customers, attending conventions where US exhibits its products, and making the rounds of golf tournaments and after-hours cocktail parties. Marc is divorced and lives in a high-rise condominium in Ann Arbor, where he has a very active social life.

Marc is aware of Arnie's feelings about him but brushes them aside as normal jealousy. He believes that if he could get Arnie to go on a golf outing with him a few times, things could be patched up. As it is, although their relationship is somewhat strained, it is not affecting either's ability to do his job.

Vice President, Administration
Neelima Shrikhande

Aged 38, Neelima Shrikhande (pronounced *Nee-LEE-ma Shree-KON-dee*) is from India. She has a master of science degree in management information systems from Stanford University. She was promoted to her present position only last year, having served as manager of the Office and Information Systems (OIS) unit at Urban Systems for four years prior to that.

Neelima is single and an ardent feminist. She is also very involved in politics and worked extensively in the unsuccessful campaign of Walter K. Mason, the Liberal Party candidate for governor of Michigan last year.

Neelima manages the division that houses both the human resources function and the office function; the office function employs a large number of clerical and secretarial workers (all of whom are female). When Dave Kaplan offered her the promotion to vice president, Neelima informed him that one of her goals would be to institute policies that would upgrade the role of females within the company. Although she gets along well with Arnie McNally, she resents Marc Kaplan's sometimes condescending attitude toward her and what she considers his chauvinistic attitude toward many of the females on his staff.

Financial Data

By year's end, assets for Urban Systems totaled $23.2 million, with net income of $1.4 million. Earnings per share for the current year were $1.08; and a dividend of $0.64 per share was paid on the 1.3 million outstanding shares (all of which are held by the two Kaplan families). This and other financial information are contained in the most recent financial statements for Urban Systems, shown in Figures 2 and 3.

FIGURE 2   Balance Sheet

Urban Systems Balance Sheet December 31, 19—

Assets		Liabilities and Shareholders' Equity	
Current Assets:		Current Liabilities:	
Cash and marketable securities	423,600	Notes payable	3,250,000
Trade receivables	4,942,400	Accounts payable	4,971,800
Inventories	5,645,100	Accrued compensation and taxes	946,100
Prepaid expenses	307,500	Other liabilities	952,500
Total Current Assets	11,318,600	Long-term debt due within one year	205,300
Other Assets	5,825,200	Total Current Liabilities	10,325,700
Property and Equipment:		Long-Term Debt	1,345,600
Land	255,300	Deferred Federal Income Taxes	1,800,500
Buildings and improvements	4,291,600	Shareholders' Equity:	
Machinery and equipment	5,749,500	Common stock—par value $1.00 per share	
Furniture and fixtures	347,100	Authorized shares: 3,000,000	
Total	10,643,500	Outstanding shares: 1,327,500	1,435,800
Less allowances for depreciation	4,558,600	Additional capital	7,147,900
Total Property and Equipment	6,084,900	Retained earnings	1,173,200
TOTAL ASSETS	23,228,700	Total Shareholders' Equity	9,756,900
		TOTAL LIABILITIES AND SHAREHOLDERS' EQUITY	23,228,700

FIGURE 3   Income Statement

Urban Systems Statement of Operations For the Year Ended December 31, 19—

Net Sales	29,750,100
Operating Costs and Expenses:	
Cost of Sales	23,026,400
Selling and Administrative Expenses	2,795,200
Interest Income—Net	(289,500)
Other Income—Net	(97,500)
Total Operating Costs and Expenses	27,434,600
Income from Continuing Operations Before Taxes	2,315,500
Provision for Federal Income Taxes:	
Current	689,900
Deferred	195,400
Total Federal Income Taxes	885,300
Net Income	1,430,200
Retained Earnings:	
Retained Earnings—January 1	1,323,600
Dividends per Share—$0.64	849,600
Retained Earnings—December 31	1,173,200
Earnings per Share	1.08

2

Work-Team Communication

An Insider's Perspective

Need a decision? Call a meeting. That's the advice of Amy Hilliard-Jones, president and founder of Hilliard-Jones Marketing Group, a firm that helps Fortune 500 businesses develop advertising, promotion, and public relations programs to reach out to African-American, Hispanic, and Asian consumers across the country. With her assistance, insurance providers, technology companies, food conglomerates, and financial services firms learn how to communicate more effectively by bridging differences in culture and language among these growing segments of the U.S. population.

Although organizations hold meetings for a variety of reasons, one of the most important reasons is to come to a decision. "Face-to-face meetings expedite decisions," maintains Hilliard-Jones. "Many times, if you have the right people at the meeting, you can get a decision right away."

Conducting a meeting with a diverse group of employees, suppliers, or customers requires facilitative leadership. "When leading a meeting with people who are not directly under your authority, it is particularly important to help all members feel they are making a contribution," says Hilliard-Jones. In such situations, she gets participants involved even before the meeting is held by soliciting suggestions for the agenda and asking what they want the meeting to accomplish. "Meetings tend to evolve," she observes, "but the leader can bring people back to the desired focus as long as an agenda and common goals have been established up front."

Hilliard-Jones also reserves at least some time for every individual to comment, which avoids potential conflict while bringing multiple viewpoints to the group's attention. "Most conflict is a result of people wanting to be heard," she says. "But no one has the right to monopolize the meeting or jeopardize a productive outcome. You've got to balance people's right to be heard with the larger goal of being productive in a democratic way." As a leader and a participant, she also understands the importance of listening. "Sometimes it's difficult to listen without having your response percolating in your mind, but you need to clear your mind and concen-

COMMUNICATION OBJECTIVES

After you have finished this chapter, you should be able to

■ Communicate effectively in small groups.

■ Explain the meaning of nonverbal messages communicated in different cultures.

■ Listen effectively in business situations.

■ Plan, conduct, and participate in a business meeting.

■ Use a professional demeanor and appropriate behavior to maintain effective working relationships.

trate on what the other person is saying." Her advice? "Treat others the way you would like to be treated. If you want other people to listen to your point of view, be sure that you are giving them the same opportunity."

Nonverbal communication is a good way to convey that you are really listening. "For example, sitting with arms folded signals that you're closed," she explains, "but sitting with arms open and eyes focused on the speaker signals that you're listening and you welcome that person's input." In meetings with participants from other cultures, Hilliard-Jones suggests paying close attention to both verbal and nonverbal communication. "Because some people are less emotive in their use of hand gestures, facial expressions, or voice inflection, you really have to be sensitive to the timing of a comment as well as the content and the intensity of the language being used."

Taking notes during a meeting helps participants and leaders remember what has been decided and what must be done next. This is especially important when deadlines loom and there is no time for a follow-up memo. During projects with tight schedules, Hilliard-Jones prefers to consult her notes and summarize the results before a meeting ends. "Taking notes during meetings can serve as a

Amy Hilliard-Jones

President and founder, Hilliard-Jones Marketing Group (Chicago, Illinois)

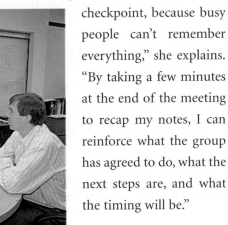

checkpoint, because busy people can't remember everything," she explains. "By taking a few minutes at the end of the meeting to recap my notes, I can reinforce what the group has agreed to do, what the next steps are, and what the timing will be."

Communicating in Work Teams

A **team** is a group of individuals who depend on one another to accomplish a common objective. Teams are often superior to individuals because they can accomplish more work, are more creative, have more information available to them, and offer more interpersonal communication dynamics. On the other hand, teams can waste time, accomplish little work, and create an environment in which interpersonal conflict can rage.

Two to seven members seems to be the most appropriate size range for most effective work teams. Small-team research indicates that five is an ideal size.[1] Smaller teams often do not have enough diversity of skills and interests to function effectively as a team, whereas larger teams may lack healthy team interaction because just a few people may dominate the discussions.

If the group is too large, members may begin to form cliques, or subgroups.

The Variables of Group Communication

Three factors—conflict, conformity, and consensus—greatly affect the efficiency with which a team operates and the amount of enjoyment members derive from it.

Conflict   Conflict is a greatly misunderstood facet of group communication. Many group leaders work hard to avoid conflict because they think it detracts from a group's goals. Their attitude is that a group experiencing conflict is not running smoothly and is destined to fail.

In fact, conflict is what group meetings are all about. One purpose of collaborating on a project is to ensure that various viewpoints are heard so that agreement as to the most appropriate course of action can emerge. Groups can use conflict productively to generate and test ideas before they are implemented. Rather than indicating that a meeting is disorderly, the presence of conflict indicates that members are actively discussing the issues. If a group does not exhibit conflict by debating ideas or questioning others, there is very little reason for it to exist. The members may as well be working individually.

Debate issues, not personalities.

Conflict, then, is the essence of group interaction. Competent leaders use conflict as a means to determine what is and what is not an acceptable idea or solution. Note, however, that the conflict we are talking about involves debate about *issues*, not about *personalities*. Interpersonal conflict can, indeed, have serious negative consequences for work teams.

Conformity   Conformity is agreement with regard to ideas, rules, or principles. Members may be encouraged to disagree about the definition of a problem or possible solutions, but certain fundamental issues—such as how the group should operate—should be agreed to by everyone.

Although group conformity and group cohesiveness are necessary for successful small-group communication, too much cohesiveness can result in what has been termed **groupthink,** the barrier to communication that results from an overemphasis on unity, which stifles opposing ideas and the free flow of information[2] (see Figure 2.1).

The pressure to conform can become so great that negative information and contrary opinions are never even brought out into the open and discussed. Thus, the group loses the advantage of hearing and considering various perspectives. In

FIGURE 2.1   **Effect of Excessive Conformity on a Group's Productivity**

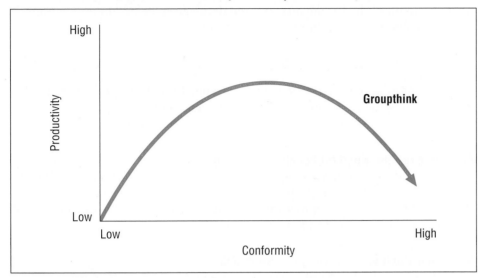

effective work-team communication, conflicts, different opinions, and questions are considered an inevitable and essential part of the collaborative process.

Consensus   Consensus means reaching a decision that best reflects the thinking of all team members. It is finding a solution that is acceptable enough that all members can support it (perhaps, though, with reservations) and that no member actively opposes it. Consensus is not necessarily a unanimous vote, or even a majority vote, because in a majority vote only the majority get something they are happy with; people in the minority may have to accept something they don't like at all.

Consensus does not mean a unanimous vote—or even necessarily a majority vote.

Not every decision, of course, needs to have the support of every member; to push for consensus on every matter would require a tremendous investment of time and energy. The group should decide ahead of time when to push for consensus— for example, when reaching decisions that have a major impact on the direction of the project or the conduct of the team.

Initial Group Goals

It is difficult to work effectively as a team if the team members do not know one another well and are not aware of each member's strengths and weaknesses, styles of working, experiences, attitudes, and the like. Thus, the first task of most new teams is to get to know one another. For small teams to function effectively, not only the task dimension but also the social dimension must be considered. Some amount of "small talk" about family, friends, current happenings, and the like before and after the meetings is natural and helps to establish a supportive and open environment. You want to be able to compliment each other without embarrassment and to disagree without fear.

The group's first task is to get to know one another.

Too often, decisions just "happen" in a team; members may go along with what they think everyone else wants. Teams should therefore discuss how they will make decisions and should develop operating rules. They should talk about what would be legitimate reasons for missing a meeting, establish a procedure for informing others of an absence beforehand and of keeping the absent member informed of what was accomplished at the meeting, and decide what being "on time" means. In short, they should develop "norms" for the team.

Giving Constructive Feedback

Giving and receiving feedback should be a part of every team's culture.

The single most important skill to have in working through any problem is the ability to give constructive feedback. There are proven methods for giving and receiving criticism that work equally well for giving and receiving praise.[3]

Acknowledge the Need for Feedback   Feedback is vital; it is the only way to find out what needs to be improved and should be an overall part of the organization's culture. Thus, your team must agree that giving and receiving feedback is an acceptable part of how you will improve the way you work together. This way, no one will be surprised when he or she receives feedback.

Give Both Positive and Negative Feedback   Many people take good work for granted and give feedback only when there are problems. Unfortunately, this habit is counterproductive. People are far more likely to pay attention to your complaints if they have also received your compliments.

Learn How to Give Feedback   Use these guidelines for compliments as well as complaints:

1. *Be descriptive.* Relate objectively what you saw or what you heard. Give specific examples: the more recent, the better.
2. *Avoid using labels.* Words like *undependable, unprofessional, irresponsible,* and *lazy* are labels we attach to behaviors. Instead, describe the behaviors and drop the labels.

A new type of human-resource tool, called 360-degree feedback, lets your boss, your peers, and your subordinates anonymously rate you on personality, values, talents, ethics, and leadership traits. The purpose is to provide you with constructive information to help you become a better manager. For Robert Saldich, CEO of Raychem, feedback from his top team allowed him to work on shortcomings he thought he had kept hidden.

3. *Don't exaggerate.* Be exact. To say, "You're always late for deadlines" is probably untrue and therefore unfair.
4. *Speak for yourself.* Don't refer to absent, anonymous people ("A lot of people here don't like it when you . . . ").
5. *Use "I" statements.* This is perhaps the most important guideline. For example, instead of saying, "You are frequently late for meetings," say, "I feel annoyed when you are late for meetings." "I" statements create an adult/peer relationship (see Figure 2.2).

"I" statements tell specifically how someone's behavior affects you.

FIGURE 2.2   Using "I" Statements When Giving Feedback

Sequence	Explanation
1. "When you . . . "	Start with a "When you . . . " statement that describes the behavior without judgment, exaggeration, labeling, attribution, or motives. Just state the facts as specifically as possible.
2. "I feel . . . "	Tell how the behavior affects you. If you need more than a word or two to describe the feeling, it's probably just some variation of joy, sorrow, anger, or fear.
3. "Because I . . . "	Now say why you are affected that way. Describe the connection between the facts you observed and the feelings they provoke in you.
(4. Pause for discussion)	Let the other person respond.
5. "I would like . . . "	Describe the change you want the other person to consider . . .
6. "Because . . . "	. . . and why you think the change will alleviate the problem.
7. "What do you think?"	Listen to the other person's response. Be prepared to discuss options and compromise on a solution.

How the feedback will work:

When you [do this], I feel [this way], because [of such and such]. What I would like you to consider is [doing X], because I think it will accomplish [Y]. What do you think?

Example:

"When you are late for meetings, I get angry because I think it is wasting the time of all the other team members and we are never able to get through our agenda items. I would like you to consider finding some way of planning your schedule that lets you get to these meetings on time. That way we can be more productive at the meetings and we can all keep to our tight schedules."

Source: From Peter R. Scholtes, *The Team Handbook,* Madison, WI: Joiner Associates, 1988, pp. 6–27. Copyright © 1988 Joiner Associates Inc. Reprinted with permission.

Solving Group Problems

Most problems can be anticipated or prevented if a group spends time developing itself into a team, getting to know one another, establishing ground rules, discussing norms for group behavior, and the like. However, no matter how much planning is done or how conscientiously team members work, group problems occasionally show up.

React to problems appropriately, consider them "group" problems, and have realistic expectations about the group process.

One of the worst tactics to take is to accept problems blindly. Problems rarely disappear on their own. However, you should neither overreact nor underreact to group problems. Some behaviors are only fleeting disruptions and can be ignored. Others are chronic and disruptive and must be resolved.

Think of each problem as a group problem. Groups should avoid the temptation to defuse conflicts by making a scapegoat of one member—for example, "We'd be finished with this report now if Sam had done his part; you never can depend on him." Rarely is one person solely responsible for the success or failure of a group effort. Examine each problem in light of what the group does to encourage or allow the behavior and what the group can do differently to encourage more constructive behavior. Because every member's role is a function of both his or her own personality and the group's personality, the group should consider how to help every person contribute more to the collaborative efforts.

Finally, be realistic. Don't assume responsibility for the happiness of others. You are responsible for behaving ethically and for treating other group members with respect, but the purpose of the group is not to develop lifelong friendships or to solve other people's time-management or personal problems.

Competent communicators welcome all contributions from group members, regardless of whether the members agree or disagree with their own views. They

Team writing and collaboration involves designing a set of measurement criteria that everyone can agree on. Hewlett-Packard's Industrial Lab investigative team needed to do just that in order to assess and report on the impact of Research and Development contributions to the company. The team's first step was to identify the core values that they shared in measuring effectiveness.

evaluate each contribution objectively and respond in a nonthreatening manner, with comments that are factual, constructive, and goal-oriented. If the atmosphere becomes tense, they make a light comment, laugh, compliment, recall previous incidents, or take other helpful actions to restore harmony and move the group forward. If interpersonal conflict appears to be developing into a more or less permanent part of the group interactions, the group should put the topic of conflict on its agenda and then devote sufficient meeting time to discussing and working through the conflict.

Team Writing

The increasing quantity and complexity of the workplace makes it difficult for any one person to have either the time or the expertise to be able to identify and solve many of the problems that arise and prepare written responses. This is especially true for long or complex documents. The differing talents, skills, and perspectives of several individuals are often needed in a joint effort to analyze a given situation and generate proposals or recommendations. Thus, team writing is becoming quite prevalent in organizations. (As a matter of fact, collaborative communication has always been much more common in organizations than many people realized.)

Writing as part of a team is a common task in contemporary organizations.

In addition to the general team-building guidelines discussed in the previous section, writing teams should follow these strategies:

Assign Tasks and Develop a Schedule   Start by determining the goals of the project and identifying the reader. Determine the components of the project, what research is needed, and when each aspect needs to be completed. Then divide the tasks equitably, based on each member's needs, interests, expertise, and commitment to the project.

Develop a work schedule— and stick to it.

Meet Regularly   Schedule regular meetings throughout the project to pool ideas, keep track of new developments, assess progress, avoid overlap and omissions, and, if necessary, to renegotiate the workload and redefine tasks. As soon as the initial data-gathering phase is complete, confer as a group to develop an outline for the finished project. This outline should show the sequence of major and subordinate topics in the document. Beware of a "data-dump," in which every bit of information gathered is dumped into the final document. All the information that you collect doesn't necessarily have to be included in the report.

Meet frequently to ensure smooth coordination of the project.

Draft the Document   The goal at this stage is not to prepare a finished product but to draft all of the content. You have two options:

■ *Assign parts to different members.* Having each member write a different part of the document provides an equitable distribution of the work and may result in a faster draft. You must ensure, however, that each member is writing in his or her area of expertise and that all are agreed on such style issues as the degree of formality, direct versus indirect organization, and use of preview and summary.

---

wordwise

Would you say that . . .

■ the U.S. trade deficit is news of considerable import?
■ conglomerates are known by the companies they keep?
■ people who sell perfume are always sticking their business into your nose?
■ jingle writers work under ad verse conditions?
■ librarians are shelf-employed?
■ a seed catalog is a kernel journal?
■ a dessert cart is a calorie gallery?
■ jargon is pros' prose?

■ *Assign one person to draft the entire document.* Assigning one member (presumably the most gifted writer) to draft the entire document helps guarantee a more consistent writing style and lessens the risk of serious omissions or duplication. You must, however, provide sufficient guidance to the writer and allow ample time for one person to complete the entire writing task.

Ensure that the final group document "speaks with one voice"—that is, it is coherent and unified.

One common pitfall in team writing is the failure to achieve a single "voice" in the project. Regardless of who prepares each individual part of the report, the final report must look and sound as though it were prepared by one writer. Think of the report as a whole, rather than as a collection of parts. Organize and present the data so that the report comes across as coherent and unified.

Revise the Draft   Be sure to allow enough time for editing the draft. This is best accomplished by providing each member with a copy of the draft beforehand (to allow time for reading and annotating) and then meeting as a group to review each section for errors in content, gaps or repetition, and effective writing style. Alternately, you may decide to use groupware software to revise your document electronically (see Spotlight 3—On Technology, pp. 44–45).

Do not neglect the final step of proofreading.

Decide who will be responsible for making the changes to each section, how the document will be formatted, and who will be responsible for proofreading the final document. Typically, one person (preferably not the typist) will be assigned to review the final draft for consistency and correctness in content, style, and format.

The Ethical Dimension of Work-Team Communication

Concentrate on group goals rather than individual goals.

Accepting membership on a team implies acceptance of certain standards of ethical behavior. One of the most basic of these is to put the good of the team ahead of personal gain. Just as the successful ball player declares, "I don't care if I score as long as my team wins," so also should the successful team player in the organization adopt the attitude "I don't care who gets the credit as long as we achieve our goal."

Elsie Cross Associates runs a three-day retreat for work-team members to raise awareness, examine racial and gender bias, and seek ways to change. According to Cross, "there is anger, shouting, and sometimes tears" at these workshops, but the goal is always constructive feedback and change.

Team members should set aside hidden agendas in their team actions and avoid advocating positions that might benefit them personally but that would not be best for the team.

Team members also have an ethical responsibility to respect the integrity and emotional needs of one another. Everyone's ideas should be treated with respect, and no action should be taken that results in a loss of self-esteem for a member.

Finally, each member has an ethical responsibility to promote the team's welfare—by contributing his or her best efforts to the team's mission and by refraining from destructive gossip, domination of meetings, and other counterproductive actions.

Nonverbal Communication

Not all the communication that occurs on work teams, or on the job in general, is spoken, heard, written, or read—that is, verbal. According to management guru Peter Drucker, "The most important thing in communication is to hear what isn't being said."[4] A nonverbal message is any message that is not written or spoken. The nonverbal message may accompany a verbal message (smiling as you greet a colleague), or it may occur alone (selecting the back seat when entering the conference room for a staff meeting). Nonverbal messages are typically more spontaneous than verbal messages, but that does not mean that they are any less important. One study has shown that only 7% of the meaning communicated by most messages comes from the verbal portion, with the remaining 93% being conveyed nonverbally.[5]

Nonverbal messages are unwritten and unspoken.

The six most common types of nonverbal communication in business are discussed in the following sections.

Body Movement

By far, the most expressive part of your body is your face—especially your eyes. Research shows that receivers tend to be quite consistent in their reading of facial expressions. In fact, many of these expressions have the same meaning across different cultures.[6] Eye contact and eye movements tell you a lot about a person, although—as we shall see later—maintaining eye contact with the person to whom you're speaking is not perceived as important (or even polite) in some cultures.

Cultures differ in the importance they attach to eye contact.

DILBERT

Using Groupware to Edit Team Writing

Once upon a time, to edit a group report you'd first print out several copies and distribute them to your team members; then they'd handwrite their comments on their copies and send them back to you. Finally, you'd manually collate the copies, make whatever changes were necessary, and print out a final copy of the report. Those days are fading fast.

Today, the advent of computer technology, and especially *groupware*, has greatly enhanced the effectiveness and efficiency of collaborative writing. **Groupware** (such as Lotus Notes) is a broad category of business software that automates information sharing and enables work teams to communicate electronically and to coordinate their efforts painlessly.

For example, using an electronic conferencing system, each group member (may be in the same room or on different continents) sits in front of a computer terminal and keyboard. Each time a member enters some information on his or her computer, that message is instantly visible on everyone's computer screen. Thus, people can fully participate in a meeting even though they are geographically remote. In addition, they can vote anonymously if desired; and all decisions and action items from the meeting are recorded electronically and can be distributed electronically. Sophisticated conferencing systems also include video cameras to transmit both verbal and nonverbal messages.

SPOTLIGHT 3

ON

TECHNOLOGY

One type of groupware, sometimes called a *group-authoring system,* is geared specifically to team writing. CommonSpace (Boston: Houghton Mifflin, Ver 1.1 ©1996), for example, is a software program that enhances the process of collaborative writing by enabling team members to comment with ease on one another's writing. The program keeps an "edit trail" of changes made, who made them, and when. Because group members can comment on both the original draft and other members' comments and raise and answer questions, such programs can reduce the need for time-consuming face-to-face meetings.

Assume, for example, your team is writing a training manual on connecting to the Internet. As the designated writer for the group, you have created the draft of your document shown on screen **a.** This draft could have been created directly in CommonSpace or it could have been created in any word processing program and then opened in CommonSpace. You then e-mail a copy of your draft to the other two

a.

```
 File  Edit  Format  Font  Style  Column  Workspaces
```

Workspace of Lesson2a.csp

Original Text

Making Sense of the Internet

   Getting on to the Internet is fairly easy. It's not as arduous a task as it used to be. Not long ago, starting to use the Internet meant exploring the depths of network hardware and software, but now, there are graphical interfaces that makes it easier to connect and use the Internet.

   The first thing you need is a provider. Once you have a provider, you're virtually connected. The "net" is not owned, so there's no one place that one can go to get information. It's scattered. There are the major online services to consider, but you may find that they are expensive and their services are sometimes incomplete.

   There are plenty of lists of providers. Several organizations and individuals have compiled lists. But many of the lists don't list every provider; some are wrong because providers also go out of business. Then there are the online lists. But to get online lists you must be online. You might try asking a friend. If a friend is on the Internet, then they can help you get lists (see "Toll Roads on the Net").

b.

```
 File  Edit  Format  Font  Style  Column  Workspaces
```

Workspace of Internet.csp

Original Text

Making Sense of the Internet

   Getting on to the Internet is fairly easy. It's not as arduous a task as it used to be. Not long ago, starting to use the Internet meant exploring the depths of network hardware and software, but now, there are graphical interfaces that makes it easier to connect and use the Internet.

   The first thing you need is a provider. Once you have a provider, you're virtually connected. The "net" is not owned, so there's no one place that one can go to get information. It's scattered. There are the major online services to consider, but you may find that they are expensive and their services are sometimes incomplete.

   There are plenty of lists of providers. Several

David's Comments

Is the report really about "Making Sense"? How about: Making the Internet Connection?

I think we need to tell them what a provider is up front. How to define? Something like: An Internet provider sells access to the Internet, typically via a local dial-up service?

team members—David Hua and Calandra Wilson. They have several options for annotating your draft.

David chooses to create a second column, in which he can comment on the original text. He highlights the text he wants to address and then types his comment in the second column. Because each comment is linked to a specific word or phrase in the original document, his comment will always appear opposite the pertinent highlighted word or phrase. As shown on page 44 (screen **b**), David's first comment is a question about the title you've given to this section of the report. After keying in his remarks, he saves the document (which now contains both the original draft and all of his comments) and e-mails it back to you.

You also e-mailed a copy of your draft to your third team member, Calandra Wilson, who prefers to do line-by-line editing. To preserve the original version intact, she first has CommonSpace make a side-by-side copy of the original text (see screen **c**) and then uses traditional word processing commands to edit the copy. Then she e-mails the complete file back to you.

You, in turn, open the document and view the annotations David and Calandra made. It's easy, of course, to follow David's comments but a little more difficult to determine what specific changes Calandra made. Therefore, you use the "compare" feature of CommonSpace (screen **d**), which identifies each change Calandra made to the original text.

Finally, you make whatever changes are needed in the original document and print out a fully formatted final copy. If you prefer, you can respond to the changes and send the file, including all annotations, back to your teammates for another round of review. When you're finished, you can save just the final document with or without the comments—or you can save all versions of the document, in case your team later changes its mind about a revision.

Source: Screens adapted from Common Space™. Copyright © 1997 by Sixth Floor Media. Used with permission of Houghton Mifflin Company.

c.

d.

Gestures are hand and upper-body movements that add important information to face-to-face interactions. As the game of charades proves, you can communicate quite a bit without using oral or written signals. More typically, gestures are used to help illustrate and reinforce your verbal message.

Body stance (posture, placement of arms and legs, distribution of weight, and the like) is another form of nonverbal communication. For example, leaning slightly toward the person you're communicating with would probably be taken as a sign of interest and involvement in the interaction. On the other hand, leaning back with arms folded across the chest might be taken (and intended) as a sign of boredom or defiance.

Physical Appearance

Our culture places great value on physical appearance. Television, newspapers, and magazines are filled with advertisements for personal-care products, and the ads typically feature attractive users of these products. Attractive people tend to be seen as more intelligent, more likable, and more persuasive than unattractive people; in addition, they earn more money.[7]

Your appearance is particularly important for making a good first impression. Although you may not be able to change some of your physical features, understanding the importance of good grooming and physical appearance can help you to emphasize your strong points. Also, your clothing, jewelry, office and home furnishings, and automobile provide information about your values, taste, heritage, conformity, status, age, sexuality, and group identification.

Voice Qualities

No one speaks in a monotone. To illustrate, read the following sentence aloud, each time emphasizing the italicized word. Note how the meaning changes with each reading.

- *You* were late. (*Answers the question "Who was late?"*)
- You *were* late. (*Responds to the other person's denial of being late.*)
- You were *late*. (*Emphasizes how late the person was.*)

Voice qualities such as volume, speed, pitch, tone, and accent carry both intentional and unintentional messages. For example, when you are nervous, you tend to speak faster and at a higher pitch than normal. People who constantly speak too softly risk being interrupted or ignored, whereas people who constantly speak too loudly are often seen as being pushy or insecure.

Time

The meaning we attach to time depends upon our status, the specific situation, and our culture.

How do you feel when you're late for an appointment? when others are late? The meaning given to time varies greatly by culture, with North American cultures being much more time conscious than South American or Middle Eastern cultures.

Time is related not only to culture but also to one's status within the organization. You would be much less likely to keep a superior waiting for an appointment than you would a subordinate. Time is also situation-specific. Although you normally might not worry about being five minutes late for a staff meeting, you would probably arrive early if you were the first presenter.

Touch

Touch is the first sense we develop, acquired even before birth. Some touches, such as those made by a physician during an examination, are purely physical; others, such as a handshake, are a friendly sign of willingness to communicate; and still others indicate intimacy. Although touching is a very important form of business communication, it is one that most people do not know how to use appropriately and effectively. The person who never touches anyone in a business setting may be seen as cold and standoffish, whereas the person who touches too frequently may cause the receiver to feel apprehensive and uncomfortable.

Space and Territory

When you are on a crowded elevator, you probably look at the floor indicator, at advertisements, at your feet, or just straight ahead. Most people in our culture are uncomfortable in such close proximity to strangers. Psychologists have identified four zones within which people in our culture interact:[8]

1. *Intimate Zone:* From physical contact to about 18 inches is where all your body movements occur; this is the area in which you move throughout the day. It is an area normally reserved for close, intimate interactions. Business associates typically enter this space infrequently and only briefly—perhaps to shake hands or pat someone on the back.
2. *Personal Zone:* This zone, extending from 18 inches to about 4 feet, is where conversation with close friends and colleagues takes place. Unlike interaction in the intimate zone, normal talking is frequent in the personal zone. Some, but not a great deal of, business interaction occurs here; for example, business lunches typically occur in this zone.
3. *Social Zone:* From 4 feet to 12 feet, the social zone is where most business exchanges occur. Informal business conferences and staff meetings occur within this space.
4. *Public Zone:* The public zone extends from 12 feet to as far as the eye can see and the ear can hear. This is the most formal zone, and the least significant interactions occur here. Because of the great distance, communication in the public zone is often one way, as from a speaker to a large audience.

Competent communicators recognize their own personal space needs and the needs of others. When communicating with people who prefer more or less space, the competent communicator makes the adjustments necessary to facilitate reaching his or her objective.

Different types of communication occur at different distances.

Diversity in Work Teams

Paying attention to the needs of others means that we recognize and accept diversity. When we talk about diversity, we mean cultural differences not only in the American and Canadian work force but also in the worldwide marketplace. The United States is a major participant in international business—both as a buyer and as a seller. This country is the world's largest importer of goods and services and the world's second largest exporter. The dominant role that the United States thus plays in the global economy does not, however, mean that international business matters are handled "the American way." Some years ago a book called *The Ugly American* condemned Americans abroad for their "Let 'em do it our way or not at all" attitude.

When we talk about culture, we mean the customary traits, attitudes, and behaviors of a group of people. **Ethnocentrism** is the belief that one's own cultural group is superior. Such an attitude hinders communication, understanding, and goodwill between trading partners. An attitude of arrogance is not only counterproductive but also unrealistic, considering the fact that the U.S. population represents less than 5% of the world population. Moreover, of the world's countries, the United States is currently fourth in population and is expected to drop to eighth place by the year 2050.[9]

International business would not be possible without international communication.

IBM's corporate work force diversity staff, headed by Ted Childs (top center) helps make sure that downsizing doesn't mean homogenization of the employee pool at Big Blue.

Another fact of life in international business is that comparatively few Americans speak a foreign language. Although English is the major language for conducting business worldwide, it would be naive to assume that it is the other person's responsibility to learn English. As a matter of fact, only about 8.5% of the world's population speak English competently (about 450 million out of a world population of 5.3 billion). This means that English-only speakers cannot communicate one-to-one with more than 90% of the people in this world.[10]

Perhaps the (unintended) implication up to this point has been that you must leave the United States and Canada in order to encounter cultures different from your own. Nothing could be further from the truth. In fact, the term *minority,* which traditionally has referred to such groups as blacks, Hispanics, and Asians, is becoming something of a misnomer. Today, minorities make up a majority of the population in one out of six U.S. cities.[11]

As illustrated by Figure 2.3, by the year 2050, America's minority groups will make up just under half of the nation's population, and non-Hispanic whites will decrease to 53% of the population, from 75% today. Consider these additional facts:[12]

- There is a 40% chance that two randomly selected North Americans will be of different racial or ethnic backgrounds.

- In 14% of U.S. homes, a language other than English is spoken.

- Of all new entrants into the work force, 43% are people of color and immigrants.

- Women and people of color will comprise 70% of the work force in the year 2000.

Clearly, the term *global village* that Marshall McLuhan coined applies to our own country as well.

Obviously, diversity will have a profound impact on our lives and will pose a growing challenge for managers. The following discussion provides useful guidance

FIGURE 2.3   America's Diverse Population

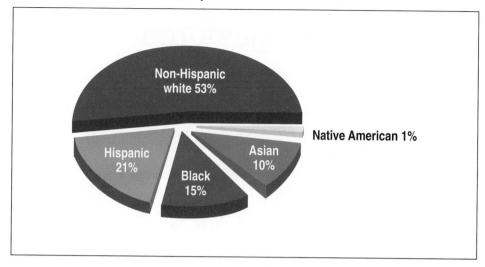

for communicating with people from different cultures—both internationally as well as domestically. Although it is helpful to be aware of cultural differences, competent communicators recognize that each member of a culture is an individual, with individual needs, perceptions, and experiences, and should be treated as such.

Cultural Differences

Each person interprets events through his or her mental filter, and that filter is based on the receiver's unique knowledge, experiences, and viewpoints. For example, the language of time is as different among cultures as the language of words. Americans, Canadians, Germans, and Japanese are very time conscious and very precise about appointments; Latin American and Arab cultures tend to be more casual about time.

Cultures differ not only in their verbal language but also in their nonverbal language. Very few nonverbal messages have universal meanings.

Businesspeople in both Asian and Latin American countries tend to favor long negotiations and slow deliberations. They exchange pleasantries at some length before getting down to business. Likewise, many non-Western cultures use the silent intervals for contemplation, whereas businesspeople from North America tend to have little tolerance for silence in business negotiations. As a result, North Americans may rush in and offer compromises and counterproposals that would have been unnecessary if they had shown more patience.

Body language, especially gestures and eye contact, also varies among cultures. For example, our sign for "okay"—forming a circle with our forefinger and thumb—means "zero" in France, "money" in Japan, and a vulgarity in Brazil. (See Figure 2.4 for some gesture guidelines distributed to volunteers at the 1996 Olympic games in Atlanta.) Americans and Canadians consider eye contact important. In Asian and many Latin American countries, however, looking a partner full in the eye is considered an irritating sign of ill breeding.

Touching behavior is very culture-specific. Many Asians do not like to be touched, except for a brief handshake in greeting. However, handshakes in much of Europe tend to last much longer than in the United States and Canada, and Europeans tend to shake hands every time they see each other, perhaps several times a day. Similarly, in much of Europe, men often kiss each other upon greeting; unless

FIGURE 2.4 **Same Sign, Diverse Meanings**

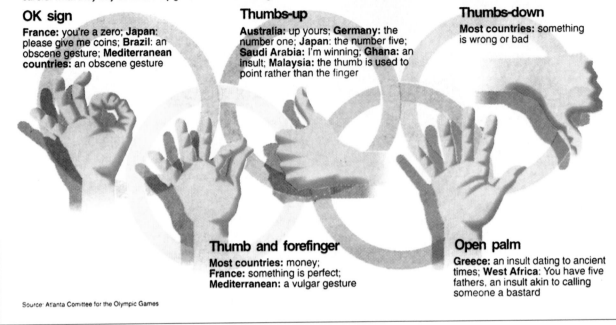

The Olympic don'ts of gestures

Olympic volunteers who will be working with international visitors are being trained to be careful what they say or what they gesture. Here's what gestures mean in other countries:

OK sign
France: you're a zero; **Japan:** please give me coins; **Brazil:** an obscene gesture; **Mediterranean countries:** an obscene gesture

Thumbs-up
Australia: up yours; **Germany:** the number one; **Japan:** the number five; **Saudi Arabia:** I'm winning; **Ghana:** an insult; **Malaysia:** the thumb is used to point rather than the finger

Thumbs-down
Most countries: something is wrong or bad

Thumb and forefinger
Most countries: money; **France:** something is perfect; **Mediterranean:** a vulgar gesture

Open palm
Greece: an insult dating to ancient times; **West Africa:** You have five fathers, an insult akin to calling someone a bastard

Source: Atlanta Comittee for the Olympic Games

Source: Atlanta Committee for Olympic Games, by Sam Ward, *USA Today.* Taken from Ben Brown, "Atlanta Out to Mind Its Manners," *USA Today,* March 14, 1996, p. 7c. Copyright © 1996 *USA Today.* Reprinted with permission.

an American or Canadian businessman is aware of this custom, he might react inappropriately.

When in doubt about how to act, follow the lead of your host.

Our feelings about space are partly an outgrowth of our culture and partly a result of geography and economics. For example, Americans and Canadians are used to wide-open spaces and tend to move about expansively, using hand and arm motions for emphasis. But in Japan, which has much smaller living and working spaces, such abrupt and extensive body movements are not typical. Likewise, Americans and Canadians tend to sit face to face, so that they can maintain eye contact, whereas the Chinese and Japanese (to whom eye contact is not important) tend to sit side by side during negotiations.

Also, the sense of personal space differs among cultures. In the United States and Canada most business exchanges occur at about five feet, within the so-called social zone discussed earlier. However, both in the Middle East and in Latin American countries, this distance is too far. Businesspeople there tend to stand close enough to feel your breath as you speak. Most Americans and Canadians tend to back away unconsciously from such close contact.

Finally, social behavior is very culture-dependent. For example, in the Japanese culture, the matter of who bows first upon meeting, how deeply the person bows, and how long the bow is held is very dependent upon one's status.

Competent communicators become familiar with such role-related behavior and also learn the customs regarding giving (and accepting) gifts, exchanging business cards, the degree of formality expected, and the accepted means of entertaining and being entertained.

Group-Oriented Behavior

The business environment in a capitalistic society such as the United States and Canada places great value on the contributions of the individual toward the success of the organization. Individual effort is often stressed more than group effort, and a competitive atmosphere prevails. In other cultures, however, originality and independence of judgment are not valued as highly as teamwork. The Japanese say, "A nail standing out will be hammered down." Thus, the Japanese go to great lengths to reach decisions through consensus, wherein every participating member, not just a majority, is able to agree.

Expect negotiations to take longer when unanimous agreement rather than majority rule is the norm.

Closely related to the concept of group-oriented behavior is the notion of saving face. The desire to "save face" simply means that neither party in a given interaction should suffer embarrassment. Human relationships are highly valued in such cultures and are embodied in the concept of *wa*, or the Japanese pursuit of harmony. This concept makes it difficult for the Japanese to say "no" to a request because it would be impolite. They are very reluctant to offend others—even if they unintentionally mislead them instead. Thus, a "yes" to a Japanese might mean "Yes, I understand you" rather than "Yes, I agree." Latin Americans also tend to avoid an outright "no" in their business dealings, preferring instead a milder, less explicit, response. In intercultural communications, one has to read between the lines, because what is left unsaid or unwritten may be just as important as what *is* said or written.

Strategies for Communicating Across Cultures

When communicating with people from different cultures, whether abroad or at home, use the following strategies.

Maintain Formality   Compared to the traditional American and Canadian culture, most other cultures value and respect a much more formal approach to business dealings. Call others by their titles and family names unless specifically asked to do otherwise. By both verbal and nonverbal clues, convey an attitude of propriety and decorum. Most other cultures do not equate formality with coldness.

Show Respect   Withhold judgment, accepting the premise that attitudes held by an entire culture are probably based on sound reasoning. Listen carefully to what is being communicated, trying to understand the other person's feelings. Learn about your host country—its geography, form of government, largest cities, culture, current events, and the like.

Showing respect is probably the easiest strategy to exhibit—and one of the most important.

Communicate Clearly   To ensure that your oral and written messages are understood, follow these guidelines:

- Avoid slang, jargon, and other figures of speech. Expressions such as "They'll eat that up" or "out in left field" are likely to confuse even a fluent English speaker.

- Be specific and illustrate your points with concrete examples.

- Provide and solicit feedback; summarize frequently; provide a written summary of the points covered in a meeting; ask your counterpart to paraphrase what has been said; encourage questions.

- Use a variety of media: handouts (distributed before the meeting to allow time for reading), audiovisual aids, models, and the like.

- Avoid attempts at humor; humor is likely to be lost on your counterpart.

- Speak plainly and slowly (but not so slowly as to appear condescending), choosing your words carefully.

Value Diversity   Those who view diversity among employees as a source of richness and strength for the organization can help bring a wide range of benefits to their organization. Whether you happen to belong to the majority culture or to one of the minority cultures where you work, you will share your work and leisure hours with people different from yourself—people who have values, mannerisms, and speech habits different from your own. This is true today, and it will be even truer in the future. The same strategies apply whether the cultural differences exist at home or abroad.

Cultural diversity provides a rich environment for solving problems and for expanding horizons.

A person who is knowledgeable about, and comfortable with, different cultures is a more effective manager because he or she can avoid misunderstandings and tap into the greater variety of viewpoints a diverse culture provides. In addition, such understanding provides personal satisfaction.

Listening

Effective communication—whether across continents or across a conference table—requires both sending and receiving messages—both transmission and reception. Whether you are making a formal presentation to 500 people or conversing with one person over lunch, your efforts will be in vain if your audience does not listen.

There is a difference between hearing and listening.

Listening involves much more than just hearing. You can hear and not listen (just as you can listen and not understand). Hearing is simply perceiving sound; sound waves strike the eardrum, sending impulses to the brain. Hearing is a passive process, whereas listening is an active process. When you *perceive* a sound, you're merely aware of it; you don't necessarily comprehend it. When you *listen*, you interpret and assign meaning to the sounds.

Consider the automobile you drive. When the car is operating normally, even though you *hear* the sound of the engine as you're driving, you're barely aware of it; you tend to tune it out. But the minute the engine begins to make a strange sound—not necessarily louder or harsher, but just *different*—you immediately tune back in, listening intently to try to discern the nature of the problem. You *heard* the normal hum of the engine but *listened* to the strange noise.

The Problem of Poor Listening Skills

Listening is the communication skill we use the most. White-collar workers typically devote at least 40% of their workday to listening. Yet immediately after hearing a ten-minute oral presentation, the average person retains only 50% of the information. Forty-eight hours later, only 25% of what was heard can be recalled.[13] Thus, listening is probably the least developed of the four verbal communication skills (writing, reading, speaking, and listening).

One of the major causes of poor listening is that most people have simply not been taught how to listen well. Think back to your early years in school. How much class time was devoted to teaching you to read and write? How many opportunities were you given to read aloud, participate in plays, or speak before a group? Chances are that reading, writing, and perhaps speaking were heavily stressed in your education. But how much formal training have you had in listening? If you're typical, the answer is "Not much."

Another factor that contributes to poor listening skill is the disparity between the speed at which we normally speak and the speed at which our brains can process data. We can think faster than we can speak—about four times faster, as a matter of fact. Thus, when listening to others, our minds begin to wander, and we lose our ability to concentrate on what is being said.

The results of ineffective listening include such problems as instructions not being followed, equipment broken from misuse, sales lost, feelings hurt, morale lowered, productivity decreased, rumors started, and health risks increased. Still, poor listening skills are not as readily apparent as poor speaking or writing skills. It's easy to spot a poor speaker or writer but much more difficult to spot a poor listener because a poor listener can fake attention. In fact, the poor listener may not even be aware of this weakness. He or she may mistake hearing for listening.

Although listening is the communication skill we use the most frequently, most people have not been taught how to listen effectively.

Keys to Better Listening

To learn to listen more effectively, whether you're involved in a one-on-one dialogue or are part of a mass audience, give the speaker your undivided attention, stay open-minded, avoid interrupting, and involve yourself in the communication.

Give the Speaker Your Undivided Attention   During a business presentation, a member of the audience may hear certain familiar themes, think, "Oh no, not again," and proceed to tune the speaker out. Or during a conference with a subordinate, an executive may make or take phone calls, doodle, play around with a pen or pencil, or do other distracting things that give the speaker the impression that what he or she has to say is unimportant or uninteresting.

Physical distractions are the easiest to eliminate. Simply shutting the door or asking your assistant to hold all calls will eliminate many interruptions during personal conferences. If you're in a meeting where the environment is noisy, the temperature too cold or hot, or the chairs uncomfortable, try to tune out the distractions rather than the speaker. Learn to ignore those annoyances over which you have no control and concentrate instead on the speaker and what he or she is saying.

Mental distractions are more difficult to eliminate. But with practice and effort, you can discipline yourself, for example, to temporarily forget about your fatigue or to put competing thoughts out of your mind so that you can give the speaker your attention.

Just as it is important for the speaker to maintain eye contact with the whole audience, it is also important for the *listener* to maintain eye contact with the speaker. Doing so sends the message that you're interested in what the speaker has to say, and the speaker will be more likely to open up to you and provide the information you need.

We talk about giving the speaker your undivided attention. Actually, it would be more accurate to say that you give the speaker's *comments* your undivided attention; that is, you focus on the content of the talk and are not overly concerned about how the talk is delivered. It is true, of course, that nonverbal clues do provide important information. However, do not be put off by the fact that the speaker may have dressed inappropriately, spoken too fast or in an unfamiliar accent, or appeared nervous. Almost always, *what* is said is more important than how it is said.

Likewise, avoid dismissing a topic simply because it is uninteresting or is presented in an uninteresting manner. "Boring" does not mean unimportant. Some information that may be boring or difficult to follow may in fact prove to be quite useful to you and thus well worth your effort to give it your full attention.

Stay Open-Minded   Regardless of whom you're listening to or what the topic is, keep your emotions in check. Listen objectively and empathetically. Be willing to accept new information and new points of view, regardless of whether they mesh with your existing beliefs. Concentrate on the content of the message rather than on its source.

Don't look at the situation as a win/lose proposition; that is, don't consider that the speaker wins and you lose if you concede the merits of his or her position. Instead, think of it as a win/win situation: the speaker wins by convincing you of the merits of his or her position, and you win by gaining new information and insights that will help you perform your duties more effectively.

Maintain neutrality as long as possible, and don't jump to conclusions too quickly. Instead, try to understand *why* the speaker is arguing a particular point of view and what facts or experience convinced the speaker to adopt this position. When you assume this empathetic frame of reference, you will likely find that you neither completely agree nor completely disagree with every point the speaker makes. This ability to evaluate the message objectively will help you gain the most from the exchange.

Don't Interrupt   Perhaps because of time pressures, we sometimes get impatient. As soon as we've figured out what a person is going to say, we tend to interrupt to finish the sentence for the speaker; this practice is especially a problem when listening to a slow speaker. Or, as soon as we can think of a counterargument, we tend to rush right in—whether or not the speaker has finished or even paused for a breath.

Such interruptions have many negative consequences. First of all, they are considered rude. Also, instead of speeding up the exchange, such interruptions tend to drag it out because they often interfere with the speaker's train of thought, causing backtracking. The most serious negative consequence, however, is the nonverbal message such an interruption sends: "I have the right to interrupt you because what I have to say is more important than what you have to say!" Is it any wonder, then, that such a message hinders effective communication?

There is a difference between listening and simply waiting to speak. Even if you're too polite to interrupt, don't simply lie in wait for the first available opportunity to barge in with your version of the truth. If you're constantly planning what you'll say next, you can hardly listen attentively to what the other person is saying.

Americans tend to have low tolerance for silence. Yet waiting a moment or two after someone has finished before you respond has several positive effects—especially in an emotional exchange. It gives the person speaking a chance to elaborate on his or her remarks, thereby drawing out further insights. It also helps create a quieter, calmer, more respectful atmosphere, one that is more conducive to solving the problem at hand.

Involve Yourself   As we have said, hearing is passive whereas listening is active. You should be *doing* something while the other person is speaking (and we don't mean doodling, staring out the window, or planning your afternoon activities).

Involve yourself mentally in what the speaker is saying.

Much of what you should be doing is mental. Summarize to yourself what the speaker is saying; create what the experts call an *internal paraphrase* of the speaker's comments. We can process information much faster than the speaker can present it, so use that extra time for active listening—ensuring that you really are hearing not only what the person is saying but the motives and implications as well.

Some listeners find it helpful to jot down points, translating their mental notes into written notes. If you do this, keep your notes brief; don't become so busy writing down the facts that you miss the message. Concentrate on the main ideas; if you get these, you'll be much more likely to remember the supporting details later. Recognize also that even if a detail or two of the speaker's message might be inaccurate or irrelevant, the major points may still be valid. Evaluate the validity of the overall argument; don't get bogged down in trivia.

Be selfish in your listening. Constantly ask yourself, How does this affect me? How can I use this information to further my goals or to help me perform my job more effectively? Personalizing the information will help you to concentrate more easily and to weigh the evidence more objectively—even if the topic is difficult to follow or uninteresting and even if the speaker has some annoying mannerisms or an unpleasant personality.

Encourage the speaker by letting him or her know that you're actively involved in the exchange. Maintain eye contact, nod in agreement, lean forward, utter encouraging phrases such as "uh huh" or "I see." In a conversation, ensure that your mental paraphrases are on target by summarizing aloud for the speaker what you think you're hearing. You can give such feedback as "So you believe . . . , is that true?" or "Do you mean that . . . ?" which in turn enables the speaker to clarify remarks, add new information, or clear up any misconceptions. Further, it tells the speaker that you're paying attention to the exchange.

Business Meetings

Much of the listening you'll do in the workplace will be in the context of business meetings. Meetings serve a wide variety of purposes in the organization. They keep members informed of events related to carrying out their duties; they provide a forum for soliciting input, solving problems, and making decisions; and they promote unity and cohesiveness among the members through social interaction.

Effective managers know how to run and participate in business meetings.

Considering these important purposes, it is not surprising that as many as 20 million meetings take place each day in America. The average executive spends 25% to 70% of his or her day in meetings—and considers about a third of them to be unproductive. No wonder, then, many managers complain that "meetingitis" has become a national plague in American business. (Someone once described a meeting as an occasion for a group of people to keep minutes and waste hours.) The typical American business meeting is a staff meeting held in a company conference room for just under two hours, with no written agenda distributed in advance.[14]

The ability to conduct and participate in meetings is a crucial managerial skill. One survey of more than 2,000 business leaders showed that executives who run a meeting well are perceived to be better managers by both their superiors and their peers.[15]

To use meetings as an effective managerial tool, you need to know not only how to run them but also when to call them and how to follow up afterward. Like so many decisions you will have to make about communication, your choices will be guided by what you hope to accomplish.

Planning the Meeting

When you add up the hourly salaries and fringe benefits of those planning and attending a meeting, the cost can be considerable. Managers must make sure they're getting their money's worth from a meeting, and that guarantee requires careful planning: identifying the purpose and determining whether a meeting is in fact necessary, preparing an agenda, deciding who should attend, and planning the logistics.

Identifying Your Purpose   The first step is always to determine your purpose. The more specific you can be, the better results you will get. A purpose such as "to discuss how to make our marketing representatives more effective" is vague and therefore not as helpful as "to decide whether to purchase cellular phones for our marketing representatives." The more focused your purpose, the easier it will be to select a means of accomplishing that purpose.

First, determine if a meeting is the best way to accomplish your goal.

Determining Whether a Meeting Is Necessary   Sometimes meetings are not the most efficient means of communication. For example, a short memo or e-mail message is more efficient than a face-to-face meeting to communicate routine information. Similarly, it doesn't make sense to use the weekly staff meeting of ten people to hold a long discussion involving only one or two of the members. A phone call or smaller meeting would accomplish that task quicker and at less cost.

However, alternative means of conveying or securing information often present their own problems. Some people don't read written messages carefully or they interpret them differently. Time is lost in transmitting and responding to written messages. And information may be garbled as it moves from person to person and from level to level.

An agenda helps focus the attention of both the leader and the participants.

Preparing an Agenda   Once you've established your specific purpose, you need to consider in more detail what topics the meeting will cover and in what order. This list of topics, or **agenda,** will accomplish two things: (1) it will help you prepare for the meeting by showing what background information you'll need, and (2) it will help you run the meeting by keeping you focused on your plan.

Knowing what topics will be discussed will also help those attending the meeting to plan for the meeting effectively—reviewing needed documents, bringing pertinent records, deciding what questions need to be raised, and the like. The survey of 2,000 business leaders mentioned earlier revealed that three-fourths of the managers consider agendas to be essential for efficient meetings; yet nearly half the meetings they attend are *not* accompanied by written agendas.[16]

Formal, recurring business meetings might follow an agenda like this one; of course, not every meeting will contain all these elements:

1. Call to order
2. Roll call (if necessary)
3. Reading and approval of minutes of previous meeting (if necessary)
4. Reports of officers and standing committees
5. Reports of special committees
6. Unfinished business

7. New business
8. Announcements
9. Program
10. Adjournment

Each item to be covered under these headings should be identified, including the speaker (if other than the chair); for example:

7. NEW BUSINESS
   a. Review of December 3 press conference
   b. Recommendation for annual charitable contribution
   c. Status of remodeling—Jan Fischer

Deciding Who Should Attend   A great number of ad hoc meetings take place each business day for the purpose of solving a specific problem. If you must decide who will attend a particular meeting, your first concern is how the participants relate to your purpose. Who will make the decision? Who will implement the decision? Who can provide needed background information? On the one hand, you want to include all who can contribute to solving the problem; on the other, you want to keep the meeting to a manageable number of people.

Everyone at the meetings should have a direct reason for being there.

Consider also how the potential group members differ in status within the organization, in knowledge about the issue, in communication skills, and in personal relationships. The greater the differences, the more difficult it will be to involve everyone in a genuine discussion aimed at solving the problem.

Don't underestimate the impact of potential group members' hidden agendas. If any member's personal goals for the meeting differ from the group goals, conflicts can arise and the quality of the resulting decisions can be impaired. Meeting separately with some of the important participants ahead of time might help to identify sources of potential dissension and provide clues for dealing with them.

Membership in recurring meetings (such as a weekly staff or committee meeting) is relatively fixed. Even for these meetings, however, the planner must decide whether outsiders will be invited to observe, participate, or simply be available as resource people.

Determining Logistics   It would be unwise to schedule a meeting that requires extensive discussion and creative problem solving at the end of the workday, when members may be exhausted emotionally and physically. Likewise, it would be counterproductive to schedule a three-hour meeting in a room equipped with uncushioned fold-up chairs, poor lighting, and extreme temperatures.

Instead, facilitate group problem solving by making intelligent choices about the timing and location of the meeting, room and seating arrangements, types of audiovisual equipment, and the like. Doing so will increase the likelihood of achieving the goals of the meeting.

Increasingly, another logistical consideration is whether to hold a face-to-face meeting or a **teleconference,** a meeting in which members in different locations are linked by simultaneous electronic communications, using camera, projection screens, microphones, and computer equipment.

Conducting the Meeting

Planning for a meeting goes a long way toward ensuring its success, but the manager's job is by no means over when the meeting begins. A manager must be a leader during the meeting, keeping the group focused on the point and encouraging participation.

An efficient leader begins and ends each meeting on time.

Punctuality   Unless a high-level member or one whose input is vital to the business at hand is tardy, make it a habit to begin every meeting on time. Doing so will send a powerful nonverbal message to chronic late arrivers that business will be conducted and decisions made whether they're present or not.

If you wait for latecomers, you send the message to those who *were* punctual that they wasted their time by being prompt. As a result, they will probably arrive late for subsequent meetings. And the habitual late arrivers will then begin arriving even later! Avoid this vicious cycle by beginning (and ending) at the appointed times.

Following the Agenda   One of the keys to a focused meeting is to follow the agenda. At formal meetings you will be expected to discuss all items on the published agenda and no items not on the agenda. The less formal the meeting, the more flexibility you have in allowing new topics to be introduced. It's always possible that new information that has a bearing on your problem may arise. To prevent discussion simply because you didn't include the item on your agenda would make it more difficult for you to achieve your purpose. But as leader of the meeting, you must make certain that new topics are directly relevant.

Leading the Meeting   Begin the meeting with a statement of your purpose and an overview of the agenda. As the meeting progresses, keep track of time. Don't let the discussion get bogged down in details.

Preventing people from talking too much or digressing from the topic requires tact. Comments like "I see your point, and that relates to what we were just discussing" can keep you on track without offending the speaker. You'll also need to encourage the participation of the quieter members of the group with comments like "John, how does this look from the perspective of your department?"

Determine which problem-solving strategy is appropriate.

If your purpose is to solve a problem, you should consider ahead of time how you will structure the discussion. The particular strategy you use (such as brainstorming or role-playing) will, of course, depend on the nature and importance of the problem and the skills of the group members. For many topics and groups, a simple discussion is all that is needed.

As leader, you'll sometimes have to resolve conflicts among members. Your first step is to make sure all members understand the facts involved and that you and everyone else understand each person's position. You then need to examine what each person's goals are and search for alternatives that will satisfy the largest number of goals.

At the end of the meeting, summarize for everyone what the meeting has accomplished. What was decided? What are the next steps? Review any assignments and make sure everyone understands his or her responsibilities.

During the meeting, someone—either an assistant, the leader, or someone the leader designates—should record what happens. That person must report objectively and not impose his or her own biases.

Parliamentary Procedure   Every group needs to adopt rules that permit the orderly transactions of business in meetings. The larger the group and the more important its mission, the more important it is to establish written rules of order (called **parliamentary procedure**). Imagine, for example, the chaos that could result if a meeting did not follow the basic rule that only one person can have the floor and speak at a time!

The basic principle of parliamentary procedure is that the minority shall be heard but that the majority shall prevail. The reference guide for parliamentary procedure—the authority used by governments, associations, and business organizations the world over—is *Robert's Rules of Order.*[17] The rationale for using parliamentary procedure is given in the preface of that classic:

In parliamentary procedure, the minority is heard and the majority prevails.

> The application of parliamentary law is the best method yet devised to enable assemblies of any size, with due regard for every member's opinion, to arrive at the general will on a maximum number of questions of varying complexity in a minimum time and under all kinds of internal climate ranging from total harmony to hardened or impassioned division of opinion.[18]

This 61-word sentence is probably as good an example as you're likely to find of a long sentence that communicates its message clearly and concisely.

Robert's Rules of Order was written in 1896 by Gen. Henry M. Robert, a U.S. Army officer who was active in many civic and educational organizations; it has been revised periodically since then. The current edition contains more than 650 pages of rules and procedures; those that are most helpful for running the typical business meeting are summarized in Figure 2.5.

Knowledge of basic parliamentary procedure is a strategic communication skill for managers. Anyone who runs a business meeting, whether at work or in connection with a professional, civic, or social organization, would do well to become familiar with the basic requirements of conducting meetings in a parliamentary manner.

Following Up the Meeting

Routine meetings may require only a short memorandum as a follow-up to what was decided. Formal meetings or meetings where controversial ideas were discussed may require a more formal summary.

Formal meetings require formal minutes of what took place.

Minutes are an official record of the proceedings; they summarize what was discussed and what decisions were made. Generally, they should emphasize what was *done* at the meeting, not what was *said* by the members. Minutes may, however, present an intelligent summary of the points of view expressed on a particular issue, without names attached, followed by the decision made. Avoid presenting minutes that are either so short they lack the "flavor" of what transpired or so long they tend to be ignored.

The first paragraph of minutes should identify the type of meeting (regular or special); the meeting date, time, and place; the presiding officer; the names of those present (or absent) if customary; and the fact that the minutes of the previous meeting were read and approved.

The minutes should be accurate, objective, and complete.

The body of the minutes should contain a separate paragraph for each topic. According to parliamentary procedure, the name of the maker of a motion, but not the seconder, should be entered in the minutes. The precise wording of motions, exactly as voted on, should also appear in minutes. It is often helpful to use the same subheadings as in the agenda. A sample portion of the minutes of a business meeting follows:

Review of December 3 Press Conference

> A videotape of the December 3 press conference conducted by Donita Doyle was viewed and discussed. Roger Eggland's motion that "Donita Doyle be commended for the professional and ethical manner in which she presented the company's view at the December 3 press conference" was adopted unanimously without debate.

FIGURE 2.5   Parliamentary Procedure for Business Meetings

To Do This:	You Say This:	Interrupt the speaker?	Need a second?	Debatable?	Amendable?	Vote needed?
Main Motion						
Make a main motion	I move that . . .	yes	yes	yes	yes	maj
Secondary Motions						
Adjourn	I move that we adjourn.	no	yes	no	no	maj
Amend a motion	I move to amend by . . .	no	yes	yes	yes	maj
Appeal a chair's ruling	I appeal the decision of the chair.	yes	yes	yes	no	maj
Ask a question	I rise to a point of information.	yes	no	no	no	none
Call for a secret ballot	I move the vote be taken by ballot.	no	yes	no	yes	maj
Call for standing or show-of-hands vote	I call for a division.	yes	no	no	no	none
Close debate	I move the previous question.	no	yes	no	no	$2/_3$
Close nominations	I move to close nominations.	no	yes	no	yes	$2/_3$
Consider parts of a motion separately	I move to divide the question.	no	yes	no	yes	$2/_3$
Lay the pending motion aside temporarily	I move to lay the question on the table.	no	yes	no	no	maj
Point out a rule violation	I rise to a point of order.	yes	no	no	no	none
Postpone to a certain time	I move to postpone the question until . . .	no	yes	yes	yes	maj
Postpone indefinitely	I move to postpone the question indefinitely.	no	yes	yes	no	maj
Raise a point of parliamentary procedure	I rise to a parliamentary inquiry.	yes	no	no	no	none
Refer a motion to a committee	I move to refer the question to . . .	no	yes	yes	yes	maj
Require that the agenda be followed	I call for orders of the day.	yes	no	no	no	none
State a request affecting one's rights	I rise to a question of privilege.	yes	no	no	no	none
Suspend the rule	I move to suspend the rule . . .	no	yes	no	no	$2/_3$
Take a recess	I move that we take a . . . recess.	no	yes	no	yes	maj
Motions That Bring a Question Again Before the Assembly						
Reconsider a previously passed motion	I move to reconsider the vote on . . .	no	yes	yes	no	maj
Revoke action taken at previous meeting	I move to rescind the motion relating to . . . adopted at the May meeting.	no	yes	yes	yes	$2/_3$ [a]
Take from the table	I move to take the question from the table.	no	yes	no	no	maj

[a]Requires a two-thirds vote if no prior notice has been given, majority vote if prior notice has been given.

Miscellaneous Notes
1. Types of motions:
   a. A main motion brings an action before the group. It may be made only when no other motion is pending and must be made and seconded before it can be discussed.
   b. A secondary motion may be made and considered while a main motion is pending and must be acted on before the main motion can be considered further.
   c. A motion that brings a question again before the assembly enables the group to reconsider an action disposed of earlier.

FIGURE 2.5   **(Continued)**

2. Special rules adopted by the group take precedence over *Robert's Rules of Order*.
3. Unless otherwise specified, a majority of the membership constitutes a quorum (the minimum number of members who must be present to transact business).
4. A vote is not required to approve the minutes of the previous meeting. They are simply accepted as read and/or distributed, or they are accepted as corrected.
5. A vote is not required to accept a committee report. However, committee recommendations that require action must be voted on. Motions made on behalf of the committee do not require a second.
6. The purpose of tabling a motion is to enable the group to consider a more urgent matter that has arisen. If the tabled motion is not taken from the table by the next regularly scheduled meeting, the question dies.
7. The purpose of postponing a motion definitely is to defer action until a later date (e.g., when more information has been gathered). The purpose of postponing a motion indefinitely is to avoid taking action on the motion, thereby killing it.
8. The motion to reconsider a previously passed motion must be made at the same meeting as the original vote and must be made by someone from the prevailing (majority) side of the original vote.
9. After a motion has been made and seconded, the chair repeats the motion before calling for discussion and again before calling for the vote.

Recommendation for Annual Charitable Contribution

Tinrah Porisupatani moved "that American Chemical donate $15,000 to a worthwhile charity operating in Essex County." Linda Peters moved to amend the motion by inserting the words "an amount not exceeding" after the word "donate." On a motion by Todd Chandler, the motion to make a donation, with the pending amendment, was referred for further study to the Social Responsibility Committee with instructions to recommend a specific amount and charity and report at the next meeting.

The last paragraph of the minutes should state the time of adjournment and, if appropriate, the time set for the next meeting. The minutes should be signed by the person preparing them. If someone other than the chair prepares the minutes, they should be read and approved by the chair before being distributed.

Guidelines for conducting business meetings are summarized in Checklist 1 (see p. 62).

Business Etiquette

Business etiquette is the practice of polite and appropriate behavior in the business setting. It dictates what behaviors are proper and under what circumstances; thus, business etiquette is really concerned with interaction between people—not meaningless ritual.

Each organization has its own rules about what is and is not considered fitting in terms of dress, ways of addressing superiors, importance of punctuality, and the like. In addition, every country and every culture has its own rules. Generally, these

Learn what is considered appropriate behavior in your organization.

✔ CHECKLIST 1   Business Meetings

Planning the Meeting

- ✔ Identify the purpose of the meeting.
- ✔ Determine whether a face-to-face meeting is the most appropriate method for achieving your purpose.
- ✔ Prepare an agenda for distribution to the participants.
- ✔ Decide who should attend the meeting.
- ✔ Determine the logistics of the meeting—timing, location, room and seating arrangements, and types of audiovisual equipment needed.
- ✔ Assign someone (even if it is yourself) the task of taking notes during the meeting. These notes should be objective, accurate, and complete.

Conducting the Meeting

- ✔ Encourage punctuality by beginning and ending the meeting on time.

- ✔ Begin each meeting by stating the purpose of the meeting and reviewing the agenda.
- ✔ Establish ground rules that permit the orderly transaction of business. Many organizations follow parliamentary procedure.
- ✔ Control the discussion to ensure that it is relevant, that a few members do not monopolize the discussion, and that all members have an opportunity to be heard.
- ✔ At the end of the meeting, summarize what was decided, what the next steps are, and what each member's responsibilities are.

Following Up the Meeting

- ✔ If the meeting was routine and informal, follow it up with a memorandum summarizing the major points of the meeting. For more formal meetings, prepare and distribute minutes.

rules are not written down but must be learned informally or through observation. Executives who follow correct business etiquette are more confident and appear more in charge; and the higher you advance in your career, the more important such behavior will become.

Business etiquette differs in many ways from social etiquette. The manager who enumerates all his or her accomplishments to the superior during a performance appraisal is simply being savvy, but if the manager does so during a social engagement, he or she is being boorish. You must be sensitive to what is appropriate under any given circumstances.

Good manners are good business; they communicate a strong positive message about you as a person. As Mark Twain once observed about etiquette, "Always do right: you will please some people and astonish the rest."

Making Introductions

The important point to remember about making introductions is simply to *make them*. The format you use is less important than the fact that you avoid the awkwardness of requiring two people to introduce themselves.

Traditionally, a man is introduced to a woman (the woman's name is said first), the lower ranking person is introduced to the higher ranking person (the higher ranking person's name is said first), and other people are introduced to the guest (the guest's name is said first). However, when introducing a newcomer to a group of people, simply mention the newcomer's name first and then go around the group introducing each person in turn.

The format for an introduction might be like this: "Helen, I'd like you to meet Carl Byrum. Carl just began working here as an account manager. Carl, this is Helen Smith, our vice president." Or, in a social situation, you might just say, "Rosa, this is

Gene Stauffer. Gene, Rosa Bennett." The appropriate response to an introduction is "How do you do, Gene?" Regardless of the gender of the two people being introduced, either may initiate the handshake—a gesture of welcome.

To help yourself remember the name of someone you've met, make a point of using his or her name when shaking hands. And using the person's name again at least once during the conversation will help fix that name in your mind. If you cannot remember someone's name, when the person approaches you, simply extend your hand and say your name. The other person will typically respond by shaking your hand and also giving his or her name.

Use a person's name in the conversation to help yourself remember it.

Whenever you greet an acquaintance whom you've met only once some time ago, introduce yourself and immediately follow it with some information to help the other person remember, unless he or she immediately recognizes you—for example, "Hello, Mr. Wise, I'm Eileen Wagoner. We met at the Grahams' party last month."

Dining

The restaurant you select for a business meal reflects on you and your organization. Choose one where the food is of top quality and the service dependable. In general, the more important your guest, the more exclusive the restaurant. If a maitre d' (headwaiter) seats you and your guest, your guest should precede you to the table. If you're seating yourselves, take the lead in locating an appropriate table. Give your guest the preferred seat, facing the window with an attractive view or facing the dining room if you're seated next to the wall.

Although customs vary, it is traditional for a man to hold the woman's chair as she is being seated and for the nearest man to rise when a woman excuses herself for a moment and when she returns. Female managers and professionals do not mistake genuine gestures of courtesy as chauvinism. Let common sense and your knowledge of the person's preferences guide your actions.

Unfold your napkin and place it in your lap immediately upon being seated. To avoid grabbing the wrong glass of water, remember "solids on the left, liquids on the right." When making a food recommendation or announcing, when asked, what you intend to order, recognize that your guest will take your choice as a guideline to suitable price ranges. Each guest should order for himself or herself at a business meal. If the server mistakenly begins by asking you, the host, for your order, simply say, "My guests will order first," thereby letting the server also know that you should get the check.

Always pass food or condiments to the right, offering items to someone else before you serve yourself. Avoid salting your food before tasting it. If asked to pass the salt or pepper, pass both together. At the conclusion of the meal, return your folded napkin to the table just before rising and leaving the table. In most parts of the country, the usual tip for standard service is 15% to 20% of the food and bar bill and 10% of the cost of wine.

Giving Gifts

Giving gifts to suppliers, customers, or workers within one's own organization is typical at many firms, especially in December during the holiday period. Although such gifts are often deeply appreciated, you must be sensitive in terms of whom you give a gift to and the type of gift you select. Most people would consider a gift appropriate if it meets these four criteria:

Avoid giving gifts that are extravagant or personal or that might be perceived as a bribe.

- *It is an impersonal gift.* Gifts that can be used in the office or in connection with one's work are nearly always appropriate.

- *It is for past favors.* Gifts should be used to thank someone for past favors, business, or performance—*not* to create obligations for the future. A gift to a prospective customer who has never ordered from you before might be interpreted as a bribe.

- *It is given to everyone in similar circumstances.* Singling out one person for a gift and ignoring others in similar positions would not only embarrass the one selected but create bad feelings among those who were ignored.

- *It is not extravagant.* A very expensive gift might make the recipient uneasy, create a sense of obligation, and call into question your motives for giving.

Although it is often the custom for a superior to give a subordinate a gift, especially one's secretary, it is less usual for the subordinate to give a personal gift to a superior. More likely, coworkers will contribute to a joint gift for the boss, again selecting one that is neither too expensive nor too personal. As always, follow local customs when giving gifts to international colleagues (see Spotlight 4—Across Cultures).

Dressing Appropriately

Different positions, different companies, and different parts of the country and world have different dress codes—some stated explicitly in the company manual, others communicated indirectly via corporate culture. In the absence of other information, you should choose well-tailored, clean, conservative clothing for the workplace (see "Dressing for Success," pp. 502–503).

Increasingly, however, dress-down days (like "Casual Fridays") are gaining popularity in U.S. business. A recent Gallup poll found that 57% of U.S. companies now allow casual dress at least once a week.[19] The adoption of these casual days has caused some confusion about what exactly is considered appropriate. These guidelines for "business casual" from Levi Strauss & Co.[20] should prove helpful:

1. Aim for a classic but understated look when selecting casual business wear. Pick clothing that is comfortable yet communicates a professional attitude. Subtle, quality accessories (such as belts, jewelry, and scarves) coordinated with an outfit can show attention to important details.
2. Combine business wardrobe items with casual attire; for example, a button-down shirt with khakis and loafers, with either a more colorful tie or scarf or just a sport coat or sweater. Ask, "Am I successfully representing myself and my company?"
3. Casual does not mean sloppy. Clothing should be clean, pressed or wrinkle-free, and without holes or frayed areas. Like suits and tailored clothing, casual business wear lasts longer and looks better with special care.
4. Keep the focus on work quality. Anything worn to the gym or beach (or to clean the garage) should be left at home. Avoid clothing that is too revealing or tight-fitting. Trendy or "high-fashion" clothing may communicate a whimsical or pretentious attitude that is not suitable for most offices. T-shirts with messages other than the company's logo are probably not a good idea. Keep clothing colors muted and coordinated to help create a professional appearance.

Gift Giving—Japanese-Style

When conducting business in Japan, there are few occasions when giving a gift is not considered appropriate. There are two occasions, however, when gift giving is mandatory—for the Japanese as well as for those doing business with the Japanese. These two occasions are *O-chugen,* which falls in midsummer, and *O-seibo,* at year's end. *O-seibo,* which can only be compared with Christmas, is an especially important gift-giving occasion, with more than $10 billion spent on gifts during this one season.

SPOTLIGHT 4

ACROSS CULTURES

What to Give

As incongruous as it might sound, your best bet in selecting a gift for your Japanese colleague is to "Buy American." Your best choices for gifts are items that either are not easily available in Japan or are quite expensive there. Anything with a prominent American label might be appropriate. Brand names such as Gucci, Ralph Lauren, and L. L. Bean are understood and valued in Japan.

Regional gifts are always popular—such as Vermont maple syrup, mugs with your city name, university sweatshirts, baseball caps from famous teams, and even subscriptions to popular American magazines. Food selections are also appropriate—including such items as fruit and preserves, cheese, beef, and wine and spirits (especially bourbon, which is a uniquely American product).

Make sure that whatever items you choose are of the highest quality, but never ostentatious. Tact is the key to successful gift giving: nothing too large and extravagant nor too small and cheap. Take your cue from your Japanese colleagues. And remember that hierarchical relationships are important. Never give the same gift (or an equally priced gift) to people at different levels in the same organization.

How to Give

The presentation of the gift may be as important as the gift itself. The gift should be wrapped attractively in top-quality gift wrap, and it is customary to transport the gift in a neat paper bag (so as not to call attention to the fact that you're bringing a gift).

When presenting the gift, extend it to the recipient with both hands (a sign of respect and humility), while making a self-deprecating comment such as "This is really nothing at all." It is customary for the recipient to then put the gift aside, unopened in the presence of the giver.

When you give a gift to a Japanese colleague, you can expect to receive one of similar value in the near future. Similarly, if you receive a gift, you will be expected to reciprocate. The Japanese (and many other Asian societies) value relationships highly, and giving gifts is one way of maintaining relationships.

Sources: Dean Foster, "Business Across Borders: International Etiquette for the Effective Global Secretary," *The Secretary,* October 1992, pp. 20–24; "Gift Giving Japanese-Style," *Business Tokyo,* November 1990, pp. 9–12; Yumiko Ono, "There's an Old Saying: Never Look for a Gift, of Course, in the Mouth," *Wall Street Journal,* December 13, 1989, p. B1.

5. Pay attention to the fit of your clothing. Pants should break just above the shoe, sleeves should reach the base of the hand and show just a bit of the cuff when a jacket is worn, and shirt collars should button comfortably without pinching or leaving gaps. Also, if a tie is worn, its tip should reach just below the bottom of the belt buckle.

6. Shoes matter. Leather shoes are generally preferable, but if athletic shoes are allowed, make sure they are clean, subtle in design, and scuff-free. Leather shoes look best when polished and in good repair. For most offices, open-toed sandals and beach thongs are not appropriate.

7. Take the day's schedule into account when dressing. If a meeting with visitors is scheduled, dress more traditionally or check to see if casual dress might be appropriate.

8. When in doubt, leave it out. Casual clothing should make the employee and coworkers work more comfortably. Ask the manager ahead of time if you have any questions.

Around the Office

Many situations occur every day in the typical office that call for common courtesy. The basis for appropriate behavior is always the golden rule: "Treat others as you yourself would like to be treated."

Drinking Coffee   If there is a container provided to pay for the coffee, do so every time you take a cup; don't force others to treat you to a cup of coffee. Also, take your turn making the coffee and cleaning the pot if that is a task performed by the group. Although in most offices it is acceptable to drink coffee or some other beverage while working, some offices have an unwritten rule against snacking at one's desk. Regardless, never eat while talking to someone in person or on the telephone.

Smoking   Most offices today have designated smoking areas, and many prohibit smoking anywhere on the premises. If you smoke, follow the rules strictly. Smoking in public anywhere is increasingly considered bad manners, not to mention a health hazard.

Follow the golden rule in your dealings with others at work.

People with Disabilities   When talking with a blind person, deal in words rather than gestures or glances. As you approach a blind person, make your presence known; and if in a group, address the person by name so that he or she will know when you're talking directly to him or her. Identify yourself and use a normal voice and speed.

When interacting with a physically disabled person, always ask before providing special assistance, and follow the person's wishes. When possible, place yourself at eye level and in front of the person to facilitate communication.

Most important, relax. Insofar as possible, forget about the disability, and treat the person as you would anyone else. That person was hired because of the contribution he or she could make to the organization—not because of the disability.

SUMMARY

Teams can accomplish more and better-quality work in less time than individuals *if* the teams function properly. Otherwise, teams can waste time and cause interpersonal conflicts. Conflict about ideas is a helpful part of the group process, whereas interpersonal conflicts are detrimental. An appropriate emphasis on consensus and conformity is productive, but too much emphasis can lead to groupthink, wherein legitimate differences of opinion are not even discussed.

At the beginning, group members should get to know one another and set operating rules. They should also acknowledge the need for positive and negative feedback and know how to give productive feedback. When problems arise, group members should react to them appropriately, consider them as group problems, and be realistic about what to expect from the group.

For group writing projects, team members should develop a work schedule and meet regularly to ensure proper coordination. Either one person can be assigned to write the draft, or the parts can be divided among group members. Everyone, however, should be involved in revising the draft.

Nonverbal communication includes body movement, physical appearance, voice qualities, time, touch, and space and territory. Cultures differ greatly in terms of how they interpret nonverbal behavior and in terms of the importance they attach to group as opposed to individual behavior. Competent communicators maintain formality, show respect, remain flexible, and write and speak clearly when communicating with people of different cultures.

Listening is the most used but least developed of the verbal communication skills. Whether listening to a formal presentation or conversing with one or two people, you can learn to listen more effectively by giving the speaker your undivided attention, staying open-minded about the speaker and the topic, avoiding interrupting the speaker, and involving yourself actively in the communication.

Planning a business meeting requires determining your purpose and deciding whether a meeting is the most efficient way of accomplishing that purpose. You must then determine your agenda, decide who should attend, and plan such logistics as timing, location, and room arrangements.

When conducting a meeting, begin with a statement of your purpose and agenda. Then follow the agenda, keeping things moving along. Control those who talk too much, and encourage those who talk too little. Use whatever strategies seem appropriate for solving problems and managing conflicts. At the end of the meeting, send a follow-up memo if needed or distribute minutes of the meeting.

Business etiquette is a guide to help people behave appropriately in business situations. To be effective in business, learn how to make introductions, conduct business lunches, give suitable gifts, dress appropriately, and maintain good working relationships around the office. Good manners are good business.

KEY TERMS

agenda	minutes
business etiquette	parliamentary procedure
ethnocentrism	team
groupthink	teleconference
groupware	

REVIEW AND DISCUSSION

1. **Communication at Hilliard-Jones Marketing Group Revisited**   As Amy Hilliard-Jones knows, meetings are a good way to bring out different viewpoints, identify potential solutions to problems, and help groups come to a consensus about what needs to be done.
   a. Should the leader hold a brainstorming session to a strict schedule? Explain your answer.
   b. Should the minutes of a problem-solving meeting name the participants who propose particular solutions? Why or why not?
   c. Why is conflict to be expected or even encouraged during a problem-solving meeting?
2. Is conflict in a team good or bad? Explain.
3. What are five points to remember when giving feedback?

4. Should you assume responsibility for the happiness of others in your group? Explain.

5. What is meant by "speaking with one voice" in a team-written document? How does a team accomplish this?

6. Give an example of a nonverbal message that reinforces a verbal message and one that contradicts a verbal message.

7. How do cultures differ in terms of time, body language, touch, and space?

8. What are four strategies for successfully communicating across cultures? Give an example of each.

9. What is the difference between listening and hearing?

10. What are the major causes and effects of poor listening skills?

11. What is meant by the tip "Be selfish in your listening"?

12. Under what circumstances is a meeting the most efficient way of accomplishing business objectives?

13. What are some ways of encouraging punctuality at a meeting?

14. What is the difference between a main motion and a secondary motion? between tabling a motion and postponing a motion?

15. What types of information should be included in minutes of a meeting and what types should be excluded?

16. How should you introduce your professor and your roommate?

17. What guidelines should you follow for giving business gifts?

EXERCISES

1. **Communication Applications at Hilliard-Jones Marketing Group**   As you saw in the chapter-opening profile, Amy Hilliard-Jones frequently conducts meetings as a way of facilitating group decisions. But planning and leading meetings that bring together diverse groups of people can be particularly challenging.

    Imagine that you are a special assistant to Hilliard-Jones. She has called a meeting for February 21 to gain agreement about the direction of a new advertising campaign for a large bank. In addition to Hilliard-Jones, participants include Ashley Goodwin, marketing director for BankUSA; Jonathan Denlinger, account manager for Horizon Advertising; and Maria Fernandez, creative director for Horizon Advertising. You have been asked to prepare a brief e-mail memo today (February 1) asking participants for their suggestions about topics to be placed on the agenda.

    a. Why would Hilliard-Jones ask participants for suggestions about the agenda in advance of the actual meeting?

    b. Who should receive this memo?

    c. What phrase will you write on the subject line of your memo?

    d. What information should you include in this memo?

2. **Work-Team Communication**   Everyone had agreed to have his or her part of the five-year marketing plan drafted by the time your team met today. What would be an appropriate response to each of the following incidents at today's meeting? Where appropriate, use the steps shown in Figure 2.2, Using "I" Statements When Giving Feedback, to compose your response.

    a. Fred did not have his part ready (although this is the first time he has been late).

    b. Thales did not have his part ready (the third time this year he has missed a deadline).

    c. Anita not only had her part completed but had also sketched out an attractive design for formatting the final document.

d. Sunggong was 45 minutes late for the meeting because his car had skidded into a ditch as a result of last night's snowstorm.

e. Elvira left a message that she would have to miss the meeting because she was working on another report, one due tomorrow.

3. **Entrepreneurship** Marty Chernov, owner of a small salvage yard employing 18 people, has an appointment with John Garrison Boyd IV, vice president of Metropolitan Bank, to discuss his application for a $35,000 business loan. What helpful guidelines can you give Marty regarding his nonverbal behavior at the conference?

4. **Diversity** Assume that you are a supervisor in a firm where one-third of the work force is Hispanic, about evenly divided between Mexican American and Cuban American. All are either U.S. citizens or legal residents. Because both groups have Spanish as their native language, can you assume that both groups have similar cultures? Do some research on both groups in terms of their typical educational backgrounds, political beliefs, job experiences, and the like. Organize your findings into a two-page report (typed, double-spaced).

5. **International** Joe arrived 15 minutes late for his appointment with Itaru Nakamura, sales manager for a small manufacturer to which Joe's firm hoped to sell parts. "Sorry to be late," he apologized, "but you know how the local drivers are. At any rate, since I'm late, let's get right down to brass tacks." Joe began to pace back and forth in the small office. "The way I see it, if you and I can come to some agreement this afternoon, we'll be able to get the rest to agree. After all, who knows more about this than you and I?" Joe sat down opposite his colleague and looked him straight in the eye. "So what do you say? Can we agree on the basics and let our assistants hammer out the details?" His colleague was silent for a few moments, then said, "Yes." Discuss Joe's intercultural skills. Specifically, what did he do wrong? What did Nakamura's response probably mean?

6. **Work-Team Communication** Working in small groups, interview at least three international students or professors, each from a different country. For each country represented, determine the types of written and oral communications common in business, the extent of technological development, problems with the English language, and examples of slang used in their native language. Prepare a written summary of your findings, proofread, revise as necessary, and submit.

7. **Listening** Your instructor will assign you a television show to watch this week—a news program, talk show, or documentary. Using the listening techniques you learned in this chapter, take notes on the important points covered in the presentation. Listen for the major themes, not the details. Write a one-page memo to your instructor summarizing the important information you heard. Should every student's paper contain basically the same information? Explain your answer.

8. **Planning a Business Meeting** Assume that you are a dean at your institution, which does not celebrate Martin Luther King, Jr.'s birthday with a paid holiday. You are seeking the support of the college's other four deans for making the third Monday in January a holiday for all college employees and students.

Prepare a memorandum, including the agenda, to the other deans. Submit both your memo and your responses to the questions to your instructor.

9. **Work-Team Communication—Conducting a Meeting**   Divide into groups of five, with each person assuming the role of a dean at your institution (see Exercise 8). Draw straws to determine who will be the dean calling the meeting and use this person's agenda. Conduct a 15- to 20-minute meeting. Following the meeting, evaluate its effectiveness. Did you achieve your objective? Explain your answer.

10. **Work-Team Writing—Conducting a Meeting**   Divide into groups of five, with each member playing the role of a president of one of the five business student organizations on campus. The dean of the School of Business has proposed requiring all students to purchase a certain brand of portable computer (student price of $1,450) before being allowed to take upper-division business courses. Your group is meeting to either support or oppose this proposal. Draw straws to determine who will be group leader. Each person other than the group leader must either make or amend a motion during the meeting.

    Conduct a 15- to 20-minute meeting on this topic, following parliamentary procedure. Do not adjourn until you have approved a motion one way or the other. After adjournment, evaluate the meeting. Discuss how efficiently it was conducted, how well each person's role was performed, and whether correct parliamentary procedure was followed. Write up your evaluation in a joint memo to your instructor.

11. **Using Business Etiquette**   Assume that you're the dean of your college. Think of three people to whom it would be appropriate to give a gift during December holidays and three people to whom it would not be appropriate to give a gift. Identify the individuals and their positions, and give reasons for your decisions. For the three people to whom you *would* give, suggest an appropriate gift, and a recommended price range.

CONTINUING CASE 2

URBAN SYSTEMS

Don't Let the Smoke Get in Your Eyes

Marc Kaplan ground his cigarette into the ashtray and thought, "Here go those save-the-earth people again." He had just read a copy of a memo that Neelima had sent to Dave Kaplan asking that smoking be prohibited throughout the premises of Urban Systems—both in Ann Arbor and in Charlotte. Neelima cited health dangers, reduced productivity, rights of nonsmokers, and damage to company property.

Marc knew he could cite some arguments also: the rights of smokers, the unfairness of imposing new restrictions that were not in place when workers were hired, the reduced productivity due to stress from not smoking or to time spent on outside smoking breaks, and the fact that other health-related productivity hazards (such as gross obesity) were not banned. He felt he could enlist the support of O. J. Drew and Wendy Janish—the other two smokers in the management offices. Arnie McNally, an ex-smoker, was an unknown.

At any rate, Dave Kaplan had decided to hold a special meeting of the executive committee, made up of himself and the three vice presidents, the following week to discuss and resolve the issue. Parliamentary procedure is followed at these meetings.

Oral and Written Communication Projects

1. Assume the role of Dave Kaplan. Compose a memo to the executive committee announcing the meeting and outlining the agenda.

2. Have four members play the roles of Dave and the three vice presidents; Dave conducts the meeting. The other class members should listen actively, take notes, and be prepared to discuss the events afterward. Each observer should also serve as the secretary and submit a set of minutes for the meeting.

Critical Thinking

3. After role-playing, discuss the situation. How did each actor feel? Was anyone arguing a position he or she didn't really agree with? Was correct parliamentary procedure followed? Was the meeting successful? Did anyone win? lose?

3

Using Technology to Access and Share Information

An Insider's Perspective

As the architect of the 3M Innovation Network (http://www.mmm.com), the multifaceted World Wide Web site for 3M, James Radford is at the forefront of the movement toward electronic access and sharing of information, both internally and externally. In his role as Interactive Business Solutions Manager, Radford is one of a team of experts who help different units within 3M apply interactive technologies to enhance two-way communication between customers and company personnel. In addition, he serves as manager of emerging technologies, examining how new waves of technologies can be coordinated with the marketing use of existing technologies to better achieve business goals.

Roughly 20,000 e-mail messages flow through the 3M Web site every year—and the count is growing dramatically as the company looks for new ways to build its brand names and reach more customers using technology. In building a foundation for tomorrow's electronic marketplace, Radford and his colleagues need to know not only what customers want but how they operate in cyberspace. "We're carefully studying how customers react to the online experience," he says. "It's important to understand how to build a relationship of trust with customers through online delivery and how to open the door to people who have never before come to us."

Fast and accurate internal communication is an important priority in a $14 billion global company with more than 70,000 employees and some 60,000 products for sale. "E-mail has become the communication tool of choice at 3M, replacing volumes of paper and fax documents as well as phone calls and some express courier service," Radford says. "Our employees are comfortable with e-mail because it's integrated into their desktop environment and they receive e-mail training starting on the first day of employment."

The company uses Lotus Notes for internal communication, so the design of each e-mail document is uniform—making the exchange of information much more efficient. "With regular use of a common format, readers learn to anticipate the visual cues," Radford explains. "Then they can move through their messages

COMMUNICATION OBJECTIVES

After you have finished this chapter, you should be able to

■ Identify the major types of electronic information sources.

■ Browse and search the Internet and World Wide Web.

■ Evaluate the quality of the electronic data you gather.

■ Communicate using word processing software, e-mail, and the telephone.

much more quickly because they know where information appears on the form." Depending on what they want to communicate, 3M employees can also enrich their e-mail messages using integrated graphics or attachments such as additional files to be transmitted along with the message.

One of the most important ongoing projects at 3M is the development of a "global enterprise data warehouse," a massive electronic storehouse of data and graphics that will be available to internal users who need to locate certain facts, figures, or images. For example, employees will be able to search the electronic image bank to select among thousands of digitized photos and graphics that are ready to be inserted into brochures, letters, videos, proposals, and reports—with just a few keystrokes. "A good data warehouse saves money and increases productivity," observes Radford. "You can reduce costs by making images available to a wider audience and by encouraging the use of images for more than one purpose. But you need to have good search capabilities to make accessing graphics and data as convenient as possible."

The 3M executive offers this advice for anyone who is looking for data online: "Start by defining the goals and the scope of the search. Then consider the source of the data," he says. "Names you can trust are important on the Internet. The chance

James Radford

Interactive Business Solutions Manager, 3M (St. Paul, Minnesota)

of finding good information improves when you go to recognized sources that have established reputations for highly accurate and current information. Ask questions and verify with a second source before using data from newer or unfamiliar sources."

Our Need to Know—Now!

Consider the following situations, all typical of those occurring thousands of times every day:

- *1* The SyQuest removable hard-disk drive Janice purchased and installed six months ago has just crashed. She needs to contact the company to determine if the disk drive is still under warranty and if so, how she can get it repaired or replaced.

- *2* Chris's boss, the director of human resources, asks her to make a hotel reservation for January 15–18 at a hotel in downtown San Francisco that charges between $150 and $250 per night.

- *3* Kim's company is trying to get ISO 2000 certification to expand its operations into central Europe. She wonders what is involved in securing such certification and what the advantages and disadvantages are.

- *4* Marc has just read an article in the *Wall Street Journal* about Auto-by-Tel, an online automobile buying service. He wonders if this would be a profitable company in which to invest his $8,500 Keogh account.

- As part of Kyle's term paper in European art history, he needs to include a color picture of the *Mona Lisa*.

- You've finally finished cramming for tomorrow's accounting exam and are ready to relax for a bit. What movies are on TV tonight?

Much of the information we need is too new to be available in printed form.

As these situations illustrate, our need for information is insatiable and unrelenting. Today, information is a mass commodity—not a scarce resource. The secret to dealing with this phenomenon is being able to access and make use of that information. As painful as it might be to contemplate, much (if not most) of your education is going to be obsolete within a few years. You will have a lifelong need to update your skills, secure relevant, accurate information, and share that information with others.

Contemporary managers need up-to-date information—and they need it now!

To the rescue comes the **Internet,** a worldwide collection of computers sitting in university labs, business offices, and government centers—all interconnected, all filled with massive amounts of information, and all accessible for free (or nearly so) to anyone with an Internet account (which includes almost all college students). The ability to access this information stored in thousands of computers worldwide and to chat with anyone around the globe at any hour of the day bestows tremendous power on anyone who knows how to retrieve, evaluate, and share that information.

Learn how to secure the information you need— whether it is a phone number, statistic, or research report.

Before you can communicate, you must, first of all, have something important to communicate. Thus, it only makes sense for us to learn how to access and share information now—before we learn about specific communication strategies. This chapter shows you how to use different forms of technology to communicate more easily, more efficiently, and more effectively.

Accessing Electronic Information

Today, in most libraries you can perform computer-assisted data searches. In fact, an entire knowledge industry has evolved in which organizations store huge

Stanley Herz is a living example of how technology can affect employment levels but boost efficiency. He laid off all seven employees at his executive-search firm and now runs the entire operation from his home, using only a computer and online data resources.

amounts of statistical, financial, and bibliographic information in the memory banks of their mainframe computers or on compact disks and then make this information available to users nationwide for a fee.

An electronic **database** is a computer-searchable collection of information on a general subject area, such as business, education, or psychology. Electronic databases are fast; you can typically collect more data electronically in an hour than would be possible in an entire day of conventional library research.

In addition, electronic databases are typically more current than printed databases; most are updated weekly or monthly. Also, each contains several years' worth of citations, whereas manual indexes require searching through individual annual volumes and monthly supplements. Finally, electronic databases are extremely flexible. You can use different search terms, combine them, and modify your search at every step.

Although you may never write another academic report after graduating from college, you *will* continue to need to locate information—for business, political, or personal reasons. Computer-assisted information retrieval has now become so widely available, economical, and easy to use that it has become a powerful tool helping managers solve problems and make decisions.

You can conduct a comprehensive search for data without ever leaving your office, via online computer searching.

CD-ROM Databases

A **CD-ROM database** is a collection of information stored on a high-capacity disk that is accessible by a microcomputer with a CD drive. One CD-ROM (compact disk—read-only memory) can hold up to 250,000 pages of text—the equivalent of 1,500 floppy disks. The advantage of using a CD-ROM database is that the collection is stored on a disk connected directly to the computer you're using. Rather than pay for a telephone hookup to the remote mainframe computer, the library or organization purchases the CD-ROM collection and its periodic updates; individual computer searches are typically free to the user.

Most of the directories and indexes available in print format are also available in CD-ROM format, although sometimes under a different name.

Online Databases

Unlike CD-ROM databases, online databases require that you be electronically connected to a remote mainframe computer.

An **online database** is a collection of information stored in a mainframe computer that is accessible by a microcomputer and a telephone hookup. A user in Bangor, Maine, for example, could use his or her computer and modem to access the ABI/Inform database by dialing up the DIALOG Information Services mainframe computer in Palo Alto, California. The user could then instruct the computer to print out a list of articles on a particular topic from its database of citations from more than 800 business and management journals.

The main advantage of using an online database is that it can be accessed anywhere a microcomputer, modem, and telephone line are available—from your office, your hotel room, even your automobile. The user can print out citations, abstracts, and sometimes even the full text of articles. If the full text is not available online, information is provided for ordering photocopies or faxes of the articles.

Online Information Services

Online information services (such as America Online, CompuServe Information Service, and the Microsoft Network) provide dial-up access to collections of information for business research, consumer needs, and entertainment (see Figure 3.1). A flat monthly fee buys unlimited use of their basic information services; other more specialized information services are available on a per-use fee.

The Internet

Chances are that the very information you need is stored somewhere on the Internet. You have to learn how to access it.

As we noted earlier, the Internet is a vast information system that connects millions of computers worldwide, allowing them to exchange all types of information and to conduct many types of business transactions, such as online banking and shopping. On the Internet, you can send and receive e-mail, transfer files between computers, search for information (our focus here), and participate in discussion groups.

It's like standing on the bridge of Starship Enterprise. Andersen Consulting's new Pegasus software program combines Web pages, news bulletins, and 3-D graphics to help work teams visualize data and reach collaborative decisions.

FIGURE 3.1 The Microsoft Network Information Service

To give you some idea of how large the Internet is, consider these statistics:[1]

- Between 2 and 4 million computers in 156 countries are now connected via the Internet.

- From 10 to 30 million people have access to the Internet (7 to 15 million in the United States alone).

- By the year 2000, there may be 1 billion Internet users, with the majority of these users connecting to the Internet from their homes.

Recall, however, our earlier discussion of the temporal nature of data. These figures are, as you read them, hopelessly out of date. (You could, of course, log on to the Internet for more up-to-date figures.)

Although numerous types of resources are available on the Internet, our interest here is in two main types: discussion resources (consisting primarily of mailing lists and newsgroups) and reference resources (consisting primarily of Gopher and the World Wide Web).

Discussion Resources

Discussion groups on the Internet allow you to participate in interactive, ongoing discussions on a particular topic with people all over the world.

A **mailing list** is a discussion group in which messages are sent directly to members via e-mail. On the Internet, these mailing lists are called *listservs*. To become a member, you must first subscribe to the list (typically by sending an e-mail message to the listserver). From then on, any messages posted to the list are automatically sent to your e-mail address. Listservs are usually created to enable members to

Mailing-list articles are sent directly to your electronic mailbox.

exchange information and views about a particular topic. Your professor, for example, may create a mailing list for your class. That way, any message posted to that mailing list either by the instructor or by one of the students is sent to (and presumably read by) all members of the class. Such a list would be discontinued at the end of the school term. Some more-or-less permanent mailing lists provide searchable archive files that contain all the old messages.

You must log on to a newsgroup to read the new messages.

A **newsgroup** is a discussion group in which messages (called *articles*) are posted at the newsgroup site. Anyone can connect to the site via an Internet *usenet* connection as frequently as desired to read any newly posted articles. Newsgroups differ from mailing lists in that newsgroup members have to "visit" the newsgroup site in order to see any new messages, whereas new messages are automatically sent as e-mail to mailing-list members. The news administrator determines how long old articles are archived (and, therefore, available for searching).

As this chapter is being written, there are in excess of 15,000 newsgroups to which you can subscribe. Some are moderated, meaning that all messages first go to an individual who reviews and screens them for appropriateness before posting them to the newsgroup. Others are unmoderated, meaning that the articles have not been screened. Newsgroups have multipart names, separated by dots, with the main topic listed first and increasingly narrow subtopics in order. Thus, the newsgroup *rec.travel.air* provides information about recreation; specifically, about travel; and even more specifically, about deals on airline tickets; *rec.travel.germany* provides information on travel to and within Germany. Figure 3.2 shows a typical newsgroup article.

FIGURE 3.2   A Reader Posting in a Newsgroup

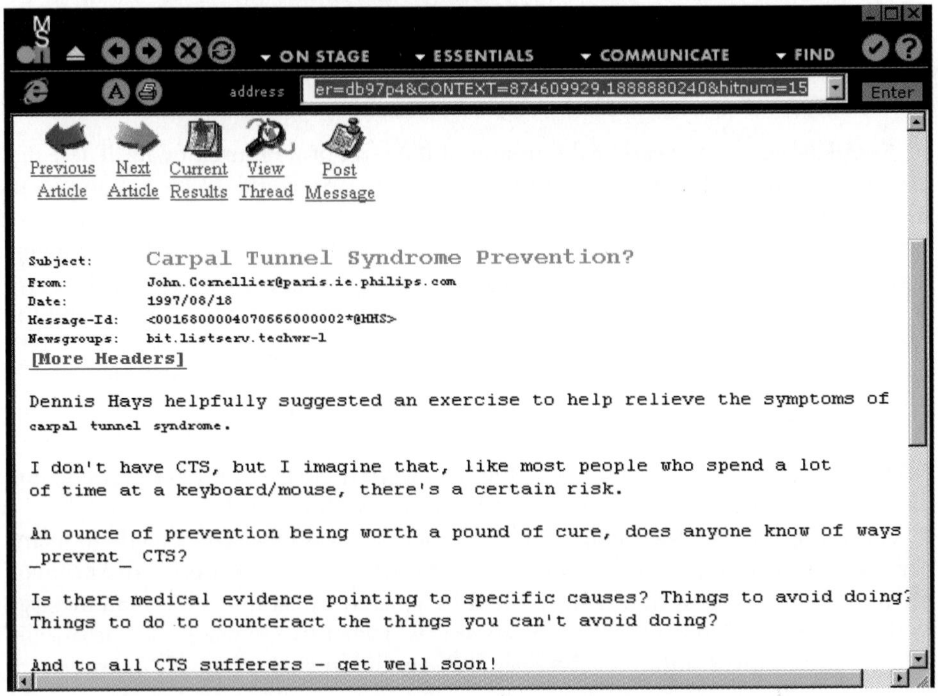

Reference Resources

Gopher is a software program that provides access to text-only documents typically stored at sites maintained by government agencies or educational institutions. Using Gopher, you can download files such as regulations, policies, reports of governmental agencies, research reports, newspaper articles, movie reviews, and weather forecasts. The entire range of information available from Gopher is known as *Gopherspace.*

Gopher was one of the original building blocks of the Internet, providing access to text-only data.

The newest and fastest-growing segment of the Internet (and the resource that is of most interest to us) is the **World Wide Web** (also known as WWW or simply the Web). Web documents, called *pages,* can contain text, graphics, sound, and video, all written in *hypertext.* Hypertext links (highlighted words or images) in the document enable the reader to explore as much or as little of a document as desired. Clicking on a hypertext link instantly opens that document (which may be on a different computer halfway around the world). These hypertext links distinguish the Web from all other Internet resources and make it such a useful and versatile tool for accessing and sharing information. Users access this information by a software program known as a *Web browser,* the most popular of which are Microsoft Internet Explorer and Netscape Navigator.

Browsing and Searching the Internet

Nobody "owns" the Internet; that is, there is no one governing authority that can make rules and impose order. Thus, it should not surprise you that the massive amount of information available on the Internet is not neatly and logically organized for easy search and retrieval. One "Internaut" describes the situation this way:

Browse (perhaps using Yahoo!) when you're not sure precisely what you're looking for. Search (perhaps using Excite) when you're looking for specific information.

> Imagine yourself having a key to the door of a large library. Unfortunately, everyone else has a key also. Everyone has free access to put anything they want in the library, wherever they want to put it. To make matters worse, there is no librarian, there is no card catalog, no computerized index, no map, and no reference staff; so after people deposit materials, there is no structure to help others locate them. The Internet is like that library—a disorganized chaotic repository of information.[2]

Fortunately, there are a variety of search sites available on the Internet to make accessing Internet resources if not painless, at least more pleasant and productive. Basically, these sites fall into two categories—*directories* for browsing the Internet and *indexes* for searching for specific information. According to *PC Magazine,* Yahoo! is the best online directory and Excite is the best search index.[3]

With a search directory, you can search deeper and deeper into a subject, gradually narrowing your focus.

Browsing the Internet   Web directories are hyperlinked lists of Web sites, hierarchically organized into topical categories and subcategories. Yahoo! is a directory of several hundred thousand Web sites submitted by human beings and sorted into categories. Clicking your way through these lists will lead you to Web site links for the subject you're investigating. Built by people rather than computers, the directories cover far less ground than Web indexes but are generally better organized.

Use Yahoo! when you need to find common information quickly and easily. If you aren't looking for something specific, try using Yahoo!'s categories to drill down and narrow your search. Yahoo! is an excellent starting point for Web searching. Its well-organized Web catalog either delivers high-quality results or sends you to a search engine to get what you want. Spotlight 5—On Technology illustrates step-by-step the process of using a search directory.

Browsing the Internet Using Yahoo!

Marisa is interested in learning if there are any relevant job openings posted online for which she might apply.

Because she's not sure where to begin, Marisa logs on to the Internet and points her Netscape Web browser to the Yahoo! search site *(www.yahoo.com).*

Although she could have typed in a search term in the Search box, when browsing, it is generally more productive to first "drill down" through the categories shown. Marisa clicks on Business and Economy.

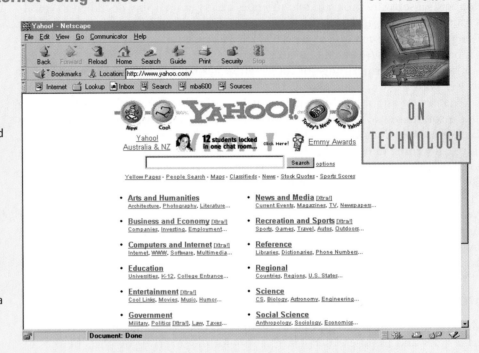

When the next level of categories appears (the subcategories under Business and Economy), she clicks on Employment.

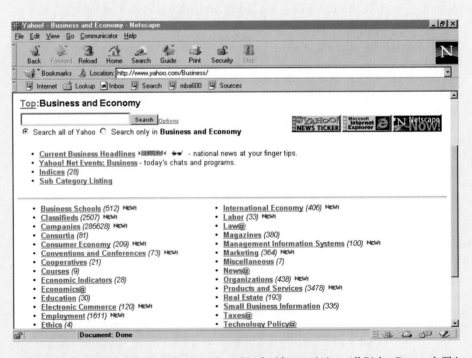

Copyright 1995 Netscape Communications Corp. Used with permission. All Rights Reserved. This electronic file or page may not be reprinted or copied without the express written permission of Netscape.

Note how Yahoo! keeps track of each level of information. You can click on any level to return to that level.

Marisa now clicks on Resumes.

After scanning the resulting list, Marisa clicks on the Best Jobs in the USA Today site.

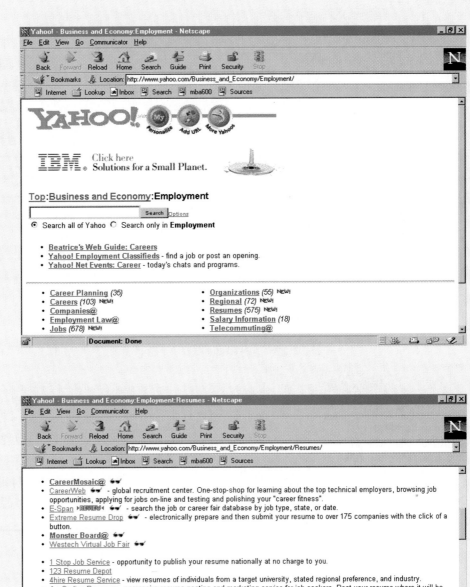

Copyright 1995 Netscape Communications Corp. Used with permission. All Rights Reserved. This electronic file or page may not be reprinted or copied without the express written permission of Netscape.

She then selects Ohio and Professional from the drop-down menus and clicks on Search Database.

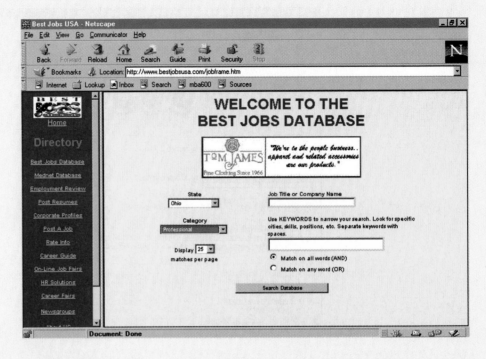

The program searches its database and lists all of the professional job openings it has on file for Ohio. Marisa clicks on the Quality Assurance position at General Electric.

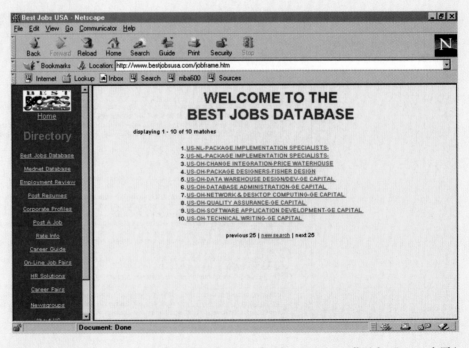

Copyright 1995 Netscape Communications Corp. Used with permission. All Rights Reserved. This electronic file or page may not be reprinted or copied without the express written permission of Netscape.

Clicking on a job opening brings up the job description and requirements.

If Marisa decides she's interested in the job, she can either fax her résumé or send it as an e-mail message to General Electric.

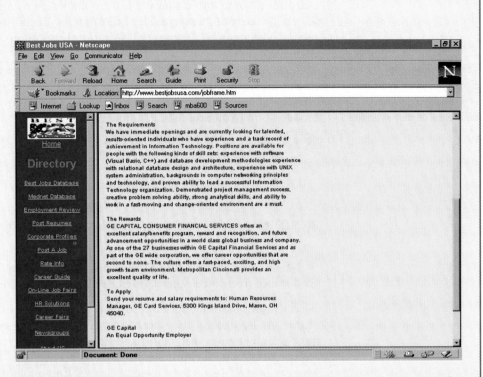

Source: Copyright 1995 Netscape Communications Corp. Used with permission. All Rights Reserved. This electronic file or page may not be reprinted or copied without the express written permission of Netscape. Text and artwork copyright ©1996 by YAHOO!, Inc. All rights reserved. YAHOO! and the YAHOO! logo are trademarks of YAHOO!, Inc.

Searching the Internet   Web indexes (for example, Excite and AltaVista) are massive, computer-generated databases containing information on millions of Web pages and usenet newsgroup articles. By entering keywords or phrases, you can retrieve lists of Web pages that contain your search term. The lists are created by *Web crawlers* (also called *robots* or *spiders*), software programs that roam the Web, looking for new sites by following links from page to page. When a spider finds a new page, it scans and indexes its contents, and follows its links to other pages. Some crawler engines create full-text indexes, while others attempt to extract only significant terms. Once your query executes, the Web search site displays the list of hits as a page containing the URLs (Universal Resource Locators, or Internet addresses) that are hyperlinked. To move directly to any particular site, simply click its URL.

Some "metasearch" indexes (such as Metacrawler) search through numerous individual search sites. These searches, naturally, take much longer than using an individual search site.

The Excite search index contains the full text of 50 million Web pages and 15,000 newsgroups. According to *PC* magazine, "Excite is a powerful search tool that handles natural-language queries with aplomb, delivers relevant hits, and offers impressive features, such as its keyword weighting."[4] Excite's primary advantage over most other search engines is its conceptual searching feature—it finds not only your keyword but also lots of concepts related to it.

The success of your Internet search will depend on how skillfully you choose your keywords (or *search terms*). Remember that the computer makes a very literal search; it will find exactly what you ask for—and nothing more. If you use the search term "secretaries," most search indexes will not find citations for the words "secretary" or "secretarial" (because it performs conceptual searches, Excite is an exception). Some indexes have a feature known as *truncation,* which allows you to search for the root of a term. Thus, a search for "secre" would retrieve "secret," "secretarial," "secretaries," "secretary," "secretion," and so on. You would then choose the entries appropriate for your purpose.

Take the time to learn basic Boolean logic; it will save you time and enhance the efficiency of your searches.

Most indexes also allow the use of logical search operators (called *Boolean logic*) in the keywords. There are four basic search operators—AND, OR, NOT, and NEAR—and as you can see, they are always typed in all capitals. The operators broaden or narrow searches as follows:

- AND for items that contain both term 1 AND term 2; AND decreases the number of hits.

- OR for items that contain either term 1 OR term 2; OR increases the number of hits.

- NOT to exclude items containing the NOT term; NOT decreases the number of hits.

- NEAR to locate only those items in which the two terms are within a given distance from each other; NEAR decreases the number of hits.

Placing quotation marks around a phrase requires the exact matching of a phrase. As in algebra, the operations inside parentheses are performed first, and most search engines read command lines from left to right. Thus, the search term "heavy metal" would eliminate the flagging of Web sites devoted to metals and ores, whereas *"metal" NOT "heavy metal*" would find *only* those sites devoted to metals and ores. Spotlight 6—On Technology illustrates step-by-step the process of using a search index.

Evaluating the Quality of Electronic Information

Don't believe everything you read!

Anyone with access to the Internet can post pretty much anything he or she wants online. There is no law, regulation, or Internet policy that states that the information posted on the Internet has to be true, objective, intelligent, or politically correct (recall that there is no central authority for managing the Internet).

The range of informational quality on the Net is enormous. Information posted by governmental and educational institutions (typically, those sites that end in ".gov" or ".edu") is most often comprehensive, accurate, and up-to-date. Most pages sponsored by commercial organizations (typically, those sites that end in ".com") are also of high quality, as long as you recognize the profit incentive for these pages; some "dot com" sites, however, are best approached with a "buyer beware" attitude. Personal home pages and those sponsored by advocacy organizations should be evaluated especially carefully for accuracy, fairness, and coverage. The same is true for usenet newsgroups and mailing lists.

You are responsible for the quality of the data in your communications.

The consequences of making decisions based upon invalid data can range from minor inconvenience to receiving a failing grade in a class to jeopardizing the financial viability of your company. You are responsible for the quality of the information you include in your correspondence, reports, and presentations. Avoid accepting something as fact just because you saw it on the Net. Evaluate your sources critically, using the questions in Checklist 2 (page 91) as a guide.

Searching the Internet Using Excite

SPOTLIGHT 6

ON TECHNOLOGY

Before deciding whether to apply for a position at General Electric, Marisa wants to learn more about the company. Because she is searching for specific information, she logs on to the Internet and points her Web browser to the Excite search site *(www.excite.com).*

In the Search box, she types "General Electric" AND Cincinnati and then clicks on Search. (By default, Excite searches the World Wide Web.)

Excite locates 1,467 documents that contain both the phrase "General Electric" and the word "Cincinnati." It lists these documents in order of relevance.

The first document listed has a relevancy score of 79% (out of 100%). Marisa clicks on it.

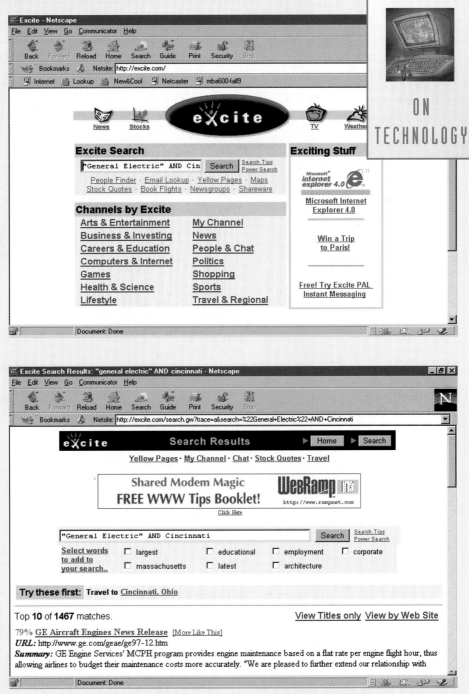

Copyright 1995 Netscape Communications Corp. Used with permission. All Rights Reserved. This electronic file or page may not be reprinted or copied without the express written permission of Netscape.

Here's a bit of information that might prove useful if Marisa interviews at GE in Cincinnati, so she prints out a copy by clicking Print on the toolbar. Then she clicks the Back button on the toolbar to return to the list of sources.

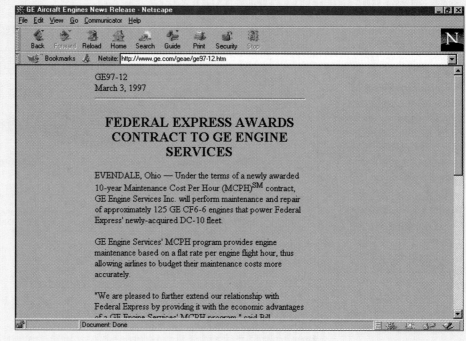

Marisa scrolls down the list of sources and clicks on one that provides information about Cincinnati.

Copyright 1995 Netscape Communications Corp. Used with permission. All Rights Reserved. This electronic file or page may not be reprinted or copied without the express written permission of Netscape.

Up comes some general information about the city in which the job is available.

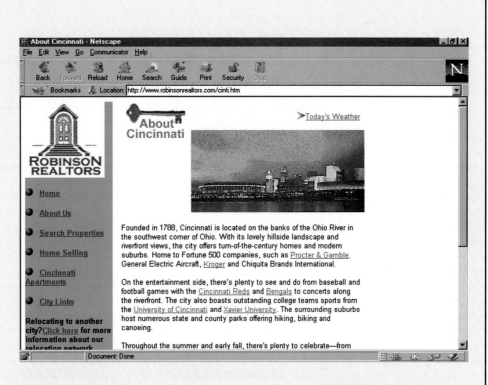

Marisa wonders if General Electric has a home page. Back on Excite's main page, she types "General Electric" AND "home page" (there are numerous other ways of locating corporate home pages as well) and clicks on Search.

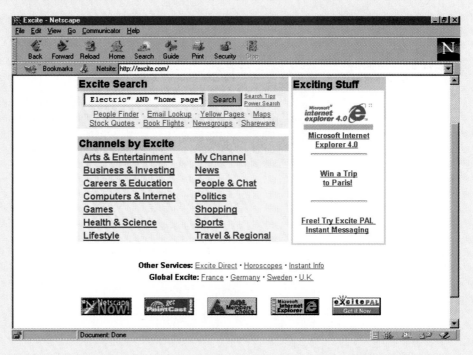

Copyright 1995 Netscape Communications Corp. Used with permission. All Rights Reserved. This electronic file or page may not be reprinted or copied without the express written permission of Netscape.

Sure enough, the second entry is what she's looking for, and she clicks on it.

At the company's home page, Marisa can read detailed information about the company, its history, and its products and can study its latest annual report.

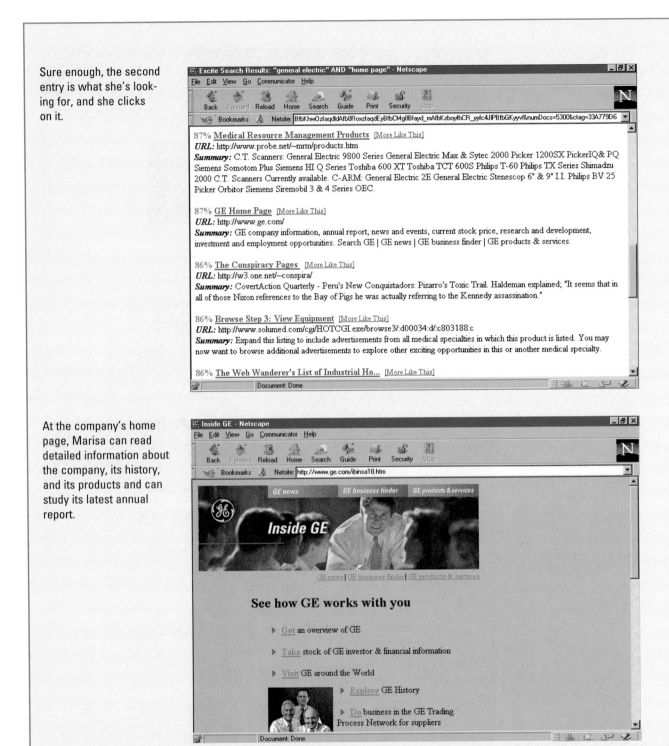

Copyright 1995 Netscape Communications Corp. Used with permission. All Rights Reserved. This electronic file or page may not be reprinted or copied without the express written permission of Netscape.

Now, Marisa goes back to Excite's home page and selects the Power Search option. Then she selects "Current News" from the "I want to search" drop-down menu and types in "General Electric" in the "My search results must contain" box.

Excite's Current News feature locates 56 recent articles about General Electric. Marisa clicks on the first one.

Copyright 1995 Netscape Communications Corp. Used with permission. All Rights Reserved. This electronic file or page may not be reprinted or copied without the express written permission of Netscape.

The top Current News hit is a recent article from *Business Week* showing General Electric has the highest market value of any international company.

Marisa then clicks the Back button on the toolbar and proceeds to scan other articles about the company, printing out those she thinks might be useful.

Copyright 1995 Netscape Communications Corp. Used with permission. All Rights Reserved. This electronic file or page may not be reprinted or copied without the express written permission of Netscape. Excite, Excite Search, City Net, and the Excite Logo are trademarks of Excite, Inc. and may be registered in various jurisdictions. Excite screen display copyright 1995–1997 Excite, Inc.

Sharing Electronic Information

Technology helps us not only access information but also share it with others. You will often incorporate the information you access electronically into your own electronic communications—correspondence, reports, phone calls, and the like (we cover business presentations in Chapter 13)—using a variety of technological innovations.

Word Processing

Touch keyboarding (typing) skills are critical in the contemporary business environment.

Word processing is the production of letters, memorandums, reports, and other documents through the use of automated electronic equipment. Most word processing today is done through the use of software programs that operate on microcomputers. The two most popular word processing programs in the business community are WordPerfect® and Microsoft Word®.

Using word processing, a writer can keyboard a message very quickly, without worrying about format or typographical errors. Then, using the various editing functions built into the software, the writer can revise, delete, add, or reposition words and sentences until the final document is ready to be printed. The document is then stored for later retrieval—most often on a removable floppy disk or on a permanent hard disk.

✔ CHECKLIST 2   Evaluating the Quality of Internet Resources

Criterion 1: Authority

☑ Is it clear who sponsors the page and what the sponsor's purpose in maintaining the page is?

☑ Is it clear who wrote the material and what the author's qualifications for writing on this topic are?

☑ Is there a way of verifying the legitimacy of the page's sponsor; that is, is there a phone number or postal address to contact for more information? (Simply an e-mail address is not enough.)

☑ If the material is protected by copyright, is the name of the copyright holder given?

Criterion 2: Accuracy

☑ Are the sources for any factual information clearly listed so they can be verified in another source?

☑ Has the sponsor provided a link to outside sources (such as product reviews or reports filed with the SEC) that can be used to verify the sponsor's claims?

☑ Is the information free of grammatical, spelling, and other typographical errors? (These kinds of errors not only indicate a lack of quality control but can actually produce inaccuracies in information.)

☑ Is statistical data in graphs and charts clearly labeled and easy to read?

☑ Does anyone monitor the accuracy of the information being published?

Criterion 3: Objectivity

☑ For any given piece of information, is it clear what the sponsor's motivation is for providing it?

☑ Is the informational content clearly separated from any advertising or opinion content?

☑ Is the point of view of the sponsor presented in a clear manner, with its arguments well supported?

Criterion 4: Currentness

☑ Are there dates on the page to indicate when the page was written, first placed on the Web, and last revised?

☑ Are there any other indications that the material is kept current?

☑ If material is presented in graphs or charts, is it clearly stated when the data was gathered?

☑ Is there an indication that the page has been completed and is not still in the process of being developed?

Source: This material was compiled from a set of five checklists created by Jan Alexander and Marsha Tate, "Teaching Critical Evaluation Skills for World Wide Web Resources," 28 Oct. 1996. http://www.widener.edu/libraries.html. (Select link "Evaluating Web Resources.") Copyright Widener University 1996. 6 Jan. 1997.

Sophisticated word processing programs can check spelling, replace a word or phrase throughout a document, automatically insert the current date and page number, generate an index, produce "original" form letters, perform mathematical calculations, copy charts and graphics from other programs (such as spreadsheets), automatically number and position footnotes and endnotes, and arrange text in columns.

Many word processing systems offer additional features designed to improve writing. An electronic thesaurus provides a list of synonyms for words. A grammar and punctuation checker calls attention to simple errors such as repeated words, numbers in incorrect format (for example, "$5,32"), and sentences not started with a capital letter. Other available features include an online style manual that you can call to the screen to review rules of grammar, punctuation, and usage; electronic

Novell Corporation's Netware software has captured around 60% of the worldwide networking market, allowing managers to share information regardless of geographical location and time differences.

outliners that provide a format the writer can fill in to outline a message; and writing analysis software that can help you analyze the extent to which a document follows the principles of clear writing.

Desktop publishing (DTP) software is a specialized form of word processing that permits users to write, assemble, and design such publications as company newsletters, brochures, and catalogs. Typically, the text is entered (keyboarded) by means of word processing software and then copied into the desktop publishing software, where it can be easily manipulated. After the document has been designed on the computer, it is typically printed out on a laser printer, which produces high-quality output, and then duplicated.

Desktop publishing software provides more advanced graphics features than word processing software, it is faster and cheaper than using a commercial printing company, and it provides users more flexibility and control of their documents. The disadvantage is that not everyone who knows how to keyboard also knows how to design a document so that the result is both effective and attractive.

Presentation software is similar to desktop publishing, except that it is used to produce audiovisual aids for presentations. By means of built-in designs called *templates,* users can create attractive and effective transparencies and slides at a reasonable cost. Transparencies can be made directly from a laser printer (either color or black and white); slides are more often prepared from the computer files by a slide-processing firm. Increasingly, presenters are projecting their audiovisuals directly from their computers, thereby avoiding the need for hard-copy output. We'll talk more about electronic presentations in Chapter 13. It is likely that the use of desktop presentation software (such as PowerPoint® and Freelance Graphics®) will increase dramatically in the years ahead.

E-mail

E-mail may be your most frequent form of written communication on the job.

Always think *before you* write.

In e-mail (electronic mail), messages are composed, transmitted, and usually read on computer screens. Messages travel through cables within the company and through telephone lines or cellular signals outside the company. E-mail delivery is almost instantaneous, although the receiver must access the computer system to know that a message is waiting. In many corporations, e-mail has almost completely replaced the traditional interoffice memorandum.

Because e-mail is often written "on the fly"—composed and sent while keyboarding—writers sometimes tend to forget about matters of formatting, correctness of expression, and courtesy. Competent communicators follow the guidelines shown in Checklist 3 to ensure that their e-mail messages achieve their objectives.

The Telephone

There are more than 285 million telephones in the world, 115 million of them in the United States. That is the equivalent of about one telephone for every two people in this country. American Telephone and Telegraph (AT&T) processes 75 million calls on these phones every single day.[5] No wonder, then, that communicating effectively by telephone is a crucial managerial skill, one that becomes increasingly important as the need for instantaneous information increases. Your telephone demeanor may be taken by the caller as the attitude of the entire organization. Every time the phone rings, your organization's future is on the line.

✔CHECKLIST 3   Effective E-mail Practices

Format

✔ **Use short lines and short paragraphs.** A short line length (perhaps 50 to 60 characters) is much easier to read than the 80-character line of most text editors. Similarly, short paragraphs (especially the first and last paragraph) are more inviting to read. Avoid formatting a long message as one solid paragraph.

✔ **Don't shout.** Use all-capital letters only for emphasis or to substitute for italicized text (such as book titles). Do NOT type your entire message in all capitals. It is a text-based form of *shouting* at your reader and is considered rude (not to mention being more difficult to read).

✔ **Proofread your message before sending.** Don't let the speed and convenience of e-mail lull you into being careless. While an occasional typo or other surface error will probably be overlooked by the reader, excessive errors or sloppy language creates an unprofessional image of the sender.

Content

✔ **Choose your recipients carefully.** Don't send a message to an entire mailing list (for example, the whole department) if it applies to only one or two people. Likewise, if you're writing to John about Joan, don't get the two confused when filling in the address line. A mistake such as this could be professionally and personally embarrassing to both you and the recipient.

✔ **Use a descriptive subject line.** Most e-mail programs allow the reader to preview all new messages by date received, sender, and subject, so the wording of the subject line may determine not only *when* but even *if* a message is read. Use a brief, but descriptive, subject.

✔ **Greet your recipient.** Downplay the seeming impersonality of computerized mail by starting your message with a friendly salutation, such as "Hi, Amos" or "Dear Mr. Fisher."

✔ **Append previous messages appropriately.** Most e-mail systems allow you to append the original message to your reply. Use this feature judiciously. Occasionally, it may be helpful for the reader to see his or her entire message replayed. More often, however, you can save the reader time by establishing the context of the original message in your reply. If necessary, quote pertinent parts of the original message. If the entire original message is needed, treat it as an appendix and insert it at the *end* of your reply—not at the beginning.

✔ **Use a direct style of writing.** Put your major idea in the first sentence or two. If the message is so sensitive or emotionally laden that a more indirect organization would be appropriate, you should reconsider whether e-mail is the most effective medium for the message.

✔ **Think twice; write once.** This variation of the carpenter's advice ("measure twice; cut once") is appropriate here. Because it is so easy to respond immediately to a message, you might be tempted to let your emotions take over. Such behavior is called "flaming" and should be avoided. Always assume the message you send will never be destroyed but will be saved permanently in somebody's computer file.

✔ **Provide an appropriate closing.** Some e-mail programs identify only the e-mail address (for example, "70511.753 @ compuserve.com") in the message header they transmit. Don't take a chance that your reader won't recognize you. Include your name, e-mail address, and any other appropriate identifying information at the end of your message.

Calling Versus Writing

Before you pick up the phone to make a call, consider whether you'll accomplish your purpose better by calling or by writing. If your message is long and complicated, it may be easier for your audience to understand in writing, and the person can refer back to the document when necessary. If you are conveying bad news, a phone call may soften the blow, whereas a letter may strengthen the force of your message. You'll need to have a clear purpose and understand the effect the form of your message will have on your audience.

Written messages, of course, provide a record of communication. Even if you decide to telephone, remember that you should often follow a call with a written note, both to make sure there has been no misunderstanding and to document your communication.

Your Telephone Voice

Your voice is a primary means of accomplishing your objective on the phone.

Much of what you have learned about body language is useless when you're talking on the phone. You cannot maintain eye contact or observe facial expression and body posture through telephone lines (yet!). That is one reason why ear-to-ear communication is often not as effective as person-to-person communication in solving difficult problems. You are, however, able to make use of such voice qualities as rate of speech and pitch to pick up nonverbal clues about the other person (and, of course, the other person is able to make use of the same information about you).

Because the person to whom you're speaking has no visual clues to augment the auditory clues, a voice that is raspy, hoarse, shrill, loud, or weak can make you sound angry, excited, depressed, or bored—even if you aren't. Therefore, try to control your voice and project a friendly, competent, enthusiastic image to the other party.

To make your voice as clear as possible, sit or stand tall and avoid chewing gum or eating while talking. If your head is tilted sideways to cradle the phone between your head and shoulder, your throat is strained and your words may sound unclear.

Greet the telephone caller with a smile—just as you would greet someone in person. Your voice sounds more pleasant when you're smiling. An experiment was once conducted in which telephone salespeople were instructed to smile when they talked to their customers on one day and to scowl on the next. The salespeople sold almost twice as much on the days they were smiling.[6]

When the phone rings, pause, shift gears mentally, smile, and then answer the phone. Some firms even attach a sticker to the phone to remind employees to smile. "Smile," the sticker says, "it might be the boss calling."

Answer promptly and courteously, providing as much helpful information as possible.

Always answer the phone by the second or third ring. Regardless of how busy you are, you do not want to give the impression that your company doesn't care about its callers. Answer clearly and slowly, giving the company's name. Remember that even if you give the same greeting fifty times a day, your callers probably hear it only once. Make sure they can understand it.

Be a good listener. Just as you would never continue writing or reading while someone speaks to you in person, do not engage in such distracting activities during phone calls. Pay attention especially to getting names correct and use the person's name during the conversation to personalize the message.

Voice Mail

Whether you love it or hate it, voice mail (for example, "Press 1 to leave a message or press 2 to speak to an operator") is here to stay. Although some callers find voice mail impersonal and irritating, most are grateful for the opportunity to leave a message when they're unable to reach their party.

Before you even make a call, recognize that you might have to leave a message (using voice mail or an answering machine), so plan your message beforehand. Be polite and get to the point quickly. Clearly define the purpose of the call and the desired action and always give your phone number—even if the caller has it on file. The calls that get returned the fastest are those that are easiest to make.

If you have voice mail on your own office phone, follow these guidelines:

wordwise

Extra: End of the World!   According to reader contributions submitted to columnist Richard Price, here's how the end of the world will be reported:

Wall Street Journal	"Dow Jones Plummets as World Ends"
Inc.	"Ten Ways You Can Profit from the Apocalypse"
Ladies Home Journal	"Lose 10 lbs. by Judgment Day with Our New Armageddon Diet"
Playboy	"Girls of the Apocalpyse"
The National Enquirer	"O.J. and Nicole, Together Again"
Sports Illustrated	"Game Over"

- Never use voice mail as a substitute for answering your phone when you are available. Your customers, suppliers, and fellow workers deserve more consideration than that.

- Record your outgoing message in your own voice and keep it short (today, almost everyone knows how to use voice mail or an answering machine). Here is an example: "Hello, this is John Smith. Please leave me a message and I'll get back to you as quickly as I can. Thank you." Change your message when you will be away from the office for an extended period of time.

- Check your messages at least daily and return calls promptly. Callers assume that you've received their messages and may interpret a lack of response as rudeness.

Cellular Phones and Paging Devices

Nothing is more disconcerting than to have your business presentation interrupted by the ringing of someone's handheld cellular phone or the beeping of someone's pager. In public locations where conversation is expected (such as in airline terminals), using a cellular phone or answering a page is appropriate. However, at formal meetings, restaurants, movies, and social occasions, you should either turn off your machine or switch it to the "silent-alert" mode (typically either a light or a vibrating device).

When calling someone on a cellular phone, get down to business quickly; both you and the recipient are paying by-the-minute charges for using the phone. And when driving, remember that safety comes first. Do not make (or even answer) a call while maneuvering in difficult traffic.

SUMMARY

Our need for information is insatiable and unrelenting. Much of the information we need can be located on an as-needed basis from electronic sources—including CD-ROMs and online information services. Increasingly, however, we are turning to the discussion and reference resources of the Internet and tapping into the massive amount of information located in its networked computers around the world. Mailing lists and newsgroups are discussion resources on the Internet that allow you to participate in interactive, ongoing discussions on a particular topic. Reference resources on the Internet include Gopher, a software program that provides access to text-only documents, and the World Wide Web, which contains pages of text, graphics, sound, and video, with hyperlinks that enable the reader to instantly jump to related topics. This information can be located by using directories (such as Yahoo!) for browsing the Internet and indexes (such as Excite) for searching for specific information.

Because the quality of the information on the Internet varies tremendously, you should seriously evaluate the information you receive before deciding whether to use it. Evaluate all information in terms of the authority of the writer and sponsoring organization and the accuracy, objectivity, and currentness of the content.

Technology has a major effect on the way we share information. Word processing offers innumerable features for improving the writing process electronically, and desktop publishing and presentation software allow communicators to assemble and design sophisticated documents. E-mail is increasingly becoming a standard vehicle for workplace communication. Competent communicators format their e-mail messages for readability and ensure that the content is clear and concise. The telephone and its related technologies (voice mail, cellular phones, and paging devices) continue to play a critical role in sharing information quickly and economically.

KEY TERMS

CD-ROM database	Internet	presentation software
database	mailing list	word processing
desktop publishing	newsgroup	World Wide Web
Gopher	online database	

REVIEW AND DISCUSSION

1. **Communication at 3M Revisited**   When James Radford and his colleagues set up the 3M Innovation Network Web site, they double-checked the data being posted and built in the capability for two-way communication between employees and cutomers.
   a. Why would people who visit 3M's Web site want reassurance that the information there is both accurate and up to date?
   b. Why would 3M invite e-mail messages from customers?
   c. Why would 3M want to register its Web site with Yahoo! and other Internet directories?
2. Which is more convenient: a CD-ROM database or an online database? Why?
3. What is the difference between a mailing list and a newsgroup on the Internet?
4. Name two types of discussion resources and two types of reference resources on the Internet.
5. What is the difference between browsing and searching the Internet?
6. What is the difference between a textbook page and an Internet "page"?
7. What criteria should be used to evaluate the quality of electronic information?
8. Why is it important to know who sponsors a Web page?
9. What is the difference between using AND and OR as operators in a search statement? Which one would likely give you more hits?
10. What components of the word processing environment are available to improve writing?
11. "I don't have to worry about spelling and typing errors because my computer has a spell-checker." Discuss the validity of this statement.
12. What is meant by "flaming" in an e-mail message?
13. Why is it important to greet the telephone caller with a smile when the caller cannot see it?

1. **Communication Applications at 3M**   Thinking about how to harness new communication technology keeps 3M's James Radford busy. He and his 3M colleagues use e-mail constantly, and the company facilitates two-way electronic communication with customers through its World Wide Web site. As an experienced user of the Internet, Radford is well aware of the need to evaluate downloaded information before he includes it in any messages to internal or external audiences.

   Assume that you are starting a summer internship with 3M. Your first assignment is to look for online sources of information about the projected growth in Internet usage during the next few years. This information will be used to estimate the increased volume in e-mail messages that will be received through 3M's World Wide Web site, so that Radford can develop a process for responding to each message in a timely manner. Search the Internet for two or three credible sources of this information and then prepare to write an e-mail memo telling Radford the results of your search.

   a. Why do you need to check the credibility of your Internet sources before sending a memo to Radford?

   b. Will you use discussion resources or reference resources (or both) in your search? Explain your answer.

   c. What sources do you find when you conduct the search and how do you know these sources are credible?

   d. What do you need to tell Radford about each source you have located?

   e. Write a descriptive subject line for your e-mail memo to Radford.

2. **Using Technology**   Assume you are the fleet manager for a magazine distributor. You have been asked to write a report on the feasibility of leasing versus purchasing your fleet of delivery vans. Give a specific example of how you might productively make use of each of these technologies in preparing your report:

   a. desktop publishing   c. Internet newsgroups   e. voice mail
   b. e-mail   d. presentation software   f. World Wide Web

3. **Searching the Internet**   Recall the six situations on page 74 that require the collection of information. Locate and download at least one article on the Internet that would help you answer each question. Then prepare a short report to your instructor describing how you collected your data; for example, the search sites you used, the keywords you used, and the amount of information you found. Include a photocopy of each Internet article as an appendix to your report.

4. **Locating Specific Information**   You have been asked to determine the feasibility of opening a frozen yogurt store in Akron, Ohio. Answer the following questions, using the latest figures available. Provide a citation for each source.

   a. What were the number of establishments and the total sales last year for TCBY, a frozen yogurt franchise?

   b. What is the population of Akron, Ohio? What percentage of this population is between the ages of 18 and 24?

   c. What is the per capita income of residents of Akron?

   d. What is the address of Everything Yogurt, a frozen yogurt franchise?

   e. What is the climate of Akron, Ohio?

   f. How many students are enrolled at the University of Akron?

   g. What is the market outlook for frozen yogurt stores nationwide?

   h. What is the most current journal or newspaper article you can find on this topic?

5. **Internet Resources**   Think of an outside interest or hobby you enjoy. Locate and subscribe to two mailing lists that relate to this topic. Remain a member long

enough to receive two articles from one or both of these lists. Then, if you desire, unsubscribe to the lists. Also locate two newsgroups associated with this topic and retrieve two articles of interest. For the same interest or hobby, locate two World Wide Web pages that provide relevant information. Submit photocopies of the six articles to your instructor.

6. **Evaluating Electronic Information**   Using the guidelines in Checklist 2 (see page 91), evaluate the quality of each of the six resources you located in Exercise 3. If you were researching this information for a business purpose, would you *not* use any of the six sources? Why? Which source (mailing lists, newsgroups, or World Wide Web) appears to have the highest-quality information?

7. **Effective E-mail Practices**   Evaluate the following e-mail message in terms of the guidelines provided in Checklist 3 (see page 93). Specifically, what would you change to make it more effective? Should this message have been sent as an e-mail message in the first place? Discuss.

8. **Telecommuting**   Assume you are an advertising copywriter for a pharmaceutical firm in Los Angeles, and your first child was born three weeks ago. Now, you wish to work out of your home for the next 12 months, staying in contact with the office through electronic communication. Prepare a list of the equipment (hardware and software) you will need and explain how you will use each piece of equipment. What advantages and disadvantages of this arrangement (called *telecommuting*) do you see for yourself? for your company?

9. **Communicating by Telephone**   Role-play the situation described below. Record the conversations for later evaluation. While two students are role-playing, the others in the class should be making notes of what goes well and what might be improved. To help simulate a telephone environment, have the two student actors sit back-to-back so that they cannot see each other or the other class members.

   Situation: You are Chris Renshaw, administrative assistant for Ronald Krugel, the marketing manager at Kraft Enterprises. Terry Plachta, an important customer whom you've never met, calls your boss with a complaint that an item ordered two weeks ago does not work as advertised. Your boss won't be back in the office until tomorrow afternoon.

10. **Evaluating Telephone Communications**   Telephone two organizations in your area. Your purpose is to speak to the director of human resources to learn how much time he or she spends in meetings each week and to get an evaluation of the effectiveness of these meetings. Call at least three times if you're not successful the first time. Leave a message if necessary. Keep a log of each person with whom you speak at each organization, and evaluate the effectiveness of that person's telephone communication skills. Finally, write a summary of what you learned about meetings in that organization. Submit both your log and your summary to your instructor.

Internet Scavenger Hunt

CONTINUING CASE 3

Well, they had their little meeting on smoking (see Continuing Case 2, p. 70). Not surprisingly, Dave ended the meeting by asking Neelima and Marc to submit memos outlining their arguments for and against a smoking ban at Urban Systems.

Neelima and Marc both had the same idea—jump on the Internet and locate some good sources. As a starting point, Neelima thought that the American Cancer Society would probably have some useful information if she could figure out how to call them. Marc expected that the tobacco companies might provide some support; he also had heard about a tobacco research institute sponsored by the tobacco companies. And both assumed they'd be able to find articles, editorials, or research studies to give them the ammunition they needed to persuade Dave.

Written Communication Projects

1. Locate at least two newsgroup articles to support Neelima's position and two to support Marc's position.

2. Locate at least three World Wide Web articles to support each position.

3. Locate a mailing address and phone number for the American Cancer Society mentioned above.

Critical Thinking

4. Evaluate each resource you located in terms of the criteria provided in Checklist 2. Would you be confident using data from all of the sources, in your memo to your boss? Why or why not?

5. Judging from just the electronic information you've uncovered, which of the two sides do you think has the stronger argument? Why?

The BusCom Online Learning Center

Your Gateway to the Internet

As we make clear in this chapter, the Internet and World Wide Web are having profound effects on the way people access, use, and disseminate information. Given the pervasive nature of this exciting new medium of communication, competent communicators the world over must constantly ensure that they have access to (and can critically evaluate) the data they need to conduct business.

This textbook is designed to provide you with the strategies and information you need to communicate effectively in the contemporary work environment. The strategies you are learning will have relevance throughout your working life. But the fast-changing nature of technology means that information can change almost instantaneously. Thus, the specific facts that you learn today may or may not be relevant tomorrow. Unfortunately, printed facts and statistics can become outdated in a matter of days.

To help you stay abreast of the information you need to function effectively in this course, in other college courses, and on the job, we have developed a unique source of information—an online learning center for business communication students. Simply point your web browser to *http://www.hmco.com/college*, your one-stop guide to the world of online business communication.

Here you will be able to explore the Internet (including how to create your own home page); locate business information; get help with writing problems; participate in enrichment exercises designed to help you gain more from this course; and get help writing résumés and cover letters, learning about available jobs and potential employers, and advertising yourself on the Web when you're looking for an internship or postcollege job.

Here also you will be able to communicate with the author and the publisher of this text and read comments from other students around the country who are taking this course, ask questions, share your perspectives on business communication and the Internet, or just check in to see what other people are thinking. You'll soon learn that the content of this site changes frequently.

In short, the BusCom Online Learning Center is *your* site on the Internet. Check it out (it's free, of course), bookmark it as one of your favorites, and use it often—to make yourself a more effective communicator.

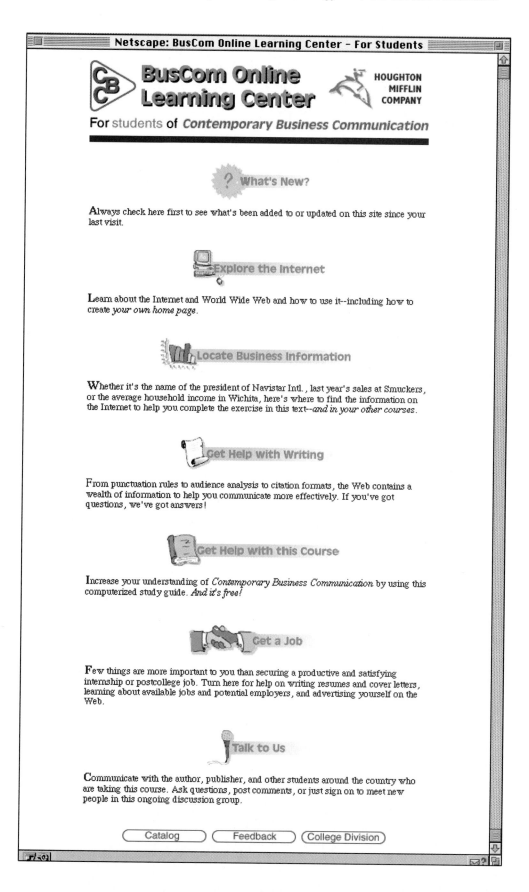

Netscape: BusCom Online Learning Center – For Students

BusCom Online Learning Center

HOUGHTON MIFFLIN COMPANY

For students of *Contemporary Business Communication*

? What's New?

Always check here first to see what's been added to or updated on this site since your last visit.

Explore the Internet

Learn about the Internet and World Wide Web and how to use it--including how to create *your own home page*.

Locate Business Information

Whether it's the name of the president of Navistar Intl., last year's sales at Smuckers, or the average household income in Wichita, here's where to find the information on the Internet to help you complete the exercise in this text--*and in your other courses*.

Get Help with Writing

From punctuation rules to audience analysis to citation formats, the Web contains a wealth of information to help you communicate more effectively. If you've got questions, we've got answers!

Get Help with this Course

Increase your understanding of *Contemporary Business Communication* by using this computerized study guide. *And it's free!*

Get a Job

Few things are more important to you than securing a productive and satisfying internship or postcollege job. Turn here for help on writing resumes and cover letters, learning about available jobs and potential employers, and advertising yourself on the Web.

Talk to Us

Communicate with the author, publisher, and other students around the country who are taking this course. Ask questions, post comments, or just sign on to meet new people in this ongoing discussion group.

(Catalog)   (Feedback)   (College Division)

Developing Your Writing Skills

4

Writing with Style: Individual Elements

An Insider's Perspective

What is it like to write for an audience of 34,000 employees spread across Canada and the United States, with branch offices around the world? Communicating with an international audience of employees is only one of the responsibilities handled by Martha Durdin, vice president of communications for Bank of Montreal. One of the largest banks in North America, Bank of Montreal owns Harris Bank in Chicago and has a stake in Grupo Financiero Bancomer in Mexico. Durdin and her staff not only prepare a bankwide employee magazine, they also work with their U.S. and Mexican counterparts to help in communicating with shareholders, media representatives, consumers, and businesses across the continent.

Although Durdin's communication responsibilities span a diversity of audiences and writing tasks, each message is planned with the "you" attitude in mind. "It's important to understand your audience and tailor the language and content so it is relevant to your readers," she advises. "Make sure that you are looking at the communication from the reader's viewpoint rather than your own viewpoint. That prevents you from getting caught up in the writing and using language that may not be familiar to your audience."

When the bank's communicators are writing for outside audiences, they are careful to define any industry jargon or acronyms that must be used. "We first spell out terms such as *automated teller machine* and show the acronym *ATM* in parentheses," says Durdin. "Then readers understand what we mean when we use the acronym later in the document." This approach is especially critical in cross-border communications, because Canadian jargon is not always the same as American jargon. For example, Canadians talk about *ABMs* (automated banking machines), while Americans talk about *ATMs*. As a result, Durdin's staff is scrupulous about matching the terminology to the audience and including definitions when needed.

At times, Durdin or her staff has to communicate a message that the reader is likely to perceive as negative. In such situations, she avoids negative language and

COMMUNICATION OBJECTIVES

After you have finished this chapter, you should be able to

■ Write clearly.

■ Prefer short, simple words.

■ Write with vigor.

■ Write concisely.

■ Prefer positive language.

■ Use a variety of sentence types.

■ Use active and passive voice appropriately.

■ Keep paragraphs unified and coherent.

■ Control paragraph length.

relies instead on positive language to get the point across. "The best way to deal with bad news is to present it clearly and get it out of the way quickly," she says. "Use positive language and try not to confuse the issue by wrapping the message around complicated language."

Martha Durdin

Vice president of communications, Bank of Montreal (Toronto, Canada)

To sharpen clarity, Bank of Montreal tests many of its written communications to be sure they are appropriate for their intended audiences. Surveys of customers and employees who receive written materials, as well as direct feedback from readers, help the bank's communicators spot potential problems and determine whether any revisions are needed. Once the communicators have refined the way they present certain information, such as a paragraph describing the bank, they can use it over and over in press releases, brochures, speeches, Internet materials, and other communications. "We may not use the information word for word in other communications," notes Durdin, "but using similar language provides consistency and allows us to capture what we are trying to express."

One of the most important communications produced by Durdin's department is Bank of Montreal's annual report to shareholders, which mixes written information with visual aids such as tables and graphs. Not long ago, the bank's chief financial officer wanted a new way to highlight the primary measures of financial performance in the upcoming annual report. Durdin's communicators and designers helped him develop an innovative, reader-friendly format. Then, to guide readers through the material, they positioned a small-scale view of the key pages (complete with arrows and notations about the main items) at the start of the section. "This format made the information more accessible," says Durdin, "and helped us to communicate the financial data more effectively."

What Do We Mean by *Style*?

If you study the five LAB (Language Arts Basics) exercises in the Reference Manual at the end of this book, you will know how to express yourself *correctly* in most business writing situations; that is, you will know how to avoid major errors in grammar, spelling, punctuation, and word usage. But a technically correct message may still not achieve its objective. For example, consider the following paragraph:

NOT: During the preceding year just past, Oxford Industries operated at a financial deficit. It closed three plants. It laid off many employees. The company's president was recently named Iowa Small Business Executive of the Year. Oxford is now endeavoring to ascertain the causes of its financial exigency. The company president said that. . . .

> *Your writing can be error-free and still lack style, but it cannot have style unless it is error-free.*

This paragraph has no grammatical, mechanical, or usage errors. But it is not clear, vigorous, or coherent. For example, consider the phrase "preceding year just past." "Preceding" *means* "just past," so why use both terms? In the second sentence, was closing the three plants the *cause* or the *result* of the financial deficit? What is the point of the sentence about the president? If you were speaking instead of writing, would you really say "endeavoring to ascertain," or would you use simpler language, like "trying to find out"? Finally, there are no transitions, or bridges, between the sentences; as a result, they don't flow smoothly.

Although the paragraph is technically correct, it lacks **style.** By style, we mean the way in which an idea is expressed (not its *substance*). Style consists of the particular words the writer uses and the manner in which those words are combined into sentences, paragraphs, and complete messages.

Now compare the first-draft paragraph above with this revised version:

> **Successful novelists like Mark Helprin (*A Winter's Tale, Ellis Island,* and *Soldier of the Great War*) write to *impress,* whereas business communicators write to *express.* Part of the beauty of fiction is that different readers glean different meanings from the same passage. Such a situation in business writing could prove disastrous.**

BUT: Last year Oxford Industries lost money and, as a result, closed three plants and laid off 200 employees. Now the company is trying to determine the causes of its problems. In an explanation to stockholders, Oxford's president, who was recently named Iowa Small Business Executive of the Year, said that. . . .

The revised version is more direct and readable. It clarifies relationships among the sentences. It uses concise, familiar language. It presents ideas in logical order. In short, it has style. Chapters 4 and 5 discuss 15 principles of effective writing style for business. Apply these principles of style as you write the letters, memos, and reports that are assigned in later chapters.

Words

1. Write clearly.
2. Prefer short, simple words.
3. Write with vigor.
4. Write concisely.
5. Prefer positive language.

Sentences

6. Use a variety of sentence types.
7. Use active and passive voice appropriately.

Paragraphs

8. Keep paragraphs unified and coherent.
9. Control paragraph length.

Overall Tone

10. Write confidently.
11. Use a courteous and sincere tone.
12. Use appropriate emphasis and subordination.
13. Use nondiscriminatory language.
14. Stress the "you" attitude.
15. Write at an appropriate level of difficulty.

While writing the first draft of a message, you should be more concerned with content than with style. Your major objective should be to get your ideas down in some form, without worrying about style and mechanics. (**Mechanics** are elements in communication that show up only in written form, including spelling, punctuation, abbreviations, capitalization, number expression, and word division.)

The more familiar you are with basic stylistic principles, the easier it will be to write your first draft and the less editing you will need to do later. So studying these principles first makes your writing process more efficient. You will then return to these principles when revising your writing to make sure that you have followed each guideline.

Principles 1–9 focus on the *parts* of the message (words, sentences, and paragraphs) and are discussed in this chapter (see Figure 4.1). Principles 10–15 focus on the tone of the *whole* message and are discussed in the next chapter. At the end of that chapter, a checklist summarizes all 15 writing principles. You should use Checklist 4 in evaluating your own style.

---

word**wise**

Spelling Problems

Teacher: How do you spell *rain?*
Student: *R-a-n-e.*
Teacher: That's the worst spell of rain we've had in a long time.

Fobia: A fear of misspelled words.

A man called the police to report a dead man in his driveway. "Where do you live?" asked the desk sergeant.

"205 Pocahontas Drive," the man replied.

There was a pause. "How do you spell *Pocahontas?*" asked the sergeant.

After another pause, the man answered, "I'll tell you what. I'll drag the body over to Elm Street and then call you back."

Style *refers to the effectiveness of the words, sentences, paragraphs, and overall tone of your message.*

Mechanics *refers to how an idea is expressed in writing.*

FIGURE 4.1 **Steps to an Effective Message**

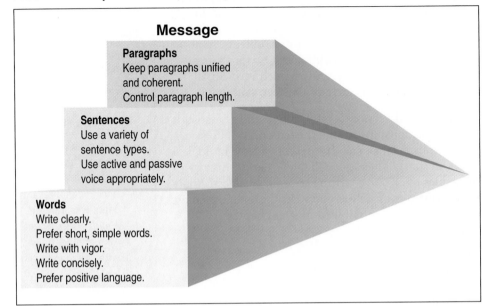

Choosing the Right Words

Individual words are our basic units of writing, the bricks with which we build meaningful messages. All writers have access to the same words. The care with which we select and combine words can make the difference between a message that achieves its objective and one that does not. Discussed below are five principles of word choice to help you write more effectively.

1. Write Clearly.

The basic guideline for writing, the one that must be present in order for the other principles to have meaning, is to write clearly—to write messages the reader can understand, depend on, and act on. You can achieve clarity by making your message accurate and complete, by using familiar words, and by avoiding dangling expressions and unnecessary jargon.

Accuracy is the most important attribute in business writing. It involves more than freedom from errors.

Be Accurate   A writer's credibility is perhaps his or her most important asset, and credibility depends greatly on the accuracy of the message. If by carelessness, lack of preparation, or a desire to manipulate, a writer misleads the reader, the damage is immediate and long-lasting. A reader who has been fooled once may not trust the writer again.

Accuracy can take many forms. The most basic is the truthful presentation of facts and figures. But accuracy involves much more. For example, consider the following sentence from a memo to a firm's financial backers:

> The executive committee of Mitchell Financial Services met on Thursday, May 28, to determine how to resolve the distribution fiasco.

Suppose, on checking, the reader learns that May 28 fell on a Wednesday this year—not on a Thursday. Immediately, the reader may suspect everything else in the message. The reader's thinking might be, "If the writer made this error that I *did* catch, how many errors that I *didn't* catch are lurking there?"

Now consider more subtle shades of truth. The sentence implies that the committee met, perhaps in an emergency session, for the *sole* purpose of resolving the distribution fiasco. But suppose this matter was only one of five agenda items being discussed at a regularly scheduled meeting. Is the statement still accurate? Suppose the actual agenda listed the topic as "Discussion of Recent Distribution Problems." Is *fiasco* the same as *problems*?

The accuracy of a message, then, depends on what is said, how it is said, and what is left unsaid (see, for example, the following section on the importance of completeness). Each writer must assess the ethical dimensions of his or her writing and use integrity, fairness, and good judgment to make sure communication is ethical.

Ethical communicators make sure the overall tone of their message is accurate.

Be Complete   Closely related to accuracy is completeness. A message that lacks important information may create inaccurate impressions. A message is complete when it contains all the information the reader needs—no more and no less—to react appropriately.

As a start, answer the five Ws; tell the reader *who, what, when, where,* and *why.* Leaving out any of this information may result either in decisions based on incomplete information or in extra follow-up correspondence to gather the needed information.

Use Familiar Words   Your message must be understood in order for someone to act on it. So you must use words that are both familiar to you (so that you will not misuse the word) and familiar to your readers.

A true story illustrates this point. A young soldier, serving in Vietnam as a typist for a general, received a report he thought the general should see. Believing that "for your edification" meant "for your information" (it actually means "for your *improvement*"), the typist wrote "Sir: For your edification" on the report and sent it to the general. Back came the general's reply: "Private: First, look up the word *edification.* Then see me for *your* edification!"

Don't assume that only long words cause confusion. Consider the following sentences:

Use language that you and your reader understand.

DILBERT

> **NOT:** The hexad worked with élan in order to redact their report and eloign their guilt.
>
> **BUT:** The six people vigorously edited their report in order to conceal their guilt.

The first version consists entirely of short words, with the longest word having just six letters and two syllables. Probably only a crossword puzzle addict, however, would be able to understand the first version; most readers would understand the second.

Long words are sometimes useful in business communication, of course, and should be used when appropriate. The larger your vocabulary and the more you know about your reader, the better equipped you will be to choose and use correctly those words that are familiar to your reader.

Avoid Dangling Expressions   A **dangling expression** is any part of a sentence that doesn't logically fit in with the rest of the sentence. Its relationship with the other parts of the sentence is unclear; it *dangles.* The two most common types of dangling expressions are misplaced modifiers and unclear antecedents.

To correct dangling expressions, (1) make the subject of the sentence the doer of the action expressed in the introductory clause; (2) move the expression closer to the word that it modifies; (3) make sure that the specific word to which a pronoun refers (its *antecedent*) is clear; or (4) otherwise revise the sentence.

> **NOT:** After reading the proposal, a few problems occurred to me. (*As written, the sentence implies that "a few problems" read the proposal.*)
>
> **BUT:** After reading the proposal, I noted a few problems.

> **NOT:** Dr. Ellis gave a presentation on the use of drugs in our auditorium. (*Are drugs being used in the auditorium?*)
>
> **BUT:** Dr. Ellis gave a presentation in our auditorium on the use of drugs.

> **NOT:** Robin explained the proposal to Joy, but she was not happy with it. (*Who was not happy—Robin or Joy?*)
>
> **BUT:** Robin explained the proposal to Joy, but Joy was not happy with it.

Jargon is sometimes appropriate and sometimes inappropriate.

Avoid Unnecessary Jargon   Jargon is technical vocabulary used within a special group. Every field has its own specialized words, and jargon offers a precise and efficient way of communicating with people in the same field. But problems arise when jargon is used to communicate with someone who does not understand it. For example, to a banker the term *CD* means a "certificate of deposit," but to a stereo buff or computer user it means a "compact disk." Even familiar words can be confusing when given a specialized meaning.

> **NOT:** Your incorrect bill was caused by a computer virus, which disabled the error-lockout function, resulting in encrypted data.
>
> **BUT:** Your incorrect bill was caused by a temporary software problem, which let unreadable data get entered into the computer.

The original sentence might be appropriate when communicating with other information specialists. In this case, a utility company was explaining to a customer why she had received a bill for "$a.00." The explanation was probably as unreadable as the bill had been!

Does the field of business communication have jargon? It does—just look at the Key Terms list at the end of each chapter. The word *jargon* itself might be considered communication jargon. In this text, such terms are first defined and then used to make communication precise and efficient. Competent writers use specialized vocabulary to communicate with specialists who understand it. And they avoid using it when their readers are not specialists.

2. Prefer Short, Simple Words.

Short and simple words are more likely to be understood, less likely to be misused, and less likely to distract the reader. Literary authors often write to *impress*; they select words to achieve a specific reader reaction, such as amusement, excitement, or anger. Business writers, on the other hand, write to *express*; they want to achieve *comprehension*. They want their readers to focus on their information, not on how they convey their information. Using short, simple words helps achieve this goal.

Short, simple words are the building blocks of effective business communication.

NOT: To recapitulate, our utilization of adulterated water precipitated the interminable delays.

BUT: To review, our use of impure water caused the endless delays.

It is true, of course, that often no short, simple word is available to convey the precise shade of meaning you want. For example, there is no one-syllable replacement for *ethnocentrism* (the belief that one's own cultural group is superior), a concept introduced in Chapter 2. Our guideline is not to use *only* short and simple words but to *prefer* short and simple words. (As Mark Twain, who was paid by the word for his writing, noted, "I never write *metropolis* for seven cents because I can get the same price for *city*. I never write *policeman* because I can get the same money for *cop*.")

Here are some examples of needlessly long words, gleaned from various business documents, with their preferred shorter substitutes shown in parentheses:

ascertain (learn)	modification (change)
endeavor (try)	recapitulate (review)
enumerate (list)	substantial (large)
fluctuate (vary)	termination (end)
indispensable (vital)	utilization (use)
initiate (start)	

You need not strike these long words totally from your written or spoken vocabulary; any one of these words, used in a clear sentence, would be acceptable. The problem is that a writer may tend to fill his or her writing with very long words when simpler ones could be used. Use long words in moderation. Heed the following advice from author Richard Lederer:[1]

When you speak and write, no law says you have to use big words. Short words are as good as long ones, and short, old words like *sun* and *grass* and *home* are best of all. A lot of small words, more than you might think, can meet your needs with a strength, grace, and charm that large words lack.

Big words can make the way dark for those who hear what you say and read what you write. They add fat to your prose. Small words are the ones we seem to have known from birth. They are like the hearth fire that warms the home, and they cast a clear light on big things: night and day, love and hate, war and peace, life and death.

Short words are bright, like sparks that glow in the night; sharp, like the blade of a knife; hot, like salt tears that scald the cheek; quick, like moths that flit from flame to flame; and terse, like the dart and sting of a bee.

If a long word says just what you want, do not fear to use it. But know that our tongue is rich in crisp, brisk, swift, short words. Make them the spine and the heart of what you speak and write. Like fast friends, they will not let you down.

Lederer practices what he preaches. All 223 words in these four paragraphs are one-syllable words!

Write to express—not to impress.

You've probably heard the advice "Write as you speak." Although not universally true, such advice is pretty close to the mark. Of course, if your conversation is peppered with redundancies, jargon, and clichés, you would not want to put such weaknesses on paper. But typical conversation uses mostly short, simple words—the kind you *do* want on paper. Don't assume that the bigger the words, the bigger the intellect. In fact, you need a large vocabulary and a well-developed word sense to select the best word. And more often than not, that word is short and simple. Write to express—not to impress.

3. Write with Vigor.

Vigorous language is specific and concrete. Limp language is filled with clichés, slang, and buzz words. Vigorous writing holds your reader's interest. But if your reader isn't even interested enough to read your message, your writing can't possibly achieve its objective. A second reason for writing with vigor has to do with language itself. Vigorous writing tends to lend vigor to the ideas presented. A good idea looks even better dressed in vigorous language, and a weak idea looks even weaker when dressed in limp language.

Concrete words present a vivid picture.

Use Specific, Concrete Language   In Chapter 1, we discussed the communication barriers caused by overabstraction and ambiguity. When possible, choose *specific* words—ones that have a definite, unambiguous meaning. Likewise, choose *concrete* words—ones that bring a definite picture to your reader's mind.

NOT: The vehicle broke down several times recently.

BUT: The delivery van broke down three times last week.

In the first version, what does the reader imagine when he or she reads the word *vehicle*—a golf cart? automobile? boat? space shuttle? Likewise, how many times is *several*—two? three? fifteen? The revised version tells precisely what happened.

Sometimes we do not need such specific information. For example, in "The president answered *several* questions from the audience and then adjourned the meeting," the specific number of questions is probably not important. But in most situations, you should watch out for words like *several, recently, a number of, substantial, a few,* and *a lot of.* You may need to be more exact.

Likewise, use the most concrete word that is appropriate; give the reader a specific mental picture of what you mean. Be sure that your terms convey as much meaning as the reader needs to react appropriately. Watch out for terms like *emotional meeting* (anger or gratitude?), *bright color* (red or yellow?), *new equipment* (postage meter or cash register?), and *change in price* (increase or decrease?).

Avoid Clichés, Slang, and Buzz Words   A **cliché** is an expression that has become monotonous through overuse. It lacks freshness and originality and may also send the unintended message that the writer couldn't be bothered to choose language geared specifically to the reader.

> **NOT:**   Enclosed please find an application form that you should return at your earliest convenience.

> **BUT:**   Please return the enclosed application form before May 15.

Here are some examples of other expressions that have become overused (even in other countries; see Spotlight 7—Across Cultures on p. 114) and that therefore sound trite and boring. Avoid them in your writing.

According to our records	It goes without saying that
Company policy requires	Needless to say
Do not hesitate to	Our records indicate that
For your information	Please be advised that
If I can be of further help	Take this opportunity to
If you have any other questions	Under separate cover

Picture a person finding "thank you for your letter" in all 15 letters he or she reads that day. How sincere and original does it sound?

As noted earlier, slang is an expression, often short-lived, that is identified with a specific group of people. If you understand each word in an expression but still don't understand what it means in context, chances are you're having trouble with a slang expression. For example, read the following sentence:

> It turns my stomach the way you can break your neck and beat your brains out around here, and they still stab you in the back.

To anyone unfamiliar with American slang (a nonnative speaker, perhaps), this sentence might seem to be about the body because it refers to the stomach, neck, brains, and back. The real meaning, of course, is something like this:

> I am really upset that this company ignores hard work and loyalty when making personnel decisions.

Avoid slang in most business writing, for several reasons. First, it is informal, and much business writing, although not formal, is still *businesslike* and calls for standard word usage. Second, slang is short-lived. A slang phrase used today may not be in use—and thus may not be familiar—in three years, when your letter is retrieved from the files for reference. Third, slang is identified with a specific group of people, and others in the general population may not understand the intended meaning. For these reasons, avoid terms such as the following in business writing:

can of worms	pay through the nose
chew out	play up to
go for broke	security blanket
hate one's guts	use your noodle
knock it off	wiped out
once-over	zonked out

A **buzz word** is an important-sounding expression used mainly to impress other people. Because buzz words are so often used by government officials and high-ranking businesspeople—people whose comments are "newsworthy"—these

Same Rules the World Over

SPOTLIGHT 7

ACROSS CULTURES

The strategies for writing effective business messages are universal. The passage below, from a business communication text for Chinese business executives, recommends substituting concise phrases for long, empty ones.

"简洁"是有客观标准的。虽然西方国家的作者之间在怎样用词才算"简洁"方面还是有争论的，不过他们的一些看法还是有一定参考价值的。现把他们所做的某些词句的"不简洁"与"简洁"的比较列在下面供参考：

不 简 洁   简 洁

Wordy	Concise	Wordy	Concise
enclosed herewith	enclosed	continuous and uninterrupted	continuous (or: uninterrupted)
enclosed you will find	enclosed is	during the year of 1971	during 1971
please be advised that	(four wasted words)	endorse on the back of this check	endorse this check
please don't hesitate to call upon us	please write us	for a price of $300	for $300
please feel free to write	please write		
prior to	before		
this is to advise you	(five wasted words)		
under separate cover	separately		
a long period of time	a long time		

Source: Ge-Lin Zhu, Chief Editor, *Practical Commercial English Handbook* (Beijing, China: Commercial Publishing Company, 1981), p. 49.

Clichés and buzz words go in and out of style too quickly to serve as effective components of written business communication.

expressions get much media attention. They become instant clichés and then go out of fashion just as quickly. At either end of their short life span, they cause communication problems. If an expression is currently being used by everyone, it sounds monotonous, lacking originality. If it is no longer being used by anyone, readers may not understand the intended meaning. Here are examples of recent "in" expressions:

bottom line	paradigm
done deal	parameter
impact (verb)	scenario
interface	user-friendly
no-brainer	vision statement

Be especially careful of turning nouns and other types of words into verbs by adding -ize. Such words as *agendize, prioritize, strategize, unionize,* and *operationalize* quickly become tiresome.

4. Write Concisely.

Businesspeople are busy people. The information revolution has created more paperwork, giving businesspeople access to more data. Having more data to analyze (but no more time in which to do so), managers want information presented in the fewest possible words. To achieve conciseness, make every word count. Avoid redundancy, wordy expressions, hidden verbs and nouns, and other "space-eaters."

Avoid Redundancy   A **redundancy** is the unnecessary repetition of an idea that has already been expressed or intimated. Eliminating the repetition contributes to conciseness.

> **NOT:** Signing both copies of the lease is a necessary requirement.
> **BUT:** Signing both copies of the lease is necessary.

> **NOT:** Combine the ingredients together.
> **BUT:** Combine the ingredients.

A *requirement* is by definition *necessary,* so only one of the words is needed. And to *combine* means to bring *together,* so using both words is redundant. Don't confuse redundancy and repetition. Repetition—using the same word more than once—is sometimes effective for emphasis. Redundancy, however, serves no purpose and should always be avoided.

Redundancy and repetition are not the same.

Some redundancies are humorous, as in the classic Samuel Goldwyn comment "Anybody who goes to a psychiatrist ought to have his head examined," or the sign in a jewelry store window, "Ears pierced while you wait," or the statement in an automobile advertisement, "Open seven days a week plus weekends." Most redundancies, however, are simply *verbiage*—excess words that consume time and space. Avoid them.

Do not use the unnecessary word *together* after such words as *assemble, combine, cooperate, gather, join, merge,* or *mix.* Do not use the unnecessary word *new* before such words as *beginner, discovery, fad, innovation,* or *progress.* And do not use the unnecessary word *up* after such words as *connect, divide, eat, lift, mix,* and *rest.* Also avoid the following common redundancies (use the words in parentheses instead):

Make every word count.

advance planning (planning)
any and all (any *or* all)
basic fundamentals   (basics *or* fundamentals)
but nevertheless (but *or* nevertheless)
each and every (each *or* every)
free gift (gift)
over again (over)
past history (history)
plan ahead (plan)
repeat again (repeat)
sum total (sum *or* total)
true facts (facts)
when and if (when *or* if)

Avoid Wordy Expressions   Although wordy expressions are not necessarily writing errors (as redundancies are), they do slow the pace of the communication and should be avoided. For example, try substituting one word for a phrase whenever possible.

Use the fewest number of words that will achieve your objective.

> **NOT:** In view of the fact that the model failed twice during the time that we tested it, we are at this point in time searching for other options.
> **BUT:** Because the model failed twice when we tested it, we are now searching for other options.

The original sentence contains 28 words; the revised sentence, 16. You've "saved" 12 words. In his delightful book *Revising Business Prose,* Richard Lanham speaks of the "lard factor": the percentage of words saved by "getting rid of the lard" in a sentence. In this case,

$$28 - 16 = 12; 12 \div 28 = 43\%$$

Thus, 43% of the original sentence was "lard," which fattened the sentence without providing any "nutrition." Lanham suggests, "Think of a lard factor (LF) of ⅓ to ½ as normal and don't stop revising until you've removed it."[2]

Here are examples of other wordy phrases and their preferred one-word substitutes in parentheses:

are of the opinion that (believe)
due to the fact that (because)
for the purpose of (for *or* to)
in order to (to)
in the event that (if)
pertaining to (about)
with regard to (about)

Avoid Hidden Verbs   A hidden verb is a verb that has been changed into a noun form, weakening the action. Verbs are action words and should convey the main action in the sentence. They provide interest and forward movement. Consider this example:

Changing verbs to nouns produces weak, uninteresting sentences.

NOT: Carl made an announcement that he will give consideration to our request.

What is the real action? It is not that Carl *made* something or that he will *give* something. The real action is hiding in the nouns: Carl *announced* and will *consider.* These two verb forms, then, should be the main verbs in the sentence.

BUT: Carl announced that he will consider our request.

Notice that the revised sentence is much more direct—and four words shorter (LF = 33%). Here are some other actions that should be conveyed by verbs instead of being hidden in nouns:

arrived at the conclusion (concluded)
came to an agreement (agreed)
gave a demonstration of (demonstrated)
gave an explanation (explained)
has a requirement for (requires)
held a meeting (met)
made a payment (paid)
performed an analysis of (analyzed)

Avoid Hidden Subjects   Like verbs, subjects play a prominent role in a sentence and should stand out, rather than being obscured by an expletive beginning. An **expletive** is an expression such as *there is* or *it is* that begins a clause or sentence and for which the pronoun has no antecedent. Because the topic of a sentence that begins with an expletive is not immediately clear, you should use such sentences sparingly in business writing. Avoiding expletives also contributes to conciseness.

A pronoun in an expletive does not stand for any noun.

NOT: There was no indication that it is necessary to include John in the meeting.

BUT: No one indicated that John should be included in the meeting.

Imply or Condense   Sometimes you do not need to explicitly state certain information; you can imply it instead. In other situations, you can use adjectives and adverbs instead of clauses to convey the needed information in a more concise format.

Some information need only be implied.

NOT: We have received your recent letter and are happy to provide the data you requested.

BUT: We are happy to provide the data you recently requested.

NOT: This brochure, which is available free of charge, will answer your questions.

BUT: This free brochure will answer your questions.

5. Prefer Positive Language.

Words that create a positive image are more likely to help you achieve your objective than are negative words. For example, you are more likely to persuade someone to do as you ask if you stress the advantages of doing so rather than the disadvantages of not doing so. Positive language also builds goodwill for you and your organization and often gives more information than negative language. Note the differences in tone and amount of information given in the following pairs of sentences:

NOT: The briefcase is not made of cheap imitation leather.

BUT: The briefcase is made of 100% belt leather for years of durable service.

NOT: We cannot ship your merchandise until we receive your check.

BUT: As soon as we receive your check, we will ship your merchandise.

NOT: I do not yet have any work experience.

BUT: My two terms as secretary of the Management Club taught me the importance of accurate recordkeeping and gave me experience in working with others.

Expressions like *cannot* and *will not* are not the only ones that convey negative messages. Other words, like *mistake, damage, failure, refuse,* and *deny,* also carry negative connotations and should be avoided when possible.

Avoid negative-sounding words.

NOT: Failure to follow the directions may cause the blender to malfunction.

BUT: Following the directions will ensure many years of carefree service from your blender.

NOT: We apologize for this error.

BUT: We appreciate your calling this matter to our attention.

NOT: We close at 7 p.m. on Fridays.

BUT: We're open until 7 p.m. on Fridays to give you time to shop after work.

The subjunctive mood sounds more hopeful than an outright refusal.

Sometimes you can avoid negative language by switching to the subjunctive mood, which uses words like *wish, if,* and *would* to refer to conditions that are impossible or improbable. Such language softens the impact of the negative message, making it more palatable to the reader. Here are two examples:

NOT: I cannot speak at your November meeting.

BUT: I wish it were possible for me to speak at your November meeting.

NOT: I cannot release the names of our clients.

BUT: Releasing the names of our clients would violate their right to privacy.

In short, stress what *is* true and what *can* be done rather than what is not true and what cannot be done. This is not to say that negative language has no place in business writing. Negative language is strong and emphatic, and sometimes you will want to use it. But unless the situation clearly calls for negative language, you are more likely to achieve your objective and to build goodwill for yourself and your organization by stressing the positive.

Because words are the building blocks for your message, choose them with care. Using short, simple words; writing with clarity, vigor, and conciseness; and using positive language will help you construct effective sentences and paragraphs.

Writing Effective Sentences

A sentence has a subject and predicate and expresses at least one complete thought. Beyond these attributes, however, sentences vary widely in style, length, and effect. They are also very flexible; writers can move sentence parts around, add and delete information, and substitute words in order to express different ideas and emphasize different points. To build effective sentences, use a variety of sentence types, and use active and passive voice appropriately.

6. Use a Variety of Sentence Types.

There are three basic sentence types—simple, compound, and complex—all of which are appropriate for business writing.

Use a simple sentence for emphasis and variety.

Simple Sentence   A **simple sentence** contains one independent clause (a clause that can stand alone as a complete thought). Because it presents a single idea and is usually (but not always) short, a simple sentence is often used for emphasis. Although a simple sentence contains only one independent clause, it may have a compound subject or compound verb (or both). All the following are simple sentences:

I quit.

Individual Retirement Accounts are a safe option.

Both Individual Retirement Accounts and Simplified Employee Pension Plans are safe and convenient options as retirement investments for the entrepreneur.

Compound Sentence   A **compound sentence** contains two or more independent clauses. Because each clause presents a complete idea, each idea receives equal emphasis. (If the two ideas are not closely related, they should be presented in two separate sentences.) Here are three compound sentences:

Use a compound sentence to show coordinate (equal) relationships.

Stacey listened, but I nodded.

Morris Technologies made a major acquisition last year, and it turned out to be a disaster.

Westmoreland Mines moved its headquarters to Prescott in 1984; however, it stayed there only five years and then moved back to Globe.

Complex Sentence   A **complex sentence** contains one independent clause and at least one dependent clause. For example, notice the first sentence below. "The scanner will save valuable input time" is an independent clause because it makes sense by itself. "Although it cost $2,150" is a dependent clause because it does not make sense by itself.

Use a complex sentence to express subordinate relationships.

Although it cost $2,150, the scanner will save valuable input time.

George Bosley, who is the new CEO at Hubbell, made the decision.

I will be moving to Austin when I assume my new position.

The dependent clause provides additional, but subordinate, information related to the independent clause. Sentences that contain two or more independent clauses and one or more dependent clauses are sometimes called *compound-complex sentences.*

Sentence Variety   Using a variety of sentence patterns and sentence lengths helps keep your writing interesting. Note how simplistic and choppy too many short sentences can be and how boring and difficult too many long sentences can be.

Too Choppy:

Golden Nugget will not purchase the Claridge Hotel. The hotel is 60 years old. The asking price was $110 million. It was not considered too high. Golden Nugget had wanted some commitments from New Jersey regulators. The regulators were unwilling to provide such commitments. Some observers believe the refusal was not the real reason for the decision. They blame the weak Atlantic City economy for the cancellation. Golden Nugget purchased the Stake House in Las Vegas in 1990. It lost money on that purchase. It does not want to repeat its mistake in Atlantic City. (*Average sentence length = 8 words*)

Too Difficult:

Golden Nugget will not purchase the Claridge Hotel, which is 60 years old, for an asking price of $110 million, which was not considered too high, because the company had wanted some commitments from New Jersey regulators, and the regulators were unwilling to provide such commitments. Some observers believe the refusal was not the real reason for the decision but rather that the weak Atlantic City economy was responsible for the cancellation; and since Golden Nugget purchased the Stake House in Las Vegas in 1990 and lost money on that purchase, it does not want to repeat its mistake in Atlantic City. (*Average sentence length = 50 words*)

Use a variety of sentence patterns and lengths.

The sentences in these paragraphs should be revised to show relationships between ideas more clearly, to keep readers interested, and to improve readability. Use simple sentences for emphasis and variety, compound sentences for coordinate (equal) relationships, and complex sentences for subordinate relationships.

More Variety:

Golden Nugget will not purchase the 60-year-old Claridge Hotel, even though the $110 million asking price was not considered too high. The company had wanted some commitments from New Jersey regulators, which the regulators were unwilling to provide. However, some observers blame the cancellation on the weak Atlantic City economy. Golden Nugget lost money on its 1990 purchase of the Stake House in Las Vegas, and it does not want to repeat its mistake in Atlantic City. (*Average sentence length = 20 words*)

The first two sentences in the revision are complex, the third sentence is simple, and the last sentence is compound. The lengths of the four sentences range from 12 to 27 words. To write effective sentences, use different sentence patterns and lengths. Most sentences in good business writing should range from 16 to 22 words.

7. Use Active and Passive Voice Appropriately.

Voice is the aspect of a verb that shows whether the subject of the sentence acts or is acted on. In the **active voice,** the subject does the action expressed by the verb. In the **passive voice,** the subject receives the action expressed by the verb.

ACTIVE: Inmac offers a full refund on all orders.
PASSIVE: A full refund on all orders is offered by Inmac.

ACTIVE: Shoemacher & Doerr audited the books in 1992.
PASSIVE: The books were audited in 1992 by Shoemacher & Doerr.

Passive sentences add some form of the verb *to be* to the main verb, so passive sentences are always somewhat longer than active sentences. In the first set of sentences just given, for example, compare *offers* in the active sentence with *is offered by* in the passive sentence.

In active sentences, the subject performs the action; in passive sentences, the subject receives the action.

In active sentences, the subject is the doer of the action; in passive sentences, the subject is the receiver of the action. And because the subject gets more emphasis than other nouns in a sentence, active sentences emphasize the doer, and passive sentences, the receiver, of the action. In the second set of sentences, either version could be considered correct, depending on whether the writer wanted to emphasize *Shoemacher & Doerr* or *the books.*

Use active sentences most of the time in business writing, just as you naturally use active sentences in most of your conversations. Note that verb *voice* (active or passive) has nothing to do with verb *tense,* which shows the time of the action. As the following sentences show, the action in both active and passive sentences can occur in the past, present, or future.

NOT: A very logical argument was presented by Hal. (*Passive voice, past tense*)
BUT: Hal presented a very logical argument. (*Active voice, past tense*)

NOT: An 18% increase will be reported by the eastern region. (*Passive voice, future tense*)

BUT: The eastern region will report an 18% increase. (*Active voice, future tense*)

Passive sentences are most appropriate when you want to emphasize the receiver of the action, when the person doing the action is either unknown or unimportant, or when you want to be tactful in conveying negative information. All the following sentences are appropriately stated in the passive voice:

Passive sentences are generally more effective than active sentences for conveying negative information.

Protective legislation was blamed for the drop in imports. (*Emphasizes the receiver of the action*)

Transportation to the construction site will be provided. (*The doer of the action not important*)

Several complaints have been received regarding the new policy. (*Tactfully conveys negative news*)

Words, sentences, and paragraphs are all building blocks of communication. You have seen how using a variety of sentence types and using active and passive voice appropriately can help make your sentences more effective. Now you are ready to combine these sentences to form logical paragraphs.

Developing Logical Paragraphs

A paragraph is a group of related sentences that focus on one main idea. The main idea is often identified in the first sentence of the paragraph, which is then known as a *topic sentence.* The body of the paragraph supports this main idea by giving more information, analysis, or examples. A paragraph is typically part of a longer message, although one paragraph can comprise the entire message, especially in such informal communications as memorandums and e-mail.

Paragraphs organize the topic into manageable units of information for the reader. Readers need a cue to tell them when they have finished a topic, so that they can pause and refocus their attention on the next topic. To serve this purpose, paragraphs must be unified and coherent, and they must be of an appropriate length.

Use a new paragraph to signal a change in direction.

8. Keep Paragraphs Unified and Coherent.

Although closely related, unity and coherence are not the same. A paragraph has *unity* when all its parts work together to develop a single idea consistently and logically. A paragraph has *coherence* when each sentence links smoothly to the sentences before and after it.

Unity   A unified paragraph gives information that is directly related to the topic, presents this information in a logical order, and leaves out irrelevant details. The following excerpt is a middle paragraph in a memorandum arguing against the proposal that Collins, a baby-food manufacturer, should expand into producing food for adults:

NOT: [1] We cannot focus our attention on both ends of the age spectrum. [2] In a recent survey, two-thirds of the under-35 age group named Collins as the first company that came to mind for the category "baby-food products." [3] For more than 50 years we have spent millions of dollars annually to identify our company as the baby-food company, and market research shows that we have been successful. [4] Last year, we introduced Peas 'N Pears, our most successful baby-food introduction ever. [5] To now seek to position ourselves as a producer of food for adults would simply be incongruous. [6] Our well-defined image in the marketplace would make producing food for adults risky.

The paragraph obviously lacks unity. Before reading further, rearrange the sentences to make the sequence of ideas more logical.

You would probably decide that the overall topic of the paragraph is Collins's well-defined image as a baby-food producer. So Sentence 6 would be the best topic sentence. You might also decide that Sentence 4 brings in extra information that weakens paragraph unity and should be left out. The most unified paragraph, then, would be Sentences 6, 3, 2, 5, and 1, as shown here:

BUT: Our well-defined image in the marketplace would make producing food for adults risky. For more than 50 years we have spent millions of dollars annually to identify our company as the baby-food company, and market research shows that we have been successful. In a recent survey, two-thirds of the under-35 age group named Collins as the first company that came to mind for the category "baby-food products." To now seek to position ourselves as a producer of food for adults would simply be incongruous. We cannot focus our attention on both ends of the age spectrum.

The topic sentence usually goes at the beginning of the paragraph.

A topic sentence is especially helpful in a long paragraph. It usually appears at the beginning of a paragraph. This position helps the writer focus on the topic, so the paragraph will have unity. And it lets the reader know immediately what the topic is.

Coherence is achieved by using transitional words, pronouns, repetition, and parallelism.

Coherence   A coherent paragraph weaves sentences together so that the discussion is integrated. The reader never needs to pause to puzzle out the relationships or reread to get the intended meaning. The major ways to achieve coherence are to use transitional words and pronouns, to repeat key words and ideas, and to use parallel structure.

Transitional words help the reader see relationships between sentences. Such words may be as simple as *first* and other indicators of sequence.

Ten years ago, Collins tried to overcome market resistance to its new line of baby clothes. First, it mounted a multimillion-dollar ad campaign featuring the Mason quintuplets. Next, it sponsored a Collins Baby look-alike contest. Then it sponsored two network specials featuring Dr. Benjamin Spock. Finally, it brought in the Madison Avenue firm of Morgan & Modine to broaden its image.

The words *first, next, then,* and *finally* clearly signal step-by-step movement. Now note the following logical transitions, aided by connecting words:

I recognize, however, that Collins cannot thrive on baby food alone. To begin with, since we already control 73% of the market, further gains will be difficult.

A coherent message is never more important than in a company's mission statement, the document that provides a framework for employees' decision making. Ortho Biotech's statement uses bulleted paragraphs to clearly identify its main points.

What's more, the current baby boom is slowing. Therefore, we must expand our product line.

Transitional words act as road signs, indicating where the message is heading and letting the reader know what to expect. Here are some commonly used transitional expressions grouped by the relationships they express:

Relationship	*Transitional Expressions*
addition	also, besides, furthermore, in addition, moreover, too
cause and effect	as a result, because, consequently, hence, so, therefore, thus
comparison	in the same way, likewise, similarly
contrast	although, but, however, in contrast, nevertheless, on the other hand, still, yet
illustration	for example, for instance, in other words, to illustrate
sequence	first, second, third, then, next, finally
summary/conclusion	at last, finally, in conclusion, to summarize, therefore
time	meanwhile, next, since, soon, then

A second way to achieve coherence is to use pronouns. Because pronouns stand for words already named, using pronouns binds sentences and ideas together. The pronouns are underlined here:

If Collins branches out with additional food products, one possibility would be a fruit snack for youngsters. Funny Fruits were tested in Columbus last summer, and <u>they</u> were a big hit. Roger Johnson, national marketing manager, says <u>he</u> hopes to build new food categories into a $200 million business. <u>He</u> is also exploring the possibility of acquiring other established name brands. <u>These</u>

acquired brands would let Collins expand faster than if <u>it</u> had to develop a new product of <u>its</u> own.

Purposeful repetition aids coherence; avoid needless repetition.

A third way to achieve coherence is to repeat key words. In a misguided attempt to appear interesting, writers sometimes use different terms for the same idea. For example, in discussing a proposed merger a writer may at different points use *merger, combination, union, association,* and *syndicate.* Or a writer may use the words *administrator, manager, supervisor,* and *executive* all to refer to the same person. Such "elegant variation" only confuses the reader, who has no way of knowing whether the writer is referring to the same concept or to slightly different variations of that concept. Avoid needless repetition, but use purposeful repetition to link ideas and thus to promote paragraph coherence. Here is a good example:

> Collins has taken several steps recently to enhance profits and project a stronger leadership position. One of these steps is streamlining operations. Collins's line of children's clothes was unprofitable, so it discontinued the line. Its four produce farms were likewise unprofitable, so it hired an outside professional team to manage them. This team eventually recommended selling the farms.

Parallelism refers to consistency.

The term **parallelism** means using similar grammatical structure for similar ideas—that is, matching adjectives with adjectives, nouns with nouns, infinitives with infinitives, and so on. Much widely quoted writing uses parallelism: for example, Julius Caesar's "I came, I saw, I conquered" and Abraham Lincoln's "government of the people, by the people, and for the people." Parallel structure smoothly links ideas and adds a pleasing rhythm to sentences and paragraphs, thereby enhancing coherence.

NOT: The new dispatcher is competent and a fast worker.
BUT: The new dispatcher is competent and fast.

NOT: The new grade of paper is lightweight, nonporous, and it is inexpensive.
BUT: The new grade of paper is lightweight, nonporous, and inexpensive.

NOT: The training program will cover
  1. Vacation and sick leaves
  2. How to resolve grievances
  3. Managing your workstation
BUT: The training program will cover
  1. Vacation and sick leaves
  2. Grievance resolution
  3. Workstation management

NOT: One management consultant recommended either selling the children's-furniture division or its conversion into a children's toy division.
BUT: One management consultant recommended either selling the children's-furniture division or converting it into a children's-toy division.

NOT: Gladys is not only proficient in word processing but also in desktop publishing.
BUT: Gladys is proficient not only in word processing but also in desktop publishing.

In the last two sets of sentences above, note that correlative conjunctions (such as *both/and, either/or,* and *not only/but also*) must be followed by words in parallel form. Be especially careful to use parallel structure in report headings that have equal weight and in numbered lists.

Ensure paragraph unity by developing only one topic per paragraph and by presenting the information in a logical order. Ensure paragraph coherence by using transitional words and pronouns, repeating key words, and using parallel structure.

9. Control Paragraph Length.

How long should a paragraph of business writing be? As with other considerations, the needs of the reader, rather than the convenience of the writer, should determine the answer. Paragraphs should help the reader by signaling a new idea as well as by providing a physical break. Long blocks of unbroken text look boring and needlessly complex. And they may unintentionally obscure an important idea buried in the middle (see Figure 4.2). On the other hand, a series of extremely short paragraphs can weaken coherence by obscuring underlying relationships.

Essentially, there are no fixed rules for paragraph length, and occasionally one- or ten-sentence paragraphs might be effective. However, most paragraphs of good business writers fall into the 60- to 80-word range—long enough for a topic sentence and three or four supporting sentences. Although a single paragraph should never discuss more than one major topic, complex topics often need to be divided into several paragraphs. Your purpose and the needs of your reader should ultimately determine paragraph length.

Excessively long paragraphs look boring and difficult.

FIGURE 4.2   The Effect of Paragraph Length on Readability

These two memorandums contain identical information. Which is more inviting to read?

SUMMARY

For business writing to achieve its objectives, it must be clear. Use short, simple, specific, and concrete words; and avoid dangling expressions, clichés, slang, buzz words, and unnecessary jargon. Write concisely: avoid redundancies, wordy expressions, and hidden subjects and verbs. Finally, prefer positive language; stress what you can do rather than what you cannot do.

To maintain reader interest, use a variety of sentence types, including simple, compound, and complex sentences. Use active voice to emphasize the doer of the action and passive voice to emphasize the receiver of the action.

Your paragraphs should be unified and coherent. Develop only one topic per paragraph, and use transitional words, pronouns, repetition, and parallelism. Although paragraphs of various lengths are desirable, most should range from 60 to 80 words. To help the reader follow your logic, avoid very long paragraphs and avoid strings of very short paragraphs.

KEY TERMS

active voice	mechanics
buzz word	parallelism
cliché	passive voice
complex sentence	redundancy
compound sentence	simple sentence
dangling expression	style
expletive	

REVIEW AND DISCUSSION

1. **Communication at Bank of Montreal Revisited**   Whether they are writing to Bank of Montreal's employees or to its customers, Martha Durdin and her staff must be sure that their messages can be understood by those who speak English as a second language.
   a. Under what circumstances might a letter to a European customer include jargon?
   b. Some of Bank of Montreal's materials are sent across the International Date Line. How can Durdin be sure that readers will understand the timing she intends to convey if she uses the words *today, yesterday,* or *tomorrow?*
   c. Why would Durdin prefer positive language when writing to a potential customer?
2. What is meant by the statement "Accuracy involves more than the truthfulness of facts and figures"?
3. Give an original example of each of the following types of expressions:

buzz word	hidden subject	jargon	slang
cliché	hidden verb	redundancy	

4. Substitute a shorter word for each of the following long words:

accordingly	commence	jurisdiction	stipulate
aggregate	consequence	materialize	transmit
analogous	finalize	perpetuate	verification
characteristics	inexhaustible		

5. Revise the following phrases, getting rid of the redundancies:

and etc.	exact same	surrounded on all sides
Easter Sunday	good benefits	personal opinion

foreign imports   mutual cooperation   same identical
important essentials   past experience   very unique
component part   refer back

6. Substitute one word for each of the following wordy expressions:

at the present time   until such time as   it would appear that
in the amount of   few in number
inasmuch as   in most cases

7. Why is positive language often more effective than negative language for achieving your objective?

8. What are the three sentence types? Under what circumstances should each type be used for best effect?

9. In business writing, about how long should the typical sentence and paragraph be? Should all sentences and paragraphs fall within these ranges? Why or why not?

10. Distinguish between active and passive voice, and discuss when each should be used.

11. What is the difference between paragraph unity and paragraph coherence?

12. List four ways to make a paragraph coherent.

13. Write a sentence illustrating parallelism.

14. Why should you avoid extremely long paragraphs?

EXERCISES

1. Communication Applications at Bank of Montreal   Martha Durdin and her staff of professional communicators at the Bank of Montreal make every word count as they write newsletters, annual reports, and other materials for both internal and external audiences. Surveys and reader feedback help the bank sharpen clarity, an important consideration when writing to employees and customers around the world.

Imagine that you are helping Durdin write a press release announcing a new checking account designed especially for college students with no monthly fees and no charge for deposits and withdrawals made at ATMs on college campuses. This press release will be sent to newspapers in college towns across the United States and Canada. Think about how you can use words, sentences, and paragraphs to explain the new account.

a. What do you want to accomplish with this press release?
b. What should you know about your audience(s) before you start to write?
c. What jargon or technical terms should you define in this press release? Why?
d. Will you use any negative language in this press release? Why or why not?
e. Write a concise headline for this press release.

For Exercises 2–7, revise the passages to address the matter of style indicated and to make the passage appropriate for a first-year college student who has never taken a communication or business course. Do not completely rewrite the passages; just correct any style problems.

2. Jargon

Regardless of the medium selected, noise may be encountered after the communication stimulus enters the receiver's filter. Such a problem occurs in both the formal and the informal communication networks. Workers experiencing ethnocentrism may have special problems with language connotations.

3. Short and Simple Words

The consultant demonstrated how our aggregate remuneration might be ameliorated by modifications in our propensities to utilize credit for compensating for services. She also endeavored to ascertain which of our characteristics were analogous to those of other entities for which she had fabricated solutions. She recommended we commence to initiate innumerable modifications in our procedures to increase cash flow, which she considers indispensable for facilitating increased corporate health.

4. Specific and Concrete Words

In an effort to stimulate sales, Mallmart is lowering prices substantially on its line of consumer items. Sometime soon, it will close most of its stores for several days to provide store personnel time to change prices. Markdowns will range from very little on its line of laundry equipment to a great deal on certain sporting equipment. Mallmart plans to rely on advertising to let people know of these price reductions. In particular, it is considering using a popular television star to publicize the new pricing strategy.

5. Clichés, Slang, and Buzz Words

At that point in time the corporate brass were under the gun; they decided to bite the bullet and let the chips fall where they may. They hired a head honcho with some street smarts who would be able to interface with the investment community. Financewise, the new top dog couldn't be beat. He was hard as nails and developed a scenario that would have the company back on its feet within six months. Now it was up to the team players to operationalize his plans.

6. Conciseness

In spite of the fact that Fox Inc. denied wrongdoing, it agreed to a settlement of the patent suit for a price of $6.3 million. Industry sources were surprised at the outcome because of the fact that the original patent had depreciated in value. In addition to the above, Fox also made an agreement to refrain from the manufacture of similar computers for a period of five years in length. It appears that with the exception of Emerson's new introductions, innovations in workstations will be few in number during the next few years.

7. Positive Language

We cannot issue a full refund at this time because you did not enclose a receipt or an authorized estimate. I'm sorry that we will have to delay your reimbursement. We are not like those insurance companies that promise you anything but then disappear when you have a claim. When we receive your receipt or estimate, we will not hold up your check. Our refusal to issue reimbursement without proper supporting evidence means that we do not have to charge you outlandish premiums for your automobile insurance.

8. Sentence Types

For each of the following lettered items, write a simple, a compound, and a complex sentence that incorporates both items of information. For the complex sentences, emphasize the first idea in each item.

a. Tim was given a promotion/Tim was assigned additional duties.

b. Eileen is our corporate counsel/Eileen will write the letter on our behalf.

9. **Sentence Variety**   Rewrite the following paragraph by varying sentence types and sentence lengths to keep the writing interesting.

> Smartfood was founded by Ann Withey, Andrew Martin, and Ken Meyers in 1984. The product was the first snack food to combine white cheddar cheese and popcorn. Ann Withey perfected the Smartfood recipe in her home kitchen after much trial and error. Smartfood sales were reportedly only $35,000 in 1985. During that time, the product was available only in New England. By 1988, sales had soared to $10 million. This attracted the attention of Frito-Lay. The snack-food giant bought Smartfood in 1989 for $15 million. Since the purchase, Frito-Lay has not tampered with the popular Smartfood formula. It has used its marketing expertise to keep sales growing, despite the growing number of challengers crowding the cheesy popcorn market.[3]

10. **Dangling Expressions, Parallel Structure, and Redundancies**   Edit the following paragraphs to eliminate grammatical errors. Do not completely rewrite the sentences; just correct any weaknesses.
    a. As a young child, his father took him on business trips both to London and Paris. These trips were before the war, when traveling was cheaper and an enjoyable experience.
    b. First and foremost, Alan Greenspan is a pragmatist. The favorable advantage of that approach is that he is able to reach a consensus of opinion on most matters. He will announce his latest agreements at a news conference at 3 p.m. in the afternoon.
    c. The reason was that business investment fell at a rate of 4% last year and spending for equipment declined. In trying to combat these declines, the Federal Reserve banks maintain excellent relations with the major financial institutions but they are still not doing as much as they had expected.

11. **Parallelism**   Determine whether the following sentences use parallel structure. Revise sentences as needed to make the structure parallel.
    a. The store is planning to install a new cash-register system that is easier to operate, easier to repair, and cheaper to maintain than the current system.
    b. According to the survey, most employees prefer either holding the employee cafeteria open later or its hours to be kept the same.
    c. The quarterback is expert not only in calling plays but also in throwing passes.
    d. Our career-guidance book will cover
        1. Writing résumés
        2. Application letters
        3. Techniques for interviewing

12. **Wordy Expressions**   Revise the following sentences to eliminate wordy phrases by substituting a single word wherever possible.
    a. Push the red button in the event that you see any smoke rising from the cooking surface.
    b. More than 40% of the people polled are of the opinion that government spending should be reduced.
    c. Please send me more information pertaining to your new line of pesticides.
    d. Due to the fact that two of the three highway lanes were closed for repairs, I was nearly 20 minutes late for my appointment.

13. **Hidden Verbs**   Revise the following sentences to eliminate hidden verbs and convey the appropriate action.
    a. After much deliberation, the group came to a decision about how to respond to the lawsuit.
    b. Although Hugh wanted to offer an explanation of his actions, his boss refused to listen.
    c. Nationwide Call Systems is performing an analysis of our calling patterns to determine how we can save money on long-distance telephone calls.

14. **Sentence Length**   Write a long sentence (40 to 50 words) that attempts to make sense. Then revise the sentence so that it contains 10 or fewer words. Finally, rewrite the sentence so that it contains 16 to 22 words. Which sentence is the most effective? Why?

15. **Active and Passive Voice**   For each of the following sentences, first identify whether the sentence is active or passive. Then, if necessary, revise the sentence to use the more effective verb voice.
    a. We will begin using the new plant in 2003, and the old plant will be converted into a warehouse.
    b. A very effective sales letter was written by Paul Mendleson. The letter will be mailed next week.
    c. You failed to verify the figures on the quarterly report. As a result, $5,500 was lost by the company.

16. **Coherence**   Put logical transitions in the blanks to give the following paragraph coherence.

    > Columbia is widening its lead over Kraft in the computer-magazine war. _____ its revenues increased 27% last year whereas Kraft's increased only 16%. _____ its audited paid circulation increased to 600,000, compared to 450,000 for Kraft. _____ Kraft was able to increase both the ad rate and the number of ad pages last year. One note of worry _____ is Kraft's decision to shut down its independent testing laboratory. Some industry leaders believe much of Kraft's success has been due to its reliable product reviews. _____ Columbia has just announced an agreement whereby Stanford University's world-famous engineering school will perform product testing for Columbia.

17. **Paragraph Length**   Read the following paragraph and determine how it might be divided into two or more shorter paragraphs to help the reader follow the complex topic being discussed.

    > Transforming a manuscript into a published book requires several steps. After the author submits the manuscript (in typewritten or computer-generated form), the copy editor makes any needed grammatical or spelling changes. The author reviews these changes to be sure that they haven't altered the meaning of any sentences or sections. Then the publisher sends the manuscript out for typesetting. Next, the author proofreads the typeset galleys and gives the publisher a list of any corrections. These corrections are incorporated into the page proofs, which show how the pages will look when printed. The author and publisher review these page proofs for any errors. Only after all corrections have been made does the book get published. From start to finish, this process can take as long as a year.

Stetsky Corrects the Boss

Amy Stetsky opened a new Microsoft Word document on her computer and adjusted the headphones of her transcribing unit. She was ready to transcribe some dictation from Dave Kaplan. The dictation was a first draft for part of a speech that Kaplan is going to deliver next month at a meeting of the Ann Arbor chapter of the Office Systems Research Association. Here's what Stetsky heard:

Extensive research shows that lighting has a direct effect on worker productivity and job satisfaction. Lighting that is of appropriate quantity and quality provides efficient comfortable illumination and a safe work environment. They also help to develop a feeling of visual comfort and an aesthetically attractive work area. Which increases job satisfaction.

Appropriate lighting makes the task more visible thus increasing both the speed and the accuracy of the work performed. Inadequate amounts of light causes poor workmanship inaccurate work and lowered production. For example one study conducted by the general industrial corporation showed that when illumination was temporarily reduced by no more than five percent the output of word processing operators decreased by twelve percent. In addition the accuracy of all the operators each of who were paid according to the number of correct lines they produced decreased by eight percentage.

An other study at the interstate national bank showed that errors in processing checks decreased by forty percent when lighting was increased. The productivity of the cash register clerks at a large outlet of united food marts was reduced by twenty eight percent when they were forced to work in reduced lighting for three weeks because of store remodeling. According to the researchers we also spoke with several clerks whom complained about headaches and eyestrain and customers whom complained about slow lines and errors in register receipts.

As a result of such vision research forward looking facilities managers human development personnel and labor unions are all beginning to monitor carefully the quality and quantity of illumination by which employees perform their jobs. Farthermore they are looking to technology to bring more flexibility more efficiency and to provide higher quality illumination for the seeing environment. In short they are looking at light in a new light!

Critical Thinking

1. How effective would this speech section be if it were delivered exactly as written?

Writing Project

2. With Mr. Kaplan's permission, Stetsky routinely edits the dictation as she keyboards it, correcting minor grammar and usage errors. As she transcribes, she also uses correct punctuation, capitalization, spelling, and word division. In short, Stetsky is a professional, and her work reflects it. Assuming the role of Stetsky, transcribe this dictation in double-spaced format (leaving one blank line between each line of type and indenting each paragraph). Make whatever editing changes are needed to correct errors in grammar, mechanics, punctuation, and usage. (If necessary, refer to the LABs in the Reference Manual at the back of the text.)

5

Writing with Style: Overall Tone

An Insider's Perspective

With an office just outside Reading, Pennsylvania, and a network of business affiliates stretching from Guatemala to Chile, Michael Penn keeps his bags packed and his passport at hand. As Regional Director for V. F. Corporation's Wrangler brand, Penn manages licensing throughout Latin America by contracting with local companies to produce and distribute apparel and accessory products under the Wrangler brand. In the course of his working day, he communicates with a wide variety of organizations, including licensees, fabric suppliers, factories, advertising agencies, and media companies, as well as government agencies and trade bureaus.

Penn regularly travels to Central and South America to meet with contacts, but he relies heavily on written communication to keep projects running smoothly between trips. "The written word is the backbone of operating a business that is more than 3,000 miles away," he says. "Telephone conversations are limited by high cost, language differences, and the problems of calling across time zones, so I prefer to send a letter by fax or e-mail. Setting down information in black and white allows me to transmit the same message to several people at the same time, which reduces the chance that the message will be misunderstood or misinterpreted."

The majority of Penn's outgoing correspondence is conducted in English, which is generally accepted as the global language of business. "Often English is not the other person's native language—and either Spanish or Portuguese is not ours—so it's much easier for us to communicate in writing," he says. Knowing that some affiliates are less comfortable answering in English, Wrangler has staff members ready to translate the few incoming documents that are written in other languages.

Using a courteous and sincere tone is especially important in Penn's work, where cultural and language differences can complicate communication. "Writing in a respectful business tone allows us to establish a good reputation and a good rapport with our contacts," he notes. He also stresses the need to keep sarcasm, anger, and other feelings out of business correspondence because emotional language can harm business relationships.

COMMUNICATION OBJECTIVES

After you have finished this chapter, you should be able to

■ Write confidently.

■ Use a courteous and sincere tone.

■ Use appropriate emphasis and subordination.

■ Use nondiscriminatory language.

■ Stress the "you" attitude.

■ Write at an appropriate level of difficulty.

When Penn sits down to write to a business affiliate, he first drafts an introduction to highlight the focus or importance of the letter. Next, he plans how he will address each individual point or question in the body of the letter. "I avoid mixing several ideas in the same sentence or paragraph because that can confuse the reader," he explains. "Without going into great detail, I explain each point, indicate what is required for response or follow-up, and state the deadline for responding." Because some readers may not fully comprehend key points the first time they are presented, Penn often reemphasizes them later in the letter, varying the words or sentence structure to help readers grasp the meaning.

Part of Penn's job is to oversee the design and building of Wrangler stores that will be operated by Latin American licensees, a process that can take six months from blueprints to grand opening. Because he can be onsite for only a few days at a time, he spends as long as five months monitoring the work of architects, builders, store owners, retail personnel, clothing factories, and advertising agencies from his Pennsylvania office. "Written communication is vital to coordinating this intricate network of activities," says Penn.

Michael Penn

Regional Director for Wrangler V. F. Corporation (Wyomissing, Pennsylvania)

As opening day approaches, Penn's fax machine will be even busier. "We may fax back and forth a dozen times a day—sometimes on an hourly basis—depending on how many problems we have to solve," he says. "Time is money. We want to help the stores open as soon as possible, and communicating in writing is the best way of keeping everyone on the same time line."

What Do We Mean by *Tone*?

Having chosen the right words to construct effective sentences and then having combined these sentences into logical paragraphs, we examine the tone of the complete message—the complete letter, memorandum, report, or the like. **Tone** in writing refers to the writer's attitude toward both the reader and the subject of the message. The overall tone of your written message affects your reader just as your tone of voice affects your listener in everyday exchanges. You also want to ensure the appropriateness of the overall tone of your electronic messages (see Spotlight 8—On Technology on page 136).

The business writer should strive for an overall tone that is confident, courteous, and sincere; that uses emphasis and subordination appropriately; that contains nondiscriminatory language; that stresses the "you" attitude; and that is written at an appropriate level of difficulty. (Style Principles 1–9 were presented in Chapter 4.)

10. Write Confidently.

If you believe in what you have written, write in such a way that your reader will also.

Your message should convey the confident attitude that you have done a competent job of communicating and that your reader will do as you ask or will accept your decision. If you believe that your explanation is complete, that your request is reasonable, or that your decision is based on sound logic, you are likely to write with confidence. Such confidence has a persuasive effect on your audience. Avoid using language that makes you sound unsure of yourself. Be especially wary of beginning sentences with "I hope," "If you agree," and similar self-conscious terms.

 If you'd like to take advantage of this offer, call our toll-free number.

 To take advantage of this offer, call our toll-free number.

NOT: I hope that you will agree that my qualifications match your job needs.

BUT: My qualifications match your job needs in the following respects.

In some situations, the best strategy is simply to omit information. For example, you should not provide the reader with excuses for denying your request, suggest that something might go wrong, or intimate that the reader might not be satisfied.

NOT: I know you are a busy person, but we would really enjoy hearing you speak.

BUT: The fact that you are involved in so many different enterprises makes your views on small business all the more relevant for our audience.

 Let us know if you experience any other problems.

BUT: Your GrassMaster lawn mower should now give you many years of trouble-free service.

Modest confidence is the best tactic.

A word of caution: Do not appear *overconfident;* that is, avoid sounding presumptuous or arrogant. Be especially wary of using such strong phrases as "I know that," or "I am sure you will agree that."

NOT: I'm sure you'll agree our offer is reasonable.

BUT: This solution should enable you to collect the data you need while still protecting the interests of our clients.

NOT: I plan to schedule an interview with you next Thursday to discuss my qualifications further.

BUT: Please let me know when I may meet with you to discuss my qualifications further.

Competent communicators are *confident* communicators. They write with conviction, yet they avoid appearing to be pushy or presumptuous.

11. Use a Courteous and Sincere Tone.

A tone of courtesy and sincerity builds goodwill for you and your organization and increases the likelihood that your message will achieve its objective. For example, lecturing the reader or filling a letter with **platitudes** (trite, obvious statements) implies a condescending attitude. Likewise, readers are likely to find offensive such expressions as "you failed to," "we find it difficult to believe that," "you surely don't expect," or "your complaint."

A platitude is a statement so obvious that including it in a message would insult the reader.

NOT: Companies like ours cannot survive unless our customers pay their bills on time.

BUT: By paying your bill before May 30, you will maintain your excellent credit history with our firm.

NOT: You sent your complaint to the wrong department. We don't handle shipping problems.

BUT: We have forwarded your letter to the shipping department. You should be hearing from them within the week.

Your reader is sophisticated enough to know when you're being sincere. To achieve a sincere tone, avoid exaggeration (especially using too many modifiers or too strong modifiers), obvious flattery, and expressions of surprise or disbelief.

Obvious flattery and exaggeration sound insincere.

NOT: Your satisfaction means more to us than making a profit, and we shall work night and day to see that we earn it.

BUT: We value your goodwill highly and have taken several specific steps to ensure your satisfaction.

NOT: I'm surprised you would question your raise, considering your overall performance last year.

BUT: Your raise was based on an objective evaluation of your performance last year.

Competent communicators use both verbal and nonverbal signals to convey courtesy and sincerity (see Spotlight 9—On Technology on page 138). However, it is difficult to fake these attitudes. The best way to achieve the desired tone is to truly assume a courteous and sincere outlook toward your reader.

Netiquette

"Netiquette" is network etiquette—a professional code of behavior for electronic communication. In other words, netiquette is a set of guidelines for behaving properly online. Follow these five guidelines to become (and remain) a welcomed member of the electronic community:

SPOTLIGHT 8

ON

TECHNOLOGY

1. **Remember that you're communicating with another human being.**

   Because of the lack of nonverbal clues (see Spotlight 9—On Technology, p. 138), it's easy to misinterpret the other person's meaning. Remember that the recipient has feelings more or less like your own. Stand up for yourself and your beliefs but be sensitive to other people's feelings. Never write something to someone on e-mail or in a discussion group that you would not say to that person in a face-to-face encounter. Avoid sending heated messages (called "flaming") even if you're provoked. As many users have learned to their dismay, e-mail can be misaddressed or forwarded—sometimes with devastating consequences.

   Also bear in mind that even though you may delete a message from your computer system, chances are that the message remains, perhaps for years, on your computer network's backup tape.

2. **Behave ethically.**

   Standards of online behavior are simply *different from*—but not lower than—those for personal behavior. Five of the "Ten Commandments for Computer Ethics," developed by the Computer Ethics Institute, concern the legal and ethical dimensions of electronic communication:

   ■ Thou shalt not use a computer to steal.

   ■ Thou shalt not use a computer to bear false witness.

   ■ Thou shalt not use or copy software for which you have not paid.

   ■ Thou shalt not use other people's computer resources without authorization.

   ■ Thou shalt not appropriate other people's intellectual output.

   Respect other people's privacy. Don't read other people's e-mail, and get permission before copying or forwarding someone's message to another party. Before inserting a hyperlink from your Web page to someone else's site, notify that person (you don't *have* to ask permission, but it's the courteous thing to do). Similarly, don't copy another's artwork (including cartoons) without securing permission.

3. **Lurk before you leap.**

   When you enter a discussion group that's new to you, take time to look around. Monitor the messages for a few days to get a sense of how the people who are already there act. Then go ahead and participate. Read the FAQs (Frequently Asked Questions, a file that contains answers to commonly asked questions). Ensure the accuracy (and relevance) of anything you post. Bad information spreads like wildfire on the Internet.

   On the other hand, after familiarizing yourself with a newsgroup, don't be afraid to share your knowledge and experiences. The Internet was founded because scientists wanted to share information, and gradually the rest of us got in on the act. So do your part to be helpful and to expand knowledge. That's why the Internet is called a *community*.

4. **Respect other people's time and bandwidth.**

   When you send a message via e-mail or a discussion group, you're taking up other people's time. Therefore, make sure the time they spend reading your message is time well spent. You're also taking up bandwidth—the information-carrying capacity of the telephone lines or networks used to transmit your message. Don't copy more people than necessary in an e-mail note, don't include a copy of the original message in your reply unless necessary, and be careful about posting the same message to more than one newsgroup. Similarly, if you host a Web home page, avoid large graphics.

Despite the information superhighway's superspeed, be patient. Don't expect instant responses to all your questions. Remember that a project that may be of extreme importance to you might be of less concern to others. If you can find the answers yourself with a little electronic digging, don't expect others to do it for you.

5. **Finally, be tolerant of other people's mistakes.**

Electronic communication can be a scary place for novices, and we were all network newbies once. So when someone makes a mistake—whether it's a spelling error, a stupid question, an irrelevant comment, or an unnecessarily long answer—be kind. If you want to be helpful, point out errors by a private e-mail message, not by public posting to a newsgroup. Give people the benefit of the doubt.

In short, netiquette, like good manners in all other situations, is based on adherence to the golden rule: Do unto others as you would have them do unto you. Communicate with others as you would like them to communicate with you.

Sources: "The Core Rules of Netiquette" (Online), Available: http://www.albion.com/netiquette/corerules.html   6   Feb. 1997; "Intranet Intellectual Property Guide" (Online), Available: http://www.abitec.com/home/IPguide.htm 6 Feb. 1997; "The Ten Commandments for Computer Ethics" (Online), Available: http://www.fau.edu/rinaldi/net/ten.html 6 Feb. 1997; "Social Climes/The Buzz: A Netiquette No-No Spams Back On-Line," *Los Angeles Times,* June 18, 1995, p. E5.

12. Use Appropriate Emphasis and Subordination.

Not all ideas are created equal. Some are more important and more persuasive than others. Assume, for example, that you have been asked to evaluate and compare the Copy Cat and the Repro 100 photocopiers and then to write a memo report recommending one for purchase. Assume that the two brands are alike in all important respects except these:

Feature	Copy Cat	Repro 100
Speed (copies per minute)	65	58
Cost	$2,750	$2,100
Enlargement/Reduction?	Yes	No

As you can see, Copy Cat has greater speed and more features. Thus, a casual observer might think you should recommend Copy Cat on the basis of its additional advantages. Suppose, however, that most of your photocopying involves fewer than five copies of each original, all of them full-sized. Under these conditions, Repro 100's lower cost outweighs Copy Cat's higher speed and additional features; you therefore decide to recommend purchasing Repro 100. If you want your recommendation to be credible, you must make sure your reader views the relative importance of each feature the same way you do. To do so, use appropriate emphasis and subordination techniques.

Let your reader know which ideas you consider most important.

Techniques of Emphasis   To emphasize an idea, use any of the following strategies (to subordinate an idea, simply use the opposite strategy):

To subordinate an idea, put it in the dependent clause.

1. Put the idea in a short, simple sentence. If you need a complex sentence to convey the needed information, put the more important idea in the independent clause. (The ideas communicated in each independent clause of a *compound* sentence receive *equal* emphasis.)

Electronic Punctuation Tones Up E-mail

Although e-mail is technically a form of written communication, sometimes its immediacy and intimacy make it more like a phone conversation than an exchange of letters or memos. But the rich nonverbal cues that are such an important and natural part of conversations (pauses, voice tone, emphasis, and the like) are missing in e-mail exchanges. Without some device to indicate tone of voice, misunderstandings might result and might lead to an abrupt or even angry response. Such a response, called *flaming*, can weaken your ability to accomplish your objective.

In most e-mail systems, it is impossible to use underlining or italics. Instead, you can begin and end a word or phrase you wish to emphasize with underscore characters— for example, "I _must have_ this report by Friday"— or with asterisks, as in "I *must have* this report by Friday." For stronger emphasis, use all capitals ("I MUST HAVE this report by Friday.") Avoid using all capitals for your entire message, however. All-capital letters are difficult to read, and they appear to be shouting.

Shortcuts are sometimes used to convey emotions. For example, typing <grin> or just <g> softens the effect of a sarcastic remark and lets the reader know you're joking. Commonly used abbreviations in e-mail include IMHO (in my humble opinion), FWIW (for what it's worth), and BTW (by the way).

SPOTLIGHT 9

ON
TECHNOLOGY

Another form of shorthand is the *smiley* or *emoticon,* which is a simple icon used to convey humor and other emotions. Common examples are :-) and :-(. When you tilt your head to the left, you can see that the colon represents the eyes and the hyphen represents the nose of a happy or sad face. Here are other examples of smileys (tilt your head to the left to get their meanings):

:´-(	I'm crying
:-X	My lips are sealed.
´:-)	I accidentally shaved off one eyebrow.
0:-)	I'm an angel.
}:->	I'm a devil.
*<|:-)	I'm Santa Claus.
=:-)	I'm a punk rocker.
:-)))	I'm overweight.

Although smileys are not appropriate for most business e-mail, occasionally they might lend just the right human touch to a particular message.

Sources: Michael E. Miller, "A Story of the Type That Turns Heads in Computer Circles," *Wall Street Journal,* September 15, 1992, pp. A1, A8; Michael E. Miller, "Sidelong Remarks That May Interest Propellerheads," *Wall Street Journal,* September 15, 1992, p. A8; Daniel Will-Harris, "Electronic Punctuation and Hieroglyphics," *PC Publishing and Presentations,* August– September 1991, p. 40.

SIMPLE   Repro 100 is the better photocopier for our purposes.

COMPLEX   Although Copy Cat is faster, 98% of our copying requires fewer than five copies per original. (*Emphasizes the fact that speed is not a crucial consideration for us.*)

2. Place the major idea first or last. The first paragraph of a message receives the most emphasis, the last paragraph receives less emphasis, and the middle paragraphs receive the least emphasis. Similarly, the middle sentences within a paragraph receive less emphasis than the first sentence in a paragraph.

The first criterion examined was cost. Copy Cat sells for $2,750 and Repro 100 sells for $2,100, or 24% less than the cost of Copy Cat.

Use emphasis and subordination ethically—or you may run into legal trouble. Mark Voorhees, publisher of *Information Law Alert*, an online newsletter, cautions online publishers to clearly differentiate between fact and opinion.

3. Use active voice to emphasize the doer of the action and passive voice to emphasize the receiver. In other words, make the noun you want to emphasize the subject of the sentence.

   ACTIVE   Repro 100 costs 24% less than Copy Cat. (*Emphasizes Repro 100 rather than Copy Cat.*)

   PASSIVE   The relative costs of the two models were compared first. (*Emphasizes the relative costs rather than the two models.*)

4. Devote more space to the idea.

   The two models were judged according to three criteria: cost, speed, and enlargement/reduction capabilities. Total cost is an important consideration for our firm because of the large number of copiers we use and our large volume of copying. Last year our firm used 358 photocopiers and duplicated more than 6.5 million pages. Thus, regardless of the speed or features of a particular model, if it is too expensive to operate, it will not serve our purposes.

5. Use language that directly implies importance, such as "most important," "major," or "primary."

   The most important factor for us is cost.

   Use terms such as "least important" or "a minor point" to subordinate an idea.

6. Use repetition (within reason).

   However, Copy Cat is expensive—expensive to purchase and expensive to operate.

7. Use mechanical means (within reason)—enumeration, underscoring, solid capitals, second color, indenting from left and right margins, or other elements of design—to emphasize key ideas.

But the most important criterion is cost, and <u>Repro 100 costs 24% *less*</u> than Copy Cat.

Use language that expresses your honest evaluation; do not mislead the reader.

The Ethical Dimension   In using emphasis and subordination, your goal should be to ensure a common frame of reference between you and your reader; you want your reader to see how important you consider each idea to be. Your goal is *not* to mislead the reader. For example, if you believe that Alternative A is the *slightly* better choice, you would certainly not want to intentionally mislead your reader into concluding that Alternative A is *clearly* the better choice. Such a tactic would be not only unethical but also unwise. Use sound business judgment and a sense of fair play to help yourself achieve your communication objectives.

13. Use Nondiscriminatory Language.

Be sensitive to your readers' feelings

Nondiscriminatory language treats everyone equally, making no unwarranted assumptions about any group of people. Using nondiscriminatory language is smart business because (1) it is the ethical thing to do and (2) we risk offending others if we do otherwise. Consider the types of bias in this report:

> The finishing plant was the scene of a confrontation today when two ladies from the morning shift accused a foreman of sexual harassment. Marta Maria Valdez, a Hispanic inspector, and Margaret Sawyer, an assembly-line worker, accused Mr. Engerrand of making suggestive comments. Mr. Engerrand, who is 62 years old and an epileptic, denied the charges and said he thought the girls were trying to gyp the company with their demand for a cash award.

Were you able to identify the following instances of bias or discriminatory language?

- The women were referred to as *ladies* and *girls,* although it is unlikely that the men in the company are referred to as *gentlemen* and *boys.*
- The term *foreman* (and all other -*man* occupational titles) has a sexist connotation.
- The two women were identified by their first and last names, without a personal title, whereas the man was identified by a personal title and last name only.
- Valdez's ethnicity, Engerrand's age, and Engerrand's disability were identified, although they were irrelevant to the situation.

Use language that implies equality.

- The word *gyp,* derived from *gypsy,* is derogatory.

Competent communicators make sure that their writing is free of sexist language and free of bias based on such factors as race, ethnicity, religion, age, sexual orientation, and disability.

Sexist Language   It makes no business sense to exclude or perhaps offend half the population by using sexist language. To avoid sexism in your writing, follow these strategies:

1. Use neutral job titles that do not imply that a job is held by only men or only women.

Instead of	*Use*
chairman	chair, chairperson
foreman	supervisor
salesman	sales representative
woman lawyer	lawyer
workman	worker, employee

2. Avoid words and phrases that unnecessarily imply gender.

Instead of	*Use*
best man for the job	best person for the job
executives and their wives	executives and their spouses
housewife	homemaker
manmade	artificial, manufactured
manpower	human resources, personnel

3. Avoid demeaning or stereotypical terms.

Instead of	*Use*
My girl will handle it.	My secretary will handle it.
Women don't like football.	Some people don't like football.
Watch your language around the ladies.	Watch your language.
Housewives like our long hours.	Our customers like our long hours.
He was a real jock.	He enjoyed all types of sports.
Each nurse supplies her own uniform.	Nurses supply their own uniforms.

Males also may be the victims of sexist language.

4. Use parallel language.

Instead of	*Use*
Joe, a broker, and his wife, a beautiful brunette	Joe, a broker, and his wife, Mary a lawyer (*or* homemaker)
Ms. Wyllie and William Poe	Ms. Wyllie and Mr. Poe
man and wife	husband and wife

5. Use appropriate personal titles and salutations.

 ▪ If a woman has a professional title, use it (Dr. Martha Ralston, the Rev. Deborah Connell).

 ▪ Follow a woman's preference in being addressed as *Miss, Mrs.,* or *Ms.*

 ▪ If a woman's marital status or her preference is unknown, use *Ms.*

 ▪ If you do not know the reader's gender, use a nonsexist salutation (Dear Investor:, Dear Friend:, Dear Customer:, Dear Policyholder:).

 ▪ If you cannot tell the reader's gender, you may use the full name in the salutation (Dear Chris Andrews:, Dear Terry Brooks:).

Follow the reader's preference to be addressed as Ms., Miss, or Mrs.

6. Whether it is appropriate to use *he* or *his* as generic pronouns in referring to males or females (e.g., "Each manager must evaluate *his* subordinates annually") is currently a matter of some debate. Proponents argue that its use is based on tradition and on the fact that no genderless alternative pronoun exists. Opponents argue that its use appears to exclude females. Although many businesspeople would not be offended by such use, some would be. The conservative approach is to avoid such usage whenever possible by adopting any of these strategies:

The generic use of he *and* him *may offend some readers.*

■ Use plural nouns and pronouns.

All managers must evaluate their subordinates annually.
But not: Each manager must evaluate their subordinates annually.

■ Use second-person pronouns (*you, your*).

You must evaluate your subordinates annually.

■ Revise the sentence.

Each manager must evaluate subordinates annually.

Excessive use of the term he or she *or* his or hers *sounds awkward.*

■ Use *his or her* (sparingly).

Each manager must evaluate his or her subordinates annually.

Other Discriminatory Language   We are all members of different groups, each of which may have different customs, values, and attitudes. If you think of your readers as individuals, rather than as stereotypical members of some particular group, you will avoid bias when communicating about race, ethnic background, religion, age, sexual orientation, and disabilities. Group membership should be mentioned only if it is clearly pertinent.

Mention group membership only if it is clearly relevant.

NOT: Richard McKenna, noted black legislator, supported our position.
BUT: Richard McKenna, noted legislator, supported our position.

NOT: Because of rising interest rates, he welshed on the deal.
BUT: Because of rising interest rates, he backed out of the deal.

NOT: Anita Voyles performed the job well for her age.
BUT: Anita Voyles performed the job well.

NOT: Patricia Barbour's lesbianism has not affected her job performance.
BUT: Patricia Barbour's job performance has been exemplary.

NOT: Mary, an epileptic, had no trouble passing the medical examination.
BUT: Mary, who has epilepsy, had no trouble passing the medical examination.
(*When the impairment is relevant, separate the impairment from the person.*)

Most of us like to think of ourselves as sensitive, caring people who do not wish to offend others; our writing and speaking should reflect this attitude. Unfortunately, some types of discriminatory language may be so deeply ingrained that using bias-free language may take a concerted effort at first. Bias will not disappear completely from our language until it disappears completely from our lives. Still, competent communicators strive to use language impartially so that readers can focus their attention on *what* is written without being offended by *how* it is written.

14. Stress the "You" Attitude.

Are you more interested in how well *you* perform in your courses or in how well your classmates perform? When you hear a television commercial, are you more interested in how the product will benefit *you* or in how your purchase of the product will benefit the advertiser? If you're like most people reading or hearing a message, your conscious or unconscious reaction is likely to be "What's in it for *me?*" Knowing that this is true provides you with a powerful strategy for structuring your messages to maximize their impact: stress the "you" attitude, not the "me" attitude.

The **"you" attitude** emphasizes what the *receiver* (either the listener or the reader) wants to know and how he or she will be affected by the message. It requires developing **empathy**—the ability to project yourself into another person's position and to understand that person's situation, feelings, motives, and needs. To avoid sounding selfish and uninterested, focus on the reader—adopt the "you" attitude.

> **NOT:**   I am shipping your order this afternoon.
>
> **BUT:**   Your order should arrive by Friday.

> **NOT:**   We will be open on Sundays from 1 to 5 p.m., beginning May 15.
>
> **BUT:**   You will be able to shop on Sundays from 1 to 5 p.m., beginning May 15.

Reader Benefits   An important component of the "you" attitude is the concept of **reader benefits**—emphasizing how the *reader* will benefit from doing as you ask. Sometimes, especially when asking a favor or refusing a request, the best we can do is to show how *someone* (not necessarily the reader) will benefit. But whenever possible, we should show how someone *other than ourselves* benefits from our request or from our decision.

> **NOT:**   We cannot afford to purchase an ad in your organization's directory.
>
> **BUT:**   Advertising exclusively on television allows us to offer consumers like you the lowest prices on their cosmetics.

> **NOT:**   Our decorative fireplace has an oak mantel and is portable.
>
> **BUT:**   Whether you're entertaining in your living room or den, you can still enjoy the ambience of a blazing fire because our decorative fireplace is portable. Simply take it with you from room to room.

Note that the revised sentences, which stress reader benefits, are longer than the original sentences—because they contain *more information*. Yet they are not verbose; that is, they do not contain unnecessary words. You can add information and still write concisely.

Exceptions   Stressing the "you" attitude focuses the attention on the reader, which is right where the attention should be—most of the time. In some situations, however, you may want to avoid focusing on the reader; these situations all involve conveying negative information. When you refuse someone's request, disagree with

---

wordwise

What's in a Name?   The following are actual baby names recorded on birth certificates:

- Heaven Leigh Joy
- Crystal Shanda Lear
- April Schauer
- Female & Tamale (twin girl and boy)
- Boya & Boyb (twin boys)
- Orangello & Lemongello (twin girls)
- Ken & Kenny (twin boys whose dad was named "Kenneth")

Write from the reader's perspective.

Answer the reader's unspoken question, "What's in it for me?*"*

In some situations you do not want to focus attention on the reader.

someone, or talk about someone's mistakes or shortcomings, avoid connecting the reader too closely with the negative information. In such situations, avoid second-person pronouns (*you* and *your*), and use passive sentences or other subordinating techniques to stress the receiver of the action rather than the doer.

NOT: You should have included more supporting evidence in your presentation.

BUT: Including more supporting evidence would have made the presentation more convincing.

NOT: You failed to return the merchandise within the 10-day period.

BUT: We are happy to give a full refund on all merchandise that is returned within ten days.

Note that neither of the revised sentences contains the word *you*. Thus, they help to separate the reader from the negative information, making the message more tactful and palatable.

15. Write at an Appropriate Level of Difficulty.

The term **readability** refers to the ease of understanding a passage based on its style of writing. You should write (and speak) at a level of readability that is appropriate for your specific audience. For example, a toy manufacturer would not use the same language in an advertisement in *Kid's World* (directed primarily to 8- to 10-year-olds) as it would use in an advertisement in *Corporate Wholesaler* (directed primarily to corporate executives).

Various readability formulas are available that estimate the complexity of a passage on the basis of an analysis of such factors as sentence length, number of

Avoid the OOSOOM (out-of-sight, out-of-mind) syndrome, warns Max Dobens, a national account manager for Swissôtel. A telecommuter himself, he cautions those working at home not to forget to communicate frequently with colleagues back at the office.

FIGURE 5.1   Readability Statistics and Explanation for a Document Typed in Microsoft Word for Windows 97

Readability Statistics	? X
Counts	
Words	387
Characters	2009
Paragraphs	15
Sentences	23
Averages	
Sentences per Paragraph	3.8
Words per Sentence	12.9
Characters per Word	4.7
Readability	
Passive Sentences	0%
Flesch Reading Ease	61.3
Flesch-Kincaid Grade Level	7.6
	OK

Flesch Reading Ease. Rates text on a 100-point scale; the higher the score, the easier it is to understand the document. For most business documents, aim for a score of approximately 50 to 70.

Flesch-Kincaid Grade Level. Rates text on a U.S. grade-school level. For example, a score of 8.0 means that an eighth grader can understand the document. For most business documents, aim for a score of 7.0 to 9.0.

The readability scores of the illustrated document indicate that it was probably meant for a typical business reader.

syllables per word, and word frequency. Most contemporary word processing programs will automatically compute readability statistics for a document you compose (see Figure 5.1).

Although applying a readability formula is helpful in judging the readability of your message, you should use the results as a guide only. You could, for example, artificially change your readability score by using shorter sentences and shorter words. But sometimes a longer word is more precise and more familiar than a shorter word. Likewise, lowering the score by using all short sentences (for example, all simple sentences) might obscure the relationships among ideas because then all ideas would receive equal emphasis.

Although readability formulas are helpful, other factors are also important.

A further caution with regard to overreliance on readability measures concerns what they do *not* measure. They do not measure the complexity and organization of the ideas or the design of the document. Perhaps, more important, they do not measure reader interest in the passage. A reader who is intently interested in what you have to say may plow through even the foggiest writing. But if you have reason to expect low reader interest, be sure to make your writing especially easy and inviting to read.

Effective Business Writing

Writing style goes beyond *correctness*. Although a letter that contains many grammatical, mechanical, or usage errors could hardly be considered effective, a letter

CHECKLIST 4   Writing with Style

Words

☑ *Write clearly.* Be accurate and complete; use familiar words; avoid dangling expressions and unnecessary jargon.

☑ *Prefer short, simple words.* They are less likely to be misused by the writer and more likely to be understood by the reader.

☑ *Write with vigor.* Use specific, concrete language; avoid clichés, slang, and buzz words.

☑ *Write concisely.* Avoid redundancy, wordy expressions, and hidden subjects and verbs.

☑ *Prefer positive language.* Stress what you can do or what is true rather than what you cannot do or what is not true.

Sentences

☑ *Use a variety of sentence types.* Use simple sentences for emphasis and variety, compound sentences for coordinate relationships, and complex sentences for subordinate relationships. Most sentences should range from 16 to 22 words.

☑ *Use active and passive voice appropriately.* Use active voice in general and to emphasize the doer of the action; use passive voice to emphasize the receiver.

Paragraphs

☑ *Keep paragraphs unified and coherent.* Develop a single idea consistently and logically; use transitional words and pronouns, repetition, and parallelism.

☑ *Control paragraph length.* Use a variety of lengths, although most paragraphs should range from 60 to 80 words.

Overall Tone

☑ *Write confidently.* Avoid sounding self-conscious (by overusing such phrases as "I think" and "I hope"), but also avoid sounding arrogant or presumptuous.

☑ *Use a courteous and sincere tone.* Avoid platitudes, exaggeration, obvious flattery, and expressions of surprise or disbelief.

☑ *Use appropriate emphasis and subordination.* Emphasize and subordinate through the use of sentence structure, position, verb voice, amount of space, language, repetition, and mechanical means.

☑ *Use nondiscriminatory language.* When communicating, avoid bias about gender, race, ethnic background, religion, age, sexual orientation, and disabilities.

☑ *Stress the "you" attitude.* Emphasize what the receiver wants to know and how the receiver will be affected by the message; stress reader benefits.

☑ *Write at an appropriate level of difficulty.* A Flesch-Kincaid grade level of 7 to 9 is generally an appropriate readability level in business writing, although many factors other than syllabic intensity and sentence length affect readability.

that contains no such errors might still be ineffective because it lacks style. Style involves choosing the right words, writing effective sentences, developing logical paragraphs, and setting an appropriate overall tone. Checklist 4 summarizes the 15 principles discussed in Chapters 4 and 5.

These principles will help you communicate your ideas clearly and effectively. They provide a solid foundation for the higher-order communication skills you will be developing in the following chapters. At first, you may find it somewhat difficult and time-consuming to constantly assess your writing according to these criteria. Their importance, however, merits the effort. Soon you will find that you are applying these principles automatically as you compose and revise messages.

SUMMARY

Competent communicators achieve their objectives by writing with confidence, courtesy, and sincerity. They recognize that not all ideas are equally important, and they use techniques of emphasis and subordination to develop a common frame of reference between writer and reader. They use nondiscriminatory language in their writing by treating everyone equally and by not making unwarranted assumptions about any group of people.

Effective writing keeps the emphasis on the reader—stressing what the reader needs to know and how the reader will be affected by the message. Effective messages are also written at an appropriate level of difficulty so that the reader can easily understand the passage, because of its style of writing.

KEY TERMS

empathy	readability	tone
nondiscriminatory language	reader benefits	"you" attitude
platitude		

REVIEW AND DISCUSSION

1. **Communication at V. F. Corporation Revisited.** In between business trips to Latin America, Michael Penn depends on written communication to keep his Wrangler projects running smoothly.
   a. Should Penn's correspondence with Latin American contacts have a high or low readability score? Why?
   b. Why is it especially important for Penn to avoid platitudes when writing to a new affiliate for the first time?
   c. Why would Penn repeat a particular point, using different words or a different sentence structure?
2. Give an example of a sentence that sounds too confident and one that doesn't sound confident enough. Then revise both sentences to make them more effective.
3. What are three means of achieving a sincere tone in a message?
4. List seven techniques for emphasizing an idea.
5. List seven techniques for subordinating an idea.
6. Why should discriminatory language be avoided in business writing?
7. Do you feel it is appropriate or inappropriate to use the pronoun *he* as a generic pronoun referring to both males and females (for example, "Each manager must ensure that *he* submits *his* reports on time")? Write a paragraph defending your position.
8. List six techniques for avoiding sexism in business writing.
9. Construct a sentence illustrating the "you" attitude.
10. Under what circumstances should the reader *not* be the focus of attention in business writing?
11. Under what circumstances might a readability formula *not* be an appropriate measure of difficulty?

EXERCISES

1. **Communication Applications at V. F. Corporation**   From his office in Pennsylvania, Michael Penn relies heavily on written communication to keep Wrangler

brand licensing projects running smoothly in Latin America. He uses a courteous, sincere tone to show respect when he writes to his business contacts. To avoid misunderstandings because of language and cultural differences, Penn restates important points—using other words.

Penn has asked you, the advertising coordinator for Wrangler's Latin American region, to write to the local advertising agency to explain the timetable for new store advertising. You will need to see the agency's initial advertising ideas four months before the opening; your legal department will need to review the campaign three months before; the agency should print the posters two months before; and the newspaper ads should be placed one month before.

a. Why are you writing this letter?
b. What do you need to know about your audience?
c. How can you stress the "you" attitude in your letter?
d. What points will you cover in your letter, and in what order?

For Exercises 2–5, revise the passages to reflect the writing principle indicated. Do not completely rewrite the passages; just correct any style problems.

2. Writing Confidently

If you believe my proposal has merit, I hope that you will allocate $50,000 for a pilot study. It's possible that this pilot study will bear out my profit estimates so that we can proceed on a permanent basis. Even though you have several other worthwhile projects to consider for funding, I know you will agree the proposal should be funded prior to January 1. Please call me before the end of the week to tell me that you've accepted my proposal.

3. Using a Courteous and Sincere Tone

You, our loyal and dedicated employees, have always been the most qualified and the most industrious in the industry. Because of your faithful and dependable service, I was quite surprised to learn yesterday that an organizational meeting for union representation was recently held here. You must realize that a company like ours cannot survive unless we hold labor costs down. I cannot believe that you don't appreciate the many benefits of working at Allied. We will immediately have to declare bankruptcy if a union is voted in. Please don't be fooled by empty rhetoric.

4. Using Nondiscriminatory Language

Mr. Timmerman argued that the 62-year-old Kathy Beviere should be replaced because she doesn't dress appropriately for her receptionist position. However, the human resources director, who is female, countered that we don't pay any of the girls in the clerical positions well enough for them to buy appropriate attire. Mr. Timmerman did acknowledge that the receptionist, who is a paraplegic, is well suited for her receptionist job. He added that he just wished she would dress more businesslike instead of wearing the colorful clothes and makeup that reflect her immigrant background.

5. Stressing the "You" Attitude

We are happy to announce that we are offering for sale an empty parcel of land at the corner of Mission and High Streets. We will be selling this parcel for $89,500, with a minimum down payment of $22,500. We have had the lot rezoned M-2 for student housing. We originally purchased this lot because of its proximity to the university and had planned to erect student housing, but our investment plans have changed. We still feel that our lot would make a profitable site for up to three 12-unit buildings.

6. **Writing Confidently**   Revise the following sentences to convey an appropriately confident attitude.

   a. Can you think of any reason not to buy a wristwatch for dressy occasions?
   b. I hope you agree that my offer provides good value for the money.
   c. Of course, I am confident that my offer provides good value for the money.
   d. You might try to find a few minutes to visit our gallery on your next visit to galleries in this area.

7. **Using Appropriate Emphasis and Subordination**   Assume that you have evaluated two candidates for the position of sales assistant. This is what you have learned:
   a. Carl Barteolli has more sales experience.
   b. Elizabeth Larson has more appropriate formal training (college degree in marketing, attendance at several three-week sales seminars, and the like).
   c. Elizabeth Larson's personality appears to mesh more closely with the prevailing corporate attitudes at your firm.

   You must write a memo to Robert Underwood, the vice president, recommending one of these candidates. First, assume that personality is the most important criterion and write a memo recommending Elizabeth Larson. Second, assume that experience is the most important criterion and write a memo recommending Carl Barteolli. Use appropriate emphasis and subordination in each message. You may make up any reasonable information needed to complete the assignment.

8. **Using Nondiscriminatory Language**   Revise the following sentences to eliminate discriminatory language.

   a. The mayor opened contract talks with the union representing local policemen.
   b. While the salesmen are at the convention, their wives will be treated to a tour of the city's landmarks.
   c. Our company gives each foreman the day off on his birthday.
   d. Our public relations director, Heather Marshall, will ask her young secretary, Bonita Carwell, to take notes during the president's speech.
   e. Both Dr. Fernandez and his assistant, Andrea Lee-McNeill, attended the new-product seminar.

9. **Writing at an Appropriate Level of Difficulty**   Select an actual paper that you have written and submitted for a course grade in this or some other course and that you have saved on disk. Use your word processing software to compute the readability of the paper. What does this score mean? If necessary, revise the passage to adjust the readability level; then recompute your score. Submit both versions and your calculations to your instructor.

10. **Using Techniques of Emphasis**   Revise each sentence by applying the indicated technique of emphasis. In each case, emphasize the problems of cold weather.

    a. Use one complex sentence.

       Outdoor workers in White Butte, North Dakota, have to battle severe winter conditions. However, outdoor workers in Atlanta, Georgia, face mild winter conditions.

    b. Make the noun you want to emphasize the subject of the sentence.

       Telephone and utility repair personnel who work outdoors have to cope with dangerous working conditions created by subzero temperatures.

    c. Use language that directly implies importance.

       Outdoor workers generally face a range of weather conditions, but frigid temperatures can pose particularly severe problems.

    d. Use repetition.

       Utilities in the northern states frequently remind outdoor workers about the cold-weather dangers of frostbite and hypothermia.

11. Stressing Reader Benefits   Revise the following sentences to emphasize reader benefits.

    a. We have been in the business of repairing sewing machines for more than 40 years.
    b. We need donations so we can expand the free-food program in this community.
    c. Company policy requires us to impose a 2% late charge when customers don't pay their bills on time.
    d. Although the refund department is open from 9 a.m. to 5 p.m., it is closed from 1 p.m. to 2 p.m. so our employees can take their lunch breaks.

12. Evaluating Writing Style   As a college student with a potentially bright future, you no doubt frequently receive letters from credit-card companies, department stores, insurance firms, and the like, soliciting your business. Select a letter that you or a colleague has received, and analyze it according to each of the 15 principles in Checklist 4. Write a statement of evaluation describing how well the letter adheres to each principle.

13. Exceptions to the "You" Attitude   Revise the following sentences, which convey negative information, to take the focus off the reader.

    a. Because you paid your bill after the due da te, you are being invoiced for an additional 2% late charge.
    b. Your proposal was sent too late for this year's competition.
    c. You forgot to include copies of last month's pay stubs with your loan application.
    d. Your report was one-sided because it did not provide enough details about the disadvantages of buying directly from the manufacturer.

Drew Drafts a Drab Memo

Here is a first-draft memo written by O. J. Drew to Arnie McNally:

MEMO TO: Arnold McNally, vice president, manufacturing

FROM: O. J. Drew, production manager

DATE: October 13, 19—

SUBJECT: Charlotte Expansion

As you will remember, when we opened our Charlotte plant, we made plans to increase capacity within three years. We're now approaching the end of our third year, and even though sales are increasing, I suggest we delay any expansion plans for another two years.

To begin with, interest rates are heading up across the board. Last week, North Carolina National Bank and Wachovia Bank both raised their prime rate quite a bit. This is the highest it has been in several years. Other big banks are likely to follow with similar increases. Both NCNB and Wachovia financed our initial efforts in Charlotte—at a lower rate. The Wall Street Journal predicts that interest rates will remain high for at least the next 18 months. A second reason for my suggestion is that present capacity is sufficient to support our present level of sales. If sales continue to grow substantially, we will continue to have sufficient capacity for three more years. We can increase production for minimal plant cost by simply adding a third shift. Adding a third shift will lower per-unit costs and enable us to convert numerous part-time positions to full-time positions, with a corresponding savings in fringe benefits. Finally, our union contract expires next year. Although our plant is automated, we still employ 95 unionized workers. These men's wage demands are high; and unless we are able to jew them down a bit, we will simply not be able to afford an expansion. I predict getting a reasonable union contract this time will be a hard nut to crack. In addition, Neelima believes that if a strike is at all possible, we won't even be using the capacity we presently have—let alone expanded capacity.

For these reasons, I recommend we delay any expansion plans for another two years at least. I hope you will agree with me. Luis Diaz does; and if you desire, we can produce a formal report of our recommendation for you to present to the board. Let me know if you have any questions.

juv

Critical Thinking

1. In terms of what you know about Arnie McNally (see Appendix to Chapter 1), assess the appropriateness of the readability of this memo for its intended audience. What factors not measured by readability formulas affect the readability of this memo?

Writing Projects

2. Analyze each paragraph, using Checklist 4 as the basis for your analysis. What effective and ineffective techniques has Drew used?
3. List each transitional expression that was used in the second paragraph to achieve coherence. Does the paragraph have unity? Explain.
4. Revise this memorandum, making whatever changes are necessary to increase its effectiveness. You may make up any needed facts as long as they are reasonable.

6

The Process of Writing

COMMUNICATION OBJECTIVES

After you have finished this chapter, you should be able to

■ Specify the purpose of your message and analyze your audience.

■ Determine what information to include and in what order to present it.

■ Compose a first draft of your message.

■ Use a variety of strategies to overcome writer's block.

■ Revise for content, style, and correctness.

■ Arrange documents in a standard format.

■ Proofread a document for content, typographical, and format errors.

An Insider's Perspective

Planning for the future is Michael Hanley's expertise. Before any company can make decisions about products, markets, distributors, or even internal structure, it needs a solid business strategy to lead the way. Hanley's role in the Integrated Strategic Services Practice at Coopers & Lybrand Consulting (CLC) is to help corporate clients plot a course for determining where they want to be in the coming years.

In this fast-paced environment, electronic communication is the most efficient way to link the firm's 70,000 employees. Even clients appreciate the speed and convenience of e-mail, notes Hanley: "We still print some documents to hand to clients, but we often send files to clients by attaching them to Internet messages." As the author of the style book that CLC employees follow when preparing written communications, he insists that e-mail to clients reflect the same level of professionalism as paper-based documents. "E-mail documents should be treated as formally as business letters, because that's what they are," he explains. "We recognize that people may have different styles, and we allow our employees some leeway. However, we draw the line at breaking the rules of punctuation, capitalization, grammar, and spelling."

Before starting a new project, Hanley writes the client a letter covering his understanding of the situation, CLC's proposed approach, the benefits that the client can expect, and the anticipated schedule, staffing, and fees. This letter may be as long as seven pages or as brief as a few paragraphs, depending on the complexity of the project. Then, as each project progresses, Hanley prepares interim reports to let the client know what has been accomplished to date, concluding with a final report that summarizes the results. Instead of using a written report format, Hanley and his colleagues make slide or electronic presentations and provide clients with multipage handouts. Each handout page consists of a title, a graphic such as a bar chart or pie chart, and supporting text, all shown in landscape orientation.

Knowing that these handouts double as reports, Hanley has developed a structure to guide CLC consultations through the preparation process. The first step is to write each slide's title in a full sentence. "We stay away from three- or four-word phrases or bullet points," he says, "because those typically aren't precise enough to carry a lot of meaning." The next step is to use the pyramid principle to arrange these sentences into a cohesive "story line" for a presentation, starting with a brief description of the client's situation and the challenge being addressed, then moving to CLC's solution and the supporting details. "The key is to show the solution, the big 'so what,' right up front," he explains. This direct organizational plan helps clients follow the logic and understand the significance of the information being presented.

Michael Hanley

Partner, Integrated Services Practice, Coopers & Lybrand Consulting (Chicago, Illinois)

The importance of establishing the story line as an outline for the report was driven home when Hanley was working on a large-scale strategy project early in his CLC career. His task was to coordinate and edit the final report of the ten consultants who had researched the problem for nearly three months. Anticipating a handout of 90 pages, he brought the consultants together a week before the report was due. Once they had agreed on the overall story line, each worked individually on his or her section, with Hanley's assistance. This process went so smoothly that the report was completed a day early. The client's reaction? "There is only one way to know if a client likes our work," notes Hanley, "and that is if they sign us up for more work. That's exactly what happened after this presentation."

An Overview of the Writing Process

When faced with a writing task, some people just start writing. They try to do everything at once, figuring out what to say and how to say it, visualizing an audience and a goal, keeping watch on spelling and grammar, and choosing their words and building sentences—all at the same time. It's not easy to keep switching back and forth from one of these distinct writing tasks to another and still make headway. In fact, unless you're an expert writer, it's harder and slower than breaking the job up into steps and completing each step in turn.

The idea of writing step by step may at first sound as if it will prolong the job, but it won't. The step of planning, for example, gives you a sense of where you want to go and that, in turn, makes getting there faster and easier. The clearer you are about your goals, the more likely your writing will accomplish those goals. And if you save a separate step for proofreading, that job will also go more smoothly and efficiently. After all, it's difficult to spot a typo while you're still trying to think up the "big ending" for your report.

There is no single "best" writing process. In fact, all good writers develop their own process that suits their own ways of tackling a problem. But one way or another, competent communicators typically perform the following five steps when faced with a business situation that calls for a written response (see Figure 6.1):

The writing process consists of planning, drafting, revising, formatting, and proofreading.

1. *Planning:* Determining what the purpose of the message is, who the reader will be, what information you need to give the reader to achieve your purpose, and in what order to present the information.
2. *Drafting:* Composing a first draft of the message.
3. *Revising:* Revising for content, style, and correctness.
4. *Formatting:* Arranging the document in an appropriate format.
5. *Proofreading:* Reviewing the document to check for content, typographical, and format errors.

The amount of time you will devote to each step depends on the complexity, length, and importance of the document. Not all steps may be needed for all writing tasks. For example, you may go through all the steps if you are writing a business plan to get funding for a small business from a bank but not if you are answering an e-mail message inviting you to a meeting. Nevertheless, these steps are a good starting point for completing a writing assignment—either in class or on the job.

Planning

Planning, the first step in writing, involves making conscious decisions about the purpose, audience, content, and organization of the message.

Purpose

The purpose should be specific enough to serve as a yardstick for judging the success of the message.

The first decision relates to the purpose of the message. If you don't know why you're writing the message (that is, if you don't know what you hope to accomplish), then later you'll have no way of knowing whether or not you've achieved your goal. In the end, what matters is not how well-crafted your message was or how

FIGURE 6.1   The Five Steps in the Writing Process

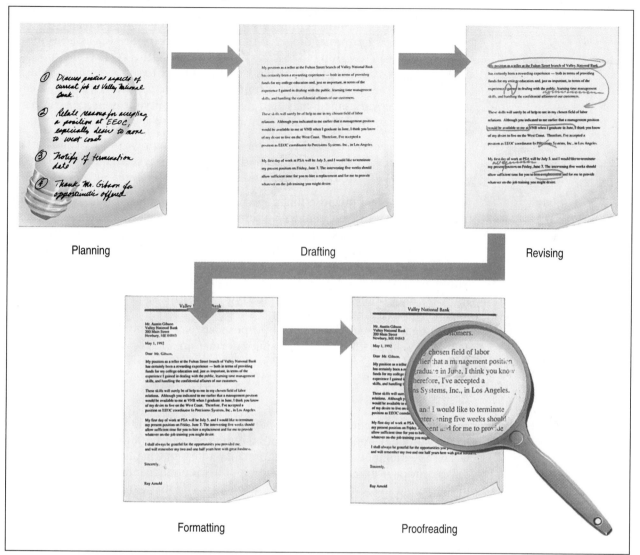

attractive it looked on the page; what matters is whether you achieved your communication objective. If you did, your communication was successful; if you did not, it was not.

Most writers find it easier to start with a general purpose and then refine the general purpose into a specific one. The specific purpose should indicate the response desired from the reader.

Assume, for example, that you are a marketing manager at Seaside Resorts, a chain of hotels along the California, Oregon, and Washington coasts. You have noted that many of the larger hotel chains have instituted "frequent-stay" plans, which, like the frequent-flier programs they are modeled after, reward repeat customers with free lodging, travel, or merchandise. You want to write a message recommending a similar plan for Seaside Resorts. Your general purpose might be this:

General Purpose: To describe the benefits of a frequent-stay plan at Seaside Resorts.

A clearly stated purpose helps you avoid including irrelevant and distracting information.

Such a goal is a good starting point, but it is not specific enough. To begin with, it doesn't identify the intended audience. Are you writing a memo to the vice president of marketing recommending this plan, or are you writing a letter to frequent business travelers recommending that they enroll in this plan? Let's assume, for the moment, that you're writing to the marketing vice president. What is she supposed to *do* as a result of reading your memo? Do you want her to simply understand what you've written? agree with you? commit resources for further research? agree to implement the plan immediately? How will you know if your message achieves its objective? Perhaps you decide that your specific purpose is this:

Specific Purpose: To persuade the marketing VP to approve the development and implementation of a frequent-stay plan for a 12-month test period in Seaside's three Oregon resorts.

Now you have a purpose that's specific enough to guide you as you write the memo and to permit you to judge, in time, whether your message achieved its goal.

In another situation, your general purpose might be to resolve a problem regarding a shipment of damaged merchandise, and your specific purpose might be to persuade the manufacturer to replace the damaged shipment at no cost to you within ten days. Or your general purpose might be to refuse a customer's claim, and your specific purpose might be to convince the customer that your refusal is reasonable and to maintain the customer's goodwill.

Having a clear-cut statement of purpose lets you focus on the content and organization, eliminating any distracting information and incorporating all relevant information.

Audience Analysis

To maximize the effectiveness of your message, you should perform an **audience analysis;** that is, you should identify the interests, needs, and personality of your receiver. Remember our discussion of mental filters in Chapter 1. Each person perceives a message differently because of his or her unique mental filter. Thus, we need to determine the level of detail, the language to be used, and the overall tone by answering the pertinent questions about audience discussed in the following sections (see Figure 6.2).

Who Is the Primary Audience?   For most correspondence, the audience is one person, which simplifies the writing task immensely. It is much easier to personalize a message addressed to one individual than a message addressed to many individuals. Sometimes, however, you will have more than one audience. In this case, you need to identify your **primary audience** (the person whose cooperation is crucial if your message is to achieve its objectives) and then your **secondary audience** (others who will also read and be affected by your message). If you can satisfy no one else, try to satisfy the needs of the primary decision maker. If possible, also satisfy the needs of any secondary audience.

If, for example, you're presenting a proposal that must be approved by the general manager but that will also require the cooperation of your colleagues in other departments, the general manager is the primary audience and your colleagues are the secondary audience. Gear your message—its content, organization, and tone—mainly to the needs of the general manager. Most often (but not always), the primary audience will be the highest-level person to whom you're addressing your communication.

FIGURE 6.2   **Questions for Audience Analysis**

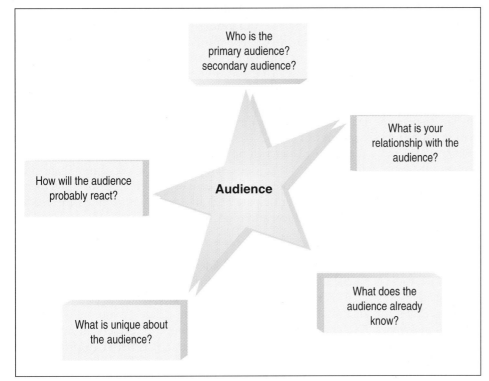

What Is Your Relationship with the Audience?   Does your audience know you? If not, you will first have to establish your credibility by assuming a reasonable tone and giving enough evidence to support your claims. Are you writing to someone inside or outside the organization? If outside, your message will often be a little more formal and will contain more background information and less jargon than if you are writing to someone inside the organization.

What is your status in the organization in relation to your audience? Communications to your superiors are obviously vital to your success in the organization. Such communications are typically a little more formal, less authoritarian in tone, and more information-filled than communications to peers or subordinates. In addition, such messages are typically "front-loaded"—that is, they use a direct organizational style and present the major idea in the first paragraph. Study your superior's own messages to get a sense of his or her preferred style and diction, and adapt your own message accordingly.

When you communicate with subordinates, be polite but not patronizing. Try to instill a sense of collaboration and of corporate ownership of your proposal. When praising or criticizing, be specific; and criticize the action—not the person. Try to praise in public but criticize in private.

How Will the Audience React?   If the reader's initial reaction to both you and your topic is likely to be *positive*, your job is relatively easy. You can use a direct approach—beginning with the most important information (for example, your conclusions or recommendations) and then supplying the needed details. If the reader's initial reaction is likely to be *neutral*, you may want to use the first few lines of the message to get the reader's attention and convince him or her that what you

Your relationship with the reader determines the tone and content of your message.

have to say is important and that your reasoning is sound. Make sure your message is short and easy to read and that any requested action is easy to take.

Suppose, however, that you expect your reader's reaction—either to your topic or to you personally—will be *negative*. Here you have a real sales job to do. If the reader shows a personal dislike of you, your best strategy is to call on external evidence and expert opinion to bolster your position. Show that others, people whom the reader is likely to know and respect, share your opinions. Use courteous, conservative language, and suggest ways the reader can cooperate without appearing to "give in"—perhaps by reminding the reader that new circumstances and new information call for new strategies.

If the expected reader reaction is negative, present lots of evidence and expert testimony.

If you anticipate that your reader will oppose your proposal, your best strategy is to supply extra evidence. Instead of one example, give two or three. Instead of quoting two external sources, quote several. Begin with the areas of agreement, stress reader benefits, and try to anticipate and answer any objections the reader might have. Through logic, evidence, and tone, build your case for the reasonableness of your position.

What Does the Audience Already Know?   Understanding the audience's present grasp of the topic is crucial to making decisions about content and writing style. You must decide how much background information is necessary, whether the use of jargon is called for, and what readability level is appropriate. If you are writing to multiple audiences, gear the amount of detail to the level of understanding of the key decision maker (the primary audience). In general, it is better to provide *too much* rather than too little information.

Determine how much information the reader needs.

What Is Unique About the Audience?   The success or failure of a message often depends on little things—the extra touches that say to the reader, "You're important, and I've taken the time to learn some things about you."

Make the reader feel important by personalizing the content.

What can you learn about the personal interests or demographic characteristics of your audience that you can build into your message? Is the reader a "take-charge"

Rich Brandwein of AT&T spin-off Lucent Technologies uses his company's Intranet, an internal version of the Internet, to provide the specific personalized information his audience needs—no more and no less.

kind of person who would prefer to have important information up front—regardless of whether the news is good or bad? What level of formality is expected? Would the reader be flattered or be put off by the use of his or her first name in the salutation? Have good things or bad things happened recently at work or at home that may affect the reader's receptivity to your message?

Competent communicators analyze their audience and then use this information to structure the content, organization, and tone of their messages.

Example of Audience Analysis   To illustrate the crucial role that audience analysis plays in communication, let's consider three different scenarios for the memo to the marketing vice president requesting a pilot test of a frequent-stay incentive program.

First, assume that Cynthia Haney, vice president of marketing and your immediate superior, will be the only reader of your memo; that is, she has the authority to approve or reject your proposal. Ms. Haney is an old hand in the hotel business, having had 20 years of managerial experience, and she respects your judgment. She has made clear that she likes directness in writing and wants the important information up front—so that she can get the major ideas first and then skim the rest of the communication as necessary. The first paragraph of your memo to her might then use a direct approach, as follows:

> The purpose of this memo is to recommend implementing a frequent-stay plan for a 12-month test period in our three Oregon resorts. This recommendation is based on a review of the policies of our competitors and on an analysis of the costs and benefits of instituting such a program. The pertinent data is presented below.

Some readers like a direct approach, regardless of the purpose of the message.

In the next scenario, assume that Haney assumed her position at Seaside Resorts just six months ago and that she is still "learning the ropes" of the hospitality industry. Up to this point, your relationship with her has been cordial, although she is probably not very familiar with your work. That being the case, the first paragraph of your memo might use an indirect approach, in which you discuss your procedures and present the evidence before making a recommendation.

> The attached *Wall Street Journal* article discusses four large hotel chains that have started frequent-stay plans. The purpose of this memo is to describe such plans and analyze their costs and benefits. Then I will recommend what action Seaside might take in this regard.

In a third scenario, suppose that instead of having confidence in your skills, Haney has given some indication that she *doesn't* yet completely trust your judgment. You might then be wise to add a second paragraph to establish your credibility.

> To gather the needed data, I studied published reports prepared by the Hotel and Restaurant Association. Then, I interviewed the person in charge of frequent-stay programs at three hotels. Finally, Dr. Kenneth Lowe, professor of

Establish credibility by showing the basis for your recommendations.

wordwise

What Word?

- What is a thirteen-letter word in which the first eight letters mean the largest and the complete word means the smallest? *Infinitesimal*
- What is a seven-letter word in which the first two letters mean a man, the first three letters mean a woman, the first four letters mean a great man, and all the letters mean a great woman? *Heroine*
- What word can be placed in any of the ten numbered positions in this sentence to produce ten sentences of different meaning? (1) I (2) helped (3) my (4) dog (5) carry (6) my (7) husband's (8) slippers (9) yesterday (10). *Only*
- What word can be repeated six times in succession in a sentence and still make sense? *That (You must understand that that "that" that that "that" refers to is another "that.")* Got that?

hospitality services at Southern Cal, reviewed and commented on my first draft. Thus, this proposal is based on a large body of data collected over two months.

As can be seen, the type of information you include in your message, the amount, and the organization reflect what you know (or can learn) about your audience.

Content

Do not start writing until you have planned what you want to say.

Once you have determined the purpose of your message and have identified the needs and interests of your audience, the next step is to decide what information to include. For some letters and simple memos, this step presents few problems. However, many communication tasks require numerous decisions about what to include. How much background information is needed? What statistical data best supports the conclusions? Is expert opinion called for? Would examples, anecdotes, or graphics aid comprehension? Will research be necessary, or do you have what you need at hand?

The trick is to include enough information that you don't lose or confuse the reader, yet to avoid including irrelevant material that wastes the reader's time and obscures the important data. Different writers use different methods for identifying what information is needed. Some simply jot down notes on the points they plan to cover. For all but the simplest communications, the one thing you should *not* do is to start drafting immediately, deciding as you write what information to include. Instead, start with at least a rudimentary outline of your message—whether it's in your head, in a well-developed outline, or in the form of notes on a piece of scratch paper.

One useful strategy is **brainstorming**—jotting down ideas, facts, possible leads, and anything else you think might be helpful in constructing your message. Aim for quantity, not quality. Don't evaluate your output until you've run out of ideas. Then begin to refine, delete, combine, and otherwise revise your ideas to form the basis for your message.

Another possible strategy is **mind mapping** (also called *clustering*), a process that avoids the step-by-step limitations of lists. Instead, you write the purpose of your message in the middle of a page and circle it. Then, as you think of possible points to add, write them down and link them by a line either to the main purpose or to another point. As you think of other details, add them where you think they might fit. This visual outline offers flexibility and encourages free thinking. Figure 6.3 shows an example of mind mapping for our frequent-stay memo.

Organization

The final step in the planning process is to establish the **organization** of the message; that is, to determine in what order to discuss each topic. After you have brainstormed or mapped out your ideas around a main idea, you need to organize them into an outline that you can use to draft your message into its most effective form.

Classification (grouping related ideas) is the first step in organizing your message. Once you've grouped related ideas, you then need to differentiate between the major and minor points so that you can line up minor ideas and evidence to support the major ideas.

FIGURE 6.3 A Sample Mind Map

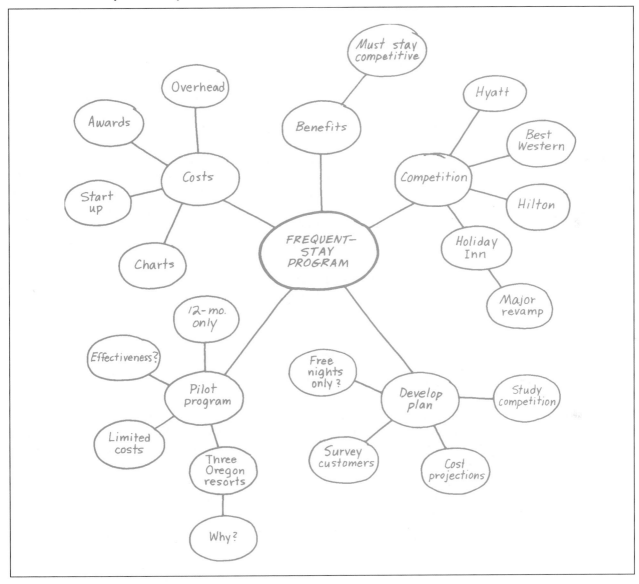

The most effective sequence for the major ideas often depends on the reaction you expect from your audience. If you expect a positive response, you may want to use a direct approach, in which the conclusion or major idea is presented first, followed by the reasons. If you expect a negative response, you may decide to use an indirect approach, in which the reasons are presented first and the conclusion after.

Because of the importance of the sequence in which topics are discussed, the recommended organization of each specific type of communication is discussed in detail in the chapters that follow. (See also Chapter 4's extensive coverage of paragraph unity, coherence, and length—all of which are important elements of organization.)

To maintain good human relations, base your organization on the expected reader reaction.

Drafting

Having now finished planning, you are ready to begin **drafting**—that is, composing a preliminary version of a message. The success of this second stage of the process depends on the attention you gave to the first stage. The warning given earlier bears repeating: don't begin writing too soon. Some people believe they have weak writing skills; when faced with a writing task, their first impulse is therefore to jump in and get it over with as quickly as possible. Avoid the rush. Follow each of the five steps of the writing process to ease the journey and improve the product.

Do not combine drafting and revising. They involve two separate skills and two separate mindsets.

Probably the most important thing to remember about drafting is to just let go—let your ideas flow as quickly as possible onto paper or computer screen, without worrying about style, correctness, or format. Separate the drafting stage from the revising stage. Although some people revise as they create, most find it easier to first get their ideas down on paper in rough-draft form, then revise. It's much easier to polish a page full of writing than a page full of *nothing*. As one writing authority has noted,

> Writing is art. Rewriting is craft. Mix the two at your peril. If you let your inner editor (who, according to popular theory, lives in the left side of your brain) into the process too early, it's liable to overpower your artist, blocking your creative flow.[1]

So avoid moving from author to editor too quickly. Your first draft is just that—a *draft*. Don't expect perfection, and don't strive for it. Concentrate, instead, on recording in narrative form all the points you identified in the planning stage. When you have finished and then begin to revise, you will likely discover that a surprising amount of your first draft is usable and will be included in your final draft.

Employ the power of positive thinking: You can write an effective message!

If a report is due in five weeks, some managers (and students) spend four weeks worrying about the task and one week (or even one long weekend) actually writing the report. Similarly, when given 45 minutes to write a letter or memo, some people spend 35 minutes anxiously staring at a blank page or blank screen and 10 minutes actually writing. These people are experiencing **writer's block**—the inability to focus on the writing process and to draft a message. The causes of writer's block are typically one or more of the following:

- *Procrastination:* Putting off what we dislike doing.

- *Impatience:* Growing tired of the naturally slow pace of the writing process.

- *Perfectionism:* Believing that our draft must be perfect the first time.

These factors naturally interfere with creativity and concentration. In addition, they undermine the writer's self-image and make him or her even more reluctant to tackle the next writing task. The treatment for writer's block lies in the strategies discussed in the following paragraphs.

1. **Choose the right environment.** The ability to concentrate on the task at hand is one of the most important components of effective writing. The best environment may *not* be the same desk where you normally do your other work. Even if you can turn off the phones and shut the door to visitors, silent distractions can bother you—a notation on your calendar reminding you of an important upcoming event, notes about a current project, even a photograph of a loved one. Many people write best in a library-type environment, with a

Although it may seem an unusual environment for inspiration, greeting card author Linda Elrod finds her personal office space conducive to writing.

low noise level, relative anonymity, and the space to spread out notes and other resources on a large table. Others find a computer room conducive to thinking and writing, with its low level of constant background noise and the presence of other people similarly engaged.

2. **Schedule a reasonable block of time.** If the writing task is short, you can block out enough time to plan, draft, and revise the entire message at one sitting. If the task is long or complex, however, schedule blocks of no more than two hours or so. After all, writing is hard work. When your time is up or your work completed, give yourself a reward—take a break or get a snack.

3. **State your purpose in writing.** Having identified your specific purpose during the planning phase, write it at the top of your blank page or tack it on the bulletin board in front of you. Keep it visible so that it will be uppermost in your consciousness as you compose.

4. **Engage in free writing.** Review your purpose and your audience; then, as a means of releasing your pent-up ideas and getting past the block, begin **free writing;** that is, write continuously for five to ten minutes, literally without stopping. Although free writing is typically considered a predrafting technique, it can also be quite useful for helping writers "unblock" their ideas.

    While free writing, don't look back and don't stop writing. If you cannot think of anything to say, simply keep repeating the last word or keep writing some sentence such as, "I'll think of something soon." Resist the temptation to evaluate what you've written. (If you're composing at a computer, you may want to darken your screen so that you won't be tempted to review what you've written thus far; this is called *invisible writing.*) At the end of five or ten minutes, take a breather, stretch and relax, read what you've written, and then start again, if necessary.

5. **Avoid the perfectionism syndrome.** Remember that the product you're producing now is a *draft*—not a final document. Don't worry about style, coherence, spelling or punctuation errors, and the like. The artist in you must create something before the editor can refine it.

6. **Think out loud.** Some people are more skilled at *speaking* their thoughts than at writing them. Picture yourself telling a colleague about what you're writing, and explain aloud the ideas you're trying to get across. Hearing your ideas will help sharpen and focus them.

You need not write the parts of a message in the order in which they will finally appear. Begin with the easiest parts.

7. **Write the easiest parts first.** The opening paragraph of a letter or memo is often the most difficult one to compose. If that is the case, skip it and begin in the middle. In a report, the procedures section may be easier to write than the recommendations. Getting *something* down on paper will give you a sense of accomplishment, and your writing may generate ideas for other sections.

Try each of these strategies for avoiding writer's block at least once; then build into your writing routine those strategies that work best for you. Just as different athletes and artists use different strategies for accomplishing their goals, so do different writers. There is no one best way, so choose what is effective for you.

Revising

Revising is the process of modifying a document to increase its effectiveness. Having the raw material—your first draft—in front of you, you can now refine it into the most effective document possible, considering its importance and the time constraints under which you are working. If possible, put your draft away for a period of time—the longer the better. Leaving time between creation and revision helps you distance yourself from your writing. If you revise immediately, the memory of what you "meant to say" rather than what you actually wrote may be so strong that it keeps you from spotting weaknesses in logic or diction.

If you're a typical writer, you will have made numerous minor revisions even as you were composing; however, as noted earlier, you should save the major revisions until later. For important writing projects, you will probably want to solicit comments about your draft from colleagues as part of the revision process.

Although we have discussed revising as the third step of the writing process, in fact it is several steps. Most writers revise first for content, then for style, and finally for correctness. All types of revision are most efficiently done from a typed copy of the draft rather than from a handwritten copy.

Revising for Content

Revise for content, style, and correctness.

After an appropriate time interval, first reread your purpose statement and then the entire draft to get an overview of your message. Ask yourself such questions as these:

■ Is the content appropriate for the purpose I've identified?

■ Will the purpose of the message be clear to the reader?

■ Have I been sensitive to the needs of the reader?

■ Is all the information necessary?

■ Is any needed information missing?

■ Is the order of presentation of the points effective?

Although it is natural to have a certain pride of authorship in your draft document, don't be afraid to make whatever changes you think will strengthen your

The process described in this chapter applies not just to writing but to preparing any form of communication. Project Director Lonnie Bunch (center)—shown here working with curators on an exhibit of American history that will travel to Japan—must consider issues of content, style, and audience to make the exhibit successful.

document—even if it means striking out whole sections and starting again from scratch. The aim is to produce a revised document in which you can have even more pride.

Revising for Style

Next, read each paragraph again (aloud, if possible), using the 15 criteria contained in Checklist 4 on page 146 as the basis for your evaluation. Reading aloud gives you a feel for the rhythm and flow of your writing. Long sentences that made sense as you wrote them may leave you out of breath when you read them aloud.

If time permits and the importance of the document merits it, try reading your message aloud to friends or colleagues, or have them read your revised draft. Ask them what is clear or unclear. Can they identify the purpose of your message? What kind of image do they get of the writer just from reading the message? Adhering to Checklist 4 (see p. 146) and securing feedback from colleagues will help you identify areas of your message that need revision.

Make sure the readability of your message is appropriate for the intended audience. Determining the readability of your draft is often a useful first step in the revision process. More important, however, is the analysis that follows the calculation. Considering what you know about your audience's interest level, educational level, and knowledge of the topic, revise the readability of your draft as appropriate.

Revising for Correctness

The final phase of revising is **editing,** the process of ensuring that writing conforms to standard English. Editing involves checking for correctness; that is, identifying problems with grammar, spelling, punctuation, and word usage. Editing should follow revision because there is no need to correct minor errors in passages that may later be revised or deleted. Writers who fail to check for grammar, mechanical, and usage errors risk losing credibility with their reader. Such errors may distract the reader, delay comprehension, cause misunderstandings, and reflect negatively on the writer's abilities.

You can write faster and revise much faster on a computer than in longhand.

All three types of revision—for content, style, and correctness—can be accomplished most efficiently on a computer (see Spotlight 10—On Technology).

Formatting

Letters are external documents that are sent to people outside the organization. Memos are internal documents that are sent to people inside the same organization as the writer. E-mail messages and reports may be either internal or external. No one format for any type of business document is universally accepted as standard; a fair amount of variation is common in industry. Detailed guidelines for the most common formatting standards are presented in the Reference Manual at the back of this text.

To some extent, technology is changing formatting standards. For example, although formatting is traditionally the next-to-last step in the writing process, you may in fact make some formatting decisions at the planning or drafting stages. For example, your word processing program has probably been set with default side margins of 1 inch, which are appropriate for most documents.

In addition, e-mail messages all look like memorandums—whether they are sent to someone inside or outside the organization. They typically contain *To:*, *From:*, *Date:*, and *Subject:* lines just as memos do, and they do not contain an inside address or complimentary closing, as is typical in letters. The important point is to use the format that is appropriate for each specific message.

Take personal responsibility for all aspects of a message that goes out under your name.

Regardless of who actually types your documents, *you* are the one who signs and submits them, so *you* must accept responsibility for not only the content but also the mechanics, format, and appearance of your documents. In addition, the increasing use of word processing means that executives now keyboard many of their own documents—without the help of an assistant.

Another advantage of standard formatting is simply that it is more efficient. Formatting the documents the same way each time means that you do not need to make individual layout decisions for every document. Thus, a standard format not only saves time but also gives a consistent appearance to the organization's documents. Finally, readers *expect* to find certain information in certain positions in a document. If the information is not there, the reader is unnecessarily distracted. For all these reasons, you should become familiar with the standard conventions for formatting documents.

Proofreading

Proofreading is the final quality-control check for your document. Remember that a reader may not know whether an incorrect word resulted from a simple typo or from the writer's ignorance of correct usage. And even one such error can have adverse effects. Being *almost perfect* is not good enough; for example, if your telephone directory were only 99% perfect, each page would contain about four wrong numbers! And imagine the embarrassment of the tax preparer who submitted supporting statements for a client's tax return that contained this direction: "Please reference *Lie 12* on Schedule C." (Would a computer's spelling checker have caught this error?) Or how about the newspaper ad that Continental Airlines ran in the

Revising on the Computer

Given the pervasive impact of technology and the amount of time contemporary managers spend using computers, every student today should develop touch-keyboarding skills of at least 30 words per minute. Today, keyboarding must be considered a crucial *communication* skill.

SPOTLIGHT 10

ON

TECHNOLOGY

Using the computer makes nearly every step of the writing process easier and more effective. Even a mediocre typist (using a hunt-and-peck style) can probably write faster at the keyboard than in longhand. Also, the fact that you can move paragraphs around lets you write the easiest parts first. Or, if you can't think of what to write in one section, you can simply space down a few lines and begin the next topic. But the point at which computers play their most effective role is during revision. For example, in addition to inserting, deleting, and changing wording, with word processing you can easily

- Move paragraphs around to achieve the most logical organization.
- Print drafts quickly (most writers find revising on paper easier than revising on a computer screen).
- Use the search-and-replace function to make a change throughout the document; for example, changing *SEC* to *Securities and Exchange Commission* throughout a ten-page document can be accomplished in one easy step.
- Use the thesaurus function to produce a list of synonyms for any highlighted word to help yourself select the word with the precise meaning that is appropriate for the particular context.
- Use the spelling function to help yourself proofread for typographical and spelling errors. (You should remember, though, that a spelling checker can only *help* you check for errors; words that are misused or errors that form a new word are not identified. Thus, most spelling checkers would not identify any problem with even a sentence as silly as "I mint too meat hem at $5 o'clock four a drinks.")

In addition, grammar and style checkers, which are now standard features of some word processing programs, identify possible examples of awkward writing, clichés, jargon, passive voice, mismatched punctuation marks, and the like. They then propose alternatives that you can accept, reject, or mark for subsequent fixing. Many of these programs are somewhat nitpicking, and many of the words and phrases they flag are, in fact, used correctly. Other genuine errors may be ignored. For example, in the grammar-checked passage shown here, Microsoft Word correctly identified the subject-verb agreement problem in the first sentence (screen a) and the nonstandard word in the second sentence (screen b). The program failed, however, to identify the misuse of the word *whom* and the missing comma after *appointment* in the second sentence. Nevertheless, for the novice writer especially, grammar checkers provide an additional aid in improving the style of business documents.

a.

Spelling and Grammar: English (United States) [?][X]

Subject-Verb Agreement:
Sherrie Smith, as well as James M. Smith, are being considered for an appointment to the FTC.

Ignore
Ignore All
Next Sentence

Suggestions:
is

Change

[?] ☑ Check grammar   Options...   Undo   Close

Sherrie Smith, as well as James M. Smith, **are** being considered for an appointment to the FTC. **Irregardless** of whom gets the appointment we'll be happy.

b.

Spelling and Grammar: English (United States) [?][X]

Non-standard Word:
Irregardless of whom gets the appointment we'll be happy.

Ignore
Ignore All
Next Sentence

Suggestions:
Regardless

Change

[?] ☑ Check grammar   Options...   Undo   Cancel

Boston Herald, in which the company advertised one-way fares from Boston to Los Angeles for $48? The actual one-way fare was *$148.* That typographical error cost Continental $4 million, because it sold 20,000 round-trip tickets at a loss of $200 each.[2]

Don't depend on having an assistant catch and correct every mistake; become a "super blooper snooper" yourself. It's your reputation that is at stake. Take responsibility for ensuring the accuracy of your communications, just as you take responsibility for your other managerial tasks. Proofread for content, typographical, and format errors.

Typographical errors may send a negative nonverbal message about the writer.

■ *Content Errors:* First, read through your document quickly, checking for content errors. Was any material omitted unintentionally? Unfortunately, writers who use word processing to move, delete, and insert material, sometimes omit passages unintentionally or duplicate the same passage in two different places in the document. In short, check to be sure that your document *makes sense.*

■ *Typographical Errors:* Next, read through your document slowly, checking for typographical errors. Watch especially for errors that form a new word; for example, "I took the figures *form* last month's reports." Such errors are difficult to spot. Also be on the lookout for repeated or omitted words. Double-check all proper names and all figures, using the original source if possible. (Don't overlook the possibility that you may have copied the words or figures incorrectly in your notes or first draft.) Professional proofreaders find that writers often overlook errors in the titles and headings of reports, in the opening and closing parts of letters and memos, and in the last paragraph of all types of documents.

■ *Format Errors:* Visually inspect the document for appropriate format. Are all the parts included and in the correct position? What will be the receiver's first impression before reading the document? Does the document look attractive on the page? Do not consider the proofreading stage complete until you are able to read through the entire document without making any changes. There is always the possibility that in correcting one error you inadvertently introduced another.

Finally, after planning, drafting, revising, formatting, and proofreading your document, transmit it—confident and satisfied, that you've taken all reasonable steps to ensure that it achieves its objectives. The steps in the writing process are summarized in Checklist 5.

Introducing the 3Ps Microwriting Activities

Beginning with this chapter, every chapter concludes with a 3Ps microwriting activity designed to illustrate important communication concepts covered in the chapter (see the following section). These short case studies of typical communication assignments include the *problem,* the *process,* and the *product* (the 3Ps). The problem defines the situation and discusses the need for a particular communication task. The process is a series of questions that provides step-by-step guidance for accomplishing the specific communication task. Finally, the product is the result—the finished document.

✔ CHECKLIST 5   **The Writing Process**

Planning

☑ Determine the purpose of the message.
 a. Make it as specific as possible.
 b. Indicate the type of response desired from the reader.

☑ Analyze the audience.
 a. Identify the audience and your relationship with this person.
 b. Determine how the audience will probably react.
 c. Determine how much the audience already knows about the topic.
 d. Determine what is unique about the audience—demographic information, interests, desired level of formality, and the like.

☑ Determine what information to include in the message, given its purpose and your analysis of the audience.

☑ Organize the information.
 a. Prefer a direct approach for routine and good-news messages and for most messages to superiors: present the major idea first, followed by supporting details.
 b. Prefer an indirect approach for persuasive and bad-news messages written to someone other than your superior: present the reasons first, followed by the major idea.

Drafting

☑ Choose a productive work environment and schedule a reasonable block of time to devote to the drafting phase.

☑ Let your ideas flow as quickly as possible, without worrying about style, correctness, or format. If helpful, write the easiest parts first.

☑ Do not expect a perfect first draft; avoid the urge to revise at this stage.

☑ If possible, leave a time gap between writing and revising the draft.

Revising

☑ Revise for content: determine whether all information is necessary, whether any needed information has been omitted, and whether the content has been presented in an appropriate sequence.

☑ Revise for style: follow the guidelines in Checklist 4 (see p. 146).

☑ Revise for correctness: use correct grammar, mechanics, punctuation, and word choice (see the Reference Manual).

Formatting

☑ Format the document according to commonly used standards (see the Reference Manual).

Proofreading

☑ Proofread for content errors, typographical errors, and format errors.

The 3Ps microwriting activities provide a practical demonstration of a particular type of communication, shown close up so that you can see the *process of writing,* not just the results. This process helps you focus on one aspect of writing at a time. Use the 3Ps microwriting steps regularly in your own writing so that your written communications will be easier to produce and more effective in their results.

Pay particular attention to the questions in the Process section, and ask yourself similar questions as you compose your own messages. Finally, read through the finished document, and note any changes made from the draft sentences composed in the Process section.

The 3Ps microwriting activities guide you step-by-step through a typical writing assignment by posing and answering relevant questions about each aspect of the message.

The 3Ps

A Simple Memo

PROBLEM

Today is December 3, 19—, and you are Alice R. Stengren, president of the Entrepreneurial Association of Reed Northern College. *EARN* is the newest of the six student organizations in the school of business and has 38 members. It was formed two years ago when the department of management instituted a major in entrepreneurship. The purposes of EARN are (1) to provide opportunities for members to learn more about entrepreneurship, primarily through monthly meetings that feature guest speakers; (2) to provide social interactions for future entrepreneurs; and (3) to promote entrepreneurship as a major or minor course of study at the college.

To further the third purpose, the association recently voted to institute an annual $1,000 EARN scholarship. The scholarship will be awarded on the basis of merit to a junior or senior business student majoring in entrepreneurship at Reed Northern. Funds for the scholarship will be raised by selling coffee and doughnuts each day from 7:30 to 10:30 A.M. in the main lobby of the School of Business building. Write a memo to Dean Richard Wilhite, asking permission to start this fundraising project in January.

PROCESS

1. What is the purpose of your memo?

   To convince the dean to let EARN sell coffee and doughnuts in the main lobby from 7:30 to 10:30 A.M. daily, beginning in January.

2. Describe your primary audience (see Figure 6.2, p. 157).

   Dean Richard Wilhite:

   ■ Former president of Wilhite Energy Systems (started the company— an entrepreneur himself)

   ■ 46 years old; has been business dean at RNC for six years (very familiar with the school and college)

   ■ Nationally known labor expert

   ■ Holds tenure in the department of management (which offers an entrepreneurship major)

   ■ Has spoken about the need to increase scholarships

   ■ Devotes a great deal of time to lobbying the legislature and raising funds (recognizes the need for fund-raising)

   ■ Doesn't know me personally but is familiar with EARN

3. Is there a secondary audience for your memo? If so, describe.

   No secondary audience.

4. Considering your purpose, what information should you include in the memo? (Either brainstorm and jot down the topics you might cover or construct a mind map.)

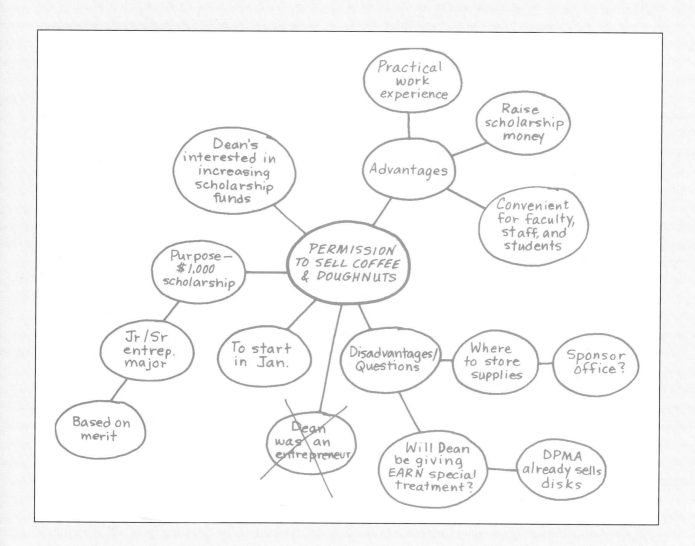

5. Jot down the major topics in the order in which you'll discuss them.

   a. Dean's interest in increasing scholarships
   b. Introduce scholarship and our fund-raising proposal
   c. Practical work experience that members will get
   d. Possible drawbacks (where to store supplies; special treatment for EARN)
   e. Other needed details
   f. Close—convenient for faculty, staff, students

6. Using the rough outline developed in Step 5, write your first draft. Concentrate on getting the needed information down. Do not worry about grammar, spelling, punctuation, transitions, unity, and the like at this stage.

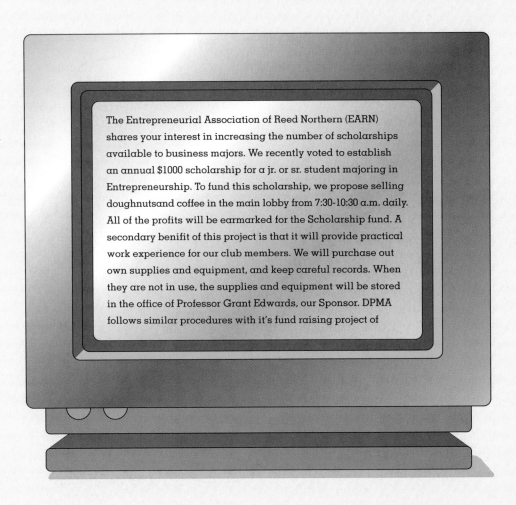

> The Entrepreneurial Association of Reed Northern (EARN) shares your interest in increasing the number of scholarships available to business majors. We recently voted to establish an annual $1000 scholarship for a jr. or sr. student majoring in Entrepreneurship. To fund this scholarship, we propose selling doughnutsand coffee in the main lobby from 7:30-10:30 a.m. daily. All of the profits will be earmarked for the Scholarship fund. A secondary benifit of this project is that it will provide practical work experience for our club members. We will purchase out own supplies and equipment, and keep careful records. When they are not in use, the supplies and equipment will be stored in the office of Professor Grant Edwards, our Sponsor. DPMA follows similar procedures with it's fund raising project of

7. Print out your draft and revise it for content, style, and correctness. (As needed, refer to the Reference Manual at the back of the book for guidance on grammar, mechanics, punctuation, and usage and to Checklist 4 on page 146 for style pointers.)

8. How will you transmit this message; that is, what format will you use?

I could, of course, send the dean an e-mail message. Given the importance of this request, however, I'll format it as a memo on our association's letterhead. That way the request will look more professional, and the dean will have a printed copy for review.

9. Format your revised draft, using a standard memo style. Then proofread.

The Entrepreneurial Association of Reed Northern (EARN) shares your interest in increasing the number of scholarships available to business majors. We recently voted to establish an annual $1,000 scholarship for a jr. or sr. student majoring in Entrepreneurship. To fund this scholarship, we propose selling doughnuts and coffee in the main lobby from 7:30/10:30 a.m. daily. All of the profits will be earmarked for the scholarship fund. A secondary benefit of this project is that it will provide practical work experience for our club members. We will purchase our own supplies and equipment and keep careful records. When they are not in use, the supplies and equipment will be stored in the office of Professor Grant Edwards, our sponsor. DPMA follows similar procedures with it's fund-raising project of selling computer disks in the main lobby.

We need your approval of this scholarship project in time for us to begin in January. This project also provides a convenient service for faculty, staff, and students.

In addition to raising new scholarship money and providing work experience for our members, we will also be providing

PRODUCT

Entrepreneurial Association of Reed Northern

102 Waldt Hall • PH: 555-1003

MEMO TO: Dean Richard Wilhite

FROM: Alice R. Stengren, President *ARS*
Entrepreneurial Association of Reed Northern

DATE: December 3, 19--

SUBJECT: Establishment of EARN Scholarship

The Entrepreneurial Association of Reed Northern (EARN) shares your interest in increasing the number of scholarships available to business majors. Toward that end, we recently voted to establish an annual $1,000 scholarship for a junior or senior student majoring in entrepreneurship. To fund this scholarship, we propose selling doughnuts and coffee in the main lobby from 7:30 to 10:30 a.m. daily. All of the profits will be earmarked for the scholarship fund.

A secondary benefit of this project is that it will provide practical work experience for our club members. We will purchase our own supplies and equipment and keep careful records. When not in use, the supplies and equipment will be stored in the office of Professor Grant Edwards, our sponsor. The Data Processing Management Association follows similar procedures with its fundraising project of selling computer disks in the main lobby.

We look forward to receiving your approval of this fund-raising project in time for us to begin in January. In addition to raising new scholarship money and providing work experience for our members, we will also be providing a convenient service for faculty, staff, and students.

EARN YOUR WAY THROUGH COLLEGE!

The writing process is a series of steps designed to produce written messages in an effective and efficient manner. These steps—planning, drafting, revising, formatting, and proofreading—are summarized in Checklist 5 (p. 169).

The amount of time devoted to each step depends on the complexity, length, and importance of the document. Not all steps may be needed for each document, the steps don't necessarily have to come in order, and one step doesn't necessarily have to be completed before the next one begins. However, you would be well advised to follow each step consciously and carefully in the beginning. Then, after gaining experience and confidence, you can adapt the process to form a writing routine that is most effective and efficient for you personally.

audience analysis

brainstorming

drafting

editing

free writing

mind mapping

organization

primary audience

revising

secondary audience

writer's block

1. **Communication at Coopers & Lybrand Consulting Revisited**   Whether Michael Hanley is using e-mail messages or written reports to communicate with clients, he never loses sight of two basic elements: who his readers are and what his goals are.
   a. What is Hanley's general purpose in writing a letter to a client before starting a new project?
   b. Identify the primary and secondary audiences for one of the multipage final reports that Hanley and his colleagues prepare at the end of a project.
   c. Describe Hanley's relationship with the primary audience for a final report prepared at the end of a project.
2. Give an example of a general purpose and a specific purpose for a particular communication task.
3. How does your relationship with the audience affect the content and tone of the message?
4. What writing strategies should you employ if you expect your audience (a subordinate) to react negatively?
5. Distinguish between a direct and an indirect organization plan.
6. What steps should precede the drafting stage? Why?
7. List eight possible strategies for overcoming writer's block.
8. Why should a time gap be left between writing a first draft and revising the draft?
9. Why is it generally not a good idea to combine the drafting and the revising stages?
10. Why should executives know how to format common business documents in a standard style?
11. Why should touch-keyboarding be considered a strategic communication skill today?
12. What three types of errors should you check for when proofreading a document?

Help Wanted

Directions: This memo is from Tim White, an assistant vice president at Irving Bank, to Jack Presley, the vice president (and White's superior). Revise the memo to make it more effective, taking into consideration the editor's marginal comments.

As you know, I'm required to give numerous speeches each year for the Irving Bank. May I have financial support and released time to attend the national convention of Toastmasters International, which meets February 3–6 in Honolulu, Hawaii? During the past six months I made 18 presentations to school groups, civic clubs, and professional organizations and expect to make even more during the next six months. Attending this convention will help me to sharpen my speaking skills. Also, since I chair the continuing education committee of Toastmasters International, I have scheduled a meeting of our committee for this convention. Since I'm not ordinarily very busy at this time of the year, my work here at Irving will not suffer during my four_day absence. Also, when I assume my new position as assistant loan officer next year, I will be required to make numerous presentations to our board of directors.

org—dir

para

rel

punc

end

list   *Consider grouping all of your reasons together into a bulleted list.*

Note: Help Wanted exercises provide you with *guided* editing practice. You must revise the document on the basis of the marginal comments, which are similar to the notes an editor (or your instructor) might make. If necessary, refer to the grading symbols on the inside back cover of this text.

EXERCISES

1. **The 3Ps Microwriting Model: Communication Applications at Coopers & Lybrand Consulting**   Michael Hanley follows all five steps in the writing process when he prepares letters and reports for clients of Coopers & Lybrand Consulting (CLC). To ensure that written messages to clients reflect the company's professional standards, he has developed specific guidelines for e-mail and paper-based documents. Before he or his colleagues send any documents to clients, they perform one last check for content, punctuation, capitalization, grammar, spelling, and format errors.

Problem

As CLC's training coordinator, you teach new employees about the company's guidelines for written communication. Because you will be training a new group of employees on February 5 (today is January 20), you need to order 50 additional copies of the guidelines from the central warehouse. Looking ahead, you also want the warehouse to be prepared to provide 250 copies of the guidelines for participants in the management training program, which starts on March 18. Prepare an e-mail memo to Betsy Dumont, Warehouse Manager, to explain your needs.

Process

a. What is the purpose of this memo?
b. Describe your audience.
c. What topics should you cover in your memo?
d. In what order should you discuss these topics?
e. What phrase will you write on the subject line of your memo?

Product

Using your knowledge of the writing process, prepare a one-page e-mail memo, inventing any reasonable data needed to complete this assignment.

2. **The 3Ps Microwriting Model: A Simple Memo**

Problem

According to a story you read in the student newspaper this morning (May 25), the president of your university has proposed to the board of trustees that beginning next year, every employee pay the same price for his or her contribution to the university's health-insurance plan—regardless of whether the employee is single, married without children, or married with children.

You are single and do not feel it is fair that single employees will be required to pay the same premium for health insurance as married employees pay for family coverage. As president of the Campus Singles Club, an organization comprised of single staff and faculty members at the university, write to the president objecting to this proposal.

Process

a. What is the purpose of your memo?
b. Describe your primary audience.
c. Is there a secondary audience for your memo? If so, describe.
d. Brainstorm for a few moments, jotting down all the points you might cover in your memo.
e. Review the points you've jotted down and then list all the points you will cover—in the order in which you will cover them.
f. Using this rough outline, compose a first draft. Don't worry for now about style, grammar, and mechanics.
g. Print out your draft and revise it for content, style, and accuracy.

Product

Format your revised draft, using plain paper and a standard memo format. Then proofread and submit to your instructor both your memo and your responses to the preceding questions. If requested to do so, submit both documents as an e-mail message to your instructor.

3. **Communication Purpose**   Compose a specific goal for each of the following communication tasks:

a. A memo to a professor asking him to change a grade.

b. A letter to MasterCard about an incorrect charge.

c. A letter to the president of a local bank thanking her for speaking at your student organization meeting.

d. A memo of reprimand to a subordinate for leaving the warehouse unlocked overnight.

4. **Communication Purpose and Reader Response**   For each of the following communication tasks, indicate the specific purpose and the desired response.

a. A letter to a state senator about a proposed state surcharge on college tuition.

b. A memo to your payroll department head about an incorrect pay check.

c. A letter to the college newspaper discussing the quality of the cafeteria food in recent months.

d. A memo to your assistant asking about the status of an overdue report.

5. **Audience Analysis**   Assume you must write a letter to your current business communication professor, asking him or her to let you take your final examination one week early so that you can attend your cousin's wedding.

a. Perform an audience analysis of your professor. List everything you know about this professor that might help you compose a more effective letter.

b. Write two good opening sentences for this letter, the first one assuming that you are an A student who has missed class only once this term and the second assuming you are a C student who has missed class six times this term.

6. **Audience Analysis Revisited**   Now assume the role of the professor (see Exercise 5) who must reply to the request of the student with the C grade who has missed class six times. You'll tell the student that you are not willing to schedule an early exam.

a. Perform an audience analysis of yourself (as the student). What do you know about yourself that would help the professor write an effective letter?

b. Should the professor use a direct or an indirect organization? Why?

c. Write the first sentence of the professor's letter.

7. **Free Writing**   As office manager for a small insurance firm, you want to buy a scanner to use with the three computers in your office. The scanner would let you input graphics (charts and pictures) into your computer documents and enter data without having to rekeyboard. A scanner operates like a photocopier: you feed a copy of a picture or a page of text into the machine, and the picture or text then appears on your computer screen, where it can be used by your word processing or other software programs.

You must write a memo, the goal of which is to convince the general manager to let you buy a scanner and related software for $1,785. Think for a few moments about ways you could use this equipment. Then free write for 10 to 15 minutes without stopping and without worrying about the quality of what you're writing. (You may first want to reread the discussion of free writing on p. 163 of this chapter.)

Now examine what you have written. If you were actually going to write the memo, how much of your output could you use after revision?

8. **Analysis of Primary and Secondary Audiences**   Assume you are a store credit manager who has decided not to approve the credit application of a person who applied at the suggestion of a neighbor working at the store. You'll have to write a letter explaining your decision, which was based on a credit report showing the applicant's tendency to pay bills two or three months late.

a. Who is the primary audience? List what you know about the primary audience. What does this audience know about credit and about your store? How will the audience probably react to the news in your letter? Should you use a formal or informal tone?

b. Who is the secondary audience? List what you know about the secondary audience, including the credit manager's relationship with the secondary audience, what that audience knows about credit, and how that audience is likely to react to the message.

c. On the basis of your audience analysis, should you use a direct or an indirect organization? Why?

d. Given the purpose of this letter, what information should you include?

9. **Mind Mapping (Clustering)**　Assume you must write a two-page, double-spaced abstract of the important points of this chapter. *Without reviewing the chapter*, prepare a mind map of the points you might want to cover.

10. **Organizing**　Prepare a rough outline for the abstract in Exercise 9, using the mind map as your guide. List the major and minor points you will cover and the order in which you will cover them. (You do not have to follow your mind map precisely; it's only for guidance.)

11. **Brainstorming and Organizing**　Assume that you are going to write a letter to your state senator about a proposed state surcharge on college tuition fees. Determine a specific purpose, and then brainstorm at least six facts, ideas, and questions you might want to raise in your letter. Next, decide which are major points and which are minor points. Once you've selected either a direct or an indirect approach, arrange the items on your list in logical order.

12. **Drafting**　Building on the process of brainstorming and organizing in Exercise 11, draft the letter to your legislator.

a. Write the specific purpose at the top of your blank page.

b. Write the easiest part of the letter first. Which part did you start with? Why?

c. Continue to draft the remaining sections of the letter. In what order did you complete your letter? Why?

d. Did you use every fact, question, or idea on your list? Explain your choices.

13. **Work-Team Communication**　You will work in groups of four for this assignment. Assume that a large shopping center is next to your campus and many day students park there for free while attending classes. The shopping center management is considering closing this lot to student use, citing the need for additional space for customer parking. The four members of your group represent four student organizations (a sorority, a fraternity, a business student organization, and a campus service organization), which have decided to write a joint letter to the manager of the shopping center, trying to convince him to maintain the status quo.

Following the five-step process outlined in this chapter, compose a one-page letter to the manager. Brainstorm to generate ideas for the content of the letter; have each member of the group call out possible points to include while one person writes down all the ideas. Don't evaluate any of the ideas until you have worked for 10 to 15 minutes. Then discuss each point listed and decide which ones to include and in what order.

Format your letter in block style. Address it to Mr. Martin Uthe, Executive Manager, Fairview Shopping Center, P.O. Box 1083, DeKalb, IL 60115. Type an envelope, sign and fold the letter, and insert it into the envelope before submitting it to your instructor.

14. **Revising**   Bring in a one-page composition you have written in the past—an essay exam response, business letter, or the like. Make sure your name is *not* on the paper. Exchange papers among several colleagues (so that you are not revising the paper of the person who is revising yours) and complete the following revision tasks:

    a. Read the paper once, revising for content. Make sure that all needed information is included, no unneeded information is included, and the information is presented in a logical sequence.

    b. Read the paper a second time, revising for style. Make sure that the words, sentences, paragraphs, and overall tone are appropriate.

    c. Read the paper a third time, revising for correctness. Make sure that grammar, mechanics, punctuation, and word choice are error-free.

    Return the paper to the writer. Then, using the revisions of your paper as a guide only (after all, *you* are the author), prepare a final version of the page. Submit both the marked-up version and the final version of your paper to your instructor.

15. **Proofreading**   Assume that you are Michael Land and you wrote and typed the following letter. Proofread the letter, using the line numbers to indicate the position of each error. Proofread for content, typographical errors, and format. For each error, indicate by a *yes* or *no* whether the error would have been identified by using a computer's spelling checker. Assume that the letter is formatted exactly as shown, but on letterhead stationery. (*Hint:* Can you find 30 content, typographical, or format errors?)

    1   April 31, 1999

    2   Mr. Thomas Johnson, Manger
    3   JoAnn @ Friends, Inc.
    4   1323 Charleston Avenue
    5   Minneapolis, MI 55402

    6   Dear Mr. Thomas:

    7   As a writing consultant, I have often aksed aud-
    8   iences to locate all teh errors in this letter.
    9   I am allways surprized if the find all the errors.
    10   The result being that we all need more practical
    11   advise in how to proof read.

    12   To avoid these types of error, you must ensure that
    13   that you review your documents carefully. I have
    14   preparred the enclosed exercises for each of you
    15   to in your efforts at JoAnne & Freinds, Inc.

    16   Would you be willing to try this out on you own
    17   workers and let me know the results.

    18   Sincerly Yours

    19   Mr. Michael Land,
    20   Writing Consultant

Two Heads Are Better Than One

Last year the office information systems (OIS) department installed a voice mail system. One of the features of this system is that users can now call over the telephone and dictate their correspondence and reports. All executives below the rank of vice president use the system. Three full-time transcriptionists in the OIS Department then transcribe the dictation using word processing software. Turnaround time is typically less than five hours.

Yesterday, Angela Harper, one of the three transcriptionists, told department head Eric Fox that she really wants to be able to spend more time with her three-year-old son. She asked about the possibility of job-sharing. She has a friend, Li Ying Yu, who has had extensive experience as a transcriptionist and who would also like to work half-time. Angela could work from 8 A.M. until noon daily, and Li Ying could work from 1 until 5 P.M. daily. Eric has had difficulty finding workers; he does not want to lose Angela.

On the plus side, if he accepts Angela's plan, he will have two highly qualified employees. If one employee is sick the other might be willing to cover for her. Two employees working only half a day would probably be more productive than one employee working the entire day, and any deficiencies in one employee might be compensated for by the other (for example, if one employee is better at handling technical vocabulary, such dictation could be saved for her). On the negative side is the fact that there might be some coordination problems (especially in the beginning), and fringe benefits will be increased somewhat (he estimates about 15%).

Eric decides to write a memo to Neelima Shrikhande recommending the concept of job-sharing for this one position. Because job-sharing would be a new company policy, he knows that his memo will ultimately be forwarded to David Kaplan for his reaction.

Critical Thinking

1. Assume the role of Eric Fox. What is the specific goal of your memo?

2. Who are the primary and secondary audiences for this memo? What do you know about the primary audience that will help you write a more effective memo?

Writing Projects

3. List the points you should cover in the memo—in order.

4. Write a draft of the memo. (You may make up any needed information, as long as it is reasonable.)

5. Revise the draft.

6. Format the memo, proofread, and submit.

Basic Correspondence

7 Routine Messages

An Insider's Perspective

In the dynamic, competitive world of stocks and bonds, no request for product information is entirely routine. At the brokerage house of PaineWebber, where the pace never slows, Gwen Salley and other investment executives have to consider each family's or company's financial situation and provide factual information while at the same time building a client relationship. In some cases, the law requires that clients receive product information (such as the prospectus for a mutual fund) before they are allowed to invest, so answering requests for product information is an important part of the daily routine at this leading Wall Street firm.

In the course of starting relationships with prospective clients and strengthening relationships with existing clients, Salley writes as many as 25 letters a day. "My business is primarily conducted through the mail and over the phone," she explains. "I use letters to prospective clients as a way of introducing myself and my firm's capabilities. Often, prospects decide on the basis of an introductory letter whether they will take my call or meet with me in the future."

Salley usually talks with people about their financial needs and goals before writing a letter with the product information they have requested. In this way, she is able to tailor her letters to demonstrate what she and PaineWebber can do for each potential investor. These letters are intended to be informational rather than sales oriented. "People don't want to be sold when they are in the process of making a financial decision," she observes. "They want letters that clearly communicate the facts and my educated recommendations in an informational style."

Knowing that businesspeople get a lot of mail, Salley strives to capture the reader's attention in the very first sentence. "The first thing I do in my letter is to recollect something from our conversation. This helps the reader recognize who is writing," she says. To show respect for her reader's time, she gets to the point quickly, using the direct organizational plan to present the most important information as early in the letter as possible.

COMMUNICATION OBJECTIVES

After you have finished this chapter, you should be able to

■ Compose a routine request.

■ Compose a routine reply.

■ Compose a routine claim letter.

■ Compose a routine adjustment letter.

■ Compose a goodwill message.

Although the purpose is to provide the requested information, this stockbroker also wants readers to feel comfortable about doing business with her and with the firm she represents. One way Salley builds goodwill is by briefly repeating some of the needs and goals that readers have mentioned during earlier conversations. "It shows that I listened and that I understood what they asked for. It's also an affirmation of the importance of their concerns."

Every letter, no matter how routine, must be factual, professional, and accurate. "The objective is to communicate my professionalism and expertise," says Salley. "My paragraphs tend to be short and full of relevant facts. Every letter has to be absolutely correct in terms of spelling, grammar, and punctuation. None of my letters can reflect sloppiness or a lack of attention to detail, because nobody wants to work with a broker who operates that way."

Over time, Salley has developed a series of descriptions and charts to use in response to frequently asked questions. Reusing this material increases her productivity and ensures that the information is presented correctly every time. But she still customizes every letter and works hard to set her correspondence apart from the other mail in an investor's mailbox. "To personalize a letter a little more, I'll sometimes jot a handwritten note at the bottom. This indicates to the reader that the letter is not just a form letter that is sent to everyone. I want readers to see that I'm willing to do the little extra things that will encourage them to start or continue a relationship with me."

Gwen Salley

Investment executive, PaineWebber (New York, New York)

Planning the Routine Message

Most of the typical manager's correspondence consists of communicating about routine matters. For example, a small-business owner asks for a catalog and credit application from a potential supplier; a manager at a large corporation sends a memo notifying employees of a change in policy; a consumer notifies a company that an ordered product arrived in damaged condition; or a government agency responds to a request for a brochure.

Although routine, such messages are of interest to the reader because the information the message contains is necessary for day-to-day operations. For example, although no company is pleased when a customer is dissatisfied with one of its products, the company *is* interested in learning about such situations so that it can correct the problem and prevent its recurrence.

The direct style presents the major idea first, followed by needed details.

When the purpose of a message is to convey routine information and our analysis of the audience indicates that the reader will probably be interested in its contents, we use a **direct organizational plan.** The main idea is stated first, followed by any needed explanation, then a friendly closing, as illustrated in Figure 7.1.

Use an indirect plan when you present negative news or anticipate reader resistance.

The advantage of using a direct organizational plan for routine correspondence is that it puts the major news first—where it stands out and gets the most attention. This saves the reader time because he or she can quickly see what the message is about by scanning the first sentence or two. The **indirect organizational plan,** in which the reasons are presented before the major idea, is often used for persuasive and bad-news messages and is covered in subsequent chapters.

FIGURE 7.1   A Typical Routine E-mail Message

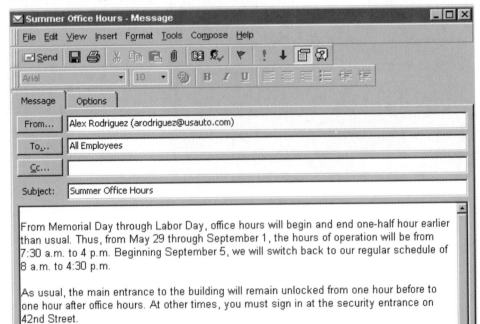

CEO William Mason (left) and his teammates at ADRA Systems have lots of reasons to smile. Sales of their company's product data management (PDM) software have rocketed 300% a quarter since it came out last year. One advantage of PDM software is that it helps to streamline the flow of routine correspondence among product designers, engineers, and manufacturing personnel.

You may transmit your message as an interoffice memorandum (written to someone in the same organization), a letter (written to someone outside the organization), or an e-mail message (written to anyone in the world with computer e-mail capability). Still, the principles of effective business writing discussed in Chapters 4–6 apply, regardless of the medium used to transmit the message.

Before learning how to write routine messages, you should know that many times a letter or memo is not the most efficient means of achieving your objective. Often a quick phone call or a walk down the hall to a colleague's office will work faster and at less expense than a letter or memo. However, when you need a permanent record of your message (or of the reader's response to your message) or when the topic requires elaboration, a written message is more effective.

For example, if you want to confirm that the staff meeting starts at 10 A.M. tomorrow, you would probably telephone a colleague. However, if you want to confirm that a colleague has agreed to share the cost of a new advertising campaign, you would probably want to have this information on file in a written memo.

Of course, not all messages are routine, as we will see in the following chapters. Messages that the reader is likely to resist require persuasion and are discussed in Chapter 8, and messages that contain bad news are discussed in Chapter 9.

Routine Requests

A request is routine if you anticipate that the reader will readily do as you ask without having to be persuaded. For example, a request for specific information about an organization's product is routine because all organizations appreciate the opportunity to promote their products. However, a request for free samples of a company's product to distribute at your store's anniversary sale might not be routine because the company might have concluded that such promotion efforts are not cost-effective; thus, you would have to *persuade* the reader to grant the request.

DILBERT

Major Idea First

Use a direct question, polite request, or statement to present your request.

When making a routine request, present the major idea—your request—clearly and directly in the first sentence or two (see, however, Spotlight 11—Across Cultures). You may use a direct question, a statement, or a polite request to present the main idea. A polite request is a statement that is phrased as a question out of courtesy but takes a period instead of a question mark, such as "May I please have your answer by May 3." Use a polite request when you expect the reader to respond by *acting* rather than by actually giving a yes-or-no answer. Always pose your request clearly and politely, and give any background information needed to set the stage. All of the following are effective routine requests:

Direct Question: Does Black & Decker offer educational discounts for public institutions making quantity purchases of tools? Blair Junior High School will soon be replacing approximately 50 portable electric drills used by our industrial arts students.

Statement: I would appreciate your letting me know how I might invest in your deferred money-market fund. As an American currently working in Bangkok, Thailand, I cannot easily take advantage of your automatic monthly deposit plan.

Polite Request: Would you please answer several questions about the work performance of Janice Henry. She has applied for the position of industrial safety officer at Inland Steel and has given your name as a reference.

Decide in advance how much detail you are seeking. If you need only a one-sentence reply, it would be unfair to word your request in such a way as to prompt the writer to provide a three-page answer. Define clearly the type of response you want and phrase your request to elicit that response.

NOT: Please explain the features of your Interact word processing program.

BUT: Does your Interact word processing program automatically number lines and paragraphs?

Do not ask more questions than are necessary. Make the questions easy to answer.

Remember that you are imposing on the goodwill of the reader. Ask as few questions as possible—and never for any information that you can reasonably get on your own. If many questions *are* necessary, number them; most readers will answer questions in the order in which you pose them and will thus be less likely to skip

When in Rome . . .

The direct organizational style is suggested for each type of message presented in this chapter. This style can be summarized in five words: *Present the major idea immediately.* American business executives have little time and patience for needless formalities and "beating around the bush."

Such is not always the case, however, when writing to someone whose culture and experiences are quite different from your own. Natives of some countries may find letters written in the direct style too harsh and abrupt, lacking in courtesy. You should therefore adapt your writing style to the expectations of the reader.

For example, an American manufacturer sent a form sales letter to many domestic and foreign retail stores, inviting inquiries about stocking its line of fishing tackle. Note the differences in two of the responses the manufacturer received, shown below.

The moral is simple. Write as your receiver expects you to write. Take a cue from his or her own writing. If the letters you receive from an international associate are written in a direct style, you may safely respond in a similar style. However, if the letters you receive are similar to the Chinese response below, you might try a more formal, less direct style when responding. Although you would not want to *adopt* the reader's style, you might need to *adapt* your own, on the basis of your analysis of the audience.

SPOTLIGHT 11

ACROSS CULTURES

Would you please send me a sample of the fishing tackle you advertised in your October 3 letter, along with price and shipping information. As a long-time retailer of fishing tackle, I would be especially interested in any items you might have for fly fishing.

Since the trout season starts in six weeks, I would appreciate having this information as soon as possible.

American Response

It was with great pleasure that we received your letter dated 3 October. We send our deepest respects and wish to inform you that Yoon Sung Fishing Tackle Company, Ltd., has been selling fishing items for 38 years.

We would be pleased to consider your merchandise. May we ask you to please send us samples, price, and shipping information. It will be a great pleasure to conduct business with your company.

Chinese Response

one unintentionally. Yes-or-no questions or short-answer questions are easy for the reader to answer; but when you need more information, use open-ended questions.

Arrange your questions in logical order (for example, order of importance, chronological order, or simple-to-complex order), word each question clearly and objectively (to avoid bias), and limit the content to one topic per question. If appropriate, assure the reader that the information provided will be treated confidentially.

Explanation and Details

Most of the time you will need to give additional explanation or details about your initial request. Include any needed background information (such as the reason for

Explain why you're making the request.

asking) either immediately before or after making the request. For example, suppose you received the polite request given earlier asking about Janice Henry's job performance. Unless you were also told that the request came from a potential employer and that Janice Henry had given your name as a reference, you might be reluctant to provide such confidential information.

Or assume that you're writing to a former employer or professor asking for a letter of recommendation. You might need to give some background about yourself to jog the reader's memory. Or you might need to justify or expand on your request. Put yourself in the reader's position. What information would you need to answer the request accurately and completely?

If possible, show how others benefit from your receiving the requested information.

A reader is more likely to cooperate if you can show how he or she will benefit from agreeing to your request. In fact, it is often the communication of such benefits that makes the message routine rather than persuasive.

> Will you please help us serve you better by answering several questions about your banking needs. We're building a branch bank in your neighborhood and would like to make it as convenient for you as possible.

In general, you should identify reader benefits when they may not be obvious to the reader, but you need not belabor the point if such benefits are obvious. For example, a memo asking employees to recycle their paper and plastic trash would probably not need to discuss the value of recycling since most readers would already be familiar with the advantages of recycling.

Friendly Closing

Close on a friendly note.

In your final paragraph, assume a friendly tone. Close by expressing appreciation for the assistance to be provided (but without seeming to take the recipient's cooperation for granted), by stating and justifying any deadlines, or by offering to reciprocate. Make your ending friendly and positive, as illustrated by the following examples:

> Please let me know if I can return the favor.

> We appreciate your providing this information, which will help us make a fairer evaluation of Janice Henry's qualifications for this position.

> May I please have the product information by October 1, when I place my Christmas wholesale orders. That way, I will be able to include Kodak products in my holiday sales.

Model 1 illustrates these guidelines for writing a routine request.

Routine Replies

Routine replies provide the information requested in the original message or otherwise comply with the writer's request. Like the original request letters, they are organized in a direct organizational style, putting the "good news"—the fact that you're responding favorably—up front.

Respond promptly so that the information will arrive in time to be used.

Probably one of the most important guidelines to follow is to answer promptly. If a potential customer asks for product information, ensure that the information arrives before the customer must make a purchase decision. Otherwise, the time it

MODEL 1 Routine Request

```
HP 340 Product Information - Composition                    _ □ ✕
File  Edit  View  Tools  Communicator  Help

  ✉        "        ▨        ✎        ▨       ⬇       ☐       ▩              N
 Send     Quote    Address   Attach   Spelling  Save   Security  Stop

 ▤   ▼  To: ▨ albertgleason@hp.com

 ✎
 ▨

 Subject: HP 340 Product Information
```

Dear Mr. Gleason:

Would you provide me with information regarding your HP 340 portable printer.
I'm interested in purchasing 34 lightweight printers that our marketing
representatives can use with their Toshiba 1200XE notebook computers when
they travel.

Specifically, I would like answers to the following four questions:

1. Is the HP 340 a laser printer?

2. Is it battery operated? Since we wish to use the printer for traveling,
    such a feature in important.

3. Does the printer have a 15-inch carriage?

4. Does it come with at least a six-month guarantee?

I would appreciate your faxing me the information I need to make a purchase
decision (Fax: 919-555-0327). I would also appreciate receiving ordering
information.

Sincerely,

Carolyn J. Ryerson, Purchasing Director
Home Security Products
Box 302, Edenton, NC 27932
Phone: 919-555-4022

This message is from a potential customer to a manufacturer.

Presents the request in the first sentence, followed by the reason for asking.

Enumerates questions for emphasis and clarity; makes questions easy to answer.

Expresses appreciation; hints at a reader benefit.

Grammar and Mechanics Notes

1 Format e-mail messages for easy readability—and always proofread before sending.   2 *Your HP 340 portable printer:* Use a period after a polite request.   3 *appreciate your faxing:* Use the possessive form of a pronoun (*your*) before a gerund (*faxing*).

took you to respond will have been wasted. Also, delaying a response might send the unintentional nonverbal message that you do not want to comply with the writer's request.

Your response should be courteous. If you appear to be acting grudgingly, you will probably lose any goodwill that a gracious response might have earned for you or your organization.

NOT: Although we do not generally provide the type of information you requested, we have decided to do so in this case.

BUT: We are happy to provide the information you requested.

Grant the request or give the requested information early in the message. Doing so not only saves the reader's time but also puts him or her in a good state of mind immediately. Although the reader may be pleased to hear that "We have received your letter of June 26," such news is not nearly so eagerly received as telling the reader that "I would be pleased to speak at your Lion's Club meeting on August 8; thanks for thinking of me." Put the good news up front—where it will receive the most emphasis.

Be sure to answer all the questions asked or implied, using objective and clearly understood language. Although it is often helpful to provide additional information or suggestions, you should never fail to at least address all the questions asked—even if your answer is not what the reader hopes to hear. Questions are usually answered in the order in which they were asked, but consider rearranging them if a different order makes more sense. Determining what your reader already knows about the topic should help you decide what information to include and how to phrase it.

The reader will probably be in a positive mood as the result of your letter, and you may consider either including some sales promotion if appropriate or building goodwill by implying such characteristics about your organization as public spirit-edness, quality products, social responsibility, or concern for employees. To be effective, sales promotion and goodwill appeals should be subtle; avoid exaggeration and do not devote too much space to such efforts.

Often the writer's questions have been asked by others many times before; in such a situation, a form letter may be the most appropriate way to respond. A **form letter** is a letter with standardized wording that is sent to different people. With word processing, it is often difficult to tell the difference between a form letter and a personal letter. If a stockholder wrote asking why your company conducted business in Cuba, a personal reply would probably be called for. However, if a potential stockholder wrote asking for a copy of your latest annual report, you might simply send an annual report, along with a form letter such as the following:

Consider using form letters for answering frequent requests.

We are happy to send you our latest annual report. Also enclosed is a copy of a recent profile of Dennison Industries contained in the June issue of *Fortune* magazine.

As you study our annual report, note the diversity of our product offerings—from men's clothing to massive earth movers. This diversity is one of the reasons we have shown a profit for each of the past 57 years. Our 5-, 10-, and 15-year income statements are shown on page 8 of the enclosed report.

Dennison Industries stock is traded on the New York Stock Exchange, listed under "DenIn." Simply call your local broker to join the 275,000 other satisfied investors in Dennison Industries common stock.

In the body of your message, refer to any enclosure and then add an enclosure notation at the bottom of the letter. Referring to a specific page of an enclosed brochure or to a particular paragraph of an enclosed document helps ensure that such enclosures will be read.

Close your letter on a positive, friendly note. Avoid such clichés as "If you have additional questions, please don't hesitate to let me know." Use original wording, personalized especially for the reader. After all, the reader might receive many letters like yours, and if he or she has already encountered "Thank you for your interest in our products" five times that day, the expression will sound trite and insincere.

Model 2 is a routine reply to the request shown in Model 1. The original request asked four questions about the printer, and the answers are as follows: (1) No, the HP 340 is not a laser printer; (2) No, it is not battery operated; (3) Yes, it does have a 15-inch carriage; and (4) No, it does not come with a six-month warranty. As you can see, only one of the four questions can be answered with an unqualified "yes," and that is the question the respondent chose to lead off with. Positive language helps soften the impact of the negative responses to the other three questions. Also, reader benefits are stressed throughout the letter. Instead of just describing the features, the writer shows how the features can benefit the reader.

Checklist 6 (p. 195)summarizes the points you should consider when writing and responding to routine requests. Use this checklist as a guide in structuring your message and in evaluating the effectiveness of your first draft. In addition, when composing messages that have legal implications, follow the strategies provided in Spotlight 12—On Law and Ethics on page 196.

> **wordwise**
>
> **Made-to-Order Convention Sites**
>
> - Accountants   *Billings, Montana*
> - Dugout canoeists   *Roanoke, Virginia*
> - Egotists   *Superior, Wisconsin*
> - Mystery writers   *Erie, Pennsylvania*
> - Plastic surgeons   *Scarsdale, New York*
> - Psychiatrists   *Normal, Illinois*
> - Voyeurs   *Topeka, Kansas*

Refer to any enclosures in your letter to make sure they are read.

Use positive language to create a positive impression.

Routine Claim Letters

A **claim letter** is written by the buyer to the seller, seeking some type of action to correct a problem with the seller's product or service. The purchaser may be an individual or an organization. A claim letter differs from a simple complaint letter in that it requests some type of adjustment (such as repairing or replacing the product). As a matter of fact, many complaint letters would probably be more successful if they carried an implied claim that the writer wanted some adjustment to be made as a result of poor service, unfair practices, or the like. The desired adjustment might be nothing more than an explanation or apology, but the mere fact that you request some direct action will increase your chances of getting a satisfactory response.

A claim letter can be considered routine if you can reasonably anticipate that the reader will comply with your request. If, for example, you ordered a shipment of shoes for your store that were advertised at $23.50 each and the wholesaler charged you $32.50 instead, you would write a routine claim letter, asking the seller to correct the error. But suppose the wholesaler marked the price down to $19.50 two days after you placed your order. Then instead of writing a routine claim letter, you

MODEL 2 **Routine Reply**

This letter responds to the request in Model 1.

Hewlett-Packard Company
PO Box 10301
Palo Alto, California 94304-0890

hp HEWLETT·
PACKARD

September 12, 19--

Ms. Carolyn J. Ryerson
Purchasing Director
Home Security Products
Box 302
Edenton, NC 27932

Dear Ms. Ryerson:

Yes, our popular HP 340 portable printer does come with a 15-inch carriage. This wider carriage will enable your representatives to print out even your most complex spread-sheets while on the road. Of course, the pinstops also adjust easily to fit standard $8^1/_2$-by-11-inch paper.

1   For quiet operation and easy portability, the HP uses ink-jet printing. This technology provides nearly the same quality output as a laser printer at less than half the cost.

2   Either plain paper or specially coated paper may be used.

3   Although many travelers use their laptop computers on a plane or in their automobiles, our research shows that they typically wait until reaching their destination to print out their documents. Thus, the HP uses AC power only, thereby reducing its weight by nearly a pound. The extra-long 12-foot power cord will let you power-up your printer easily no matter where the electrical outlet is hidden. And our 30-day warranty, standard in the computer industry, ensures the reliability and trouble-free service that our customers have come to expect of all HP products.

4   To order or take the HP 340 for a test drive, call your local Computerland (Phone: 800-555-2189). They will show you how to increase your productivity while increasing your luggage weight by only about 4 pounds.

Sincerely yours,

Albert Gleason

Albert Gleason
Sales Manager

juc
By Fax

Printed on recycled paper

Begins by answering the "yes" question first.

Answers all questions, using positive language and pointing out the benefits of each feature.

Uses paragraphs instead of enumeration to answer each question because each answer requires elaboration.

Gives important purchase information; closes on a forward-looking note.

Grammar and Mechanics Notes

1 *ink-jet printing:* Hyphenate a compound adjective before a noun.   2 *specially coated paper:* Do not hyphenate a compound adjective if the first word ends in *-ly*. 3 *its:* Do not confuse *its* (the possessive pronoun) with *it's* (the contraction for *it is*). 4 *a test drive,:* Place a comma after an introductory expression.

✔ CHECKLIST 6   Routine Requests and Replies

Routine Requests	Routine Replies
☑ Present the major request in the first sentence or two, preceded or followed by reasons for making the request.	☑ Answer promptly and graciously.
☑ Provide any needed explanation or details.	☑ Grant the request or begin giving the requested information in the first sentence or two.
☑ Phrase each question so that it is clear, is easy to answer, and covers only one topic. Ask as few questions as possible, but if several questions are necessary, number them and arrange them in logical order.	☑ Address all questions asked or implied; include additional information or suggestions if that would be helpful.
☑ If appropriate, incorporate reader benefits and promise confidentiality.	☑ Include subtle sales promotion if appropriate.
	☑ Consider developing a form letter for frequent requests.
☑ Close on a friendly note by expressing appreciation, justifying any necessary deadlines, offering to reciprocate, or otherwise making your ending personal and original.	☑ Refer to any items you enclose with the letter, and insert an enclosure notation at the bottom.
	☑ Close on a positive and friendly note, use original wording, and avoid such clichés as "If you have any further questions, please let me know."

might want to write a persuasive letter, trying to convince the wholesaler to give you the lower price. (Persuasive letters are discussed in the next chapter.)

Contemporary corporate culture places a premium on product quality and customer service, and most companies make a genuine effort to settle claims from customers. They want to know if their customers are dissatisfied with their products so that they can correct the situation. A dissatisfied customer may not only refuse to purchase additional products from the offending company but may also tell others about the bad experience. One study of consumers showed that the typical dissatisfied customer tells nine or ten other people about the incident and that each of them, in turn, tells four or five more people. The typical satisfied customer, on the other hand, recommends the product or service to four or five other people.[1]

Write your claim letter promptly—as soon as you've identified a problem. Delaying unnecessarily might not only push you past the warranty date but might also raise suspicions about the validity of your claim; the more recent the purchase, the more valid your claim will appear.

Although some consumer advocates suggest addressing your claim letter to the company president, business courtesy argues for first giving the company's order department or customer relations department an opportunity to solve the problem. Such departments are designed to handle these problems most efficiently; and their employees are the most knowledgeable about specific company policies and procedures, product history, warranty information, decisions in similar cases, and the like. Only if your claim is not settled satisfactorily at this level should you then appeal to a higher level of management in the company.

Although you may be frustrated or angry as a result of the situation, remember that the person to whom you're writing was not *personally* responsible for your problem. Be courteous and avoid emotional language. Assume that the company is

Assume a courteous tone; avoid emotionalism.

Messages with Legal Implications

All written messages carry certain legal implications. For example, if you knowingly write something false about a company that results in damages to that company's reputation or financial well-being, you are guilty of libel. Therefore, in all messages ensure that your information is accurate and that your message does not violate any federal or state laws.

Some types of messages have special legal implications. Follow these guidelines when writing letters of recomendation, letters rejecting a job applicant, and memos containing personnel evaluations.

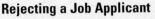

Writing a Letter of Recommendation

1. Be fair—to yourself, to the prospective employer, to the applicant whom you're recommending, and to the other applicants for the same position.
2. Begin by giving the name of the applicant, the position for which the applicant is applying, and the nature and length of your relationship with the applicant.
3. Label the information "confidential," and state that you were asked to provide this information.
4. Discuss only job-related traits and behaviors, be as objective as possible, and support your statements with specific examples.
5. If writing a recommendation for a specific position, answer all questions asked and gear your comments to the applicant's qualifications for the particular job.
6. Present any negative information in such a way that the reader will perceive it with the same

degree of importance that you do.
7. Close by giving an overall summary of your evaluation.

Rejecting a Job Applicant

1. Keep the letter short; the candidate is anxious to learn whether your decision is "yes" or "no."
2. Provide a short, supportive buffer, perhaps mentioning some specific positive comment about the candidate's résumé or interview.
3. Indicate that another candidate was chosen (not that the reader was *not* chosen), and briefly explain why.
4. Close on an off-the-topic note, perhaps thanking the reader for applying or extending best wishes.

Writing a Personnel Evaluation

1. Be fair—to yourself, to the employee, and to the organization.
2. Discuss only job-related behaviors and traits.
3. Document any praise or criticism with specific examples; avoid exaggeration.
4. Ensure that any negative information receives only the appropriate amount of emphasis.
5. Emphasize the improvement aspect of the evaluation; that is, state specifically what steps should be taken to improve performance.
6. Close with an overall summary of your evaluation or with a friendly, forward-looking comment.

reasonable and will do as you reasonably ask. Avoid any hint of anger, sarcasm, threat, or exaggeration. A reader who becomes angry as a result of the strong language in your claim letter will be less likely to do as you ask. Instead, using factual and unemotional language, begin your routine claim letter directly, telling exactly what the problem is.

 You should be ashamed at your dishonest advertising for the videotape *Safety Is Job One.*

 The videotape *Safety Is Job One* that I rented for $125 from your company last week lived up to our expectations in every way but one.

The customer-service representatives at consumer-products companies spend much time handling customer questions and concerns. Simple claims can often be handled over the phone, but most claims (and adjustments) should be in writing—to provide a written trail for reference.

NOT: I am disgusted at the way United Express cheated me out of $12.50 last week. What a rip-off!

BUT: An overnight letter that I mailed on December 3 did not arrive the next day, as promised by United Express.

After you have identified the problem, begin your explanation. Provide as much background information as necessary—dates, model numbers, amounts, photocopies of canceled checks or correspondence, and the like. Use a confident tone and logic (rather than emotion) to present your case. Write in an impersonal style, avoiding the use of *you* pronouns so as not to link your reader too closely to the negative news.

Provide needed details.

NOT: I delivered this letter to *you* sometime in the early afternoon on December 3. Although *you* promised to deliver it by 3 P.M. the next day, *you* failed to do so.

BUT: As shown on the enclosed copy of my receipt, I delivered this letter to United Express at 3:30 P.M. on December 3. According to the sign prominently displayed in the office, any package received by 4 P.M. is guaranteed to arrive by 3 P.M. the following business day.

Tell exactly what went wrong and how you were inconvenienced. If it is true and relevant, mention something positive about the company or its products to make your letter appear reasonable.

If possible, mention something positive about the product.

According to the enclosed receipt, my letter was not delivered until 8:30 A.M. on December 5. Because the letter contained material needed for a dinner meeting on December 4, it arrived too late to be of any use. This is not the type of on-time service I've routinely received from United Express during the eight years I've been using your delivery system.

Finally, tell what type of adjustment you expect. Do you want the company to replace the product, repair it, issue a refund, simply apologize, or what? End the letter on a confident note.

> I would appreciate your refunding my $12.50, thereby reestablishing my confidence in United Express.

In some situations, you may not know what type of adjustment is reasonable; then, you would leave it up to the reader to suggest an appropriate course of action. This might be the situation when you suffered no monetary loss but simply wish to avoid an unpleasant situation in the future (such as discourteous service, long lines, or ordering the wrong model because of having received incomplete or misleading information).

> Please let me know how I might avoid this problem in the future.

Model 3 illustrates a routine claim letter about a defective product, asking for a specific remedy.

Routine Adjustment Letter

An adjustment letter responds to a claim letter.

An **adjustment letter** is written to inform a customer of the action taken in response to the customer's claim letter. Few people bother to write a claim letter unless they have a real problem, so most claims that companies receive are legitimate and are adjusted according to the individual situation. If the action taken is what the customer asked for or expected, a routine adjustment letter using the direct organizational plan would be written.

You should note that *anyone* in an organization may be called upon to write claim and adjustment letters—not just those working in purchasing or sales or customer service. For example, an accounting manager may send (and receive) a letter complaining of poor service from an employee.

Overall Tone

Adopt a gracious, confident tone for your adjustment letters.

A claim represents a possible loss of goodwill and confidence in your company or its products. Because the customer is upset, the overall tone of your adjustment letter is crucial. Since you have already decided to honor the claim, your best strategy is to adopt a gracious, trusting tone. Give your customer the benefit of the doubt. It does not make sense to adopt a grudging or resentful tone and risk losing whatever goodwill you might have gained from granting the adjustment.

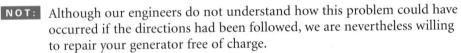

NOT: Although our engineers do not understand how this problem could have occurred if the directions had been followed, we are nevertheless willing to repair your generator free of charge.

BUT: We are happy to repair your generator free of charge. Within ten days, a factory representative will call you to schedule a convenient time to make the repair.

Your overall tone should show confidence both in the reader's honesty and in the essential worth of your own company and its products. To the extent possible, use

MODEL 3   Routine Claim—Remedy Specified

This claim letter is about a defective product.

Rubbermaid

April 15, 19--

Customer Relations Representative
Color-Vu Graphics
P.O. Box 210742
Dallas, TX 75211-7036

1   Dear Customer Relations Representative:

Subject: Poor Quality of Slides from Invoice 4073

The poor quality of the 13 color slides you processed for me on April 8 made them unsuitable for use in my recent presentation to 200 marketing representatives. As a result, I had to use black-and-white transparencies instead.

2   The enclosed slide is typical of all 13 slides from this order. As you can see, the colors
3   often run together and the type is fuzzy. The slides are not equivalent in quality to those illustrated in the Color-Vu advertisement on page 154 of the April *Business Management*.

I have already given the presentation for which these slides were made, so redeveloping them would not solve the problem. Because I have not yet paid your Invoice 4073 for $176.50, dated April 12, would you please cancel this charge. If you would like me to return the other 12 slides, I shall be happy to do so.

4   I know that despite one's best efforts, mistakes will occasionally happen, and I am confident that you will correct this problem promptly.

Sincerely,

Claire D. Scriven

Claire D. Scriven
Marketing Manager

ric
Enclosure

Rubbermaid Incorporated
1147 Akron Road, Wooster, Ohio 44691-6000 ¥ 330 264-6464 ¥ www.rubbermaid.com

Identifies the problem immediately and tells how the writer was inconvenienced.

Provides the needed details in a nonemotional, businesslike manner.

Identifies and justifies the specific remedy requested.

Closes on a confident note.

Grammar and Mechanics Notes

1 If an addressee's name is unknown, you may use a title in both the inside address and the salutation.   2 *run together and:* Do not insert any punctuation before the *and* separating the two independent clauses because the second clause, "the type is fuzzy," is so short.   3 April *Business Management:* Italicize or underline magazine titles.   4 *occasionally:* Note that this word has two *c*'s and one *s*.

Avoid using negative language when describing the basis for the claim.

neutral or positive language in referring to the claim (for example, write "the situation" instead of "your complaint"). Also avoid appearing to doubt the reader. Instead of saying "you claim that," use more neutral wording, such as "you state that."

Finally, respond promptly. Your customer is already upset; the longer this anger remains, the more difficult it will be to overcome.

Good News First

Nothing that you are likely to tell the reader will be more welcome than the fact that you are granting the claim, so put this news up front—in the very first sentence if possible. The details and background information will come later, as illustrated by the following examples:

> A new copy of the *American World Dictionary* is on its way to your office, and I assure you that no pages are missing from this copy. I checked it myself!

> The enclosed $17.50 check reimburses you for your company's delayed overnight letter. Thank you for bringing this matter to my attention.

> Thanks to you, we have undertaken a new training program for our housekeeping staff. Please use the enclosed coupon for two nights' free stay at the Ambassador to see for yourself the difference your letter has made.

It is appropriate to apologize for serious problems.

It is often appropriate to thank the reader for giving you an opportunity to resolve the situation, but what about apologizing? An apology, which tends to emphasize the negative aspects of the situation, is probably not necessary for small, routine claims that are promptly resolved to the customer's satisfaction. Instead, emphasize the positive aspects and look forward to future transactions. If, however, the customer has been severely inconvenienced or embarrassed and the company is clearly at fault, a sincere apology would be in order. In such a situation, first give the good news and then apologize in a businesslike manner; avoid repeating the apology in the closing lines.

> I have contracted with a local mason to rebuild your home's brick walkway, which our driver mistakenly damaged on February 23. I am truly sorry for the inconvenience this situation has caused you and am grateful for your understanding.

Explanation

After presenting the "good news," you must educate your reader as to why the problem occurred and, if appropriate, what steps you've taken to make sure it doesn't recur. Explain the situation in sufficient detail to be believable, but don't belabor the reason for the problem. Emphasize the fact that you stand behind your products. Avoid using negative language, don't pass the buck, and don't hide behind a "mistakes-will-happen" attitude.

Explain specifically, but briefly, what went wrong.

> Let me explain what happened. On December 4, the plane that had your letter in its cargo bay could not land at O'Hare Airport because of a snowstorm and was diverted to Detroit. Although our Detroit personnel worked overtime to reload the mail onto a delivery truck, which was then driven to Chicago, the shipment did not arrive until early on December 5.

Because the reader's faith in your products has been shaken, you also have a sales job to do. You must build into your letter **resale**—that is, information that reestablishes the customer's confidence in the product purchased or in the company that sells the product. In order to be believable, do *not* promise that the problem will never happen again; that's unrealistic. Do, however, use specific language, including facts and figures when possible.

Use resale to reassure the customer of the worth of your products.

NOT: We have taken steps to ensure that this situation will not happen again.

BUT: Fortunately, such incidents are rare. For example, even considering bad weather, airline strikes, and the like, United Express has maintained an on-time delivery record of 97.6% during the past 12 months. No other delivery service even comes close to this record.

Sometimes you may decide to honor a claim even when the customer is at fault—perhaps because the writer has been a good customer for many years or represents important potential business. In such situations, your beginning paragraph should still convey the good news that you're honoring the claim, but you might temper the enthusiasm a bit. And in the explanatory paragraphs, you would tactfully communicate to the reader the facts surrounding the case—that the reader is at fault, the product was misused, the warranty has expired, or whatever the situation requires.

If the customer is at fault, explain in tactful, impersonal language how to avoid such problems in the future.

On the one hand, it is necessary to inform the reader of the circumstances so that he or she won't keep repeating the problem. On the other hand, if you do so in an insulting manner, you will lose the reader's goodwill. Instead, use impersonal, tactful language, taking special pains not to lecture the reader or sound condescending. For example, in the second paragraph that follows, note that the pronoun *you* is not used at all when explaining the misuse of the equipment.

Because we value your friendship, we are pleased to repair your Braniff 250 copier free of charge. Our maintenance technician tells me that she took care of the problem on September 15.

Your machine's register indicated that 9,832 copies had been made since the copier was installed on July 18. The Braniff 250 is designed for low-level office use—fewer than 1,500 copies per month. If you find that you will continue to experience high-volume usage, may I suggest trading up to the Braniff 300, which will easily handle your needs. We will gladly offer you $1,300 as a trade-in allowance.

Positive, Forward-Looking Closing

End your letter on a positive note. Do not refer to the problem again, do not apologize again, do not suggest the possibility of future problems, and do not imply that the reader might still be upset. Instead, use strategies that imply a continuing relationship with the customer, such as including additional resale, a comment about the satisfaction the reader will receive from the repaired product or improved service, or appreciation for the reader's interest in your products.

Do not mention the claim in the closing. Instead, look to the future.

Include sales promotion only if you are confident that your adjustment has restored the customer's confidence in your product or service; otherwise, it might backfire. If used, sales promotion should be subtle and should involve a new product or accessory rather than promoting a new or improved model of what the reader has already bought.

> **NOT:** Again, I apologize for the delay in delivering your letter. If you experience such problems again, please don't hesitate to write.
>
> **BUT:** We have enjoyed serving your delivery needs for the past eight years, Ms. Clarke, and look forward to many more years of service.
>
> **OR:** If you're the type of person who has frequent crash deadlines, Ms. Clarke, you will probably be interested in our eight-hour delivery service. It is described in the enclosed brochure.

Model 4 illustrates an adjustment letter, and Checklist 7 summarizes the guidelines for writing routine claim and adjustment letters.

Goodwill Messages

A **goodwill message** is one that is sent strictly out of a sense of kindness and friendliness. Examples include messages conveying congratulations, appreciation, and sympathy. These messages achieve their goodwill objective precisely because they have no true business objective. To include even subtle sales promotion in such messages would defeat their purpose. Recipients are quick to see through such efforts. Letters that include sales promotion or resale are *sales* letters, as might be expected, and are covered elsewhere in this text.

That is not to say, however, that business advantages do not accrue from such efforts. People naturally like to deal with businesses and with people who are friendly and who take the time to comment on noteworthy occasions. The point is that such business advantages are strictly incidental to the real purpose of extending a friendly gesture.

Progressive companies promote goodwill both within their organization and within the local community. Although many of these messages are verbal, they can be nonverbal as well. McDonald's, for example, has built numerous "Ronald McDonald House" residences for seriously ill children and their families. This one is located across from a hospital in Long Branch, New Jersey.

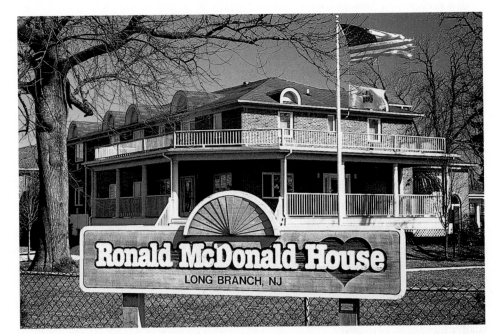

MODEL 4 Adjustment Letter

This adjustment letter responds to the claim letter in Model 3.

COLOR-VU GRAPHICS
The Media Specialists

April 22, 19--

1 Ms.Claire Scriven
Marketing Manager
Rubbermaid Incorporated
1147 Akron Road
Wooster, Ohio 44691-6000

Dear Ms. Scriven:

2 Color-Vu Graphics is, of course, happy to cancel the $176.50 charge for Invoice 4073. I appreciate your taking the time to write and send us a sample slide (you may simply
3 discard the other slides).

4 Upon receiving your letter, I immediately sent your slide to our quality-control personnel for closer examination. They agreed with you that the slide should have been redeveloped before it left our processing lab. We have now revised our procedures to ensure that before each slide leaves our lab, it is inspected by someone other than the person preparing it.

To better serve the media needs of our corporate customers, we are installing the Kodak 1120 processor, the most sophisticated development system available. Thus, when you send us your next order, you'll see that your slides are of even higher quality than those in the *Business Management* advertisement that impressed you.

Sincerely yours,

David Foster

David Foster
Customer Relations

ied

P.O. Box 210742 • Dallas, TX 75211 • 214-555-0932

Tells immediately that the adjustment is being made; thanks the reader.

Explains briefly, but specifically, what happened.

Looks forward to a continuing relationship with the customer; does not mention the problem again.

Grammar and Mechanics Notes

1 Type the position title either on the same line as the person's name or, as here, on a line by itself. 2 *Invoice 4073:* Capitalize a noun that precedes a number. 3 *slides).:* Place the period outside the closing parenthesis unless the entire sentence is in parentheses. 4 *personnel:* Do not confuse *personnel* (employees) with *personal* (private).

✔ CHECKLIST 7   Routine Claim and Adjustment Letters

Routine Claim Letters

☑ Write your claim letter promptly—as soon as you've identified a problem. Try to determine the name of the appropriate individual to whom to write; if that is not possible, address your letter to the customer relations department.

☑ Strive for an overall tone of courtesy and confidence; avoid anger, sarcasm, threats, and exaggeration. If true and relevant, mention something positive about the company or its products somewhere in the letter.

☑ Begin the letter directly, identifying the problem immediately.

☑ Provide as much detail as necessary. Using impersonal language, tell specifically what went wrong and how you were inconvenienced.

☑ If appropriate, tell what type of adjustment you expect—replacement, repair, refund, or apology. End on a confident note.

Routine Adjustment Letters

☑ Respond promptly; your customer is already upset.

☑ Begin the letter directly, telling the reader immediately what adjustment is being made.

☑ Adopt a courteous tone. Use neutral or positive language throughout.

☑ If appropriate, somewhere in the letter thank the reader for writing, and apologize if the customer has been severely inconvenienced or embarrassed because of your company's actions.

☑ In a forthright manner, explain the reason for the problem in sufficient detail to be believable, but don't belabor the point. If appropriate, tell what steps you've taken to prevent a recurrence of the problem.

☑ Provide information that reestablishes your customer's confidence in the product or your company. Be specific enough to be believable.

☑ If the customer was at fault, explain in impersonal and tactful language the facts surrounding the case.

☑ Close on a positive note. Include additional resale, subtle sales promotion, appreciation for the reader's interest in your products, or some other strategy that implies customer satisfaction and the expectation of a continuing relationship.

Often the gesture could be accomplished by telephoning instead of by writing—especially for minor occasions. But a written message, either in place of or in addition to the phone call, is more thoughtful, more appreciated, and more permanent. And because it requires extra effort and the recipient will receive fewer of them, a written message is much more meaningful than a telephone message.

General Guidelines

Five guidelines for goodwill messages: be prompt, direct, sincere, specific, and brief.

To ensure that your goodwill messages achieve their desired effect, follow these five guidelines:

1. *Be prompt.* Too often, people consider writing a goodwill message but then put it off until it is too late. The most meaningful messages are those received while the reason for them is still fresh in the reader's mind.
2. *Be direct.* State the major idea in the first sentence or two, even for sympathy notes; since the reader already knows the bad news, you don't need to shelter him or her from it.

3. *Be sincere.* Avoid language that is too flowery or too strong. Use a conversational tone, as if you were speaking to the person directly, and focus on the reader—not on yourself. Take special care to spell names correctly and to make sure your facts are accurate.
4. *Be specific.* If you're thanking or complimenting someone, mention a specific incident or anecdote. Personalize your message to avoid having it sound like a form letter.
5. *Be brief.* You don't need two pages (or, likely, even one full page) to get your point across. Often a personal note card is more appropriate than full-sized business stationery.

Congratulatory Messages

Congratulatory notes should be sent for major business achievements—receiving a promotion, announcing a retirement, winning an award, opening a new branch, celebrating an anniversary, and the like. Such notes are also appropriate for personal milestones—engagements, weddings, births, graduations, and other noteworthy occasions. Congratulatory notes should be written both to employees within the company and to customers, suppliers, and others outside the firm with whom you have a relationship.

> Congratulations, Tom, on your election to the presidency of the United Way of Alberta County. I was happy to see the announcement in this morning's newspaper and to learn of your plans for the upcoming campaign.
>
> Best wishes for a successful fund drive. This important community effort surely deserves everyone's full support.

Thank-You Notes

A note of thanks or appreciation is often valued more than a monetary reward. A handwritten thank-you note is especially appreciated today, when people routinely receive so many "personalized" computer-generated messages. A handwritten note assures the reader that you are offering sincere and genuine thanks, rather than simply sending out a form letter. And if you take the trouble to send a photocopy of your typed note to the person's supervisor, the recipient will be twice blessed.

Thank-you notes are expected in some situations; they are unexpected (and therefore much appreciated) in others.

Thank-you notes (either typed or handwritten) should be sent whenever someone does you a favor—gives you a gift, writes a letter of recommendation for you, comes to your support unexpectedly, gives a speech or appears on a panel, and so on. Don't forget that customers and suppliers like to be recognized as well. Unexpected thank-you notes are often the most appreciated—to the salesperson, instructor, secretary, copy center operator, restaurant server, receptionist, or anyone else who provided service beyond the call of duty.

> Thank you so much, Alice, for serving on the panel of suppliers for our new-employee orientation program. Your comments on scheduling problems and your suggestions for alleviating them were especially helpful. They were the kind of information that only an experienced pro like you could give.
>
> I think you could tell from the comments and many questions that your remarks were well received by our new employees. Thanks again for your professional contributions.

Sympathy Notes

Expressions of sympathy or condolence to a person who has experienced pain, grief, or misfortune are especially difficult to write but are also especially appreciated. People who have experienced serious health problems, a severe business setback, or the death of a loved one need to know that others are thinking of them and that they are not alone.

Begin by expressing sympathy, offer some personal memory of the deceased, and close by offering comfort.

Some of the most difficult messages to write are those expressing sympathy over someone's death. These notes should be handwritten, when possible. They should not avoid mentioning the death, but they need not dwell on it. Most sympathy notes are short. Begin with an expression of sympathy, mention some specific quality or personal reminiscence about the deceased, and then close with an expression of comfort and affection. An offer to help, if genuine, would be appropriate (see Model 5).

MODEL 5 Goodwill Message

This goodwill message expresses sympathy to the husband of a coworker over his wife's death.

1

~ Robert B. Meyers ~

April 3, 19—

2 Dear Ralph,

I was deeply saddened to learn of Jane's sudden death. It was certainly a great shock to her many friends and colleagues.

Jane had a well-earned reputation here for her top-notch negotiating skills and for her endearing sense of humor. She was an accomplished manager and a good friend, and I shall miss her greatly.

3 If I can help smooth the way in your dealings with our human resources office, I would be honored to help. Please call me on my private line (555-1036) if there is anything I can do.

Affectionately,
Bob

H Ψ C
Executive Vice President

Begins with an expression of sympathy.

Mentions some specific quality or personal reminiscence.

Closes with a genuine offer of help.

Grammar and Mechanics Notes

1 Use either company letterhead or personal stationery for sympathy notes.
2 Insert a comma (instead of a colon) after the salutation of a personal letter.
3 Handwrite the sympathy note, if possible.

The 3Ps

A Routine Adjustment Letter

PROBLEM

You are Kathryn Smith, a correspondent in the customer service department of Home Depot, a large home-supply store. This morning (May 25, 19—), you received the following letter from Mrs. Henrietta Daniels, an angry customer:

Dear Customer Service Manager:

I am really upset at the poor-quality shades that you sell. Two months ago I purchased two pairs of your pleated fabric shades in Wedgewood Blue at $35.99 each for my two bathroom windows. A copy of my $74.32 bill is enclosed.

The color has already begun to fade from these shades. I couldn't believe it when I checked and found that they now look tie-dyed! That is not the look I wish for my home.

Since these shades did not provide the type of wear that I paid for, please refund my $74.32.

Sincerely,

Was this an *effective* claim letter?

You take Mrs. Daniels's itemized bill down to the sales floor and find the model of shades she purchased. You can only conclude that Mrs. Daniels's home has large bathroom windows because the only size this particular shade comes in is 64 inches long by 32 inches wide. And printed right on the tag attached to the shade is this caution: "Warning: The imported fabric in this shade makes them unsuitable for use in areas of high humidity." Clearly, these shades were not made for bathroom use. You call up Mrs. Daniels's account on your computer and find that she has been a loyal customer for many years. You decide, therefore, to refund her $74.32, even though she misused the product. Write the adjustment letter (Mrs. Henrietta Daniels, 117 Pine Forest Drive, Atlanta, GA 30345).

PROCESS

1. What is the purpose of your letter?

   To refund Mrs. Daniels's money, tactfully explain that you were not at fault, and retain her goodwill.

2. Describe your audience.

   - An important customer

   - Angry at you at the present time

   - Now believes your product is of poor quality

   - May be the type of person who doesn't read instructions carefully

3. List in the appropriate order the topics you'll discuss.

   a. Give the refund.

   b. Explain that the shades weren't intended for bathroom use.

   c. Promote your cotton and polyester bathroom curtains.

4. Write a gracious opening sentence for your letter that tells Mrs. Daniels you're refunding the $74.32. Be warm and positive in granting her request. Remember, however, that she was at fault; therefore, do not be overly enthusiastic.

   You have been a valued and faithful customer of ours for several years, Mrs. Daniels, and we are therefore refunding your $74.32.

5. Write the sentence that explains how the shades were misused. Use tactful, neutral, and impersonal language, avoiding the use of second-person pronouns (*you* and *your*).

   As the tag attached to the shades explains, the fine imported woven material used in these shades reflects sunlight without fading but will not withstand the high humidity typical of bathrooms.

6. Now write your closing paragraph, in which you promote your cotton and polyester bathroom curtains.

   For the elegant look and durable service you want in your bathroom, please consider the cotton and polyester bathroom curtains shown in the enclosed brochure. They come in Wedgewood Blue and can be custom-ordered in the exact size you desire.

PRODUCT

2455 Paces Ferry Road, N.W.   •   Atlanta, GA 30339-4024
(770)433-8211

May 25, 19--

Mrs. Henrietta Daniels
117 Pine Forest Drive
Atlanta, GA 30345

Dear Mrs. Daniels:

You have been a valued customer of ours for several years, and we are, therefore, refunding your $74.32. A check for that amount is enclosed. You can simply
return the blue shades to our customer service window the next time you stop
by Home Depot.

As the tag attached to the shades explains, the fine imported woven material
used in these shades reflects sunlight without fading but will not withstand
the high humidity typically found in bathrooms. However, when these shades
are used on windows in living rooms, dining rooms, and bedrooms, they will
provide many years of beautiful and carefree service.

For the elegant look and durable service you want in your bathroom, please
consider the cotton and polyester bathroom curtains shown in the enclosed
brochure. They come in Wedgewood Blue and can be custom-ordered in the
exact size you require. Please come in and let us show them to you.

Sincerely,

Kathryn Smith

Kathryn Smith
Customer Service Department

jmr
Enclosures

U S A
36 USC 380
Proud Sponsor

Most business writing tasks involve routine matters in which the writer conveys either positive or routine information that is of interest to the reader. Such situations call for a direct organizational plan in which the major purpose of the message is presented first. The major idea is followed by any needed background information or additional explanation, and the message ends on a friendly, forward-looking note.

Guidelines for writing routine requests and routine replies are summarized in Checklist 6. Guidelines for writing routine claim letters and routine adjustment letters are summarized in Checklist 7. Use both checklists in composing such messages and in revising your drafts.

Goodwill messages include congratulatory messages, thank-you notes, and sympathy notes. The important points to remember for all of these are to write promptly, using a direct pattern, and to be sincere, specific, and brief. Rather than serving an overt business purpose, these notes are written out of a sense of kindness and friendliness.

KEY TERMS

adjustment letter

claim letter

direct organizational plan

form letter

goodwill message

indirect organizational plan

resale

REVIEW AND DISCUSSION

1. **Communication at PaineWebber Revisited**

   Although most of the 25 letters Gwen Salley writes every day are routine messages answering questions about products and services offered by PaineWebber, she is careful to tailor each to the needs of the reader.

   a. When Salley is writing in response to routine requests for information, should she use the direct or the indirect organizational plan for her letters? Why?

   b. Should Salley provide product information to a long-time customer in a letter or a memo? Why?

   c. Is a form letter an appropriate way for Salley to answer requests from people who are not yet her clients?

2. Explain the basic parts of the direct organizational plan. For what types of messages is this plan appropriate?

3. Assume you need information from a bank about interest rates for a 90-day loan for your small business. Write three versions of the first sentence of your letter, using (a) a direct question, (b) a polite request, and (c) a statement.

4. What guidelines should you follow when asking questions in a routine request?

5. Why should routine requests be answered promptly?

6. Critique each of the following first sentences of a routine reply:

   a. Your letter of November 23 has been referred to me for reply.

   b. Although we will not be able to help you with remodeling your factory, we can provide expert remodeling service for your office area.

   c. Our trained architects and interior designers can provide a complete remodeling plan for your office area.

   d. Thank you for inquiring about our comprehensive remodeling services.

7. Compose an appropriate last sentence for your routine reply for the situation referred to in Exercise 6.

8. Under what circumstances is a form letter desirable for answering routine inquiries?

9. How does a claim letter differ from a complaint letter?

10. Why should claim letters be written promptly? Why should they be answered promptly?

11. What should be the overall tone of the claim letter? of the adjustment letter?

12. Under what circumstances would the direct organizational plan *not* be appropriate for a claim letter? for an adjustment letter?

13. Under what circumstances should you apologize in an adjustment letter?

14. How does an adjustment letter in which the company is at fault differ from an adjustment letter in which the customer is at fault?

15. What is the difference between *resale* and *sales promotion?*

16. Assume you've agreed to replace a customer's broken CD player that has been sent to you for inspection. Compose an appropriate last sentence for this adjustment letter.

17. Why is it not appropriate to include sales promotion in a goodwill message?

Help Wanted

Directions: This letter is from Claire Scriven, marketing manager at American Homes, to Philip Williams, general manager of the Ambassador Hotel. Revise the letter to make it more effective, taking into consideration the editor's marginal comments.

Dear Mr. Williams:

Any positive aspects you can mention?

I feel sure you will want to know about our recent <u>horrible</u>   *tone*

treatment at your hotel. Our sales representatives who stayed there

thought your housekeeping service was substandard.

spec   We rented <u>many rooms in April</u> for our annual marketing

managers' conference. When a few representatives complained about

word   the housekeeping service, I explored the matter <u>farther</u>. Here's what I

learned:

1. Six people commented that at least one lamp in their room had a burned-out light bulb.

int — How were you inconvenienced?

2. Twelve people commented that their rooms sometimes were not cleaned until after 5 p.m., even though they were out of the room all day.

end — Be more specific and courteous.

3. Others spoke about the general uncleanliness of their rooms. What on earth happened?

sp   <u>Sincerly,</u>

EXERCISES

1. **The 3Ps Microwriting Model: Communication Applications at PaineWebber**

   Most of the 25 letters Gwen Salley writes every day are routine messages answering questions about products and services offered by PaineWebber. Because the ultimate goal is to establish or strengthen relationships with customers and prospects, she and other investment executives are careful to tailor their letters to the needs and interests of their readers.

   Problem

   As Gwen Salley's assistant, you are writing a letter in response to a call for information about opening an IRA retirement account. The caller, Joseph Bianchi, has never had an IRA account, so he needs to receive an application form and a booklet about IRAs. A few days after you send your letter, Salley plans to follow up by calling Bianchi to ask about his retirement goals so she can suggest appropriate investment opportunities for his consideration.

   Process

   a. What is the purpose of your letter?
   b. Describe your audience.
   c. List in the appropriate order the topics to be discussed.
   d. Write an opening paragraph for this letter, letting Mr. Bianchi know the purpose of the letter and setting the tone for the establishment of an ongoing relationship.
   e. Write a sentence referring to the items you are enclosing with the letter.
   f. Write a closing paragraph indicating when, how, and why Salley will follow up.

   Product

   Using your knowledge of routine messages, write this letter to Joseph Bianchi (9018 West Third Street, Bartlett, TN 38101).

2. **The 3Ps Microwriting Model: A Claim Letter for a Defective Product**

   Problem

   You are J. R. McCord, purchasing agent for People's Energy Company. On February 3 you ordered a box of four laser cartridges for your Sampson Model 25 printers at $69.35 each, plus $6.85 shipping and handling—total price of $284.25. The catalog description for this cartridge (Part No. 02-8R01656) stated, "Fits Epson and Xerox printers and most compatibles." Since the Sampson is advertised as a Xerox clone printer, you assumed the cartridges would fit. When the order arrived, you discovered that the cartridges didn't fit your Sampson. Although the cartridge is the same shape, it is about ¼ inch thicker and won't seat properly on the spindles.

   You believe that your supplier's misleading advertising caused you to order the wrong model cartridge. You'd like the company to either refund the $284.25 you paid on its Invoice 95-076 or replace the cartridges with ones that do work with your printers. You'll be happy to return all four cartridges if the company will give you instructions for doing so.

   Write your routine claim letter.

   Process

   a. What is the purpose of your letter?
   b. Describe your audience.

c. Write the first sentence of your letter, in which you identify the problem. Strive for an overall tone of courtesy and confidence.

d. Using impersonal language, write the middle section of the letter, in which you tell specifically what went wrong and how you were inconvenienced by the problem.

e. Write the last paragraph of the letter, in which you identify the type of adjustment you expect and also perhaps mention some positive aspect of the company or its products.

Product

Revise, format, and proofread your letter, which should be addressed to the Customer Service Department of Nationwide Office Supply, located at 2640 Kerper Boulevard in Dubuque, IA 52001. Submit to your instructor both your responses to the process questions and your final letter.

3. **Routine Request—Product Information**   Luis St. Jean is a famous design house in France with annual sales of $1.2 billion in clothing, perfume, scarves, and other designer items. Each year it prepares more than 150 original designs for its seasonal collections. As head buyer for Cindy's, an upscale women's clothing store at Mall of America in Minneapolis, you think you might like to begin offering LSJ's line of perfume. You need to know more about pricing, types of perfume offered, minimum ordering quantities, marketing assistance provided by LSJ, and the like. You'd also like to know if you can have exclusive marketing rights to LSJ perfumes in the Minneapolis area and whether you would have to carry LSJ's complete line (you don't think the most expensive perfumes would be big sellers).

Write to Mr. Henri Vixier, License Supervisor, Luis St. Jean, 90513 Cergy, Pointoise Cedex, France, seeking answers to your questions.

4. **Routine Request—Membership Information**   Although your part-time job is only temporary while you finish college, your boss wants you to gain more experience in public speaking and has suggested that you join Toastmasters International, an organization devoted to helping its members practice and improve their public-speaking skills. You are interested in determining whether your town has a local chapter and, if so, the time and place of meetings, the amount of annual dues, and the like.

Compose an e-mail message to Toastmasters International (e-mail address: *tminfo@toastmasters.org*) asking several specific pertinent questions. E-mail a copy of your message to your instructor. Follow your instructor's direction regarding whether to mail your message to Toastmasters.

5. **Routine Request—Letter of Recommendation**   As part of your application papers for a one-semester internship at American Express, you are asked to include a letter of recommendation from one of your business professors. You made a good grade in MGT 382: Wage and Salary Administration, which you took three semesters ago from Dr. Dennis Thavinet in the management department at your university. You liked the course so well that you missed class only twice (for good reasons). Although you were not one of the most vocal members in class, Dr. Thavinet did commend you for your group project. American Express (at 1850 East Camelback Road, Phoenix, AZ 85017) wants to know especially about your ability to work well with others.

Compose (but do not send) an e-mail message to Dr. Thavinet (*djthavinet@marsu.edu*), asking for a letter of recommendation. You would like him to respond within one week.

6. **Routine Request—Product Information**   Choose an advertisement from a newspaper or magazine for a product or service about which you have some interest. The ad probably does not have sufficient space to provide all the information you need to make an intelligent purchase decision. Write to the company (if necessary, locate its address using one of the directories available in your library or on the Internet), asking at least three questions about the product. Be sure to mention where you learned about the product. Try to encourage a prompt response.

Attach a copy of the ad to your letter and submit both to your instructor. Your instructor may ask you to mail the letter so that the class can later compare the types of responses received from different companies.

7. **Routine Response—Student Information**   As the dean of admissions for Eastern State University, you have received a letter from Linda O'Kelly, a first-year student at the State University of New York, 665 Catskill Hall, Oswego, NY 13126. She is interested in transferring to your school, but she has a number of questions about the courses and the transfer requirements. Here are her questions and the answers:
   a. *Does the school offer an undergraduate degree in environmental engineering?* Yes, the school initiated this program two years ago.
   b. *What are the requirements for transfer students?* Transfer students must have at least a 2.75 first-year GPA to be considered for admission as sophomores.
   c. *Can all courses taken at another school be transferred for credit?* No, only courses for which Eastern State has an equivalent offering are accepted for credit.

Your school accepts only a few transfer students each semester, but you don't want to discourage Ms. O'Kelly (who may be among the few accepted). Respond to her letter and mention that you are sending additional information (such as a college catalog) in a separate package.

8. **Routine Response—Product Information**   As the business manager for Maison Richard, a 200-seat restaurant in Seattle, you received an inquiry from Chris Shearing, 1926 Second Avenue, Seattle, WA 98101. She had several questions about the meat and fish served in your restaurant. Here are her questions and the answers:
   a. *Are the cattle from which your beef comes allowed to roam freely on an open range instead of being fattened in cramped feedlots?* No, allowing free-roaming would increase the muscle tissue in the beef, making it less tender.
   b. *Are the cattle fed antibiotics and hormones?* Yes, to ensure a healthy animal and to promote faster growth.
   c. *Do your trout come from lakes and streams?* No, they're farm-grown, which is more economical and results in less disease.

Ms. Shearing is a well-known animal-rights activist, and you want to present your case as positively as possible to avoid the loss of her goodwill and any negative publicity that might result. Respond to her letter, supplying whatever other appropriate information you feel is reasonable.

9. **Routine Response—Form Letter**   You are the executive producer for "The Sherry Show," a popular syndicated morning talk show featuring Sherry Baker as host. The show features interviews and panel discussions on a wide variety of current topics.

Because Sherry takes questions and comments from the audience, it is important to have a full house each day. When the show started two years ago, you had trouble filling the 150-seat studio. Now, however, you get more ticket requests than you can accommodate. Anyone wanting a ticket must write at least four months ahead and can request no more than four tickets (which are free). The show tapes from 9:30 until 11 A.M. Monday through Friday each week. Tickets are for reserved seats, but any seats not occupied by 9 A.M. are released on a first-come, first-served basis. Studio doors close promptly at 9:15 each morning and do not reopen until the show ends at 11 A.M. Children under age 12 are not admitted.

Write a form letter telling people how to order tickets and conveying other needed information. The letter will be sent to anyone who requests ticket information.

10. **Work-Team Communication—Routine Response**   You are a member of the Presidents' Council, an organization made up of the presidents of each student organization on campus. You just received a memorandum from Dr. Robin H. Hill, dean of students, wanting to know what types of social projects the student organizations on campus have been engaged in during the past year. The dean must report to the board of trustees on the important role played by student organizations—both in the life of the university and community and in the development of student leadership and social skills. She wants to include such information as student-run programs on drug and alcohol abuse, community service, and fund-raising.

Working in groups of four, identify and summarize the types of social projects that student organizations at your institution have completed this year. Then organize and synthesize your findings into a one-page memo to Dr. Hill. After writing your first draft, have each member review and comment on the draft. Then revise as needed and submit. Use only factual data for this assignment.

11. **Claim Letter—Incorrectly Personalized Product**   You are the marketing manager for Statewide Telemarketing, a company that conducts telemarketing campaigns on behalf of local banks, department stores, and insurance agencies. To advertise your company, you recently ordered 500 dark blue personalized pens from Midwest Stationery, a local stationery store. In turn, the store sent the order to a Chicago manufacturer, which stamped your firm's name on the pens and shipped the order directly to your office. However, when the pens arrived, the personalization was incorrectly spelled "Statwide Telemarketing." When you called the stationery store, the salesperson instructed you to write directly to the manufacturer and to include your original order along with one of the pens.

Write to the manufacturer, Prairie Pens, at 7140 Rush Street, Chicago, IL 60611, to request a replacement order. You are willing to return the pens but not to pay the postage; you think the manufacturer should pay for any return postage. You plan to distribute these pens at a convention next month, so you would like the replacement order to arrive within two weeks.

12. **Claim Letter—Inaccurate Reporting**   As the marketing manager for ReSolve, a basic computer spreadsheet program for Windows, you were pleased that your product was reviewed in the current issue of *Computing Trends.* The review praised your product for its "lightning-fast speed and convenient user interface." You were not pleased, however, that your product was downgraded because it lacked high-level graphics capability. The reviewer compared ReSolve with full-featured spreadsheet programs costing, on average, $200 more than your program. No wonder, then, that your program rated a 6.6 out of 10, coming in third out of the five pro-

grams reviewed. If your program had been compared with similar low-level programs, you feel certain that ReSolve would have easily come out on top.

Although you do not want to get the magazine upset with your company (Software Entrepreneurs, Inc.), you do feel that it should compare apples with apples and should conduct another review of your program. Write to Roberta J. Horton, their review editor, at 200 Public Square in Cleveland, OH 44114, and tell her so.

13. **Claim Letter—Poor Service**   As the owner of Parker Central, a small plumbing business, you try to instill in all your employees a *customer-first* attitude. Therefore, you were quite put off by your own treatment yesterday (July 13) at the hands of the receptionist at Englehard Investment Service (231 East 50 Street, Indianapolis, IN 46205). You showed up 20 minutes early for your 2:30 P.M. appointment with Jack Nutley, an investment counselor with the firm. You were meeting with him for the first time to discuss setting up a Simplified Employee Pension (SEP) plan for your 20 employees.

To begin with, the receptionist ignored you for at least five minutes until she finished the last paragraph of a document she was typing. Then, after finding out whom you wanted to see, she did not even call Jack's office to announce your arrival until 2:30 P.M. Finally, you learned that Jack had just become ill and had to go to the doctor. So you wasted half an afternoon and were also insulted by the receptionist's rude treatment.

You decide to write to Jack Nutley about the receptionist's office behavior. Your *claim* is for better service in the future. You want him to know that if you are going to continue to be treated in such a manner, you have no interest in doing business with his firm. Write the claim letter.

14. **Adjustment Letter—Company at Fault**   Assume the role of customer service representative at Nationwide Office Supply (see Exercise 2). You've received Mr. McCord's letter (People's Energy Company, Wheatley Road, Old Westbury, NY 11568). You've done some background investigation and have learned that what the customer said is true—the Sampson Model 25 *is* a Xerox clone and your catalog *does* state that this cartridge fits Xerox printers and most compatibles. The problem came about because the Model 25, Sampson's newest model, was introduced shortly after your catalog went to press. This model's spindle is slightly shorter than previous Sampson models.

Unfortunately, you do not carry in your inventory a cartridge that will fit the Sampson Model 25. The customer should return the case COD, marking on the address label "Return Authorization 95-076R." In the meantime, you've authorized a refund of $284.25; Mr. McCord should receive the check within ten days. Convey this information to Mr. McCord.

15. **Adjustment Letter—Customer at Fault**   Assume the role of customer service representative at Nationwide Office Supply (see Exercises 2 and 14). You've done some background investigation and have learned that Mr. McCord was somewhat mistaken in stating that the Sampson Model 25 is a Xerox clone. What Sampson advertises instead is that the Model 25 uses the same character set as Xerox printers; this means that all fonts available from Xerox can also be downloaded to the Model 25. Sampson neither states nor implies that Xerox-compatible cartridges or other supplies will fit its machines.

Because the customer made an innocent mistake and you will be able to resell the unused cartridges, you decide to honor his claim anyway. He should return the case prepaid, marking on the address label "Return Authorization 95-076R." In the meantime, you're shipping him four cartridges (Part No. 02-9R32732) that *will* work on the Model 25; he can expect to receive them within ten days. You're also enclosing your summer catalog.

16. **Adjustment Letter—Company at Fault**   Assume that you are the customer service representative at Prairie Pens who receives the claim letter from Ann Marie Thompson of Statewide Telemarketing, 25830 West Oaklawn Drive, Springdale, AR 72764 (see Exercise 11). You track down the original production order and discover that the person responsible for setting type for the screen made an error. Although you can screen another 500 pens and ship them in one day, your warehouse is out of dark blue pens. You do have royal blue pens, so you decide to substitute these and charge Statewide 25% less than they were billed for their first-choice color. You plan to cancel the first invoice and prepare a new invoice with the lower price, which should go a long way toward softening the error.

   Although the customer offered to return the faulty shipment, you have no use for these personalized pens. However, you can turn these unwanted pens into a gesture of goodwill. When you write to Statewide, note that you will not bill the customer for these pens and suggest that the customer keep the pens for office use. Let Ms. Thompson know—in a letter you will send by fax—what you are doing to solve her problem, and assure her that the new pens will be shipped tomorrow.

17. **Adjustment Letter—Form Letter**   As the new review editor at *Computing Trends* (see Exercise 12), you've already come to expect that whenever products are panned in your magazine, you can expect a negative reaction from the developers. You're happy to hear from them, however, because they sometimes bring to light additional information that your readers will find helpful. Unless the review contained a factual error, your policy is to publish the letters in the "Feedback" column in a future issue. (In this particular instance, you compared ReSolve with the full-featured spreadsheets because that is exactly how Software Entrepreneurs, Inc., advertises the program.)

   You review most major software products once yearly in your state-of-the-art computer labs, using criteria established by your readers. Write a form letter that you can send to product developers who write to complain about the review of their products, giving them this information.

18. **Adjustment Letter—Form Letter**   Assume the role of fulfillment representative at Paperbacks by Post, a book club that automatically mails members a selected paperback every month unless they send back a postcard declining the shipment. Although the system works well most of the time, occasionally a member receives a book even after returning the refusal postcard. In such cases, your company asks the member to take the parcel to the post office, which will return it at company expense. You also cancel the invoice and send the member a discount coupon toward future selections.

   Write a form letter that you can send to members who complain about receiving an unwanted shipment. Advise them to act promptly, posting returns no later than two weeks after receipt.

19. **Goodwill Letter—Appreciation**   Think of a recent speech you have heard and enjoyed—perhaps by a speaker at a student organization meeting, a speaker sponsored by your university, a guest speaker in class, or some similar presentation. If necessary, do some research to locate a correct mailing address for this person. Then write this person a letter of appreciation, letting him or her know how much you enjoyed and benefited from his or her remarks. (If you have not heard a speech you enjoyed lately, write a former professor, expressing appreciation for what you learned in class.) Use only actual data for this assignment.

**CONTINUING
CASE 7**

The Case of the Missing Briefcase

It was Friday afternoon and Paul Yu was determined to take care of all pending correspondence before leaving for the weekend. On Tuesday, he had received a memo from Maurice Potts, an Urban Systems sales representative, that said in part:

> Last week I made a sales presentation to Albany Electronics and carried two briefcases with me—my regular case plus a second case filled with handouts and brochures.

At the conclusion of my presentation, I distributed the handouts and brochures, picked up my regular briefcase and left—completely forgetting about my second case. When I discovered the following morning what had happened, I immediately called Albany Electronics, but they have been unable to locate the missing case.

This leather briefcase was two months old and cost $287.50 (see the attached sales slip). Since the Urban Systems policy manual states that employees will be reimbursed for all reasonable costs of carrying out their assigned duties, may I please be reimbursed for the $287.50 lost briefcase.

Paul had been thinking about this situation all week; he had even discussed it with Marc, but Marc told him to make whatever decision he thought reasonable. On the one hand, Maurice is a good sales representative. And the policy manual does contain the exact sentence Maurice quoted. On the other hand, Paul does not feel that US should be responsible for such obvious mistakes as this; assuming responsibility for such mistakes would not only be expensive but also might encourage padded expense accounts.

Finally, Paul decides to do two things. First, he'll write a memo to the sales staff, interpreting more fully company policy. Policy 14.2 is entitled *Reimbursement of Expenses,* and Paragraph 14.2.b states, "With the approval of their supervisors, employees will be reimbursed for all reasonable costs of carrying out their assigned duties." Paul wants the sales staff to know that in the future he intends to interpret this policy to mean that any personal property that is stolen will be reimbursed at its present value (not its replacement value) if reasonable care has been taken to secure such property, if the incident is reported within three days, and if the value of the property can be determined. Lost or damaged personal property will normally not be reimbursed, no matter what the reason. Any sales representative may, of course, appeal Paul's decisions to the vice president of marketing.

Second, because the present policy may not have been sufficiently clear, Paul will write a memo to Maurice and agree to reimburse him $287.50 for the briefcase. He'll also enclose a copy of the new policy memo he is sending out to the sales staff.

Critical Thinking

1. How reasonable was Maurice Potts's claim? Was the intent of the policy clear? Should Paul have reimbursed him? Why or why not?

2. How reasonable is Paul's interpretation of the company policy?

Writing Projects

3. Compose the two documents that Paul intends to write: the memo to the sales staff and the memo to Maurice Potts. Format them in an appropriate style.

8

Persuasive Messages

An Insider's Perspective

When Jim Waltman sits down to draft a persuasive message, a lot is riding on his words. As Director of Refuges and Wildlife for the nonprofit Wilderness Society, Waltman uses communication to promote the conservation of America's national wildlife refuges and endangered species. To influence the attitudes and actions of government leaders, company executives, and the general public, he writes letters, posts messages on the World Wide Web, and talks with reporters from newspapers, magazines, television, and radio. In addition, he regularly enlists the assistance of The Wilderness Society's 259,000 members in persuading members of Congress to protect wetlands, forests, rivers, or deserts from threats such as encroaching development.

Before writing a persuasive message, Waltman and his colleagues at the Society analyze the audience to determine how much people know and how people feel about an issue. He can get a better idea of what may interest his readers by looking at demographic data (such as age) as well as social and cultural data (such as locally popular outdoor activities). "Understanding the needs and concerns of people in each part of the country helps us target messages by region," he says. "For example, knowing the favorite outdoor sport in an area allows us to write persuasively about how participants will be affected by an environmental issue in that region."

When Congress is considering a bill that affects the environment, Waltman will research the views of members of the Senate and the House of Representatives so he can plan his messages accordingly. "When we're trying to influence public policy, we have to look at how the votes stack up and where we need to do more work in urging support and better understanding of the special places we're trying to protect," he explains. In addition to communicating his organization's position to legislators, he uses letters and media exposure to persuade voters to take action.

Waltman generally relies on a combination of logical and emotional appeals to create interest and add impact to his persuasive arguments. "We've learned to take a broader, more sophisticated approach," he says, "and we've become more skilled at

<aside>
COMMUNICATION OBJECTIVES

After you have finished this chapter, you should be able to

■ Decide when to use a direct or an indirect organizational plan for persuasive messages.

■ Compose a persuasive message promoting an idea.

■ Compose a persuasive message requesting a favor.

■ Compose a persuasive claim.

■ Compose a sales letter.
</aside>

explaining the economics as well as the ecology of an environmental issue." He cites expert opinions, statistics, and examples to support his arguments; he also includes photos in brochures and speeches to visually reinforce what may be lost if the audience doesn't act.

To capture the audience's attention at the beginning of a persuasive letter, Waltman stresses the local angle on a particular issue. "The goal is to make readers understand that something they care about is at stake," he notes. "We let them know that they have the power to make a difference, and we suggest a few ways that they can help." Then, to make it easy for readers to take action, he provides all the information that readers need, including contact names, addresses, phone and fax numbers, and e-mail addresses, when available.

Not long ago, The Wilderness Society successfully used persuasive messages to defend the Endangered Species Act. Using letters, posters, magazine articles, and other techniques, Waltman and his colleagues explained that imperiled animals and plants promise to be an important source of medicines in the coming years, as dangerous diseases continue to emerge and evolve. "Protecting the natural world is the best medicine for our own future health," he says. Preprinted labels bearing this message went out to all members, with the request that they wrap the labels around empty medicine bottles and ship the bottles to members of Congress. Soon afterward, thousands of medicine bottles landed in Washington—and the result was stronger Congressional support for the Endangered Species Act.

Jim Waltman

Director of Refuges and Wildlife, The Wilderness Society (Washington, D.C.)

Jim Waltman hiking in the Arctic National Wildlife Refuge in Alaska; The Wilderness Society opposes proposals to open this area to oil drilling.

Planning the Persuasive Message

Persuasion is the process of motivating someone to take a specific action or to support a particular idea. Persuasion motivates someone to believe something or to do something that he or she would not otherwise have done. Every day many people try to persuade you to do certain things or to believe certain ideas. Likewise, you have many opportunities to persuade others each day.

As an executive, you will also need to persuade others to do as you want. You may need to persuade a superior to adopt a certain proposal, a supplier to refund the purchase price of a defective product, or a potential customer to buy your product or service. In a sense, *all* business communication involves persuasion. Even if your primary purpose is to inform, you still want your reader to accept your perspective and to believe the information you present.

Persuasion is necessary when the other person initially resists your efforts.

The essence of persuasion is overcoming initial resistance. The reader may resist your efforts for any number of reasons. Your proposal may require the reader to spend time or money—at the very least, you're asking for his or her time to *read* your message. Or the reader may have had bad experiences in the past with similar requests or may hold opinions that predispose him or her against your request.

Your job in writing a persuasive message, then, is to talk your readers into something, to convince them that your point of view is the most appropriate one. You'll have the best chance of succeeding if you tailor your message to your audience, provide your readers with reasons they will find convincing, and anticipate and deflect or disarm their objections. Such tailor-made writing requires careful planning; you need to define your purpose clearly and analyze your audience.

Purpose

Decide specifically what you want the reader to do as a result of your message.

The purpose of a persuasive message is to motivate the reader to agree with you or to do as you ask. Unless you are clear about the specific results you wish to achieve, you won't be able to plan an effective strategy that will achieve your goals.

Suppose, for example, you want to convince your superior to adopt a complex proposal. The purpose of your memo might be to persuade your superior to either (1) adopt your proposal, (2) approve a pilot test of the proposal, or (3) schedule a meeting where you can present your proposal in person and answer any questions. Achieving any one of these three goals may require a different strategy. Similarly, if you're writing a sales letter, you must determine whether your purpose is to actually make a sale, to get the reader to request more information, or to schedule a sales call. Again, your specific goal determines your strategy.

Knowing your purpose lets you know what kind of information to include in your persuasive message. "Knowledge is power" and never is this saying truer than when writing persuasive messages. In order to write effectively about an idea or product, you must know the idea or product intimately. If you're promoting an idea, consider all the ramifications of your proposal.

■ Are there competing proposals that should be considered?

■ What are the implications for the organization if your proposal is adopted and it *fails*?

■ How does your proposal fit in with the existing plans and direction of the organization?

Writers of persuasive messages must know their audience and personalize their message to best meet the needs and interests of the audience. Sometimes the intended audience is so diverse that different messages are warranted. Here, New York City's main post office promotes its first-class phone card in five languages on colorful banners.

If you're promoting a product, how is the product made, marketed, operated, and maintained? You also need to learn this same information about your competition's products so you can determine the major differences between yours and theirs.

Audience Analysis

The more you're able to promote the features of your idea or product as satisfying a *specific* need of your audience, the more persuasive your message will be. Suppose, for example, you're promoting a line of men's shoes; you should stress different features, depending upon your audience.

Young executive:	stylish . . . comes in various shades of black and brown . . . a perfect accessory to your business wardrobe
Mid-career executive:	perfect detailing . . . 12-hour comfort . . . stays sharp-looking through days of travel
Retired executive:	economical . . . comfortable . . . a no-nonsense type of shoe

The point to remember is to know your audience and to personalize your message to best meet its needs and interests. Use the "you" attitude to achieve the results you want. When sending a form letter to perhaps thousands of readers, your approach cannot, of necessity, be as personal. Nevertheless, you should still strive to make the approach as personal as possible.

Knowledge and Attitude of the Reader   What does the reader already know about the topic? Determining this will tell you how much background information you should include. What is the reader's predisposition toward the topic? If it is negative, then where one or two reasons might ordinarily suffice, you will need to give more. Initial resistance also calls for more objective, verifiable evidence than if the reader were initially neutral. You also need to learn *why* the reader is resistant so that you can tailor your arguments to overcome those specific objections.

Show how your reader will be affected by your proposal.

Effect on the Reader   How will your proposal affect the reader? If the reader is being asked to commit resources (time or money), discuss the rewards for doing so. If the reader is being asked to endorse some proposal, provide enough specific information to enable the reader to make an informed decision. The reader wants to know "What's in it for me?" *You* are already convinced of the wisdom of your proposal. Your job is to let the reader know the benefits of doing as you ask.

To be persuasive, you must present *specific, believable* evidence. However, one of the worst mistakes you could make would be to simply describe the features of the product or list the advantages of doing as you ask. Instead, put yourself in the reader's place. Discuss how the reader will benefit from your proposal. Emphasize the *reader* rather than the product or idea you're promoting.

> **NOT:**   The San Diego Accounting Society would like you to speak to us on the topic of expensing versus capitalizing 401-C assets.
>
> **BUT:**   Speaking to the San Diego Accounting Society would enable you to present your firm's views on the controversial topic of expensing versus capitalizing 401-C assets.

Sometimes your readers won't benefit *directly* from doing as you ask. If you are trying to entice your employees to contribute to the United Way, for example, it would be difficult to discuss direct reader benefits. In such situations, discuss the *indirect* benefits of reader participation; for example, show how someone other than you, the solicitor of the funds, will benefit.

Discussing indirect benefits prevents your request from sounding selfish.

> Your contribution will enable inner-city youngsters, many of whom have never even been outside the city of Columbus, to see pandas living and thriving in their natural habitat.

A reader who trusts you is more likely to trust your message.

Writer Credibility   What is your credibility with the reader? The more trustworthy you are, the more trustworthy your message will appear. Credibility comes from many sources. You may be perceived as being credible by virtue of the position you hold or by virtue of being a well-known authority. Or you may achieve credibility for your proposal by supplying convincing evidence, such as facts and statistics that can be verified.

Suppose, for example, you have worked in an advertising production department and have extensive experience with color reproduction. If you are writing a memo to a colleague suggesting that certain photos will not reproduce clearly and should therefore be replaced, you probably don't need to explain your expertise. Your colleague is likely to believe you. But if you are writing a letter to the photographer, who does not know you, you would probably want to discuss past incidents that lead you to conclude the photos should be replaced.

Organizing a Persuasive Request

A persuasive request seeks to motivate the reader to accept your idea (rather than to buy your product). The purpose of your message and your knowledge of the reader will help determine the content of your message and the sequence in which you discuss each topic.

Determining How to Start the Message

In the past, it was common practice to organize *all* persuasive messages by using an indirect organizational plan—presenting the rationale first, followed by the major idea (the request for action)—and this plan is still used for many persuasive messages. However, writers today should determine which organizational plan (direct or indirect) will help them better achieve their objectives.

Direct Plan—Present the Major Idea First   Most superiors prefer to have memos from their subordinates organized in the direct style introduced in Chapter 7. Thus, when writing persuasive memos that travel up the organization, you should generally present the main idea (your recommendation) first, followed by the supporting evidence. The direct organizational plan saves time and immediately satisfies the reader's curiosity about your purpose. To get readers to accept your proposal when using the direct plan, present your recommendation along with the criteria or brief rationale in the first paragraph.

Prefer the direct plan when writing persuasive messages to your superior.

> **NOT:**   I recommend we hold our Pittsburgh sales meeting at the Mark-Congress Hotel.

> **BUT:**   I have evaluated three hotels as possible meeting sites for our Pittsburgh sales conference and recommend we meet at the Mark-Congress Hotel. As discussed below, the Mark-Congress is centrally located, has the best meeting facilities, and is moderately priced.

In general, prefer the direct organizational plan for persuasive messages when any of the following conditions apply:

- You are writing to superiors within the organization.

- Your audience is predisposed to listen objectively to your request.

- The proposal does not require strong persuasion (that is, there are no major obstacles present).

- The proposal is long or complex (a reader may become impatient if your main point is buried in a long report).

- You know that your reader prefers the direct approach.

Indirect Plan—Gain the Reader's Attention First   Unfortunately, many times your readers will initially resist your suggestions. Your job then is to explain the merits of your proposal and show how the reader will benefit from doing as you ask. Because a reluctant reader is more likely to agree to an idea *after* he or she understands its merits, your plan of organization is to convince the reader before asking for action.

Thus, you should use the indirect organizational plan when writing to subordinates, when strong persuasion is needed, or when you know that your reader prefers the indirect plan. When using the indirect plan, you delay asking for action until after you've presented your reasons. A subject line is therefore not generally used in persuasive letters. If a subject line is a standard part of the heading for your organization's memorandums, make it neutral. Don't announce your purpose immediately, but rather, lead up to it gradually.

NOT: SUBJECT: Proposal to Sell the Roper Division

BUT: SUBJECT: Analysis of Roper Division Profitability

The first test of a good opening sentence in a persuasive request is whether it is interesting enough to catch and keep the reader's attention. It won't matter how much evidence you have marshaled to support your case if the recipient does not bother to continue reading carefully after the first sentence.

A **rhetorical question** is often effective as an opening sentence. A rhetorical question is asked strictly to get the reader thinking about the topic of your message; a literal answer is not expected. Of course, questions with obvious answers are not effective motivators for further reading and, in fact, may insult the reader's intelligence. Similarly, yes-or-no questions rarely make good lead-ins because pondering an answer doesn't require much thought.

NOT: How would you like to save our department $7,500 yearly?

BUT: What do you think the labor costs are for changing just one light bulb? $2? $5? More?

NOT: Did you know that the Hartford Community Fund is more than 50 years old?

BUT: What do Tina Turner and the Hartford Community Fund have in common?

Sometimes an unusual fact or unexpected statement will draw the reader into the message. At other times, you might want to select some statement about which the reader and writer will agree—to immediately establish some common ground.

Our company spent more money on janitorial service last year than on research and development.

A five-year-old boy taught me an important lesson last week.

Automotive News calls your 6-year/60,000 mile warranty the best in the business. (*opening for a claim letter*)

The opening statement must be relevant.

Your opening statement must also be relevant to the purpose of your message. If it is too far off the topic or misleads the reader, you risk losing goodwill, and the reader may simply stop reading. At the very least, the reader will feel confused or deceived, making persuasion more difficult.

Keep your opening statement short. Often an opening paragraph of just one sentence will make the message inviting to read. Few readers have the patience to wade through a long introduction to figure out the purpose of the message. In summary, make the opening for a persuasive message written in the indirect organizational plan interesting, relevant, and short. The purpose is to make sure your reader gets to the body of your message.

Creating Interest and Justifying Your Request

Regardless of whether your opening is written in a direct or indirect style, you must now begin the process of convincing the reader that your request is reasonable. This process may require several paragraphs of discussion, depending on how much evidence you think will be needed to convince the reader. Because it takes more space to state *why* something should be done than simply to state *that* it should be done, persuasive requests are typically longer than other types of messages.

To convince your readers, you must be objective, specific, logical, and reasonable. Avoid emotionalism, obvious flattery, insincerity, and exaggeration. Let your evidence carry the weight of your argument.

Provide convincing evidence and use a reasonable tone.

NOT: Locating our plant in Suffolk instead of in Norfolk would result in considerable savings.

BUT: Locating our plant in Suffolk instead of in Norfolk would result in annual savings of nearly $175,000, as shown in Table 3.

NOT: Why should it take a thousand phone calls to convince your computer to credit my account for $38.50?

BUT: Even after five phone calls over the past three weeks, I find that $38.50 has still not been credited to my account.

The type of evidence you present depends, of course, on the circumstances. The usual types of evidence are these:

■ *Facts and statistics: Facts* are objective statements whose truth can be verified; *statistics* are facts consisting of numbers. Both must be relevant and accurate. For example, statistics that were accurate five years ago may no longer be accurate today.

■ *Expert opinion:* Testimony from authorities on the topic might be presented if their input is relevant and, if necessary, you can supply the experts' credentials.

■ *Examples:* Specific cases or incidents used to illustrate the point under discussion should be relevant, representative, and complete.

Present the benefits (either direct or indirect) that will accompany the adoption of your proposal, and provide enough background and objective evidence to enable the reader to make an informed decision.

Dealing with Obstacles

Ignoring any obvious obstacles to granting your request would provide the reader a ready excuse to refuse your request. Assume, for example, that you're trying to persuade a supplier to provide an in-store demonstrator of the firm's products—even though you know it's against their company policy to do so. If you ignore this factor, you're simply inviting the reader to respond that company policy prohibits granting your request. Instead, your strategy should be to show that *even considering such an obstacle,* your request is still reasonable, perhaps as follows:

Last year we sold 356 of your Golden Microwave ovens. We believe the extensive publicity our sale will generate (as well as our previous sales performance) justifies your temporarily setting aside your policy and providing an in-store demonstrator. The ease of use and the actual cooked results that your representative will be able to display are sure to increase the sales of your microwaves.

Note the reader benefits in the last sentence.

If you're asking someone to speak to a professional organization but are unable to provide an honorarium, emphasize the free publicity the speaker will receive and the impact that the speaker's remarks will have on the audience. If you're asking for

How Can You Collect Money That Is Due You?

The primary purpose of collection messages is to collect past-due accounts. The secondary purpose is to retain the debtor's goodwill. The collection process usually begins with the mailing of the monthly statement, and the vast majority of accounts are paid by the due date. For those that are not, companies often use a four-stage series of messages: reminder, inquiry, appeal, and ultimatum (more than one message may be sent at any one of these stages).

SPOTLIGHT 13

ON LAW AND ETHICS

For All Collection Letters

1. Ensure that the information is accurate and that your message follows all federal and state laws regarding collection practices.
2. Adopt a tone of reasonableness and helpfulness; avoid anger.
3. Send letters promptly and—if payment doesn't result—at systematic intervals, so that the debt is never out of the reader's mind.
4. In every letter include the reader's account number, the amount owed, and a postpaid envelope.

Reminder Stage

1. Assume the reader has simply overlooked paying.
2. Avoid embarrassing the customer by sending a personal letter. Instead, send a second copy of the bill or an impersonal form letter.

Inquiry Stage

1. Assume the reader is deliberately not paying because of some unusual circumstance.
2. Send a short, personalized letter, written in the direct pattern.

3. Remind the reader that payment is late, ask why the account hasn't been paid, and solicit either payment or a plan for payment.
4. Don't provide excuses and don't suggest that the reader has merely overlooked payment.

Appeal Stage

1. Assume the reader must be persuaded to pay.
2. Write a persuasive letter—in the indirect pattern.
3. Select one central appeal to use and stress it throughout the letter. The most effective appeals (in increasing order of forcefulness) are resale, fair play, pride, self-interest, and fear.
4. Make the opening attention-getter interesting, short, and related to the central appeal.
5. In the middle section, continue to stress the central appeal, using reader benefits and positive language to motivate payment.
6. Close by directly asking for payment, combining your request with another reader benefit.

Ultimatum Stage

1. Assume the reader has no intention of paying.
2. Write in a direct pattern; at this point, maintaining goodwill is less important than securing payment.
3. In a polite and businesslike manner, explain exactly what you intend to do if the bill is not paid. Review the efforts you've already made to collect.
4. Give the reader one last opportunity to pay, setting a specific deadline.

confidential information, discuss how you will treat it as such. If you're asking for a large donation, explain how payment can be made on the installment plan or by payroll deduction and point out the tax-deductible feature of the donation. (See Spotlight 13—On Law and Ethics for tips on asking for money that is due you.)

Even though you must address the major obstacles, do *not* emphasize them. Subordinate this discussion by devoting relatively little space to it, by dealing with obstacles in the same sentence as a reader benefit, or by putting the discussion in the middle of a paragraph. Regardless of how you do it, show the reader that you're aware of the obvious obstacles and that despite them, your proposal still has merit.

Motivating Action

Although your request has been stated (direct organizational plan) or implied (indirect organizational plan) earlier, give a direct statement of the request late in the message—after most of the background information and reader benefits have been thoroughly covered. Make the specific action that you want clear and easy to take. For example, if the reader agrees to do as you ask, how is he or she to let you know? Will a phone call suffice, or is a written reply necessary? If a phone call is adequate, have you provided a phone number? If you're asking for a favor that requires a written response, have you included a stamped, addressed envelope?

Ask for the desired action in a confident tone. If your request or proposal is reasonable, there is no need to apologize, and you surely do not want to supply the reader with excuses for refusing. Take whatever steps you can to ensure a prompt reply.

NOT: I know you're a busy person, but I would appreciate your completing this questionnaire.

BUT: So that this information will be available for the financial managers attending our fall conference, I would appreciate your returning the questionnaire by May 15.

Note the indirect benefit implied.

NOT: If you agree this proposal is worthwhile, please let me know by June 1.

BUT: To enable us to have this plan in place before the opening of our new branch on June 1, simply initial this memo and return it to me.

Note the motivation for a prompt reply.

Checklist 8 (on page 230) summarizes guidelines to use in writing persuasive requests. Although you will not be able to use all these suggestions in each persuasive request, you should use them as an overall framework for structuring your persuasive message.

Common Types of Persuasive Requests

In many ways, writing a persuasive request is more difficult than writing a sales letter because reader benefits are not always so obvious in persuasive requests. This section provides specific strategies and examples for selling an idea, requesting a favor, and writing a persuasive claim letter.

Selling an Idea

You will have many opportunities to use your education and experience to help solve problems faced by your organization. On the job you will frequently write letters or memorandums proposing one alternative over another, suggesting a new procedure, or in some other way recommending some course of action. Organize such messages logically, showing what the problem is, how you intend to solve the

---

✔ CHECKLIST 8   **Persuasive Requests**

Determine How to Start the Message

✔ **Direct Plan**—Use a direct organizational plan when writing to superiors, when your audience is predisposed to listen objectively to your request, when the proposal does not require strong persuasion, when the proposal is long or complex, or when you know your reader prefers the direct approach. Present the recommendation, along with the criteria or brief rationale, in the first paragraph.

✔ **Indirect Plan**—Use an indirect organizational plan when writing to subordinates, when strong persuasion is needed, or when you know your reader prefers the indirect approach. Start by gaining the reader's attention.

  a. Make the first sentence motivate the reader to continue reading. Use, for example, a rhetorical question, unusual fact, unexpected statement, or common-ground statement.

  b. Keep the opening paragraph short (often just one sentence), relevant to the message, and, when appropriate, related to a reader benefit.

Create Interest and Justify Your Request

✔ Devote the major part of your message to justifying your request. Give enough background and evidence to enable the reader to make an informed decision.

✔ Use facts and statistics, expert opinion, and examples to support your proposal. Ensure that the evidence is accurate, relevant, representative, and complete.

✔ Use an objective, logical, reasonable, and sincere tone. Avoid obvious flattery, emotionalism, and exaggeration.

✔ Present the evidence in terms of either direct or indirect reader benefits.

Minimize Obstacles

✔ Do not ignore obstacles or any negative aspects of your request. Instead, show that even considering them, your request is still reasonable.

✔ Subordinate the discussion of obstacles by position and amount of space devoted to the topic.

Ask Confidently for Action

✔ State (or restate) the specific request late in the message—after most of the benefits have been discussed.

✔ Make the desired action clear and easy for the reader to take, use a confident tone, do not apologize, and do not supply excuses.

✔ End on a forward-looking note, continuing to stress reader benefits.

---

problem, and why your solution is sound. Write in an objective style and provide evidence to support your claims.

The memo in Model 6 illustrates the selling of an idea. In this case, a marketing supervisor for an auto-parts supplier is asking the vice president to reassign parking spaces to give preference to those employees driving American-made cars. Because the memo is written to his superior, the writer uses a direct organizational style.

Requesting a Favor

Favors require persuasion because the reader gets nothing tangible in return.

It has often been said that the wheels of industry are greased with favors. The giving and receiving of favors makes success more likely and makes life in general more agreeable.

MODEL 6   Persuasive Request—Selling an Idea

This persuasive memo uses the direct plan because the memo travels up the organization.

+ Timkin   ━1034 York Road
+ Electrical   ━Baltimore, MD 21204
+ Systems   ━Phone: 301-555-1086

1
MEMO TO: Elliott Lamborn, Vice President

FROM: Jenson J. Peterson, Marketing Supervisor *JJP*

DATE: October 3, 19--

SUBJECT: Proposal to Reassign Parking Lots

As one means of emphasizing our support for the American auto industry, I propose that the close-in parking lots around our headquarters be restricted to use by cars manufactured primarily in the United States.

2
Whenever customers from the auto industry visit our headquarters, they must either drive by or walk through Parking Lots A and B, those nearest the building. When they do, they will see, as our staff did during a recent inspection, that approximately 30% of our employees drive foreign-made cars—despite the fact that nearly all our business comes from the American auto industry.

I recognize, of course, that many factors go into the decision to purchase a particular car. However, a purchasing agent from Embassy told me last week, "How can you expect us to support you when you don't support us?" This executive was not asking us specifically to promote Embassy cars— just American-made cars. (Though determining whether a particular car is primarily American-made or foreign-made might be difficult for the average consumer, you can be sure that our auto-industry customers know the difference.)

The purpose of this memo, then, is to seek approval to have Parking Lots A and B and Rows 1-5 of the Executive Parking Lot restricted to use by American-made cars. The Maintenance Department estimates that it will need four weeks and about $500 to make the needed signs.

Our labor contract requires union approval of any changes in working conditions. However, Sally Marsh, our shop steward, has told me that she would be willing to discuss this matter— especially if similar restrictions are imposed on the Executive Parking Lot.

3
Since our quarterly marketing managers' meeting will be held on November 8-10, I look forward to being able to announce the new plan to them then. By approving this change, you will be sending a powerful positive message to headquarters visitors: Our employees believe in the products we sell.

urs

Begins by introducing the recommendation, along with a brief rationale.

Provides a smooth transition to the necessary background information. Cites statistics and external testimony for credibility.

Repeats the recommendation after presenting most of the rationale.
Neutralizes an obvious obstacle.

Closes on a positive, confident note; motivates prompt action.

Grammar and Mechanics Notes

1 If you need the space for a long one-page memo, begin typing the heading lines 1 inch from the top (instead of 2 inches) or begin 2 or 3 lines below the letterhead.   2 30%: Use figures and the % sign in business correspondence.   3 *managers' meeting:* Place the apostrophe *after* the s to form the possessive of a plural noun (*managers*).

MODEL 7   Persuasive Request—Asking a Favor

This persuasive request uses the indirect plan because the writer does not know the reader personally and because strong persuasion is needed.

BALTIMORE PENTIUM USER'S GROUP

B

P.O. Box 1038 • Baltimore, MD 21204 • 301-555-9879

January 15, 19--

Ms. Tanya Porratt, President
The Office Training Group
1800 Ten Hills Road, Suite B
Boston, MA 02145

Dear Ms. Porratt:

"Desktop publishing has been around for 100 years."

Opens by quoting the reader, thus complimenting her.

1   This comment of yours in a recent interview published in the *Boston Globe* certainly made me sit up and think. After all, the first desktop publishing software was introduced only in 1986—certainly not 100 years ago.

Intimates the request; provides the necessary background information.

2   Members of the Baltimore Pentium User's Group would enjoy and benefit from hearing a respected DTP professional who has been actively involved in the field since its inception. As the speaker at our annual banquet at the Baltimore Park Plaza Hotel on April 25, you would be able to present your ideas on DTP to our 200 members. You would, of course, be our guest for the banquet, which begins at 7 p.m. Your 45-minute presentation would begin at 8:30 p.m.

Subordinates a potential obstacle by putting it in the dependent clause of a sentence.

Closes with a restatement of a reader benefit.

We will reimburse you for air travel and hotel accommodations. Although our nonprofit association is unable to offer an honorarium, we do offer an opportunity to introduce your firm and to present your ideas to representatives of every major company in the Baltimore metropolitan area.

3   We would like to announce your speech as the lead article in our next newsletter, which goes to press on March 23. Won't you please use the enclosed postal card to let us know that you can come. We will have a large, enthusiastic audience of decision-makers waiting to hear you.

Cordially,

Magda D. Lyon

Magda D. Lyon
Banquet Chairperson

rk
Enclosure

Grammar and Mechanics Notes

1 *Boston Globe:* Either italicize or underline the titles of separately published works, such as newspapers, magazines, or books.   2 *its:* Use no apostrophe when the pronoun *it* is used to show possession.   3 *that you can come.:* Use a period after a courteous request.

A request for a favor differs from a routine request in that routine requests are granted almost automatically, whereas favors require persuasion. For example, asking a colleague to trade places with you on the program for the monthly managers' meeting might be considered a routine request. Asking the same colleague to prepare and give your presentation for you would more likely be a favor, requiring some persuasion.

Although friends and close colleagues often do each other favors as a matter of course, many times in business the granting of a favor might not be so automatic—especially if you don't know the person to whom you're writing. In such situations, you will want to begin your request with an attention-getter and stress the reader benefits from granting the favor.

Discuss at least one reader benefit before making your request. Explain why the favor is being asked and continue to show how the reader (or someone else) will benefit from the favor. Keep a positive, confident tone throughout, and make the action clear and easy to take.

Often the favor is requested because the reader is an expert on some topic. If that is the case, you may legitimately make a complimentary remark about the reader. Make sure, however, that your compliment sounds sincere. Readers are rightfully suspicious, for example, when they read in a form letter that they have been specifically chosen to participate in some project. ("Me and how many thousands of others" they might wonder.) On the other hand, such a compliment in a letter that is obviously personally typed and signed has much more credibility.

For a sincere tone, make any flattering comments unique to the reader.

The most important factor to remember in asking for a favor has to do with the favor itself rather than with the writing process. Keep your request reasonable. Don't ask someone else to do something that you can or should do for yourself.

Model 7 illustrates a persuasive request, asking for a favor. The reader and writer do not know each other, which makes persuasion a little more challenging and which calls for an indirect organizational plan. Reader benefits (the opportunity to promote the reader's firm and the flattering prospect of being the center of attention) are included.

Writing a Persuasive Claim

As discussed in Chapter 7, most claim letters are routine letters and should be written using a direct plan of organization—stating the problem early in the letter. Because it is to the company's benefit to keep its clientele happy, most reasonable claims are settled to the customer's satisfaction. Therefore, persuasion is not ordinarily necessary.

Suppose, however, that you wrote a routine claim letter and the company, for some reason, denied your claim. If you still feel that your original claim is legitimate, you might then write a *persuasive* claim letter—using all the techniques discussed earlier in this chapter for writing persuasive requests. Or assume that your new photocopier broke three days after the warranty period expired. The company is not legally obligated to honor your claim, but you may decide to try to persuade them to do so anyway.

---

wordwise

Business Directory   Names of actual companies and the businesses they're in:

■ *Amazing Grates*	Fireplace accessories store
■ *Brilliant Deductions*	Accounting firm
■ *Curl Up and Dye*	Beauty shop
■ *Madison Hair Garden*	Beauty shop in Madison, Connecticut
■ *Royal Flush*	Plumbing company
■ *Tanks a Lot*	Tropical fish store
■ *Tender Lubing Care*	Auto diagnostic service
■ *Too Good To Be Threw*	Consignment shop

Avoid showing anger.

Showing anger in your persuasive claim letter would be counterproductive, even if the company turned down your original claim. The goal of your letter is not to vent your anger but to solve a problem. And that is more likely to happen when a calm atmosphere prevails.

As in a routine claim letter, you will need to explain in sufficient detail precisely what the problem is, how it came about, and how you want the reader to solve the problem. Use a calm, objective, courteous tone, avoiding anger and exaggeration. Although similar in some respects to a routine claim letter, the persuasive claim differs in two important ways: it has an attention-getting opening and it presents more evidence.

Attention-Getting Opening   Recall that you begin a routine claim letter by stating the problem. This type of opening would not be wise for a persuasive claim, because the reader may conclude the claim is unreasonable until he or she gets to your rationale.

NOT: Would you please repair my Marlow 203 copier without charge, even though the 90-day warranty expired last week.

BUT: We took a chance and lost! We bet that the Marlow 203 we purchased from you 96 days ago would prove to be as reliable as the other ten Marlows our firm uses.

The original opening is counterproductive, providing a ready excuse for denying the claim. The revised version holds off making the request until enough background information has been provided. Note also the personal relationship the writer is beginning to establish with the reader in the revised version—discussing not only that the company owns ten other Marlow copiers but also that the other copiers have all been very reliable. Such an understanding tone will make the reader more likely to grant the request.

More Evidence   Because your claim either is nonroutine or has been rejected once, you will need to present as much convincing evidence as possible. Explain fully the basis for your claim; then request a specific adjustment.

In a courteous manner, provide complete details.

Model 8 illustrates these guidelines for writing a persuasive claim letter.

Writing a Sales Letter

The heart of most business is sales—selling a product or service. Much of a company's sales effort is accomplished through the writing of effective sales letters—either individual letters for individual sales or form letters for large-scale sales.

In large companies, the writing of sales letters is centered in the marketing or advertising department and is a highly specialized task performed by advertising copywriters and marketing consultants. Within a few years after graduation, however, a growing number of college students opt to own their own businesses. These start-up companies are typically quite small, with only a few employees.

In such a situation, the company must mount an aggressive sales effort in order to develop business, but the company is often too small to hire a full-time copywriter or marketing consultant. Thus, the owner usually ends up writing these sales letters, which are vital to the ongoing health of the firm. So no matter where

Small-business owners often write their own sales letters.

MODEL 8 Persuasive Claim

This persuasive claim letter uses the indirect plan because the writer does not personally know the reader and thus cannot expect the favor to be granted automatically.

June 18, 19--

Customer Services Supervisor
Northern Airlines, Inc.
P.O. Box 6001
Denver, CO 80240

Dear Customer Services Supervisor:

I think you will agree that a relaxing 90-minute flight on Northern Airlines is more enjoyable than a grueling six-hour automobile trip.

Begins on a warm and relevant note.

1 Yet, on June 2, my wife and I found ourselves doing just that—driving from Saginaw, Michigan, to Indianapolis—in the middle of the night and in the company of three tired children.

Provides a smooth transition from the opening sentence.

2 We had made reservations on Northern Flight 126 a month earlier. To obtain the cheapest fare ($136 per ticket), we had purchased nonrefundable tickets. When we arrived at the airport, we were told that Flight 126, scheduled to depart at 8 p.m. had been canceled. Your gate agent (Ms. Nixon) had graciously rebooked us on the next available flight, leaving at 9:45 the next morning.

Provides the necessary background information.

Since the purpose of our trip was to attend a family wedding on June 3, we had no choice but to cancel our rebooked flight and to drive to Indianapolis instead. When we tried to turn in our tickets for a refund, Ms. Nixon informed us that because the flight had been canceled due to inclement weather, she would be unable to credit my American Express charge card.

Tells exactly what the problem is in a neutral, courteous tone.

3 As a frequent flier on Northern, I've experienced firsthand the "Welcome Aboard!" feeling that is the basis for your current advertising campaign; and I believe you will want to extend that same taken-care-of feeling to your ticket operations as well. Please credit my American Express charge card (Account No. 4102 817 171) for the $680 cost of the five tickets, thus putting out the welcome mat again for my family.

Provides a rationale for granting the claim; asks confidently for specific action; mentions the reader benefit of keeping a satisfied customer.

Sincerely,

Oliver J. Arbin (signature)

Oliver J. Arbin
4 518 Thompson Street
Saginaw, MI 48607

Grammar and Mechanics Notes

1 *just that—driving:* If your keyboard doesn't have a dash, type two hyphens (--) with no space before or after.   **2** *nonrefundable:* Write most *non-* words solid—without a hyphen. **3** *taken-care-of feeling:* Hyphenate a compound adjective that comes before a noun.   **4** For personal business letters on plain paper, type your address below your name.

you intend to work, the chances are that at some point you will need to write sales letters.

The indirect organizational plan is used for sales letters. It is sometimes called the *AIDA* plan, because you first gain the reader's *attention,* then create *interest* in and *desire* for the benefits of your product, and finally motivate *action.*

Selecting a Central Selling Theme

Your first step is to become thoroughly familiar with your product, its competition, and your intended audience. Then, you must select a **central selling theme** for your letter. Most products have numerous features that you will want to introduce and discuss. For your letter to make a real impact, however, you need to have a single theme running through your letter—a major reader benefit that you introduce early and emphasize throughout the letter. One noted copywriting consultant calls this principle a basic law of direct-mail advertising and labels it $E^2 = 0$, meaning that when you try to emphasize *everything,* you end up emphasizing *nothing.*[1]

It would be unrealistic to expect your reader to remember five different features that you mention about your product. In any case, you have only a short time to make a lasting impression on your reader. Use that time wisely to emphasize what you think is the most compelling benefit from owning your product. Two means of achieving this emphasis are *position* and *repetition.* Introduce your central selling theme early (in the opening sentence if possible), and keep referring to it throughout the letter.

Gaining the Reader's Attention

Review the earlier section on gaining the reader's attention when writing persuasive requests.

A reply to a request for product information from a potential customer is called a **solicited sales letter.** An **unsolicited sales letter,** on the other hand, is a letter promoting a firm's products that is mailed to potential customers who have not expressed any interest in the product. (Unsolicited sales letters are also called *prospecting letters.*)

Because most sales letters are unsolicited, you have only a line or two in which to grab the reader's attention. Unless a sales letter is addressed to the reader personally and is obviously not a form letter, the reader is likely to just skim it—either out of curiosity or because the opening sentence was especially intriguing.

Most readers will scan the opening even of a form letter, perhaps just to learn what product is being promoted. If you can capture their attention in these first few lines, they may continue reading. Otherwise, all your efforts will have been wasted. The following types of opening sentences have proven effective for sales letters.

Technique	Example
Rhetorical question	What is the difference between extravagance and luxury? (*promoting a high-priced car*)
Thought-provoking statement	Most of what we had to say about business this morning was unprintable! (*promoting an early-morning television news program*)
Unusual fact	If your family is typical, you will wash one ton of laundry this year. (*promoting a laundry detergent*)

Current event	The new Arrow assembly plant will bring 1,700 new families to White Rock within three years. (*promoting a real estate company*)
Anecdote	During six years of college, the one experience that helped me the most did not even occur in the classroom. (*promoting a weekly business magazine*)
Direct challenge	Drop the enclosed Pointer pen on the floor, writing tip first, and then sign your name with it. (*promoting a no-blot ball point pen*)

As in persuasive requests, the opening of a sales letter should be interesting, short, and original. When possible, incorporate the central selling theme into your opening; and avoid irrelevant, obvious, or timeworn statements.

Many attention-getting openings consist of a one-sentence paragraph.

If you have received an inquiry from a potential customer about your product, you know that the person is already at least mildly interested in the product. Therefore, when you write solicited sales letters, an attention-getting opening is not as crucial. In such a situation, you might begin by expressing appreciation for the customer's inquiry and then start introducing the central selling theme.

Creating Interest and Building Desire

If your opening sentence is directly related to your product, the transition to the discussion of features and reader benefits will be smooth and logical. Make sure that the first sentence of the following paragraph relates directly to the idea introduced in your opening sentence. Unrelated ideas will make the reader pause and feel puzzled.

Interpreting Features   The major part of your letter (typically, several paragraphs) will probably be devoted to creating interest and building desire for your product. You should not only describe the product and its features but, more important, *interpret* these features by showing specifically how each will benefit the reader. Make the reader—not the product—the subject of most of your sentences.

Devote several paragraphs to interpreting the product's features.

Marketers refer to the benefit a user receives from a product or service as the **derived benefit.** As Charles Revson, founder of the Revlon cosmetics company, once said, "In our factory we make lipstick; in our advertising we sell hope."[2]

NOT: The JT Laser II prints at the speed of ten pages per minute.

BUT: After pressing the print key, you'll barely have time to reach over and retrieve the page from the bin. The JT Laser II's print speed of ten pages per minute is twice that of the typical printer.

NOT: Masco binoculars zoom from 3 to 12 power.

BUT: With Masco binoculars, you can look a ruby-throated hummingbird squarely in the eye at 300 feet and see it blink.

Although emphasizing the derived benefit rather than product features is generally the preferred strategy, there are two situations that call for emphasizing product features instead: when promoting a product to experts and when promoting expensive equipment. For example, if the car you're promoting to sports car enthusiasts achieves a maximum torque of 138 ft.-lbs. at 3,000 rpm or produces 145 hp at

To be effective, your persuasive message must be believable. Avoid emotionalism, obvious flattery, insincerity, and exaggeration. Rely instead on specific evidence—such as facts and figures. Ensure, however, that your facts and figures are relevant and accurate.

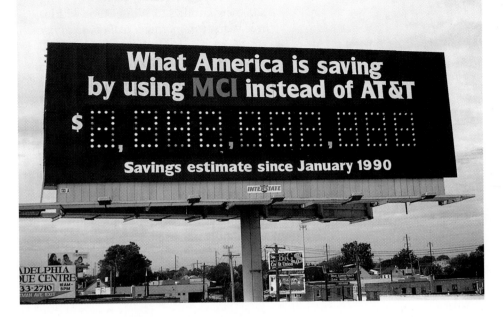

5,500 rpm, tell the reader that. You would sound condescending trying to interpret to such experts what this means.

Using Vivid Language   Use action-packed verbs when talking about the product's features and benefits. Within reason, use colorful adjectives and adverbs, being careful to avoid a hard-sell approach. Finally, to convey a dynamic image, use positive language, stressing what your product *is,* rather than what it is *not.*

  The paper tray is designed to hold 200 sheets.

  The paper tray holds 200 sheets—enough to last the busy executive a full week without reloading.

  The Terminator snowblower is not one of those lightweight models.

  The Terminator's 4.5 hp engine is 50% more powerful than the standard 3.0 hp engine used in most snowblowers.

Maintain credibility by providing specific facts and figures.

Using Objective, Ethical Language   To be convincing, you must present specific, objective evidence. Simply saying that a product is great is not enough. You must provide evidence to show *why* or *how* it is great. Here is where you'll use all the data you gathered before you started to write. Avoid generalities, unsupported superlatives and claims, and too many or too strong adjectives and adverbs.

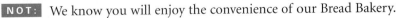 At $395, the Sherwood moped is the best buy on the market.

BUT: The May 1995 *Independent Consumer* rated the $395 Sherwood moped the year's best buy.

Positive statements by independent agencies lend powerful support.

NOT: We know you will enjoy the convenience of our Bread Bakery.

BUT: Our Bread Bakery comes with one feature we don't think you'll ever use: a 30-day, no-questions-asked return policy.

What May You Say in a Sales Letter?

May I say that our product is the best on the market?

Yes. You may legally express an opinion about your product; this is called *puffery.* You may not, however, make a claim that can be proven false, such as saying that your product is cheaper than a competing product when, in fact, your product is not cheaper.

The typist mistakenly typed the price of our product as $19.95, instead of the correct price of $29.95. Do I have to sell it for $19.95?

No. You are not legally responsible for an honest mistake, as long as your intent was not to deceive the buyer.

May I include a sample of my product with my letter and require the reader to either send payment or return the product at my expense?

No. Readers do not have to pay for or return any unordered goods. They may legally treat them as a gift from you.

I want to send a sales letter promoting our rock music to high school students. May I legally accept orders from minors?

Yes. You may accept their orders, and if you do, you are legally bound to honor the contract. However,

SPOTLIGHT 14

ON LAW
AND ETHICS

until they reach the age of adulthood (18 years in some states and 21 years in others), minors may legally cancel a contract and return the merchandise to you.

I want to sell the furniture in my showroom that has small knicks and scratches on it. If I state in my sales letter that all sales are final and sale items are marked "as is," do I have to issue refunds to anyone who complains?

No. By using the term "as is," you tell the consumer that you are not promising new merchandise.

Without my knowledge, my assistant wrote a letter in which she promised a customer a 10% price break; such a price reduction is clearly against store policy. Do we have to honor my assistant's price?

Yes. Your assistant was acting as your agent, and her promise is legally binding on your firm.

Sources: Ronald A. Anderson, Ivan Fox, and David P. Twomey, *Business Law and the Legal Environment,* 14th ed. South-Western, Cincinnati, OH, 1990; Gordon W. Brown, Edward E. Byers, and Mary Ann Lawlor, *Business Law: With UCC Applications,* 7th ed. McGraw-Hill, New York, 1989; Neil Story and Lynn Ward, *American Business Law and the Regulatory Environment,* South-Western, Cincinnati, OH, 1989.

Although the law allows you to promote your product aggressively, there are certain legal and ethical constraints under which you will want to operate. The guidelines provided in Spotlight 14—On Law and Ethics apply to American law and customs. When operating in the international environment, you should follow local laws and customs.

Focusing on the Central Selling Theme   The recurring theme of your letter should be the one feature that sets your product apart from the competition. If your reader remembers nothing else about your product, this one feature is what you want him or her to remember. Whenever possible, unify the features under one umbrella theme—whether the theme is convenience, ease of use, flexibility, price, or some other distinguishing characteristic around which you can build your case.

Discussing and fully interpreting these features may take a considerable amount of space; and some readers may be unwilling to read through a long sales letter.

However, those who do will be more motivated to respond favorably. The test of an effective sales letter is the number of sales it generates—*not* the number of people who read the letter.

Mentioning Price   If price is your central selling theme, introduce it early and emphasize it often. In most cases, however, price is not the central selling theme and should therefore be subordinated. Introduce the price late in the message, after most of the advantages of owning the product have been discussed. To subordinate price, state it in a long complex or compound sentence, perhaps in a sentence that also mentions a reader benefit.

> You'll consider the $250 cost of this spreadsheet seminar repaid in full the very next time your boss asks you to revise the quarterly sales budget—on a Friday afternoon!

Sometimes it is helpful to present the price in terms of small units, for example, showing how subscribing to a weekly magazine costs less than $1 per week, rather than $50 a year. Or compare the price to that of a familiar object—"about what you'd pay for your morning newspaper or cup of coffee."

Use techniques of subordination when mentioning price.

Referring to Enclosures   Sometimes, some of the features of a product or service are best displayed in a brochure that you can enclose with the sales letter. Subordinate your reference to the enclosure, and refer to some specific item in the enclosure to increase the likelihood of its being read.

> Note the porcelain robin's detailed coloring on the actual-size photograph on page 2 of the enclosed brochure.

> Use the enclosed order blank to send us your order today. Within three weeks, you will be enjoying this museum-quality sculpture in your own home.

Motivating Action

Although the purpose of your letter should be apparent right from the start, delay making your specific request until late in the letter—after you have created interest and built desire for the product. Then state the specific action you want.

If the desired action is an actual sale, make the action easy to take by including a toll-free number, enclosing an order blank, accepting credit cards, and the like. For high-priced items, it would be unreasonable to expect to make an actual sale by mail. Probably no one has read a sales letter promoting a new automobile and then phoned in an order for the car. For such items, your goal is to get the reader to take just a small step toward purchasing—sending for more information, stopping by the dealer for a demonstration, or asking a sales representative to call. Again, make the step easy for the reader to take.

Provide an incentive for prompt action by, for example, offering a gift to the first 100 people who respond or stressing the need to buy early while there is still a good selection, before the holiday rush, or during the three-day sale. Make your push for action *gently,* however. Any tactic that smacks of high-pressure selling at this point is likely to increase reader resistance.

Use confident language when asking for action, avoiding such hesitant phrases as "If you want to save money" or "I hope you agree that this product will save you time." When asking the reader to part with money, it is always a good idea to mention a reader benefit in the same sentence.

✔ CHECKLIST 9   Sales Letters

Prepare

☑ Learn as much as possible about the product, the competition, and the audience.

☑ Select a central selling theme—your product's most distinguishing feature.

Gain the Reader's Attention

☑ Make your opening brief, interesting, and original. Avoid obvious, misleading, and irrelevant statements.

☑ Use any of these openings: rhetorical question, thought-provoking statement, unusual fact, current event, anecdote, direct challenge, or some similar attention-getting device.

☑ Introduce (or at least lead up to) the central selling theme in the opening.

☑ If the letter is in response to a customer inquiry, begin by expressing appreciation for the inquiry and introduce the central selling theme.

Create Interest and Build Desire

☑ Make the introduction of the product follow naturally from the attention-getter.

☑ *Interpret* the features of the product; instead of just describing the features, show how the reader will benefit from each feature. Let the reader picture owning, using, and enjoying the product.

☑ Use action-packed, positive, and objective language. Provide convincing evidence to support your claims—specific facts and figures, independent product reviews, endorsements, and so on.

☑ Continue to stress the central selling theme throughout.

☑ Subordinate price (unless price is the central selling theme). State price in small terms, in a long sentence, or in a sentence that talks about benefits.

Motivate Action

☑ Make the desired action clear and easy to take.

☑ Ask confidently, avoiding the hesitant "If you'd like to" or "I hope you agree that."

☑ Encourage prompt action (but avoid a hard-sell approach).

☑ End your letter with a reminder of a reader benefit.

NOT: Hurry! Hurry! Hurry! These sale prices won't be in effect long.

NOT: If you agree that this ice cream maker will make your summers more enjoyable, you can place your order by telephone.

BUT: To have your Jiffy Ice Cream Maker available for use during the upcoming July 4 weekend, simply call our toll-free number today.

Push confidently, but gently, for prompt action.

Consider putting an important marketing point in a postscript (P.S.). Some marketing studies have shown that a postscript notation is the most-often-read part of a sales letter.[3] It can be as long or as short as needed, but it should contain new and interesting information.

P.S. If you stop in for a demonstration before May 1, you'll walk out with a free box of color transparencies (retail value $21.95)—just for trying Up Front, the new presentation software program by Acme Products.

These guidelines for writing an effective sales letter are illustrated in Model 9 (see page 242) and summarized in Checklist 9. As always, the test of the effectiveness of a message is whether it achieves its goal. Use whatever information you have available (especially in terms of audience analysis) to help your letter achieve its goal.

MODEL 9 Sales Letter

Home Security Products
Box 302, Edenton, NC 27932
919-555-4022

Starts with a rhetorical
question.

Introduces need for safety
and security as the central
selling theme.

Presents specific evidence
and discusses it in terms of
reader benefits.

Emphasizes *you* instead of
the product in most
sentences.

Subordinates price in a long
sentence that also discusses
benefits.

Makes the desired action
clear and easy to take; ends
with a reader benefit.

1

2   Dear Homeowner:

Do you view your home as an investment or as your castle? Is it primarily a tax write-off
or a place of refuge—a place where you can find comfort and respite from workday stress?

Most of us view our homes as places where we can feel safe from outside intrusions. Thus,
we feel threatened by government statistics showing that 5.3% of all U.S. households were
burglarized last year. How can we protect ourselves?

Today, there's a simple and dependable alarm that protects up to 2,500 square feet of your
home. Just plug in the Safescan Home Alarm system, adjust the sensitivity to the size of
your room, and turn the key. You then have 30 seconds to leave and 15 seconds to switch
off the alarm once you return.

Worried that your dog might trigger the alarm? You needn't be, because Safescan's micro-
3   processor screens out normal sounds like crying babies, outside traffic, and rain. But hostile
noises like breaking glass and splintering wood trigger the alarm. The 105-decibel siren is
loud enough to alert neighbors and to drive away even the most determined burglar.

What if a smart burglar disconnects the electricity to your home or pulls the plug? No
problem, because built-in batteries assure that Safescan operates through power failures up
to 24 hours, and batteries recharge automatically. Best of all, installation couldn't be easier.
Simply mount the 4-pound unit on a wall (we supply the four screws), and plug it in.
Nothing could be faster.

Finally, there is a $259 home alarm that you can trust; and the one-year warranty and ten-
day return policy ensure your complete satisfaction.

Last year, 3.2 million burglaries occurred in the United States, but you can now tip the odds
back in your favor. To order the Safescan Home Alarm System, use your credit card now
and call our operator toll-free at 800-555-2914. Within ten days, Safescan will be guarding
your home, giving you peace of mind.

Sincerely yours,

Jeffrey Parret
National Sales Manager

Grammar and Mechanics Notes

1 In general, omit the date and inside address in form sales letters.   2 *Dear Homeowner:*
Note the generic salutation.   3 *crying babies, outside traffic, and:* Separate items in a series
by commas.

The 3Ps

A Sales Letter

You are the proprietor of Lee's Consumer Products, a small retail store located in the Fiesta Mall, 1200 Dobson Road, Mesa, AZ 85201. You are the exclusive dealer for Voice Note, a recorder that allows you to record messages to yourself rather than scribbling them on scraps of paper.

The recorder is $2^1/_2 \times 1 \times {}^1/_2$ inches, weighs 3 ounces, and is made in Japan from sturdy plastic. It records messages up to 30 seconds long and holds 10 minutes of dictation. A lock button prevents recording over a message. After the message has been played back, the loop-to-loop tape automatically resets for use the next time. The Voice Note is operated by pressing the Record button and speaking. It runs on two AAA batteries that are included and comes with a 90-day warranty and a 30-day full-refund policy.

To promote this product, you decide to try a direct-mail campaign directed at the business community. You purchase a mailing list containing the names and addresses of the 800 members of the Phoenix Athletic Club, a downtown facility used by businesspeople for lunch, after-work drinks, exercise, and social affairs. The club has racquetball and tennis courts, an indoor pool, and exercise rooms. Its yearly membership fee is $3,000. You decide to send these 800 members a form letter promoting the Voice Note for $29. You'll include your local phone number (555-2394) for placing credit-card orders by phone, or the readers may stop by the store to purchase the recorder in person.

PROCESS

1. Describe your audience.

   ■ Business men and women

   ■ Active (sports and exercise facilities)

   ■ Upscale (can afford $3,000 annual membership)

   ■ Probably very busy professionally and socially

2. What will be your central selling theme?

   Convenience/portability is the unique benefit of Voice Note.

3. Write an attention-getter that is original, interesting, and short; that is reader-oriented; that relates to the product; and, if possible, that introduces the central selling theme.

   You're driving home on the freeway in bumper-to-bumper traffic when the solution to a nagging problem facing you at work suddenly pops into your head. But by the time you get home 30 minutes later, your good idea has vanished.

4. Jot down the features you might discuss and the reader benefits associated with each feature.

   Size is $2\frac{1}{2} \times 1 \times \frac{1}{2}$ inches, weighs 3 oz.: *smaller and lighter than a microcassette recorder; fits in shirt pocket or purse; easy to use on the go.*

   Records 30-second messages—up to 10 minutes' worth: *room enough for most "to-do" messages—20 different reminders.*

   Press record button and then speak; lock function prevents overrecording: *Easy to use, even in car; not a lot of buttons to fiddle with.*

   Powered by two AAA batteries (included): *real portability.*

5. Write the sentence that mentions price. (Since price is not the central selling theme, it should be subordinated.)

   The Voice Note's price of $29 is less than you'd pay for a bulky microcassette recorder that is much less convenient for on-the-go use.

6. What action are you seeking from the reader?

   To purchase the Voice Note.

7. How can you motivate prompt action?

   Make the action easy to take; offer warranty and guarantee satisfaction; stress that the sooner you buy, the sooner you'll enjoy using it.

Lee's
Consumer
Products

Fiesta Mall
1200 Dobson Road
Mesa, AZ 85201
602-555-6372

Dear Club Member:

You leave the Athletic Club and are heading home on the freeway in bumper-to-bumper traffic when the solution to a nagging problem at work suddenly pops into your head. But by the time you get home 30 minutes later, your good idea has vanished.

Next time, carry Voice Note, the 3-ounce recorder that allows you to record reminders to yourself on the go. Now you can "jot" down your ideas as soon as they occur: while jogging, waiting at the bank, or lying in bed at 3 a.m. As you know, inspiration often strikes far from a pad and pencil!

Much smaller than a microcassette ($2^1/2$ x 1 x $^1/2$ inches), Voice Note slips into your shirt pocket or purse. And there aren't a lot of buttons to fiddle with. Just press Record and speak. A lock button prevents overrecording your earlier messages.

You can record up to 20 different messages of 30 seconds each—"to do" messages like "Call Richard about the Hewlett contract" or "Place order for 200 shares of SRP stock" or even "Pick up Jenny from soccer practice at 5:30." After playback, the tape automatically resets for immediate use.

For true portability, the Voice Note is powered by two AAA batteries (included). Your satisfaction is guaranteed by our 90-day warranty and 30-day full-refund policy.

The Voice Note's price of $29 is less than you'd pay for a bulky microcassette recorder that is much less convenient for on-the-go use. For credit-card orders, simply call us at 555-2394. Or stop by our retail store at Fiesta Mall for a personal demonstration. The next time you need to pick up a quart of milk on the way home, make a Voice Note. You won't come home empty-handed.

Sincerely,

Richard E. Lee

Richard E. Lee
Proprietor

cd

SUMMARY

The ability to write persuasively is crucial for success in business. In order to write persuasively, you must overcome the reader's initial resistance, establish your own credibility, and develop an appeal that meets a need of the reader. You must also become thoroughly familiar with your reader so that you can translate the advantages of your idea or the features of your product into specific reader benefits.

When writing to superiors, use a direct writing style, giving the proposal or recommendation, along with the criteria or a brief rationale, in the first paragraph. For most other persuasive messages, prefer an indirect writing style. First gain the reader's attention by using an opening paragraph that is relevant, interesting, and short.

For persuasive requests, devote the majority of the message to discussing the merits of your proposal and showing specifically how your proposal meets some need of the reader. Provide evidence that is accurate, relevant, representative, and complete. Discuss and minimize any obstacles to your proposal. For sales letters, introduce a central selling theme early and build on it throughout the message. Devote most of the message to showing how the reader will specifically benefit from owning the product. Subordinate the price, unless price is the central selling theme.

For all types of persuasive messages, end on a confident, positive note, making sure the reader knows what action is desired and making the action easy to take. Persuasive messages are often longer than other types of messages because of the need to present convincing evidence. By taking the space needed to support your statements with specific facts and figures, you'll increase your ability to persuade your readers.

KEY TERMS

central selling theme	persuasion	solicited sales letter
derived benefit	rhetorical question	unsolicited sales letter

REVIEW AND DISCUSSION

1. **Communication at The Wilderness Society Revisited**   Before Jim Waltman starts to draft a persuasive message on behalf of The Wilderness Society, he thinks carefully about his readers' attitudes and viewpoints.
   a. Would a direct or an indirect organizational plan be more appropriate when writing to prospective members who have never received a letter from The Wilderness Society?
   b. How can The Wilderness Society establish credibility with an audience that has not been involved with the organization in the past?
   c. What might Waltman say in a letter to justify a request for members of Congress to strengthen the Endangered Species Act?
2. What is meant by the term *persuasion?*
3. Why might the reader initially resist your persuasive efforts?
4. What are the sources of writer credibility?
5. Give an example of a direct reader benefit and an indirect benefit.
6. What should you know about your reader before beginning to write a persuasive letter?
7. Under what circumstances should a direct organizational plan be used for a persuasive request?
8. What are some characteristics of an effective attention-getter?
9. How should the writer deal with obstacles to his or her proposal?
10. Why are persuasive messages often longer than other types of messages?

11. Why is showing anger a poor strategy in a persuasive claim letter?
12. What is a central selling theme? Why is it important in a sales letter?
13. Why should the reader instead of the product be the focus of attention in a sales letter?
14. What are some techniques for subordinating the price in a sales letter?

Help Wanted

Directions: This form letter is from Gwendolyn Douglas, sales manager at Shop-at-Home Appliances, to all of their customers. Revise the letter to make it more effective, taking into consideration the editor's marginal comments.

should you date your form letter?

October 5, 19—

Dear Shop-at-Home Customer:

How would you like to save big bucks on the purchase of your next refrigerator?

Avoid rhetorical questions with obvious answers.

tran

Solve your frozen-food problems by buying a new Penguin refrigerator. The advanced technology built into the Penguin guarantees automatic temperature control so that you don't have to check or reset the thermostat. And the Penguin is worry-free, thanks to a ten-year warranty on parts and labor.

In addition, the Penguin comes with these features:

How much does it cost?

- 10 cubic feet of food storage
- a door rack that stores 12 bottles in an upright position
- five attractive colors

int — How do these features benefit the customer?

This roomy, efficient refrigerator safely stores your frozen foods for only pennies per day. And by ordering before September 1, you can save even more because we've slashed our everyday low price by 20%.

Would a customer really buy a refrigerator without first inspecting it?

Stop the waste that comes from throwing away spoiled frozen foods and start saving money today. Call us toll-free at 800-555-8755, to order your new Penguin.

punct

Sincerely,

E X E R C I S E S

1. **The 3Ps Microwriting Model: Communication Applications at The Wilderness Society**
   Jim Waltman uses written communication to muster public support for national wildlife refuges and endangered species around the United States. He helps his readers understand how the broader issues relate to local concerns, and he supports

his arguments with facts and expert opinions. To encourage readers to take action, Waltman provides detailed information about whom to contact—and how.

Problem

Assume the role of Waltman's assistant. On January 29, the U.S. Senate will vote on funding for a wildlife refuge in Texas where several endangered animal species now flourish. In addition, the rare plants on this site are being tested by scientists in search of new medicines to treat burns and skin diseases, with promising results. Although there is some pressure to cut funding, you believe that more senators will support full funding for this refuge if they hear from their constituents. You are therefore writing a letter today (January 6) to ask members for their help in urging the Senate to fully fund this refuge.

Process

a. Describe your audience.
b. Should you use a direct or indirect organizational plan for this letter? Why?
c. List the points you will make to support your request to members.
d. Write an opening sentence for your letter.
e. What obstacle might prevent your readers from taking the requested action?
f. Write a sentence to address this obstacle (subordinate this discussion).
g. Write the closing paragraph of your letter, in which you restate your request and end on a forward-looking note.

Product

Using your knowledge of persuasive messages, draft a letter to members, inventing any reasonable data needed to complete this assignment.

2. **The 3Ps Microwriting Model: A Persuasive Message—Selling an Idea**

Problem

You are O. B. Presley, a sales representative for Midland Medical Supplies. Like most of the other 38 Midland reps, you are on the road three or four days a week, promoting your products to hospitals, clinics, and physicians in private practice. Three years ago, Midland purchased 8-pound laptop computers for all sales reps. These computers simplified your job immensely, especially in terms of filing call reports. Each evening in your hotel room you keyboard the report, showing to whom you spoke, their experiences with your products, what they'd like to see changed, and the like. You then submit these reports, along with actual orders, electronically to headquarters via the computer's built-in modem.

It occurs to you that you could be more productive by replacing your bulky laptop with a notebook computer and built-in portable printer. That way, whenever a customer wanted a specification sheet for a new product, you could electronically retrieve the information from the company's mainframe computer and print it out on the spot for the customer. You're sure you'd get additional sales as a result.

The specific system you're interested in is the Canon NoteJet, a Pentium-based notebook computer that has a built-in modem and ink-jet printer. The entire system weighs just 7.7 pounds and sells for $2,499 with 16MB of RAM and a 200MB hard disk. The only problem is that you don't know what to do with your present laptop computer. There's not much demand for used laptops, especially for three-year-old 8-pounders. Still, you think notebooks would be a good investment for all sales reps. Send a memo to Charles J. Redding, national sales manager, trying to sell him on the idea.

Process

a. Describe your audience.

b. Should you use a direct or indirect organizational plan? Why?

c. Write the opening sentence of your memo.

d. List the reasons you might discuss for your proposal—including any reader benefits associated with each reason.

e. What is an obstacle that might prevent you from achieving your objective?

f. Write a sentence that addresses this obstacle (subordinate this discussion).

g. Write the last paragraph of your memo, in which you state (or restate) your request. Make the action easy for the reader to take, ask confidently, and end on a forward-looking note.

Product

Draft, revise, format, and proofread your memo. Then submit both your responses to the process questions and your revised memo to your instructor.

3. Selling an Idea—Indirect Organizational Plan   Refer to Exercise 2. Assume that you (O. B. Presley) are relatively new on the job and have not yet earned the trust of the national sales manager. In addition, you know that Redding is not a big fan of technology. Therefore, you decide to write your memo using an indirect organizational plan. Write the memo.

4. Selling an Idea—Direct Organizational Plan   You are the night manager for White Mountain Gas, a 24-hour, self-service gasoline station on a New Hampshire highway. The station owner, Adam Bream, has asked you to survey customers about the new credit-card-activated pumps that he is considering installing. This pump would authorize a sale and release the gasoline hose when the customer inserted a credit card; after the customer finished using the hose, the pump would automatically shut off and print a receipt. Bream wants to know what customers think before he goes ahead.

You have talked with 300 customers over the course of two weeks, and more than three-quarters of them liked the idea: they *don't* like having to walk to the office to pay, and the new pump sounds as if it would be faster. But at least 35 people expressed concern over learning how to use the pump, and another 20 or so said they never pay by credit card. These people were worried that attendants might not be available for assistance and cash transactions after the new pumps were installed.

On the basis of your research, you want to recommend that the station install the pumps. To help reluctant customers, you think, extra attendants should be on hand for the first two months. You also want your boss to be aware that some people were worried about not being able to pay cash for their gas. Using a direct organizational plan, write a persuasive memo to Bream about your recommendations.

5. Selling an Idea—Oversized Dressing Rooms   You are Robert Kilcline, a merchandising manager at Lordstrom, Inc., a women's clothing store in Seattle. Your firm has decided to open a new store in Fashion Square Mall, an upscale department store on the north side. Retail space is quite expensive in this mall (nearly 50% more expensive than at your other locations), so Lordstrom facility engineers are trying to make every inch of space count.

Despite the costs, you feel that to be competitive in this mall, you will have to offer superior customer service. You already offer a no-questions-asked return policy, abundant inventory to ensure a complete selection of sizes and colors, and a harpist who performs on the main floor from 11 A.M. until 2 P.M. daily. But you think that the new store should also have oversized dressing rooms—ones large enough to hold a comfortable chair, garment rack, and adjustable three-sided mirrors. You want your customers to be able to make their selections in comfort.

You estimate that adding the furnishings and additional 20 square feet per dressing room in the new store will add $18,500 to the construction costs, plus $155 to the monthly lease. Present your ideas in a memo to your boss, Rebecca Lordstrom, executive vice president.

6. **Requesting a Favor—Field Trip**   You are David Pearson, owner and manager of Jack 'n Jill Preschool. During the next few weeks, you will be discussing food and nutrition with the youngsters; and you want to end the unit by having the children walk to the nearby Salad Haven, take a tour of the kitchens, and then make their own salads for lunch from the restaurant's popular salad bar. Of course, each family would pay for their child's meal. In fact, to help make the visit easier, you'll collect the money beforehand and pay the cashier for everyone at once. You will ask several parents to come with you to help supervise the 23 children, ages three through five, although they will probably need some extra help from the salad-bar attendants. You can come any day during the week of October 10–14. State regulations require that the children eat lunch between 11 A.M. and 12:30 P.M.

Write to Donna Jo Luse (Manager, Salad Haven, 28 Grenvale Road, Westminster, MD 21157) asking for permission to make the field trip.

7. **Requesting a Favor—Celebrity Donation**   Coming out of the movie theater after watching the Academy Award–winning movie *Rocky Mountain Adventure,* starring Robert Forte, you suddenly have an idea. As executive director of the Wilderness Fund, you've been searching for an unusual raffle prize for your upcoming fundraiser. You wonder whether you could persuade Robert Forte to donate some item used in this popular movie (perhaps a stage prop or costume item) for the raffle. The Wilderness Fund is an 8,000-member nonprofit agency dedicated to preserving forest lands—the very type of lands photographed so beautifully in Forte's latest movie. Write to the actor at Century Studios, 590 North Vermont Avenue, Los Angeles, CA 90004.

8. **Writing a Persuasive Claim—Azaleas**   You are Vera Malcolm, the facilities manager for Public Service Company of Arkansas. In preparation for the recent dedication of your new hydroelectric plant, you spruced up the grounds near the viewing stand. As part of the stage decorations, you ordered ten potted azaleas at $28.50 each (plus $10.50 shipping) from Jackson-Parsons Nurseries (410 Wick Avenue, Youngstown, OH 44555) on February 3. The bushes were guaranteed to arrive in show condition—ready to burst into bloom within three days—or your money would be cheerfully refunded.

The plants arrived in healthy condition but were in their final days (perhaps hours) of flowering—certainly in no shape to display at the dedication. You decided, instead, to plant the azaleas as part of your permanent landscaping. Because the plants arrived only three days before the dedication, you had to purchase substitute azaleas from the local florist—at a much higher price. In fact, you ended up paying $436 for the florist plants—$140.50 more than the Jackson-Parsons price. You feel that the nursery was responsible for your having to incur the additional expenditure. Write a letter asking Jackson-Parsons to reimburse your company for the $140.50.

9. **Writing a Persuasive Claim—Inaccurate Reporting**   As the CEO of Software Entrepreneurs, Inc., you just received a memo from the marketing manager for your ReSolve spreadsheet program. The manager had written to the review editor at *Computing Trends* protesting inaccurate reporting; the reply (from Roberta J.

Horton) was a form letter describing the magazine's policy on product reviews (see Exercises 12 and 17 of Chapter 7). Although you are glad to know that your product will be included in the yearly software review, you agree with your marketing manager that the editor made an error in downgrading your program. Apparently the reviewer worked with the original version of ReSolve and not with the improved version that was released one month before the review appeared. The new version is so powerful that it outperforms the competition on nearly every test used by the reviewer to determine product rankings.

Because magazine deadlines require that articles be completed well in advance of the printing date, you realize that the magazine could not possibly have included the improved version in their tests. However, you would like the review editor to print a small item noting the availability of the improved ReSolve in an upcoming issue. Write to Horton with this request.

10. **Writing a Persuasive Claim—Ripped Suit**   After a hurried taxi ride from LaGuardia Airport to the Marriott Marquis Hotel on May 15, you barely made it to your 2 P.M. appointment. You did not realize until you sat down at the conference table that you had ripped the pants of your $450 suit on an exposed spring in the taxi seat. The next day, your tailor tells you there is no way to repair the rip invisibly, so the suit is, in effect, now useless. Since you've owned the suit for a year, you don't expect the taxi company to reimburse you for $450, but you do think reimbursement of $200 is reasonable. From your taxi receipt, you learn that you took Taxi 1145 belonging to Empire State Taxi (50 West 77th Street, New York, NY 10024). Since this is a personal claim, write your letter on plain paper, using your own return address.

11. **Writing a Persuasive Claim—Defective Product**   Assume the role of J. R. McCord again, purchasing agent at People's Energy Company (see Exercises 2 and 14 of Chapter 7). Because Nationwide Office Supply believes you were at fault, it refused your initial routine claim. However, you've been a good customer for many years; last year, in fact, you purchased $5,800 worth of office supplies from Nationwide. In addition, since you've not used the printer cartridges, they could be resold easily. Thus, you've decided to write Nationwide again, this time adding persuasion to your claim letter.

12. **Selling a Product—Letter Critique**   Select a sales letter that you or a friend has received. Critique the letter, noting the specific ways that it does and does not follow the guidelines discussed in this chapter (see especially Checklists 8 and 9). Then revise the letter to remedy any weaknesses. Submit the original letter and your revised version to your instructor, along with a memo explaining the rationale for your revisions.

13. **Selling a Product—Work Boots**   As sales manager for Industrial Footwear, Inc., send a form sales letter advertising your Durham work boot to 3,000 members of Local 147 of the Building Trades Union. Local 147 is made up primarily of construction workers on high-rise buildings in Houston, Texas.

The Durham is an 8-inch, waterproof insulated boot, made of oil-tanned cowhide. It exceeds the guidelines for steel-toe protection issued by the American National Standards Institute (ANSI). The Durham has an all-rubber heel that provides firm footing, and its steel shanks provide additional support for arches and heels. It comes in whole sizes 7–13 in black or brown at a price of $79, plus $4.50 shipping. The price is guaranteed for the next 30 days. There is a one-year, no-questions-asked warranty.

Select a suitable salutation for your form letter and omit the date and inside address. The purpose of the letter is to motivate readers to order the boot by using the enclosed order blank or by calling your toll-free order number, 800-555-2993.

14. **Writing a Solicited Sales Letter—Real Estate**   As a realtor in the local franchise of National Home Sales, you receive a letter from Ms. Edith Willis (667 Rising Hills Drive, Xenia, OH 45385). Her letter states, in part,

> I am a single mother of two young children who is being transferred to your town and wish to purchase a three-bedroom condominium in a nice area in the price range of $100,000 to $125,000. I would be able to make a down payment of up to $25,000. Would you please write me, letting me know whether you have any property available that would fit my needs.

Although the housing market in your small town is tight, you do have a condominium available that might suit her needs. It has three bedrooms plus a finished basement, is air-conditioned (important in your part of the country), and is four years old. The neighborhood elementary school is considered the best in town; the only drawback is that the condominium is next door to a large but attractive apartment building. The home is listed for $119,900.

Send Ms. Willis a photograph and fact sheet on the listing. The purpose of your letter is to encourage her to phone you at 602-555-3459 to make an appointment to visit your office so that you can personally show her this and perhaps other properties you have available.

15. **Work-Team Communication—Selling a Product**   Select an ad from a newspaper or journal published within the past month. Working in groups of three or four, write an unsolicited form sales letter for the advertised product, to be signed by the sales manager. (You may need to gather additional information about the product, perhaps from the Internet.) The audience for your letter will be either the students or the faculty at your institution (you decide which). Include only actual data about the product and about the audience. Submit a copy of both the advertisement and your letter.

16. **Selling a Service—Small Business**   While studying for your bar exams, you decide to start a part-time business delivering singing telegrams throughout the Atlanta metropolitan area. For a flat fee of $50, you'll personally deliver a greeting card and sing any song (in good taste) of the customer's choice—using either the actual wording of the song or special lyrics composed by the customer. You promote your company (Musical Messages) for birthdays, anniversaries, graduations, promotions, and other special occasions. Send a form letter to a random sample of Atlanta's residents, promoting your service. The purpose of your letter is to persuade the reader to call you at 404-555-9831 to order a singing telegram. Orders must be prepaid (no credit cards), and you require seven days' notice.

17. **Form Letter—Selling for Charity**   As the director of fund-raising for the Buckeye Bread Basket, a Cleveland, Ohio, charity that buys food for people in need, you are starting a new program. You plan to sell holiday greeting cards to raise money for your annual Thanksgiving Day dinner. This year, more than 400 needy people (including singles and families) are expected to attend the dinner. An Ohio artist created the original watercolor scene on the cards, which come in boxes of 10, with green envelopes. People who buy the cards are able to take a tax deduction for their donations; the money from the sale of a single box can feed a hungry family of four on Thanksgiving.

Write a form letter that will persuade people to order your cards. The price is $12 per box, plus $1 postage and handling, and orders can be placed using the enclosed form and return envelope.

CONTINUING CASE 8

Flying High at Urban Systems

Neelima, Jean, and Larry were analyzing the quarterly expense report. "Look at line item 415," Neelima said. "Air-travel expenses have increased 28% from last year. Is there any room for savings there?"

"Jean and I were discussing that earlier," Larry said. "I think we should begin requiring our people to join all the frequent-flyer programs so that after they fly 20,000 to 30,000 miles on any one airline, they get a free ticket. Then we should require them to use that free ticket the next time they have to take a business trip for us."

"I disagree," Jean said. "To begin with, there's no easy way to enforce the requirement. Who's going to keep track of how many miles each person flies on each airline and when a free flight coupon is due that person? It would make us appear to be Big Brother, looking over their shoulders all the time.

"In addition, our people put in long hours on the road. If they can get a free ticket and occasionally are able to take their spouses along with them, what's the big deal? They're happier and probably end up doing a better job for us."

"Still," Larry countered, "company resources were used to purchase the original tickets, so logically the free tickets belong to the company. And why should our people who travel get free tickets, compliments of the company, when those who don't travel do not get free tickets?"

Jean was ready with a counterargument, but Neelima put an end to the discussion: "Both of you think about the matter some more and let me have a memo by next week giving me your position. Then I'll decide."

Critical Thinking

1. Jot down all the reasons you can think of for and against Larry's proposition—including any reasons that might not have been discussed at the meeting. What are the benefits associated with each reason? Has this topic been covered on the Internet?

Writing Projects

2. Assume the role of Larry. Write a memo to Neelima trying to persuade her to begin requiring employees to use their frequent-flyer miles toward business travel. Knowing that Jean will be writing a memo arguing the opposing viewpoint—that employees should be able to use their free airline tickets for personal use—try to counteract her possible arguments.

3. Now assume the role of Jean. Write a memo to Neelima arguing for the status quo. Try to anticipate and counteract Larry's likely arguments.

9

Bad-News Messages

An Insider's Perspective

Open disclosure is the way Howard High deals with messages about potential problems. High is Strategic Communications Manager for Intel, the global leader in making microprocessors for personal computers. As a company spokesperson, he shares information about the $21 billion company and its products with reporters from U.S. and foreign business publications. Intel products are definitely high-tech; they're also high-profile, thanks to the "Intel Inside" brand-building campaign that has established the company's worldwide reputation for quality.

As Intel adds innovative features and more processing power to new chips, it faces the challenge of managing public perceptions and expectations of product performance to prevent disappointment. This is where insightful audience analysis and open disclosure pay off. "Chip products are extremely complex," comments High. "Although our chips are becoming better and better, we try to communicate to the buying public that there are limitations, so that people do not expect absolute perfection."

For example, if a chip's actual performance differs from the original specifications, Intel notes the differences on an "errata list" that is circulated to dealers and computer users through the World Wide Web and other sources. Not everyone wants to study the technical details, but Intel provides complete information so that those who are interested can find out what they need to know. "We didn't do this in the past," explains High, "but now we realize that making this information available takes away the potential for a negative reaction. We would rather err on the side of being open and truthful so people don't ask, 'Why didn't you tell us about this problem? Why did you keep this a secret?'"

When he has to communicate a bad-news message about a problem that may affect a large number of customers, High will take additional steps to publicize the issue. "We would probably involve a senior-level manager as the spokesperson or the quoted source in the news release and, if necessary, hold an audio conference call

COMMUNICATION OBJECTIVES

After you have finished this chapter, you should be able to

■ Decide when to use a direct or an indirect organizational plan for bad-news messages.

■ Compose a message that rejects an idea.

■ Compose a message that refuses a favor.

■ Compose a message that refuses a claim.

■ Compose an announcement that conveys bad news.

with reporters to explain the situation," he says. He also arranges for speedy replies to customers who write or e-mail the company to express their concerns.

Even when more research is needed to resolve the problem, Intel does not delay in communicating a bad-news message. "As long as you indicate that you are continuing to look for answers, open communication will show people that you are working hard to bring the problem to a successful conclusion," High says. "But if people feel blocked from understanding the problem—let alone the solution—you may be setting up an adversarial situation."

Intel's customer-focused communication policy was influenced by the 1994 media coverage of a technical problem with the original Pentium processor chip. After the chip was introduced, internal analysis showed that it had a floating-point error problem. Believing that the flaw would affect few customers, Intel fixed the problem but did not publicize it. Then a college professor doing sophisticated mathematical calculations found and discussed the problem with colleagues via the Internet. Business reporters who read the Internet messages called Intel and were told that the problem had been fixed and that newer versions of the chip would soon be available. Then a television reporter picked up the story, which sparked widespread media interest. Initially, Intel announced that it would selectively

replace the chips, based on the company's determination of how each customer was using his or her computer. However, a firestorm of customer protests convinced Intel to change its policy, and within 30 days, it had a global process for providing free replacement chips on request.

This experience gave Intel new insights into handling bad-news messages. "As a company, we learned how to change the way we manage this kind of communication," High observes. "Now we really understand the importance of looking at these issues from our customers' perspective."

Howard High

Strategic Communications Manager, Intel Corporation (Santa Clara, California)

Planning the Bad-News Message

At some point in our lives we have all probably been both the relayers and the recipients of bad news. And just as most people find it difficult to accept bad news, they also find it difficult to convey bad news. Therefore, like persuasive messages, bad-news messages require careful planning. How you write your messages won't change the news you have to convey, but it may determine whether your reader accepts your decision as reasonable—or goes away mad.

Your purpose in writing a bad-news message is twofold: first, to say "no" or to convey bad news; and second, to retain the reader's goodwill. To accomplish these goals, you must communicate your message politely, clearly, and firmly. And you must show the reader that you've seriously considered the request but that as a matter of fairness and good business practice, you must deny the request.

Your objectives are to convey the bad news and retain the reader's goodwill.

Sometimes you can achieve your purpose better with a phone call or personal visit than with a written message. A phone call is often appropriate when the reader will not be personally disappointed in the outcome, and a personal visit is often called for when you are giving a subordinate negative news of considerable consequence. Frequently, though, a written message is most appropriate because it lets you control more carefully the wording, sequence, and pace of the ideas presented. In addition, it provides a permanent record of what was communicated.

Organizing to Suit Your Audience

The reader's needs, expectations, and personality—as well as the writer's relationship with the reader—will largely determine the content and organization of a bad-news message. Thus you need to put yourself in the place of the reader.

To decide whether to use the direct or the indirect plan for refusing a request, check the sender's original message. If the original message was written in the direct style, the sender may have considered it a routine request, and you would be safe in answering in the direct style. If the original message was written in the indirect style, the sender probably considered it a persuasive request, and you should consider answering in the indirect style. (However, memorandums written to one's superior are typically written in the direct style, regardless of whether the reader considers the original request routine or persuasive.)

For example, a memo telling employees that the company cafeteria will be closed for one day to permit installation of new equipment can be written directly and in a paragraph or two. A memo telling employees that the company cafeteria will be closed permanently and that employees will now have to go outside for lunch (and pay higher prices) would require more explanation and should probably be written in the indirect style.

Direct Plan—Present the Bad News Immediately   As discussed in Chapter 7, many requests are routine; the writer simply wants a yes-or-no decision and wants to hear it in a direct manner. Similarly, if an announcement of bad news is not likely to generate an emotional response from readers, you should use a direct approach. The direct plan for bad-news messages is basically the same plan used for routine messages discussed in Chapter 7: present the major idea (the bad news) up front. To help readers accept your decision when using the direct plan, present a brief rationale along with the bad news in the first paragraph.

Companies like Kiwi Airlines that are forced to declare Chapter 11 bankruptcy face a real challenge in conveying bad news. They must try to keep employees, creditors, customers, and stockholders content long enough for the company to get back on its feet financially.

NOT: The annual company picnic originally scheduled for August 3 at Riverside Park has been canceled.

BUT: Because ongoing construction at Riverside Park might present safety hazards to our employees and their families, the annual company picnic originally scheduled for August 3 has been canceled.

As usual, state the message in language as positive as possible, while still maintaining honesty.

NOT: Our departmental compliance report will be late next month.

NOT: I am pleased to announce that our departmental compliance report will be submitted on March 15.

BUT: The extra time required to resolve the Baton Rouge refinery problem means that our departmental compliance report will be submitted on March 15 rather than on March 1.

Then follow with any needed explanation and a friendly closing. The direct organizational plan should be used under the following circumstances:

- The bad news involves a small, insignificant matter and can be considered routine. If the reader is not likely to be emotionally involved and thus not seriously disappointed by the decision, use the direct approach.

- The reader prefers directness. Superiors typically prefer that *all* messages from subordinates be written in the direct style.

- The reader expects a "no" response. For example, mid-career job applicants know that job offers at their level are typically made by phone and job rejections by letter. Thus, upon receiving a letter from the prospective employer, the applicant expects a "no" response; under these circumstances, delaying the inevitable only causes ill will and makes the writer look less than forthright.

- The writer wants to emphasize the negative news. Suppose that you have already refused a request once and the reader writes a second time; under these

Prefer the direct organizational plan for communicating bad news to your superior.

In some situations, it is necessary to emphasize the bad news.

circumstances, a forceful "no" might be in order. Or consider the situation where negative information is to be included in a form letter—perhaps as an insert in a monthly statement. Because the reader might otherwise discard or only skim an "unimportant-looking" message, you should consider placing the bad news up front—where it will be noticed.

- The reader-writer relationship is at either extreme—either very close or very poor. Consider using the direct approach if the relationship is either so friendly that you can assume the continued goodwill of the reader or so strained and suspicious that the reader may think he or she is being given the runaround if the bad news is buried in the middle.

Direct messages are not necessarily shorter than indirect messages.

A message organized according to a direct plan is not necessarily any shorter than one organized according to an indirect plan. Both types of message may contain the same basic information but simply in a different order. For example, assume that the program chairman of the Downtown Marketing Club has written to ask you to be the luncheon speaker at the March 8 meeting, but because of a prior commitment, you must decline. If you have a close relationship with the reader, you might choose the direct approach, as follows:

> Except for the fact that I'll be in Mexico on March 8, I would have enjoyed speaking to the Downtown Marketing Club. As you know, Hansdorf Industries is opening an outlet in Nogales, and I'll be there March 7–14 interviewing marketing representatives and setting up sales territories.
>
> If, however, you find yourself in need of a speaker during the summer months, please keep me in mind. My travel schedule thus far is quite light during June, July, and August.
>
> As a long-time member of the Downtown Marketing Club, I've enjoyed and benefited from the luncheon speakers the club sponsors each month. Best wishes, Roger, for a successful year as program chairperson. (*114 words*)

Now assume the same situation, except that you do not know the reader. This time, you might choose the indirect approach, as follows:

> As a long-time member of the Downtown Marketing Club, I've enjoyed and benefited from the luncheon speakers the club sponsors each month. Monica Foote's December talk on the pitfalls of international marketing was especially interesting and helpful.
>
> As you may have read in the newspaper, Hansdorf Industries is opening an outlet in Nogales, Mexico, and I'll be there March 7–14 interviewing marketing representatives and setting up sales territories. Thus, you will need to select another speaker for your March 8 meeting.
>
> If you find yourself in need of a speaker during the summer months, Mr. Caine, please keep me in mind. My travel schedule thus far is quite light during June, July, and August. (*113 words*)

Complex situations typically call for an indirect organizational pattern and require more explanation than simpler situations.

Direct messages are often shorter than indirect messages only because the direct plan is often used for *simpler* situations, which require little explanation and background information.

Indirect Plan—Buffer the Bad News   Because the preceding conditions are *not* true for many bad-news situations, you will often want to use an indirect plan—especially when giving bad news to

- Subordinates

- Customers

- Readers who prefer the indirect approach

- Readers you don't know[1]

With the indirect approach, you present the reasons first, then the negative news. This approach emphasizes the *reasons* for the bad news, rather than the bad news itself.

Suppose, for example, a subordinate expects a "yes" answer upon opening your memo. Putting the negative news in the first sentence might be too harsh and emphatic, and your decision might sound unreasonable until the reader has heard the rationale. In such a situation, you should begin with a neutral and relevant statement—one that helps establish or strengthen the reader-writer relationship. Such a statement serves as a **buffer** between the reader and the bad news that will follow.

A buffer lessens the impact of bad news.

Recall the earlier situation, introduced in Chapter 8, in which the owner of an appliance store wrote one of its suppliers, asking the supplier to provide an in-store demonstrator of the firm's products (even though it was against the company's policy to do so). In Chapter 8 we assumed the role of the appliance store owner and wrote a persuasive message. Now let's assume the role of the supplier, who, for good business reasons, must refuse the request. Because we're writing to a good customer, we decide to use an indirect plan. We might start our message by using any of the following types of buffers:

Buffer Type	Example
Agreement	We both recognize the promotional possibilities that often accompany big anniversary sales such as yours.
Appreciation	Thanks for letting us know of your success in selling Golden Microwaves. (*However, avoid thanking the reader for asking you to do something that you're going to refuse to do; such expressions of appreciation sound insincere.*)
Compliment	Congratulations on having served the community of Greenville for ten years.
Facts	Three-fourths of the Golden distributors who held anniversary sales last year reported at least a 6% increase in annual sales of our home products.
General principle	We believe in furnishing Golden distributors a wide range of support in promoting our products.
Good news	Golden's upcoming 20%-off sale will be heavily advertised and will certainly provide increased traffic for your February anniversary sale.
Understanding	I wish to assure you of Golden's desire to help make your anniversary sale successful.

Note these characteristics of an effective opening buffer for bad-news messages:

1. It is *neutral*. To serve as a true buffer, the opening must not convey the negative news immediately. On the other hand, guard against implying that the request will be *granted*, thus building up the reader for a big letdown.

A buffer should be neutral, relevant, supportive, interesting, and short.

Not neutral:	Stores like Parker Brothers benefit from Golden's policy of not providing in-store demonstrators for our line of microwave ovens.
Misleading:	Your tenth-anniversary sale would be a great opportunity for Golden to promote its products.

Relevant buffers provide a smooth transition to the discussion of reasons.

2. It is *relevant*. The danger with starting *too* far from the topic is that the reader might not recognize that the letter is in response to his or her request. In addition, an irrelevant opening seems to avoid the issue, thus sounding insincere or self-serving. To show relevance and to personalize the opening, you might include some reference to the reader's letter in your first sentence. A relevant opening provides a smooth transition to the reasons that follow.

Irrelevant:	Golden's new apartment-sized microwave oven means that young couples, retirees, and even students can enjoy the convenience of microwave cooking.

3. It is *supportive*. The purpose of the opening is to help establish compatibility between reader and writer. If the opening is controversial or seems to lecture the reader, it will not achieve its purpose.

Unsupportive:	You must realize how expensive it would be to supply an in-house demonstrator for anniversary sales such as yours.

4. It is *interesting*. Although buffer openings are not substitutes for the strong attention-getters that are used in persuasive messages, they should nevertheless be interesting enough to motivate the recipient to continue reading. Therefore, avoid giving obvious information.

Obvious:	We have received your letter requesting an in-store demonstrator for your upcoming tenth-anniversary sale.

5. Finally, it is *short*. Readers get impatient if they have to wait too long to get to the major point of the message.

Too long:	As you may remember, for many years Golden provided in-store demonstrators for our line of microwave ovens. We were happy to do this because we felt that customers needed to see the spectacular results of our new browning element, which made microwaved food look as if it had just come from a regular oven. We discontinued this practice five years ago because . . .

Ethical communicators use a buffer *not* in an attempt to manipulate or confuse the reader but in a sincere effort to help the reader accept the disappointing information in an objective manner.

Justifying Your Decision

Presumably, you reached your negative decision by analyzing all the relevant information. Whether you began in a direct or an indirect manner, now explain your analysis to help convince the reader that your decision is reasonable. The major part of your message should thus focus on the reasons rather than on the bad news itself.

For routine bad-news messages (that is, those written in a direct approach), the reasons can probably be stated concisely and matter-of-factly. Indirectly written messages, however, require more careful planning—because the stakes are typically greater.

Provide a smooth transition from the opening buffer and present the reasons honestly and convincingly. If possible, explain how the reasons benefit the reader or, at least, benefit someone other than you. Thus, refusing to exchange a worn garment might enable you to offer better-quality merchandise to your customers, raising the price of your product might enable you to switch to nonpolluting energy for manufacturing it, or refusing to provide copies of company documents might protect the confidentiality of customer transactions. Presenting reader benefits keeps your decision from sounding selfish.

wordwise	
Self-Canceling Phrases (*Oxymorons***)**	
■ Terribly nice	■ Work party
■ Loose tights	■ Rolling stop
■ Standard options	■ Numb feeling
■ Loyal opposition	■ Live recording
■ Paid volunteers	■ Authentic replica
■ Mournful optimist	■ Deafening silence

Sometimes, however, granting the request is simply not in the company's own best interests. In such situations, don't "manufacture" reader benefits; instead, just provide whatever short explanation you can and let it go at that.

> Because this data would be of strategic importance to our competitors, we treat it as confidential. Similar information about our entire industry (SIC Code 1473), however, is collected in the annual *U.S. Census of Manufacturing*. These census reports are available in most public and university libraries.

Show the reader that your decision was a *business* decision, not a personal one. Show that the request was taken seriously, and don't hide behind company policy. If the policy is a sound one, it was established for good reasons; therefore, explain the rationale for the policy.

NOT: Company policy prohibits our providing an in-store demonstrator for your tenth-anniversary sale.

BUT: A survey of our dealers three years ago indicated they felt the space taken up by in-store demonstrators and the resulting traffic problems were not worth the effort; they were also concerned about the legal implications of having someone cooking in their stores.

The reasons justifying your decision should take up the major part of the message, but be concise or your readers may become impatient. Do not belabor a point and do not provide more background than is necessary. If you have several reasons for refusing a request, present the strongest ones first—where they will receive the most emphasis. If possible, avoid mentioning any weak reasons. If the reader feels he or she can effectively rebut even one of your arguments, you're simply raising false hopes and inviting needless correspondence. Finally, be aware of the ethical and legal aspects of your decisions and your justification of your decisions (see Spotlight 15—On Law and Ethics, page 262).

Giving the Bad News

The bad news is communicated up front in directly written messages. And even in an indirectly written message, if you have done a convincing job of explaining the

Ten Reasons to Consult Your Lawyer

SPOTLIGHT 15

ON LAW

AND ETHICS

Because memos, letters, and corporate communications may be used as evidence against you or your organization in a court of law, it is often wise to check with a lawyer to make sure that what you write doesn't violate state or federal law. You should consult legal counsel when a document that you have written

1. Commits you to a legally binding contract.
2. Commits you to a warranty or guarantee of a product or service.
3. Makes an advertising claim.
4. Amends or modifies corporate policy.
5. Requests documents from an attorney.
6. Makes a statement to an insurance adjuster, the police, or a government agency.
7. Reports an accident involving a product, service, or employee.
8. Concerns the termination of an employee.
9. Concerns workers' compensation or insurance matters.
10. Concerns any product or process that will affect the environment.

The reader should be able to infer the bad news before it is presented.

reasons, the bad news itself will come as no surprise; the decision will appear logical and reasonable—indeed the *only* logical and reasonable decision that could have been made under the circumstances.

To retain the reader's goodwill, state the bad news in positive or neutral language, stressing what you *are* able to do rather than what you are not able to do. Avoid, for example, such words and phrases as "cannot," "are not able to," "impossible," "unfortunately," "sorry," and "must refuse." To subordinate the bad news, put it in the middle of a paragraph, and include in the same sentence (or immediately afterward) additional discussion of reasons.

> In response to these dealer concerns, we eliminated in-store demonstrations and now advertise exclusively in the print media. Doing so has enabled us to begin featuring a two-page spread in each major Sunday newspaper, including your local paper, the *Greenville Courier*.

When using the indirect plan, phrase the bad news in impersonal language, avoiding the use of *you* and *your*. The objective is to distance the reader from the bad news so that it will not be perceived as a personal rejection. So as not to point out the bad news that lies ahead, avoid using *but* and *however* to introduce it. The fact is, most readers won't remember what was written before the *but*—only what was written after it.

You do not need to apologize for making a rational business decision.

Resist any temptation to apologize for your decision. You may reasonably assume that if the reader were faced with the same options and had the same information available, he or she would act in a similar way. There is no reason to apologize for any reasonable business decision.

In some situations, the refusal can be implied, making a direct statement of refusal unnecessary. But don't be evasive. If you think a positive, subordinated refusal might be misunderstood, go ahead and state it directly. However, even under these circumstances, you should use impersonal language and include reader benefits.

When conveying news with a negative implication, a direct, open attitude is often effective because it helps establish credibility. A woman sued McDonald's (and won) based on the fact that she burned herself on their hot coffee. Now, many McDonald's restaurants warn customers to be careful. As usual, open communication leads to better results than closed communication.

Closing on a Pleasant Note

Any refusal, even when handled skillfully, has negative overtones. Therefore, you need to end your message on a more pleasant note. Make your closing original, friendly, and positive by using any of the following techniques. Avoid referring again to the bad news.

Do not refer to the bad news in the closing.

Technique	*Example*
Best wishes	Best wishes for success with your tenth-anniversary sale. We have certainly enjoyed our ten-year relationship with Parker Brothers and look forward to continuing to serve your needs in the future.
Counterproposal	To provide increased publicity for your tenth-anniversary sale, we would be happy to include a special 2-by-6-inch boxed notice of your sale in the *Greenville Courier* edition of our ad on Sunday, February 8. Just send us your camera-ready copy by January 26.
Other sources of help	A dealer in South Carolina switched from using in-store demonstrators to

showing a video continuously during his microwave sale. He used the 10-minute film *Twenty-Minute Dinners with Pizzazz* (available for $45 from the Microwave Research Institute, P.O. Box 800, Chicago, IL 60625) and reported a very favorable reaction from customers.

Resale or subtle sales promotion

You can be sure that the new Golden Mini-Micro we're introducing in January will draw many customers to your store during your anniversary sale.

Close the letter on a positive, friendly, helpful note.

To sound sincere and helpful, make your ending original. If you provide a counterproposal or offer other sources of help, provide all the information the reader needs to follow through. If you include sales promotion, make it subtle and reader-oriented. Avoid statements such as the following:

Problem to Avoid	*Example of Problem*
Apologizing	Again, I am sorry that we were unable to grant this request.
Anticipating problems	If you run into any problems, please write me directly.
Inviting needless communication	If you have any further questions, please let me know.
Referring again to bad news	Although we are unable to supply an in-store demonstrator, we do wish you much success in your tenth-anniversary sale.
Repeating a cliché	If we can be of any further help, please don't hesitate to call on us.
Revealing doubt	I trust that you now understand why we made this decision.
Sounding selfish	Don't forget to feature Golden microwaves prominently in your anniversary display.

In short, the last idea the reader hears from you should be positive, friendly, and helpful. Checklist 10 summarizes guidelines for writing bad-news letters. The rest of this chapter discusses strategies for writing bad-news replies and bad-news announcements.

Bad-News Replies

Despite the skill with which a persuasive message is written, circumstances of which the reader is unaware may require a negative response. Your organization's well-being (and your own) may depend on the skill with which you are able to refuse a request and still maintain the goodwill of the reader.

✓ CHECKLIST 10   Bad-News Messages

Determine How to Start the Message

☑ **Direct Plan**—Use a direct organizational plan when the bad news is insignificant, the reader prefers directness (such as your superior) or expects a "no" response, the writer wants to emphasize the bad news, or the reader-writer relationship is either extremely close or extremely poor. Present the bad news (see "Give the Bad News" at right), along with a brief rationale, in the first paragraph.

☑ **Indirect Plan**—Use an indirect organizational plan when writing to subordinates, customers, readers who prefer the indirect plan, or readers you don't know. Start by buffering the bad news, following these guidelines:

   a. Remember the purpose: to establish a common ground with the reader.
   b. Select an opening statement that is neutral, relevant, supportive, interesting, and short.
   c. Consider establishing a point of agreement, expressing appreciation, giving a sincere compliment, presenting a fact or general principle, giving good news, or showing understanding.
   d. Provide a smooth transition from the buffer to the reasons that follow.

Justify Your Decision

☑ If possible, stress reasons that benefit someone other than yourself.

☑ State reasons in positive language.

☑ Avoid relying on "company policy"; instead, explain the reason behind the policy.

☑ State reasons concisely to avoid reader impatience. Do not overexplain.

☑ Present the strongest reasons first; avoid discussing weak reasons.

Give the Bad News

☑ If using the indirect plan, subordinate the bad news by putting it in the middle of a paragraph and including additional discussion of reasons.

☑ Present the bad news as a logical outcome of the reasons given.

☑ State the bad news in positive and impersonal language. Avoid terms such as *cannot* and *your*.

☑ Do not apologize.

☑ Make the refusal definite—by implication if possible; otherwise, by stating it directly.

Close on a Positive Note

☑ Make your closing original, friendly, off the topic of the bad news, and positive.

☑ Consider expressing best wishes, offering a counterproposal, suggesting other sources of help, or building in resale or subtle sales promotion.

☑ Avoid anticipating problems, apologizing, inviting needless communication, referring to the bad news, repeating a cliché, revealing doubt, or sounding selfish.

Rejecting an Idea

One of the more challenging bad-news messages to write is one that rejects someone's idea or proposal. Put yourself in the role of the person making the suggestion. He or she has probably spent a considerable amount of time in developing the idea, studying its feasibility, perhaps doing some research, and, of course, writing the original persuasive message.

Consider, for example, the persuasive memo presented in Model 6 on page 231, in which Jenson Peterson tries to persuade Elliott Lamborn to restrict the nearest parking lots to American-built automobiles. Peterson obviously thinks his idea has merit. He went to the trouble of having his staff count the number of foreign-made automobiles in the lots, getting a cost estimate for making the change, and contacting the union representative to get the union's position. Finally, he organized all his information into an effectively written memo.

Having invested that much time and energy in the proposal, Peterson probably feels quite strongly that his proposal is valid, and he likely expects Lamborn to approve it. If—or in this case *when*—his proposal is rejected, Peterson will be surprised and disappointed.

Because Lamborn is Peterson's superior, he could send Peterson a directly written memo saying in effect, "I have considered your proposal and must reject it." But Peterson is obviously intelligent and enterprising, and Lamborn does not want to discourage future initiatives on his part. As with all such bad-news replies, then, Lamborn's twin objectives are to refuse the proposal and retain Peterson's goodwill.

Rejecting someone's idea requires extreme tact and sound reasons.

To be successful, Lamborn has an educating job to do. He must give Peterson the reasons for the rejection, reasons of which Peterson is probably unaware. He must also show that he recognizes Peterson's proposal as carefully considered and that the rejection is based on business—not personal—considerations.

Given the amount of effort Peterson has put into this project, Lamborn's memo will be most effective if written in the indirect pattern. This pattern will let Lamborn move his subordinate gradually into agreeing that the proposal is not in the best interests of the firm.

Lamborn's memo rejecting Peterson's proposal is shown in Model 10. Although we label this memo a bad-news message, actually it is also a *persuasive* message. Like all bad-news messages, the memo seeks to persuade the reader that the writer's position is reasonable.

Refusing a Favor

Many favors are asked and granted almost automatically. Doing routine favors for others in the organization shows a cooperative spirit, and a spirit of reciprocity often prevails—we recognize that the person asking us for a favor today may be the person from whom we'll need a favor next week. Sometimes, however, for business or personal reasons, we are not able to accommodate the other person and must decline an invitation or a request for a favor.

The type of message written to refuse a favor depends on the particular circumstances. Occasionally, someone asks a "big" favor—perhaps one involving a major investment of time or resources. In that case, the person has probably written a thoughtful, reasoned message trying to persuade you to do as he or she asks. If you must refuse such a significant request, you should probably present your refusal indirectly, following the guidelines given earlier.

When refusing routine requests, give the refusal in the first paragraph.

Most requests for favors, however, are routine, and a routine request should receive a routine response; that is, a response written in the direct organizational plan. A colleague asking you to attend a meeting in her place, a superior asking you to serve on a committee, or a business associate inviting you to lunch is not going to be deeply disappointed if you decline. The writer probably has not spent a great deal of energy composing the request; the main thing he or she wants to know from you is "yes" or "no."

In such situations, give your refusal in the first paragraph, but avoid curtness and coldness. Courtesy demands that you buffer the bad news somewhat and that you at least give a quick, reasonable rationale for declining. Although the refusal itself might not lose the reader's goodwill, a poorly written refusal message might!

MODEL 10 Bad-News Reply—Rejecting an Idea

This memo responds to the persuasive request in Model 6 (see page 231).

+ Timkin   —1034 York Road
+ Electrical   —Baltimore, MD 21204
+ Systems   —Phone: 301-555-1086

MEMO TO: Jenson J. Peterson, Marketing Supervisor

FROM: Elliott Lamborn, Vice President *E L*

DATE: October 15, 19--

SUBJECT: Parking Lot Proposal

1   Your October 3 memo certainly enlightened me regarding the automobile buying habits of our employees. I had no idea that one-third of our workers drive foreign-made cars.

The increasing popularity of foreign-made cars recently led Timkin management to conclude that we should extend our promotional thrust to take advantage of this expanding market. President Wrede has appointed a task force to determine how we might enter the Japanese, German, and English auto markets. In fact, our newest long-range plan, which will be presented to the board next week, estimates that within five years international sales will account for 18% to 20% of Timkin's sales.

Our successful entry into the international automotive market will mean that many of the foreign-made automobiles Timkin employees drive will, in fact, have Timkin electrical systems. Thus, our firm will benefit from the continuing presence of these cars in all our lots.

2   Your memo got me to thinking, Jenson, that we might be missing an opportunity to promote our products to headquarters visitors. Would you please develop some type of awareness campaign (perhaps a bumper sticker for employee cars that contains a Timkin electrical system or some type of billboard) that shows our employees support the products we sell. I would appreciate having a memo from you with your ideas by
3   November 3 so that I might include this project in next year's marketing campaign.

amp

Uses a neutrally worded subject line.
Starts with a supportive buffer; the second sentence provides a smooth transition to the reason.

Begins discussing the reason.

Presents the refusal in the last sentence of the paragraph, using positive and impersonal language.
Closes on a forward-looking, off-the-topic note.

Grammar and Mechanics Notes

1 *one-third:* Spell out and hyphenate fractions.   2 *thinking, Jenson, that:* Set off nouns of direct address *(Jenson)* with commas.   3 *year's:* Use apostrophe plus *s* to form the possessive of a singular noun *(year)*.

The e-mail message in Model 11 declines a request to serve on a corporate committee and is written using a direct plan.

Assume for a moment, however, that Peter Carmichael had decided, instead, that his best strategy would be to write the message (Model 11) in the indirect pattern, explaining his rationale before refusing. His opening buffer might then have been as follows:

> Like you, I believe our new Executive-in-Residence program will prove to be effective for both Utah State and the executives who participate.

Refusing a Claim

The indirect plan is almost always used when refusing an adjustment request because the reader (the dissatisfied customer) is emotionally involved in the situation. The customer is already upset by the failure of the product to live up to expectations. If you refuse the claim immediately, you risk losing the customer's goodwill. And, as noted previously, every dissatisfied customer tells nine or ten people about the bad experience and they, in turn, each tell four or five others. Clearly, you want to avoid the ripple effect of such situations.

The tone of your refusal must convey respect and consideration for the customer—even when the customer is at fault. To separate the reader from the refusal, begin with a buffer, using one of the techniques presented earlier (for example, showing understanding).

> Frequent travelers like you depend on luggage that "can take it"—luggage that will hold up for many years under normal use.

Use impersonal, neutral language to explain the basis for the refusal.

When explaining the reasons for denying the claim, do not accuse or lecture the reader. At the same time, however, don't appear to accept responsibility for the problem if the customer is at fault. In impersonal, neutral language, explain why the claim is being denied.

NOT: The reason the handles ripped off your Sebastian luggage is that you overloaded it. The tag on the luggage clearly states that you should use the luggage only for clothing, with a maximum of 40 pounds. However, our engineers concluded that you had put at least 65 pounds of items in the luggage.

BUT: On receiving your piece of Sebastian luggage, we sent it to our testing department. The engineers there found stretch marks on the leather and a frayed nylon stitching cord. They concluded that such wear could have been caused only by contents weighing substantially more than the 40-pound maximum weight that is stated on the luggage tag. Such use is beyond the "normal wear and tear" covered in our warranty.

Note that in the second example, the pronoun *you* is not used at all when discussing the bad news. By using third-person pronouns and the passive voice, the example avoids directly accusing the reader of misusing the product. The actual refusal, given in the last sentence, is conveyed in neutral language.

An offer of a compromise, however small, helps retain the reader's goodwill.

As with other bad-news messages, close on a friendly, forward-looking note. If you can offer a compromise, it will take the sting out of the rejection and show the customer that you are reasonable. It will also help the customer save face. Be careful, however, that your offer does not imply any assumption of responsibility on

MODEL 11 Bad-News Reply—Refusing a Favor

```
┌─────────────────────────────────────────────────────────────────────┐
│ ✉ Your Memo of May 9, 19-- - Message                      _ □ ✕      │
├─────────────────────────────────────────────────────────────────────┤
│  File  Edit  View  Insert  Format  Tools  Compose  Help               │
├─────────────────────────────────────────────────────────────────────┤
│  ⊟Send  💾 🖨  ✂ 🗐 📋 📎  📖 🔍  ▼  !  ↓  🗐 🔲                       │
├─────────────────────────────────────────────────────────────────────┤
│  Arial            ▼  10  ▼  🎨  B  I  U   ≡ ≡ ≡ ⋮≡ ⋲ ⋺               │
├─────────────────────────────────────────────────────────────────────┤
│ ┌──────────┬──────────┐                                               │
│ │ Message  │ Options  │                                               │
│ ├──────────┴──────────┴───────────────────────────────────┐          │
│                                                                        │
│  ┌────────┐                                                            │
│  │  To... │  Wanda K. Berenson <Berenson@KempMan>         1          │
│  └────────┘                                                            │
│  ┌────────┐                                                            │
│  │  Cc... │  Fay Lee <Lee@KempMan>                        2          │
│  └────────┘                                                            │
│  Subject:   Your Memo of May 9, 19--                                   │
│                                                                        │
│  Hi, Wanda:                                                            │
│                                                                        │
│  You did such a good job of explaining the merits of our new          │
│  Executive-in-Residence program that I've tentatively decided to      │
│  apply for the program myself. To keep my options open, then, I       │
│  must ask you to select someone else to serve on the evaluation       │
│  committee.                                                           │
│                                                                        │
│  Since I may be an applicant myself, I believe it would be            │
│  inappropriate for me to suggest an alternative committee member.     │
│                                                                        │
│  I will know by July 1 whether my workload for the fall semester      │
│  will allow me to apply. If I decide not to apply, I'll be back in     │
│  touch with you then to see if there is some way I can assist you     │
│  in getting this important program off to a successful start.         │
│                                                                        │
│  Peter                                                                 │
│                                                                        │
└─────────────────────────────────────────────────────────────────────┘
```

Gives a quick reason, immediately followed by the refusal.

Provides additional details.

Closes on a helpful note.

Grammar and Mechanics Notes

1 Most e-mail programs will automatically insert the *From:* line in the header.   2 Use the copy line *(Cc:)* to indicate who else received a copy of the message.   3 *July 1 whether:* Do not use a comma after an incomplete date.

your part. The compromise can either come before or be a part of the closing. For example,

> Although we replace luggage only when it is damaged in normal use, our repair shop tells me the damaged handle can easily be replaced. We would be happy to do so for $39.50, including return shipping. If you will simply initial this letter and return it to us in the enclosed, addressed envelope, we will return your repaired luggage within four weeks.

Somewhere in your letter you might also include a subtle pitch for resale. The customer has had a negative experience with your product. If you want your reader to continue to be a customer, you might restate some of the benefits that led him or her to buy the product in the first place. But use this technique carefully; a strong pitch may simply annoy an already unhappy customer.

Consider the persuasive request written by Oliver Arbin presented in Model 8 on p. 235. Mr. Arbin, as you may remember, was upset that his family's flight to Indianapolis was canceled and that they were thus forced to make a six-hour drive instead. He wanted a refund of the $680 cost of his five nonrefundable tickets. It appears, on further investigation, that Mr. Arbin was not completely forthright. The letter refusing his claim request is shown in Model 12.

Bad-News Announcements

Bad-news announcements are not in response to any request.

The previous section discussed strategies for writing negative replies. Often, however, the bad news we have to present involves a new situation; that is, it is not in response to another message. And quite often, these messages go to a large audience, as, for example, when you're announcing a major price increase or new rules and regulations. Such announcements may be either internal (addressed to employees) or external (addressed to customers, news media, stockholders, and the like).

As with other bad-news messages, you must decide whether to use the direct or the indirect plan of organization. Be guided by the effect the bad news will have on the recipients and on your relationship with them.

Bad News About Normal Operations

Assume that management has decided a price increase of 10% is justified on the Danforth cabin tent you manufacture. This price increase requires that you notify your order department, your wholesalers, and finally, a special retail customer.

To notify the order department of the price change (a routine matter), you would probably send a memo or e-mail message like this, written in the direct pattern:

> Effective March 1, the regular price of our Danforth cabin tent (Item R-885) changes from $149.99 to $164.99, an increase of 10%. Any order postmarked before March 1 should be billed at the lower price, regardless of when the order is actually shipped.
>
> The new price will be shown in our spring catalog, and a notice is being sent immediately to all wholesalers. If you receive orders postmarked after March 1 but showing the old price, please notify the wholesaler before filling the order.

MODEL 12 Bad-News Reply—Refusing a Claim

NORTHERN

A I R L I N E S

June 27, 19--

Mr. Oliver J. Arbin
518 Thompson Street
Saginaw, MI 48607

1   Dear Mr. Arbin

We make no money when our customers are forced to take long trips by car rather
than by flying Northern Airlines; and when that happens, we want to find out why.

A review of the June 2 log of the aborted Flight 126 shows that it was scheduled to
depart at 8 p.m. and was cancelled at 7:10 p.m. because of inclement weather. Passen-
2   gers were asked to remain in the boarding area; those who did were rebooked on Flight
3321, which departed at 9:15 p.m. Flight 3321 arrived in Indianapolis at 10:40 p.m.,
just 75 minutes later than the scheduled arrival of Flight 126. Given these circumstances,
Ms. Lois Nixon, the ticket agent, was correct in disallowing any refund on nonrefundable
tickets.

Since you indicated that you're a frequent traveler on Northern, I've asked our Scheduling Department to add you to the mailing list to receive a complimentary subscription
to our quarterly Saginaw flight schedule. A copy of the current schedule is enclosed.
From now on, you'll be sure to know exactly when every Northern flight arrives at and
departs from Tri-Cities Airport.

Sincerely

Madelyn Masarani

Madelyn Masarani
Service Representative

eta
3   Enclosure

P.O. BOX 6001, DENVER, CO 80240 • (303) 555-3990 • FAX (303) 555-3992

---

*This letter responds to the
persuasive claim in
Model 8 on page 235.*

Opens on an agreeable
and relevant note.

Begins the explanation;
presents the refusal in
impersonal language.

Closes on a helpful note;
assumes that the reader
will continue to fly on
Northern.

Grammar and Mechanics Notes

1 Insert no punctuation after the salutation and complimentary closing when using open
punctuation.   2 *boarding area;:* Use a semicolon to separate two closely related independent clauses not connected by a conjunction.   3 Use an enclosure notation to alert the
recipient to look for some inserted material.

If the reader will not be disappointed, present the bad news directly.

The preceding message reflects the fact that the price increase will have minor negative consequences to the order department. Therefore, the news is given directly—in the first sentence—followed by the details. Because the person receiving this memorandum will not be personally disappointed in the news, you don't need to explain the price increase.

However, you also need to notify your wholesalers of this price increase. How will they react? They probably will not be personally disappointed because price increases are common in business and come as no surprise; thus a direct message is called for. But wholesalers *do* have a choice about where to buy tents for resale, so you need to justify your price increase.

A reason may be presented first—even in a message written in a direct pattern.

Because of the prolonged strike in South African mines, we now must purchase the chrome used in our Danforth cabin tent elsewhere at a higher cost. Thus, effective March 1, the regular price of the Danforth tent (Item R-885) will change from $149.99 to $164.99.

As a courtesy to our wholesalers, however, we are billing any orders postmarked prior to March 1 at the old price of $149.99. Use the enclosed form or call our toll-free number (800-555-9843) to place your order for what *American Camper* calls the "sock-it-to-me" tent.

Note how the bad news is cushioned by (1) presenting the reason first—a reason that is clearly beyond your control; (2) selling at the old price until March 1; and (3) including resale in the closing paragraph.

Finally, you need to write a third message about the price increase. For the past two years, you have had an exclusive marketing agreement with the Association for Backpackers and Campers. They promote the Danforth cabin tent in each issue of *Field News,* their quarterly magazine, at no cost to you in exchange for your offering their members the wholesale price of $149.99 (instead of the retail price, which is about 35% higher).

ABC selected the Danforth tent because of its quality *and* because of this attractive price arrangement, and you want to make sure that your price increase does not endanger this relationship. Thus, you write an indirect-pattern letter, in which your major emphasis is on the reasons, not the results.

If the reader must be persuaded of the reasonableness of your decision, use the indirect approach.

The popularity of the Danforth cabin tent that you feature in each issue of *Field News* is based on our exclusive use of a chrome frame. Chrome is twice as strong as aluminum, yet weighs about the same.

Because of the prolonged strike in South African mines, we were faced with the choice of either switching to aluminum or securing the needed chrome elsewhere at a higher cost. We elected to continue using chrome in our tent. This decision to maintain quality has resulted in a change in the wholesale price of the Danforth cabin tent (Item R-885) from $149.99 to $164.99.

The Danforth tent promotion in the spring issue of *Field News* should be changed to reflect this new price. Since the spring issue usually arrives the last week of February, we will bill any orders postmarked before March 1 at the lower price of $149.99.

We have enjoyed the opportunity to serve ABC members and extend best wishes to your organization for another successful year of providing such valuable service to American backpackers and campers.

Another situation that calls for indirect organization is one in which a change in organizational policy will adversely affect employees. It is just as important, of course, to retain the goodwill of employees as it is to retain that of customers. Acceptance of a new policy depends not only on the reasons for the policy but also on the skill with which the reasons are communicated. An example of such a situation is shown in Model 13 on page 274.

When dealing with issues that are of such personal interest to the reader, don't hurry your discussion. Take as much space as necessary to show the reader that your decision was not made in haste, that you considered all options, and that the reader's interests were taken into account.

Explain thoroughly the basis for your decision.

Note, especially, the use of personal and impersonal language throughout the memo. When discussing insurance programs that will be retained (third paragraph), *you* and *your* are used extensively. When discussing the program that will be dropped (fourth paragraph), impersonal language is used instead. The purpose is to closely associate the readers with the good news and to separate them from the bad news. Such deliberate use of language does not manipulate the reader; it simply uses good human relations to bring the reader to an understanding and appreciation of the writer's position.

Bad News About the Organization

If your organization is experiencing serious problems, your employees, customers, and stockholders should hear the news from you—not from newspaper accounts or through the grapevine. For extremely serious problems that receive widespread attention (for example, product recalls, unexpected operating deficits, or legal problems), the company's public relations department will probably issue a news release.

Often, some type of correspondence is also necessary. For example, owners of recalled products must be notified, customers must be notified if an impending strike will affect delivery dates, and employees must be notified if they will be affected by plant closings or layoffs. To show that these situations are receiving attention from top management, such messages should generally come from a high-level official.

Show that the situation is receiving top-management attention.

If the situation about which you are writing has news value, assume that your communication may find its way to a reporter's desk. Thus, make sure not only that the overall tone of the letter is appropriate but also that individual sentences of the letter cannot be misinterpreted if they are lifted out of context.

Throughout your message, choose each word with care. In general, avoid using words with negative connotations and emphasize those with positive connotations. Effective communication techniques can help you control the emphasis, subordination, and tone of your *own* message; however, you cannot do so for a news item that quotes individual parts of your message. For example, note the following misinterpretation, in a published news item, of a sentence from a company president's letter.

News item: Although other drilling companies in the area erect 8-foot fences around their excavation sites, Owens-Ohio President Robert Leach admitted in a letter to stockholders yesterday that "our company does not require fences around these sites."

Write in such a way as not to be misinterpreted.

MODEL 13 Bad-News Announcement—Memo

Danforth Recreational Industries

TO: All Danforth Employees

FROM: Mary Louis Lytle, Vice President   *M U*

DATE: July 8, 19--

1   **RE:**   Change in Insurance Coverage

2   Thanks to you, President Adams will announce a 13% increase in sales for the year that ended June 30. Six of the seven divisions met or exceeded their sales quotas for the year. What an example of the Danforth spirit!

Our pleasure at the 13% increase in sales is somewhat tempered by a corresponding increase in expenditures for the year. In studying the reasons for this increase, we found that fringe benefits, especially insurance, were the largest contributor. Medical insurance costs increased 23% last year and have risen 58% in the past three years.

In order to continue providing needed coverage for our employees and their families and still hold costs to a reasonable level, we've analyzed the use and cost of each component of our program. We learned that last year 89% of you used your health insurance at least once, with the average being 12 family-member consultations per year. Clearly, your health insurance is important to you and, therefore, to us. Similarly, although only 6% used your major medical insurance for hospital care last year, protecting our employees from devastating health-care costs remains a top priority for us.

The other major component of our medical insurance program is dental. Here we found that only 9% of our employees used this coverage last year; yet dental insurance represented 19% of our total medical insurance costs. We believe the funds now being used for dental care for a small minority of our employees can better be used to pay the escalating costs of health and major-medical coverage for all our employees. Thus, effective next January 1, all company-paid insurance programs will include only health and major-medical coverage. Although dental coverage will be discontinued at that time, all requests for reimbursement for dental bills submitted on or before December 31 will be paid at the normal rates.

3   The Benefits Office will hold an open forum on July 28 from 2 to 3 p.m. in the second-floor auditorium to solicit your views on all areas of employee benefits. Please come prepared with questions and comments on pensions, vacations, medical insurance, stock-option plans, and other areas of interest. Your input will enable us to continue to provide our family of employees the kind of protection and options you deserve.

ama

Sidebar annotations:

Uses a neutral subject line.

Begins with a compliment.

Provides a smooth transition to the explanation; uses figures for believability.

Uses the overall welfare of all employees as the reader benefit; presents the good news before the bad.

Implies that fairness demands a change; subordinates the bad news in the middle of a long paragraph.

Closes by discussing a different, but related, topic.

Grammar and Mechanics Notes

1 You may use *RE:* instead of *SUBJECT:* in the memo heading.   2 *President Adams:* Capitalize a title that is used before a name.   3 *3 p.m.:* Use figures to express time; type the abbreviation *p.m.* in lowercase letters, with no space after the internal period.

President's actual statement: Unlike several other firms in the area, we have always had a strict policy of not allowing any digging in residential areas. In fact, all our excavation sites are at least 2 miles from any paved road and are well marked by 10-foot signs. Because these sites are so isolated, our company does not require fences around these sites.

The last sentence of the president's statement would have been more effective had it been worded in positive, impersonal language.

Fences are unnecessary in such isolated sites and, in fact, can cause safety hazards of their own. For example, . . .

If the reader has already learned about the situation from other sources, your best strategy is to use a direct organizational pattern. In a spirit of helpfulness and forthrightness, confirm the bad news quickly and begin immediately to provide the necessary information to help the reader understand the situation. For example,

As you entered the building this morning, you may have seen the evidence of a burglary last night. The purpose of this memo is to let you know exactly what happened and to outline steps we are taking to ensure the continued safety of our employees who work during evening hours.

If the reader is hearing the news for the first time, your best strategy is to use the indirect pattern, using a buffer opening and stressing the most positive aspects of the situation (in this case, the steps you're taking to prevent a recurrence of the problem).

Employees in our data-entry and maintenance departments who work at night perform a valuable service for Martin Company, and their safety and well-being are of prime concern to us. In that spirit, I would like to discuss with you several steps we are taking as a result of. . . .

Model 14 on page 276 shows a letter written to alert customers to the possibility of a demonstration outside the site of a meeting announcing a new product. By showing a respectful attitude toward the demonstrators and by avoiding emotional language, the writer is able to convey the bad news with a minimum of fuss. And the fact that each customer received a personally typed letter from the president is in itself reassuring.

This letter also illustrates another common aspect of bad-news messages: occasionally, you may have to defend positions with which you personally disagree. Your disagreement may be strategic (it's not a smart move at this time) or philosophical (we shouldn't be selling and promoting this product). The issue, of course, goes much deeper than communicating. If you and your organization's philosophies consistently do not mesh, you might be happier finding employment in a more compatible environment. If you decide to stay, however, you should have no qualms about defending any legal and ethical position the organization decides to take.

Being a part of the management team sometimes requires that you support decisions with which you personally disagree.

MODEL 14 Bad-News Announcement—Personal Letter

A personal letter from the president draws the needed attention.

≡ **PACIFIC LABORATORIES**   *A LIFE-LABS COMPANY*

1   November 8, 19--

Ms. Michelle Loftis
Planning Department
Crosslanes Pharmacies
1842 Le Purc Boulevard
El Toro, CA 92630

Dear Ms. Loftis:

Uses sales promotion for the opening buffer.

The breakthrough in over-the-counter birth control that Pacific Laboratories will announce at 3 p.m. on December 5 at the Park Inn will present a very substantial marketing opportunity for Crosslanes Pharmacies. I'm pleased you can be with us for the announcement.

Presents the company in a favorable light by using a reasoned and even-handed approach.

2   Like many scientific breakthroughs, our new product is generating quite a bit of interest in the media. Already, 12 newspapers and television stations have requested and been granted permission to cover this product announcement. We welcome such coverage and believe that an open discussion of such products will lead to more informed decisions by consumers.

Treats the news of the expected demonstrations (the bad news) objectively and unemotionally.

3   In the same spirit, we have taken no steps to prevent any demonstrations outside the Park Inn on that day. It is likely that some pro-life and anti-abortion groups will march and distribute leaflets. So long as they do so peacefully, they are perfectly within their rights. We also are within our rights to hold a meeting without disruption, and there will be adequate security personnel on hand to ensure that everything runs smoothly. We do ask that you bring your original invitation (or this letter) to identify yourself, and we suggest that you use the Broad Street entrance to the hotel.

Closes with additional sales promotion and reader benefits.

We look forward to showing off the efforts of five years of research by our staff. The safety, convenience, and ease of use of this product will make it a very popular item on your pharmacy shelves.

Sincerely,

Stephen Lynch

Stephen Lynch
President

jel

924 Ninth Street, Santa Monica, CA 90403 • (415) 555-2389

Grammar and Mechanics Notes

1 Begin the date and closing lines at the center point when using a modified block style of letter.   2 *coverage and:* Do not insert a comma before the conjunction *(and)* because what follows is not an independent clause.   3 *runs smoothly:* Use an adverb *(smoothly)* instead of an adjective *(smooth)* to modify a verb.

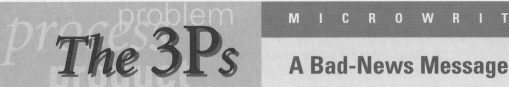
You are a facilities manager at General Mills. Your firm recently constructed a new administrative building on a five-acre lot, and you've landscaped the unused four acres with lighted walkways, fountains, and ponds for employees to enjoy during their lunch hours and before and after work. Your lovely campus-like site is one of the few such locations within the city limits.

Joan Bradley, the mayor of your city, is running for reelection. She has written to you asking permission to hold a campaign fund-raiser on your grounds on July 7 from 8 p.m. until midnight. This event will be for "heavy" contributors; up to 150 people, each paying $500, are expected. Her reelection committee will take care of all catering, security, and cleanup.

You do not want to become involved in this event for numerous reasons. Write to the mayor (The Honorable Joan Bradley, Mayor of Clarkfield, Clarkfield, MN 56223) and decline her request.

1. Describe your primary audience.

   ■ Very important person (don't want to offend her)

   ■ Holds political views different from my own

   ■ Possibility of her losing the election (don't want to appear to be backing a loser)

2. Describe your secondary audience.

   ■ The 150 big contributors (What will be their reaction to my refusal?)

   ■ The other candidates (do not wish to offend anyone who might become the next mayor)

3. Brainstorm: List as many reasons as you can think of why you might refuse her request. Then, after you've come up with several, determine which one will be most effective. Underline that reason.

   ■ Other sites in the city offering a more suitable environment for the event

   ■ Would have to provide the same favor for every other candidate

   ■ <u>Possible harm to lawn, plants, and animals</u>

   ■ Company policy that prohibits outside use

4. Write your buffer opening—neutral, relevant, supportive, interesting, and short.

   Thank you for your kind comments about our lovely grounds. Our staff has been able to create an environment in which plants and animals not normally found in the Midwest are able to thrive.

5. Now skip to the actual refusal itself. Write the statement in which you refuse the request—making it positive, subordinated, and unselfish.

   To protect this delicate environment, we restrict the use of these grounds to company employees.

6. Write the closing for your letter—original, friendly, off the topic of the refusal, and positive. *Suggestions:* best wishes, counterproposal, other sources of help, or subtle resale.

   As an alternative, may I suggest the beautiful grounds at the Minnesota Educational Consortium on Lapeer Street. They were designed with a Minnesota motif by Larry Miller, the designer for our grounds.

General Mills
General Offices

Post Office Box 1113
Minneapolis, Minnesota 55440

May 20, 19--

The Honorable Joan Bradley
Mayor of Clarkfield
Clarkfield, MN 56223

Dear Mayor Bradley:

Thank you for your kind comments about our lovely grounds. Our staff has been able to create an environment here in which plants and animals not normally found in the Midwest are able to thrive.

For example, after much effort, we have finally been able to attract a family of Eastern Bluebirds to our site. At this very moment, the female is sitting on three eggs, and various members of our staff unobtrusively check on her progress each day.

Similar efforts have resulted in the successful introduction of beautiful but sensitive flowers, shrubs, and marsh grasses. To protect this delicate environment, we restrict the use of these grounds to company employees, many whom have contributed ideas, plants, and time in developing the grounds.

As an alternative, may I suggest the beautiful grounds at the Minnesota Educational Consortium on Lapeer Street. They were designed with a Minnesota motif by Larry Miller, the designer for our grounds. Various public events have been held there without damage to the environment. Susan Siebold, their executive director (555-9832), is the person to contact about using MEC's facilities.

Sincerely,

J. W. Hudson

J.W. Hudson
Facilities Manager

tma

General Offices at Number One General Mills Boulevard

SUMMARY

When writing a bad-news message, your goal is to convey the bad news and, at the same time, keep the reader's goodwill. A direct organizational plan is recommended when you are writing to superiors, when the bad news involves a small, insignificant matter, or when you want to emphasize the bad news. When using the direct plan, state the bad news in positive language in the first paragraph, perhaps preceded or followed by a short buffer or a reason for the decision. Then present the explanation or reasons, and close on a friendly and positive note.

When writing to subordinates, customers, or people you don't know, you should generally use an indirect plan. This approach begins with a buffer—a neutral and relevant statement that helps establish or strengthen the reader-writer relationship. Then follows the explanation of or reasons for the bad news. The reasons should be logical and, when possible, should identify a reader benefit. The bad news should be subordinated, using positive and impersonal language; apologies are not necessary. The closing should be friendly, positive, and off the topic.

Depending on the individual circumstances, either the direct or the indirect pattern may be used to reject an idea, refuse a favor, deny a claim, or present bad news about normal operations or about the organization itself.

KEY TERM

buffer

REVIEW AND DISCUSSION

1. **Communication at Intel Corporation Revisited**   As an Intel spokesperson, Howard High uses open disclosure to let the public know about any problems that might affect the company's microprocessor products for personal computers.
   a. Should High use the direct or indirect pattern in a memo to employees about a problem with a new chip?
   b. What opening buffer might High use in a bad-news letter to dealers about a delay in shipping chips because severe flooding has washed out roads around the manufacturing plant?
   c. Should High apologize for the flooding problem? If so, where?
2. What are the two objectives of a bad-news message?
3. Under what conditions should a direct plan of organization be used for bad-news messages?
4. Why are direct messages often shorter than indirect messages?
5. Indicate whether a direct or an indirect message would be more effective when writing to
   a. A colleague, refusing her offer of a free ride to your upcoming sales conference because you have to go a day early.
   b. Employees, telling them that for the first time no vacations may be scheduled during July and August.
   c. Your superior, informing him that the quarterly employee newsletter will be three days late because the offset machine broke down.
   d. The sales staff, informing them that their sales quotas will be increased by 8% for the coming year.
   e. Stockholders, informing them of an impending federal investigation of your vice chairperson.
6. Why is the opening sentence of an indirect message called a "buffer"?

7. List the five characteristics of an effective buffer.
8. Critique each of the following buffers; then revise them to correct the weaknesses.

   a. Thank you so much for asking me to serve on the employee relations committee.

   b. You can always depend on Meyers to honor claims for damaged merchandise.

   c. I wish I could grant your request to mail your organization's newsletter from our mailroom.

9. Critique each of the following reasons or explanations for refusing; then revise them to correct the weaknesses.

   a. Unfortunately, the cost of participating in this project is prohibitive; furthermore, . . .

   b. You can surely understand that participating in this project would be prohibitively expensive.

   c. That is why company policy prohibits all such endeavors.

10. You wish to refuse a worker's request to use the microcomputer at her desk after hours to compose a newsletter for a charitable organization to which she belongs. Write the statement in which you actually say "no."

11. What techniques are effective for the closing of a bad-news message? What techniques should you avoid?

12. Write an effective closing sentence for a letter in which you have refused to honor a claim for a damaged dress because it was improperly laundered.

Help Wanted

Directions: This letter is from Kenneth C. Collins, a travel agent at Galactic Travel & Leisure, to Rita Warren, a customer. Revise the letter to make it more effective, taking into consideration the editor's marginal comments.

Use a neutral subject line.

Dear Ms. Warren

Subject: Cancelation of Tokyo Trip

    The charter trip to Tokyo that was scheduled to depart on March 23 has been canceled.   *org—*

    Our customers have enjoyed the <u>convience</u> of   *sp* taking charter flights directly from our city airport for nearly 25 years. However, because of the current strike by airport personnel, airport management has decided to cancel all scheduled charter flights until further notice.

frag

If you prefer, we will refund your deposit in full. <u>Or transfer</u> your reservations to an identical Tokyo trip we are organizing for May 2–10. Please call us toll-free at 800-555-2863 to let us know your

sp

preference. If we <u>donot year</u> from you by Friday, March 20, we will automatically send out your refund check.

Sincerely

EXERCISES

1. The 3Ps Microwriting Model: Communication Applications at Intel   Taking the customers' perspective helps Howard High craft bad-news messages when Intel has to announce a problem. The company is careful to keep customers—and the media—informed about any problems as soon as they are discovered. This open disclosure policy allows High and his colleagues to minimize the possibility of a negative reaction to bad news.

Problem

Imagine that Intel is adding a variety of speed-enhancing features to the next generation of its Pentium Pro chip. To allow for extensive testing of these features, the new chip will not be available until March, four weeks later than originally announced. As an Intel communication specialist, you have been asked to convey this information in a letter to the production manager of Compaq, which buys Intel chips to install in its PCs. Although the delay may be disappointing, Compaq should know that the testing will bring out any flaws that need to be addressed before the new (and substantially improved) chips are shipped.

Process
a. Describe your audience.
b. Should you use a direct or indirect organizational plan for this letter? Why?
c. Write your buffer opening, bearing in mind the need to retain Compaq's goodwill despite the delay.
d. What points should you make in discussing the reason for this delay?
e. Write the closing of your letter, striving for a positive, supportive tone.

Product

Using your knowledge of bad-news messages, draft this letter to John Cullinan, Production Manager, Compaq (P.O. Box 69200, Houston, TX 77269-2000).

2. The 3Ps Microwriting Model: A Claims Refusal

Problem

You have just received a claim letter from John Stodel (306 Hyde Court, Kirkwood, MO 63122-4541). Mr. Stodel purchased a Clipper lawn mower (Model 306-B) from you two years ago. For the third time, he has written a claim letter requesting that you repair his $486 mower for free because its self-propelling mechanism stopped working after 15 months of use. Twice already, you've sent polite adjustment letters, denying the claim on the basis that the Model 306-B comes with a one-year warranty and the repair does not fall within the warranty period. You don't want to be rude, but you wish he would stop writing to you about a matter that you've already settled. Let him know.

Process

a. What is the purpose of your message?
b. Describe your audience.
c. Should you use a direct or indirect organizational plan? Why?
d. Write the first sentence of your letter. Be firm and businesslike—but polite and respectful. Remember that you want to retain the customer's goodwill.
e. How much space should you devote to discussing the reasons for your refusal to honor the claim? Why?
f. Write the last sentence of your letter. Again, strive for a firm, businesslike, polite, and respectful tone.

Product

Draft, revise, format, and proofread your letter. Then submit both your answers to the process questions and your revised letter to your instructor.

3. **Rejecting an Idea—Notebook Computer**   You are Charles J. Redding, and you have received the memo written by O. B. Presley (Exercise 2 of Chapter 8). You have, of course, considered all kinds of options to make the sales representatives more productive—notebook computers with built-in printers, cellular telephones for their cars, computerized answering and call-forwarding services, and the like. The fact is that your firm simply cannot afford them for every sales representative. And some of the less energetic representatives clearly do not need them. Instead, your company's philosophy is to pay your representatives top salary and commission and then have them purchase out of their commission earnings whatever "extra" devices or services they deem worthwhile.

You have, however, checked with your purchasing department and found that your corporate price for the Canon NoteJet is $1,850, instead of the retail price of $2,499 Presley quoted. You would be happy to have the company purchase this machine for Presley and deduct the cost from his commission check. Even though Presley will be disappointed in what you have to say, send him a memo conveying this information.

4. **Refusing an Application—McDonald's Franchise**   As the director of franchise operations for McDonald's, Inc., you must evaluate the hundreds of applications for franchises you receive each month. Today you received an application from Maxine Denton, who is developing a large shopping-center complex in Austin, Texas. Her corporation wants to open a McDonald's restaurant in her shopping center. Of course, they will have no trouble coming up with the initial investment. And they will select a qualified manager who will then go through McDonald's extensive training and orientation course.

But McDonald's has a policy against granting franchises to corporations, real estate developers, and other absentee owners. They want their owners to manage their stores personally. They prefer high-energy types who will devote their careers to their restaurant and not be involved in numerous other business ventures. Write to Ms. Denton (she's the president of Lone Star Development Corporation, P.O. Box 1086, Houston, TX 77001), turning down her application.

5. **Refusing a Request—Product Review**   You are Hal Burk, the product reviewer for Computing Trends who received the letter from Heather Lawson, CEO of Software Entrepreneurs, Inc. (see Exercise 9 of Chapter 8). You are accustomed to software firms' being upset about product reviews; no matter when you test a product, the improved version is almost certain to be released soon afterward. If you waited for the improved version of every product you want to test, you would never be able to write a review. Instead, you test the version of each product that consumers are able to buy in their local stores at the time the review is conducted.

You will not test the new ReSolve until you conduct the next scheduled review of spreadsheet programs, in nine months. Space limitations do not permit you to include new product announcements on the review page, but the magazine does have a special feature section for such information. Write a letter to Lawson to convey your position.

6. **Refusing an Idea—Oversized Dressing Rooms**   You are Rebecca Lordstrom (see Exercise 5 of Chapter 8), and you certainly appreciate Robert Kilcline's memo recommending oversized dressing rooms for your new store in Fashion Square Mall. Robert has always been very customer-conscious, a trait you try to instill and nurture in all your employees.

After checking with the facility planner for the new store, you find that the Fashion Square Mall management has only a certain amount of space available for your store. Thus, any space taken up by the dressing rooms would have to be at the expense of the public store areas.

Write a memo to Robert, giving him this information. Perhaps he can suggest other ways instead to enhance customer service.

7. **Refusing a Favor—Summer Internship**   Assume the role of vice president of operations for Kolor Kosmetics, a small manufacturer in Biloxi, Mississippi. One of your colleagues from the local chamber of commerce, Dr. Andrea T. Mazzi, has written asking whether your firm can provide a summer internship in your department for her son Peter, a college sophomore who is interested in a manufacturing career. Kolor Kosmetics has no provisions for temporary summer employees and does not currently operate an internship program. Further, the factory shuts down for a two-week vacation every July.

Write Dr. Mazzi (at 3930 Lyman Turnpike, Biloxi, MS 39530) to let her know this information. Perhaps there are other ways that her son can gain firsthand experience in manufacturing during the summer.

8. **Refusing a Favor—Field Trip**   You are Donna Jo Luse and you have received the letter written by David Pearson (see Exercise 6 of Chapter 8). Lunch is, of course, your busiest time, and no one has the time then (or the patience) to provide a tour of the kitchens and help 23 youngsters make their salads. Perhaps, instead, they could come for a tour and snack midmorning or midafternoon. Write to Mr. Pearson (Jack 'n Jill Preschool, 113 Grenvale Road, Westminster, MD 21157), refusing his request.

9. Refusing Business—Hotel Reservation   You are the manager of the Daytona 100, a 100-room hotel in Daytona, Florida, that caters to businesspeople. You've received a reservation from Alpha Kappa Psi fraternity at Ball State University to rent 24 double rooms during their spring break (April 6–13). They have offered to send a $1,000 deposit to guarantee the rooms if necessary.

As a former AKPsi, you know that these are responsible students who would cause no problems. You also recognize that when these students graduate and assume positions in industry, they are the very type of people you hope will use your hotel. However, because of previous bad experiences, you now have a strict policy against accepting reservations from student groups. Write to the AKPsi treasurer (Scott Rovan, 40 Cypress Grove Court, No. 25, Muncie, IN 47304), conveying this information.

10. Refusing a Claim—No Refund   Once again, assume you are the fulfillment representative at Paperbacks by Post (see Exercise 18 of Chapter 7). Roberto Valazquez has written to request that you take back a book he received three months ago. The problem is not the book itself, which he read and enjoyed, but the value for the money. He complains that the book is too short (162 pages) to justify the amount he paid ($10.95). Valazquez wants his money back, and he also wants the book club to refund the cost of shipping the book back.

This is the fourth time in five months that Valazquez has returned a book. Each time he had a different complaint—once he didn't like the cover illustration, another time he found the language offensive—and you agreed to send him his refunds. At this point, however, you believe that he is simply reading the books and then making up an excuse to avoid paying for them. You decide not to refund his money on this occasion (the number of pages and price of the book were both clearly noted in the announcement Valazquez received before the book was shipped). You also decide to cancel his membership. Write him a letter (at 717 North Walnut Street, Jacksonville, FL 32241) to let him know your decisions.

11. Refusing a Claim—Azaleas   You are a customer service representative for Jackson-Parsons Nurseries and have received the letter written by Vera Malcolm (see Exercise 8 of Chapter 8). Jackson-Parsons goes to great expense to use only the highest-quality patented stock and to pack each order in dampened sphagnum moss. However, there is no way that any nursery can control the care that plants receive on reaching their destination. Your obligation in this matter clearly ended when Ms. Malcolm did not notify you of the problem immediately. If she had, you would have cheerfully refunded her money. But evidently the azaleas are now thriving where they were planted, and you feel you have no further obligation. Tell this to Ms. Malcolm in a letter (Public Service Company of Arkansas, 189 Blackwood Lane, Little Rock, AR 72207).

12. Work-Team Communication—Writing an AIDS Policy   Working in teams of three or four, assume the role of the grievance committee of your union. Your small company has its first known case of an employee with AIDS. The employee, an assistant manager (nonunion position), has indicated that she intends to continue working as long as she is physically able. The company has upheld her right to do so.

You've received a memo signed by six union members who work in her department, objecting to her continued presence at work. They are worried about the risks of contracting the disease from a coworker. Although they have compassion for the assistant manager, they want the union to step in and require that she either resign or be reassigned so that union members do not have to interact with her in the course of completing their own work.

Your committee does some research on the topic and based on your findings decides not to intervene in this matter. Do the research and write a memo to Katherine Kellendorf, chair of the Committee of Concerned Workers, giving her your decision.

13. **Declining an Invitation—Dinner**   You are the purchasing manager at your firm and have received an e-mail message from Barbara Sorrels, one of your firm's major suppliers. She will be in town on October 13 and would like to take you out to dinner that evening. However, you have an early-morning flight on October 14 to Kansas City and will need to pack and make last-minute preparations on the evening of the 13th. Write to Ms. Sorrels (bsorrels@aol.com), declining her invitation.

14. **Declining an Invitation—Public Speaking**   You are Tanya Porratt, president of The Office Training Group. You just received an invitation from Magda D. Lyon to address a dinner meeting of the Baltimore Pentium Users' Group (see Model 7 on page 232). In the past, you frequently accepted such invitations. However, your firm is in the process of being purchased by Triton Technology Corporation, and for the time being you have new rules to follow: you cannot speak in public until the merger has been completed. Because you are unsure of the final date, you are refusing all speaking engagements until October. Tell this to Lyon in a letter.

15. **Bad-News Announcement—Undercharge**   The Wade & Roe law firm is an important customer of your delicatessen. Almost every day you receive a large lunch order from their receptionist, which you deliver to their premises. They pay their bill monthly. In recording their January payment of $348.50, you discover you made an error in billing them. You sent them a bill for $348.50 when, in fact, their charges totaled $438.50. Write them a letter, explaining the matter and requesting payment of the remaining $90 (Fred Walsh, Office Manager, Wade & Roe, Suite 350, North Serrano Place, Los Angeles, CA 90004).

16. **Bad-News Announcement—No Inventory**   Put yourself in the shoes of Alan Teison, the director of distribution for Nu-Shu Sneakers, the best-selling children's sneaker in the United States. Because of this popularity, the company is struggling to keep up with soaring demand. Although you are pleased that sales are so strong, you are concerned that you often lack sufficient inventory to fill every order you receive. Unfortunately, due to temporary stock-outs, some stores will have to wait. One unlucky store is Step Out (212 E. Main Street, Wheat Ridge, CO 80034).

Write to Lily Greenhill, the store manager, explaining that the three styles she ordered are out of stock but you will fill her order as soon as your inventory is replenished. The next shipment from your factory is due in four weeks, so you expect to deliver back-ordered merchandise within five weeks. That date still allows Greenhill time to promote her (your) products for back-to-school wear.

17. **Bad-News Announcement—No Renewal**   Assume the role of Gene Harley, the leasing manager of Northern Plaza. You have decided not to renew the lease of T-Shirts Plus, which operates a tiny T-shirt decorating outlet in the mall. Three times in the past 13 months, the store's employees have left their heat-transfer machinery switched on after closing. Each time, the smoke activated the mall's smoke alarms and brought the fire department to the mall during the late-night hours. Although no damage has occurred, your insurance agent warns that the mall's rates will rise if this situation continues.

The lease that T-Shirts Plus signed five years ago specifies that either party can decide not to renew. All that is required is written notification to the other party at least 90 days in advance of the yearly anniversary of the contract date. By writing this week, you will be providing adequate notice. Convey this information to the store's manager, Henry D. Curtis (at Northern Plaza, Brook Parkway North, Cranbrook, British Columbia, V1C 2Z3, Canada).

18. **Bad-News Announcement—Accounting**   As budget specialist, send an e-mail message to all departments telling them that beginning July 1, all unused balances in their departmental budgets will revert to the organization's central fund. Previously, departments were permitted to carry forward unspent funds to the new year. However, this has caused problems in budgeting and forecasting. Any purchase orders processed by June 10 will be charged against this year's budget; those processed after that date will be charged against the new budget.

19. **Bad-News Announcement—No Party**   Nobody likes a party more than Edgar Dunkirk, the president of Rockabilly Enterprises. In the early days, the company's holiday parties were legendary for their splendid food arrangements and outstanding entertainment (featuring the label's popular singing stars). Employees performed elaborate skits and competed for valuable prizes that included color television sets and videocassette recorders. These days, however, sales of the company's country and rockabilly recordings are down. In fact, Dunkirk recently had to lay off 150 of the company's 350 employees, the most severe austerity measure in the company's history.

    Because so many employees had to be let go, including some who had helped Dunkirk found the company a decade ago, the president has decided that a lavish party would be inappropriate. He has therefore canceled the traditional holiday party. As Dunkirk's vice president of personnel, you must prepare a memo conveying this information to Rockabilly's employees.

20. **Bad-News Announcement—Fringe Benefits**   When your organization moved to its new building in Dallas three years ago, you negotiated a contract with the Universal Self-Parking garage a half-block away to provide free parking to all employees at Grade Level 11 or above. Your rationale was that these managerial employees often work long hours and that convenient, free parking was a justifiable fringe benefit.

    Universal has just notified you that when your contract expires in three months, the monthly fee will increase by 15%. Given the state of the economy and your organization's declining profits, you feel that not only can you not afford the 15% increase but you must, reluctantly, discontinue the free parking altogether.

    Therefore, beginning January 1, all employees must locate and pay for their own parking. Your organization continues to promote ride sharing; and the receptionist has copies of the city bus schedule—a bus stops a block from your building. Write a memo to these managerial employees giving them the information.

21. **Bad-News Announcement—Product Recall**   You have received two reports that users of your ten-stitch portable sewing machine, Sew-Now, have been injured when the needle broke off while sewing. One person was sewing lined denim and the other was sewing drapery fabric—neither of which should have been used on this small machine. Fortunately, neither injury was serious. Although your firm accepts no responsibility for these injuries, you decide to recall all Sew-Now machines to have a stronger needle installed.

    Owners should take their machines to the store where they purchased them. These stores have been notified and already have a supply of the replacement needles. The needle can be replaced while the customer waits. Or users can ship their machines to you prepaid (Betsy Ross Sewing Machine Company, 168 West 17th

Avenue, Columbus, OH 43210). Other than for shipping, there is no cost to the user.

Prepare a form letter that will go out to the 1,750 Sew-Now purchasers. Customers can call your toll-free number (800-555-9821) if they have questions.

CONTINUING
CASE 9

No Such Thing as a Free Flight

Neelima has now received the memos she requested from Jean and Larry regarding the frequent-flyer program (see Continuing Case 8 in Chapter 8). She has thought about the issue quite a bit and discussed it with Marc, Arnie, and Dave.

It seems to her that Larry has the more convincing argument: Company funds *were* used to purchase the tickets; therefore, the company logically owns the free tickets its employees earned. In addition, allowing traveling employees to keep their free tickets in effect amounts to an additional fringe benefit that equally hard-working nontraveling employees do not receive. So Neelima decides to begin requiring US employees to use their frequent-flyer free tickets for business travel rather than personal travel.

Now she needs to write to Jean and Larry to communicate her decision. Larry, of course, will be pleased; Jean will be extremely disappointed—not only because she believes her position to be correct but because she will feel threatened by being turned down by her superior. Jean was promoted to her present position only several months ago and is still a little unsure of her abilities.

Neelima also needs to issue a policy memo to all employees outlining the new program. The system will have to operate on trust; she does not intend to act as "Big Brother," policing the program and verifying mileage. Each employee will be required to join the frequent-flyer program for any airline he or she uses in connection with business travel. Employees can use different versions of their names if they also have a frequent-flyer number for their nonbusiness travel.

The expense report form will be revised to include a check-off question that asks if their frequent-flyer mileage for the flight was recorded. The clerk in OIS who makes all flight reservations will be instructed to ask each manager requesting tickets if he or she has accumulated enough miles on any airline to receive a free flight. Other details can be worked out.

Although many employees, especially those in marketing and R & D who travel extensively, will be upset, Neelima is confident her decision is reasonable and in the best interests of Urban Systems.

Critical Thinking

1. Should Neelima send Jean and Larry a joint memo or separate memos? Why?

Writing Projects

2. Write the needed memos: to Jean and Larry (either a joint memo or separate memos, depending on your response to Question 1) and to the staff.

3. Assume that Urban Systems employees do *not* travel extensively and that Neelima's memo outlining the new restrictions will be considered a routine policy announcement. Write a second version of this memo to the staff using the direct pattern.

Report Writing

10 Planning the Report

An Insider's Perspective

Talking with reporters from CNN, the *Los Angeles Times,* and *Newsweek* is all in a day's work for Janis Lamar. As director of external communications for Experian, an international supplier of information about consumer and business credit, direct marketing, and real estate, it is Lamar's role to field media inquiries and help top management communicate the company's positions to the press. On any given day, she and her team may be writing a news release about a new product or providing facts for a journalist's feature story on consumer credit reporting.

Although most of Lamar's responsibilities involve crafting messages, her duties do not end when the microphones are turned off or the newspaper goes to print. She and her team continuously track how many times the company is mentioned in the media—as many as 2,000 mentions per year—and examine the context as well as the content of each mention. Then, every six months, she prepares an analytical report for an internal audience of 70 top executives, discussing both the details of Experian's media exposure and the meaning of that exposure for the company and its competitive situation.

"This media analysis report serves as a measure of the return on investment of our company's media relations efforts," explains Lamar. "It's also a way to benchmark our media coverage against that of our competitors." In addition, the report shows how a single interview with a key wire service reporter can lead to multiple newspaper stories around the country; such a demonstration helps company executives understand the importance of carefully selecting among interview opportunities.

In planning and writing this report, Lamar takes into consideration her audience's level of knowledge and interest in the subject. "Our executives are not media experts, so I try to keep jargon to a minimum," she says. "When I do use jargon, I either provide an example to clarify or I explain the meaning." In one recent report, Lamar referred to a "pull quote" and included a specific example to show readers exactly what she was talking about. "More information never hurts," she observes. "I've never found anybody who is insulted by clarity and completeness."

COMMUNICATION OBJECTIVES

After you have finished this chapter, you should be able to

■ Describe four common characteristics of business reports.

■ Describe four common types of business reports.

■ Identify the three major purposes of business reports.

■ Analyze the audience for business reports.

■ Evaluate the quality of data already available.

■ Discuss the need for managing reports in the organization.

To speed busy readers through the main points of the 10-page report, Lamar presents the major findings in a one-page executive summary, written after she completes the body of the report. Knowing that her readers are most interested in media coverage of the company's business activities, she presents that information directly following the summary. She also highlights the number of media mentions in bold type to call attention to these measurements. But numbers alone do not tell the whole story, Lamar stresses, which is why she works hard to write a report that will hold her readers' attention. "My readers have many documents competing for their attention," she notes. "I can use color commentary that's appropriate to the subject to make my report a bit more entertaining than a financial report."

Janis Lamar

Director of External Communications, Experian (Orange, California)

Lamar initiated the media analysis report several years ago in response to management's complaint that competitors seemed to be getting more media attention. As she began collecting and analyzing data on media coverage of the industry, she found that Experian was actually getting much more media attention than competitors. Since then, the report has evolved into a valuable early warning system, alerting management to emerging issues of public importance. According

to Lamar, "This report is a very good leading indicator of potential problems. When readers see the totality of media coverage of a particular issue, it makes an impact—and opens the door for changes in company practices or procedures to address that issue."

Who Reads and Writes Reports?

Consider the following routine informational needs of management and other human resources in a large, complex, and perhaps multinational organization:

- A sales manager at headquarters uses information provided by the field representatives to make sales projections.

- A vice president asks subordinates to gather and analyze information needed to make an operational decision.

- A human resources supervisor relies on the firm's legal staff to interpret government requirements for completing a compliance report.

- A manager prepares a proposal for the company to bid on a government project.

- An administrator informs all subordinates about a new company policy on hiring temporary personnel.

A wide variety of reports help managers solve problems.

These common situations show why a wide variety of reports have become such a basic part of the typical management information system (MIS). Because constraints are imposed by geographical separation, time pressures, and lack of technical expertise, managers must rely on others to provide the information, analysis, and recommendations they need for making decisions and solving problems. Because reports travel upward, downward, and laterally within the organization, reading and writing reports is a typical part of nearly every manager's duties.

Reports can range from a fill-in form to a one-page letter or memo to a multivolume manuscript. For our purposes, we define a business report as an orderly and objective presentation of information that helps in decision making and problem solving. Note the different parts of our definition.

- The report must be *orderly* so that the reader can locate the needed information quickly.

- It must be *objective* because the reader will use the report to make decisions that affect the health and welfare of the organization.

- It must present *information*—facts, data. Where subjective judgments are required, as in drawing conclusions and making recommendations, they must be presented ethically and be based squarely on the information presented in the report.

- Finally, the report must aid in *decision making* and *problem solving.* There is a practical, "need-to-know" dimension in business reports that is sometimes missing in scientific and academic reports. Business reports must provide the specific information that management and other personnel need to make a decision or solve a problem. This goal should be uppermost in the writer's mind during all phases of the reporting process.

Characteristics of Business Reports

To better understand your role as a reporter of business information, consider the four following characteristics of business reports:

1. Reports vary widely—in length, complexity, formality, and format.
2. The quality of the report process affects the quality of the final product.
3. Accuracy is the most important trait of a report.
4. Reports are often a collaborative effort.

Let's examine each of these characteristics further.

Reports Vary Widely

There is no such document as a standard report—in length, complexity, formality, or format. The sales representative who spends five minutes completing a half-page call report showing which customers were contacted has completed a report. Likewise, the team of designers, engineers, and marketing personnel who spend six months preparing a six-volume proposal to submit to the U.S. Department of Defense has completed a report. The typical report lies somewhere in between. One analysis of 383 actual business reports found that 36% were one page, 37% were two to three pages, and 27% were four or more pages long.[1]

The typical business report is 1–3 pages long and written in narrative format.

Most reports are written using a standard narrative (manuscript) format, but reports may also be in the form of letters, memos, or preprinted forms. In addition to the body, a report may include such preliminary (prefatory) parts as a cover letter, title page, table of contents, and executive summary. Supplemental parts may include a list of references, appendixes, and an index.

Although reports may be either oral or written, most important reports are written; even most oral reports are written initially. In other words, many reports are first written and then presented orally. Having the report available in written format is important for several reasons: (1) the written report provides a permanent record, (2) it can be read and reread as needed, and (3) the reader can control the pace—rereading the complex parts, marking the important points, and skipping some sections.

The Quality of the Process Affects the Quality of the Product

Writing a report involves much more than "writing a report." As contradictory as this statement might seem, consider a fairly routine report assignment—determining whether to recommend the purchase of Brand A, B, or C overhead projector for your organization's conference room. Before you can begin to write your recommendation, you must do your homework. At a minimum, you must (1) determine what technical features are most important to the users of the machines; (2) evaluate each brand in terms of these features; (3) compare the brands on such characteristics as cost, maintenance, reliability, and ease of use; and (4) draw a conclusion about which brand to recommend.

A report may be well written and still contain faulty data.

If at any step you make a mistake, your report will be worse than useless; it will contain errors that the reader will in turn rely on to make a decision. Suppose you interviewed only 2 of the 50 managers who will be using the new projector. The needs of these 2 managers may not be typical of the needs of the other 48. For example, both of these managers may need color projection, whereas the other 48 may need only black and white. Or suppose you failed to consider the amount of downtime required by each brand. Regardless of its features, no machine can meet the needs of its users when it is inoperable.

As such situations show, your report itself (the end product of your efforts) can be well written and well designed, with appropriate charts and tables; yet if the process by which the information was assembled and analyzed was defective, erroneous, or incomplete, the report will be also. The final product can be only as good as the weakest link in the chain of events leading up to the report.

As indicated in Checklist 11, the reporting process involves planning, data gathering and analysis, and writing. We cover the two major components of the planning stage—defining the purpose of the report and analyzing the audience—later in this chapter. The other steps are discussed in the following chapters.

Accuracy Is the Most Important Trait

Your most important job is to ensure that the information you transmit is correct.

No report weakness—including making major grammatical mistakes, misspelling the name of the report reader, or missing the deadline for submitting the report—is as serious as communicating inaccurate information. It's a basic tenet of management that bad information leads to bad decisions. And in such situations, the bearer of the "bad" news will surely suffer the consequences.

Suppose that while conducting the research for the overhead projector report, you inadvertently noted that the bulbs for Brand A had a 100-hour life when, in fact, they have a 300-hour life. If operating costs were a major criterion, your final recommendation might be incorrect because of this simple careless error. It doesn't even matter how the error occurred—whether you made it or the typist made it. You are responsible for the project, and the praise or criticism of the results of your efforts will fall on you.

To achieve accuracy, follow these guidelines:

1. *Report all the relevant facts.* Errors of *omission* are just as serious as errors of *commission.* Don't mislead the reader by reporting just those facts that tend to support your position.

   NOT: During the two-year period of 1993–1994, our return on investment averaged 13%.

   BUT: Our return on investment was 34% in 1993 but − 8% in 1994, for an average of 13%.

2. *Use emphasis and subordination appropriately.* Your goal is to help the reader see the relative importance of the points you discuss. If you honestly think a certain idea is of minor importance, subordinate it—regardless of whether it reinforces or weakens your ultimate conclusion. Don't emphasize a point simply because it reinforces your position, and don't subordinate a point simply because it weakens your position.

3. *Give enough evidence to support your conclusions.* Make sure that your sources are accurate, reliable, and objective and that there is enough evidence to support your position. Sometimes your evidence (the data you gather) may be so sparse or of such questionable quality that you are unable to draw a valid conclusion. If so, simply present the findings and don't draw a conclusion. To give the reader confidence in your statements, discuss your procedures thoroughly and cite all your sources.

4. *Avoid letting personal biases and unfounded opinions influence your interpretation and presentation of the data.* Sometimes you will be asked to draw conclusions and to make recommendations, and such judgments inherently involve a certain amount of subjectivity. But you must make a special effort to look at the data objectively and to base your conclusions solely on the data. Avoid letting your personal feelings influence the outcomes. Sometimes the use of a single word can unintentionally convey bias.

✔ CHECKLIST 11   **The Reporting Process**

Planning

☑ Define the purpose of the report.
- Determine why the issue is important; what use will be made of the report; and what the time, resource, and length constraints are.
- Decide whether the purpose is to inform, analyze, or recommend.
- Using neutral language, construct a one-sentence problem statement, perhaps in question form.

☑ Define the audience for the report.
- Is the report for an internal or an external reader?
- Did the reader authorize the report or is it voluntary?
- What is the level of knowledge and interest of the reader?

Data Gathering and Analysis

☑ Determine what data will be required.
- Factor the problem statement into its component parts, perhaps stating each sub-problem as a question.
- Determine what data will be needed to answer each subproblem.

☑ Decide which methods to use to collect the needed data.
- Ensure that any secondary data used is current, accurate, complete, free from bias and misinterpretation, and relevant.
- If secondary data is not available, determine the most efficient means of collecting the needed data.

☑ Collect the data.
- Ensure that all informational needs have been identified.
- Allot sufficient time to gather the needed data.
- Ensure that the collection methods will produce valid and reliable data.

☑ Compile the data in a systematic and logical form, organizing it according to the sub-problems.

☑ Analyze each bit of data individually at first and then in conjunction with every other bit of data. Finally, look at all the data together to try to discern trends, contradictions, unexpected findings, areas for further investigation, and the like.

☑ Construct appropriate visual aids.

Writing

☑ Draft the report.
- Consider the needs of the reader and the nature of the problem.
- Determine the organization, length, formality, and format of the report.
- Make sure the report is clear, complete, objective, and credible.

☑ Revise the report for content, style, and correctness.

☑ Use generally accepted formatting conventions to format the report in an attractive, efficient, and effective style.

☑ Proofread to ensure that the report reflects the highest standards of scholarship, critical thinking, and care.

NOT: The accounting supervisor *claimed* the error was unintentional.

BUT: The accounting supervisor *stated* the error was unintentional.

Reports Are Often a Collaborative Effort

Short, informal reports are usually a one-person effort. But many recurring reports in an organization are multiperson efforts. It is not likely, for example, that general management would ask a single person to study the feasibility of entering the generic-product market. Instead, a combination of talents would be needed—marketing, manufacturing, personnel, and the like.

Complex reports require the talents of many people.

At Motorola's Communication (or Comm) Sector, employees and managers brainstorm to develop improvements for two-way radios. This scene is typical in business where a combination of talents joins to produce a collaborative report.

Such joint efforts require well-defined organizational skills, time management, close coordination, and a real spirit of cooperation. Although more difficult to manage than individually written reports, team-written reports offer these advantages:

- They draw on the diverse experiences and talents of many members.

- They increase each manager's awareness of other viewpoints.

- They typically result in higher-quality output than might be the case if a single person worked alone on a complex assignment.

- They can produce a final product in less time than would be possible otherwise.

- They help develop important networking contacts.

- They provide valuable experience in working with small groups.

Common Types of Reports

Management needs comprehensive, up-to-date, accurate, and understandable information to achieve the organization's goals. Much of this information is communicated in the form of reports. The most common types of business reports are periodic reports, proposals, policies and procedures, and situational reports. Each of these types is discussed and illustrated in the following sections.

Periodic Reports

Periodic reports are recurring routine reports submitted at regular intervals.

Three common types of periodic reports are routine management reports, compliance reports, and progress reports.

Routine Management Reports   Every organization requires its own set of recurring reports to provide the knowledge base from which decisions are made and problems are solved. Some of these routine management reports are statistical, consisting sometimes of just computer printouts; other management reports are primarily narrative. Routine management reports range from accounting, financial, and sales updates to various personnel and equipment reports.

Compliance Reports   Many state and federal government agencies require companies doing business with them to file reports showing that they are complying with regulations in such areas as affirmative action, contacts with foreign firms, labor relations, occupational safety, financial dealings, and environmental concerns. Completing these compliance reports is often mostly a matter of gathering the needed data and reporting it honestly and completely. Typically, very little analysis of the data is required.

Progress Reports   Interim progress reports are often used to report the status of long-term projects. They are submitted periodically to management for internal projects, to the customer for external projects, and to the investor for an accounting of venture capital expenditures. Typically, these narrative reports (1) tell what has been accomplished since the last progress report, (2) document how well the project is adhering to the schedule and budget, (3) describe any problems encountered and how they were solved, and (4) outline future plans (see Model 15 on pp. 298–299).

Proposals

A **proposal** is a written report that seeks to persuade a reader from outside the organization to do as the writer wishes (internal proposals are a form of situational report and are discussed in a following section). For example, a manager may write a proposal that seeks to persuade a potential customer to purchase goods or services from the writer's firm, persuade the federal government to locate a new research facility in the headquarters city of the writer's firm, or persuade a foundation to fund a project to be undertaken by the writer's firm.

Proposals may be solicited or unsolicited. Government agencies and many large commercial firms routinely solicit proposals from potential suppliers. For example, the government might publish an RFP (request for proposal) stating its intention to purchase 5,000 microcomputers, giving detailed specifications regarding the features it needs on these computers, and inviting prospective suppliers to bid on the project. Similarly, the computer manufacturer that submits the successful bid might itself publish an RFP to invite parts manufacturers to bid on supplying some component the manufacturer needs for these computers.

Both solicited and unsolicited proposals require persuasion.

The unsolicited proposal differs from the solicited proposal in that the former typically requires more background information and more persuasion. Because the reader may not be familiar with the project, the writer must present more evidence to convince the reader of the merits of the proposal.

The proposal reader is typically outside the organization. The format for these external documents may be a letter report, a manuscript report, or even a form report, with the form supplied by the soliciting organization. If the soliciting organization does not supply a form, it will likely specify in detailed language the format required for the proposal. Obviously, the reader's instructions should be followed explicitly. Despite the merits of a proposal, failure to follow such guidelines may be sufficient reason for the evaluator to reject it.

MODEL 15   Progress Report

This progress report is submitted in letter format.

May 9, 19--

Mr. Ellis Shephard, Chief
Manufacturing Department
Columbia-Collins, Inc.
680 Fourth Avenue
Louisville, KY 40202

Dear Mr. Shepard:

Begins by giving the purpose and an overall summary.

This letter brings you up to date on the status of the construction of your new warehouse on Lafayette Street. As you will see, construction is on schedule and within budget, with no major problems foreseen.

Provides a brief background of the project.

Background: On January 3, 19--, Columbia-Collins contracted with Davenport Construction Company to construct a 48' x 96' frame warehouse at 136 Lafayette Street. Turn-key price was $96,500, with construction to begin on March 10 and to be completed no later than July 20. We agreed to provide interim progress reports on April 10, May 10, and June 10.

Identifies the work completed, in progress, and still to be done.

Work Completed to Date: We have now completed the following jobs:

1. By February 20, all of the plans had been approved by the appropriate regulatory agencies.

2. The foundation was poured on March 27.

1 3. The exterior of the building, including asphalt roofing and aluminum siding, was completed on April 23.

Uses enumerations to make the items stand out.

2 **Work in Progress:** The following work has been started but has not yet been completed:

3 1. The dry-wallers are installing the interior walls and partitions; they should be fininshed by the end of next week.

2. The electricians are installing the lighting, alarm system, outlets, and other electrical requirements.

3. The plumbers have installed the necessary fixtures in the washrooms and are installing the Amana high-energy-efficient heating/cooling unit.

Davenport Construction Company
144 North Limestone • Lexington, KY 40507 • (606) 555-9935

Grammar and Mechanics Notes

1 *exterior . . . was:* Ignore intervening words when establishing subject/verb agreement. 2 *been started but:* Do not insert a comma between parts of a compound predicate. 3 *partitions; they:* Connect two closely related independent clauses with a semicolon—not a comma.

MODEL 15 (CONTINUED)

4   Mr. Ellis Shephard
     Page 2
     May 9, 19--

5   **Work to Be Completed:** From now until July 20, we will be completing these tasks:

1. The vinyl flooring will be installed by June 23.

2. The painters are scheduled to paint the interior on July 1-3.

3. The modular rack storage system is scheduled to be installed by July 15.

4. The landscaper will install all landscaping by July 15, including exterior lighting and an underground sprinkler system.

5. The city inspector and fire marshal will perform a final inspection on July 17.

Anticipated Problems or Decisions to Be Made: Listed below are a minor problem regarding a shipment delay and a decision that we need from you:

1. The modular rack storage system was ordered on April 3 and should have been delivered two weeks ago. I've spoken with our supplier and she assures me that the system will be delivered by May 12. If so, we should have no problems installing it on schedule.

2. By June 25, you will need to make a final color selection for the interior walls. The plan calls for one color. In making your selection, you might want to remember that the exterior of the warehouse is Colonial Blue (a pale blue), and the metal storage system is putty.

We appreciate the opportunity to build this facility for you and are sure you will enjoy using it. I will provide you another update in June.

                    Sincerely,

                    Mark Handorf

                    Mark Handorf
                    Project Supervisor

jit

Margin notes:

Uses first- and second-person pronouns (appropriate in a letter or memo report).

Identifies problems and needed decisions.

Closes on a goodwill note.

Grammar and Mechanics Notes

4 Type the second page on plain paper, with a 1-inch top margin and a heading that identifies the recipient, page number, and date.   5 Use your word processing program's enumeration or bullet feature to format lists automatically.

Researchers at successful companies like Gillette are constantly developing proposals for new products to satisfy fast-changing consumer tastes. As part of one proposal that was accepted by management, every day, 200 Gillette employees lather up their faces and scrape away the 15/1000th of an inch their 10,000 whiskers have grown over the previous 24 hours. These volunteers evaluate razors of the future for sharpness of blade, smoothness of glide, and ease of handling.

Proposals are persuasive reports written to an external audience.

When writing a proposal, the writer must keep in mind that the proposal may become legally binding on the writer and his or her organization. In spelling out exactly what the writer's organization will provide, when, under what circumstances, and at what price, the proposal report writer creates the *offer* part of a contract which, if accepted, becomes binding on his or her firm.

Proposals are persuasive documents, and all the techniques you learned about persuasion in letter and memo writing apply equally here:

■ Give ample, credible evidence for all statements.

■ Do not exaggerate.

■ Provide examples, expert testimony, and specific facts and figures to support your statements.

■ Use simple, straightforward, and direct language, preferring simple sentences and the active voice.

■ Stress reader benefits. Remember that you are asking for something, usually a commitment of money; let the reader know what he or she will get in return.

Obviously, having a good idea is not enough. You must be able to present that idea clearly and convincingly so that it will be accepted. The benefits of clear and persuasive writing go far beyond the immediate goal of securing approval for your current project. A well-written proposal increases both your visibility and your credibility with the reader and with the company on whose behalf you wrote the proposal.

Although proposals vary in length, organization, complexity, and format, the following sections are typical:

1. *Background:* Introduce the problem you're addressing and discuss why it merits the reader's consideration. Provide enough background information to show that a problem exists and that you have a viable solution.
2. *Objectives:* Provide specific information about what the outcomes of the project will be. Be specific and honest in discussing what the reader will get in return for a commitment of resources.
3. *Procedures:* Discuss in detail exactly how you will achieve these objectives. Include a step-by-step discussion of what will be done, when, and exactly how much each component or phase will cost.
4. *Qualifications:* Show how you, your organization, and any others who would

Provide all the objective information the reader needs to make a decision.

be involved in conducting this project are qualified to do so. If appropriate, include testimonials or other external evidence to support your claims.

5. *Request for approval:* Directly ask for approval of your proposal. Depending on the reader's needs, this request could come either at the beginning or at the end of the proposal.

6. *Supporting data:* Include as an appendix to your proposal any relevant but supplementary information that might bolster your arguments.

As with all persuasive writing, the use of clear and objective language, ample evidence, and logical organization will help you achieve your goals. An example of a proposal for a small project is shown in Model 16 (see pp. 302–303).

Policies and Procedures

Policies are broad operating guidelines that govern the general direction and activities of an organization; **procedures** are the recommended methods or sequential steps to follow when performing a specific activity. Thus, an organization's attitude toward promoting from within the firm would constitute a *policy,* and the steps to be taken to apply for a promotion would constitute a *procedure.* Policy statements are typically written by top management; procedures are typically written by the managers and supervisors who are involved in the day-to-day operation of the organization.

Begin a policy statement by setting the stage; that is, justify the need for a policy. Your justification should be general enough that the policy covers a broad range of situations but not so general that it has no real "teeth." Ensure that the reader knows exactly who is covered by the policy, what is required, and any other needed information. Finally, show how the reader, the organization, or *someone* benefits from this policy.

Avoid making policies so general that they are of little practical help.

Write procedures in a businesslike but not formal manner, using the active voice. Imagine that you are explaining the procedure orally to someone. Go step by step through the process, explaining, when necessary, what should *not* be done as well as what should be done. Try to put yourself in the reader's shoes. How much background information is needed; how much jargon can safely be used; what reading level is appropriate? Anticipate questions and problems. Show and tell; that is, use pictures and diagrams as appropriate.

Write procedures in a businesslike, step-by-step format.

Don't assume that the reader knows anything about the process, but likewise don't assume that the reader is completely ignorant. Since it would be impossible to answer every conceivable question, concentrate on the high-risk components— those tasks that are difficult to perform or that have serious safety or financial implications if performed incorrectly.

Minimize the amount of conceptual information included, concentrating instead on the practical information. (Remember that a person can learn to drive a car safely without needing to learn how the engine actually propels the car forward.) Usually, numbered steps are appropriate, but use a narrative approach if it seems more effective.

After you have written a draft, have several employees who are typical of those who will use the document read and comment on it. If the document is a policy, ask them questions to see if they really understand the policy. If it is a procedure, have them follow the steps to see if they work. Revise as necessary.

Have typical users review and edit drafts of policies and procedures.

An example of a policy is given in Model 17 (see p. 304) and a procedure, in Model 18 (see p. 305). Could you follow this procedure and get the desired results?

MODEL 16 Proposal

This solicited proposal seeks to persuade an organization to sponsor a workshop.

September 16, 19--

Ms. Carolyn Soule, Employee Manager
Everglades National Corporation
1407 Lincoln Road, Suite 15
Miami, FL 33139

The Writing Doctor

P.O. Box 1036 • West Palm Beach, FL 33402
(813) 555-1036

Dear Ms. Soule:

1   Subject: Proposal for an In-House Workshop on Business Writing

Begins by identifying the purpose of the letter.

I enjoyed discussing with you the business writing workshops you intend to sponsor for the engineering staff at Everglades National Corporation. As you requested, I am submitting this proposal to conduct a two-day workshop.

BACKGROUND

Provides specific examples to show that a need exists.

2   On September 4-5, I interviewed four engineers at your organization and analyzed samples of their writing. My research indicates that your engineers are typical of many highly trained specialists who know exactly what they want to say but sometimes do not structure their communications in the most effective manner. Problems with audience analysis, organization, and overall writing style were especially apparent when they were communicating with nonspecialists either inside or outside the organization.

Suggests a reasonable solution.

3   Because your engineers devote much of their time to written communications, a workshop that teaches writing as a process should prove especially helpful. Thus, I propose that you sponsor a two-day writing workshop that I will develop entitled "The Process of Business Writing." The workshop could be held during any two days between November 26 and December 10; the two dates need not be consecutive.

OBJECTIVES

Tells exactly what the proposal should accomplish.

The workshop would help your engineers achieve these objectives:

1. Specify the purpose of a message and perform an audience analysis.

2. Determine what information to include and in what order to present it.

3. Choose the right words and construct effective sentences and logical paragraphs.

4   4. Set an appropriate overall tone by using confident, courteous, and sincere language; using appropriate emphasis and subordination; and stressing the "you" attitude.

Grammar and Mechanics Notes

1 Leave one blank line before and after a subject line.   2 *highly trained specialists:* Do not hyphenate a compound modifier when the first word (an adverb) ends in *-ly*.   3 *Business Writing.":* Place the period inside the closing quotation marks.   4 *language; using:* Separate these items in a series with semicolons because the first item contains internal commas; note that all three items are in parallel form.

MODEL 16 (CONTINUED)

Ms. Carolyn Soule
Page 2
September 16, 19--

PROCEDURES

The enclosed outline shows the coverage of the course. The workshop would require a meeting room with participants seated at tables, an overhead projector, and a chalkboard or some other writing surface. The program would be divided into four half-day segments, each lasting three hours. The first two hours would be devoted to discussing the topics listed, followed by a 15-minute break. The final hour would consist of group and individual writing assignments, with appropriate guidance and feedback.

5   My fee for teaching the two-day workshop would be $2,000, plus expenses (including photocopying handouts, automobile mileage, and lunch on the workshop days). Your organization would be responsible for arranging and providing the morning and afternoon refreshments and lunch for the participants.

QUALIFICATIONS

I would be responsible for planning and conducting the workshop. As you can see from the enclosed data sheet, I've had 15 years of consulting experience in business communications and have spoken and written widely on the topic. You may contact any of the individuals listed in the consulting section of the data sheet to learn their reactions to my previous presentations.

SUMMARY

6   My experience in working with professionals such as your engineers has taught me that they recognize the value of effective business communications and are motivated to improve their writing skills. The course should help your engineers become more effective communicators and more effective managers for Everglades.

I wish you much success in your efforts to upgrade the writing skills of your professional staff. Please call me at 555-1036 to let me know your reactions to this proposal.

7   Sincerely yours,

Ann Skarzinski

Ann Skarzinski, President

mje
Enclosures

Provides enough details to enable the reader to understand what is planned.

Discusses costs in an open and confident manner.

Highlights only the most relevant information from the enclosed data sheet.

Shows how the reader will benefit from doing as asked.

Closes on a friendly, confident note.

Grammar and Mechanics Notes

5 *$2,000:* Omit the decimal point and zeroes for even amounts of money. Use a comma in all numerals of four or more digits except years.   6 *engineers has:* Use the singular verb *(has)* because the subject is *experience,* not *engineers.*   7 *Sincerely yours,:* Capitalize only the first word of a complimentary closing.

MODEL 17 Policy

Provides in the heading the necessary background information for filing and locating the policy.

[CENTRAL MICHIGAN UNIVERSITY seal] **STANDARD PRACTICE CODE**	**SUBJECT:** Alcohol
	EFFECTIVE DATE: May 1, 1995
CENTRAL MICHIGAN UNIVERSITY	**NUMBER:** U-803 **PAGE:** 1 **OF:** 1

SUBJECT: Alcohol

APPLIES TO: All Faculty, Staff, and Student Employees

Tells who is affected by the policy.

Central Michigan University (CMU) is committed to providing a workplace that is free from the unauthorized or unlawful manufacture, distribution, dispensation, or possession of beverage alcohol.

Introduces the topic and provides a setting.

Uses an appropriate balance between general and specific language to describe the policy.

It is the intent of CMU to provide a healthful, safe, and secure work environment. No employee will report to work evidencing any effects of alcohol consumption. Use of beverage alcohol is limited to those locations approved by CMU policy or licensed by the State of Michigan. Violations of this policy will result in disciplinary action, up to and including dismissal pursuant to university procedures relating to employee discipline.

All university employees will, as a condition of employment, abide by the terms of this policy.

Shows a caring attitude by closing with a discussion of reader benefits.

CMU supports programs aimed at the prevention of alcohol abuse by its employees. CMU's Employee Assistance Program provides preventative programs, counseling for employees experiencing alcohol dependency problems, and assistance for problems related to alcohol abuse. Such counseling is confidential and unrelated to performance evaluations. Leaves of absence to obtain treatment may be obtained under the medical-leave provision of the appropriate labor agreeement, employee handbook, or policy.

Grammar and Mechanics Note

Each organization usually has its own specific style for formatting policy statements. This organization uses a preprinted form.

MODEL 18 **Procedure**

PROCEDURE FOR HIRING A TEMPORARY EMPLOYEE

Actor	Action
Requester	1. Requests a temporary employee with specific, specialized skills by filling out Form 722, "Request for a Temporary Employee."
	2. Secures manager's approval.
	3. Sends four copies of Form 722 to buyer of special services in the Purchasing Department.
Buyer of Special Services	4. Sends all four copies to the labor analyst in the Budget Control Department.
Labor Analyst	5. Checks overtime figures of regular employees in the department or section.
	6. If there is a question, contacts manager to learn of any upcoming increased workload.
	7. If satisfied that the specific people and skills are necessary, checks budget.
	8. If funds are available, approves Form 722, returns three copies to buyer, files the fourth copy.
Buyer of Special Services	9. Notifies outside temporary help contractor by telephone and follows up the same day with a confirming letter.
	10. Negotiates a mutually agreeable effective date.
	11. Contacts both Personnel and Furniture/Equipment sections by phone, telling them of the number of people, the effective dates, and the equipment requirements.
Personnel	12. Notifies Security, Badges, and Gate Guards.
	13. Returns one copy of Form 722 to the requester.
	14. Provides a temporary ID.
Contractor of Temporary Help Services	15. Furnishes assigned employee or employees with information on the job description, effective date, and the individual to whom to report.
Temporary Employee	16. Reports to receptionist one half-hour early on effective day.

A step-by-step outline of who (Actor) does what (Action) when temporary help is hired. Uses a descriptive title.

Begins with the act that starts the process and ends with the final result.

Contains only essential information.

Details clearly and concisely what steps are necessary and in what order.

Maintains parallel structure (complete sentences are not necessary).

Grammar and Mechanics Note

The format used is optional. This procedure uses a *playscript* format that clearly specifies what role each person plays in the process.

Situational Reports

Situational reports are one-of-a-kind reports.

In any organization, unique problems and opportunities appear that require one-time-only reports. Many of these situations call for information to be gathered and analyzed and for recommendations to be made. These so-called *situational reports* are perhaps the most challenging for the report writer. Because they involve a unique event, the writer has no previous reports to use as a guide; he or she must decide what types of information and how much information are needed and how best to organize and present the findings.

A sample situational report is shown in Model 19. The guidelines presented in the upcoming report chapters are especially applicable to situational reports because of the many decisions that surround these one-of-a-kind projects.

Purposes of Reports

At the outset, you need to determine why you are writing the report. Business reports generally aim to inform, analyze, or recommend.

Informing

Informational reports present information without analyzing it.

Informational reports relate objectively the facts and events surrounding a particular situation. No attempt is made to analyze and interpret the data, draw conclusions, or recommend a course of action. Most periodic reports, as well as policies and procedures, are examples of informational reports. In most cases, these types of reports are the easiest to complete. The report writer's major interest is in presenting all of the relevant information objectively, accurately, and clearly, while refraining from including unsolicited analysis and recommendations.

Analyzing

Analytical reports interpret the information.

One step in complexity above the informational report is the analytical report, which not only presents the information but also analyzes it. Data by itself may be meaningless; it must be put into some context before readers can make use of it. As social forecaster John Naisbitt has remarked, "We are drowning in information, but starved for knowledge."[2]

Consider, for example, this informational statement: "Sales for the quarter ending June 30 were $780,000." Was this performance good or bad? We cannot possibly know unless the writer *analyzes* the information for us. Here are two possible interpretations of this statement:

> Sales for the quarter ending June 30 were $780,000, up 7% from the previous quarter. This strong showing was achieved despite an industry-wide slump and may be attributed to the new "Tell One—Sell One" campaign we introduced in January.

> Sales for the quarter ending June 30 were $780,000, a decline of 5.5% from the same quarter last year. All regions experienced a 3% to 5% *increase* except for the western region, which experienced an 18% decrease in sales. John Manilow, western regional manager, attributes his area's sharp drop in sales to the budgetary problems now being experienced by the state governments in California and Arizona.

MODEL 19 Situational Report

This situational report is shown in manuscript format.

THE FEASIBILITY OF A MIXED-USE DEVELOPMENT IN PHOENIX

David M. Beall

1 Mixed-use development (MXD) is a form of real estate that integrates three or more land uses (e.g., office, retail, hotel, residential, and recreational) in a high-density configuration with uninterrupted circulation from one component to another. Interviews with seven local real estate developers and bankers and documents available from the Greater Phoenix Chamber of Commerce provided information on the feasibility of constructing a mixed-use development in Phoenix.

Begins by introducing the topic and discussing the procedures used. This report uses the indirect pattern, saving the recommendations until the end.

Low Land Prices and Low-Density Population Weaken MXD Potential

2 Land prices are a key economic factor in real estate development. High prices force developers to develop land with highly intensive uses to justify land costs. The much more expensive cost of an MXD makes economic sense only when high land prices justify the investment. Land prices in Phoenix, however, are relatively low compared to prices in other major U.S. cities. The Galleria in Houston and the Metrocenter in Phoenix are similar-sized developments that offer an excellent comparison of how land prices dictate development intensity. The Galleria site cost $85,000 per acre; six years later, the Metrocenter site cost only $10,000 per acre (Rogers, 1992, p. 148).

Is organized according to the criteria used to solve the problem.

Uses the author-date format for citing references (see Reference Manual).

Successful MXDs tend to be located in high-density urban cores. The Phoenix market, on the other hand, is a low-density environment, as reflected by its horizontal urban form. Approximately 67% of the Phoenix housing stock is single-family homes, and relatively few commerical buildings reach over six stories high ("Inside Phoenix," 1996).

3 **Financing Would Be Difficult**

The area bankers interviewed are reluctant to become involved with a new type of large-scale commercial development. Instead, they prefer to sponsor projects with which they have had experience. According to one banker, "A bank is only as successful as its last loan" (Weiss, 1997, p. 36). The bankers believe the economic risks associated with developing an MXD outweigh the rewards. They cite such adverse factors as high development costs, complexity, and lack of expertise (Allen, 1996; Gorman, 1994).

Davenport Should Delay MXD Project

Because of Phoenix's relatively low land costs and low-density population and the difficulty of securing financing, Davenport should not pursue a mixed-use development in the Phoenix area now. However, because the Southwest is growing so rapidly, Davenport should reevaluate the Phoenix market in three years.

Closes by making a recommendation based on the findings presented.

Grammar and Mechanics Notes

1 *real estate developers:* Do not hyphenate a compound noun *(real estate)* that comes before another noun *(developers).*   2 *site:* location *(cite:* "to quote"; *sight:* "to view").   3 Be consistent in formatting report side headings; there is no one standard format (other than consistency). This report uses "talking" headings, which identify both the topic and the major conclusion of each section.

The report writer must be careful that any conclusions drawn are reasonable, valid, and fully supported by the data presented. Although the writer must attempt to avoid inserting his or her own biases or preexisting opinions into the report, analysis and interpretation can never be completely objective. The report writer makes numerous decisions that call for subjective evaluations. Note the difference in effect of the following two statements, which contain the same information but in reversed order:

Original:

Although it is too early to determine the effectiveness of Mundrake's efforts, he believes the steps he is taking will bring Limerick's absentee rate down to the industry average of 3.6% by December.

Reversed:

Although Mundrake believes the steps he is taking will bring Limerick's absentee rate down to the industry average of 3.6% by December, it is too early to determine the effectiveness of his efforts.

The original order leaves a confident impression of the probable success of the steps taken, whereas the reversed order leaves a much more skeptical impression.

Recommending

Recommendation reports propose a course of action.

Recommendation reports add the element of endorsing a specific course of action (see, for example, the situational report in Model 19). The writer presents the relevant information, interprets it, and then suggests a plan of attack. The important point is that you must let the *data* be the basis for any conclusions you draw and any recommendations you make. You want to analyze and present your data so that the truth, the whole truth, and nothing but the truth emerges. In other words, avoid the temptation of beginning with a preconceived idea and then marshaling and manipulating data to support it.

In a sense, your final recommendation is only the tip of the iceberg, but it is a very visible tip. The logic, clarity, and strength of your recommendation can have major implications for your career and for your organization's well-being.

Audience Analysis

The audience for a report—the reader or readers—is typically homogeneous. Many times, of course, the audience is one person; but even when it is not, the audience usually consists of people with similar levels of expertise, background knowledge, and the like. Thus, you can, and should, develop your report to take into account the needs of your reader. In doing so, you will need to consider the following elements.

Internal Versus External Audiences

Internal reports are generally less formal and contain less background information than external reports.

Internal reports are written for readers within the organization and are usually less formal than external reports, for which the reader might be a customer, potential customer, or government agency. Internal reports also typically require less background information and can safely use more technical vocabulary than external reports, which are often more sensitive to public relations issues.

Internal reports are also directional and are aimed at the writer's superiors, peers, or subordinates. The strategy used must be appropriate for the audience's position. For example, reports often have a costs-and-profits tone when directed to superiors, a conversational tone when directed to peers, and an emphatic tone when directed to subordinates.

Authorized Versus Voluntary Reports

Authorized reports are written at the specific request of some higher authority. Thus, the reader has an inherent interest in the report. Voluntary reports, on the other hand, are prepared on the writer's own initiative. Therefore, the reader needs more background information and frequently more persuasive evidence than do readers of authorized reports.

Voluntary reports require more background information and more persuasion than authorized reports.

Authorized reports may be either periodic or special. Periodic reports are submitted on a recurring, systematic basis. Very often they are form reports, with space provided for specific items of information. Readers of periodic reports need little introductory or background information because of the report's recurring nature. Readers of special, one-time reports, on the other hand, need more explanatory material because of the uniqueness of the report.

Level of Knowledge and Interest

Is the reader already familiar with your topic? Will he or she understand the terms used, or will you need to define them? If you have a heterogeneous audience for your report, striking an appropriate balance in level of detail given will require careful planning.

Gear the amount of information presented and the order in which it is presented to the needs of the reader.

Most reports are written in the direct pattern, with the major conclusions and recommendations given up front (but see, however, Spotlight 16—Across Cultures). This is especially true when you know the reader is interested in your project or is likely to agree with your opinions and judgments. Reports that make a recommendation with which the reader may disagree are often written in the indirect pattern because you want the reader to study the reasons first. The reader will be more likely to accept or at least consider the recommendation if he or she has first had an opportunity to study its rationale.

What Data Is Already Available?

Before collecting any data, you must define the report purpose and analyze the intended audience. Then you must determine what data is needed to solve the problem. (*Note:* The term *data* is technically the plural form of *datum* and therefore requires a plural verb when referring to several individual items of data. In most cases in this text, however, the term is used in the sense of a collective noun and takes a singular verb.) Sometimes the data you need will be in your mind or in documents you already have at hand, sometimes it will be in documents located elsewhere, and sometimes the data is not available at all but must be generated by you.

Start the data-collection phase by **factoring** your problem; that is, by breaking it down into its component parts so that you will know what data you need to collect. The easiest way to do this is to think about what questions you need to answer

Determine what questions must be answered in order to solve your report problem.

Context in International Reports

Most business reports are written for a relatively homogeneous audience. However, in the international arena the reader and writer often have different cultural viewpoints. The greater the amount of knowledge, perceptions, and attitudes the reader and writer share (that is, the higher the *context* of the communication exchange), the less important it is for report writers to directly express *everything* they wish to communicate. Conversely, the less the reader and writer have in common, the more they need to convey every nuance of their meaning explicitly through words—that is, the less they can assume to be implicitly understood.

Contexting can be categorized as either high or low. When report writers have considerable knowledge and experience in common with their readers, their reports are generally *highly contexted*. In highly contexted reports, what the writer chooses *not* to put into words is still essential to understanding the actual message intended. But the writer assumes that what is not said is actually *already understood.*

When report writers rely relatively little on shared knowledge and experience, their report is *low contexted.* As a result, in low-context exchanges more information must be explicitly stated than in high-context ones. Thus, low-context cultures tend to rely on *direct* communication; they often consider the indirect pattern a waste of time or a strain on the receiver's patience. High-context cultures, on the other hand, tend to rely on *indirect* communication to smooth over interpersonal differences and to keep from losing face in a conflict situation. They often consider directness rude and offensive.

To a large extent, contexting is a culturally learned behavior, with the degree of context varying from culture to culture. As shown below, Germans and German-speaking Swiss tend to be low-context cultures (all important information is explicitly stated), whereas the Japanese, Arabic, and Latin American people tend to be high-context cultures (much important information is implicitly assumed).

As Stella Ting-Toomey has noted, "In the HCC [high-context culture] system, what is not said is sometimes more important than what is said. In contrast, in the LCC [low-context culture] system, words represent truth and power."

Competent communicators ensure that the degree of explicitness, the amount of detail, and the assumptions built into their reports match the context expectations of their audience.

SPOTLIGHT 16

ACROSS CULTURES

Importance of Context in Different Cultures

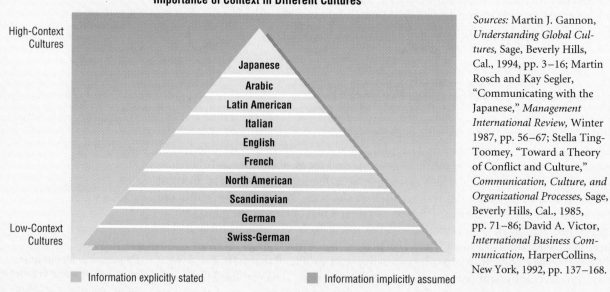

High-Context Cultures

- Japanese
- Arabic
- Latin American
- Italian
- English
- French
- North American
- Scandinavian
- German
- Swiss-German

Low-Context Cultures

■ Information explicitly stated   ■ Information implicitly assumed

Sources: Martin J. Gannon, *Understanding Global Cultures,* Sage, Beverly Hills, Cal., 1994, pp. 3–16; Martin Rosch and Kay Segler, "Communicating with the Japanese," *Management International Review,* Winter 1987, pp. 56–67; Stella Ting-Toomey, "Toward a Theory of Conflict and Culture," *Communication, Culture, and Organizational Processes,* Sage, Beverly Hills, Cal., 1985, pp. 71–86; David A. Victor, *International Business Communication,* HarperCollins, New York, 1992, pp. 137–168.

before you can solve the problem. The answers to these questions will ultimately provide the answer to the overall problem you're trying to solve, and the question topics may, in fact, ultimately serve as the major divisions of your report.

Research and report writing are a cost, just like other corporate expenses. Thus, you should use data-collection methods that will provide the needed data with the least expenditure of time and money but at the level of completeness, accuracy, and precision needed to solve your problem. There is a break-even point to data collection. You do not want to provide a $100 answer to a $5 question, but neither do you want to provide a $5 answer to a $100 question.

> ### wordwise
>
> **Newspaper Nicknames**
>
> - Dallas Morning Snooze *(Dallas Morning News)*
> - Halifax Chronically Horrid *(Halifax Chronicle-Herald)*
> - Kent Wretched Courier *(Kent Record-Courier)*
> - Raleigh Nuisance & Disturber *(Raleigh News & Observer)*
> - Rochester Compost-Bulletin *(Rochester Post-Bulletin)*
> - San Jose Murky News *(San Jose Mercury News)*
> - Springfield Nuisance *(Springfield News-Sun)*

Common Types of Data

The two major types of data you will collect are secondary and primary data. **Secondary data** is data collected by someone else for some other purpose; it may be published or unpublished. Published data includes any material that is widely disseminated, including the following:

- World Wide Web and other Internet resources
- Journal, magazine, and newspaper articles (*Note:* Technically, a *journal* is a scholarly periodical published by a professional association or a university, and a *magazine* is a commercial periodical published by a for-profit organization. Although the distinction is sometimes useful in evaluating secondary sources, the two terms are used interchangeably in this chapter to refer to any periodical publication.) These articles may be located in print format or may be retrieved from an electronic database (see Spotlight 17—on Technology).
- Books
- Brochures and pamphlets
- Technical reports

Unpublished secondary data includes any material that is not widely disseminated, including the following:

- Company records (such as financial records, personnel data, and minutes of previous correspondence and reports)
- Legal documents (such as court records and minutes of regulatory hearings)
- Personal records (such as diaries, receipts, and checkbook registers)
- Medical records

Nearly all reporting tasks use secondary data.

Primary data is collected by the researcher to solve the specific problem at hand. Because you are collecting the data yourself, you have more control over its accuracy, completeness, objectivity, and relevance. The three main methods of primary data collection are surveys (questionnaires, interviews, and telephone inquiries), observation, and experimentation.

Although secondary and primary data are both important sources for business reports, we usually start our data collection by reviewing the data that is already available. Not all report situations require collecting new (primary) data, but it would be unusual to write a report that did not use some type of secondary data.

Sample Online Search Session

User dials an information retrieval service and is connected to the database.

SIGN ON   7:18:23   07/02/95

(1/74–3/95)

SEARCH MODE–ENTER QUERY

No.	Request	Documents
1	banking–industry.de	8394
2	management.de	61847
3	women.de	2994
4	1 and 2 and 3	21
5	p 4 1/1	

Steps 1–3: User asks the computer to search for three terms. Computer responds by telling how many documents contain that term as a descriptor.

Step 4: User asks for all documents containing all three terms; computer locates 21 such documents.

Step 5: User asks computer to print (p) the first document (1/1) from the 4th search (4). Computer lists author (AU), title (TI), source (SO), descriptors (DE), abstract (AB), service that sells a photocopy of the document (AV), and the accession number (AC)—the number used to identify the document.

AU: Shinar–Eva–H.

TI: Sexual Stereotypes of Occupations

SO: J. Voc. Behavior. VOL: v20n8. PAG: 102–110, 9 pages. Aug 1994.

DE: Role-stereotypes. Personnel-management. Women. Banking-industry. Manufacturing-industry. Retail-industry.

AB: The strength of sexual stereotypes attached to 129 occupations was measured by having 60 male and 60 female subjects rank these jobs as masculine, feminine, or neutral. An extremely high correlation between male and female subjects' mean ratings of the sex appropriateness of the given occupations indicates that sex labeling of occupations is a deeply ingrained feature in attitudes toward the world of work. The results showed that those occupations stereotypically associated with high levels of competence, rationality, and assertion are viewed as masculine, whereas those associated with dependency, passivity, nurturance, and interpersonal warmth are perceived as feminine occupations. For example, bank tellers, elementary school teachers, and librarians had high feminine ratings, whereas bankers, doctors, politicians, and professional athletes had high masculine ratings. The notion that males continue to stereotype while females have more liberated views is not supported.

AV: ABI/INFORM

AC: 0120–5582

END OF REQUEST

SEARCH MODE–ENTER QUERY
    bye

User signs off. Computer shows search took 8 minutes and 26 seconds, or 0.141 hour.

*CONNECT TIME: 0:08:26 HH:MM:SS 0.141 DEC HRS

SESSION 17208

Studying what is already known about a topic and what remains to be learned makes the reporting process more efficient because the report writer can then concentrate scarce resources on generating new information rather than rediscovering existing information. Also, studying secondary data can provide sources for additional information, suggest methods of primary research, or give clues for questionnaire items—that is, provide guidance for primary research. For these reasons, our discussion of data collection first focuses on secondary sources.

Secondary data is neither better nor worse than primary data; it's simply *different*. The source of the data is not as important as its quality and its relevance for your particular purpose. The major advantages of using secondary data are economic: using secondary data is less costly and less time-consuming than collecting primary data. The disadvantages relate not only to the availability of sufficient secondary data but also to the quality of the data that is available. Never use any data before you have evaluated its appropriateness for the intended purpose.

Much secondary data is available on the World Wide Web, but users must always evaluate the data to ensure that it is accurate, relevant, up-to-date, and objective. Here a user searches for scientific information on the Web at CERN, the European particle physics laboratory near Geneva, Switzerland. The World Wide Web was created by CERN computer scientists and started services in 1989.

Evaluating Secondary Data

By definition, secondary data was gathered for some purpose other than your particular report needs. Therefore, the categories used, the population sampled, and the analyses reported might not be appropriate for your use. In Chapter 3 we discussed guidelines for evaluating the quality of electronic data (see Checklist 2 on p. 91). In addition, ask yourself the following questions about any secondary sources you're thinking about incorporating into your report.

What Was the Purpose of the Study?   If the study was undertaken to genuinely find the answer to a question or problem, you can have more confidence about the accuracy and objectivity of the results than if, for example, the study was undertaken merely to prove a point. People seeking honest answers to honest questions are more likely to select their samples carefully, to ask clear and unbiased questions, and to analyze the data appropriately.

Be wary of secondary data if the researcher had a vested interest in the outcome of the study. For example, you would probably have more faith in a study extolling the merits of the Hubbard automobile that had been conducted by *Consumer Reports* than one conducted by Hubbard Motors, Inc.

Avoid using biased data in your report.

How Was the Data Collected?   Were appropriate procedures used? Although you may not be an experienced researcher yourself, your reading of secondary data will likely alert you to certain standard research procedures that should be followed. For example, common sense should tell you that if you are interested in learning the reactions of all factory workers in your organization to a particular proposal, you would not gather data from just the newly hired workers. Likewise, if a questionnaire was sent to all the factory workers and only 10% responded, you would probably not be able to conclude that the opinions of these few respondents represented the views of all the workers.

How Was the Data Analyzed?   As we shall see in Chapter 11, different types of data lend themselves to different types of analyses. Sometimes the low number of responses to a particular question or ambiguity in the question itself prevents us from drawing any valid conclusions.

In some situations, even though the analysis was appropriate for the original study, it may not be appropriate for your particular purposes. For example, suppose you're interested in the reactions of teenagers and the only available secondary data used the category "under 21 years of age." You would not know whether the responses came mostly from those younger than 13 years old, those 13 to 19 years old (your target group), or those older than 19 years old.

How Consistent Is the Data with That from Other Studies?   When you find the same general conclusions in several independent sources, you can have greater confidence in the data. On the other hand, if four studies of a particular topic reached one conclusion and a fifth study reached an opposite conclusion, you would need to scrutinize the fifth study carefully before accepting its findings.

Generally, the more consensus you find in secondary data, the more trustworthy the data.

Avoid accepting something as true simply because you read it in print or saw it on the Internet. Because the reader of your report will be making decisions based on the data you present, take care that the data in your report is accurate.

How Old Is the Data?   Data that was true at the time it was collected might or might not be true today. A job-satisfaction study completed at your organization last year may have yielded accurate data then. But if in the meantime your organization has merged with another company, moved its headquarters, or been torn by a strike, the job-satisfaction data may have no relevance today. On the other hand, some data may still be accurate years after its collection. For example, a thorough study of the origins of the labor movement in the United States may have almost permanent validity.

Your data must pass these five tests, whether it comes from company records or published sources. Data that fails even one of these tests should probably be discarded and not used in your report. At the very least, such data requires extra scrutiny and perhaps extra explanation in the report itself if you do choose to use it.

Managing Reports

Throughout this chapter we have made a strong case for the increasingly important role that business reports play in the successful management of the contemporary organization. However, too much of a good thing is a bad thing. Without proper management, reports, especially computer printouts, can backfire, becoming a nuisance and contributing to information overload.

With the increasing availability of data and the ease with which that data can be manipulated, copied, and distributed, managers sometimes tend to generate every type of report possible and then submit them all to higher-level management. Some managers seem to devote more energy to generating reports than to analyzing and making use of their contents.

Thus, someone in the organization—preferably someone in higher management—should be assigned the task of controlling reports. Periodically (typically, annually) this individual should make an inventory of all recurring reports and determine the continuing usefulness of each one. Some reports may be eliminated altogether, some modified, others merged, and, where justified, new reports authorized.

Ensure that all reports serve a specific purpose, that only needed information is included, and that all recipients actually need the report.

This review process will guarantee that business reports continue to serve management rather than vice versa. With or without such controls, all managers should ensure that the reports they write serve some actual purpose, stick to that purpose, and avoid including extraneous computer data just because it's easily available.

8) In answer to your letter, I have given birth to a boy weighing ten pounds. I hope this is satisfactory.

9) I am forwarding my marriage certificate and three sons one of which is a mistake as you can see.

10) My husband got his project cut off two weeks ago and I haven't had any relief since.

11) You have changed my little boy to a girl. Will this make any difference?

12) In accordance with you instructions I have given birth to twins in the enclosed envelope.

13) I want my money as quick as I can get it. I've been in bed with the doctor for two weeks and he doesn't do me any good. If things don't improve, I will have to send for another doctor.

11) All articles that coruscate with resplendence are not truly auriferous. *All that glitters is not gold.*

12) Where the are visible vapors ignited carbonaceous materials, there is conflagration. *when there is smoke there will rise*

13) Selectivity on the part of mendicants must be interdicted. *Besars can't be Choosers.*

14) A plethora of individuals with expertise in culinary techniques vitiate the potable concoction produced by steeping certain comestibles. *To many cooks spoil the plate.*

15) Eleemosynary deeds have their incipience intramurally. *Charity begins at home.*

16) Male cadavers are incapable of yielding testimony. *Dead men tells no tales.*

PROBLEM

Y ou and your colleagues who teach business communication at Valley State College are interested in setting up a business writer's hotline—a telephone service that will provide answers to grammar, mechanics, and format questions from people who call in. You see this as a way of providing a much-needed service to local businesspeople, as well as a way of providing positive public relations for your institution.

Each faculty member is willing to donate time to answer the phones, but you will need funds for telephone lines, answering machines, reference books, advertising, and the like. You decide to apply for a grant from the A. C. Reynolds Foundation to fund the project for one year. After that, if the hotline is successful, you will either reapply for funds or ask the Valley State College administration to fund the continuing costs. For requests for less than $3,000, the foundation requires a simple narrative report explaining and justifying the request.

PROCESS

1. What is the background of the problem?

Every writer has occasional questions about writing style but may not have a reference book or style manual available to answer the questions. We know there is a need for such a service because we frequently get calls from people on campus with these questions. Although several grammar hotlines operate nationally, none is available within a 200-mile radius of Portland.

2. What will be the outcome of the project?

A telephone service that will be available free of charge 24 hours a day to answer any question regarding business writing.

3. Describe the audience for this report and the implications for structuring your report.

The A. C. Reynolds Foundation makes grants to nonprofit organizations in the Portland area, mostly for small projects of less than $10,000 each. Because of the foundation's small size and personal orientation, a direct and personal (rather than scholarly) writing style should be used. Since there is no reason to expect that the foundation holds a negative attitude toward this project, the proposal will be written in a direct pattern—the request for funds will be made at the beginning of the report.

4. Describe how the hotline will work.

a. A faculty member will answer phoned-in questions each weekday from 10 a.m. until 2 p.m. Questions phoned in at other times will be recorded on an answering machine.

b. A phone line with a call-forwarding feature will be installed.

315

    c. The faculty will agree on which books should serve as the standards of reference.

    d. The faculty will attempt to answer any reasonable question about grammar, mechanics, format, and the like but will not review or edit anyone's writing and will not answer questions requiring extensive research.

5. What are the advantages of this project?

    a. Enhancing the college's reputation as an asset to the community.

    b. Providing a genuine service to business writers.

    c. Aiding business productivity by decreasing communication problems.

    d. Helping the business communication faculty stay abreast of their fields.

6. What will the project cost?

The faculty members will donate their time. Two copies of each of the reference books needed will cost $123.50. The telephone line will cost $61.30 monthly, and the long-distance charges for returning calls are estimated at $55 monthly. An answering machine costs $119.50. Monthly advertisements in the campus newspaper and in the local newspaper are estimated at $62.50.

7. What are the qualifications of those involved in this project?

Each of the 12 faculty members has a doctoral degree and has taught business communication and related courses an average of eight years.

THE BUSINESS WRITER'S HOTLINE

A Proposal Submitted by Professor Steve Harland
Valley State College of Portland, Oregon
March 15, 19--

All business writers have occasional questions about writing style. Indeed, the business communication faculty at Valley State College frequently receives calls asking questions about punctuation, subject-verb agreement, the correct format for business correspondence, and the like. Although several grammar hotlines operate nationwide to answer such questions, none is presently available within a 200-mile radius of Portland.

Thus, the business communication faculty of Valley State College requests that a grant for $2,388.60 be awarded for the purpose of establishing and operating a Business Writer's Hotline for one year to benefit the Portland community and Valley State College students, faculty, and staff.

Outcome of the Project

The project will fund the establishment and operation of a Business Writer's Hotline in which qualified faculty members answer telephone inquiries from business writers on the subject of grammar, mechanics, and format. The service will operate at no cost to users and will be available each day that Valley State College is in session. This hotline will

1. Increase business productivity by lessening the chance that an error in writing will cause communication problems, needless delays, or even incorrect decisions.

2. Provide a service to business writers (including college students, faculty, staff, businesspeople, and the general community) who presently have no convenient way of getting their questions answered.

3. Enhance the college's reputation as an asset to the local community.

Procedures

When school is in session, a faculty member will be available to answer any phoned-in questions every weekday from 10 a.m. until 2 p.m. Questions phoned in at other times will be recorded on an answering machine, with a telephone response provided by the end of the next working day.

A dedicated telephone line with a call-forwarding feature will be installed. Faculty members on duty can simply have the calls forwarded to their offices so that they can work on other matters when no phone calls are being received.

PRODUCT

2

Faculty consultants will attempt to answer any reasonable question regarding grammar, mechanics (including punctuation and spelling), document format, and the like. They will not review or edit anyone's writing and will not be available to answer questions that require extensive research. Three books will serve as the standard references: *The Chicago Manual of Style*, *The Associated Press Stylebook and Libel Manual*, and *The American Heritage Dictionary*.

The hotline will begin operating the first day of the school year after the award of the grant and will continue for one year. A small ad announcing the availability of this service will be placed monthly in the *Valley State Voice* and in the *Portland Herald*.

A detailed log will be maintained showing the amount of use and types of questions answered. These records will show whether the service is fulfilling a need and whether a need exists for additional collegiate education or industry training in business writing.

Budget

The following budget is projected for the Business Writer's Hotline for the first year of operation:

Purchase of two copies each of three reference books	$ 123.50
Purchase of one telephone-answering machine	119.50
Rental of one telephone line (12 mo. @ $61.30)	735.60
Long-distance charges (12 mo. estimated @ $55)	660.00
Newspaper advertisements (12 mo. @ 62.50)	750.00
Total	$ 2,388.60

Note: The faculty consultants will provide their time at no cost to the project.

Personnel Qualifications

Each of the 12 faculty members who will act as a voluntary consultant has a doctoral degree and an average of eight years of experience teaching business communication and related courses. Thus, the faculty members have had much experience in answering the types of questions likely to be encountered.

Summary

The establishment of a Business Writer's Hotline will increase the communication skills and the quality of writing of the local community. The recurring cost of $2,145.60 is less than $10 per day and 40 cents per hour for the 45 weeks of 24-hour service. This cost is a small amount to pay for the benefits that will be provided to area business writers, the college, and the faculty volunteers.

SUMMARY

Reading and writing reports is a typical part of nearly every manager's duties. Reports vary greatly in length, complexity, formality, and format, and many are collaborative efforts. Accuracy is the most important trait of all reports, and the quality of the process affects the quality of the final product.

The most common types of reports are periodic reports (including routine management, compliance, and progress reports), proposals, policies and procedures, and situational reports. The purpose of each type of report may be either to inform, to analyze, or to recommend. Because the audience for a specific report is typically homogeneous, you should develop your report to take into account the reader's needs—in terms of level of knowledge and interest, internal versus external readers, and authorized versus voluntary reports.

Secondary data is data collected by others for their own specific purposes. Therefore, the researcher who wants to use secondary data for his or her own study must first evaluate it in terms of why and how the data was collected, how it was analyzed, how consistent the data is with that found in other studies, and how old the data is.

Reports can become a drain on the organization's resources if they are not controlled. Management should therefore periodically inventory and review all reports to ensure that only needed reports are being generated and distributed and that they contain the information needed to help solve problems and make decisions.

KEY TERMS

factoring	primary data	proposal
policy	procedure	secondary data

REVIEW AND DISCUSSION

1. **Communication at Experian Revisited** Janis Lamar's reports support management decision-making by analyzing Experian's return on investment in media relations and comparing the company's media coverage with competitors' coverage.
   a. Is Lamar's media analysis report a periodic report, a proposal, or a situational report?
   b. Should Lamar include copies of all the articles analyzed as supporting data for each report? Why or why not?
   c. Are the articles collected for a media analysis report secondary or primary data?
2. Why are business reports so important to the contemporary organization?
3. Define and give an example of each of the four types of common business reports.
4. What is meant by the statement "There is no such document as a standard report"?
5. What is meant by the statement "Writing a report involves much more than writing a report"?
6. What are the advantages of collaboratively written reports?
7. Give four guidelines for achieving accuracy in a report.
8. Describe three types of situational reports.
9. Give an example of a solicited proposal and an unsolicited proposal.
10. What sections are typical in a proposal?
11. Give an example of a policy and a related procedure.
12. How much detail should be given in a procedure?
13. Why is secondary data an important part of most research?
14. What criteria should be used to evaluate the quality of secondary data?
15. Why should reports be controlled?

Help Wanted

This is a draft of a procedure for handling a bomb threat. Revise the document to make it more effective, taking into consideration the editor's marginal comments.

In the event of a telephoned bomb threat, you should note the exact time of the call and the exact words used by the caller. Listen carefully for any identifiable voice characteristics and background sound.

It's generally best to number every step in a procedure.

Ask the caller these questions:

In this order?

1. When the bomb is going to explode.
2. Where is the bomb?
3. What it looks like

par

4. What will cause it to explode?
5. Did you place the bomb? Why?
6. Where you're calling from
7. What is your address?
8. What is your name?

sp

After recieving the bomb threat, dial 911 to advise Public Safety of the threat. Then advice the appropriate department administrator of the threat.

word

Who decides whether or not to evacuate?

If the facility is evacuated, do not reenter the building until Public Safety announces the "All-Clear" signal.

While bomb threats are most often received by telephone, it may also come via note, U.S. mail, voice mail, or e-mail. In each case, great caution should be taken not to touch or otherwise compromise or destroy the physical evidence that may be present on the message.

agr

act

1. **The 3Ps Microwriting Model: Communication Applications at Experian**   Janis Lamar's media analysis reports examine Experian's media exposure over the previous six months, look at the coverage received by competing firms, and identify emerging issues that the company may need to address. Because Experian's managers often make decisions based on Lamar's reports, she places a premium on accuracy and carefully defines the purpose and the audience before she gathers and analyzes the data and then drafts each report.

Problem

As a media relations consultant working with Experian, you have just learned that the company received extensive coverage in this week's issue of *Time* magazine. Lamar requests that you write a brief informational report summarizing the key points for the company's top managers. Reading the article, you see that it explains how consumer credit reporting operates, how Experian maintains a database of consumer credit files, how consumers can view their own credit files, and how banks and retailers access Experian's files electronically to obtain the payment history of people who are applying for new credit cards or loans. Overall, the reporter takes an objective approach and seems particularly impressed with Experian's sophisticated database technology. However, the article also raises questions about personal privacy in this computer age, and you think this is an important public issue for management to consider.

Process

a. What is the purpose of your report?
b. Describe your audience.
c. What points will you cover and in what order?
d. Which point(s) should you emphasize? Why?
e. Compose the specific headings for this report.
f. Draft an opening paragraph to introduce the report and bring the highlights to your readers' attention.

Product

Using your knowledge of reports, prepare a two-page report in memorandum format, inventing any reasonable data needed to complete this assignment.

2. **The 3Ps Microwriting Model: A Proposal—Starting a Student-Run Business**

Problem

You are the president of the Hospitality Services Association, a campus organization made up of students planning careers in hotel and motel management, tourism, and the like. You've just received a copy of a memo from the provost at your university addressed to the presidents of all campus organizations. The university is seeking proposals from student organizations to run a part-time business, tentatively named University Hosts, which would provide local services and organize various events for campus visitors.

For example, when the admissions office lets University Hosts know that a prospective student and his or her family will be visiting the campus, UH would immediately contact the family and offer to provide any reasonable service to help campus visitors enjoy their stay and receive a favorable impression of the institution. The service would be aimed at potential students and their families, alumni, donors, prospective faculty and staff members, and visiting legislators.

You feel that HSA would be the most logical organization to run this enterprise for the university. Your executive council has authorized you to submit a proposal to the provost. Personnel time (to be supplied by student members of HSA) would be billed at $10 per hour; a 10% surcharge would be added to the actual cost of all services provided (for example, tickets to campus or local events); automobile expenses would be billed at 22 cents per mile; and other charges would be billed at actual cost. Depending on the purpose of the campus visits, costs of the services would be billed either to the university or to the actual clients.

Process

a. What is the purpose of your report?
b. Describe your audience.
c. Is this a solicited or unsolicited proposal?
d. List the major advantages of this project and indicate how someone other than HSA will benefit from each advantage.
e. What costs are involved?
f. What qualifies HSA members to operate this business?
g. Will you request approval for this project at the beginning or end of your proposal? Why?
h. Compose an effective first sentence for your proposal.
i. What topics will you cover and in what order? Compose the specific headings for each topic.

Product

Prepare a three- to five-page typed proposal in memorandum format and submit it, along with your answers to the process questions, to your instructor. (You may invent any reasonable data needed.)

3. **Small Business—Reporting Needs**   Interview the owner/operator of a small business (10 to 50 employees) in your area. Determine the extent and types of reports written and received by employees in this firm. Write a memo report to your instructor summarizing your findings.

4. **Progress Report—Market Analysis**   Your market research firm, National Collegiate Solutions, Inc. (NCSI), was recently hired by Archway Publications, a publisher of teen magazines. Edgar Martin, Archway's vice president of marketing, wants you to analyze the market for a proposed monthly magazine geared toward college students. As director of research for NCSI, you agreed to submit a progress report at the end of each month. It's April 30 (you started the project on April 5), so it's time to tell Martin what your firm has accomplished so far.

First, you developed an interview form to gather data on what college students like and dislike about the magazines currently available. After testing this interview form on 35 students to be sure the questions were correctly phrased, you made appropriate revisions and obtained Archway's approval of the final instrument. Then you began the lengthy process of conducting 50 face-to-face interviews on each of 12 campuses across the country. By April 29, you had scheduled and completed the 50 interviews on three campuses; you expect to schedule and complete the remainder of the interviews by June 1. All interviews are going according to schedule. You plan to submit a brief synopsis of your findings by June 6, and by June 20 you will submit a full report including conclusions and recommendations.

Using a letter format, write a progress report to Martin, whose company is located at 15097 Dana Avenue, Cincinnati, OH 45207.

5. **Work-Team Communication—Common Report Types**   Four types of business reports were identified in this chapter. Working in a group of three to five students, obtain a sample of three report types, perhaps from someone at the university or where you work. Analyze these reports for such factors as the following:
   a. Purpose (to inform, analyze, or recommend)
   b. Target audience
   c. Length, format, and degree of formality
   d. Clarity, completeness, and accuracy of the information
   e. Authorship (individual or work-team)
   Write a two-page memo report to your instructor summarizing your findings.

6. **Work-Team Communication—Situational Report**   You are one member of a four-student team that has volunteered to look into the advantages and disadvantages of extending the college library's hours the week before each long break and the final week of each term or semester. You have heard some students complain that the evening hours are too short; they would especially like to see the library open later during periods when most students are working on research papers, examinations, and projects. Of course, longer hours would have an effect on payroll, staff scheduling, and other aspects of the library's operation. Your team will examine the issues, report your findings, and suggest how the administration might proceed.

   Team up with three other students to plan a situational report for your school's head of administrative services. Prepare a one- to two-page memo to your instructor indicating the purpose of your report, the audience, and the data that you will gather. Also list the issues you expect to examine. Will this situational report include recommendations? Why or why not?

7. **Procedure—Giving Directions**   As director of the student union at your institution, you frequently receive calls from for-profit and nonprofit organizations inquiring about reserving a room for special meetings. Sometimes these organizations want food service such as a meal or refreshments, sometimes they want a cash bar, and at other times they simply want an attractive meeting room. Of course, they're also interested in the cost, availability of parking, use of audiovisual equipment, deadlines, forms that need to be completed, and the like.

   Prepare a procedure that can be distributed to inquirers that will answer their most frequent questions and that will take them through the reservation process from initial inquiry through paying the final bill (if there is one). Use the actual practices in effect at your institution. Decide on an effective format for the written procedure report.

8. **Policy—Using University Facilities**   Refer to Exercise 7. Assume that your institution is establishing a policy that only nonprofit organizations may reserve meeting rooms on campus and that reservations by any on-campus groups take precedence over those from off-campus groups. The reason for this policy is to avoid competing with local commercial establishments and to prevent overcrowding of campus facilities. Prepare a policy statement (University Policy No. 403) for the board of trustees to consider at its next meeting.

9. **Audience Analysis—Curriculum**   The dean of your school of business has asked you, as president of the leading business honorary society on campus, to write a report evaluating the advantages and disadvantages of adding another required English course to the curriculum for all business majors.

Write out what you know (or can learn) about the dean that will help make your report more effective. Include such considerations as internal versus external audience, authorized versus voluntary report, and level of knowledge and interest of the reader. Discuss specifically how each item of information will influence your decisions about content, format, organization, and the like.

10. **Audience Analysis—Market Research**   Resume the role of director of research for National Collegiate Solutions, Inc. (see Exercise 4). Now that all the student interviews have been completed and the data analyzed, you are planning the final report of your findings, conclusions, and recommendations. Analyze your audience for this report. Is the audience internal or external? Is this a solicited or unsolicited report? What is the level of interest of the reader? Should you use a formal or informal style? Will you use a memo, letter, or manuscript format for this report? What organizational plan is appropriate? Prepare a one- to two-page summary of your answers to these questions.

11. **Report Management—Large Business**   Interview the records manager at a large business in your area (personally or by phone). Determine what policies the organization follows to control reports, especially recurring reports, in terms of need, frequency, length, distribution, and the like. Write a memo to your instructor summarizing your findings.

12. **Managing Reports—Control Policy**   Assume the role of the records manager you interviewed in Exercise 11 above. Your new boss, Cathy Saunders, has been reviewing the various recurring reports generated by managers in the organization. Although you have successfully controlled these reports in the past, Saunders believes that as the company grows, more reports (both needed and unneeded) will inevitably emerge. She asks you to prepare a policy statement to govern the addition of new reports. Using what you learned from your interview and from this chapter, write a policy statement directed to all company managers. Supply any reasonable information to complete this assignment.

13. **Managing Reports—Procedures**   Your policy statement about new reports (see Exercise 12 above) prompts several inquiries from managers who are uncertain about how to go about discontinuing a recurring report that doesn't seem to be needed anymore. When does a report become obsolete? For example, several departments or managers at several levels may be simply accustomed to seeing a given report, even if they no longer need it, but there may be one manager who actually needs and uses the information in the report. You decide to prepare a procedure that describes the steps to take before discontinuing a recurring report. Consider both the writer's and the readers' needs for information. What can you do before distributing your procedure statement to determine whether it is reasonable and appropriate?

The Copy Cat

Larry Haas has been surprised to learn when examining the quarterly departmental statements that photocopying costs have more than doubled from the previous quarter. In talking over the problem with others, he has learned that some workers photocopy nearly everything on their small departmental photocopier (there are five of these convenient, but relatively inefficient, copiers at headquarters) and other workers copy only small jobs on the departmental copiers and send larger jobs to the copy center, one of the departments managed by Eric Fox.

Jobs that are too big or too complicated for even the copy center to manage are sent to a local print shop. Some departments do the sending on their own; others rely on the copy center to do it. Regardless of where the copying is done, the individual department is charged for the job. From a company point of view, however, Larry is interested in ensuring that each job is completed in the most cost-effective way possible.

An additional problem that Larry has discovered is that the company's lax attitude about using the departmental photocopiers may have given the erroneous impression that employees have permission to photocopy personal documents. He has heard of numerous instances regarding the copying of personal insurance forms, recipes, sports stories, even kids' homework.

In speaking with the manager of the copy center, Larry learns that departmental copiers are designed for small jobs—no more than 30 copies of an original and no more than 20 originals per job. Any larger job should be sent to the copy center, which will decide whether to do the job in-house or send it outside. Generally, the in-house center handles one-color jobs on 8$\frac{1}{2}$-by-11-inch paper and up to 2,000 copies. Any job requiring more copies, more than one color, special binding, photographs, or the like is sent to the print shop.

Larry decides that a policy is needed on photocopying. And several specific procedures need to be established to accomplish the legitimate photocopying efficiently.

Critical Thinking

1. Taking into account the absence of any formal organizational policy, what are the ethical implications of employees' copying personal insurance forms, recipes, sports stories, and the like on the office copier?

Writing Projects

2. Write a policy statement (General Guideline 72) on the topic of photocopying. You may assume any reasonable information needed.

3. Once a job is submitted to the copy center, a procedure must be in place for deciding whether it's an in-house or outside job. Write a procedure that covers the situation from when the job reaches the copy center until it is returned to the requester.

11 Collecting and Analyzing Data

An Insider's Perspective

Domino's Pizza has an enormous appetite for data, as Chris Wall well knows. In his role as Senior Director of Consumer Research and Business Analysis, Wall is always on the go, collecting and analyzing data to help Domino's maintain its position as the world's leading pizza delivery company. With more than 5,600 stores in more than fifty countries, the company sells over 226 million pizzas every year. To fuel sales growth, Domino's managers need accurate, up-to-date information about consumer needs, product sales, and competitive moves. As a result, Wall and his group are constantly gathering and interpreting data to support management decisions about everything from introducing new products to boosting customer satisfaction.

As he investigates customer preferences and satisfaction with Domino's food and service, Wall and his team arrange to collect data directly from customers, usually by telephone. "We have a research firm conducting telephone interviews with customers who have purchased our products during the past twenty-four hours," Wall says. Domino's market researchers design questionnaires to make it as easy for customers to respond as it is to tally the answers. For example, some Domino's questionnaires present answers expressed as numbers on a five- or seven-point scale.

There are times, however, when more in-depth information is needed. In such cases, Domino's customers are invited to answer questions in their own words. During satisfaction surveys, for example, such answers can reveal specifics about what customers like and don't like—and what changes need to be made. Wall explains, "We report the responses verbatim so our store managers can see exactly what their customers are saying. If a customer says, 'I ordered a mushroom pizza but I got a pepperoni pizza,' that is something our store managers can address." Although compiling and interpreting these responses takes time and skill, the results are valuable because they reveal information that might otherwise not be captured. Before launching a new product, Domino's gathers data by asking selected groups of

COMMUNICATION OBJECTIVES

After you have finished this chapter, you should be able to

■ Develop an effective questionnaire and cover letter.

■ Conduct a data-gathering interview.

■ Construct clear, concise, and accurate tables.

■ Determine the most effective chart form and construct any needed charts.

■ Interpret the data for the report reader.

people about the concept and the taste. Before introducing the Roma Herb–flavored crust pizza, for example, the company elicited comments from groups of consumers, analyzed the results, and then invited other groups to taste and discuss various samples. Finally, the company tested actual customer response by offering the product in a limited number of stores before making it available throughout the United States. Domino's electronically collects sales data from all its stores to find out which pizza sizes, toppings, and crusts are selling. In addition, for general information about the overall pizza market and competitive trends, Wall looks to secondary sources. However, he is careful to consider the source before he uses any secondary data. "Just because it's in print or in a database doesn't mean that the information is accurate," he notes. "It could be right, but you need to be very cautious if you're not personally familiar with the source."

Chris Wall

Senior Director of Consumer Research and Business Analysis, Domino's Pizza (Ann Arbor, Michigan)

Once all the information has been gathered and analyzed, Wall and his team prepare a report or a presentation to communicate the results to management. Sum-

marizing the key findings and recommendations up front allows managers to see at a glance what happened in the study and what else has to be done; details are included after the summary, supported by graphs, charts, and tables. "Even though we may have been collecting data for months and have huge reams of material," Wall says, "we boil it all down to a one- or two-page summary so executives can get right to the meat."

Collecting Data Through Questionnaires

Despite your best efforts, you will sometimes find that not enough high-quality secondary data is available to solve your problem. In such a situation, you will probably need to collect primary data.

A **survey** is a data-collection method that gathers information through questionnaires, telephone inquiries, or interviews. The **questionnaire** (a written instrument containing questions designed to obtain information from the individual being surveyed) is the most frequently used method in business research. The researcher can economically get a representative sampling over a large geographical area. After all, it costs no more to mail a questionnaire across the country than across the street.

Don't confuse the terms survey *and* questionnaire: *you* conduct *a survey by* administering *a questionnaire.*

Also, the anonymity of a questionnaire increases the validity of some responses. Certain personal and economic data may be given more completely and honestly when the respondent remains unidentified. In addition, no interviewer is present to possibly bias the results. Finally, respondents can answer at a time convenient for them, which is not always the case with telephone or interview studies.

The main disadvantage of surveys is a low response rate.

The big disadvantage of mail questionnaires is the low response rate, and those who do respond may not be representative (typical) of the population. Indeed, extensive research has shown that respondents tend to be better educated, have higher social status, be more intelligent, have higher need for social approval, and be more sociable than those who choose not to respond.[1] Thus, mail questionnaires should be used only under certain conditions:

- *When the desired information can be provided easily and quickly.* Questionnaires should contain mostly yes-or-no questions, check-off alternatives, or one- to two-word fill-in responses. People tend not to return questionnaires that call for lengthy or complex responses.

- *When the target audience is homogeneous.* To ensure a high response rate, your study must interest the respondents and you must use language they understand. It is difficult to construct a questionnaire that would be clearly and uniformly understood by people with widely differing interests, education, and socioeconomic backgrounds.

- *When sufficient time is available.* Three to four weeks is generally required from questionnaire mailing to final returns—including follow-ups of the nonrespondents. A telephone survey, on the other hand, can often be completed in one day.

Constructing the Questionnaire

Because the target audience's time is valuable, make sure that every question you ask is necessary—that it is essential to help you solve your problem and that you cannot acquire the information from other sources (such as through library or online research). Guidelines for constructing a questionnaire are provided in Checklist 12. Some of the more important points are illustrated in the following paragraphs.

The question should not yield clues to the "correct" answer.

Your language must be clear, precise, and understandable so that the questionnaire yields valid and reliable data. Moreover, each question must be neutral (unbiased). Consider the following question:

✔ CHECKLIST 12   Questionnaires

Content

☑ Do not ask for information that is easily available elsewhere.

☑ Have a purpose for each question. Make sure that all questions directly help you to solve your problem. Avoid asking for unimportant or merely "interesting" information.

☑ Use precise wording so that no question can possibly be misunderstood. Use clear, simple language, and define any term that may be unfamiliar to the respondent or that you are using in a special way.

☑ Use neutrally worded questions and deal with only one topic per question. Avoid loaded, leading, or multifaceted questions.

☑ Ensure that the response choices are both exhaustive and mutually exclusive (that is, that there is an appropriate response for every one and that there are no overlapping categories).

☑ Be especially careful about asking sensitive questions, such as information about age, salary, or morals. Consider using broad categories for such questions (instead of narrow, more specific categories).

☑ Pilot-test your questionnaire on a few people to ensure that all questions function as intended. Revise as needed.

Organization

☑ Arrange the questions in some logical order. Group together all questions that deal with a particular topic. If your questionnaire is long, divide it into sections.

☑ Arrange the alternatives for each question in some logical order—such as numerical, chronological, or alphabetical.

☑ Give the questionnaire a descriptive title, provide whatever directions are necessary, and include your name and return address somewhere on the questionnaire.

Format

☑ Use an easy-to-answer format. Check-off questions draw the most responses and are easiest to answer and tabulate. Use free-response items only when absolutely necessary.

☑ To increase the likelihood that your target audience will cooperate and take your study seriously, ensure that your questionnaire has a professional appearance:
- Use a simple and attractive format, allowing for plenty of white (blank) space.
- Ensure that the questionnaire is free from errors in grammar, spelling, and style.
- Use a high-quality printer and make high-quality photocopies.

NOT: Do you think our company should open an on-site child-care center as a means of ensuring the welfare of our employees' small children?
___ yes
___ no

   This wording of the question obviously favors the "pro" side, thereby biasing the responses. A more neutral question is needed if valid responses are to result.

BUT: Which one of the following possible additional fringe benefits would you most prefer?
___ a dental insurance plan
___ an on-site child-care center
___ three personal-leave days annually
___ other (please specify: _____)

Note several things about this question. First, it is more neutral than the original version; no "right" answer is apparent. Second, the alternatives are arranged in alphabetical order. To avoid possibly biasing the responses, always arrange the alternatives in some logical order—alphabetical, numerical, chronological, or the like.

Finally, note that an "other" category is provided; it always goes last and is accompanied by the request to "please specify." Suppose the one fringe benefit that the vast majority of employees really wanted most was for the company to increase its pension contributions. If the "other" category were missing, the researcher would never learn that important information.

Ensure that your categories are *exhaustive* (that is, that they include all possible alternatives), by including an "other" category if necessary. Also be certain that each question contains a single idea. Note the following question:

Ask only one question in each item.

NOT: Our company should spend less money on advertising and more money on research and development.
___ agree
___ disagree

Suppose the respondent believes that the company should spend more (or less) money on advertising *and* on research and development? How is he or she supposed to answer? The solution is to put each of the two ideas in a separate question.

Finally, ensure that your categories are *mutually exclusive;* that is, that there are no overlapping categories.

NOT: In your opinion, what is the major cause of high employee turnover?
___ lack of air-conditioning
___ noncompetitive financial package
___ poor fringe benefits
___ poor working conditions
___ weak management

The problem with this item is that the "lack of air-conditioning" category overlaps with the "poor working conditions" category, and "noncompetitive financial package" overlaps with "poor fringe benefits." And all four of these probably overlap with "weak management." Such intermingling of categories will thoroughly confuse the respondent and yield unreliable survey results.

Recognize that respondents may be hesitant to answer sensitive questions (regarding age, salary, morals, and the like). Even worse, they may deliberately provide *inaccurate* responses. When it is necessary to gather such data, ensure that the respondent understands that the questionnaire is anonymous (by prominently discussing that fact in the cover letter). Respondents tend to be more cooperative in answering such questions when broad categories are used. Accurate estimates provided by broad categories are preferable to precise data that is incorrect.

NOT: What is your annual gross salary? $ _____

BUT: Please check the category that best describes your annual salary:
___ Less than $15,000
___ $15,000–$25,000
___ $25,001–$50,000
___ More than $50,000

Simply checking a broad range of figures might be less threatening than having to write in an exact figure.

Note that the use of the number "$25,001" in the third category is necessary to avoid overlap with the figure "$25,000" in the second category; remember that the categories must be mutually exclusive.

Even experienced researchers find it difficult to spot ambiguities or other problems in their own questionnaires. If time permits, administer the draft questionnaire to a small sample of potential respondents and then revise it as necessary. At a minimum, ask a colleague to edit your instrument with a critical eye. The sample questionnaire shown in Model 20 (on pp. 332–333) illustrates a variety of question types, along with clear directions and efficient format.

Writing the Cover Letter

Unless you intend to distribute the questionnaires personally (in which case, you would be able to explain the purpose and procedures in person), include a cover letter like the one shown in Model 21 (on p. 334) with your questionnaire. The cover letter should be written as a regular persuasive letter (see Chapter 8). Your job is to convince the reader that it's worth taking the time to complete the questionnaire.

Collecting Data Through Interviews

Personal interviews are generally considered to be the most valid method of survey research. In a personal interview, the interviewer can probe, ask for clarification, clear up any misunderstandings immediately, ensure that all questions are answered completely, and pursue unexpected avenues. Thus, data resulting from an interview is often of a higher quality than data resulting from a questionnaire.

Although expensive to conduct, personal interviews are most appropriate for gathering in-depth or complex data.

Personal interviews are most appropriate when in-depth information is desired. The interview permits open-ended questions and gives the respondent free rein to answer as he or she desires. Respondents are likely to *say* more than they will write. Research into topics such as motives, deeply held feelings, and complex issues simply does not lend itself to the objective questions that are found in most questionnaires.

There are, however, several problems with interviews. Interview research is expensive; it is time-consuming to schedule the interviews, conduct them, and analyze the subjective data that flows from them. Also, in-depth interviewing requires specially trained and experienced interviewers.

Second, the interviewer can consciously or unconsciously bias the results—by not recording the answers exactly, for instance, or showing a favorable or unfavorable reaction to a response, or hurrying through parts of the interview. Different interviewers may experience the same situation and "see" different things. Thus, analyzing interview data is often more difficult than analyzing questionnaire data. The subjective nature of the data given and of the data received affects the validity of the research.

Finally, a personal interview is not appropriate for eliciting information of a sensitive nature. Questions about age, salary, personal beliefs, and the like should not be used in face-to-face questioning where anonymity is not possible. (The alert interviewer can, however, sometimes get an estimate of these variables by carefully observing the interviewee and his or her environment.)

In most situations, the sample for a questionnaire study is selected so that each member is typical of the population. However, interviewees are often selected for just the opposite reason: they may have *unique* expertise or experiences to share,

MODEL 20 Questionnaire

This questionnaire uses a variety of response formats.

Uses a descriptive title.

Provides clear directions.

Uses check-off responses for Questions 1–3.

Uses fill-in-the-blank responses for Question 4.

Uses ranking responses for Question 8.

1

STUDENT USE OF COMPUTERS AT CMU

This survey is being conducted as part of a research project for BEOA 249 (Business Communication). Please complete this questionnaire only if you (a) are a full-time junior or senior student at CMU, (b) attended CMU last semester, and (c) have declared a major.

A. DESCRIPTIVE INFORMATION

2   1. Grade level: 2. Gender: 3. Age:
      ___ junior   ___ female   ___ 20 or younger
      ___ senior   ___ male   ___ 21-24
                                                  ___ 25 or older

4. Are you pursuing a teaching or nonteaching major?
    ___ teaching *(Please write in the name of your major:* _____)
    ___ nonteaching *(Please write in the name of your major:* _____)

5. College where major is located:
    ___ Arts and Sciences   ___ Education
    ___ Business   ___ Other *(Please specify:* _____)

6. Did you use a computer in a CMU computer lab last semester either as a course requirement or for personal use?
    ___ yes *(Please continue with Question 7.)*
    ___ no *(Please disregard the following questions and return the questionnaire to the researcher.)*

B. TYPE AND EXTENT OF COMPUTER USE

7. During the last semester, which type of microcomputer did you use *most frequently?*
    ___ IBM or compatible
    ___ Macintosh
    ___ other *(Please specify:* _____)

8. Which on-campus computer labs were most convenient for completing your out-of-class computer assignments? Please rank from 1 *(most)* to 4 *(least)* the convenience of each lab; *write in* the appropriate number in each blank.
    ___ business lab   ___ library lab
    ___ dormitory lab   ___ student center lab

3   9. Listed on the next page are different types of computer software. For each, first check the type of use you made of this software at any time during the previous semester. You may check both *Required* and *Personal* if appropriate. An example of personal use would be typing a term paper using word processing software—if such use were not required. Then, if you used this type of software, check the total number of hours of use during the semester, including both in-class and out-of-class use.

Grammar and Mechanics Notes

1 Make the title and section headings stand out through the use of bold type and perhaps a larger font size.   2 If space is at a premium, group shorter questions on the same line (as in Questions 1–3).   3 Although not always possible (as illustrated here), try to avoid splitting a question between two pages.

MODEL 20 *(Continued)*

Question 9 (cont'd)

Type of Software	None	Type of Use Required	Personal	Amount of Use <5 Hrs	5-10 Hrs	>10 Hrs
EXAMPLE: Games	—	—	✓	—	—	✓
Accounting/Financial	—	—	—	—	—	—
Database	—	—	—	—	—	—
Educational (tutorial)	—	—	—	—	—	—
Graphics/Presentation	—	—	—	—	—	—
Programming	—	—	—	—	—	—
Spreadsheet	—	—	—	—	—	—
Word processing	—	—	—	—	—	—
Other (*please specify:* _____)	—	—	—	—	—	—

Provides clear directions and an example for the complex check-off responses in Question 9.

Lists alternatives in alphabetical (or some other logical) order.

C. STUDENT OPINIONS

Please check whether you agree with, have no opinion about, or disagree with each of the following statements.

	Agree	No Opinion	Disagree
10. Considering my major, I am receiving adequate training in the use of computers.	—	—	—
11. The computer equipment at CMU is not up to date.	—	—	—
12. I have to wait an unreasonable length of time to get onto a computer in the lab.	—	—	—
13. I enjoy working with computers.	—	—	—
14. Most instructors provide adequate instruction in the use of the software they require.	—	—	—
15. Lab attendants are not as helpful as they should be.	—	—	—

Uses attitude-scale responses for Questions 10–15; this section contains a combination of positive and negative statements.

D. IMPROVEMENTS NEEDED

16. If you could make *one* suggestion to the university administration to improve computer services at CMU, what would that suggestion be?

_____

_____

_____

Saves the open-ended question for last.

Thanks for your help. Please return the completed questionnaire in the enclosed campus envelope to Matt Jones, 105 Woldt Hall.

Gives name and address of the researcher.

Grammar and Mechanics Notes

5 Label different sections if the questionnaire is more than one or two pages long.   6 Provide sufficient space for the respondent to answer open-ended questions.

MODEL 21 **Questionnaire Cover Letter**

This cover letter would accompany the questionnaire shown in Model 20.

CENTRAL METROPOLITAN UNIVERSITY

P.O. Box 0049 ¥ Fairbanks, Alaska 99701

February 8, 19--

1   Dear Fellow Student:

"Oh no—not another computer project!"

Have you ever felt this way during the first day of class when the instructor makes the course assignments? Or, instead, do you sometimes wonder, "Why is the instructor
2   making us do this project manually when it would be so much easier to do on a computer?"

Either way, here is your chance to provide the CMU administration with your views on student computer use at Central Metropolitan University. This research project is a class project for BEOA 249 (Business Communication), and the results will be shared with Dr. Dan Rulong, vice president for academic computing.

If you are a full-time junior or senior student, attended CMU last semester, and have
3   declared a major, please take five minutes to complete this questionnaire. Then simply return it by February 19 in the enclosed envelope. You'll be doing yourself and your fellow students a big favor.

Sincerely,

Matt Jones, Project Leader
105 Woldt Hall

Enclosures

Begins with a short attention-getter.

Provides a smooth transition to the purpose of the letter.

Provides reasons for cooperating.

Makes the requested action easy to take.

Grammar and Mechanics Notes

1 *Dear Fellow Student:* Use a generic salutation for form letters that are not individually prepared.   **2** *on a computer?":* Position the question mark *inside* the closing quotation mark if the entire quoted matter is a question.   **3** The word *questionnaire* contains two *n*'s and one *r*.

and the data they provide will serve as "expert testimony" and not be tabulated and generalized to the population.

Types of Questions

In most ways, your interview questions should follow the guidelines given in Checklist 12 on page 339 for questionnaire items; they should be clear and unbiased and deal with only one topic per question. However, because of the increased complexity of many interview topics, you now have other choices to make.

Open Versus Closed Questions   Open-ended questions allow the interviewee flexibility in responding, whereas closed questions limit the subject matter of the response:

Open:	What is your opinion of the NAFTA trade treaty?
Closed:	How much of your firm's business is attributable to international sales?

Use both open-ended and closed questions.

Open questions expose the interviewee's priorities and frame of reference and may uncover information that the interviewer may never have thought to ask about. Interviewees like open questions because they are easy to answer (there is no wrong answer), and they give recognition to the interviewee—by letting him or her talk through ideas while the interviewer listens intently. The drawbacks to open questions are that they are time-consuming and the responses may be rambling, difficult to record, and difficult to tabulate later.

Closed questions save time and are very useful when you know exactly what type of information you want, when you intend to tabulate the responses, and when the responses don't require elaborate explanation by the interviewee. The amount of interview information that can be obtained by closed questions, however, is fairly restricted; if all your questions lend themselves to the closed format, a questionnaire would probably yield just as valid results for much less expense.

In actual practice, the interviewer usually uses both open and closed questions, often following up a closed question with an open one.

Closed:	Do you agree or disagree with the proposal?
Open:	Why?

Closed:	Will it have any effect on your own firm?
Open:	In what way?

Direct Versus Indirect Questions   Most questions may be asked directly. In threatening or sensitive situations, however, you may want to resort to indirect questions, which are less threatening because they let the interviewee camouflage his or her response.

Direct:	How would you evaluate your boss's people skills?
Indirect:	How do you think most people in this department would evaluate the boss's people skills?

word wise

How's Business?

- "Beastly," said the zookeeper.

- "Cheesy, in a whey," said the dairy farmer.

- "It's hard to beat," said the drummer.

- "Just sew-sew," said the dressmaker.

- "Knot bad," said the sailor.

- "Pretty much up in the air," said the pilot.

- "We're forging on," said the counterfeiter.

Personal interviews are generally the most valid method of survey research because the interviewer can probe, ask for clarification, clear up any misunderstandings immediately, and pursue unexpected leads. The interviewer must, however, ensure that he or she does not consciously or unconsciously bias the results. Global polling organizations such as Gallup, shown here, train their interviewers very carefully to ensure unbiased results.

Conducting the Interview

As an interviewer, you must wear two hats—that of an observer and that of a participant. You participate by asking questions, but you must also analyze the responses to ensure that the interviewee is indeed answering the question asked and to determine if follow-up questions are needed. Fulfilling this dual role requires concentration, preparation, and flexibility.

Listening in an interview involves much more than simply hearing what is being said.

To secure the greatest cooperation from interviewees, you should make them feel comfortable and important. (They are!) The first few minutes of the interview are crucial for establishing rapport. Begin with a warm greeting; reintroduce yourself; and explain again the purpose of the interview, how the information will be used, and how much time will be required.

It is difficult to listen actively if you are busy taking notes.

One of the barriers to effective listening during an interview is the need for note taking. Keep note taking to a minimum by using a small portable cassette recorder when possible. Always get permission first, assuring the interviewee that the purpose is to make certain that he or she is not misquoted and to let you give his or her responses your full attention. Keep the recorder out of sight (perhaps on the floor beside you) so that the interviewee is not constantly reminded that his or her remarks are being recorded. Test the recording level beforehand to ensure that the responses will be audible.

Always use an **interview guide**—a list of questions to ask, with suggested wording and possible follow-up questions. Mark off each question as it is asked *and* answered (don't assume that just because a question was asked, it was answered). Nothing is more embarrassing than repeating a question that has already been answered, and nothing is more frustrating than learning after the interview is over that you failed to ask an important question.

Provide smooth transitions when moving from topic to topic by using periodic summaries of what has been covered and previews of what will be covered next; for example,

We've covered the start-up and initial funding for your firm. Next, I'd like to investigate any problems your firm experienced during its early years.

Follow up a point if the interviewee's response is inadequate in some way; for example, the interviewee may have consciously or unconsciously failed to answer all or part of a question, given inaccurate information, or given a response you did not understand completely. When the response needs amplification, you can probe by asking for more information, by asking for clarification, or simply by repeating the question.

Indicate when the interview is over—either by a direct statement or by such nonverbal gestures as putting your papers away or standing up. Experienced interviewers often end an interview by asking these two questions:

Is there some question you think I should have asked that I didn't ask? (*to uncover unexpected information*)

May I call you if I need to verify some information? (*to enable the checking of some fact or spelling or to ask a quick follow-up question*)

Leave the interviewee with a sense of accomplishment by quickly summarizing the important points you've gathered (to show that you've listened) or by restating how the information will be used. Finally, express appreciation once more for the time granted.

Constructing Tables

At some point in the reporting process, you will have gathered enough data from your secondary and primary sources to enable you to solve your problem. (It is always possible, of course, that at any point during data analysis and report writing you may find that you need additional information on a topic.)

Tables are often the most economical way of presenting numerical data.

Your job at this point, then, is to convert your raw data, which might be represented by your notes, photocopies of journal articles, completed questionnaires, audiotapes of interviews, computer printouts, and the like, into *information*—meaningful facts, statistics, and conclusions—that will help the reader of your report make a decision. In addition to interpreting your findings in narrative form, you will also likely prepare some **visual aids**—tables, charts, photographs, or other graphic materials—to aid comprehension and add interest.

Analysis and interpretation turn data into information.

Data analysis is not a step that can be accomplished at one sitting. The more familiar you become with the data and the more you pore over it, the more different things you will see. Data analysis is usually the part of the report process that requires the most time as well as the most skill. The more insight you can provide the reader about the *meaning* of the data you've collected and presented, the more helpful your report will be.

A **table** is an orderly arrangement of data into columns and rows (see Model 22 on p. 338). It represents the most basic form of statistical analysis and is useful for showing a large amount of numerical data in a small space. A table presents numerical data more efficiently and more interestingly than narrative text and provides more information than a graph, though with less visual impact. Because of its orderly arrangement of information into vertical columns and horizontal rows, a table also permits easy comparison of figures. However, trends are more obvious when presented in graphs.

MODEL 22 **Table**

Use tables to present a large amount of data clearly and concisely.

the market leader for all of 1997 and for the first two quarters of 1998 as well, based primarily on governmental sales. As it has for the past three years, the Eastern Region led the company's sales force, as shown in Table 14.

Table number
Title
Subtitle (optional)

1

Table 14
1998 APEX SALES LEADERS BY REGION
As of December 15

Column Heading

Region	Sales Leader	Sales*	Yearly Change
Eastern	Ronald Miller	$17.5	13.4%
Western			
Continental	Dorothy Cheung	13.6	–2.1
Hawaii/Alaska	David Kane	3.2	4.0
Midwestern	C.J. Peri-Watts	9.7	4.6
Southern	Rita Rosales	8.2	–5.2
Plains	B.B. Cody	6.0	15.8
Average		$9.7	5.1%

Body

2

3

Source (optional)

Source: *Insurance Leaders DataQuest* (New York: Insurance Institute of North America, 1998), pp. 143–179.

Footnote (optional)

*In millions.

4

The sales leaders in two of the regions (Western and Southern) experienced decreased sales, even though they remained the top producers in their respective regions. The reason

Grammar and Mechanics Notes

1 Position the table below the first paragraph that makes reference to the table. A variety of table formats are appropriate, but be consistent throughout the report.   **2** Unless the column heading clearly indicates that the amounts represent dollars or percentages, insert the dollar sign before or the percent sign after the first number and before or after a total or average amount.   **3** Align word columns at the left; align number columns either at the right (for whole numbers) or on the decimal point.   **4** Leave the same amount of space (2–3 blank lines) before and after the table.

Figure 11.1 shows a computer printout of an attitude-scale item (Question 9) on a questionnaire and the corresponding table constructed from this printout. Apex Company, a manufacturer of consumer products headquartered in Des Moines, Iowa, is considering building an addition to its factory there and wants to gauge local opinion before making a commitment.

Consider first the computer printout at the top of Figure 11.1 and the meaning of each column.

- *Value Label:* Shows the five alternatives given on the questionnaire.

- *Value:* Shows the code used to identify each of these five alternatives.

- *Frequency:* Shows the number of respondents who checked each alternative.

- *Pct:* Shows the percentage of each response, based on the total number of respondents ($N = 274$), including those who left this particular item blank.

- *Valid Pct:* Shows the percentage of each response, based on the total number of respondents who actually answered this particular question ($N = 271$).

- *Cum Pct:* Shows the cumulative percentage—that is, the sum of this response plus those above it (for example, 79.7% of the respondents either agreed or strongly agreed with the statement).

The researcher must determine whether the "Pct" or "Valid Pct" column is more appropriate for the analysis. In most cases, the "Valid Pct" column, which ignores any blank responses, would be the one to choose. That is the case in Table 4, shown in the lower half of Figure 11.1.

Your reader must be able to understand each table on its own, without having to read the surrounding text. Thus, at a minimum, each table should contain a table number, a descriptive but concise title, column headings, and body (the items under

The reader should be able to understand the table without having to refer to the text.

Arlene DeCandia, founder of the Minneapolis conference center Riverwood Metro Business Resort, uses spreadsheets to back up her loan proposals. She tracks not only her business but also the business she has to turn away. Presenting this data in spreadsheets gives the bank hard data to support her plans for expansion.

FIGURE 11.1 **From Computer Printout to Report Table**

Computer Printout

Q.9   "APEX COMPANY IS AN ASSET TO OUR COMMUNITY"

VALUE LABEL	VALUE	FREQUENCY	PCT	VALID PCT	CUM PCT
Strongly agree	1	41	15.0	15.1	15.1
Agree	2	175	63.8	64.6	79.7
No opinion	3	34	12.4	12.6	92.3
Disagree	4	15	5.5	5.5	97.8
Strongly disagree	5	6	2.2	2.2	100.0
	•	3	1.1	MISSING	
TOTAL		274	100.0	100.0	100.0
VALID CASES	271		MISSING CASES 3		

Corresponding Report Table

TABLE 4.   **Response to Statement, "Apex Company is an asset to our community."**

Response	No.	Pct.
Strongly agree	41	15
Agree	175	65
No opinion	34	13
Disagree	15	5
Strongly disagree	6	2
Total	271	100

each column heading). If you need footnotes to explain individual items within the table, put them immediately below the body of the table, not at the bottom of the page. Similarly, if the table is based on secondary data, type a source note below the body, giving the appropriate citation. Common abbreviations and symbols are acceptable in tables.

Cross-tabulation analysis enables you to look at two or more groups of data simultaneously.

Cross-Tabulation Analysis

In some cases, the simple question-by-question tabulation illustrated in Table 4 of Figure 11.1 would be sufficient analysis for the reader's purpose. However, in most cases such simple tabulations would not yield all the "secrets" the data holds. Most data can be further analyzed through **cross-tabulation,** a process by which two or more pieces of data are analyzed together. For example, because of the types of products Apex manufactures, you might suspect that different subgroups of respondents would hold different views of the company. Therefore, you can combine Question 9 with questions about marital status, gender, and age, as shown in Figure 11.2.

FIGURE 11.2 Cross-Tabulation Analysis

TABLE 4.   Response to Statement, "Apex Company is an asset to our community."

	Total		Marital Status		Gender		Age			
	Total	Pct.	Married	Single	Male	Female	Under 21	21–35	36–50	Over 50
Strongly Agree	41	15.1%	14.0%	17.6%	15.7%	10.4%	21.7%	8.4%	12.0%	28.4%
Agree	175	64.6%	67.5%	58.8%	67.6%	46.3%	47.8%	65.1%	69.1%	61.0%
No Opinion	34	12.6%	11.2%	15.4%	11.4%	20.9%	17.5%	13.0%	14.3%	9.2%
Disagree	15	5.5%	5.1%	5.5%	4.0%	13.4%	13.0%	8.4%	4.0%	0.7%
Strongly Disagree	6	2.2%	2.2%	2.7%	1.3%	9.0%	0.0%	5.1%	0.6%	0.7%
Total	271	100.0%	100.0%	100.0%	100.0%	100.0%	100.0%	100.0%	100.0%	100.0%

This table shows not only the total responses (both the number and the percentages) but also the percentage responses for the subgroups according to marital status, gender, and age. A quick "eyeballing" of the table shows that there do not seem to be any major differences in the perceptions of married versus single respondents. However, there does seem to be a fairly sizable difference between male and female respondents: males have a much more positive view of the company than do females.

If the table in Figure 11.2 were one of only a few tables in your report, it would be just fine the way it is shown. However, suppose the statement "Apex Company is an asset to our community" is one of a dozen attitude items, each of which requires a similar table. It is probably too much to expect the reader to study a dozen similar tables; in such a situation, you should consider simplifying the table.

There are a number of ways to simplify a table. You should recognize right from the start, however, that whenever you simplify a table (that is, whenever you merge rows or columns or simply delete data), your table loses some of its detail. The goal in simplifying is to gain more in comprehensibility than you lose in specificity. Your knowledge of the reader and his or her needs will help you determine how much detail to present.

Sometimes tabular data needs to be condensed for easier and faster comprehension.

With that in mind, consider the simplified version of this table shown in Figure 11.3. The two positive responses ("strongly agree" and "agree") have been combined

FIGURE 11.3 Simplified Table

TABLE 4.   Response to Statement, "Apex Company is an asset to our community." (*N* = 271; all figures in %)

	Total	Marital Status		Gender		Age		
	Total	Married	Single	Male	Female	Under 21	21–50	Over 50
Agree	80	82	77	83	57	69	77	90
No opinion	12	11	15	12	21	18	14	9
Disagree	8	7	8	5	22	13	9	1
Total	100	100	100	100	100	100	100	100

into one "agree" row, as have the two negative responses. Combining not only simplifies the table but also prevents some possible interpretation problems. Given the original table in Figure 11.2, for example, would you consider the following statement to be accurate: "Less than half of the females agree that Apex Company is an asset to their community"? Technically, the statement is accurate, since the 46.3% who "agree" is *less* than half. However, the statement leaves an incorrect impression because more than half of the females (57%—those who "agree" *and* who "strongly agree") believe Apex Company is an asset to their community. This conclusion is made clear in Figure 11.3.

Note also that the two center age groups ("21–35" and "36–50") have been combined into one age group ("21–50"). Because the company's products are geared mainly to this large age group, the company wanted to compare the responses of this important group with the responses of the less important younger and older groups.

More data is not always better than less data.

Two other changes help simplify the table. First, only percentages are provided, which eliminates the need for the percentage sign after each number (interested readers can compute the raw numbers for themselves since the sample size is shown in the table subtitle). Second, each percentage is rounded to its nearest whole—a practice recommended for most business reports when presenting percentages that total 100%.

Follow these practices when rounding numbers:

- Any number with a decimal less than .50 gets rounded *down* to the next nearest whole number; any number with a decimal greater than .50 gets rounded *up.*

- Odd numbers with a decimal of exactly .50 get rounded *up;* even numbers with a decimal of exactly .50 get rounded *down.*

- If your table shows the total percentages and your rounding efforts result in totals that do not equal 100% (such as 99% or 101%), you have the option of either (1) showing the actual resulting totals or (2) readjusting one of the rounded numbers (presumably, the one that will cause the least distortion to the number) to "force" a 100% total. Thus, 86.4%, which would normally be rounded to 86%, might need to be rounded to 87% to force a 100% total. This practice is often used in business reports.

This simplification of Table 4 has deleted two of the ten columns and two of the five rows—for a net decrease of 49% in the number of individual bits of data presented. When this reduction is multiplied by the number of similar tables in the report, the net effect is rather dramatic.

Arranging Data in Tables

Arrange the data in logical format—usually from high to low.

As discussed earlier, the check-off alternatives in your questionnaire items should be arranged in some logical order, most often either numerical or alphabetical, to avoid possibly biasing the responses. Once you have the data in hand, however, it is often helpful to the reader if you rearrange the data from high to low.

In Figure 11.4, for example, the categories have been rearranged from their original *alphabetical* order in the questionnaire to *descending* order in the report table. Note also that the four smallest categories have been combined into a miscellaneous category, which always goes last, regardless of its size. Finally, note the position and format of the table footnote, which is used to explain an entry in the table.

FIGURE 11.4 Arranging Data in Tables

From This Survey Response:

6. In which of the following categories of clerical workers do you expect to hire additional workers within the next three years? (Check all that apply.)

211	bookkeepers and accounting clerks
31	computer operators
30	data-entry keyers
24	file clerks
247	general office clerks
78	receptionists and information clerks
323	secretaries
7	statistical clerks
107	typists and word processors

To This Report Table:

TABLE 2.   COMPANIES PLANNING TO HIRE ADDITIONAL CLERICAL WORKERS
(BY CATEGORY)

Category	No.	Pct.[*]
Secretaries	323	99
General office clerks	247	76
Bookkeepers and accounting clerks	211	65
Typists and word processors	107	33
Receptionists and information clerks	78	24
Miscellaneous	92	28
Total	326	

[*]Answers total more than 100% because of multiple responses.

Preparing Charts

The appropriate use of well-designed charts and graphs (technically, *graphs* are shown on graph paper; however, the two terms are used interchangeably) can aid in reader comprehension, emphasize certain data, create interest, and save time and space because the reader can perceive immediately the essential meaning of large masses of statistical data.

Because of their visual impact, charts receive more emphasis than tables or narrative text. Therefore, you should save them for presenting information that is important and that can best be grasped visually—for example, when the overall picture is more important than the individual numbers. Also recognize that the more charts your report contains, the less impact each individual chart will have.

The cardinal rule for designing charts is to keep them simple. Trying to cram too much information into one chart will only confuse the reader and lessen the impact of the graphic. Well-designed charts have only one interpretation, and that interpretation should be clear immediately; the reader shouldn't have to study the chart at length or refer to the surrounding text.

Keep charts simple. Immediate comprehension is the goal.

Regardless of their type, label all your charts as *figures,* and assign them consecutive numbers, separate from table numbers. Although tables are captioned at the top, charts may be captioned at the top or bottom. Charts used alone (for example, as an overhead transparency or slide) are typically captioned at the top. Charts preceded or followed by text or containing an explanatory paragraph are typically captioned at the bottom. As with tables, you may use commonly understood abbreviations.

Today, many microcomputer software programs are able to generate special charts automatically from data contained in spreadsheets or from data entered at the keyboard. The professional appearance and ready availability of such charts often make up for the loss of flexibility in designing graphics precisely to your wishes.

The main types of charts used in business reports and presentations are line charts, bar charts, and pie charts.

Line Charts

A **line chart** is a graph based on a grid of uniformly spaced horizontal and vertical lines. The vertical dimension represents values; the horizontal dimension represents time. Line charts are useful for showing changes in data over long periods of time and for emphasizing the movement of the data—the trends. (Model 23 on page 345 shows three kinds of line charts.) Both axes should be marked off at equal intervals and clearly labeled. The vertical axis should begin with zero, even when all the amounts are quite large. In some situations, it may be desirable to show a break in the intervals, as illustrated in Model 23B. Fluctuations of the line over time indicate variations in the trend; the distance of the line from the horizontal axis indicates quantity.

More than one variable may be plotted on the same chart (see Model 23A). For example, both sales and net profits can be plotted on one chart, using either different-colored lines or different types of lines (solid, dotted, and dashed, for example) to avoid confusion. Each line should be labeled clearly.

A variation of the line chart is the area (or surface) chart, which uses shading to emphasize the overall picture of the trend (see Model 23B). A second variation is the segmented area chart, which contains several bands that depict the components of the total trend (see Model 23C). Because the individual components cannot be read accurately, the segmented area chart should be used only to give an overall picture.

Bar Charts

A **bar chart** is a graph with horizontal or vertical bars representing values. Bar charts are one of the most useful, simple, and popular graphic techniques. They are particularly appropriate for comparing the magnitude or size of items, either at a specified time or over a period of time (see Model 24 on p. 346). The vertical bar chart (sometimes called a *column chart*) is typically used for portraying a time series when the emphasis is on the individual amounts rather than on the trends (see Model 24A).

Bar charts compare the magnitude of items. Use vertical bars for comparing items over time.

The bars should all be the same width, with the length changing to reflect the value of each item. The spacing between the bars should generally be about half the width of the bars themselves.

MODEL 23 Line Charts

A. Simple Line Chart

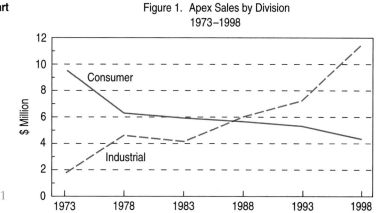

Figure 1. Apex Sales by Division
1973–1998

B. Area Chart

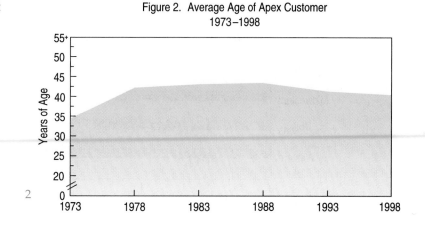

Figure 2. Average Age of Apex Customer
1973–1998

C. Segmented Area Chart

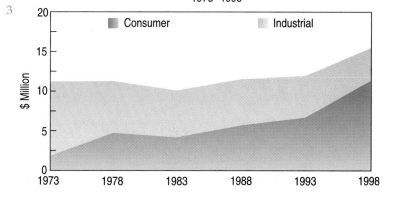

Figure 3. Apex Sales by Division
1973–1998

Grammar and Mechanics Notes

1 Start the vertical axis at the zero point.   2 Use slash marks if necessary to indicate a break in an interval.   3 Clearly differentiate between two trend lines, and label each.

MODEL 24 Bar Charts

A. Vertical Bar Chart, or Column Chart

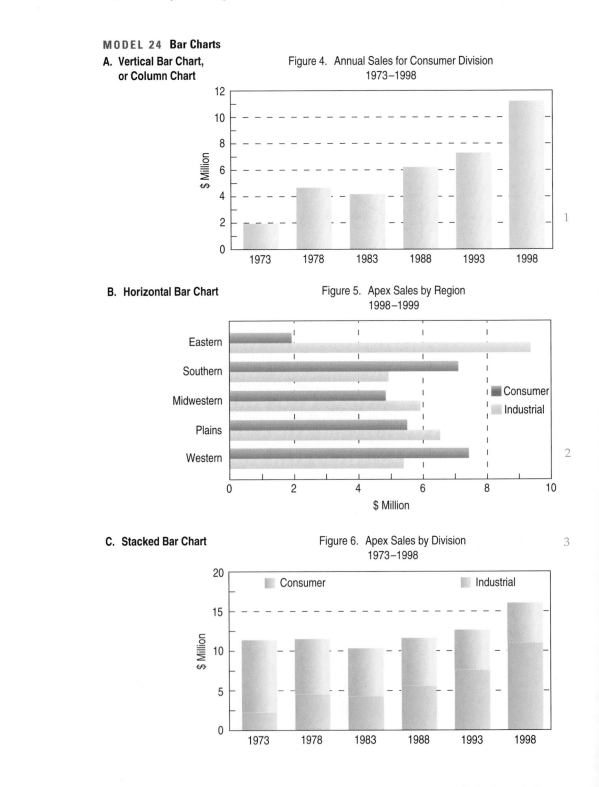

Figure 4. Annual Sales for Consumer Division
1973–1998

1

B. Horizontal Bar Chart

Figure 5. Apex Sales by Region
1998–1999

2

C. Stacked Bar Chart

Figure 6. Apex Sales by Division
1973–1998

3

Grammar and Mechanics Notes

1 Make all bars the same width; show value differences by varying the length or height.
2 Position the bars either vertically or horizontally.   3 Label all charts (regardless of type) as "figures"; place the figure number and title either above or below the chart.

Alec Mackenzie, whose book *The Time Trap* started the time-management boom in 1972 and has sold over half a million copies in 12 languages, makes extensive use of charts when giving his time-management seminars. Effective charts increase audience interest and save time by helping the reader or listener perceive immediately the essential meaning of large masses of data.

Bars may be grouped to compare several variables over a period of time (see Model 24B) or may be stacked to show component parts of several variables (see Model 24C). As with tables, the bars should be arranged in some logical order. If space permits, include the actual value of each bar for quicker comprehension.

Pie Charts

A **pie chart** is a circle graph whose area is divided into component wedges (see Model 25 on p. 348). It compares the relative parts that make up a whole. Some software charting programs permit you to "drag out" a particular wedge of the pie chart for special emphasis.

Although pie charts rank very high in popular appeal, graphics specialists hold them in somewhat lower esteem because of their lack of precision and because of the difficulty in differentiating more than a few categories, and in comparing component values across several pie charts. However, pie charts are useful for showing how component parts add up to make a total when the whole contains three to five component parts. A chart is generally not needed for presenting only two component parts; more than five can present visual difficulties in perceiving the relative value of each wedge.

It is customary to begin "slicing" the pie at the 12 o'clock position and move clockwise in some logical order (often in order of descending size). When used, a miscellaneous category goes last, regardless of its size. The labels should be placed either inside each wedge, directly opposite the wedge but outside the pie, or in a legend or key.

It is also customary to include the percentages or other values represented by each wedge and to distinguish each wedge by shading, cross-hatched lines, different colors, or some similar device.

MODEL 25 Pie Charts

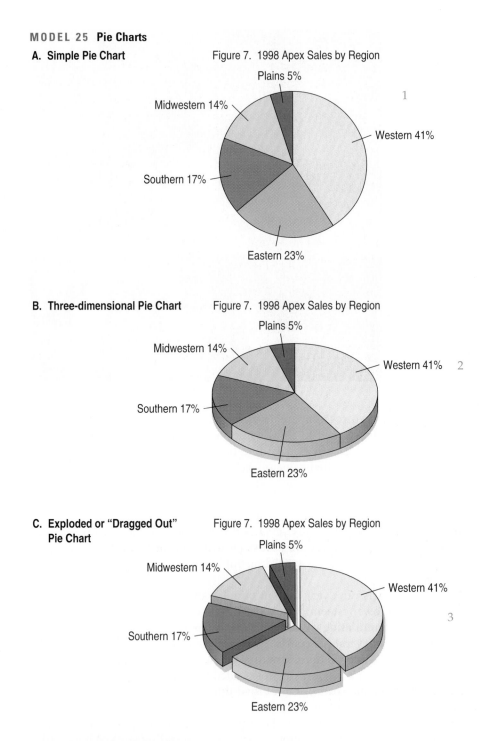

A. Simple Pie Chart

Figure 7. 1998 Apex Sales by Region

Plains 5%
Midwestern 14%
Western 41%
Southern 17%
Eastern 23%

1

B. Three-dimensional Pie Chart

Figure 7. 1998 Apex Sales by Region

Plains 5%
Midwestern 14%
Western 41%
Southern 17%
Eastern 23%

2

C. Exploded or "Dragged Out" Pie Chart

Figure 7. 1998 Apex Sales by Region

Plains 5%
Midwestern 14%
Western 41%
Southern 17%
Eastern 23%

3

Grammar and Mechanics Notes

1 Begin slicing the pie at the 12 o'clock position and move clockwise in a logical order; the order here is by size.   **2** Provide the percentage or other value shown by each wedge.   **3** Generally use between 3 and 5 wedges.

Three-dimensional graphics, although attention grabbing, are difficult to interpret because they are often used to display only two-dimensional data (horizontal and vertical), with the third dimension (depth) having no significance. Similarly, three-dimensional pie charts, which are shown slanted away from the viewer rather than vertically, can be misleading because of perspective—the slices farthest away appear smaller than they actually are. Such graphics are quite effective for gaining attention and providing a general impression but are less effective for conveying the precise meanings needed in business communications.

Checklist 13 on page 350 summarizes the most important points to consider when constructing tables and charts.

A Word of Caution

As the name *visual aids* implies, charts act as a *help*—not a substitute—for the narrative presentation and interpretation. Never use visual aids simply to make your report "look prettier."

Do not overuse visual aids; they will detract from your message.

Recent research indicates that the format of the data (tables versus graphs) has little effect on the quality of the decisions made when the task requires a thorough analysis of financial data; both formats are judged to be equally effective. Managers appear to have more confidence in their decisions when such decisions are based on data from tables alone as opposed to data from graphs alone, but managers have the most confidence when both formats are used.[2]

These research findings indicate that graphic devices should be used as an *adjunct* to textual and tabular presentations. Although most numerical data can be presented more efficiently in tables, the competent business communicator uses charts to call attention to particular findings. Rarely should the same data be presented in both tabular and graphic formats.

In *The Visual Display of Quantitative Information*, Edward Tufte warns against *chartjunk*—charts that call attention to themselves instead of to the information they contain.[3] With the ready availability and ease of use of computer graphics, the temptation might be to "overvisualize" your report. Avoid using too many, too large, too garish, or too complicated charts. If the impact is not immediate or if interpretations vary, the chart loses its effectiveness. As with all other aspects of the report project, the visual aids must contribute directly to telling your story more effectively. Avoid chartjunk; strive to *express*—not to *impress*.

Interpreting Data

When analyzing the data, you must first determine whether the data does, in fact, solve your problem. It would make no sense to prepare elaborate tables and other visual aids if your data is irrelevant, incomplete, or inaccurate. To help yourself make this initial evaluation of your data, assume for the sake of simplicity that you have gathered only three bits of information—a paraphrase from a secondary source, a chart you developed, and a computer printout, labeled Findings A, B, and C, respectively (see Figure 11.5). Now, you are ready to analyze this data.

First, look at each piece of data in isolation (Step 1). If Finding A were the only piece of data you collected, what would it mean in terms of solving the problem? What conclusions, if any, could you draw from this one bit of data? Follow the same

Determine the meaning of each finding by itself, in conjunction with each other finding, and in conjunction with all other findings.

✔ CHECKLIST 13   Visual Aids

Tables

- ☑ Use tables to present a large amount of numerical data in a small space and to permit easy comparisons of figures.

- ☑ Number tables consecutively and use concise but descriptive table titles and column headings.

- ☑ Ensure that the table is understandable by itself—without reference to the accompanying narrative.

- ☑ Arrange the rows of the table in some logical order (most often, in descending order).

- ☑ Combine smaller, less important categories into a miscellaneous category and put it last.

- ☑ Use cross-tabulation analysis to compare different subgroups.

- ☑ Use only as much detail as necessary; for example, rounding figures off to the nearest whole increases comprehension. Align decimals (if used) vertically on the decimal point.

- ☑ Use abbreviations and symbols as needed.

- ☑ Ensure that the units (dollars, percentages, or tons, for example) are identified clearly.

Charts

- ☑ Use charts only when they will help the reader interpret the data better—never just to make the report "look prettier."

- ☑ Label all charts as *figures,* and assign them consecutive numbers (separate from table numbers).

- ☑ Keep charts simple. Strive for a single, immediate, correct interpretation, and keep the reader's attention on the *data* in the chart rather than on the chart itself.

- ☑ Prefer two-dimensional charts; use three-dimensional charts only when generating interest is more important than precision.

- ☑ Use the most appropriate type of chart to achieve your objectives. Three of the most popular types of business charts are line, bar, and pie charts.

Line Charts: Use line charts to show changes in data over a period of time and to emphasize the movement of the data—the trends.
- ■ Use the vertical axis to represent amount and the horizontal axis to represent time.
- ■ Mark off both axes at equal intervals and clearly label them.
- ■ Begin the vertical axis at zero; if necessary, use slash marks (//) to show a break in the interval.
- ■ If you plot more than one variable on a chart, clearly distinguish between the lines and label each clearly.

Bar Charts: Use bar charts to compare the magnitude or relative size of items (rather than the trend over time), either at a specified time or over a period of time.
- ■ Make all bars the same width; the length varies to reflect the value of each item.
- ■ Arrange the bars in a logical order and clearly label each.

Pie Charts: Use pie charts to compare the relative parts that make up a whole.
- ■ Begin slicing the pie at the 12 o'clock position, moving clockwise in a logical order.
- ■ Label each wedge of the pie, indicate its value, and clearly differentiate the wedges.

process for Findings B and C, examining each in isolation, without considering any other data.

Then look at each piece of data in combination with the other bits (Step 2). For example, by itself Finding A might lead to one conclusion, but when viewed in conjunction with B and C, it might take on a different shade of meaning. In other words, does adding Findings B and C to your data pool *reinforce* your initial

FIGURE 11.5 **The Three Steps in Interpreting Data**

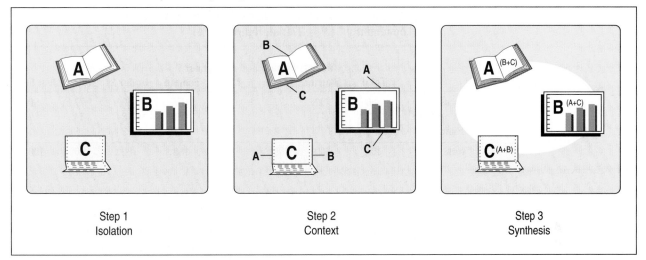

Step 1	Step 2	Step 3
Isolation	Context	Synthesis

conclusion? If so, you can use stronger language in drawing your conclusion. Or does it *weaken* your initial conclusion? If so, you might wish to qualify your conclusion with less certain language or refrain from drawing any conclusion at all.

Finally, synthesize all the information you've collected (Step 3). When you consider all the facts and their relationships together, what do they mean? For example, if Findings A, B, and C all point in the same direction, you might be able to define a trend. More important, you must determine whether all the data taken together provides an accurate and complete answer to your problem statement. If it does, you're then ready to begin the detailed analysis and presentation that will help the reader understand your findings. If it does not, you must backtrack and start the research process again.

Making Sense of the Data

As a report writer, you cannot simply present the raw data without interpreting it. The data in your tables and charts helps to solve a problem, and the report writer must make the connection between that data and the solution to the problem. In the report narrative, you need not discuss *all* the data in the tables and charts; that would be boring and insulting to the reader. But you must determine what you think the important implications of your data are, and then you must identify and discuss them for the reader.

Don't just present tables and figures. Interpret their important points.

What types of important points do you look for? Almost always, the most important finding is the overall response to a question (rather than the responses of the cross-tabulation subgroups). And almost always the category within the question that receives the largest response is the most important point. So discuss this question and this category first. Let's take another look at Apex's Table 4 presented earlier in Figure 11.3 and repeated on page 352 in Figure 11.6.

In Table 4, the major finding is this: four-fifths of the respondents believe that Apex Company is an asset to their community. Note that if you give the exact figure given in the table (here, 80%), you can use less precise language in the narrative—"four-fifths" in this case, or in other cases "one in four," "a slight majority,"

FIGURE 11.6 **Simplified Table**

TABLE 4. Response to Statement, "Apex Company is an asset to our community." (*N* = 271; all figures in %)

| | Total | Marital Status | | Gender | | Age | | |
		Married	Single	Male	Female	Under 21	21–50	Over 50
Agree	80	82	77	83	57	69	77	90
No opinion	12	11	15	12	21	18	14	9
Disagree	8	7	8	5	22	13	9	1
Total	100	100	100	100	100	100	100	100

At a minimum, discuss the overall response and any important cross-tab findings.

and the like. Doing so helps you avoid presenting facts and figures too quickly. Pace your analysis because the reader will not be able to comprehend data that is presented too quickly or in too concentrated a format.

Once you've discussed the overall finding, begin discussing the cross-tabulation data as necessary. Look for trends, unexpected findings, data that reinforces or contradicts other tables, extreme values, data that raises questions, and the like. If these are important, discuss them. In our example, there were no major differences in the responses by marital status, so you would probably not need to discuss them. However, you would need to discuss the big difference in responses between males and females. If possible, present data or draw any valid conclusions regarding the *reasons* for these differences.

Finally, point out the trend that is evident with regard to age: the older the respondent, the more positive the response. If it's important enough, you might display this trend in a graph for more visual effect.

Sometimes you will want to include descriptive statistics (such as the mean, median, range, and standard deviation). At other times, the nature of your data will necessitate the use of inference testing—to determine whether the differences found in your sample data are also likely to exist in the population. By now, you probably know more about the topic on which you're writing than the reader knows. Assist the reader, then, by pointing out the important implications, findings, and relationships of your data. Help your reader reach the same conclusions you have reached.

The Ethical Dimension

Everyone involved in the reporting situation has a responsibility to act in an ethical manner.

In gathering, analyzing, reporting, and disseminating data, everyone involved has both rights and obligations. For example, the researcher (1) has the right to expect that respondents will be truthful in their responses and (2) has an obligation not to deceive the respondent. Similarly, the organization that is paying for the research (1) has the right to expect that the researcher will provide valid and reliable information and (2) has an obligation not to misuse that data.

Emerging technology will no doubt provide even greater ethical dilemmas (see Spotlight 18—On Law and Ethics). If your research and corresponding report are to help solve problems and aid in decision making, all parties involved must use common sense, good judgment, and goodwill to make the project successful.

When Is a Picture *Not* Worth a Thousand Words?

"Seeing is believing" may no longer be the case. Granted, commercial photographers have long used the airbrush to touch up portraits, wedding scenes, and advertising layouts, but only recently has the technology to manipulate photos come to the desktop computer. Today, any computer user, with the appropriate software, can electronically alter photographs—even to the extent that they no longer reflect reality.

As an indication of the extent to which photographs can be manipulated, the cover of a *Texas Monthly* magazine showed former Texas governor Ann Richards in a computer-altered photograph. The head of Ms. Richards had been electronically superimposed on the body of a biker.

It does not take a wide stretch of the imagination to ponder the ethical dilemmas report writers may soon face. Suppose, as an adjunct to your report on the status of a building project, you use a digital camera to take a photo of the partially completed building. The digital camera stores the image directly on a compact disk rather than on film. You pop the CD into your personal computer and view the image on the screen. You notice that a worker is standing next to the building, providing a distraction. So you use your software to digitally remove the worker from the image. Then you notice that the sign on the building, which contained a typographical error, had not been fixed when you took the photo (it has since been corrected). Should you digitally correct it on the photo? How about changing the color of the building's exterior, which you plan to paint next week?

By allowing us to capture, store, and manipulate photographs, emerging computer technology is going to have an enormous impact on business communications.

Sources: Sean Callahan, "Eye Tech," *Forbes ASAP*, Spring 1993, pp. 57–67; Jane Hundertmark, "When Enhancement Is Deception," *Publish*, October 1991, pp. 51–55; Jim Meade, "Graphics That Tell the Truth," *Personal Computing*, January 1989, pp. 79–84; Daryl Moen, "Misinformation Graphics," *Aldus Magazine*, January/February 1990, pp. 62–63.

The 3Ps

PROBLEM

You are Martha Halpern, assistant store manager for Just Pool Supplies, a small firm in San Antonio, Texas. You have been asked by Joe Cox, store owner, to determine the feasibility of expanding into the spa supply business. To help yourself determine whether there is a sufficient demand for spa (hot tub) supplies, you decide to develop and administer a short questionnaire to potential customers.

PROCESS

1. What is the purpose of your questionnaire?

   To determine whether there are enough potential customers to make it profitable for us to expand into the spa supply business.

2. Who is your audience?

   The theoretical population for my study would be all spa owners in the San Antonio area. However, because our major business will still be pool supplies, I'll assume that most of my spa supply business would come from my present pool supply customers.

   Thus, the real population for my survey will be the approximately 1,500 present customers that I have on my mailing list. I don't need to contact every customer, only a representative sample. I'll have my database program generate address labels for every fifth customer.

3. What information do you need from these customers?

   a. Whether they presently own a spa or intend to purchase one in the near future

   b. Where they typically purchase their spa supplies

   c. How much money they typically spend on spa supplies each year

   d. How satisfied they are with their suppliers

   e. What the likelihood is that they'd switch their spa supply business to us

   f. How many spa supply firms are located in the area

4. Is all this information necessary? Can any of it be secured elsewhere?

   I can probably determine the number of spa supply firms and their volume of business from secondary data or from the local chamber of commerce, so I won't need to address that question (3f) in my survey. All of the other information is needed and none of it can be obtained elsewhere.

5. Do any of these questions ask for sensitive information, or are any of them difficult to answer?

   No. The question asking about the amount of money spent on spa supplies depends a little on memory; but since most people buy spa supplies only four or five times a year, respondents should be able to provide a fairly accurate estimate.

6. Is there any logical order to the questions in Item 3?

The question about spa ownership must come first, because respondents cannot answer the other questions unless they own a spa. In reviewing the other questions, I think the logical order appears to be a, c, b, d, and e.

7. Will the questionnaire require a cover letter?

Yes, because it will be mailed to the respondents, instead of being administered personally. I'll use my word processing program to generate personalized form letters to each of the customers selected.

PRODUCT

Cover Letter

P.O. Box 2277 San Antonio, TX 78298
Phone: (512) 555-0083 Fax: (512) 555-2994

February 22, 19--

Mr. Frederic J. Diehl
Rio Rancho Estates
1876 Anderson Road
San Antonio, TX 79299

Dear Mr. Diehl:

We miss you during the winter!

Although you're a frequent shopper at Just Pool Supplies during the summer months when you're using your pool, we miss having the opportunity to serve you during the rest of the year. Therefore, we're considering adding a complete line of spa supplies to our inventory.

Would you please help us make this decision by answering the enclosed five questions and then returning this form to us in the enclosed stamped envelope.

Thanks for sharing your views with us. We look forward to seeing you during our traditional Pool Party Sale in March.

Sincerely,

Martha Halpern

Martha Halpern
Assistant Manager

swm
Enclosures

Questionnaire

SPA SUPPLIES

1. Do you presently own a spa?
   ____ yes
   ____ no (Please skip the remaining questions and return this form to us
   in the enclosed envelope.)

2. Considering the number of times you purchased spa supplies last year and
   the average amount of each purchase, how much do you estimate you spent
   on spa supplies last year (include all types of purchases—chemicals, accessories, decorative items, and the like).
   ____ less than $100
   ____ $100–$300
   ____ $301–$500
   ____ more than $500

3. Where did you purchase <u>most</u> of your spa supplies last year? (Please check
   only one.)
   ____ at a general-merchandise store (e.g., Kmart or Sears)
   ____ at a pool- or spa- supply store
   ____ from a mail-order firm
   ____ other (please specify: _____)

4. How satisfied were you with each of these factors at the store where you
   purchased most of your spa supplies?

Factor	Very Satisfied	Satisfied	Very Dissatisfied
Customer service	____	____	____
Hours of operation	____	____	____
Location of store	____	____	____
Prices	____	____	____
Quality of products	____	____	____
Quantity of products	____	____	____

5. If Just Pool Supplies were to sell spa supplies, how likely would you be to
   purchase most of your spa supplies there, assuming that the quality, selection, and pricing would be similar to those for their pool supplies.
   ____ very likely
   ____ somewhat likely
   ____ don't know
   ____ somewhat unlikely
   ____ very unlikely

*Thanks for your cooperation. Please return the completed questionnaire in the enclosed envelope
to Martha Halpern, Just Pool Supplies, P.O. Box 2277, San Antonio, TX 78298.*

SUMMARY

Primary data is collected by various survey methods, primarily questionnaires, telephone inquiries, and interviews. Mail questionnaires are an economical and convenient way to gather primary data when the desired information can be supplied easily and quickly. Care should be taken to ensure that all questions are necessary, clearly worded, complete, and unbiased. The questions and their alternatives should be organized in a logical order, the directions should be clear, and the overall format should be attractive and efficient. The cover letter should be a persuasive letter explaining why it is in the reader's interest to answer the survey.

Personal interviews are preferable to questionnaires when the information desired is complex or requires extensive explanation or elaboration. The interviewer must determine whether to use open or closed questions and whether to use direct or indirect questions. The use of a cassette recorder will enable the interviewer to minimize note taking, thereby enabling him or her to listen more attentively.

Data is converted into information by careful analysis and is interpreted in the report in narrative form and by visual aids. Each table you construct from the data should be interpretable by itself, without reference to the text. Often you will want to analyze two or more fields of data together in the same table to help identify relationships. Include only as much data in a table as is helpful, keeping the table as simple as possible. Arrange the data in logical order, most often in order of descending value. Do not analyze every figure from the table in your narrative. Instead, interpret the important points from the table, pointing out the major findings, trends, contradictions, and the like.

Use well-designed line, bar, and pie charts to aid in reader comprehension, emphasize certain data, create interest, and save time and space. Avoid using too many, too large, too garish, or too complicated charts. Also avoid misrepresenting your information. The competent reporter of business information is an ethical reporter of business information.

KEY TERMS

bar chart	line chart	survey
cross-tabulation	pie chart	table
interview guide	questionnaire	visual aids

REVIEW AND DISCUSSION

1. **Communication at Domino's Pizza Revisited**   Chris Wall's job is to gather and analyze data to support the decisions that Domino's managers must make about new products, competitive strategy, and customer satisfaction.
   a. Why would Wall and his staff prefer to interview customers by telephone soon after they have ordered from Domino's, rather than mailing a questionnaire to these customers?
   b. Would Wall be likely to obtain accurate data about consumers' income if he groups answers into broad categories or asks respondents for specific amounts? Why?
   c. Would open-ended or closed questions be more useful when gathering data about consumers' reactions to a new pizza crust? Why?
2. Compose a questionnaire item using each of the following formats:
   a. Check-off response
   b. Fill-in-the-blank
   c. Ranking
   d. Attitude-scale
   e. Open-ended

3. Assume that you want to survey local rental-unit owners regarding the market for student housing. Compose the first sentence of the cover letter that will accompany your questionnaire.

4. Under what circumstances is it better to use a personal interview instead of a questionnaire?

5. Assume you wish to interview the vice president for student affairs at your college regarding the adequacy of student housing on campus. Compose an appropriate interview question in each of the following formats:

   a. Open
   b. Closed
   c. Direct
   d. Indirect

6. Why is probing sometimes necessary during an interview? How can it be accomplished?

7. What are the advantages of presenting numerical data in tables as opposed to presenting the data in narrative form?

8. Assume you have surveyed a sample of students at your institution to determine their career objectives and expectations. List three possible cross-tabulation analyses that might be appropriate for this study.

9. In what order should data be arranged in tables?

10. What types of visual aid would probably be most appropriate for each of the following situations? Explain your decisions.

    a. Data showing the percentage breakdown of employees by ethnic background.
    b. Data showing the state-by-state analysis of market share for the company's major product.
    c. A news release announcing the appointment of a new executive vice president.
    d. Data showing the number of employees by year from 1993 to 1998.
    e. An explanation of how to replace the cartridge in a laser printer.
    f. Data showing the average number of employees per department last year.

11. What types of material from a table should be discussed in the narrative of the report? What types of material need not be discussed?

12. List one right and one obligation of the researcher and of the organization sponsoring the research.

Help Wanted

Directions: This is a draft page of a student questionnaire. Revise the document to make it more effective, taking into consideration the editor's marginal comments.

Keep questions neutral. Are yes/no the only two possible answers?

QUESTIONNAIRE

1. Do you like living in the dorm?

   _____ yes

   _____ no

More descriptive title?

2. Please rank the importance of the following possible reasons that made you decide to live in the dorm, with 1 representing the most important reason and 5 representing the least important reason.

Logical order of alternatives?

_____ cost

_____ proximity to campus

_____ social environment

plur

_____ <u>parents</u> preference

_____ availability of cafeteria

3. How much money do you spend on social activities each week?

$_____

spec— What do you mean by "social activities"? Can you provide check-off alternatives?

Alternatives are neither exhaustive nor mutually exclusive.

4. What is your estimate of your parents' combined yearly income?

_____ $10,000–$20,000

_____ $20,000–$35,000

_____ $35,000–$75,000

_____ $75,000–$125,000

5. In which dorm do you live? _____

Check-off alternatives?

6. In what year was it built? _____

You can find the answer to this question yourself.

7. What is your classification?

Logical order for alternatives? Are these the only possibilities?

Arrange Questions 1–7 in a more logical sequence.

_____ freshman

_____ junior

_____ senior

_____ sophomore

EXERCISES

1. **The 3 Ps Microwriting Model: Communication Applications at Domino's Pizza**   Chris Wall and his researchers are expert at gathering and interpreting information to help Domino's managers make decisions about products, competitive strategies, and customer satisfaction. They often use telephone surveys or face-to-face interviews to determine customer needs, likes, and dislikes in more detail.

Problem

As a member of Chris Wall's staff, you have been asked to design a questionnaire for a telephone survey of customers who recently tried a new pizza topping that is being tested in one store before it is offered across the United States. The purpose of the survey is to uncover customer reaction to the topping.

Process

a. Brainstorm about possible questions to include in this survey. What specific information will each question uncover? What might Domino's management be able to do as a result of knowing the answer to each question?
b. Choose the most appropriate questions and arrange them in a logical order.
c. Edit the wording of each question for clarity. Is every question bias-free? Does each deal with only one element?
d. Consider how to format each question for the respondents' convenience in answering. Which questions should be open-ended and which should be closed?
e. Looking at your questionnaire, estimate how long each telephone interview will take. Do you need to revise or eliminate some questions or change some of the formats to speed up the interview so respondents will be more willing to participate?

Product

Using your knowledge of data collection and analysis, prepare, format, and proofread a suitable questionnaire. Submit your questionnaire and the answers to the process questions to your instructor.

2. The 3 Ps Microwriting Model: A Questionnaire

Problem

The dean of your school of business has asked you, as director of the Bureau of Business Research at your college, to survey typical businesses in your state that have hired your business graduates within the past five years. The purpose of the survey is to determine whether your business graduates have competent communication skills.

Process

a. Brainstorm for 10 minutes. List every possible question you might ask these businesses; don't worry at this point about the wording of the questions or their sequence.
b. Review your questions. Are all of them necessary? Can any of the information be secured elsewhere?
c. Edit your questions to ensure that they are clear and unbiased.
d. Arrange the questions in some logical order.
e. Where possible, format each question with check-off responses, arranging the responses in some logical order.
f. Do any of the questions ask for sensitive information, or are any of them difficult to answer? If so, how will you handle these questions?
g. What information other than the questions themselves should you include on the questionnaire?
h. Should you add a questionnaire cover letter?

Product

Draft, revise, format, and proofread your questionnaire. Submit both your questionnaire and your answers to the process questions to your instructor.

Note: For Exercises 3 and 4, assume that you have been asked to write a report on the feasibility of opening a frozen yogurt store in Akron, Ohio. (Your instructor may substitute a different product or different city for these assignments.)

3. Work-Team Communication—Questionnaire   Since the student body at the University of Akron would provide a major source of potential customers for your yogurt store, you decide to survey the students to gather relevant data. Working in a group

of four or five, develop a two-page questionnaire and a cover letter that you will mail to a sample of these students.

Ensure that the content and appearance of the questionnaire follow the guidelines given in Checklist 12. Pilot-test your questionnaire and cover letter on a small sample of students; then revise as necessary and submit to your instructor.

4. **Primary Data—Interview**   You decide to get some firsthand information from the owner-manager of a premium ice cream or frozen yogurt store in your area (such as Dairy Queen, Baskin-Robbins, TCBY, or I Can't Believe It's Yogurt). Think of the type of information he or she might be able to provide that would help you solve your research problem. Then prepare an interview guide, listing questions in a logical order and noting possible follow-up questions.

Schedule an interview with the owner-manager and conduct the interview, recording it on tape. Write up your findings in a one- or two-page memo report to your instructor. Retain your tape of the interview until after this assignment has been returned to you.

Work-Team Research: Exercises 5–9 are based on the survey results shown in Figure 11.7. Next year Broadway Productions will move its headquarters from Manhattan to Stamford, Connecticut, in the building where Tri-City Bank occupies the first floor. The bank hopes to secure many Broadway Productions employees as customers and has conducted a survey to determine their banking habits. The handwritten figures on the questionnaire show the number of respondents who checked each alternative.

5. **Constructing Tables**
   a. Is a table needed to present the information in Question 1?
   b. Would any cross-tabulation analyses help readers understand the data in this questionnaire? Explain.
   c. Construct a table that presents the important information from Question 4 of the questionnaire in a logical, helpful, and efficient manner. Give the table an appropriate title and arrange it in final report format.

6. **Interpreting Data**
   a. Give a one- or two-sentence interpretation of the data for each of the five questions.
   b. Assume you need to present the important information from this questionnaire in one paragraph of no more than 50 or 60 words. Compose this summary paragraph.

7. **Constructing Charts**   You decide to use a chart rather than a table to convey the data in Question 4 of the questionnaire.
   a. Can you use a line chart to present the data? Why or why not? If a line chart is appropriate, construct it and label the vertical and horizontal axes.
   b. Can you use a bar chart to present the data? Why or why not? If a bar chart is appropriate, construct it, arranging the bars in a logical order and clearly labeling each bar as well as the vertical axis.
   c. Can you use a pie chart to present the data? Why or why not? If a pie chart is appropriate, construct it, label each wedge, and clearly differentiate the wedges.

8. **Constructing Charts**   You want to construct a visual aid to emphasize the proportion of respondents who have changed banks within the past three years. Calculate this percentage using the survey results. Decide which type of chart would most effectively convey this information. Then construct the chart, using appropriate values and helpful labels.

FIGURE 11.7 **Survey Results**

BROADWAY PRODUCTIONS SURVEY

1. Do you currently have an account at Tri-City Bank?
   _58_ yes
   _170_ no

2. At which of the following institutions do you currently have an account?
   (Please check all that apply.)
   _201_ commercial bank
   _52_ employee credit union
   _75_ savings and loan association
   _6_ other (please specify: _____)
   _18_ none

3. In terms of convenience, which one of the following bank locations do you consider
   most important in selecting your main bank?
   _70_ near home
   _102_ near office
   _12_ near shopping
   _31_ on way to and from work
   _13_ other (please specify: _____)

4. How important do you consider each of the following banking services?

	Very Important	Somewhat Important	Not Important
Bank credit card	88	132	8
Check-guarantee card	74	32	122
Convenient ATM machines	143	56	29
Drive-in service	148	47	33
Free checking	219	9	0
Overdraft privileges	20	187	21
Personal banker	40	32	156
Telephone transfer	6	20	202
Trust department	13	45	170

5. If you have changed banks within the past three years, what was the major reason
   for the change?
   _33_ relocation of residence
   _4_ relocation of bank
   _18_ dissatisfaction with bank service
   _7_ other (please specify: _____)

Thank you so much for your cooperation. Please return this questionnaire in the enclosed envelope to Customer Service Department, Tri-City Bank, P.O. Box 1086, Stamford, CT 06902.

9. **Interpreting Data**   Looking at the results of Question 6, Tri-City Bank managers decide to find out more about the problems with bank service that have caused 18 Broadway Productions employees to change financial institutions. The results of a second study show that 7 people were dissatisfied with the monthly service charges, 5 people felt the fees for returned checks were too high, 3 were annoyed about chronically long lines at the teller windows, and 3 found their branch's banking hours inconvenient. How would you arrange these responses into two meaningful categories? Referring to the two categories, write a brief paragraph summarizing the survey results.

10. **Misrepresenting Data—Interpreting a Table**   The following sentences interpret the table in Figure 11.6 on page 352. Analyze each sentence to determine whether it represents the data in the table accurately.

    a. Males and females alike believe Apex is an asset to the community.
    b. More than one-fifth of the females (22%) did not respond.
    c. Age and the generation gap bring about different beliefs.
    d. Married males over age 50 had the most positive opinions.
    e. Females disagree more than males—probably because most of the workers at Apex are male.
    f. Female respondents tend to disagree with the statement.
    g. Apex should be proud of the fact that four-fifths of the residents believe the company is an asset to the community.
    h. Thirteen percent of the younger residents have doubts about whether Apex is an asset to the community.
    i. More single than married residents didn't care or had no opinion about the topic.
    j. Overall, the residents believe that 8% of the company is not an asset to the community.

11. **Misrepresenting Data—Interpreting Charts**   Examine the following interpretations of the data shown in Model 23, page 345. Indicate whether each statement accurately represents the data in those charts.

    a. The industrial sector has provided most of Apex's sales and profits since 1993.
    b. The average age of Apex customers has increased since 1973.
    c. The average age of Apex customers reached a peak of 45 in 1988.
    d. Nearly half of Apex's sales in 1998 were to the industrial sector.
    e. More than half of Apex's sales in 1993 were to the industrial sector.
    f. Nearly half of Apex's sales in 1973 were to the consumer sector.
    g. The decline in Apex's consumer sales is due to the increase in the average age of the firm's consumer customers.
    h. Sales to the industrial sector have risen steadily since 1973.
    i. Sales to the consumer sector have fallen steadily since 1973.

12. **Misrepresenting Data—Use of Statistics**   Politicians, businesspeople, and others love to quote statistics to support their viewpoints. Locate three news stories in which someone quotes statistics to support a particular case. Then find an unbiased source that either confirms or refutes those statistics. Write a memo to your instructor discussing your findings. Include a photocopy of both the original news articles and your supporting statistics.

The Keyboard Strikes Back

The manufacturing facility in Charlotte employs three data-entry operators who work full-time keyboarding production, personnel, and inventory data into a terminal. This data is then sent over telephone lines to the Urban Systems minicomputer, where it becomes part of the corporate database for financial, production, and personnel management.

As required by the labor agreement, in addition to a one-hour lunch period, these three operators receive two 15-minute breaks daily; they may take them at any convenient time, once in the morning and once in the afternoon. Otherwise, they generally work at their keyboards all day.

Last year, Arlene Berkowitz, one of the operators, was absent from work for two weeks for a condition diagnosed as carpal tunnel syndrome, a neuromuscular disorder of the tendons and tissue in the wrists caused by repeated hand motions. Her symptoms included a dull ache in the wrist and excruciating pain in the shoulder and neck. Her doctor treated her with anti-inflammatory medicine and a cortisone injection, and she has had no further problems. However, just last week a second data-entry operator experienced similar symptoms; her doctor diagnosed her ailment as "repeated-motion illness" or RSI (repetitive stress injury) and referred to it informally as the "VDT (video display terminal) disease."

Because the company anticipates further automation in the future, with more data-entry operators to be hired, Jean Tate asked her assistant, Pat Robbins, to gather additional information on this condition. In fact, Jean wants Pat to survey all workers at US who use a computer to determine the type and degree of their use and to identify any related health problems. Once the extent of the problem is known, she wants Pat to make any appropriate recommendations regarding the work environment—posture, furniture, work habits, rest breaks, and the like—that will alleviate this problem.

Critical Thinking

1. Assume the role of Pat Robbins. Define the problem of the report and then identify the component subparts (that is, *factor* the problem).

2. What are the ethical implications of this case?

Writing Projects

3. Search the appropriate sources and identify five relevant journal articles and five Internet resources on this topic. Photocopy or download each article and save them for a future assignment. Evaluate each article using the criteria given in this chapter; write a one-paragraph summary of your *evaluation* of each article. Make notes of these articles.

4. Develop an employee questionnaire that elicits the information Jean asked for, plus whatever additional information you believe would be helpful, based on your reading of the journal articles and Internet sources you located. In lieu of a cover letter, include a short introductory paragraph at the top of the questionnaire explaining the purpose of the study and giving any needed directions.

12 Writing the Report

An Insider's Perspective

Before members of the U.S. Congress vote on legislation related to dietary supplements, food labeling, or the school lunch program, they learn about the issues by reading informational reports written by Donna V. Porter and her colleagues in the Congressional Research Service (CRS), which is part of the Library of Congress. Dr. Porter is a specialist in life sciences, and her job is to research and prepare reports that provide senators and representatives with the background they need to make informed decisions about legislation.

Based on scientific studies and meticulous documentation, each of Dr. Porter's reports serves as an unbiased, nonpartisan review of a particular issue, with no recommendations or advocacy positions expressed. "The Congressional Research Service has high credibility because it provides balanced reports," she says. "No matter which side of the debate members of Congress may support, it's important for them to understand all the arguments on the other side as well."

Reports on scientific topics, such as nutrition, require the use of technical terms that Dr. Porter both defines and explains for her readers. "An important part of my job is to translate the science into understandable language for the lay person," she notes. Her reports provide explanations in the text or footnotes, so readers do not have to check a glossary or an appendix to understand unfamiliar terms. Knowing that Capitol Hill readers contend with an alphabet soup of acronyms, she is also careful to spell out any acronyms the first time they appear.

Many of her reports are long and detailed. "I think one comprehensive report that covers everything about an issue is much more valuable than a series of short reports, because members of Congress are often unaware of the complexities of an issue," observes Dr. Porter. Reports longer than six pages include a one-page summary to highlight the key issues and indicate where more details can be found. This way, readers who are initially interested in one question, such as whether to require whole milk in the school lunch program, can look up other related questions, such as whether the potential for allergic reactions warrants a banning of peanut products in schools.

COMMUNICATION OBJECTIVES

After you have finished this chapter, you should be able to

■ Determine an appropriate report structure based on the needs of the reader and the nature of the report problem.

■ Organize a report in a logical manner.

■ Develop an effective report outline.

■ Write each part of a report body and all supplementary pages.

■ Use an effective writing style.

■ Provide appropriate documentation when quoting, paraphrasing, or summarizing someone else's work.

■ Revise a report for content, style, and correctness.

■ Format a report for readability and consistency.

■ Proofread a report to ensure that it reflects pride of authorship.

An outline is essential when writing these lengthy reports. "I start every report with a generic outline that covers the background of the issue, the science behind it, the activities of regulatory agencies and Congress, and the position of the various interested parties," she explains. "Then I keep a running list of important points that I want to incorporate somewhere in the text."

Once she completes a report, she searches for typographical and spelling errors and has a colleague read the report as a final check for clarity before CRS review. "What may have seemed clear when I was writing may not be understood by the uninitiated," Dr. Porter stresses. "That's why it's important to ask someone who is detached from the issue to read and critique a report."

Many CRS reports are written in anticipation of legislative hearings or votes. The school lunch program, for example, must be reauthorized by Congress approximately every five years, which involves reconsideration of certain nutrition issues. Therefore, Dr. Porter prepares a comprehensive report on nutrition issues in advance of the reauthorization deadline. When senators and representatives participate in hearings on school lunch proposals, such as allowing yogurt as an alternative to meat, these reports present a broader perspective of the overall situation. According to Dr. Porter, "None of these issues are black and white or easy to resolve. Our reports help members of Congress understand the advantages and disadvantages of a given policy proposal before they vote."

Donna Porter

Specialist in Life Sciences, Congressional Research Service (Washington, D.C.)

Planning

As we have seen throughout our study of business communication, the writing process consists of planning, drafting, revising, formatting, and proofreading. You follow this same process when writing a report.

Although much of the planning in the report process is, of necessity, done even before collecting the data, the written presentation of the results requires its own stage of planning. You need to make decisions about the structure of the report, the organization of the content, and the framework of the headings before and as you write.

Determining the Report Structure

The physical structure of the report and such general traits as complexity, degree of formality, and length depend on the audience for the report and the nature of the problem that the report addresses. The three most common formats for a report are manuscript, memorandum, and letter format.

Most reports are formatted as manuscripts, memos, or letters.

Manuscript reports, the most formal of the three, are formatted in narrative (paragraph) style, with headings and subheadings separating the different sections. If the problem that the report addresses is complex and has serious consequences, the report will likely follow a manuscript format and a formal writing style. A formal writing style typically avoids the use of first- and second-person pronouns, such as *I* and *you*. In addition, the more formal the report, the more supplementary parts are included (such as a table of contents, executive summary, and appendix) and, therefore, the longer the report.

Memorandum and letter reports contain the standard correspondence parts (for example, lines identifying the names of the sender and receiver). They use a more informal writing style and may or may not contain headings and subheadings. Compare the informal, simple, and short report in memo format shown in Model 26 with the formal, complex, and long report (only the first page is shown) in manuscript format shown in Model 27 (see p. 370).

So that your written presentation will have an overall sense of proportion and unity, decide beforehand on the complexity, formality, length, and format of the report. The "right" decision depends on the needs and desires of the reader.

Organizing the Report

A sculptor creating a statue of someone doesn't necessarily start at the head and work down to the feet in lock-step fashion. Instead, he or she may first create part of the torso, then part of the head, then another part of the torso, and so on. Likewise, a movie director may film segments of the movie out of narrative order. But in the end, both creations are put together in such a way as to show unity, order, logic, and beauty.

Similarly, you may have organized the collection and analysis of data in a way that suited the investigation of various subtopics of the problem. But now that it is time to put the results of your work together into a written presentation, you may need a *new* organization, one that integrates the whole and takes into account what you have learned through your research.

Planning your written presentation to show unity, order, logic, and yes, even beauty involves selecting an organizational basis for the findings (the data you've

MODEL 26   **Informal Memorandum Report**

The memo format indicates the reader is someone from within the firm.

ALL SYSTEMS GO!!!   ***Moving Company***

2443 South Canton • Mesa, AZ 85202   **(602) 555-0143**

MEMO TO: Hiram Cooper, Director of Marketing

FROM: Barbara Novak, Sales Assistant *B.N.*

DATE: August 9, 19--

SUBJECT: Yellow Pages Advertising

I believe we should continue purchasing a quarter-page ad in the Mountain Bell Yellow Pages. My recommendation is based on the conclusion that Yellow Pages advertising has produced more inquiries than any other method of advertising and has increased net profits, especially in the local residential market.

A Pilot Test Was Set Up
On March 1 you asked me to conduct a three-month test of the effectiveness of Yellow Pages advertising. I subsequently purchased a quarter-page ad for the edition of the Yellow Pages that was distributed the week of June 2-6. For six weeks thereafter, we queried all telephone and walk-in customers to determine how they had learned about our company. I also compared the percentage of signed contracts resulting from each source. Precise before-and-after sales data could not be generated because of other factors that affect sales for each period (for example, time of year and other promotional campaigns).

Results Were Positive
My analysis of the data shows that 38% of the callers after June 2-6 first learned about our company from the Yellow Pages. The next highest source was referrals and repeat business, which accounted for 26% of the calls. In addition, 21% of the Yellow Pages inquiries resulted in signed contracts, as compared with our 19% overall average.

The new business that resulted from this advertising substantially affects the local residential market (11%-12% increase), has some effect on the commercial market (5%-6% increase), and has little or no effect on the long-haul or large-job market (0%-2% increase). Our last quarterly sales report indicated that the residential market accounts for 78% of our total sales.

We Should Continue Advertising
Based on the $358 monthly cost of our quarter-page ad, each dollar of ad cost is producing $3.77 in sales revenue and $0.983 toward product margin. These results clearly support the continuation of our Yellow Pages advertising. I would be happy to discuss the results of this research with you in more detail and to provide the supporting statistical data if you wish.

jeo

Uses a direct organizational style: the recommendation and conclusions are given first, followed by the supporting evidence.

Uses talking headings to reinforce the direct plan.

Uses informal language; makes extensive use of first- and second-person pronouns such as I, me, we, and you.

Does not include the detailed statistical information but makes it available if needed.

Grammar and Mechanics Note

See the Reference Manual at the end of the text for guidance on how to format memorandums.

MODEL 27   **Formal Manuscript Report**

The first page of a formal manuscript report is shown.

THE EFFECTIVENESS OF YELLOW PAGES ADVERTISING

FOR ALL SYSTEMS GO COMPANY

Barbara Novak, Sales Assistant

Uses an indirect organizational style: the conclusions and recommendations will be given after the supporting data is presented.

According to Mountain Bell, display advertising typically accounts for 55% of total sales for a firm in the moving business (Dye, 1997, p.17). Thus, Hiram Cooper, director of marketing, requested a three-month test be conducted of the effectiveness of Yellow Pages advertising for All Systems Go. This report describes the procedures used to gather the data and the results obtained. Based on the data, a recommendation is made regarding the continuation of Yellow Pages advertising.

A quarter-page ad was purchased in the edition of the Mountain Bell Yellow Pages that was distributed the week of June 2-6. For the six-week period encompassing June 9-July 17, all telephone and walk-in customers were queried to determine how they had learned about the company.

Uses formal language; avoids first- and second-person pronouns.

One delimitation of this study was that precise before-and-after sales data could not be generated because of other factors that affected sales for each period (for example, time of year and other promotional campaigns).

Findings

The findings of this study are reported in terms of the sources of information for learning about All Systems Go, the amount of new business generated, and a cost-benefits comparison for Yellow Pages advertising.

Sources of Information

Uses visual aids (such as tables and charts) and multi-level headings, which are typical of formal reports.

As shown in Table 1, 38% of the callers during the test period first learned about All Systems Go from the Yellow Pages display. The second highest source was referrals

Grammar and Mechanics Note

See the Reference Manual at the end of the text for guidance on how to format manuscript reports.

collected and analyzed) and developing an outline. You must decide in what order to present each piece of the puzzle and when to "spill the beans"—when to present your overall **conclusions** (the answers to the research questions raised in the introduction) and any recommendations you may wish to make.

As shown in Figure 12.1, the four most common bases for organizing your findings are *time, location, importance,* and *criteria.* There are, of course, other patterns for organizing data; for example, you can move from the known to the unknown or from the simple to the complex. The purpose of the report (information, analysis, or recommendation), the nature of the problem, and your knowledge of the reader will help you select the organizational framework that will be most useful.

Most reports are organized by time, location, importance, or criteria.

Time   The use of chronology, or time sequence, is appropriate for agendas, minutes of meetings, programs, many status reports, and similar projects. Discussing events in the order in which they occurred or in the order in which they will or should occur is an efficient way to organize many informational reports—those whose purpose is simply to inform.

FIGURE 12.1 How Should You Organize the Data?

Basis: Time *Format:* Noun Phrases	A. EASTERN ELECTRONICS: A CASE STUDY 1. Start-up of firm: 1990 2. Rapid expansion: 1990–93 3. Industry-wide slowdown: 1994 4. Retrenchment: 1995–96 5. Return to profitability: 1997
Basis: Location *Format:* Participial Phrases	B. RENOVATION NEEDS 1. Expanding the mailroom 2. Modernizing the reception area 3. Installing a humidity system in Warehouse C 4. Repaving the north parking lot
Basis: Importance *Format:* Partial Statements	C. PROGRESS REPORT ON AUTOMATION PROJECT 1. Conversion on budget 2. Time schedule slipped one month 3. Branch offices added to project 4. Software programs upgraded
Basis: Criteria *Format:* Statements	D. EVALUATION OF APPLICANTS FOR COMMUNICATIONS DIRECTOR 1. Sefcik has higher professional training. 2. Jenson has more relevant work experience. 3. Jenson's written work samples are more effective.
Format: Questions	E. ESTABLISHING A POLICY ON AIDS IN THE WORKPLACE 1. What are the firm's legal and social responsibilities? 2. What policies have other firms established? 3. What policies are needed to deal with the needs of AIDS-infected employees? 4. What policies are needed to deal with the concerns of noninfected employees? 5. How should these policies be implemented?

Despite its usefulness and simplicity, time sequence should not be overused. Because events *occur* one after another, chronology is often the most efficient way to *record* data, but it may not be the most efficient way to *present* that data to your readers. Assume, for example, that you are writing a progress report on a recruiting trip you made to four college campuses. Each day you interviewed candidates for the three positions you have open. The first passage, given in time sequence, requires too much work of the reader. The second version saves the reader time.

NOT: On Monday morning, I interviewed one candidate for the budget-analyst position and two candidates for the junior-accountant position. Then, in the afternoon, I interviewed two candidates for the asset-manager position and another for the budget-analyst position. Finally, on Tuesday, I interviewed another candidate for budget analyst and two for junior accountant.

BUT: On Monday and Tuesday, I interviewed three candidates for the budget-analyst position, four for the junior-accountant position, and two for the asset-manager position.

Obviously, a blow-by-blow description is not necessarily the most efficient means of communicating information to the reader—sometimes it forces the reader to do too much work. Organize your information in time sequence only when it is important for the reader to know the sequence in which events occurred.

Location   Like the use of time sequence, the use of location as the basis for or-ganizing a report is often appropriate for simple informational reports. Discussing topics according to their geographical or physical location (for example, describing an office layout) may be the most efficient way to present the data. Again, however, be sure that such an organizational plan helps the reader process the information most efficiently and that it is not merely the easiest way for you to report the data. Decisions should be based on reader needs rather than on writer convenience.

Importance   For the busy reader, the most efficient organizational plan may be to have the most important topic discussed first, followed in order by topics of decreasing importance. The reader then gets the major idea up front and can skim the less important information as desired or needed. This organizational plan is routinely used by newspapers, where the most important points are discussed in the lead paragraph.

For some types of reports, especially recommendation reports, the opposite plan might be used effectively. If you've analyzed four alternatives and will recommend the implementation of Alternative 4, you might first present each of the other alternatives in turn and show why they're *not* feasible. Then, you save your "trump card" until last, thus making the alternative you're recommending the freshest in the reader's mind because it is the last one read. If you use this option, make sure that you effectively "slay all the dragons" except your own, so that the reader will agree that your recommendation is the most logical one.

The most logical organization for most analytical and recommendation reports is by criteria.

Criteria   For most analytical and recommendation reports, where the purpose is to analyze the data and possibly recommend a solution, the most logical arrangement is to organize the data by criteria. One of the important steps in the reporting process is to develop hypotheses regarding causes of or solutions for the problem you're exploring. This process requires factoring, or breaking down, your problem into its component sub-problems. These factors, or criteria, then, become the bases for organizing the report.

In Example D in Figure 12.1, for instance, the three factors presented—professional training, work experience, and written work samples—are the bases on which you will evaluate each candidate. Thus, they should also form the bases for presenting the data. By focusing attention on the criteria, you help lead the reader to the same conclusion you reached. Thus, organizing data by criteria is an especially effective organizational plan when the reader might be initially resistant to your recommendations.

If you're evaluating three sites for a new facility, for example, avoid the temptation to use the *locations* of these sites as the report headings. Such an organizational plan focuses attention on the sites themselves instead of the criteria by which you evaluated them and on which you based your recommendations. Instead, use the criteria as the headings. Similarly, avoid using "Advantages" and "Disadvantages" as headings. Keep your reader in step with you by helping the reader focus on the same topics— the criteria—that you focused on during the research and analysis phases of your project.

In actual practice, you might use a combination of these organizational plans. For instance, you might organize your first-level headings by criteria but your second-level headings in simple-to-complex order. Or you might organize your first-level headings by criteria but present these criteria in their order of importance. Competent communicators select an organizational plan with a view toward helping the reader comprehend and appreciate the information and viewpoints being presented in the most efficient manner possible.

Presenting Conclusions and Recommendations   Once you've decided how to organize the findings of your study, you must decide where to present the conclusions and any recommendations that have resulted from these findings. The differences among findings, conclusions, and recommendations can be illustrated by the following examples:

Finding:	The computer monitor sometimes goes blank during operation.
Finding:	Nonsense data sometimes appears on the screen for no reason.
Conclusion:	The computer is broken.
Recommendation:	We should repair the computer before May 3, when payroll processing begins.
Finding:	Our Statesville branch has lost money four out of the past five years.
Conclusion:	Our Statesville branch is not profitable.
Recommendation:	We should close our Statesville branch.

In general, prefer the direct plan (conclusions and recommendations first) for business reports.

wordwise

Books by the Numbers

- *Bonfire of the Vanities* uses 2,343 exclamation points.
- Winston Churchill's biography contains 9.2 million words.
- *Mahabharata* is the longest poem—220,000 lines.
- Leo Tolstoy's wife hand-copied his *War and Peace* seven different times.
- Agatha Christie is the all-time best-selling novelist, having sold more than a billion books.
- The letter *e* is the most frequently occurring letter in the English language; yet in 1939, E. V. Wright wrote a novel, *Gadsby,* that does not contain the letter *e* anywhere within its 50,000 words.

The conclusions answer the research questions raised in the introduction.

Academic reports and many business reports have traditionally presented the conclusions and recommendations of a study at the end of the report, the rationale being that conclusions cannot logically be drawn until the data has been presented and analyzed; similarly, recommendations cannot be made until conclusions have been drawn.

Models 26 and 27, presented earlier, illustrate the two approaches. The informal memo report presents the conclusions and recommendations in the first paragraph; the formal manuscript report delays such presentation until after the findings have been presented and analyzed.

Although hard and fast rules cannot be given for when to use the direct and indirect organizational plans in reports, some guidance can be given. Generally, it is better to use the direct organizational plan (in which the conclusions and recommendations are presented at the beginning of the report) when

- The reader prefers the direct plan for reports.

- The reader will be receptive to your conclusions and recommendations.

- The reader can evaluate the information in the report more efficiently if the conclusions and recommendations are given up front.

- You have no specific reason to prefer the indirect pattern.

Similarly, the indirect plan (in which the evidence is presented first, followed by conclusions and recommendations) is more appropriate when

- The reader prefers the indirect plan for reports.

- The reader will be initially uninterested in or resistant to the conclusions and recommendations.

- The topic is so complex that detailed explanations and discussions are needed in order for the conclusions and recommendations to be understood and accepted.

The decision isn't necessarily an either/or situation. Instead of putting all the conclusions and recommendations either first or last, you may choose to split them up, discussing each in the appropriate subsection of your report. Similarly, even though you write a report using an indirect plan, you may add an executive summary or letter of transmittal that communicates the conclusions and recommendations to the reader before the report itself has been read.

Outlining the Report

Although we've not used the term *outlining* thus far, whenever we've talked about organizing, we've actually been talking about outlining as well. For example, early in the report process you factored your problem statement into its component subproblems. Thus, your problem statement and subproblems served as your first working outline.

Many business writers find it useful at this point in the report process to construct a more formal outline. A formal outline provides an orderly visual representation of the report, showing clearly which points are to be covered, in what order they are to be covered, and what the relationship of each is to the rest of the report. The purpose of the outline is to guide you, the writer, in structuring your report logically and efficiently. Consider it a working draft, subject to being revised as you compose the report.

The outline provides a concise visual picture of the structure of your report.

Use the working title of your report as the title of your outline. Then use upper-case roman numerals for the major headings, uppercase letters for first-level sub-headings, arabic numerals for second-level subheadings, and lowercase letters for third-level subheadings. Only rarely will you need to use all four levels of headings. Model 28 on page 376 shows an outline for a formal report.

As part of the process of developing a formal outline, you should compose the actual wording for your headings and decide how many headings you will need. Headings play an important role in helping to focus the reader's attention and in helping your report achieve unity and coherence, so plan them carefully, and revise them as needed as you work toward a final version of your report.

Talking Versus Generic Headings   **Talking headings** identify not only the topic of the section but also the major conclusion. For instance, Example C in Figure 12.1 on page 371 uses talking headings to indicate not only that the first section of the report is about the budget for the conversion but also that the conversion is proceeding on budget.

Use descriptive and parallel headings for unity and coherence.

Talking headings, which are typically used in newspapers and magazines, are often also useful for business reports, where they can serve as a preview or executive summary of the entire report. They are especially useful when directness is desired—the reader can simply skim the headings in the report (or in the table of contents) and get an overview of the topics covered and each topic's conclusions.

Generic headings, on the other hand, identify only the topic of the section, without giving the conclusion. Most formal reports and any report written in an indirect pattern would use generic headings, similar to the headings used for Examples A and B in Figure 12.1 and used throughout Model 28.

Parellelism   As illustrated in Figure 12.1, you have wide leeway in selecting the formats of headings you wish to use in your report. Noun phrases are probably the most common form of heading, but you may also choose participial phrases, partial statements (in which a verb is missing—the kind often used in newspaper headlines), statements, or questions. Perhaps there are other forms you might choose as well.

Regardless of the form of heading you select, be consistent within each level of heading. If the first major heading (a first-level heading) is a noun phrase, all first-level headings should be noun phrases. If the first major heading is a talking heading, the others should be too. As you move from level to level, you may switch to another form of heading if it would be more appropriate. Again, however, the headings within the same level must be parallel.

Length and Number of Headings   Four to eight words is about the right length for most headings. Headings that are too long lose some of their effectiveness; the shorter the heading, the more emphasis it receives. Yet headings that are too short are ineffective because they do not convey enough meaning.

Similarly, choose an appropriate number of headings. Having too many headings weakens the unity of a report—they chop the report up too much, making it look more like an outline than a discussion. Having too few headings, however, confronts the reader with page after page of solid copy, without the chance to stop periodically and refocus attention on the topic.

Use headings to break up a long report and refocus the reader's attention.

In general, consider having at least one heading or visual aid to break up each single-spaced page or each two consecutive, double-spaced pages. Make your report inviting to read.

MODEL 28   Report Outline

This report uses generic, not talking, headings.

Uses the working title of the report as the outline title.

STAFF EMPLOYEES' EVALUATION OF THE BENEFIT PROGRAM

AT ATLANTIC STATE UNIVERSITY

David Riggins

1   **I. INTRODUCTION**

    A. Purpose and Scope
    B. Procedures

Organizes the findings by criteria.

    II. FINDINGS

2   A. Knowledge of Benefits
        1. Familiarity with Benefits
        2. Present Methods of Communication

Contains at least two items in each level of subdivision.

            a. Formal Channels
            b. Informal Channels
        3. Preferred Methods of Communication
    B. Opinions of Present Benefits
        1. Importance of Benefits
        2. Satisfaction with Benefits
    C. Desirability of Additional Benefits

Uses parallel structure (noun phrases are used for each heading and subheading).

    III. SUMMARY, CONCLUSIONS, AND RECOMMENDATIONS

    A. Summary of the Problem and Procedures
    B. Summary of the Findings
    C. Conclusions and Recommendations

    APPENDIX

3   A. Cover Letter
    B. Questionnaire

Grammar and Mechanics Notes

1 Align the roman numerals vertically on the periods.   2 Type each entry in upper- and lowercase letters.   3 Identify each appendix item by letter.

Balance   Maintain a sense of balance within and among sections. It would be unusual to give one section of a report eight subsections (eight second-level headings) and give the following section none. Similarly, it would be unusual to have one section ten pages long and another section only half a page long. Also, ensure that the most important ideas are in the highest levels of headings. If you're discussing four criteria for a topic, for example, all four of these should be in the same level of heading—presumably in first-level headings.

When you do divide a section into subsections, it must have at least two subsections. You cannot logically have just one second-level heading within a section because when you divide something, it divides into more than one "piece."

Drafting

Although it is the last step of a long and sometimes complex process, the written presentation of your research is the only evidence your reader has of the effort you have invested in the project. The success or failure of all your work depends on this physical evidence. Prepare the written report carefully to bring out the full significance of your data and to help the reader reach a decision and solve a problem.

Everything that you learned in Chapter 6 about the writing process applies directly to report writing—choosing a productive work environment; scheduling a reasonable block of time to devote to the drafting phase; letting ideas flow quickly during the drafting stage, without worrying about style, correctness, or format; and revising for content, style, correctness, and readability. However, report writing requires several additional considerations as well.

Drafting the Body

The report body consists of the introduction, the findings, and the summary, conclusions, and recommendations. As stated earlier, the conclusions may go first or last in the report. Each part may be a separate chapter in long reports or a major section in shorter reports.

Introduction   The introduction sets the stage for understanding the findings that follow. In this section, present such information as the following:

The introduction presents the information the reader needs to make use of the findings.

- Background of the problem

- Need for the study

- Authorization for the report

- Hypotheses or problem statement and subproblems

- Definition of terms (if needed)

- Procedures used to gather and analyze the data

The actual topics and amount of detail presented in the introductory section will depend on the complexity of the report and the needs of the reader. For example, if the procedures are extensive, you may want to place them in a separate section, with their own first-level heading. Here is an example of an introductory section for a formal report.

Team writing is quite prevalent in organizations because the increasing quantity and complexity of the workplace makes it difficult for any one person to have either the time or the expertise to solve many of the problems that arise and prepare a written report. Regardless of who prepares each individual part of the report, the final document must look and sound as though it were prepared by one writer. Here a work team is shown reviewing each section of their report for errors in content, gaps or repetition, and effective writing style.

Employee benefits are a rapidly growing and an increasingly important form of employee compensation for both profit and nonprofit organizations. According to a recent U.S. Chamber of Commerce survey, benefits now constitute 37% of all payroll costs, averaging $9,732 yearly for each employee (Berelson, 1995, p. 183). Thus, on the basis of cost alone, an organization's benefit program must be carefully monitored and evaluated.

To ensure that the benefit program for Atlantic State University's 2,500 staff personnel is operating as effectively as possible, David Riggins, director of personnel, authorized this report on October 15, 1997.

Purpose and Scope

Specifically, the following problem statement was addressed in this study: What are the opinions of staff employees at Atlantic State University regarding their employee benefits? To answer this question, the following subproblems were addressed:

1. How knowledgeable are the employees about the benefit program?
2. What are the employees' opinions of the value of the benefits presently available?
3. What benefits, if any, would the employees like to have added to the program?

This study attempted to determine employee preferences only. The question of whether employee preferences are economically feasible is not within the scope of this study.

Procedures

A list of the 2,489 staff employees who are eligible for benefits was generated from the October 15 payroll run. By means of a 10% systematic sample, 250 employees were selected for the survey. On November 3, each of the selected employees was sent the cover letter and questionnaire shown in Appendixes A and B via campus mail. A total of 206 employees completed usable questionnaires, for a response rate of 82%.

In addition to the questionnaire data, personal interviews were held with Lois White, compensation specialist at ASU; Roger Ray, chair of the Staff Personnel Committee at ASU; and Lewis Rigby, director of the State Personnel Board. The primary data provided by the survey and personal interviews was then analyzed and compared with findings from secondary sources to determine the staff employees' opinions of the benefits program at ASU.

Findings   The findings of the study represent the major contribution of the report and make up the largest section of the report. Discuss and interpret any relevant primary and secondary data you gathered. Organize this section using one of the plans discussed earlier (for example, by time, location, importance, or criteria). Using objective language, present the information clearly, concisely, and accurately.

Don't just present your findings; analyze and interpret them for the reader.

Many reports will display numerical information in tables and figures (such as bar, line, or pie charts). The information in such displays should be self-explanatory; that is, readers should understand it without having to refer to the text. Nevertheless, all tables and figures must be mentioned and explained in the text so that the text, too, is self-explanatory. All text references should be by number (for example, "as shown in Table 4")—never by a phrase such as "as shown below," because the table or figure might actually appear at the top of the following page.

Summarize the important information from the display (see Figure 12.2). Give enough interpretation to help the reader comprehend the table or figure, but don't repeat all the information it contains. Discussing display information in the narrative *emphasizes* that information, so discuss only what merits such emphasis.

The table or figure should be placed immediately below the first paragraph of text in which the reference to the display occurs. (Of course, if the display contains supplementary information, you may place it in an appendix rather than in the body of the report itself.) Avoid splitting a table or figure between two pages. If not enough space is available on the page for the display, continue with the text to the bottom of the page and then place the display at the very top of the following page.

For all primary and secondary data, point out important items, implications, trends, contradictions, unexpected findings, similarities and differences, and the like. Use emphasis, subordination, preview, summary, and transition to make the report read clearly and smoothly. Keep the reader's needs and desires uppermost in mind as you organize, present, and discuss the information.

Summary, Conclusions, and Recommendations   A one- or two-page report may need only a one-sentence or one-paragraph summary. Longer or more complex reports, however, should include a more extensive summary. Briefly review the problem and the procedures used to solve the problem, and provide an overview of the major findings. Repeating the main points or arguments immediately before presenting the conclusions and recommendations reinforces the reasonableness of those conclusions and recommendations. To avoid monotony when summarizing, use wording that is different from the original presentation.

Findings lead to conclusions; conclusions lead to recommendations.

FIGURE 12.2   Presenting and Analyzing Tables in Reports

Recent studies (Egan, 1995; Ignatio, 1996) have shown that employees' satisfaction with benefits is directly correlated with their knowledge of such benefits. Thus, the ASU staff employees were asked to rate their level of familiarity with each benefit. As shown in Table 2, most staff employees believe that most benefits have been adequately communicated to them.

TABLE 2.   EMPLOYEE LEVEL OF FAMILIARITY WITH ASU'S BENEFIT PROGRAM

Benefit	Level of Familiarity				
	Familiar	Unfamiliar	Undecided	No Resp.	Total
Sick leave	94%	4%	1%	1%	100%
Vacation	94%	4%	1%	1%	100%
Paid holidays	92%	4%	3%	1%	100%
Hospital/Medical ins.	90%	7%	2%	0%	100%
Life insurance	84%	10%	5%	1%	100%
Retirement	84%	11%	4%	1%	100%
Long-term disability ins.	55%	33%	12%	1%	100%
Auto insurance	36%	57%	6%	15%	100%

At least four-fifths of the employees are familiar with all major benefits except for long-term disability insurance, which is familiar to only a slight majority. The low level of knowledge about auto insurance (36% familiarity) may be explained by the fact that this benefit started just six weeks before the survey was taken.

If your report only analyzes the information presented and does not make recommendations, you might label the final section of the report "Summary" or "Summary and Conclusions," as appropriate. If your report includes both conclusions and recommendations, ensure that the conclusions stem directly from your findings and that the recommendations stem directly from the conclusions. Provide ample evidence to support all your conclusions and recommendations. An example of a closing section of a report is shown below.

Conclusions and Recommendations

These findings show that staff employees at Atlantic State University are extremely knowledgeable about all benefits except long-term disability and automobile insurance; however, a majority would prefer to have an individualized benefit statement instead of the brochures now used to explain the benefit program. They consider paid time off the most important benefit and automobile insurance the least important. A majority are satisfied with all benefits, although retirement benefits generated substantial dissatisfaction. The only additional benefit desired by a majority of the employees is compensation for unused sick leave.

The following recommendations are based on these conclusions:

1. Determine the feasibility of generating an annual individualized benefit statement for each staff employee.
2. Reevaluate the attractiveness of the automobile insurance benefit in one year to determine staff employees' knowledge about, use of, and desire for this benefit. Consider the feasibility of substituting compensation for unused sick leave for the automobile insurance benefit.
3. Conduct a follow-up study of the retirement benefits at ASU to determine how competitive they are with those offered by comparable public and private institutions.

End your report with an overall concluding statement that provides a definite sense of project completion. Don't leave your reader wondering if additional pages will follow.

These recommendations, as well as the findings of this study, should help the university administration ensure that its benefit program is accomplishing its stated objectives of attracting and retaining high-quality employees and meeting their needs once employed.

Drafting the Supplementary Sections

The length, formality, and complexity of the report, as well as the needs of the reader, affect the number of report parts that precede and follow the body of the report. Use any of the following components that will help you achieve your report objectives. Each of these parts is illustrated in the Reference Manual at the end of the text.

Title Page   A title page is typically used for reports typed in manuscript (as opposed to letter or memorandum) format. It shows such information as the title of the report, the names (and perhaps titles and departments) of the reader and writer, and the date the report was transmitted to the reader. Other information may be included at the writer's discretion. The information on the title page should be arranged attractively on the page.

Transmittal Document   Formal reports and all reports that are not hand-delivered to the reader should be accompanied by a transmittal document. As its name implies, a **transmittal document** conveys the report to the reader. If the reader is outside the organization, you would use a transmittal letter; if the reader is within the organization, you would typically use a transmittal memo. Whether the report is written in formal or informal style, use a conversational, personal style of writing for the transmittal document.

Because the completion of the report assignment is good news (whether the information it contains is good or bad news), use the direct organizational plan. Begin by actually transmitting the report. Briefly discuss any needed background information, and perhaps give an overview of the conclusions and recommendations of the report (unless you want the reader to read the evidence supporting these conclusions and recommendations first). Include any other information that will help the reader understand, appreciate, and make use of the information presented in the report. End with such goodwill features as an expression of appreciation for being given the report assignment, an offer of willingness to discuss the report further, or perhaps an offer of assistance in the future.

Write the transmittal memo or letter in a direct pattern.

Here is the report on our staff benefit program that you requested on October 15.

The report shows that the staff is familiar with and values most of the benefits we offer. At the end of the report, I've made several recommendations regarding issuing individualized benefit statements annually and determining the usefulness of the automobile insurance benefit, the feasibility of offering compensation for unused sick leave, and the competitiveness of our retirement program.

I enjoyed working on this assignment, Dave, and learned quite a bit from my analysis that will help me during the upcoming labor negotiations. Please let me know if you have any questions about the report.

The letter or memo may simply be transmitted along with the report, or it may be a part of the report. In the latter case, it is placed immediately after the title page but before the executive summary or table of contents.

The report summary may be read more carefully than the report itself.

Executive Summary   An **executive summary**, also called an *abstract* or *synopsis,* is a condensed version of the body of the report (including introduction, findings, and any conclusions or recommendations). Although some readers may simply scan the report itself, most will read the executive summary carefully. Like the transmittal document, the executive summary is an optional part of the report. It is especially appropriate when the conclusions and recommendations will be welcomed by the reader, when the report is long, or when you know your reader appreciates having such information up front.

Because the purpose of the executive summary is to save the reader time, the summary should be short—generally no more than 10% of the length of the report. The summary should contain the same emphasis as the report itself and should be independent of the report; that is, you should not refer to the report itself in the summary. Assume that the person reading the summary will not have a chance to read the whole report, so include as much useful information as possible.

Use the same writing style for the summary as you used in the report. Position the summary immediately before the table of contents.

Table of Contents   Long reports with many headings and subheadings usually benefit from a table of contents. The wording used in the headings in the table of contents must be identical to the wording used in the headings in the body of the report. Typically, only two or three levels of headings are included in the table of contents—even if more levels are used in the body of the report. The page numbers identify the page on which the section heading appears, even though the section itself may comprise many pages. Obviously, the table of contents cannot be written until after the report itself has been typed.

An appendix might include supplementary reference material not important enough to go in the body of the report.

Appendix   The appendix is an optional report part that contains supplementary information or documents. For example, in an appendix you might include a copy of the questionnaire and cover letter used to collect data, supplementary tables, forms, or computer printouts that might be helpful to the reader but that are not important enough to include in the body of the report. Label each appendix separately, by letter—for example, "Appendix A: Questionnaire" and "Appendix B: Cover Letter." In the body of the report, refer by letter to any items placed in an appendix.

References   The reference list contains the complete record of any secondary sources cited in the report. Different disciplines use different formats for citing these references; whichever you choose, be consistent and include enough information that the reader can easily locate any source if he or she wants to.

A good indication of a report writer's scholarship is the accuracy of the reference list—in terms of both content and format—so proofread this part of your report carefully. The reference list is the very last section of the report.

Developing an Effective Writing Style

You can enhance the effectiveness of your written reports by paying attention to your writing style.

Tone   Regardless of the structure of your report, the writing style used is typically more objective and less conversational than, for example, the style of an informal memorandum. Avoid colloquial expressions, attempts at humor, subjectivity, bias, and exaggeration.

NOT: The company *hit the jackpot* with its new MRP program.

BUT: The new MRP program saved the company $125,000 the first year.

NOT: He *claimed* that half of his projects involved name-brand advertising.

BUT: He stated that half of his projects involved name-brand advertising.

Pronouns   For most business reports, the use of first- and second-person pronouns is not only acceptable but also quite helpful for achieving an effective writing style. Formal language, however, focuses attention on the information being conveyed instead of on the writer; therefore, reports written in the formal style should use third-person pronouns and avoid using *I, we,* and *you.*

First- and second-person pronouns can be used appropriately in most business reports.

You can avoid the awkward substitute "the writer" by recasting the sentence. Most often, it is evident that the writer is the person doing the action communicated.

Informal:	I recommend that the project be canceled.
Awkward:	The writer recommends that the project be canceled.
Formal:	The project should be canceled.

Using the passive voice is a common device for avoiding the use of *I* in formal reports, but doing so weakens the impact. Instead, recast the sentence to avoid undue use of the passive voice.

Informal:	I interviewed Jan Smith.
Passive:	Jan Smith was interviewed.
Formal:	In a personal interview, Jan Smith stated . . .

You may also want to avoid using *he* as a generic pronoun when referring to an unidentified person. Chapter 5 discusses many ways to avoid such discriminatory language.

Verb Tense   Use the verb tense (past, present, or future) that is appropriate at the time the reader *reads* the report—not necessarily at the time that you *wrote* the report. Use past tense to describe procedures and to describe the findings of other studies already completed, but use present tense for conclusions from those studies.

When possible, use the stronger present tense to present the data from your study. The rationale for doing so is that we assume our findings continue to be true;

Verb tenses should reflect the reader's (not the writer's) time frame.

thus, the use of the present tense is justified. (If we cannot assume the continuing truth of any findings, we should probably not use them in the study.)

NOT: These findings *will be discussed* later in this report.

BUT: These findings *are discussed* later in the report. (*But:* These findings *were discussed* earlier in this report.)

NOT: Three-fourths of the managers *responded* that they *believed* quality circles *were* effective at the plant.

BUT: Three-fourths of the managers *believe* that quality circles *are* effective at the plant.

Procedure:	Nearly 500 people *responded* to this survey.
Finding:	Only 11% of the managers *received* any specific training on the new procedure.
Conclusion:	Most managers *do not receive* any specific training on the new procedure.

Use emphasis and subordination ethically—not to pressure the reader.

Emphasis and Subordination   Only rarely does all the data consistently point to one conclusion. More likely, you will have a mixed bag of data from which you will have to evaluate the relative merits of each point. For your report to achieve its objective, the reader must evaluate the importance of each point the same way you did. At the very least, your reader must be *aware* of the importance you attached to each point. Therefore, you should employ the emphasis and subordination techniques learned in Chapter 5 when discussing your findings.

By making sure that the amount of space devoted to a topic reflects the importance of that topic, by carefully positioning your major ideas, and by using language that directly tells what is more and less important, you can help ensure that you and your reader are on the same wavelength when your reader analyzes the data.

Use emphasis and subordination to let the reader know what you consider most and least important—but *not* to unduly sway the reader. If the data honestly leads to a strong, definite conclusion, then by all means make your conclusion strong and definite. But if the data permits only a tentative conclusion, then say so.

Use previews, summaries, and transitions to achieve coherence and unity.

Coherence   One of the difficulties of writing any long document—especially when the document is drafted in sections and then put together—is making the finished product read smoothly and coherently, like a unified presentation rather than a cut-and-paste job. The problem is even greater for team-written reports (see "Team Writing" on p. 40 of Chapter 2).

One effective way to achieve coherence in a report is to use previews, summaries, and transitions regularly. At the beginning of each major section, preview what is discussed in that section. At the conclusion of each section, summarize what was presented and provide a smooth transition to the next topic. For long sections, the preview, summary, and transition might each be a separate paragraph; for short sections, a sentence might suffice.

Note how preview, summary, and transition are used in the following example of a report section opening and closing.

Training of System Users

The training program can be evaluated in terms of the opinions of the users and in terms of the cost of training in proportion to the cost of the system itself. . . . *(After this topic preview, several paragraphs follow that discuss the opinions of the users and the cost of the training program.)*

Even though a slight majority of users now feel competent in using the system, the training provided falls far short of the 20% of total system cost recommended by experts. This low level of training may have affected the precision of the data generated by the MRP system. *(The first sentence contains the summary of this section; the second, the transition to the next.)*

Don't depend on your heading structure for coherence. Your report should read smoothly and coherently without the headings. Avoid repeating the exact words of the heading in the subsequent narrative, and avoid using the heading as part of the narrative.

`NOT:` **THE TWO DEPARTMENTS SHOULD BE MERGED.** The reason is that there is a duplication of services.

`NOT:` **THE TWO DEPARTMENTS SHOULD BE MERGED.** The two departments should be merged. The reason is that there is a duplication of services.

`BUT:` **THE TWO DEPARTMENTS SHOULD BE MERGED.** Merging the two departments would eliminate the duplication of services.

Always introduce a topic before dividing it into subtopics. Thus, you should never have one heading following another without some intervening text. Preview for the reader how the topic will be divided before you actually make the division.

Paraphrasing Versus Direct Quotation

When including the ideas of another person in your report, avoid the temptation to become lazy and simply repeat everything in the author's exact words. It is unlikely that the problem you're trying to solve and the problem discussed by the author mesh exactly. More than likely, you'll need to take bits and pieces of information from numerous sources and integrate them into a context appropriate for your specific purposes.

A **paraphrase** is a summary or restatement of a passage in your own words. A **direct quotation,** on the other hand, contains the exact words of another. Use direct quotations (always enclosed in quotation marks) only for definitions or for text that is so precise, clear, or otherwise noteworthy that it cannot be improved on. Most of your references to secondary data should be in the form of paraphrases. Paraphrasing involves more than just rearranging the words or leaving out a word or two. It requires, instead, that you understand the writer's idea and then restate it in your own language.

Documenting Your Sources

Documentation is the identification of sources by giving credit to another person, either in the text or in the reference list, for using his or her words or ideas. You may, of course, use the words and ideas of others, provided such use is properly documented; in fact, for many business reports such secondary information may be the *only* data you use. You must, however, provide appropriate documentation whenever you quote, paraphrase, or summarize someone else's work (see Spotlight 19— On Law and Ethics on p. 386).

Who Said So?

Plagiarism is a potential problem for anyone who writes. For example, the head of Harvard University's psychiatric hospital resigned when it was found he had committed plagiarism in four papers he published. A nationally known minister was accused of plagiarizing numerous sections from someone else's book to include in his own popular book. A director of the Cooley Law School resigned immediately after admitting he used "substantial unattributed quotations" in a law-review article. Problems of dishonesty in research have, in fact, become so serious that the federal government has issued specific rules designed to police scientific fraud by researchers.

SPOTLIGHT 19

ON LAW
AND ETHICS

also verify any information you include in a report, regardless of who said it. For example, according to the book *They Never Said It,* despite widespread belief, Voltaire never said, "I disapprove of what you say, but I will defend to the death your right to say it"; Leo Durocher never said, "Nice guys finish last"; and W. C. Fields never said, "Anybody who hates children and dogs can't be all bad."

Similarly, James Cagney never used the line "You dirty rat," nor did Humphrey Bogart say, "Play it again, Sam," in any of his films. And Sherlock Holmes never uttered "Elementary, my dear Watson" in any of A. Conan Doyle's novels.

Check Your Sources

Business writers have also been guilty of shoddy scholarship. In *Pacific Rim Trade,* a book published by the American Management Association, the writers stated that Lakewood Industries, a small Minnesota firm, sells the most chopsticks in Japan. *Forbes* magazine investigated and found that the company doesn't sell the most chopsticks in Japan, never did, and never will. In fact, the three-year-old firm went bankrupt trying to perfect a technique for manufacturing the chopsticks.

You can, of course, go too far in the other direction and provide excessive documentation. Such a practice not only is distracting but also leaves the impression that the writer is not an original thinker. As an example of excessive documentation, a study of criminal procedure published in the *Georgetown Law Journal* was accompanied by 3,917 footnotes!

In addition to citing your sources, you should

Give Credit Where Credit is Due

As a competent communicator, you must give appropriate credit to your sources and ensure the accuracy of your data. Make certain that you have answered completely and fairly the question, "Who said so?" Your organization's reputation and welfare—not to mention your own—demand no less.

Sources: Kenneth H. Bacon, "U.S. Issues Rules Aimed at Policing Fraud in Research," *Wall Street Journal,* August 9, 1989, p. B3; Paul M. Barrett, "To Read This Story in Full, Don't Forget to See the Footnotes," *Wall Street Journal,* May 10, 1988, p. 1; Paul Boller and John George, *They Never Said It,* Oxford University Press, Oxford, England, 1989; Christopher Cook, "Judge Reportedly Plagiarized in Article," *Detroit Free Press,* March 19, 1989, p. 3A; John Harris, "Chop-Stuck," *Forbes,* August 21, 1989, p. 14; Ralph Keyes, "The Greatest Quotes Never Said," *Reader's Digest,* June 1993, pp. 97–100; Rob Stein, "Plagiarism Charges End in Departure at Harvard," *Detroit Free Press,* November 29, 1988, p. 8A.

Plagiarism is the use of another person's words or ideas without giving proper credit. Writings are considered the writer's legal property; someone else who wrongfully uses such property is guilty of theft. Plagiarism, therefore, carries stiff penalties. In the classroom, the penalty ranges from failure in a course to expulsion from school. On the job, the penalty for plagiarism ranges from loss of credibility to loss of employment.

What Needs to Be Documented   Except as noted here, all material in your report that comes from secondary sources must be documented; that is, enough information about the original source must be given to enable the reader to locate the source if he or she so desires. If the secondary source is published (for example, a journal article), the documentation should appear as a reference citation. If the source is unpublished, sufficient documentation can generally be given in the narrative, making a formal citation unnecessary, as illustrated below:

> According to Board Policy 91-18b, all position vacancies above the level of C-3 must be posted internally at least two weeks prior to being advertised.

> The contractor's letter of May 23, 1997, stated, "We agree to modify Blueprint 3884 by widening the southeast entrance from 10 feet to 12 feet 6 inches for a total additional charge of $273.50."

Occasionally, enough information can be given in the narrative so that a formal citation is unnecessary even for published sources. This format is most appropriate when only one or two sources are used in a report.

> Widmark made this very argument in a guest editorial entitled "Here We Go Again" in the May 4, 1997, *Wall Street Journal* (p. A12).

Once a study has been cited once, it may be mentioned again in continuous discussion on the same page or even on the next pages without further citation if no ambiguity results. If several pages intervene or if ambiguity might result, the citation should be given again.

What Does *Not* Need to Be Documented   The use of two types of material by others does not need to be documented: (1) facts that are common knowledge to the readers of your report and (2) facts that can be verified easily.

> Apple Computer is a large manufacturer of microcomputers.

> The stock market closed at 6,506 on November 8.

But such statements as "Sales of the original Macintosh were disappointing" and "Only 4,000 Macintosh computers were sold in 1984" would need to be documented. If in doubt about whether you need to document, provide the citation.

Forms of Documentation   The three major forms for documenting the ideas, information, and quotations of other people in a report are endnotes, footnotes, and author-date references (see the Reference Manual at the back of this text for examples and formatting conventions). Let the nature of the report and the needs of the reader dictate the documentation method used. Regardless of the method you select, ensure that the citations are accurate, complete, and consistently formatted and that your bibliography format is compatible with your documentation format.

1. *Endnotes:* The endnote format uses superscript (raised) numbers to identify secondary sources in the text and then provides the actual citations in a numbered list entitled "Notes" at the end of the report. The endnotes are numbered consecutively throughout the report. Some readers prefer the endnote format because it avoids the clutter of footnotes and because it's easy to use.

In the past, using endnotes for a long or complex report was somewhat risky because of the possibility of introducing errors when revising text. Every time text with a reference was inserted, deleted, or moved, all following endnote references in the text and in the list at the back of the report had to be renumbered. Today, however, most word processors have an endnote feature that automatically numbers and keeps track of endnote references. Still, some readers prefer one of the other formats because endnotes provide no clues in the text regarding the source.

Provide a reference citation for material that came from others, unless that material is common knowledge or can be verified easily.

Standard citation formats are footnotes, endnotes, and author-year citations.

Word processing has simplified the generation of endnotes and footnotes.

2. *Footnotes:* For years, footnotes were the traditional method of citing sources, especially in academic reports. A bibliographic footnote provides the complete reference at the bottom of the page on which the citation occurs in the text. Thus, a reader interested in exploring the source does not have to turn to the back of the report. Today's word processors can format footnotes almost painlessly—automatically numbering and positioning each note correctly. Some readers, however, find the presence of footnotes on the text page distracting.

The author-date format is preferred by many users of business reports.

3. *Author-Date Format:* Many business report readers prefer the author-date format of documentation, regarding the method as a reasonable compromise between endnotes (which provide *no* reference information on the text page) and footnotes (which provide *all* the reference information on the text page). In the author-date format, the writer inserts at an appropriate point in the text the last name of the author and the year of publication in parentheses. Complete bibliographic information is then included in the Notes or Reference section at the end of the report.

Distortion by Omission

It would be unethical to leave an inaccurate impression, even when what you do report is true. Sins of omission are as serious as sins of commission. Distortion by omission can occur when using quotations out of context, when omitting certain relevant background information, or when including only the most extreme or most interesting data.

It would be inappropriate, for example, to quote extensively from a survey that was conducted 15 years ago without first establishing for the reader that the findings are still valid. Likewise, it would be inappropriate to quote a finding from one study and not discuss the fact that four similar studies reached opposite conclusions.

Do not use quotations out of context.

Be especially careful to quote and paraphrase accurately from interview sources. Provide enough information to ensure that the passage reflects the interviewee's *intention.* Here are examples of possible distortions:

Original Quotation:	"I think the Lancelot is an excellent car for anyone who does not need to worry about fuel economy."
Distortion:	Johnson stated that the Lancelot "is an excellent car."
Worse Distortion:	Johnson stated that the Lancelot "is an excellent car for anyone."
Worst Distortion:	Johnson stated that the Lancelot "is an excellent car *for anyone!*"

Revising

Once you have produced a first draft of your report, put it away for a few days. Doing so will enable you to view the draft with a fresh perspective and perhaps find a more effective means of communicating your ideas to the reader. Don't try to correct all problems in one review. Instead, look at this process as having three steps—revising first for content, then for style, and finally for correctness.

Revise first for content. Make sure you've included sufficient information to support each point, that you've included no extraneous information (regardless of how interesting it might be), that all the information is accurate, and that the

Though she presents her reports on the air instead of on paper, revising is just as important for newscaster Anna Martinez of KVUE-TV in Austin, Texas, as it is for those preparing written reports. Because the amount of air time she can devote to each story is often decided at the last minute, Martinez must be able to cut or expand quickly while keeping her main points clearly focused for her audience.

information is presented in an efficient and logical sequence. Keep the purpose of the report and the reader's needs and desires in mind as you review for content.

Once you're satisfied with the content of the report, revise for style (refer to Checklist 4: Writing with Style on p. 146). Ensure that your writing is clear and that you have used short, simple, vigorous, and concise words. Check to see that you have used a variety of sentence types and have relied on active and passive voice appropriately. Do your paragraphs have unity and coherence, and are they of reasonable length? Have you maintained an overall tone of confidence, courtesy, sincerity, and objectivity? Finally, review your draft to ensure that you have used nondiscriminatory language and appropriate emphasis and subordination.

After you're confident about the content and style of your draft, revise once more for correctness. This revision step, known as *editing*, identifies and resolves any problems with grammar, spelling, punctuation, and word usage—the topics covered in the LABs in the Reference Manual at the back of this text. Do not risk losing credibility with the reader by careless English usage. If possible, have a colleague review your draft to catch any errors you may have overlooked.

Edit for grammar, spelling, punctuation, and word usage.

Formatting

The physical format of your report (margins, spacing, and the like) depends to a certain extent on the length and complexity of the report and the format preferred by either the organization or the reader.

General Formatting Guidelines

Consistency and readability are the hallmarks of an effective format. For example, be sure that all your first-level headings are formatted consistently; if they are not, the reader may not be able to tell which headings are superior or subordinate to

Adopt a consistent, logical format, keeping the needs of the reader in mind.

other headings. Regardless of the format used, make sure the reader can instantly tell which are major headings and which are minor headings. You can differentiate among headings by using different fonts, font sizes, styles (such as bold or italic), and horizontal placement.

If the organization or reader has a preferred format style, use it. Otherwise, follow the report formatting guidelines provided in the Reference Manual at the back of this text.

Enhancing Reports Through Document Design

Contemporary word processing software makes it easy for writers to take the report process one step further—that is, to *design* their business reports for maximum impact and effectiveness. Although the product is always more important than the packaging, there is no denying the fact that an attractively formatted document, with legible type and plenty of white space, will help you achieve your report objectives.

With that in mind, consider the following nine design guidelines, which are illustrated in Spotlight 20—On Technology. Both versions of the Spotlight report contain the same information. Compare the typed version with the designed version for impact and readability.

Use a simple, consistent design.

1. Keep It Simple.   The most important guideline is to use a simple, clean, and consistent design. It would be distracting, for example, to use many different type styles and sizes in the same document. Instead, select one serif typeface (*serifs* are the small strokes at the tops and bottoms of characters, such as the "feet" at the bottom of a *T;* sans serif typefaces have no such ornamental strokes) for the body of your report and one sans serif typeface for headings and subheadings. One popular combination is Times Roman for body type and Helvetica (or Arial) for special treatments such as headings, subheadings, and captions for figures.

> This is an example of Times Roman in 11-point type. Because the serifs aid in readability, Times Roman is a good choice for the body of your report.

> **This is an example of Helvetica in 11-point type. Because it contrasts nicely with Times Roman, Helvetica is a good choice for headings.**

Similarly, it would be distracting if a reader is accustomed to seeing lists arranged in a certain format but then encounters a list formatted differently. The reader would have to pause to figure out what is different, and why. Make sure that whatever decisions you initially make about margins, spacing, headings, and the like are followed consistently throughout your report.

The empty space on a page also communicates.

2. Use White Space to Advantage.   Use generous top, bottom, and side margins to make your report inviting to read. Consider white space (the blank sections of the report) as part of your overall design. In general, the more white space, the better. Break up long paragraphs into shorter ones, and leave generous space before and after headings. Also separate lengthy areas of text with subheadings. Subheadings not only break up solid blocks of type but also enhance readability by periodically providing signals for the reader.

Designing Business Reports

Typewritten Version

**STAFF EMPLOYEES' EVALUATION OF THE BENEFIT PROGRAM
AT ATLANTIC STATE UNIVERSITY**

Employee benefits are a rapidly growing and an increasingly important form of employee compensation for both profit and nonprofit organizations. According to a recent U.S. Chamber of Commerce survey, roll costs, averagin 1995, p. 183). Thus zation's benefit pr evaluated.

To ensure that the k sity's 2,500 staff possible, David Rig this report on Octol

Purpose and Scope

Specifically, the f in this study: What Atlantic State Unive this question, the :
1. How knowledgeal program?
2. What are the er benefits now a
3. What benefits, added to the p:

This study attempted Whether the preferer in the scope of the

Procedures

A list of the 2,489 fits was generated :

Designed Version

**Staff Employees' Evaluation
of the Benefit Program
at Atlantic State University**

EMPLOYEE BENEFITS ARE a rapidly growing and an increasingly important form of employee compensation for both profit and nonprofit organizations. According to a recent U.S. Chamber of Commerce survey, benefits now constitute 37% of all payroll costs, averaging $9,732 yearly for each employee (Berelson, 1995, p. 183). Thus, on the basis of cost alone, an organization's benefit program must be carefully monitored and evaluated.

To ensure that the benefit program for Atlantic State University's 2,500 staff personnel is operating as effectively as possible, David Riggins, director of personnel, authorized this report on October 15, 1997.

Purpose and Scope

Specifically, the following problem statement was addressed in this study: What are the opinions of staff employees at Atlantic State University regarding their benefits? To answer this question, the following subproblems were addressed:

- How knowledgeable are the employees about the benefit program?
- What are the employees' opinions of the value of the benefits now available?
- What benefits, if any, would the employees like to have added to the program?

This study attempted to determine employee preferences only. Whether the preferences are economically feasible is not within the scope of the study.

Procedures

A list of the 2,489 staff employees who are eligible for benefits was generated from the October 15 payroll run. By means of a 10% systematic sample, 250 employees were selected for the survey. On November 3, each of the selected employees was sent the cover letter and questionnaire shown in Appendixes A and B via campus mail. A total of 206 employees completed questionnaires, for a response rate of 82%.

In addition to the questionnaire data, personal interviews were held with Lois White, compensation specialist at ASU; Roger Ray, chair of the Staff Personnel Committee at ASU; and Lewis Rigby, director of the State Personnel Board. The primary data provided by the survey and personal interviews was then analyzed and compared with findings from secondary sources to determine the staff

3. Select a Suitable Line Length and Type Size.   Line length can have a major impact on the readability of a document. Lines that are too short weaken coherence because they needlessly disrupt the normal horizontal pattern of reading. Lines that are too long cause readers to lose their place when they return to the beginning of the next line. In general, use a line no shorter than 25 characters and no longer than 65 to 75 characters for business documents. Although one column is standard for business reports, any business document can also be typed in two or three columns on a standard-sized page.

For the body of most business reports, select a type size between 10 points (elite size) and 12 points (pica size); 1 point equals $1/72$ of an inch. Proportionately larger type should be used for headings and subheadings.

4. Determine an Appropriate Justification Format.   All text lines in the body of your report should be left-justified; that is, they should all begin at the left margin. However, the end of each line may be either right-justified (sometimes called *full justification)* or ragged right. In general, a justified line presents a clean, formal look, whereas a ragged-right line gives an informal, casual appearance. In addition, you should limit your use of full justification to documents printed on laser printers.

Use full justification for a formal appearance and an uneven right margin for an informal appearance.

This is an example of a justified column, which produces even left and right margins. You should always have the hyphenation feature of your word processor turned on when justifying your lines.

This is an example of a column with a ragged-right margin; that is, one where the lines end unevenly. Ragged-right lines do not typically require as many distracting hyphenations as justified lines of type.

5. Format Paragraphs Correctly.   Business reports prepared on a typewriter may be single- or double-spaced. Designed documents use only single spacing. New paragraphs are indicated either by leaving a blank line before the paragraph or by indenting the first line. Do not, however, both indent *and* leave a blank line; that would be too much. Even when paragraphs are indented, designed documents typically do not indent the first line of a paragraph that immediately follows a heading or subheading; it is obvious that what follows a heading is a new paragraph.

Writers sometimes use various techniques at the start of a document to engage the reader immediately: beginning the first word of the document with an extra-large, decorative letter; typing the first three or four words in solid capitals; or setting the first paragraph in larger type than the rest of the document. The purpose of such techniques is to make the copy attractive and inviting to read.

Use special emphasis techniques sparingly.

6. Emphasize Words and Ideas Appropriately.   On a typewriter, underlining and solid capitals were about the only way to emphasize a word or idea. Thus, report headings and subheadings were traditionally formatted in one of these two styles.

Designed documents, however, have a variety of techniques readily available—larger type size, boldface lettering, and italic type, for example. Any of these techniques is preferable to underlining and solid capitals. Solid capitals are appropriate only for very short headings. Unlike lowercase letters, capital letters are all the same size and are therefore more difficult to read. Also avoid using nonstandard type styles, such as outline or shadow type, in business reports; they provide visual clutter and are distracting.

Use boldface for strong emphasis and italic for medium emphasis in the body of a report. Both boldface and italic type, along with a larger type size, may be used for headings and subheadings; just be sure your main headings stand out more than your subheadings. When headings are displayed prominently, they may be typed in upper- and lowercase letters or with only the first word and proper names in uppercase. Any of the following three styles would be appropriate for a report heading:

Opinions of Present Benefits

Opinions of Present Benefits

Opinions of present benefits

7. Format Lists for Readability.   Because lists or enumerations are surrounded by white space, with each item by itself on a separate line, they tend to stand out more than when the same material is presented in narrative form. You have the choice of using either numbered lists or bulleted lists. Number your lists when *sequence* is important ("Here are the five steps for requesting temporary help") or when the list is long and numbering will help when referring to a specific point. When sequence is not important and the list is short, use bullets (small squares or circles) to call attention to each item. Keep the bullets small and close to the items they relate to. For both numbered and bulleted lists, either a hanging style or a first-line-indented style may be used. Both of the following lists are formatted appropriately:

Use numbered lists when order is important; otherwise, use bulleted lists.

To insert a chart into your report file, follow these steps:

1. Create the chart using a graphics or spreadsheet program, such as Harvard Graphics or Lotus 1-2-3.
2. Open your report file.
3. Use your word processor's command to insert the graphic.
4. Resize the graphic so that it is in proper scale and position it below the paragraph where it is introduced.

Each typeface can vary in a number of important ways:

- Posture: Roman (vertical) and italic (oblique)

- Weight: Hairline, thin, light, book, regular, medium, demibold, bold, heavy, black, and ultra

- Width: Condensed, regular, and expanded

- Size: Text (all type sizes up to 12 points) and display (type sizes larger than 12 points)

DILBERT

Use graphics only when they help you achieve your report objectives.

8. Use Graphics—In Moderation.   When used in moderation, graphics can add interest and aid comprehension. This is especially the case when using charts and tables. In addition, writers today can make use of files of computerized drawings, called *clip art,* that can be electronically inserted into their documents:

New ARW Labor Contract Approved

We're happy to report that management and Local 123 of the ARW will announce agreement on a new three-year contract this afternoon at a press conference in the second-floor conference room. Annice Hall,

To be effective, such clip art must be used sparingly and be well drawn, relevant, and in proper scale. Unless you are certain that a particular piece of clip art will help you tell your story more effectively, save clip art for more informal communications such as company newsletters and advertising documents. Most business reports should have a dignified, businesslike appearance.

Horizontal and vertical lines (called *rules*), another graphic device, can also be used in moderation to separate different elements of the document. Horizontal rules can be narrow or wide; vertical rules (sometimes used to separate columns) should be very narrow. If horizontal rules are used at the top and bottom of a page, the top rule is generally wider than the bottom.

9. Have Fun!   Just as the arrival of the personal computer gave the average manager easy access to strategic information, so also has the arrival of desktop publishing and document design given the average businessperson more control over the documents he or she produces. You don't have to be an artist to *design* your documents. The features you'll need are available on any contemporary word processing or desktop publishing program. Buy a book or two on basic design, and perhaps subscribe to one of the many desktop or personal publishing magazines. Begin to pay attention to the layout and design of professionally prepared documents, and learn from them. Be creative and don't be afraid to experiment. And, most important, have fun! Document design is empowering—to you and your ideas.

Proofreading

Do not risk destroying your credibility by failing to proofread carefully.

First impressions are important. Even before reading the first line of your report, the reader will have formed an initial impression of the report—and of *you.* Make this impression a positive one by ensuring that the report carries with it a professional appearance.

After making all your revisions and formatting the various pages, give each page one final proofreading. Check closely for typographical errors. Check for appearance. Have you arranged the pages in correct order and stapled them neatly? If you're submitting a photocopy, are all the copies legible and of even darkness? Is each page free of wrinkles and smudges?

If you formatted the report on a computer, ensure that in moving passages about, you did not inadvertently delete a line or two or repeat a passage. Run the spelling checker a final time after making all changes. (Remember, however, that a spelling checker will not locate an incorrect word that is spelled correctly.) If you have a grammar software program, evaluate your writing electronically. The grammar checker will check for use of passive voice, sentence length, misuse of words, unmatched punctuation (for example, an opening parenthesis not followed by a closing parenthesis), and readability. Use every aid at your disposal to ensure that your report reflects the highest standards of scholarship, critical thinking, and care.

In short, let your pride of authorship show through in every facet of your report. Appearances and details count. Review your entire document to ensure that you can answer "yes" to every question contained in Checklist 14: Reviewing Your Report Draft (p. 396).

CHECKLIST 14   Reviewing Your Report Draft

Introduction

☑ Is the report title accurate, descriptive, and honest?

☑ Is the research problem or the purpose of the study stated clearly and accurately?

☑ Is the scope of the study identified?

☑ Are all technical terms, or any terms used in a special way, defined?

☑ Are the procedures discussed in sufficient detail?

☑ Are any questionable decisions justified?

Findings

☑ Is the data analyzed completely, accurately, and appropriately?

☑ Is the analysis free of bias and misrepresentation?

☑ Is the data interpreted (its importance and implications discussed) rather than just presented?

☑ Are all calculations correct?

☑ Is all relevant data included and all irrelevant data excluded?

☑ Are visual aids correct, needed, clear, appropriately sized and positioned, and correctly labeled?

Summary, Conclusions, and Recommendations

☑ Is the wording used in the summary different from that used earlier to present the data initially?

☑ Are the conclusions drawn supported by ample, credible evidence?

☑ Do the conclusions answer the questions or issues raised in the introduction?

☑ Are the recommendations reasonable in light of the conclusions?

☑ Does the report end with a sense of completion and convey an impression that the project is important?

Supplementary Pages

☑ Is the executive summary short, descriptive, and in proportion to the report itself?

☑ Is the table of contents accurate, with correct page numbers and wording that is identical to that used in the report headings?

☑ Is any appended material properly labeled and referred to in the body of the report?

☑ Is the reference list accurate, complete, and in an appropriate format?

Writing Style and Format

☑ Does the overall report take into account the needs and desires of the reader?

☑ Is the material properly organized?

☑ Are the headings descriptive, parallel, and appropriate in number?

☑ Are emphasis and subordination used effectively?

☑ Does each major section contain a preview, summary, and transition?

☑ Has proper verb tense been used throughout?

☑ Has an appropriate level of formality been used?

☑ Are all references to secondary sources properly documented?

☑ Is each needed report part included and in an appropriate format?

☑ Is the length of the report appropriate?

☑ Are the paragraphs of an appropriate length?

☑ If the report is formatted on a computer, have the principles of document design been followed to enhance the report's effectiveness?

☑ Is the report free from spelling, grammar, and punctuation errors?

☑ Does the overall report provide a positive first impression and reflect care, neatness, and scholarship?

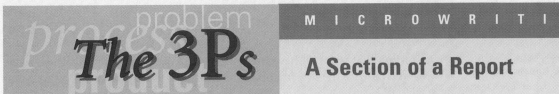
You are a manager at a software-development house that publishes communication software for the HAL and Pear microcomputers. Together, these two computers comprise about 90% of the business market. In 1998, you were asked to survey users of communication software—a repeat of a similar study you undertook in 1993.

You conducted the survey using the same questionnaire and same procedures from the 1993 study. Now you've gathered the data, along with the comparable data collected in 1993, and have organized it roughly into draft tables, one of which is shown in Figure 12.3. You're now ready to put this table into final report format and analyze its contents.

FIGURE 12.3 Draft Table

Q. From what source did you obtain your last software program?

Source	1993 Total		1993 HAL		1993 Pear		1998 Total		1998 HAL		1998 Pear	
	N	%	N	%	N	%	N	%	N	%	N	%
Mail-order company	28	21.2	24	26.1	4	10.0	60	41.1	25	30.9	35	53.9
Online bulletin board	3	2.3	2	2.2	1	2.5	4	2.7	2	2.5	2	3.1
Retail outlet	70	53.0	46	50.0	24	60.0	63	43.2	44	54.3	19	29.2
Software publisher	9	6.8	4	4.3	5	12.5	10	6.8	4	4.9	6	9.2
Unauthorized copy	21	15.9	15	16.3	6	15.0	6	4.1	3	3.7	3	4.6
Other	1	.8	1	1.1	0	0.0	3	2.1	3	3.7	0	0.0
Total	132	100.0	92	100.0	40	100.0	146	100.0	81	100.0	65	100.0

1. Table Format

a. Examine the format of your draft table—the arrangement of columns and rows. Should you change anything for the final table?

First, the year columns (1993 and 1998) should be reversed. The new data is more important than the old data, so putting it first will emphasize it.

Second, the rows need to be rearranged. They're now in alphabetical order but should be rearranged in descending order according to the first amount column—the 1998 total column. Doing this will put the most important data first in the table.

b. Assuming that you will have many tables in your final report, is there some way to condense the information in this table without undue loss of precision or detail?

Although the number of respondents is important, the readers of my report will be much more interested in the percentages. Therefore, I'll give only the total number of respondents for each column and put that figure immediately under each column heading.

Also, I see immediately that very few people obtained their software from online bulletin boards either in 1993 or 1998, so I'll combine that category with the "Other" category.

These changes are shown below.

FIGURE 12.4   Report Table

Source	1998			1993		
	Total (N = 146)	HAL (N = 81)	Pear (N = 65)	Total (N = 132)	HAL (N = 92)	Pear (N = 40)
Retail outlet	43	54	29	53	50	60
Mail-order company	41	31	54	21	26	10
Software publisher	7	5	9	7	4	13
Unauthorized copy	4	3	5	16	17	15
Other	5	7	3	3	3	2
Total	100	100	100	100	100	100

2. **Table Interpretation**

a. Study the table in Figure 12.4. If you had space to make only one statement about this table, what would it be?

Retail outlets and mail-order companies are equally important sources for obtaining software, together accounting for more than four-fifths of all sources.

b. What other 1998 data should you discuss in your narrative?

HAL and Pear users obtain their software in different ways: the majority of HAL users obtain theirs from retail outlets whereas the majority of Pear users obtain theirs from mail-order firms.

c. What should you point out in comparing 1998 data with 1993 data?

The market share for retail outlets decreased by almost 20% from 1993 to 1998 while the market share for mail-order companies almost doubled, increasing by 95%.

Also, the use of unauthorized copies appears to be decreasing (although the actual figures are probably somewhat higher than these self-reported figures).

3. **Report Writing**

a. Develop an effective talking heading and an effective generic heading for this section of the report. Which one will you use?

    Talking Heading: **MAIL ORDERS CATCHING UP WITH RETAIL SALES**

    Generic Heading: **SOURCES OF SOFTWARE PURCHASES**

    Because I do not know personally the readers of the report and their preferences, I'll make the conservative choice and use a generic heading.

b. Compose an effective topic (preview) sentence for this section.

    Respondents were asked to indicate the source of the last software program they purchased.

c. Where will you position the table for this section?

    At the end of the first paragraph that refers to the table.

d. What verb tense will you use in this section?

    Past tense for the procedures; present tense for the findings.

e. Assume that the next report section discusses the cost of software. Compose an effective summary/transition sentence for this section of the report.

    Perhaps the increasing reliance on mail-order purchases is one reason why the cost of communication software has decreased since 1993.

PRODUCT

SOURCES OF SOFTWARE PURCHASES

Respondents were asked to indicate the source of the last software program they purchased. As shown in Table 8, retail outlets and mail-order companies are now equally important sources for obtaining software, together accounting for more than four-fifths of all sources. HAL and Pear users obtain their software in different ways: the majority of HAL users obtain theirs from retail outlets whereas the majority of Pear users obtain theirs from mail-order firms.

TABLE 8. SOURCE OF LAST SOFTWARE PROGRAM
(In percentages)

Source	1998			1993		
	Total (N = 146)	HAL (N = 81)	Pear (N = 65)	Total (N = 132)	HAL (N = 92)	Pear (N = 40)
Retail outlet	43	54	29	53	50	60
Mail-order co.	41	31	54	21	26	10
Software pub.	7	5	9	7	4	13
Unauthor. copy	4	3	5	16	17	15
Other	5	7	3	3	3	2
Total	100	100	100	100	100	100

Retail outlets have decreased in popularity (down 10%) since 1993, while mail-order companies have dramatically increased in popularity (up 20%). Also, the use of unauthorized copies appears to be decreasing (although the actual figure is probably somewhat higher than these self-reported figures).

Perhaps the increasing reliance on mail-order purchases is one reason that the cost of communication software has declined since 1993.

COST OF SOFTWARE

. . .

The most common report formats are manuscript (for formal reports) and letter or memorandum (for informal reports). The most common plans for organizing the findings of a study are by time, location, importance, and criteria. Conclusions should be presented at the beginning of the report unless the reader prefers the indirect plan, the reader will not be receptive toward the conclusions, or the topic is complex. Report headings should be composed carefully—in terms of their type, parallelism, length, and number.

The body of the report consists of the introduction, findings (the major part of the report), and, as needed, the summary, conclusions, and recommendations. Long, formal reports might also require such supplementary components as a title page, transmittal document, executive summary, table of contents, appendix, and reference list.

Use an objective writing style, appropriate pronouns, and verb tenses that reflect the reader's time frame (rather than the writer's). Use emphasis and subordination techniques to help alert the reader to what you consider important; and use preview, summary, and transitional devices to help maintain coherence.

Use direct quotations sparingly; most references to secondary data should be paraphrases. Provide appropriate documentation whenever you quote, paraphrase, or summarize someone else's work by using endnotes, footnotes, or the author-date method of citation. Do not omit important, relevant information from the report.

Delay revising the report until a few days after completing the first draft. Revise in three distinct steps: first for content, then for style, and finally for correctness.

The report's format should enhance the report's appearance and readability and should be based on the organization's and reader's preferences. Unless directed otherwise, follow generally accepted formatting guidelines for margins, report headings, and pagination. Use a simple, consistent design and make generous use of white space. Select an appropriate line length, type size, justification format, and punctuation style; format paragraphs and lists correctly; use graphics in moderation, if needed; and emphasize words and ideas appropriately.

After all revisions and formatting have been completed, give each page one final proofreading. Make sure the final report reflects the highest standards of scholarship, critical thinking, and pride of authorship.

conclusions	paraphrase
direct quotation	plagiarism
documentation	talking heading
executive summary	transmittal document
generic heading	

1. **Communication at Congressional Research Service Revisited** ■ Donna Porter and her colleagues in the Congressional Research Service write reports that help elected officials learn more about the background of legislative issues.
   a. Would Dr. Porter use formal or informal language in a report to members of Congress? Why?
   b. Dr. Porter's reports are informational only; should they be organized according to the direct or the indirect plan? Explain.
   c. Why is documentation important in a report submitted to the U.S. Congress?

2. What factors influence the format and general traits of a report?
3. Give an example of a report topic for which it would be most logical to organize the findings by (a) time, (b) location, (c) importance, and (d) criteria.
4. Under what circumstances should a direct versus an indirect organizational pattern be used for presenting conclusions and recommendations?
5. Assume that your report evaluating three business texts discusses the following topics (the author of the book that rated highest in each category is shown in parentheses):
   a. Content and organization (Bates)
   b. What types of supplementary aids (such as transparencies and student guide) are available (Bates)
   c. How much the book costs (Arnold)
   d. What kind of national reputation the author has (Bates)
   e. Whether the book is up to date in its content coverage (Carroll)
      Compose two sets of headings for these five sections, first generic headings, then talking headings. Make sure each set of headings is parallel.
6. What is the difference between merely *presenting* data and *analyzing* data? Give an example.
7. What verb tense (past, present, or future) should be used for presenting the following information from a study on the effectiveness of a new accounting software program?
   a. A preview of the topics covered in the following section
   b. The procedures of this study
   c. The conclusion regarding the effectiveness of the program
   d. Recommendations for conducting a follow-up study
   e. A discussion of the product reviews contained in computer magazines
8. Assume you surveyed your firm's 50 sales representatives in April. Your survey results showed that they felt left out of the product-planning phase. As a result, you're recommending that the sales manager (the reader of your report) include a two-hour session on this topic at the next sales conference. Write a paragraph presenting this information, first using an informal writing style and then using a formal writing style.
9. Describe some techniques that can be used to emphasize and subordinate findings in a report. What is the appropriate use of such techniques?
10. Give an example of a fact that does and one that does not need to be documented by a citation.
11. What are the advantages and disadvantages of each of the three documentation methods discussed in this chapter?
12. Why should a report not be revised immediately after it is written?
13. Why is white space important in a document?
14. What special proofreading steps should you take if you formatted your report on a computer?

Help
Wanted

Directions: This is a draft page of a report. Revise the document to make it more effective, taking into consideration the editor's marginal comments.

The purchase of a digital camera would enable the Marketing Department to take photographs of our products and transfer them directly to the computer. *frag* Thus, making the process of producing ad layouts faster, easier, and more economical, since no purchase or processing of film is involved.

TABLE 1   Low-Priced Digital Cameras

Camera	Price	Weight	Minimum Focus	No. of Images	Battery	Image Quality
Apple QuickTake	$600	16 oz.	4 in.	16	AA lith	Good
Canon PowerShoot	$950	14 oz.	4 in.	4	NiCad	Outstand
Casio QV	$400	7 oz.	7 in.	96	AA lith	Poor
Epson PhotoPC	$400	27 oz.	24 in.	16	AA alk	Good
Kodak DC 40	$600	16 oz.	48 in.	48	AA alk	Good
Olympus D-200	$600	10 oz.	8 in.	20	AA alk	Outstand

word Marketing personnel agree that high image quality is the most important criteria and the ability to take close-up shots of our products is second in importance. As shown in the table above, of the cameras currently available that cost less than $1,000, the Canon or Olympus would be the most appropriate.

Given the three-hundred-fifty-dollar price differential, the Marketing Department recommends the purchase of two Olympus D-200 cameras.

Position the table at the end of this paragraph.

Because image quality, minimum focus, and cost are the most important criteria, put these columns first—and arrange the rows in order of image quality.

Refer to tables by number—not by position.

num

EXERCISES

1. **The 3Ps microwriting model: Communication Applications at the Congressional Research Service** When Dr. Donna Porter writes an informational report for members of Congress, she gathers and analyzes the data in a systematic way. However, none of the reports prepared by Porter and her colleagues are allowed to include recommendations. As a result, CRS reports have gained a reputation for being unbiased, which is why they are valuable to elected officials who need to weigh all the arguments before they vote on a piece of legislation.

   Problem

   Imagine that changes to the school lunch program are being debated in Congress. Several senators have asked the CRS for a report comparing the nutritional value of a serving of yogurt with the nutritional value of a serving of meat. This comparison will help the senators consider whether the school lunch program should allow the substitution of yogurt for meat. As a research assistant in Dr. Porter's office, you have been assigned to prepare this report.

   Process

   a. What is the purpose of your report?
   b. Describe your audience.
   c. What data do you need to gather and analyze for this report?
   d. What points will you cover and in what order?
   e. What organizational plan will you use? Why?
   f. Draft an opening paragraph to introduce the report and bring the highlights to your readers' attention.

   Product

   Using your knowledge of reports, research and prepare a two-page report in memorandum format.

2. **The 3Ps Microwriting Model: A Report Section**

   Problem

   Review Exercise 5C of Chapter 11 (p. 361). You have constructed your report table and analyzed the data. Now you are ready to write this section of the report.

   Process

   a. Compose an effective talking heading and an effective generic heading for this section of the report. Which one will you use?
   b. Compose an effective topic sentence for this section.
   c. Compose the sentence that contains your recommendation.
   d. Assume that the next section of the report discusses reasons for changing banks. Compose an effective summary/transition sentence for this section of the report.

   Product

   Prepare this section of your report (one to three paragraphs). Include the table in the appropriate position. Submit both your report section and your responses to the process activities to your instructor.

3. **Organizing the Report—Government Report** From the library or a government source, obtain a copy of a recent federal, state, or local government report about an important issue such as crime, education, or immigration. Analyze the organiza-

tional structure of the report, and write a memo to your instructor answering the following questions:

a. What is the purpose of the report?

b. Who is the intended audience?

c. Were the findings organized according to time, location, importance, or criteria? How does the choice of organizational basis relate to the purpose of the report?

d. Does the report use the indirect or direct organizational plan?

e. List the main conclusion(s) and indicate where in the report this information was presented.

f. List the recommendation(s) and indicate where in the report this information was presented.

g. Prepare an outline of the report. Are all headings in the report parallel? If not, suggest appropriate changes.

4. Report Section—Secondary Statistical Data Furnished   You are the vice president of marketing for Excelsior, a small manufacturer located in Asheboro, North Carolina. Although your firm manufactures consumer products such as toothpaste, plastic food wrap, and floor wax, you have the capability of manufacturing numerous different types of small, inexpensive products. The CEO of your firm has asked you to prepare an extensive report on the feasibility of Excelsior's entering the international market.

One strategy that you're considering is the possibility of becoming a supplier for a large multinational company. As part of your research, you have located data on the world's 100 largest public companies (see Figure 12.5). You are interested, first, in the nonbanking firms in this group that have the largest sales, and second, in the percentage change in sales from the previous year. (You are not interested in market value and profit data because they are too much affected by extraneous market conditions that are irrelevant to your purposes, and you are not interested in banks, mortgage companies, and holding companies because they would not be potential purchasers of your products.)

Compose the section of your report that presents and discusses this data. Include a table of the 25 largest firms (in terms of 1995 sales) that meet your criteria. Discuss the data in terms of the largest companies, their countries of origin, changes in sales from the previous year, and similar factors. Format the section in appropriate report format (beginning with page 5 of your report), provide an effective heading for this section, a topic sentence, summary, and transition to the next section, which discusses the largest companies in terms of the major products they sell.

5. Supplementary Sections—Going International   Resume the role of vice president of marketing for Excelsior (see Exercise 4 above). Your report to Victor Trillingham, Excelsior's CEO, needs several supplementary sections.

a. Assuming that the report will be submitted tomorrow, prepare a title page.

b. Using the data you analyzed in Exercise 4, draw conclusions and make recommendations. Then write a transmittal memo to accompany this report. Include brief statements of your conclusions and recommendations.

c. Decide whether you need an appendix; if so, note what it should contain.

6. Short Memorandum Report—New Analysis   Excelsior's CEO has read your report (see Exercise 5 above). He would like the data on the 25 companies you identified as potential purchasers analyzed from a different perspective: he wants you to group the companies according to the country in which they are based. Put the data into a

FIGURE 12.5 The World's 100 Largest Public Companies

Ranked by market value as of July 31, 1996, as determined by Morgan Stanley Capital International Perspective

(In millions of U.S. dollars; financial data at Dec. 31, 1995; exchange rates; percentage changes based on home currencies)

RANK 1996	RANK 1995	COMPANY (COUNTRY)	MARKET VALUE	FISCAL 1995 SALES*	PERCENT CHANGE FROM 1994	FISCAL 1995 PROFIT	PERCENT CHANGE FROM 1994
1	3	General Electric (U.S.)	$136,515	$70,028	17%	$6,573	11%
2	2	Royal Dutch/Shell (Netherlands/U.K.)	128,206	108,050	12	6,792	7
3	6	CocaCola (U.S.)	117,258	18,018	11	2,986	17
4	1	NTT (Japan)	113,609	68,247	5	740	53
5	4	Exxon (U.S.)	102,161	107,893	8	6,470	27
6	10	Bank of Tokyo-Mitsubishi (Japan)	98,191	498,803	3	245	47
7	7	Toyota Motor (Japan)	91,519	78,726[1]	N.A.	1,279	N.A.
8	17	Philip Morris (U.S.)	86,424	53,139	–1	5,478	16
9	5	AT&T (U.S.)	83,960	79,609	6	5,519	13
10	13	Merck (U.S.)	78,163	16,681	11	3,335	11
11	11	Roche Holding (Switzerland)	71,078	12,794	0	2,931	18
12	20	Microsoft (U.S.)	70,519	5,937	28	1,453	27
13	22	Johnson & Johnson (U.S.)	63,628	18,842	20	2,403	20
14	19	Intel (U.S.)	61,783	16,202	41	3,566	29
15	21	Procter & Gamble (U.S.)	61,219	33,434	10	2,645	20
16	14	IBM (U.S.)	58,015	71,940	12	6,018	103
17	12	Sumitomo Bank (Japan)	57,685	516,828	–2	–2,751	N.A.[2]
18	8	Fuji Bank (Japan)	57,016	517,951	–3	45	–86
19	16	Wal-Mart Stores (U.S.)	55,045	82,494	22	2,681	15
20	18	Dai-Ichi Kangyo Bank (Japan)	52,633	524,465	4	272	141
21	9	Industrial Bank of Japan (Japan)	50,896	396,086	–4	288	36
22	25	British Petroleum (U.K.)	50,807	56,056	9	3,127	31
23	15	Sanwa Bank (Japan)	50,567	504,292	–3	217	–51
24	35	PepsiCo (U.S.)	50,068	30,421	7	1,606	–10
25	26	Glaxo Wellcome (U.K.)	48,801	16,286[3]	N.A.	3,793	N.A.
26	41	DuPont (U.S.)	45,259	36,508	7	3,293	21
27	28	Nestle (Switzerland)	45,023	49,089	–1	2,536	N.A.
28	30	Hewlett-Packard (U.S.)	44,871	31,519	26	2,433	52
29	48	Pfizer (U.S.)	44,723	10,021	26	1,554	22
30	38	American International Group (U.S.)	44,548	25,874[4]	16	2,510	15
31	42	Bristol-Myers Squibb (U.S.)	43,563	13,767	15	2,600	12
32	32	Mobil (U.S.)	43,477	64,713	10	2,846	62
33	37	HSBC Holdings (U.K.)	43,058	352,146	13	3,822	20
34	60	Sandoz (Switzerland)	42,250	13,248	–4	1,790	19
35	24	Allianz Holding (Germany)	40,946	42,240[5]	9	1,058	–58
36	45	BellSouth (U.S.)	40,762	17,886	6	1,564	–28
37	44	GTE (U.S.)	40,047	19,957	2	2,538	11
38	68	Citicorp (U.S.)	39,288	256,853	3	3,464	1
39	60	Walt Disney (U.S.)	38,617	18,908	17	988	3
40	34	Unilever (Netherlands/U.K.)	38,429	49,720	–3	2,324	–14
41	52	Ford Motor (U.S.)	38,027	137,137	7	4,139	–28
42	47	Chevron (U.S.)	37,772	31,322	3	1,962	17
43	51	Singapore Telecommunications (Singapore)	37,340	2,486	10	937	10
44	36	General Motors (U.S.)	36,863	160,273	8	5,972	23
45	43	Matsushita Electric Industrial (Japan)	36,672	67,356	5	877	270
46	—	ENI (Italy)	35,923	35,299	10	2,727	35
47	70	American Home Products (U.S.)	35,905	13,376	N.A.	1,482	N.A.
48	31	British Telecom (U.K.)	35,290	21,565	2	2,687	–2
49	64	Federal National Mortgage (U.S.)	34,671	316,550	16	2,156	1
50	49	Abbott Laboratories (U.S.)	34,414	10,012	9	1,689	11
51	33	Nomura Securities (Japan)	$34,395	$104,337	7%	$ –177	N.A.[2]
52	84	Ciba-Geigy (Switzerland)	34,387	17,989	– 6	1,874	13%
53	29	Tokyo Electric Power (Japan)	34,352	48,495	N.A.	839	N.A.
54	27	Sakura Bank (Japan)	33,517	484,606	– 7	217	– 2
55	46	Amoco (U.S.)	33,226	27,066	4	2,159	25
56	—	Cisco Systems (U.S.)	32,663	1,979	59	421	34
57	58	McDonald's (U.S.)	32,428	9,795	18	1,427	17
58	23	Motorola (U.S.)	32,000	27,037	22	1,781	14
59	77	Eli Lilly (U.S.)	30,941	6,764	18	1,307	10
60	59	Ameritech (U.S.)	30,714	13,428	7	1,966	17
61	78	Boeing (U.S.)	30,629	19,515	– 11	783	– 9
62	39	Hitachi (Japan)	30,375	73,601	3	1,104	67
63	—	Chase Manhattan (U.S.)	30,249	303,989	77	2,970	19
64	54	SBC Communications (U.S.)	29,773	12,670	9	1,889	15
65	53	Siemens (Germany)	29,537	62,016	5	1,296	30
66	71	Smithkline Beecham Group (U.K.)	29,254	10,885	8	1,436	7
67	92	BankAmerica (U.S.)	28,990	232,446	8	2,664	22
68	69	Mitsubishi Heavy Industries (Japan)	28,599	27,614	2	755	– 2
69	—	Gillette (U.S.)	28,365	6,795	12	824	18
70	—	Lloyds TSB Group (U.K.)	27,831	204,548	80	2,011	N.A.[2]
71	67	Daimler-Benz (Germany)	27,334	72,346	– 1	–3,713	18
72	72	Minnesota Mining & Mfg. (U.S.)	27,211	13,460	– 11	1,306	8
73	56	Seven-Eleven (Japan)	26,417	13,497[6]	9	480[6]	6
74	—	Oracle (U.S.)	26,233	2,967	48	442	56
75	57	Asahi Bank (Japan)	25,903	272,115	4	176	– 12
76	55	Broken Hill Proprietary (Australia)	25,897	13,195	7	1,203	26
77	66	Bell Atlantic (U.S.)	25,878	13,430	– 3	1,699	21
78	—	NationsBank (U.S.)	25,755	187,298	10	1,950	15
79	—	Electronic Data Systems (U.S.)	25,621	12,246	N.A.	795	N.A.
80	86	Astra (Sweden)	25,613	5,402	28	1,322	29
81	62	Tokai Bank (Japan)	25,519	314,728	– 4	45	– 86
82	99	Eastman Kodak (U.S.)	25,342	14,980	10	1,252	N.A.
83	74	Deutsche Bank (Germany)	25,301	480,082	20	1,485	59
84	63	Schweiz Bankgesellschaft (Switzerland)	25,083	336,144	19	1,454	4
85	91	Veba (Germany)	24,843	46,338	7	1,338	40
86	61	B.A.T. Industries (U.K.)	24,246	23,131	22	2,379	22
87	85	Home Depot (U.S.)	24,121	12,477	35	605	32
88	76	Ito-Yokado (Japan)	24,010	27,908	0	691	21
89	—	Bayer (Germany)	23,708	31,147	3	1,673	22
90	88	Sony (Japan)	23,666	33,616	8	–2,844	N.A.[2]
91	—	Lucent Technologies (U.S.)	23,556	21,413	8	962	100
92	47	Honda Motor (Japan)	23,553	38,449	3	596	160
93	—	ING Groep (Netherlands)	23,441	247,194	10	1,624	15
94	94	Seibu Railway (Japan)	22,939	5,342	5	– 22	N.A.[2]
95	75	Nippon Steel (Japan)	22,918	27,930	5	–38	N.A.[2]
96	82	Columbia/HCA Healthcare (U.S.)	22,814	17,695	22	1,299	26
97	—	Sun Hung Kai Properties (Hong Kong)	22,557	2,567	12	1,340	18
98	65	Texaco USA (U.S.)	22,456	36,787	10	1,367	40
99	—	Kansai Electric Power (Japan)	22,374	24,638	N.A.	427	N.A.
100	—	Wells Fargo (U.S.)	22,333	116,061	117	1,549	N.A.

*Net premiums written are used instead of sales for insurance companies, except where otherwise specified. Assets are used instead of sales for other financial companies and are calculated without contingent liabilities and Treasury stock items.

[1]Fiscal year change from June 30 to March 31. 1995 results for 9 months [2]Results to 1995 and/or 1994 are losses [3]Fiscal year change from June 30 to December 31;

[1]1995 results are for 18 months [2]1995 results for 9 months [4]American International Group sales shown equal reported total revenue; net premiums earned totaled $19.44 million (+14%) [5]Sales shown for Allianz and Assicurazioni Generali equal net premiums earned only [6]Based on nonconsolidated results

NA = Not available

NOTE: Rank calculated for Royal Dutch/Shell Group by combining market value of Netherland's Royal Dutch Petroleum and Britain's Shell Transport & Trading. Rank calculated for Unilever by combining market value of Netherland's Unilever NV and Britain's Unilever PLC. Sales and profits are for combined companies.

Source: Reprinted by permission of The Wall Street Journal. ©1996 Dow Jones & Company, Inc. All Rights Reserved Worldwide.

table and, from your findings, draw conclusions about the geographic concentration of prospects. Write a brief memorandum report to the CEO; include your table and your conclusion.

7. **Secondary Data—International Competition**   Excelsior CEO Victor Trillingham (see Exercises 4, 5, and 6) is concerned about the international activities of Nestlé, which competes with Excelsior in the United States and would be a formidable rival in international markets. Conduct secondary research on the Internet to uncover the answers to Trillingham's questions (see p. 406).
   a.   In how many countries does Nestlé sell its products? List the countries.
   b.   What percentage of Nestlé's overall sales are made outside the United States?
   c.   What companies (if any) has Nestlé acquired during the past 12 months?
   d.   What major new consumer products has Nestlé introduced in the United States during the past 12 months?

   Using talking headings, outline an informational report in manuscript format to present your findings. Prepare visual aids to convey the answers to Questions 7a and b. Include a reference list of secondary sources used in your research. Then draft a transmittal memorandum to Trillingham (assume that the report will be submitted next Monday).

8. **Report Section—Document Design**   Reformat the report section shown on page 400 to incorporate the elements of document design discussed in this chapter. You may edit the report as needed, as long as you do not change the basic information.

9. **Short Formal Report—Primary and Secondary Statistical Data Furnished**   North Star is a producer of consumer products with annual sales of $847.2 million. It has 4.5% of the consumer market for its six consumer products (soap, deodorant, ammonia, chili, canned ham, and frozen vegetables).

   On July 8 of this year, Paul Gettisfield, sales manager, asked you, a product manager, to study the feasibility of North Star's entering the generic-products market. Generic products are products that do not have brand names but instead carry a plain generic label, such as "Paper Towels." Generic products are typically not advertised; they involve less packaging, less processing, and cheaper ingredients than brand names; and they compete both with private brands (those distributed solely by individual store chains such as A&P and Kroger) and with national brands (those available for sale at all grocery stores and advertised nationally). At the present time, North Star produces only national brands.

   Paul specifically asked you *not* to explore whether North Star had the necessary plant capacity. He wanted you only to provide up-to-date information on the generic market in general and to explore likely consumer acceptance of generic brands for the products North Star produces. He is quite interested in learning the results of your research.

   In August you conducted a mail survey of 1,500 consumers in the three states (California, Texas, and Arizona) that constitute your largest market. Responses were received from 832 consumers to the following questions; responses are provided for all 832 consumers and for the 237 largest consumers (those who indicated that they did 51% to 100% of their household shopping):

   > Have you purchased a food generic product (such as canned fruit or vegetables) in the last month?
   >   All consumers: 36% yes, 64% no
   >   Largest consumers: 29% yes, 71% no

Was this the first time you had purchased a food generic product?
All consumers: 18% yes, 82% no
Largest consumers: 20% yes, 80% no

Have you purchased a nonfood generic product (such as paper towels or soap) in the last month?
All consumers: 60% yes, 40% no
Largest consumers: 59% yes, 41% no

Was this the first time you had purchased a nonfood generic product?
All consumers: 5% yes, 95% no
Largest consumers: 7% yes, 93% no

If you could save at least 30% by purchasing a generic brand rather than a national brand, would you purchase a generic brand of any of the following products?
Bar of soap: 43% yes, 57% no, 0% don't use this product
Deodorant: 31% yes, 67% no, 2% don't use this product
Ammonia: 80% yes, 10% no, 10% don't use this product
Chili: 34% yes, 52% no, 14% don't use this product
Canned ham: 19% yes, 44% no, 37% don't use this product
Frozen vegetables: 54% yes, 30% no, 16% don't use this product

You also asked the local North Star sales representatives to audit 20 randomly selected chain supermarkets in each of these three states in August. Personal observation showed that 39 of the stores stocked generic brands, 37 of these 39 stocked 100 or more generic items, and 15 had separate generic-product sections. All but 3 of the 60 stores stocked all six products that North Star produces.

In gathering your data, you also made the following notes from three secondary sources:

1. *Hammond's Market Reports*, Gary, IN, 1998, pp. 1027–1030: This annual index lists various information for more than 2,000 consumer products. The percentages of market share for the six products North Star produces are as follows:

	1990	1994	1998
Generic brands	1.5%	2.6%	7.3%
Private labels	31.6%	30.7%	27.8%
National brands	66.9%	66.7%	64.9%

2. H. R. Nolan, "No-Name Brands: An Update," *Supermarket Management*, April 1997, pp. 31–37.

   a. Generic brands are typically priced 30% to 50% below national brands. (p. 31)
   b. Consumers require a 36% saving on a bar of soap and 40% savings on deodorant to motivate them to switch to a generic. (p. 32)
   c. Consumer awareness of generics has tripled since 1978. (p. 33)
   d. "The easiest way to become a no-name store is to ignore no-name brands." (direct quotation from p. 33)
   e. Many leading brand manufacturers feel compelled to produce the lower-profit generic brands because either the market has grown too

big to ignore or the inroads generic brands have made on their own brands have left them with idle capacity. (p. 35)

3. Edward J. Rauch and Pamela G. McCleary, "National Brands to Play a Bit Part in the Future," *Grocery Business*, Fall 1996, pp. 118–120.

    a. Eight out of ten food-chain officers believe their costs will rise more than their prices this year. (p. 118)

    b. Generics are now available in 84% of the stores nationwide and account for about 4% of the store space. (p. 118)

    c. "Supermarket executives foresee a drop in shelf space allocated to brand products and an increase in the space allocated to generics and private labels. Many experts predict that supermarkets will ultimately carry no more than the top two brands in a category plus a private label and a generic label." (direct quotation from p. 119)

    d. Today, 37% of the grocery stores have switched from paper bags to the less expensive plastic bags for packaging customer purchases, even though the plastic bags are nonbiodegradable. (p. 119)

    e. Starting from nearly zero in 1977, generics have acquired 7% of the $275 billion grocery market. Many observers predict they will go up to 25% by the turn of the century. (p. 120)

Analyze the data, prepare whatever visual aids would be helpful, and then write a formal report for Gettisfield. Include any supplementary report pages you think would be helpful.

10. Memorandum Report—Primary Statistical Data Furnished   You are a systems analyst, reporting to Hilda Brandt, vice president of information services at General Resources, Inc. The executive vice president of GRI has asked Brandt to develop a style and procedures manual for all internally produced office documents.

In preparation for this task, Brandt has asked you to analyze the documents prepared at GRI offices to determine the kinds of documents typed, the input source for these documents, the amount of time required to type each document, and the number of copies made of each. She then asked you to prepare an informal memorandum report, summarizing your findings.

For a period of one week, you asked a random sample of 100 office workers to make an extra copy of the first item they typed at their computers after 9 A.M., 11 A.M., and 2 P.M. each day and to complete a short form answering several questions about the document. A total of 531 documents were submitted for analysis—173 letters, 77 memos, 21 reports, 222 forms, and 18 miscellaneous other items.

Analyze the data contained in Figure 12.6, prepare whatever visual aids would be helpful (keep them simple for this memo report), and then write the requested analytical report.

11. Short Memorandum Report—Nonstatistical Data Furnished   You are the research assistant for Congresswoman Anna Murray. A constituent has written her asking that she introduce legislation to ban telephone call identification. Congresswoman Murray sent you the letter with this handwritten message attached: "I really don't know much about this telephone service. Please research it and prepare a short informal report (no tables, charts, or footnotes, please) so that I can make an informed decision about this matter. Should I or should I not introduce legislation to ban this type of telephone service?"

FIGURE 12.6 **Analysis of GRI Documents**

Origin of Typing Tasks, Classified by Kind of Item

Origin		Forms	Letters	Memos	Reports	Tables	Other	Totals
		Kind of Item						
Handwritten— not on same form	No. %	66 29.7%	44 25.4%	17 22.1%	8 38.1%	12 60.0%	9 50.0%	156 29.4%
Handwritten— on same form	No. %	56 25.2%	2 1.2%	4 5.2%		3 15.0%		65 12.2%
Typed and handwritten	No. %	16 7.2%	15 8.7%	7 9.1%	3 14.3%	2 10.0%	3 16.7%	46 8.7%
All typed	No. %	21 9.5%	35 20.2%	15 19.5%	6 28.6%		4 22.2%	81 15.3%
Shorthand dictation	No. %	4 1.8%	36 20.8%	16 20.8%	1 4.8%			57 10.7%
Machine dictation	No. %	3 1.4%	8 4.6%	12 15.6%	3 14.3%			26 4.9%
Self-composed	No. %	29 13.1%	33 19.1%	6 7.8%			2 11.1%	70 13.2%
Other	No. %	27 12.2%				3 15.0%		30 5.6%
Totals	No. %	222 41.8%	173 32.6%	77 14.5%	21 4.0%	20 3.8%	18 3.4%	531 100.0%

Amount of Time Required by Office Workers to Type Items, Classified by Kind of Item

Minutes required		Forms	Letters	Memos	Reports	Tables	Other	Totals
		Kind of Item						
Less than 5	No. %	144 64.9%	72 41.6%	40 51.9%	2 9.5%		4 22.2%	262 49.3%
5–9	No. %	37 16.7%	77 44.5%	17 22.1%	4 19.0%	9 45.0%	5 27.8%	149 28.1%
10 or more	No. %	41 18.5%	24 13.9%	20 26.0%	15 71.4%	11 55.0%	9 50.0%	120 22.6%
Totals	No. %	222 41.8%	173 32.6%	77 14.5%	21 4.0%	20 3.8%	18 3.4%	531 100.0%

You've talked to numerous people at the telephone company and have read brochures, magazine articles, and editorials about this topic. You've jotted down the following notes—in no particular order:

a. Automatic number identification (ANI): A telephone service that displays the phone number of the person calling you.

b. You can use ANI to decide which calls you want to answer and simply ignore the others.

c. It can threaten the privacy and personal safety of users.

FIGURE 12.6   (Continued)

Number of Copies of Typed Items Required (Including Original), Classified by Kind of Item								
Number of copies (including original)		**Kind of Item**						
		Forms	**Letters**	**Memos**	**Reports**	**Tables**	**Other**	**Totals**
1 (original only)	No.	27	9	5	1	2	4	48
	%	12.2%	5.2%	6.5%	4.8%	10.0%	22.2%	9.0%
2	No.	35	88	15	5	6		149
	%	15.8%	50.9%	19.5%	23.8%	30.0%		28.1%
3–4	No.	82	56	22	4	1	6	171
	%	36.9%	32.4%	28.6%	19.0%	5.0%	33.3%	32.2%
5 or more	No.	78	20	35	11	11	8	163
	%	35.1%	11.6%	45.5%	52.4%	55.0%	44.4%	30.7%
Totals	No.	222	173	77	21	20	18	531
	%	41.8%	32.6%	14.5%	4.0%	3.8%	3.4%	100.0%

d. Every caller's number would be displayed—even those with unpublished numbers who have paid extra for their privacy.

e. Delivery businesses (taxis and pizzerias, for example) can use ANI to ensure that telephone orders are legitimate.

f. The device that displays the callers' numbers costs up to $80.

g. Emergency services can use the number to dispatch help quickly for people who may be too panicky to give an address.

h. Customer service agents at your local utility or your stockbroker can immediately call up your file when you call to serve you more efficiently. A computer can even be programmed to do this automatically as soon as your call goes through.

i. ANI allows businesses to record the number of every caller—and perhaps even to sell your number to telemarketers.

j. New Jersey Bell Telephone Co. began the service after learning that a whopping 1.2 million of their customers had received threatening or obscene calls.

k. If you receive a threatening, obscene, or harassing call, you can record the number to notify the police or phone company without their having to tap your phone. (You can even call the person back yourself, although that might not be wise.)

l. People who make calls from their homes may have legitimate reasons for not wanting their private numbers revealed—law enforcement officers, doctors, psychiatrists, or social workers, for example.

m. New Jersey Bell reported that phone-trace requests in Hudson County dropped 49% after ANI was established—even though only 2.3% of its customers used it.

n. It's now available in a growing number of states.

o. You can even program ANI to prevent your phone from receiving calls from a specified number, thus preventing harassers from repeatedly calling your number from the same phone.

p. Runaway children might be scared to call home for fear of being traced.

q. Only a few states require a feature that lets callers prevent their numbers from being displayed (which defeats the whole purpose of the service).

r. New Jersey Bell says complaints about obscene or harassing phone calls have dropped nearly 50% since it began offering ANI.

s. You can refuse to answer telephone sales pitches that come in the middle of dinner.

t. It threatens the privacy of individuals who call suicide-prevention, drug-treatment, AIDS, and abortion-counseling hotlines.

u. It took 23 years to catch and convict Bobby Gene Stice, who used the telephone for two decades to terrorize thousands of California women. ANI could have stopped him in a day.

v. The service charge for the ANI feature is as much as $8.50 monthly.

Organize and analyze the data, and then write the requested recommendation report. Use whatever report headings would be helpful.

12. **Work-Team Communication—Long Formal Report Requiring Additional Research**
Assume that your group of four has been asked by Jim Miller, executive vice president of Jefferson Industries, to write an exploratory report on the feasibility of Jefferson's opening a frozen yogurt store in Akron, Ohio. If the preliminary data your group gathers warrants further exploration of this project, a professional venture-consultant group will be hired to conduct an in-depth, "dollars-and-cents" study. Your job, then, is to recommend whether such an expensive follow-up study is warranted. Assume that Jefferson has the financial resources to support such a venture if it looks promising.

You can immediately think of several areas you'll want to explore: the general market outlook for frozen yogurt stores, the demographic makeup of Akron (home of the University of Akron), the local economic climate, franchise opportunities in the industry, and the like. Undoubtedly, other topics (or criteria) will surface as you brainstorm the problem.

Working as a group, carry through the entire research process for this project—planning the study, collecting the data, organizing and analyzing the data, and writing the report. (*Note:* If you gathered any data by completing the exercises at the end of Chapter 11, integrate that data into your study as needed.)

Write the body of the report using formal language, organize the study by criteria, and place the conclusions and recommendations at the end. Include a title page, transmittal memo (addressed to James H. Miller), executive summary, table of contents, and reference list (use the author-date method of citation).

Regardless of how your group decides to divide up the work, everyone should review and comment on the draft of the final report. If different members write different parts, edit as needed to ensure that the report reads smoothly and coherently.

Note: For Exercises 13–17 follow the desires of your instructor (the audience) in terms of length, format, degree of formality, number of report parts, and the like.

13. **Secondary Data—Electronic Communications** You are a technical specialist for a small pharmaceutical firm located in Bayamon, Puerto Rico. Chris Rice, director of information services, is exploring the feasibility of various ways of connecting your employees to the Internet. She has asked you to prepare a background report on this topic. You know, for example, that you can connect via modem, satellite, and ISDN line. Are there other ways? What are the advantages and disadvantages of

each? How much will each cost? Since this is a background information report, you will not make any recommendations regarding which alternative your organization should choose.

14. **Secondary Data—The Female Manager**   Using the appropriate business indexes (print or computer), identify three women who are presidents or CEOs of companies listed on the New York Stock Exchange. Provide information on their backgrounds. Did they make it to the top by rising through the ranks, by starting the firm, by taking over from another family member, or in some other manner?

Analyze the effectiveness of these three individuals. How profitable are the firms they head in relation to others in the industry? Are their firms more or less profitable now than when they assumed the top job? Finally, try to uncover data regarding their management styles—how they see their role, how they relate to their employees, problems they've experienced, and the like.

From your study of these three individuals, are there any valid conclusions you can draw? Write a report objectively presenting and analyzing the information you've gathered.

15. **Secondary Data—Keyboarding Skills**   You are the director of training for an aerospace firm located in Seattle, Washington. Your superior, Charles R. Underwood, personnel manager, is concerned that so many of the firm's 2,000 white-collar employees use their computers for hours a day but still do not know how to touch-keyboard. He believes the hunt-and-peck method is inefficient and increases the possibility of making errors when inputting data, thus lowering its reliability.

He has asked you to recommend a software program that teaches the user how to type. He is specifically interested in a program that is IBM-compatible, is geared to adults, is educationally sound, and can be learned on an individual basis without an instructor present.

Identify and evaluate three to five keyboarding software programs that meet these criteria, and write a report recommending the best one to Underwood. Justify your choice.

16. **Primary Data—Career Choices**   Explore a career position in which you are interested. Determine the job outlook, present level of employment, salary trends, typical duties, working conditions, educational or experience requirements, and the like. If possible, interview someone holding this position to gain firsthand impressions. Then write up your findings in a report to your instructor. Include at least five secondary sources and at least one table or visual aid in your report.

17. **Primary Data—Intercultural Dimensions**   To what extent does network and cable television accurately portray members of cultural, ethnic, and racial minorities? To what extent are they portrayed at all during prime time (8 P.M. to 11 P.M.)? In what types of roles are they shown, and what is their relationship with nonminority characters? As assistant to the director of public relations of the National Minority Alliance, you are interested in such questions.

Locate and review at least three journal articles on this topic. Then develop a definition of the term *minority*. Randomly select and view at least ten prime-time television shows, and develop a form for recording the needed data on minority representation in these shows. As part of your research, compare the proportion of minority members in this country with their representation on prime-time television. Integrate your primary and secondary data into a report. Use objective language, being careful to present ample data to support any conclusions or recommendations you may make.

18. Primary Data—Student Living Arrangements   Darlene Anderson, a real estate developer and president of Anderson and Associates, is exploring the feasibility of building a large student-apartment complex on a lot her firm owns two blocks from campus. Even though the city planning commission believes there is already enough student housing, Anderson thinks she can succeed if she addresses specific problems of present housing. She has asked you, her executive assistant, to survey students to determine their views of off-campus living. Specifically, she wants you to develop a ranked listing of the most important attributes of student housing. How important to students are such criteria as price, location (access to campus, shopping, public transportation, and the like), space and layout, furnishings (furnished versus unfurnished), social activities, parking, pets policy, and the like?

In addition, the architect has drawn a plan that features the following options: private hotel-like rooms (sleeping and sitting area and private bath but no kitchen); private one-room efficiency apartments; one-bedroom two-person apartments; and four-bedroom four-person apartments. Which of these arrangements would students most likely rent, given their present economic situation? Would another alternative be more appealing to them?

Develop a questionnaire and administer it to a sample of students. Then analyze the data and write a report for Anderson.

**CONTINUING
CASE 12**

Reporting—A Pain in the Wrist

Review the Continuing Case account at the end of Chapter 11, in which Jean Tate asked Pat Robbins to write a report on carpal tunnel syndrome, a neuromuscular wrist ailment caused by repeated hand motions as in typing.

Now, administer the questionnaire you developed in Chapter 11 to a sample of at least 50 clerical workers at your institution, where you work, or at some other office. For the purposes of this assignment, assume that the responses you receive were actually those from Urban Systems clerical workers. Then analyze the questionnaire data carefully. Construct whatever tables and charts would be helpful to the reader.

Critical Thinking

1. Considering the findings from your questionnaire and the secondary sources you checked, what does all this information mean in terms of your problem statement?

2. For each subproblem you specified (see Chapter 11), what conclusion can you draw? In view of each of these individual conclusions, what overall conclusion is merited? In view of your individual and overall conclusions, what recommendations are appropriate?

Writing Project

3. Prepare a recommendation report in manuscript format for Tate. Use formal language for the body of the report, organize the study by criteria, and place the conclusions and recommendations at the end. Include a title page, transmittal memo, executive summary, table of contents, abstract, appendix (copy of the questionnaire), and reference list (use the author-date method of citation).

PART FIVE

Oral and Employment Communication

13 Business Presentations

COMMUNICATION OBJECTIVES

After you have finished this chapter, you should be able to

- Describe the important role that business presentations play in the organization.

- Plan a presentation by determining its purpose, analyzing the audience, and determining the timing and method of delivery.

- Write a presentation by collecting the data and organizing it in a logical format.

- Develop effective visual aids for a presentation.

- Practice a presentation to develop an effective speaking style.

- Deliver a presentation in a clear, confident, and efficient manner.

- Plan and deliver a team presentation.

An Insider's Perspective

David Hancock wants to add a cruise vacation to every traveler's itinerary. As Director of Field Sales for Royal Caribbean Cruises, Hancock works with 87 district sales managers and 20 telemarketing representatives who provide travel agents with the information they need to sell Royal Caribbean cruises. From three-day cruises to extended 14-day trips, more than 1 million passengers annually set sail on Royal Caribbean ships to the Caribbean, the Bahamas, Bermuda, Alaska, Mexico, Europe, or the Far East. Because 98% of the cruise line's business comes through travel agents, effective communication with this audience is critical.

A week or two before Hancock is scheduled to speak to a travel agent group, he sets aside time to analyze the audience and plan the presentation. "By finding out about the size of the audience, their level of knowledge, and their objectives, I can tailor my presentation to fit their needs," he says. Even when he is planning to cover much the same information that he has included in talks to other groups, Hancock is careful to adjust the content for each audience's interests.

In addition, by analyzing his audience, he can determine whether industry-specific terms will be understood. "When I used to talk about an 'outside cabin,' there was a chance that some people in the audience might think the cabin was literally outside on the deck somewhere," Hancock notes. "So if people in the audience don't know much about my topic, I bring it down to their level by using everyday language." As a result, he now uses the term 'ocean-view cabin' to describe a cabin with a porthole, picture window, or balcony.

The way Hancock handles questions depends on the size of the audience. When he speaks to large groups, he invites questions only at the end, which helps him stay on schedule and avoid interrupting the flow of the talk. However, when addressing a smaller audience, he will often take questions at any time during the presentation. He prepares in advance for audience questions by sitting down with colleagues to "do a bit of role playing and see if we can come up with questions that we're not used to answering."

Hancock uses slides, overhead transparencies, or electronic slide presentations when he addresses a group, although he prefers electronic slide presentations because he can quickly and easily make changes. Depending on the audience and the purpose of the presentation, some of his slides will show key points in bullet form, while others will show graphics or photos. Pictures of the ships, the facilities, and the destinations are especially useful when Hancock wants to describe the experience to people who have never taken cruises. In his experience, visual aids don't just convey information, they also reinforce it. "When the audience can see a visual aid and hear me talk about it at the same time, retention levels are better," he says.

Specialized visual aids can allow the audience to experience what words can only hint at. For example, Royal Caribbean has been expanding its offerings of three- and four-day cruises and adding optional land packages at resort hotels, targeting first-time cruisers and vacationers who want a quick getaway. To encourage travel agents to sell these packages, Hancock has been talking to industry groups all around the United States. During a recent presentation to 800 travel agents, he showed slides and

then stepped aside for a live performance of the Royal Caribbean Corporate Theater dancers. "We wanted to demonstrate the professional quality of our entertainment with a high-impact, memorable presentation," he says. The audience got the message—and Royal Caribbean's ships are now busier than ever.

David Hancock

Director of Field Sales
Royal Caribbean Cruises
(Miami, Florida)

The Role of Business Presentations

Almost everyone in business is required to give a presentation occasionally.

Anyone who plans a career in sales, training, or education expects to make many oral presentations to customers, employees, or students each week. What you may not realize, though, is that just about *everyone* in business will probably give at least one major presentation and many smaller ones each year, to customers, superiors, subordinates, or colleagues—not to mention presentations at PTA meetings, home-owners' association meetings, civic clubs, and the like.

The costs of ineffective presentations are immense. With many executives earning $100,000 or more a year, a presentation that discusses ideas incompletely and inefficiently wastes time and money. Sales are lost, vital information is not communicated, training programs fail, policies are not implemented, and profits fall.

Written Versus Oral Presentations

Written reports and oral presentations both play important roles in helping an organization achieve its objectives. An oral presentation may be made either in conjunction with or in place of a written report. Effective communicators must recognize the advantages and disadvantages of presenting business information orally.[1]

Oral presentations provide immediate feedback, allow speaker control, and require little work of the audience.

Advantages of Oral Presentations   Probably the most important advantage of oral presentations is the *immediate feedback* that is possible from the audience. Questions can be answered and decisions can be made on the spot. In addition, the speaker can pick up cues from the audience regarding how well they understand and agree with his or her points and then can adjust content and delivery accordingly.

A second advantage concerns *speaker control.* A written report may never even be read, let alone studied carefully. But speakers have a captive audience. They can control the pace of the presentation, question the audience to ensure attention and understanding, and use nonverbal cues such as pauses, gestures, and changes in voice speed and volume to add emphasis. In addition, visual aids used in an oral presentation are often more effective than those used in a written report.

A third advantage of the oral presentation has to do with the listener: presentations are simply *less work for the audience.* Listening is less strenuous and often more enjoyable than reading. The written report presents mostly verbal clues, whereas the oral presentation is filled with a variety of verbal and nonverbal clues to make comprehension easier and more interesting.

Oral presentations do not provide a permanent record and often are very expensive.

Disadvantages of Oral Presentations   Considering the advantages of immediate feedback, speaker control, and reduced audience effort, why isn't *all* business information communicated orally? The major reason is that oral presentations are *impermanent.* They "disappear," and within hours of delivery much of the information presented has been forgotten. Also, listeners have only one opportunity to understand what they're hearing. In contrast, the written report provides a permanent record that can be reread and referred to in the future.

Oral presentations may also be very *expensive.* It is much more cost-effective to have 1,000 managers scattered around the country read a written report than to have them hear the same information in a mass meeting. In addition to the expense, the sheer logistics of assembling such a large group can be overpowering. Furthermore, the visual aids used in oral presentations are often more expensive than those used in written reports (which is perhaps one reason that they're also typically more effective). For example, a color slide of a graph or chart costs many times more to produce than a black-and-white paper copy that has been printed directly from the computer.

It's not surprising, then, that many presentations include both an oral and a written component. As a business communicator, you'll need to weigh a number of factors when you decide whether to communicate orally or in writing: the complexity of the material, the size of the audience, your need for immediate feedback, and the cost of the presentation, among others.

The Process of Making a Business Presentation

As you will remember, we followed a specific process when learning to communicate business information in written form; the process consisted of planning, drafting, revising, formatting, and finally proofreading the written document. We follow a similar logical process for making an oral presentation.

The presentation process requires planning, organizing, developing visual aids, practicing, and delivering the presentation.

1. *Planning:* Determining the purpose of the presentation, analyzing the audience, and determining the timing and method of delivery.
2. *Organizing:* Collecting the data and outlining it in a logical order.
3. *Developing visual aids:* Selecting the appropriate type, number, and content of visual aids.
4. *Practicing:* Rehearsing by simulating the actual presentation conditions as closely as possible.
5. *Delivering:* Dressing appropriately, maintaining friendly eye contact, speaking in an effective manner, and answering questions confidently.

Planning the Presentation

When assigned the task of making a business presentation, your first impulse might be to sit down at your desk or computer and begin writing. Resist the temptation. As in written communications, several important steps precede the actual writing. These steps involve determining the purpose of the presentation, analyzing the audience, planning the timing of the presentation, and selecting a delivery method.

In addition to helping you decide what to include in your presentation, these planning tasks will give you important information about the degree of formality appropriate for the situation. The more formal the presentation, the more time you'll devote to the project. In general, complex topics or proposals with "high stakes" demand more formal presentations, with well-planned visuals, a carefully thought-out organizational plan, and extensive research. Likewise, the larger the audience and the greater the audience's opposition to your ideas, the more formal the presentation should be. A presentation you will deliver more than once is likely to be more formal than a one-time speech, as is a presentation on a complex topic. Finally, if the audience is made up of nationals from other countries, you will need to take their needs and expectations into consideration and will probably prepare a more formal presentation (see Spotlight 21—Across Cultures on p. 420).

Purpose

Keeping your purpose uppermost in mind helps you decide what information to include and what to omit, in what order to present this information, and which

Presenting Abroad

Increasingly, managers are being required to make presentations abroad to nationals from other countries. Many of the principles discussed in this chapter hold true; however, those discussed in Chapter 2 regarding international communications also apply. Because each culture is different, we cannot make broad generalizations. The following discussion, then, simply points out some factors you will want to be aware of as you try to make your presentation appropriate for the specific country.

SPOTLIGHT 21

ACROSS CULTURES

Planning the Presentation

Planning the presentation should really begin with deciding *who* should make the presentation. In the Japanese culture, age is highly respected and the credibility of a younger presenter, regardless of his or her expertise or communication skills, may be questioned by an older audience. Similarly, female presenters may experience difficulty in some Middle Eastern countries.

The culture also affects the content and organization of your presentation, and you should adopt a strategy that will help you accomplish your goal. In their book *Managing Cultural Differences,* Harris and Moran recommend the following dual strategy—one that reflects both your culture and the host country's:

1. Describe the problem as understood by both cultures.
2. Analyze the problem from two cultural perspectives.
3. Identify the cause(s) of the problem from both viewpoints.
4. Solve the problem through cooperative strategies.
5. Determine if the solution is working multiculturally.

Well-planned visual aids and printed handouts are especially desirable in helping an audience for whom English is a second language to follow your presentation. The use of examples and frequent pre-view and summary is also helpful. Know the customs and attitudes of your audience. For example, beginning a presentation with a joke, discussing incidents from one's private life, or holding a question-and-answer period might or might not be considered appropriate.

Giving the Presentation

In many cultures, a formal presentation will be expected, with the presenter speaking from a full script and using elaborate visual aids. Some audiences may misinterpret an extemporaneous speech given from notes as implying the speaker didn't respect the audience enough to prepare his or her remarks fully.

Writing out your remarks in full beforehand will also help you plan your choice of words carefully. Restrict your vocabulary to the most common English words and your word meanings to the most common ones. Avoid using jargon and slang in your speech, and also avoid clichés.

Speak slowly and clearly, using short, simple sentences, and keep gestures to a minimum. Do not be surprised if some members of the audience do not look at you directly as you speak. Eye contact is not as important in some cultures as it is to many Americans. If possible, try to include some phrase from the local language in your remarks. When using overhead and slide projectors, the American custom is normally to stand next to the projector, whereas the European custom is to present while seated, with the projector alongside on a low table.

An overall attitude of sensitivity, empathy, respect, and flexibility will help you achieve success in giving presentations—both here and abroad.

Sources: Philip R. Harris and Robert T. Moran, *Managing Cultural Differences,* 2d ed., Gulf Publishing, Houston, 1987; Dona Z. Meilach, "Visually Speaking," *Presentation Products Magazine,* undated supplement, pp. A–L; Robert T. Moran, "Tips on Making Speeches to International Audiences," *International Management,* April 1989, p. 59.

points to emphasize and subordinate. Most business presentations have one of these four purposes:

Most presentations seek either to report, explain, persuade, or motivate.

- *Reporting:* Updating the audience on some project or event.

- *Explaining:* Detailing how to carry out a procedure or how to operate a new piece of equipment.

- *Persuading:* Convincing the listeners to purchase something or to accept an idea you're presenting.

- *Motivating:* Inspiring the listeners to take some action.

Assume, for example, that you have been asked to make a short oral presentation on the topic of absenteeism at the Limerick Generating Station. If you're speaking to the management committee, your purpose would be to *report* the results of your research. Using a logical organization, you would discuss the effects of the problem on productivity, its causes, and possible solutions.

If you're speaking to the union personnel, however, your purpose might be to *motivate* the employees to reduce their absenteeism. You might then briefly discuss the extent of the problem, devote your major efforts to showing how the employees ultimately benefit from lower absenteeism, and finally introduce a monthly recognition program.

After your presentation is over, your purpose provides a criterion—the *only* important criterion—by which to judge the success of your presentation. In other words, did the management committee understand the results of your research? Were the union members motivated to reduce their absenteeism? No matter how well or how poorly you spoke and no matter how impressive or ineffective your visual aids, the important question is whether or not you accomplished your purpose.

Audience Analysis

In addition to identifying such demographic factors as the size, age, and organizational status of your audience, you will also need to determine their level of knowledge about your topic and their psychological needs (values, attitudes, and beliefs). These factors provide clues to everything from the overall content, tone, and types of examples you should use to the types of questions to expect and even the way you should dress.

Analyze the audience in terms of demographics, level of knowledge, and psychological needs.

The principles by which you analyze your audience are the same as those we discussed in the chapters on writing letters, memos, and reports. Consider the effect of your message on your audience and your credibility with them. The key is to put yourself in your audience's place so that you can anticipate their questions and reactions. The "you" attitude applies to oral as well as to written communication.

The larger your audience, the more formal your presentation will be. When you speak to a large group, you should speak more loudly and more slowly and use more emphatic gestures and larger visuals. Usually, you should allow questions only at the end of your talk. If you're speaking to a small group, you can be more flexible about questions, and your tone and gestures will be more like those used in normal conversation. Furthermore, when presenting to small groups, your options in terms of visual aids increase.

Large audiences require a more formal presentation.

If your audience is unfamiliar with your topic, you will need to use clear, easy-to-understand language, with extensive visual aids and many examples. If the audience is more knowledgeable, you can proceed at a faster pace. Suppose, however,

Just about *every* professional can expect to give at least one major presentation and many smaller ones each year. Knowing your audience—their technical expertise, level of interest in the topic, and even their feelings about you, the speaker—is critical to achieving your objectives. Here a physician uses slides to illustrate a lecture on gall bladders to the hospital staff.

that you have an audience composed of both novices and experts. One option, of course, would be to separate the two groups and to give two presentations—each geared to the level of that particular audience.

If the gulf in understanding is not quite that wide, you should determine who the key decision maker is in the group—frequently, but not always, the highest-ranking member present—and then provide a level of detail necessary to secure that person's understanding. Take time especially to understand this decision maker's needs, objectives, and interests as they relate to your objective.

The audience's psychological needs will also affect your presentation. If, for example, you think your listeners will be hostile—either to you personally or to your message—then you'll have to oversell yourself or your idea. Instead of giving one or two examples, you'll need to give several. In addition to establishing your own credibility, you may need to quote other experts to bolster your case.

In the presentation on absenteeism discussed earlier, the first audience was the management committee. They have very high organizational status and probably expect a somewhat formal presentation. Although they may not be very familiar with the specific problem, they are very familiar with the organization overall and are probably quite interested in the bottom-line implications of the problem.

Regarding the second presentation, however, the union members are probably a more heterogeneous group than the management committee. Thus, you must make sure the language and examples used are appropriate for a broad range of knowledge, interests, and attitudes. In addition, you'll probably want to use a more informal, conversational style for the presentation.

Sample overhead transparencies that might be used for each of these two presentations are shown in Figure 13.1.

FIGURE 13.1   The Audience and Purpose Determine the Content

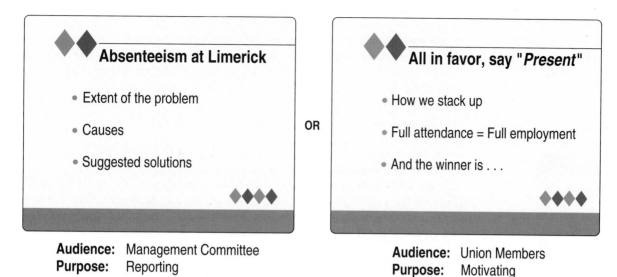

Absenteeism at Limerick	**All in favor, say "*Present*"**
• Extent of the problem	• How we stack up
• Causes	• Full attendance = Full employment
• Suggested solutions	• And the winner is . . .

OR

Audience: Management Committee
Purpose: Reporting

Audience: Union Members
Purpose: Motivating

Once you've identified your audience, it is often helpful to meet with key people before your presentation, especially with the key decision makers. These meetings can help you predispose the audience in your favor or, at the very least, help you discover sources of opposition. Knowing ahead of time about their concerns will let you build relevant information into your presentation to address those concerns.

Timing of the Presentation

Often the timing of a presentation is beyond your control. If you've been asked to update the management committee about the absenteeism problem and the committee typically meets at 2 p.m. the first Tuesday of each month, that is the precise time you must be available. Sometimes, however, you will have some flexibility. For example, if you want to present a proposal for a pet project to several managers whose cooperation is crucial for your success, you will be in charge of scheduling the meeting.

Time the presentation to allow adequate preparation and to avoid rushed periods.

Consider two factors when scheduling presentations. First, allow yourself enough time to prepare—including gathering data, writing and revising, producing visual aids, and practicing the presentation. Second, consider the needs of your audience. Avoid times when they will be away or be so occupied with other matters that they will not be able to concentrate on your presentation. In general, early or midmorning presentations are preferable to late afternoon sessions. Try to avoid giving a presentation immediately before lunch, when the audience may be hungry or eager to make lunch appointments, or, worse, immediately after lunch, when the audience may be late or not very alert.

Delivery Method

At some point during your planning, you must decide on the method of delivery—that is, will you speak without any formal preparation, memorize your speech, read it, or speak from notes? Your choice will be determined by the answers to such questions as, How long is your talk? How complex is the content? How formal is the presentation? And, what method (or combination of methods) are you most comfortable with?

*Anticipate and plan for
situations when you may be
asked to make impromptu
remarks.*

Speaking Impromptu   It is possible, of course, that during the course of a meeting or in conjunction with another person's presentation, you may unexpectedly be asked to come to the podium to "say a few words about" or "bring us up to date on" some topic. In truth, most such situations are not completely unexpected; you can often predict when you may be called on and should prepare accordingly. (Remember the words of Mark Twain: "It takes three weeks to prepare a good impromptu speech.")

If, in fact, you truly have no warning, stay calm. You would not have been called on unless you had something positive to contribute. Remember also that the audience knows you are giving impromptu remarks, so they won't expect the same polish as for a prepared presentation. There is no need to apologize. Keep to the topic, limiting your remarks to those areas in which you do have some expertise or insight, and speak for no more than a few minutes.

*Of the three common
methods of presentation
(memorizing, reading, and
speaking from notes), the last
is the most common for
business presentations.*

Memorizing   Unless a presentation is short and significant, memorizing an entire speech is risky, not to mention time-consuming. You always run the risk (a very real one if you're nervous) of forgetting your lines and thus ruining your entire presentation if you have no notes to fall back on. In addition, memorized presentations often sound mechanical and do not let you adapt the material to the needs of the audience. However, memorizing the first or last section of your presentation, a telling quotation, or a humorous story may be extremely effective for presenting a key part of your talk.

Reading   Reading speeches is quite common in academic settings, where a professor or researcher might be asked to read a paper at a professional conference. Writing out a speech and reading from the prepared text is helpful if you're dealing with a highly complex or technical topic, if the subject is controversial (making a

The marketing managers at Random House publishing company meet weekly to hear informal presentations of sales campaigns for new product introductions. Although informal presentations like these may require less preparation, less practice, and less-elaborate visual aids than a formal "stand-up" presentation, they are no less important in conducting the organization's business.

statement to the press, for example), or if you have a lot of information to present in a short time. Such delivery is *not* recommended for most business settings because the presenter's eyes are typically too much on the paper and not enough on the audience, because spontaneity and flexibility are lost, and because, after all, if the speech is going to be read word for word, why not just duplicate and distribute it to the audience for them to read at their leisure?

Speaking from Notes   By far the most common (and generally the most effective) method for business presentations is speaking from prepared notes, such as an outline. The notes contain key phrases rather than complete sentences, and you compose the exact wording as you speak. Although you may occasionally stumble in choosing a word, the spontaneous, conversational quality and the close audience rapport that result are generally superior to those of other presentation methods. The notes help ensure that you will cover all the material and in a logical order; yet this method provides enough flexibility that you can adapt your remarks in reaction to verbal and nonverbal cues from the audience.

The specific content and format of the notes is not important; choose whatever works best for you. Some people use a formal outline on full sheets of paper; others prefer notes jotted on index cards. Some use complete sentences; others, short phrases. If desirable, include notes to yourself, such as when to pause, what phrases to emphasize, and when to change a slide or transparency.

Whether you use full sheets or index cards, be sure to number each page (in case the pages are dropped). For ease in moving from sheet to sheet or card to card, write on just one side and do not staple. Typed copy is better than handwritten copy and large type is better than small type. Type your notes in standard upper- and lowercase letters rather than in all capitals, which are more difficult to read because all the letters are the same size.

Use larger type and upper- and lowercase letters for outline notes.

Examples of excerpts from a written report, a complete script for an oral presentation, and outline notes for an oral presentation are shown in Figure 13.2 (see p. 426). Note several things about the content and format of the excerpts:

- Both the complete script and the outline notes are typed in larger type for ease of reading, and both contain prompts showing when to display each visual aid (slide).

- The complete script is written in a more informal, conversational style than the written report and uses a shorter line length and extra spacing between paragraphs (to help the speaker find his or her place easily).

- The outline notes contain mostly phrases, with each subtopic indented to show its relationship to the main idea.

Of course, you can tailor any combination of these methods to suit your needs. Some people, especially those who give speeches only occasionally, do best by writing out the entire speech and then practicing it until they can recite whole paragraphs or thoughts with ease. Doing so enables them to maintain eye contact with the audience. Some insert delivery cues, indicating when to pause, smile, make a gesture, display a visual aid, slow down, and the like.

Some professionals start off by writing out the entire speech and then practice extensively from the prepared script. Only after they are thoroughly familiar with their verbatim script do they condense it into an outline and then speak from the outline. Whatever method you use, the key to a successful delivery is practice, practice, practice.

FIGURE 13.2   Complete Script Versus Outline Notes

**Original Written
Report Page**

Note the formal language.

> The staff employees were asked to rate their level of familiarity with each benefit. As shown in Table 1, most staff employees believe that most benefits have been adequately communicated to them.
>
> At least three-fourths of the employees are familiar with all major benefits except for long-term disability insurance, which is familiar to only a slight majority. The low level of knowledge about automobile insurance can be explained by the fact that this benefit had been in effect for only six weeks at the time of the survey.
>
> In general, benefit familiarity is not related to length of employment at ASU. Most employees are familiar with most benefits, regardless of their length of employment. However, as shown in Figure 1, the one benefit for which this is not true is life insurance. The longer a person has been employed at ASU, the more likely he or she is to know about this benefit.

**Excerpt of a Complete
Script of an Oral
Presentation**

Note the conversational
language, larger type size,
and shorter line length.

> We asked our employees how familiar they are with our benefits. (SLIDE 1). As you can see, most employees know about most of our benefits.
>
> At least three-fourths of them are familiar with all but two of our benefits, and those two are long-term disability and automobile insurance. Only a slight majority know about our long-term disability insurance, and slightly more than a third know about our automobile insurance. As you may remember, we began offering automobile insurance just six weeks before conducting this survey.
>
> In general, there's no correlation between how long employees have worked here and how familiar they are with our benefits. Most employees are familiar with our benefits, no matter how long they've worked here.

**Outline Notes for
an Oral Presentation**

Note the incomplete
sentences and abbreviations.

> **FAMILIARITY WITH BENEFITS—SLIDE 1**
>
> - Most know about most benefits
> - + 3/4 know about all but 2 benefits:
>   —Long-term disability = slight majority
>   —Auto insur = +1/3 (begun 6 wks before survey)
>
> - No correlation between employment length & familiarity
>   —Not true for life insur—SLIDE 2
>   —Life insur: Longer employment = more familiarity

Organizing the Presentation

For most presentations, the best way to begin is simply to brainstorm: write down every point you can think of that might be included in your presentation. Don't worry about the order or format—just get it all down. During the next several days, carry a pen and paper with you so that you can jot down random thoughts as they occur—during a meeting, at lunch, going to and from work, or in the evening at home.

Later, separate your notes into three categories: opening, body, and ending. As you begin to analyze and organize your material, you may find that you need additional information. You may need to retrieve records from files, consult with a colleague, visit your corporate or local library to fill in the gaps, or perhaps go online to retrieve data from the World Wide Web.

The Opening

The purpose of the opening is to capture the interest of your audience, and the first 90 seconds of your presentation are crucial. The audience will be observing every detail about you—your dress, posture, facial features, and voice qualities, as well as what you're actually saying—for clues about you and your topic, and they will be making preliminary judgments accordingly.

Your opening should introduce the topic, identify the purpose, and preview the presentation.

Begin immediately to establish rapport and build a relationship with your audience—not just for the duration of your presentation but for the long term. If you're making a proposal, you need not only the audience's attention during your presentation but also their cooperation later to implement your proposal. Because the opening is so crucial, many professionals write out the entire opening and practice it word for word until they almost know it by heart.

The kind of opening that will be effective depends on your topic, how well you know the audience, and how well they know you. If, for example, you're giving a status report on a project about which you've reported before, you can immediately announce your main points (for example, that the project is on schedule and proceeding as planned) and go immediately to the body of your remarks. If, however, you're presenting a new proposal to your superiors, you'll first have to introduce the topic and provide background information.

If most of the listeners don't know you, you'll first have to gain their attention with a creative opening. The following types of attention-getting openings have proven successful for business presentations; the examples given are for the presentation to union employees on the topic of absenteeism:

- *Quote a well-known person:* "Comedian Woody Allen once noted that 90% of the job is just showing up."

- *Ask a question:* "If we were able to cut our absenteeism rate by half during the coming six months, exactly how much do you think that would mean for each of us in our end-of-year bonus checks?"

- *Present a hypothetical situation:* "Assume that as you were leaving home this morning to put in a full day at work, your son came up to you and said he was too tired to go to school because he had stayed up so late last night watching 'Wrestle Mania.' What would be your reaction?"

- *Relate an appropriate anecdote, story, joke, or personal experience:* "George, a friend of mine who had recently changed jobs, happened to meet his former

Effective openings include a quotation, question, hypothetical situation, story, startling fact, or visual aid.

boss on the street and asked her whom she had hired to fill his vacancy. 'George,' his former boss said, 'when you left, you didn't *leave* any vacancy!' Perhaps the reason George didn't leave any vacancy was that. . . ."

- *Give a startling fact:* "During the next 24 hours, American industry will lose $136 million because of absenteeism."

- *Use a dramatic prop or visual aid:* (holding up a paper clip) "What do you think is the *true* cost of this paper clip to our company?"

Don't apologize or make excuses (for example, "I wish I had had more time to prepare my remarks today" or "I'm not really much of a speaker"). The audience may agree with you! At any rate, you'll turn them off immediately and weaken your credibility.

Your opening should lead into the body of your presentation by previewing your remarks: "Today, I'll cover four main points. First, . . ." Let the audience know the scope of your remarks. For example, if you're discussing the pros and cons of a plant closing from a strictly dollars-and-cents standpoint, advise the audience immediately that your analysis does not include political or human relations considerations. If you don't first define the scope of your remarks, you may invite needless questions and second-guessing during your presentation.

For most business presentations, let the audience know up front what you expect of them. Are you simply presenting information for them to absorb, or will the audience be expected to react to your remarks? Are you asking for their endorsement, their resources, their help, or what? Let the audience know what their role will be so that they can then place your remarks in perspective.

The Body

The body of your presentation conveys the real content. Here you'll develop the points you introduced in the opening, giving background information, specific evidence, examples, implications, consequences, and other needed information.

Organize the body logically, according to your topic and audience needs.

Choose a Logical Sequence   Just as you do when writing a letter or report, choose an organizational plan that suits your purpose and your audience's needs. The most commonly used organizational plans are these:

- *Criteria:* Introduce each criterion in turn and show how well each alternative meets that criterion (typically used for presenting proposals).

- *Direct sequence:* Give the major conclusions first, followed by the supporting details (typically used for presenting routine information).

- *Indirect sequence:* Present the reasons first, followed by the major conclusion (typically used for persuasive presentations).

- *Chronology:* Present the points in the order in which they occurred (typically used in status reports or when reporting on some event).

- *Cause/effect/solution:* Present the sources and consequences of some problem and then pose a solution.

- *Order of importance:* Arrange the points in order of importance and then pose each point as a question and answer it (an effective way of ensuring that the audience can follow your arguments).

■ *Elimination of alternatives:* List all alternatives and then gradually eliminate each one until only one option remains—the one you're recommending.

Whatever organizational plan you choose, make sure your audience knows at the outset where you're going and is able to follow your organization. In a written document, signposts such as headings tell the reader how the parts fit together. In an oral presentation, you must compensate for the lack of such aids by using frequent and clear transitions that tell your listeners where you are. Pace your presentation of data so that you do not lose your audience.

Establish Your Credibility   Convince the listener that you've done a thorough job of collecting and analyzing the data and that your points are reasonable. Support your arguments with credible evidence—statistics, actual experiences, examples, and support from experts. Use objective language; let the data—not exaggeration or emotion—persuade the audience. Be guided by the same principles you use when writing a persuasive letter or report.

Avoid saturating your presentation with so many facts and figures that your audience won't be able to absorb them. Regardless of their relevance, statistics will not strengthen your presentation if the audience is unable to digest all the data. A more effective tactic is to prepare handouts of detailed statistical data to distribute for review at a later time.

Deal with Negative Information   It would be unusual if *all* the data you've collected and analyzed supports your proposal. (If that were the case, persuasion would not be needed.) What should you do, then, about negative information, which, if presented, might weaken your argument? You cannot simply ignore negative information. To do so would surely open up a host of questions and subsequent doubts that would seriously weaken your position.

Do not ignore negative information.

Think about your own analysis of the data. Despite the negative information, you still concluded that your solution has merit. Your tactic, then, is to present all the important information—pro and con—and to show through your analysis and discussion that your recommendations are still valid, in spite of the disadvantages and drawbacks. Use the techniques you learned in Chapter 5 about emphasis and subordination to let your listeners know which points you considered major and which you considered minor.

Although you should discuss the important negative points, you may safely omit discussing minor ones. You must, however, be prepared to discuss these minor negative points if any questions about them arise at the conclusion of your presentation.

The Ending

The ending of your presentation is your last opportunity to achieve your objective. Don't waste it. A presentation without a strong ending is like a joke without a punch line.

Finish on a strong, upbeat note, leaving your audience with a clear and simple message.

wordwise

Geography Lesson

■ In Maine, you can drive through China, Denmark, Mexico, New Sweden, Norway, Peru, and Poland.

■ On a U.S. map, you'll find 28 cities named Madison, 25 named Clinton, 23 named Washington, 22 named Monroe, 19 named Jackson, and 19 named Lincoln (but none named Harding or Eisenhower).

■ Pennsylvania has three cities named for taverns: King of Prussia, Bird-in-Hand, and Red Lion.

■ Mole Hill, West Virginia, changed its name to Mountain.

Your closing should summarize the main points of your presentation, especially if it has been a long one. Even if the members of your audience have had an easy time following the structure of your talk, they won't necessarily remember all your important points. Let the audience know the significance of what you've said. Draw conclusions, make recommendations, or outline the next steps to take. Leave the audience with a clear and simple message.

To add punch to your ending, you may want to use one of the same techniques discussed for opening a presentation. You might tell a story, make a personal appeal, or issue a challenge. However, resist the temptation to end with a quotation. It won't sound dramatic enough. Besides, you want your listeners to remember *your* words and thoughts—not someone else's. Also avoid fading out with a weak "That's about all I have to say" or "I see that our time is running out."

After you've developed some experience in giving presentations, you will be able to judge fairly accurately how long to spend on each point in order to finish on time. Until then, practice your presentation with a stopwatch. If necessary, insert reminders at critical points in your notes indicating where you should be at what point in time. Avoid having to drop important sections or rush through the conclusion of your presentation because you misjudged your timing.

Because your audience will remember best what they hear last, think of your ending as one of the most important parts of your presentation. Finish on a strong, upbeat note. If you've used a projector during your presentation, turn it off and turn the room lights on so that *you* are the center of attention. Also remember that no one ever lost any friends by finishing a minute or two ahead of schedule. As Toastmasters International puts it, "Get up, speak up, shut up, and sit down."

The Use of Humor in Business Presentations

Memory research indicates that when ideas are presented with humor, the audience not only is able to recall more details of the presentation but also is able to retain the information longer.[2]

Use humor if it is appropriate and you are adept at telling humorous stories.

Most of us are not capable of being a Jerry Seinfeld or Rosie O'Donnell, even if we wanted to be. If you know you do not tell humorous stories well, the moment you're in front of an audience is not the time to try to rectify that situation. Both you and your audience will suffer. If, however, you feel that you can use humor effectively, doing so might add just the appropriate touch to your presentation.

Jokes, puns, satire, and especially, amusing real-life incidents are just a few examples of humor, all of which serve to form a bond between speaker and audience. Humor can be used anywhere in a presentation—in the opening to get attention, in the body to add interest, or in the closing to drive home a point. Humor should, of course, be avoided if the topic is very serious or has negative consequences for the audience.

If you tell a funny story, it must always be appropriate to the situation and in good taste. Never tell an off-color or sexist joke; never use offensive language; never single out an ethnic, racial, or religious group; and never use a dialect or foreign accent in telling a story. Such tactics are always in bad taste. The best stories are directed at yourself; they show that you are human and can laugh at yourself.

Before telling a humorous story, make sure you understand it and think it's funny. Then personalize it for your own style of speaking and for the particular situation. Avoid beginning jokes by saying, "I heard a funny story the other day about. . . ." A major element of humor is surprise, so don't warn the audience a joke is coming. If you do, they're mentally preparing for a funny punch line, and you may disappoint them. If, on the other hand, you're already halfway into the story before the audience even realizes it's a joke, your chances of success are greater.

Resist the temptation to laugh at your own stories. A slight smile is more effective. Wait for the (hoped-for) laughter to subside; then continue your presentation by relating the punch line to the topic at hand.

Regardless of your expertise as a joke teller, do not use humor too frequently. Humor is a means to an end—not an end in itself. When all is said and done, you don't want your audience to remember that you were funny. You want them to remember that what you had to say was important and made sense.

Developing Appropriate Visual Aids

Today's audiences are accustomed to multimedia events that bombard the senses. They often assume that any formal presentation must be accompanied by some visual element, whether it is a flipchart, overhead transparency, slide, film, videotape, or actual model.

Visual aids are relatively simple to create (see Spotlight 22—On Technology; see p. 432) and help the audience understand the presentation, especially if it includes complex or statistical material. A University of Pennsylvania study found that presenters who used visual aids were successful in persuading 67% of their audience, whereas those who did not use them persuaded only 50% of their audience. In addition, meetings in which visual aids were used were 28% shorter than those with no such aids. Similarly, a University of Minnesota study found that the use of graphics increased a presenter's persuasiveness by 43%. Presenters who used visual aids were also perceived as being more professional, better prepared, and more interesting than the group who didn't use visual aids.[3]

Types of Visual Aids

Transparencies for overhead projection are probably the most commonly used visual aid in business presentations. Inexpensive, easy to produce, and simple to update, they can be used without darkening the room and while you face the audience. Thus, your audience can see to take notes, and you can maintain eye contact with them. Thanks to presentation software, overhead transparencies can now make use of color, designed fonts, charts, and artwork, instead of being limited to hard-to-read and overcrowded typewriter type.

Transparencies, slides, and handouts are the most common visual aids.

Although 35-mm slides are best projected in a somewhat darkened room, their high quality adds a distinctly professional touch to a presentation, and they can be used with very large audiences. However, slides lack the flexibility of transparencies; it is difficult to review an earlier slide or skip forward several slides during a presentation. Slides are moderately expensive to produce and require somewhat more preparation time than transparencies. However, the use of computer-generated slides is decreasing both the cost and production time.

Electronic slide presentations are the newest medium for visual aids. They consist of slides shown directly from a computer and projected onto a screen by use of a projector or a display panel sitting on top of an overhead projector. Because the

Desktop Presentations

Desktop presentation software is a special type of software that combines the functions of outline, word processing, and graphics programs into one easy-to-use program that enables you to design professional-looking overhead transparencies and 35-mm slides easily, as well as produce miniature print copies to use as audience handouts.

Presentation programs come with slide and transparency templates—that is, built-in designs that specify such features as background and font colors, borders, and the size, face, and position of type. Templates are available for title slides, bulleted lists, all types of charts, and illustrations. These templates, which can be changed, ensure a professional and consistent appearance.

SPOTLIGHT 22

ON TECHNOLOGY

Users can type in ideas for the visuals and easily revise and sort them. The user can then either create charts or illustrations from within the program or insert charts created in a spreadsheet program.

When everything is perfect, the user either prints them out on a color printer (for color transparencies) or uses a modem and communication software program to send the data file electronically to a film processing company. The finished slides and transparencies are shipped back to the user within 24 hours, at a cost of a few dollars per visual. (Black-and-white transparencies can, of course, be produced directly from a laser printer.) Alternately, the speaker can give an electronic presentation by projecting the slides directly from the computer.

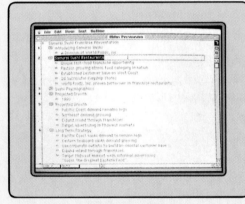

Outline your ideas.

View the finished slides.

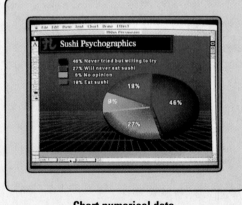

Chart numerical data.

Produce speaker notes and handouts.

slide images come directly from the computer file, actual transparencies and slides do not have to be made. Electronic presentations enable you to easily add multimedia effects to your presentation—if doing so helps you tell your story more effectively. You could, for example, show a short video, move text across the screen, or play background sound effects. Electronic slide presentations also provide more flexibility than traditional slide presentations, but they do require high-powered projectors for best results.

Handouts—printed copies of notes, tables, or illustrations—are often important in helping the audience follow a presentation. In addition, they provide a permanent record of the major points of the presentation and reduce or eliminate the need for note taking. Handouts are especially helpful for presenting complex information such as detailed statistical tables, which would be ineffective if projected as a slide or transparency.

The comparative features of these and other types of visual aids are shown in Figure 13.3.

Preparing Visual Aids

The key to effective visual aids is to use them only when needed, keep them simple and readable, and ensure they're of the highest quality.

Avoid using too many visual aids. Novice presenters sometimes use them as a crutch. Such overuse keeps the emphasis on the visual aid rather than on the presenter. Use visual aids only when they will help the audience grasp an important point, and remove them when they're no longer needed. One or two relevant, helpful visual aids are better than an entire armload of irrelevant ones—no matter how attractive they are.

Visual aids should be used only when needed, and should be simple, readable, and of high quality.

One of the most common mistakes presenters make in developing visual aids is to simply photocopy tables or illustrations from reports, printouts, or journals and project them on a screen. Print graphics usually contain far too much information to serve effectively as presentation graphics. Using print graphics in a presentation will often do more to hinder your presentation than to help it.

As a general rule, each slide or transparency should contain no more than 40 characters per line, no more than six or seven lines per visual, and no more than

FIGURE 13.3   Criteria for Selecting Visual Aids

Criteria	Electronic presentations	Transparencies	35-mm slides	Films	Videotape	Flipcharts	Handouts
Quality	Good	Good	Excellent	Excellent	Excellent	Poor	Good
Cost	Moderate	Low	Moderate	High	High	Low	Low
Ease of use	Difficult	Easy	Moderate	Moderate	Easy	Easy	Easy
Ease of preparation	Easy	Easy	Moderate	Difficult	Difficult	Easy	Easy
Ease of updating	Easy	Easy	Moderate	Difficult	Difficult	N/A	Easy
Degrees of formality	Formal	Either	Formal	Either	Either	Informal	Either
Adaptability to audience size	Moderate	Excellent	Excellent	Excellent	Moderate	Poor	Moderate
Dependence on equipment	High	Moderate	Moderate	Moderate	Moderate	Low	None

Bill Gates, founder of Microsoft Corporation and, acording to *Forbes* magazine, the richest person in America, uses PowerPoint®, the software presentation program developed by his company, to make a point at a national computer conference.

three columns of data. Use upper- and lowercase letters (rather than all capitals) in a large, simple typeface and plenty of white (empty) space. Use bulleted lists to show a group of related items that have no specific order and numbered lists to show related items in a specific order.

Establish a color scheme and stay with it for all your visual aids; that is, use the same background color for each slide or transparency. For handouts and overheads, use dark type on a light background; for slides, use light type on a dark background.

If you do not keep your visual aids clear and simple, your audience can easily become overwhelmed, with their attention drawn to the technology rather than to the content. As always, seek to *express*—not to *impress*. With visual aids, less is more.

The only real way to ensure that your visual aids are readable is to test them beforehand from the back seat of the room in which you will be presenting. If that is not possible, follow these guidelines: the smallest image projected on the screen should be 1 inch tall for each 30 feet of viewing distance, and no one should be seated farther from the screen than ten times the height of the projected image. Thus, if you're projecting onto a screen 6 feet high, the back seat should be no farther than 60 feet from the screen, and the projector should be positioned so that the projected letters are at least 2 inches tall.

The quality of your visual aids sends a nonverbal message about your competence and your respect for your audience. Just as you don't want your audience's attention distracted by the razzle-dazzle of your slides, neither do you want their attention distracted by poor quality. If the visual aid isn't readable or attractive, don't use it.

Using Visual Aids

Practice using your visual aids smoothly and effectively.

Even the best visual aid will not be effective if it is not used properly during the presentation or if the equipment doesn't work. Using equipment smoothly does not come naturally; it takes practice and a keen awareness of audience needs, especially when using a slide or overhead projector. If you have the option of positioning the projection equipment (slide or overhead projector) and screen, ensure that the image is readable from every seat and that neither you nor the projector blocks anyone's view (see Figure 13.4).

Confirm that your equipment is in top working order and that you know how to operate it and how to secure a spare bulb or spare machine quickly if one becomes necessary. Adjust the projector and focus the image so that it is clearly readable from the farthest seat. However, do not make the image larger than necessary; the presenter should be the center of attention. The image should be a square or rectangle. Avoid the common keystoning effect (where the top of the image is wider than the bottom) by tilting the top of the screen forward slightly toward the projector.

When using slide projectors, have a blank opaque slide or a generic title slide as the last slide so that the audience is not suddenly hit with a bright flash of light when you finish your presentation. And with all types of projectors, avoid walking in front of the projected image.

Try to avoid problems. Lock your slides in place in the tray; number your slides and transparencies so that they can be restored quickly if dropped; have your film already threaded into the projector; clean the overhead projector glass before using it; tape to the lectern the device used to advance the slides to avoid having it tumble off; and have an extra bulb handy (and know how to insert it). Finally, be prepared to give your presentation without visual aids if that should become necessary.

Be prepared to give your presentation without visual aids if necessary.

With practice, you can learn to stand to the side of the screen, facing the audience with your feet pointed toward them. Then, when you need to refer to an item on the screen, point with either a finger, pointer, or pen. Turn your body from the waist, keeping your feet pointed toward the audience. Doing so enables you to maintain better eye contact with the audience as well as better control of the presentation.

FIGURE 13.4   Positioning the Projector Correctly

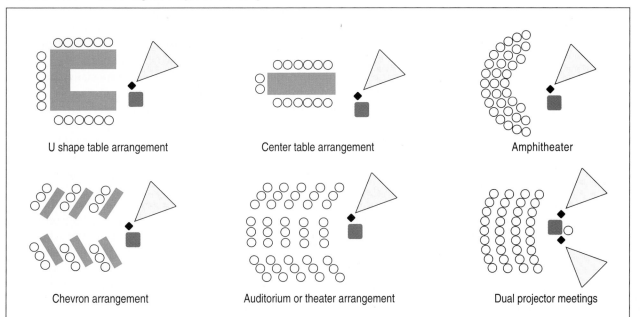

U shape table arrangement   Center table arrangement   Amphitheater

Chevron arrangement   Auditorium or theater arrangement   Dual projector meetings

Distribute handouts before your presentation if they contain information the audience will need during your presentation. Otherwise, distribute them at the end of your presentation (to avoid distracting the audience from your remarks). Do, however, alert the audience at the start that you will be distributing a printed summary of your remarks so that people won't take unneeded notes.

Practicing the Presentation

Use appropriate language, voice qualities, gestures, and posture.

The language of oral presentations must be simple. Because the listener has only one chance to comprehend the information presented, shorter sentences and simpler vocabulary should be used for oral presentations than for written presentations. Presenters have trouble articulating long, involved sentences with complex vocabulary, and listeners have trouble understanding them. A long sentence that reads easily on paper may leave the speaker breathless when he or she says it aloud. Avoid such traps. Use short, simple sentences and a conversational style. Use contractions freely, and avoid using words that you may have trouble pronouncing. (Compare, for example, the different styles used in the excerpts from the written report and the oral presentation script shown in Figure 13.2 on p. 426.)

Use frequent preview, summary, transition, and repetition to help your audience follow your presentation. The old advice to preachers is just as pertinent for business presenters: "Tell them what you're going to tell them, tell them, and then tell them what you told them."

Whether you plan to speak from a complete script or from notes or an outline, begin practicing by simulating the conditions of the meeting room as closely as possible. Always practice standing, with your notes at the same level and angle as at a podium, and use any visual aids that will be a part of your presentation.

Videotaping your rehearsal can help you review and modify your voice qualities, gestures, and speech content. If videotaping is not possible, two good substitutes are a large mirror and a tape recorder. The mirror can help you judge the appropriateness of your posture, facial expressions, and gestures. Remember that 55% of your credibility with an audience comes from your body language, 38% comes from your voice qualities, and only 7% comes from the actual words you use.[4] Play back the tape several times, paying attention to your voice qualities (especially speed and pitch), pauses, grouping of words and phrases, and pronunciation.

Speak in a conversational tone, but at a slightly slower rate than normally used in conversation. For interest and to fit the situation, vary both the volume and the rate of speaking, slowing down when presenting important or complex information and speeding up when summarizing. Use periodic pauses to emphasize important points. Use correct diction, avoid slurring or dropping off the endings of words, and practice pronouncing difficult names.

Occasional hand and arm gestures are important for adding interest and emphasis, but only if they are appropriate and appear natural. If you never "talk with your hands" in normal conversation, it is unlikely you will do so naturally while presenting. Avoid annoying and distracting mannerisms and gestures, such as jingling coins or keys in your pocket; coughing or clearing your throat excessively; wildly waving your hands; gripping the lectern tightly; nervously swaying or pacing; playing with jewelry, pens, or paper clips; or peppering your remarks with "and uh" or "you know."

Practice smiling occasionally, standing tall and naturally, with the body balanced on both feet. Rest your hands on the podium, by your side, or in any natural, quiet position. Your voice and demeanor should reflect professionalism, enthusiasm, and self-confidence.

Delivering the Presentation

Your clothing is a part of the message you communicate to your audience, so dress appropriately—in comfortable and businesslike attire. Try to dress just slightly better than the average member of your audience; the audience will be complimented by your efforts.

Dress comfortably—just slightly dressier than your audience.

If you're speaking after a meal, eat lightly, avoiding heavy sauces, desserts, and alcoholic beverages. As you're being introduced, take several deep breaths to clear your mind, walk confidently to the front of the room, take enough time to arrange yourself and your notes, look slowly around you, establish eye contact with several members of the audience, and then, in a loud, clear voice, begin your presentation.

In most environments, a microphone is not needed if you're speaking to a group smaller than 150 people—10 to 12 rows of people. Your voice should carry that far. Not using a microphone gives you more freedom to move about and avoids problems with audio feedback and volume adjustments. If you will need to use a microphone, test it beforehand to see how it operates and to determine the appropriate setting and height; the microphone normally should be 4 to 6 inches from your mouth.

You should know your presentation well enough that you can maintain eye contact easily with your audience, taking care to include members in all corners of the room. If you lose your place in your notes or script, relax and take as much time as you need to regroup.

If your mind actually does go blank, try to keep talking—even if you repeat what you've just said. The audience will probably think you intentionally repeated the information for emphasis, and the extra time may jog your memory. If this doesn't work, simply skip ahead to another part of your presentation that you do remember; then come back later to the part you omitted.

Stage Fright

For some people, making a presentation is accompanied by such symptoms as these:

- Gasping for air
- Feeling faint or nauseated ("butterflies in the stomach")
- Having shaking hands or legs and sweaty palms
- Feeling the heart beat rapidly and loudly
- Speaking too rapidly and in a high-pitched voice

If you've ever experienced any of these symptoms, take comfort in the fact that you're not alone. Fear of giving a speech is the Number 1 fear of most Americans. In a national poll of 3,000 people, 42% said the one thing they're most afraid of in life—even more than having cancer or a heart attack—is giving a speech.[5]

Fortunately, behavior-modification experts have found that of the full range of anxiety disorders, people can most predictably overcome their fear of public speaking.[6]

Recognize that you have been asked to make a presentation because someone obviously thinks you have something important to say. You should feel complimented. Unless you are an exceptionally good or exceptionally bad speaker, the audience will more likely remember *what* you say than how you say it. Most of us fall somewhere between these two extremes as presenters.

To avoid anxiety, practice, develop a positive attitude, and concentrate on friendly faces.

The best way to minimize any lingering anxiety is to overprepare. For the anxious presenter, there is no such thing as overpractice. The more familiar you are with the content of your speech and the more trial runs you've made, the better you'll be able to concentrate on your delivery once you're actually in front of the group. You may want to memorize the first several sentences of your presentation just so you can approach those critical first moments (when anxiety is highest) with more confidence.

Before your presentation, take a short walk to relax your body. While waiting for your presentation to begin, let your arms drop loosely by your sides and shake your wrists gently, all the while breathing deeply several times. As you begin to speak, look for friendly faces in the crowd, and concentrate on them initially.

Some nervousness, of course, is good. It gets the adrenalin flowing and gives your speech an edge. If you do find that you're exceedingly nervous as you begin your speech, don't say something like, "I'm so nervous this morning, my hands are shaking." Probably your audience hadn't noticed; but as soon as you bring it to their attention, their eyes will immediately move to your shaking hands, thus creating a needless distraction and weakening your credibility.

Finally, the professional who is anxious about speaking in public should consider taking a public speaking course or joining Toastmasters International, the world's oldest and largest nonprofit educational organization. The purpose of Toastmasters is to improve the speaking skills of its members. They meet weekly or monthly and deliver prepared speeches, evaluate one another's oral presentations, give impromptu talks, develop their listening skills, conduct meetings, and learn parliamentary procedure.

Answering Questions

Plan your answers to possible questions ahead of time.

One advantage of oral presentations over written reports is the opportunity to engage in two-way communication. The question-and-answer session is a vital part of your presentation; plan for it accordingly.

Normally, you should announce at the beginning of your presentation that you will be happy to answer any questions when you're through. Holding questions until the end prevents you from being interrupted and losing your train of thought or possibly running out of time and not being able to complete your prepared remarks. Also, there is always the possibility that the listener's question will be answered in the course of your presentation.

The exception to a questions-at-the-end policy is when your topic is so complex that a listener's question must be answered immediately if he or she is to follow the rest of the presentation. Another exception is informal (and generally small) meetings, where questions and comments naturally occur throughout the presentation.

As you prepare your presentation, anticipate what questions you might expect from the audience. Make a list of them and think through possible answers. If necessary, make notes to refer to while answering. If your list of questions is very long, you should probably consider revising your presentation to incorporate some of the answers into your prepared remarks.

Always listen carefully to the question; repeat it, if necessary, for the benefit of the entire audience; and look at the entire audience as you answer—not just at the questioner. Treat each questioner with unfailing courtesy. If the question is antagonistic, be firm but fair and polite.

If you don't know the answer to a question, freely say so and promise to have the answer within a specific period. Then write down the question to remind yourself to find the answer later. Do not risk embarrassing another member of the audience by referring the question to him or her.

If your call for questions results in absolute silence, you may conclude either that you did a superb job of explaining your topic or that no one wishes to be the first to ask a question. If you suspect the latter, to break the ice, you might start the questions yourself, by saying something like, "One question I'm frequently asked that might interest you is. . . ." Or you may ask the program chair ahead of time to be prepared to ask the first question if no one in the audience begins.

After the presentation is over and you're back in your office, evaluate your performance using the guidelines presented in Checklist 15 (see p. 440) so that you can benefit from the experience. What seemed to work well and what not so well? Analyze each aspect of your performance—from initial research through delivery. Regardless of how well the presentation went, vow to improve your performance next time.

Work-Team Presentations

Work-team presentations are quite common for communicating about complex projects. For example, when presenting the organization's marketing plan to management or when updating the five-year plan, it is unlikely that any one person has the expertise or time to prepare the entire presentation. Instead, a cooperative effort would be most effective.

Work-team presentations, whether written or oral, require extensive planning, close coordination, and a measure of maturity and goodwill. If you are responsible for coordinating such efforts, allow enough time and assign responsibilities on the basis of individual talents and time constraints.

Your major criterion for making assignments is what division of duties will result in the most effective presentation. Some members may be better at collecting and analyzing the information to be presented, others may be better at developing the visual aids, and others may be better at delivering the presentation. Everyone need not share equally in each aspect of the project. As coordinator, you should ensure that all efforts are recognized publicly and equally during the actual presentation, regardless of how much "podium time" each person is assigned.

Make individual assignments for work-team presentations based on individual strengths and preferences.

Just as people have different writing styles, they also have different speaking styles, and you must ensure that your overall presentation has coherence and unity—that it sounds as if it were prepared and given by one individual. Thus, the group members should decide beforehand the most appropriate tone, format, organization, style for visual aids, manner of dress, format for handling questions, and similar factors that will help the presentation flow smoothly from topic to topic and from speaker to speaker.

✔ CHECKLIST 15   The Oral Presentation Process

Planning

☑ Determine if an oral presentation will be more effective than a written report.

☑ Determine your purpose: what response do you want from your audience?

☑ Analyze your audience in terms of demographic factors, level of knowledge, and psychological needs.

☑ If possible, schedule the presentation to permit adequate preparation and to avoid inconvenience for the audience.

☑ Select an appropriate delivery method.

Organizing

☑ Brainstorm. Write down every point you think you might cover in the presentation.

☑ Separate your notes into the opening, body, and ending. Gather additional data if needed.

☑ Write an effective opening that introduces the topic, discusses the points you'll cover, and tells the audience what you hope will happen as a result of your presentation.

☑ In the body, develop the points fully, giving background data, evidence, and examples.
  a. Organize the points logically.
  b. To maintain credibility, discuss any major negative points and be prepared to discuss any minor negative points.
  c. Pace the presentation of data to avoid presenting facts and figures too quickly.

☑ Finish on a strong, upbeat note by summarizing your main points, adding a personal appeal, drawing conclusions and making recommenda-tions, discussing what needs to be done next, or using some other logical closing.

☑ Use humor only when appropriate and only if you are effective at telling humorous stories.

☑ Ensure that your visual aids are needed, simple, easily readable, and of the highest quality.

Practicing

☑ Rehearse your presentation extensively, simulating the actual speaking conditions as much as possible and using your visual aids.

☑ Use simple language and short sentences, with frequent preview, summary, transition, and repetition.

☑ Stand tall and naturally, and speak in a loud, clear, enthusiastic, and friendly voice. Vary the rate and volume of your voice.

☑ Use correct diction and appropriate gestures.

Delivering

☑ Dress appropriately—in comfortable, businesslike, conservative clothing.

☑ Use a microphone effectively.

☑ Maintain eye contact with the audience, including all corners of the room in your gaze.

☑ To avoid anxiety, practice extensively, develop a positive attitude, and concentrate on the friendly faces in the audience.

☑ Plan your answers to possible questions ahead of time. Listen to each question carefully and address your answer to the entire audience.

A full-scale rehearsal—in the room where the presentation will be made and using all visual aids—is crucial. If possible, it should be videotaped for later analy-sis by the entire group. Critiquing the performance of a colleague requires tact, empathy, and goodwill; and accepting such feedback requires grace and maturity. For the entire presentation to succeed, each individual element must also suc-ceed. And if it does, each contributor shares in the success and any rewards that may result.

Y‌ou are Matt Kromer, an information specialist at Lewis & Smith, a large import/export firm in San Francisco. Your company publishes three major external documents—a quarterly customer newsletter, a semiannual catalog, and an annual report. All three are currently prepared by an outside printing company. However, the decision was recently made to switch to some form of in-house publishing for these publications.

Your superior asked you to research the question of whether your firm should use word processing or desktop publishing software for these documents. Considering the importance of these external documents, you have been asked to make a formal 20-minute presentation of your findings and recommendations to the firm's administrative committee.

1. What is the purpose of your presentation?

   To present the findings from my research, to recommend a type of software program, and to persuade the audience that my recommendations are sound.

2. Describe your audience.

   The administrative committee consists of the five managers (including my superior) who report to the vice president for administration. I have met them all, but with the exception of my own superior, I do not know any of them well.

   Their role will be to make the final decision regarding which type of software program to use. Once that decision has been made, the actual users will decide which brand to purchase. Four of the five managers are casual users of word processing software. They've all likely heard of desktop publishing but have never used it.

3. What type of presentation will be most appropriate?

   This will be a normal business presentation to a small audience, so I'll speak from notes and use transparencies. Because I have only 20 minutes to present, I'll hold off answering questions until the end—to make sure I have enough time to cover the needed information.

4. What kind of data have you collected for your presentation?

   I studied each publication's formatting requirements, analyzed the features of the most popular word processing (Final Word) and desktop publishing (Personal Editor) programs, and spoke with a colleague from a firm that recently began publishing its documents in-house.

   On the basis of the criteria of cost, ease of use, and features, I'll recommend the use of word processing software to publish our three documents.

5. How will you organize the data?

   First I'll present the background information. Then I could organize my research data by presenting the advantages and disadvantages of each type of program. However, I think it would be more effective to organize my findings by criteria instead; that is, I will show how each program rates in terms of cost, ease of use, and features.

6. Outline an effective opening section for your presentation.

   a. <u>Introduction:</u> "Freedom of the Press" (Computer software now gives us the freedom to publish our own documents at lower cost and with greater flexibility.)

   b. <u>Purpose:</u> to recommend whether to use WP or DTP software

   c. <u>Organization:</u> by criteria (cost, ease of use, and features)

   d. <u>Audience role:</u> to make the final decision

7. How will you handle negative information?

   Although I'm recommending word processing software, the desktop publishing program has more features. However, I'll show that (a) we don't necessarily need those features and (b) those features make the program more difficult to learn.

8. What types of visual aids will you use?

   ■ <u>Slides</u> (in the form of an electronic presentation)

      a. Two slides at the beginning—to preview the topic and to illustrate our three publications

      b. Two in the middle—to compare the costs and features of the two programs

      c. Two at the end—to give my recommendations and to show what needs to be done next

   ■ <u>Handout</u>

      A one-page handout showing miniature copies of the six slides—as a summary of my important points and for future reference.

9. How will you practice your presentation?

   I'll do a dry run in the conference room where I'll be speaking, standing where I'll actually be giving the presentation and using my computer and projector. I'll also set up a cassette recorder at the far end of the conference table to tape my practice presentation to ensure that I can be heard, to check for clarity and voice qualities, and to time my presentation. I'll also practice answering any questions I think the managers might ask.

PRODUCT

SELECTING DESKTOP PUBLISHING SOFTWARE
Presented to the Administrative Committee
Matt Kromer, 10/3/--

I. OPENING

A. I'd like to talk to you today about <u>freedom of the press</u>—specifically about our recent decision to switch to in-house publishing. And though our publications won't be completely "free," desktop publishing <u>will</u> provide us with more flexibility—at a greatly reduced cost.

B. <u>Purpose of presentation</u>: To recommend whether to use word processing or desktop publishing software to publish our company newsletter, catalog, and annual report.

SLIDE 1 — FREEDOM OF THE PRESS

C. <u>Preview</u>:

   1. Background information

   2. Criteria for decision:
      a. Cost
      b. Ease of use
      c. Features

   3. My recommendation

D. <u>Your job</u>: To make final decision regarding which type of software to support. You will <u>not</u> decide which brand of software; that decision will be left up to the users.

E. Will be happy to answer any questions at the conclusion of my remarks. Also have handout of my slides to distribute later.

Provides identifying information in the opening—in case of loss or for future reference.

Uses an attention-getting opening that is written verbatim for a stress-free start.

Uses the opening to give the purpose, preview the topics, and identify the audience's role.

Alerts the audience to prevent interrupting questions and unnecessary note taking.

Grammar and Mechanics Notes

Type the outline in large upper- and lowercase letters, either on individual note cards or on full sheets of paper. Leave plenty of white space between sections so that you can easily find your place.

Marks the slide references for easy identification.

II. BODY

SLIDE 2 — PUBLICATIONS

A. Background:

1. We publish 3 major external documents, all of which have strategic marketing value:

    a. Newsletter: *The Forum*, sent quarterly to 2,000 customers; 8 pp; 1-color (black) on ivory stock, with brown masthead; photos and line art.

    b. Catalog: Semiannual; 36-42 pp; 1-color (black) interior with 4-color cover; 4,000 copies.

    c. Annual report: Annual; 24-28 pp; 1-color (blue) interior on gray stock with 4-color cover; 1,500 copies.

2. All 3 presently prepared by Medallion Printing Company

3. Research:

    a. Analyzed each publication to determine formatting requirements.

    b. Analyzed features of Final Word, the WP program we presently support, and Personal Editor, the most popular DTP software program (other DTP programs have similar features).

    c. Spoke with Paula Henning from Crown Busch; her co. began producing their documents in-house using DTP last year.

B. Criteria:

Discusses research procedures to help establish credibility.

Organizes the main part of the speech body by the criteria used for making the decision.

Grammar and Mechanics Notes

You do not have to write your presentation notes in parallel format; no one will see them but you. You may need complete sentences to jog your memory for some parts but only partial sentences, individual words, or abbreviations for other parts. Underline important points for easy referral.

SLIDE 3 — COST COMPARISON

1. <u>Cost:</u>

   a. Either program will require
      (1) One flatbed scanner and software to be shared by all: cost—$1,450.
      (2) One digital (filmless) camera to be shared by all: cost—$995.

   b. Final Word: $295 list; $245 mail order. But we already own.

   c. Personal Editor: $195 list; $175 mail order; cost for 3 copies—$525.

   d. Conclusion: Personal Editor costs $525 more than Final Word.

2. <u>Ease of use:</u>

   a. <u>Final Word:</u>
      (1) Operators already know how to use because they use it every day for routine typing.
      (2) $1/2$ day seminar must be developed to teach advanced features needed for DTP (taught by local community college faculty member); cost—$500.

   b. <u>Personal Editor:</u>
      (1) Difficult to learn to use because of its many features. However, once learned, many features are easier to implement than on Final Word.
      (2) Danger of forgetting and having to relearn because Personal Editor will be used infrequently.
      (3) 2-day seminar must be developed to teach the new software program (taught by local community college faculty member); cost—$2,000.

   c. In summary, Personal Editor costs $2,000 more than Final Word.

Presents both positive and negative information and discusses the importance and implications of each feature.

SLIDE 4 — FEATURE COMPARISON

   3. Features:

       a. Font flexibility: Both have.

       b. Column feature: Both have.

       c. Import/manipulate graphics: Both have; Personal Editor has more options.

       d. Color separations: Personal Editor has; Final Word does not (don't need now; may need in the future).

       e. Predesigned templates: Both have; Personal Editor permits more elaborate designs (not needed).

       f. Ease of revisions (important criterion): Both allow, but easier in Final Word (which has full WP features).

III. CLOSING

SLIDE 5 — RECOMMENDATION

   A. Recommendation: Final Word

     1. Cheaper

     2. Easier to use/less training needed

     3. Has all the features we presently need

Puts the final recommendation and the rationale on a slide—for emphasis.

SLIDE 6 — SCHEDULE

B. Schedule:

Today: Make decision regarding software

November: Purchase and install hardware and software

December: Conduct user training

January: Begin producing 3 documents in-house

C. Conclusion:

Our entry into desktop publishing is an exciting project because it gives us greater control over our publications at less cost. In addition, DTP will open up opportunities for even more publishing projects in the future to help us better fulfill our corporate mission.

Closes by giving the recommendation and telling what happens next. Ends on a confident, forward-looking note.

HANDOUT — SELECTING DESKTOP PUBLISHING SOFTWARE

IV. QUESTIONS

Follows presentation by a question-and-answer session.

NOTES *(To be taken during presentation)*

Leaves room for taking notes during question-and-answer session.

Grammar and Mechanics Notes

You would no doubt have to insert some last-minute handwritten changes in your final outline prior to actually giving the presentation.

Actual documents can be scanned into the computer, sized to fit, and positioned as desired.

Tables and charts are created easily using presentation software.

During the presentation, each bulleted point and each schedule line is projected one at a time—for emphasis.

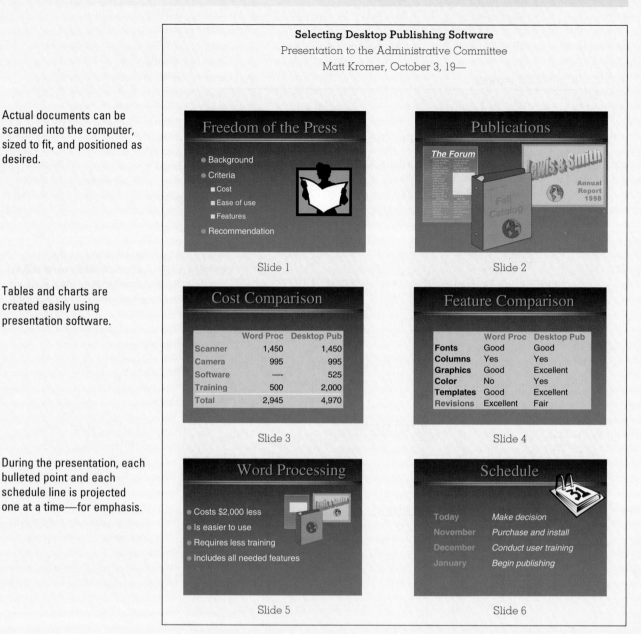

Selecting Desktop Publishing Software
Presentation to the Administrative Committee
Matt Kromer, October 3, 19—

Slide 1

Slide 2

Slide 3

Slide 4

Slide 5

Slide 6

Grammar and Mechanics Notes

This presentation uses the "Double Lines" template in Microsoft PowerPoint®. All font faces, sizes, and locations are preselected for you. Do not try to crowd too much information on each slide.

Oral business presentations are a vital part of the contemporary organization because they provide immediate feedback, give the presenter full control of the situation, and require less audience effort than do written presentations. However, oral presentations are also impermanent and expensive, and the speaker-controlled pace means that some people in the audience may not be able to keep up with the flow of information. Managers need to develop their presentation skills in order to take advantage of these strengths and to minimize these weaknesses.

Planning the presentation requires determining the purpose, analyzing the audience, and planning the timing and method of presentation appropriate for the situation. Organizing the presentation requires developing an effective opening, developing each point logically in the middle, and closing on a strong, confident note. Visual aids should be relevant, simple, easily readable, and of high quality. Practice your presentation as much as necessary. When actually delivering the presentation, dress appropriately, speak in a clear and confident manner, and maintain eye contact with the audience. Evaluate your performance afterward to ensure that your presentation skills improve with each opportunity to speak.

When making a work-team presentation, allow enough time to prepare, assign responsibilities on the basis of individual talents, and rehearse sufficiently to ensure that the overall presentation has coherence and unity.

1. **Communication at Royal Caribbean Cruises Revisited**   Before David Hancock makes a presentation to travel agents, he is careful to analyze his audience and consider whether industry jargon will be understood. He prefers electronic slide presentations because he can quickly and easily make revisions.
   a. What are the advantages and disadvantages of revising electronic presentations right up to the start of the presentation?
   b. Why would Hancock be willing to take questions at any time during a talk to a small group?
   c. Why would Hancock ask colleagues to bring up questions that he might be asked by an outside audience?
2. What are the advantages and disadvantages of oral presentations as opposed to written reports?
3. Identify and give an example of each of the four principal purposes of oral presentations.
4. Give an example of a business situation in which it would be appropriate to deliver a presentation (a) by reading the speech and (b) by speaking from notes.
5. What types of information should be presented in the opening section of a presentation?
6. List seven possible plans for organizing the body of a presentation.
7. What types of humor are appropriate in a business presentation, and under what circumstances should humor be used?
8. What criteria should be used for deciding whether to use visual aids in a business presentation?
9. What are the specific advantages of using transparencies, 35-mm slides, electronic presentations, and handouts for a business presentation?
10. What type of language is most appropriate for business presentations?

11. What voice qualities are important when presenting business information orally?
12. What are some effective strategies for dealing with stage fright?
13. Why is it best to delay audience questions until the end of a presentation? Under what circumstances is this strategy not recommended?
14. Explain the meaning of Mark Twain's observation, "It takes three weeks to prepare a good impromptu speech."
15. What special considerations must be addressed when preparing a work-team presentation?

Help Wanted

This is a draft of three slides for a presentation (see the Help Wanted exercise in Chapter 12). Revise the slides to make them more effective, taking into consideration the editor's marginal comments. You may use any template design you wish.

Use upper- and lowercase letters—much easier to read.

Clip art is of a videocamera—not a digital camera. Select another image—and make it smaller.

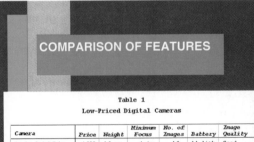

Table is _much_ too small and _much_ too detailed. Simplify and enlarge.

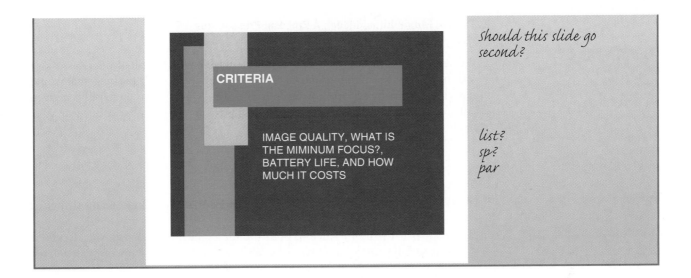

EXERCISES

1. **The 3Ps Microwriting Model: Communication Applications at Royal Caribbean Cruises**
   When David Hancock plans a presentation to travel agents, he determines the purpose, analyzes the audience, and thinks about the questions he is likely to be asked. Then he uses slides, overhead transparencies, or electronic slide presentations to illustrate his talk.

   Problem

   You are a district sales manager at Royal Caribbean Cruises. To promote sales of a new three-day cruise from Miami, you are preparing a presentation to 200 travel agents. Most of these agents have sold longer Royal Caribbean cruises in the past, although this is their first introduction to the shorter cruise. You believe that the new cruise will appeal to people who have never been on a cruise as well as to people who can get away for only a few days. You are scheduled to speak for no more than five minutes.

   Process

   a. What is the purpose of your presentation?
   b. Describe your audience.
   c. What level of knowledge is your audience likely to have about your topic?
   d. How will you capture your audience's attention in the first minute of your presentation? Draft your opening section.
   e. What points will you cover in the body of your speech, and in what order? How will you link these points to audience benefits?
   f. Write a closing section that summarizes your points and reinforces the purpose of your presentation.

   Product

   Using your knowledge of oral presentations, prepare a complete presentation outline for this speech.

2. **The 3Ps Microwriting Model: A Proposal Presentation**

   Problem

   Review Exercise 2 of Chapter 10 (page 321), in which the Hospitality Services Association at your university proposes to start University Hosts, a business that would provide hospitality services for campus visitors. Assume that you have been given 10 minutes to present your proposal orally to the President's Council at your institution.

   Process

   a. What is the purpose of your presentation?
   b. Describe your audience.
   c. What type of delivery would be most appropriate—reading, memorizing, or speaking from notes?
   d. Because of the importance of both the topic and the audience, you decide to write in full your opening remarks. Write a 1 to 1½ minute opening section for your presentation. Include an attention-getter.
   e. Outline the topics you will discuss and the order in which you will discuss them. Be sure to include reader benefits.
   f. Write a 1 to 1½ minute closing section for your presentation.
   g. Prepare rough drafts of the slides you will use for your presentation.

   Product

   Prepare (a) a complete presentation outline, including where the slides will be used and (b) final paper copies of the slides for the presentation.

3. **Understanding the Role of Business Presentations**   Interview two businesspeople in your community who hold positions in your area of interest to learn more about their experiences in making oral presentations. Write a memorandum to your instructor summarizing what you've learned. You may want to ask such questions as the following:
   a. How important has the ability to make effective oral presentations been to your career?
   b. What kinds of oral presentations do you make in and out of the office and how often?
   c. How do you typically prepare for them?
   d. What kinds of audiovisual aids do you use?

4. **Evaluating a Presentation**   Attend a presentation given by a businessperson, perhaps a speaker at an event sponsored by a campus business organization or one of the business or professional organizations in your community. Critique the speaker's presentation in light of what you've learned in this chapter, and submit a memorandum report to your instructor.

5. **Planning a Presentation**   You decided at the last minute to apply to the graduate school at your institution to work toward an MBA degree. Even though you have a 3.4 GPA (on a 4.0 scale), you were denied admission because you had not taken the GMAT, which is a prerequisite for admission. You have, however, been given 10 minutes to appear before the Graduate Council to try to convince them to grant you a temporary waiver of this requirement and permit you to enroll in MBA classes next term, during which time you will take the GMAT. The Graduate Council consists of the director of the MBA program and two senior faculty members, one of whom is your business communication professor.

a. What is the purpose of your presentation?
b. What do you know or what can you surmise about your audience that might help you prepare a more effective presentation?
c. What considerations affect the timing of your presentation?
d. What method of delivery should you use?

6. **Planning the Visual Element**   You are the trainer for an in-house survey course in effective advertising techniques that is being offered to franchise owners of your Mexican fast-food chain. As part of the course, you are scheduled to present a 30-minute session on writing effective sales letters; and you decide to use the sales-letter section of Chapter 8 in this text (beginning on page 234) as the basis for your presentation.

   Prepare four to six transparency masters that you might use for your presentation to the 25 participants. Submit full-sized photocopies of the transparencies (rather than the transparencies themselves) to your instructor.

7. **Presenting Research Data**   Review the analytical or recommendation report you prepared in Chapter 12. Assume that you have been given 15 minutes to present the important information from your written report to a committee of your superiors who will not have an opportunity to read the written report.
   a. Write your presentation notes, using either full sheets of paper or note cards.
   b. Develop four to six slides to use during your presentation.
   c. Practice your presentation several times—at least once in the classroom where you will actually give it.
   d. Give your presentation to the class.
   Your instructor may ask the audience to evaluate each presentation in terms of the effectiveness of its contents, use of visual aids, and delivery.

8. **Presenting Narrative Information**   Locate two journal articles on some aspect of business communication (the topics in the table of contents of this text will provide clues for searching). The two articles should be about the same topic. Integrate the important information from both articles, and present your findings to the class in a 5-minute presentation. Include at least one visual aid in your presentation. Prepare a one-page abstract that synthesizes the important information from both articles, and distribute it as a handout to the class after your presentation. Submit to your instructor (a) a photocopy of each article, (b) a copy of your presentation notes, (c) a copy of your visual aids, and (d) a copy of your handout.

9. **Presenting Negative Information**   Your library should have copies of the latest annual reports from many Fortune 500 companies. Select an annual report from a company that lost money last year. Assuming the role of that company's CEO, prepare and give a 10-minute presentation designed for a breakfast meeting of the New York Investment Council, a group made up of institutional investors and large private investors. Your purpose is to persuade the audience that your organization is still a good investment. Assume that the audience will have already seen a copy of your annual report. Select two visual aids contained in the annual report and simplify them as necessary for use in your oral presentation.

10. **Work-Team Presentation**   Divide into teams of four or five students. Your instructor will assign you to either the pro or the con side of one of the following topics:

- Drug testing should/should not be mandatory for all employees.

- All forms of smoking should/should not be banned completely from the workplace.

- Employers should/should not provide flextime (flexible working hours) for all office employees.

- Employers should/should not provide on-site child-care facilities for the preschool children of their employees.

- Employees who deal extensively with the public should/should not be required to wear a company uniform.

- Employers should/should not have the right to hire the most qualified employees without regard to affirmative action guidelines.

Assume that your employee group has been asked to present its views to a management committee that will make the final decision regarding your topic. The presentations will be given as follows:

a. Each side (beginning with the pro side) will have 8 minutes to present its views.
b. Each side will then have 3 minutes to confer.
c. Each side (beginning with the con side) will deliver a 2-minute rebuttal—to refute the arguments and answer the issues raised by the other side.
d. Each side (beginning with the pro side) will give a 1-minute summary.
e. The management committee (the rest of the class) will then vote by secret ballot regarding which side (pro or con) presented its case more effectively.

Gather whatever data you think will be helpful to your case, organize it, prepare suitable visual aids, and divide up the speaking roles as you deem best. (*Hint:* It might be helpful to gather information on both the pro and the con sides of the issue in preparation for the rebuttal session, which will be given impromptu.)

11. **Presenting to an International Audience**   The west coast manager of Honda has approached your school of business about the possibility of sending 30 of its Japanese managers to your institution to pursue a three-month intensive course in written and oral business communication. The purpose of the course is to make the Japanese managers better able to interact with their American counterparts.

    You, the assistant provost at your institution, have been asked to give a 6- to 8-minute presentation to the four Japanese executives who will decide whether to fund this program at your institution. The purpose of your presentation is to convince them to select your school.

    Because of the care with which you will want to select your wording for this international audience and because of the high stakes involved, you decide to prepare a full script of your presentation (approximately 1,000 words), along with several overhead transparencies. Submit your script and transparency masters to your instructor.

12. **Evaluating Your Oral Communication Skills**   Arrange to have videotaped one of the oral presentations that you prepared and delivered for this chapter. (Either use your institution's audiovisual services or have a colleague videotape your presentation, using a personal camcorder.) Review the tape and evaluate your performance, using each of the criteria given in Checklist 15 (p. 440).

Prepare a memorandum to your instructor in which you objectively discuss the strengths and weaknesses of your presentation. Your grade for this assignment will be based on your *evaluation* of your presentation—not on the presentation itself. Submit both the videotape and the memorandum to your instructor.

CONTINUING
CASE 13

The Typists Who Lost Their Touch

Review the Continuing Case presented at the ends of Chapters 11 and 12. As you recall, in response to increasing sick-leave among data-entry personnel, Jean Tate asked Pat Robbins to write a report on carpal tunnel syndrome, a neuromuscular wrist injury caused by repeated hand motions such as those used in typing. Assume the role of Pat Robbins. You have now been asked to present the results of your research in a 20-minute session to the executive committee, composed of Dave Kaplan and the three vice presidents. This is your first opportunity to speak to this high-ranking group, and the speech is on a topic about which you developed strong feelings over the past few months as you researched the topic in depth.

Critical Thinking

1. Analyze your audience. Specifically, what do you know (or what can you learn) about each of the executive committee members that will affect your presentation?

2. How will your strong feelings about this topic affect your presentation—either positively or negatively?

Speaking/Writing Projects

Prepare as many of the following projects as are assigned by your instructor. (*Note:* If you did not conduct any primary research for this project, base your presentation on secondary data.)

3. Write your presentation notes, using either full sheets of paper or note cards.

4. Develop five to eight visual aids to use during your presentation.

5. Arrange to have a full-scale practice session of your presentation videotaped. Evaluate your taped practice session in light of the guidelines presented in this chapter. Prepare a memo to your instructor critiquing your performance. Submit both your memo and the videotape.

6. Divide into groups of five students, with each student in turn giving his or her presentation to the other four. Each presenter should conduct a question-and-answer session immediately after each presentation. Be prepared to ask a question of the presenter and to answer any questions directed to you when you present. Prepare a memo to your instructor critiquing the performance of each presenter.

14 Your Résumé and Job-Application Letter

COMMUNICATION OBJECTIVES

After you have finished this chapter, you should be able to

■ Analyze your interests, strengths, weaknesses, and preferred lifestyle as the first step in choosing a career.

■ Research possible professions, demographic trends, industries, and prospective employers.

■ Determine the appropriate length and format for your résumé.

■ Determine the appropriate content for your résumé.

■ Format a résumé for accurate scanning into a computer database.

■ Compose solicited and unsolicited job-application letters.

An Insider's Perspective

Before electronic résumés, Paul Orvos used to receive mailbags full of résumés and job-application letters. Orvos is the Corporate Manager of Employment for Computer Sciences Corporation (CSC), a $5.6 billion company that provides management consulting and information solutions to businesses and government agencies. With nearly 44,000 employees and aggressive plans for global expansion, CSC is growing so fast that Orvos and his colleagues can no longer read each of the résumés they receive every year—many from college graduates starting their careers. Instead, CSC has gone paperless, requesting that applicants submit electronic résumés directly to the company's database, which stores tens of thousands of résumés for screening and consideration when openings arise.

Receiving, storing, and searching résumés electronically makes good business sense, Orvos stresses. "In this technology age, business moves at such a rapid pace that our need for information is much more immediate. We're also spread across the country and around the world, so we use electronic networks to efficiently share resources among the many parts of the organization. We can't easily ship 5,000 paper résumés to an employment manager and expect that all the résumés will be read." So these days, when CSC managers want to fill an open position, they search the companywide résumé database to quickly and conveniently identify likely candidates.

Submitting an electronic résumé makes sense for the applicant as well. "The job-seeker has the added benefit of broader exposure within the organization, compared with more limited exposure when a résumé is submitted by mail or by fax," Orvos explains, "and there's no delay in accessing the electronic résumé. Just seconds after the résumé is sent from the job-seeker's home or office computer, it is instantly available throughout the company."

Although CSC indicates in its employment ads and on its World Wide Web site (http://www.csc.com) that electronic résumés in ASCII (text) format are preferred, it will scan paper résumés so they can be entered into the database. Because no one actually reads the résumés before they are stored in the database, the look of the résumé is far less important than the content. "The days of fancy fonts, underscoring, and bold type are gone," says Orvos. "Content is what counts today." However, grammar and mechanics are still important: "Double- and triple-check your grammar, spelling, and punctuation, because employers view résumés as samples of the quality of work they can expect from you."

When an opening occurs, CSC managers search the résumé database by indicating any number of keywords that define the functional roles and experience needed for that job. Only résumés that contain those keywords will turn up in such a search, which is why Orvos recommends that job-seekers use appropriate descriptive nouns in their electronic résumés. "The keywords vary from employer to employer and from industry to industry," he says. "Generally, your résumé should include nouns that describe your specific functional role, such as programmer or engineer, as well as nouns that describe your experience, such as knowledge of particular programming languages or software packages."

Whether you submit your résumé on paper or electronically, be sure to include more than the bare bones of your job history and functional responsibilities. "While that information is important, it's only half of what an employer needs to see," explains Orvos. "What's missing is the applicant's assessment of what has been learned on each job or project. Every experience is a learning experience. If the applicant's background has little relation to an employer's business, the résumé should stress communication skills, mediation skills, organizational skills, or time-management skills, as well as other skills that translate across business and industry lines."

Paul Orvos

Corporate Manager of Employment, Computer Sciences Corporation (Falls Church, Virginia)

Planning Your Career

Communication skills play an important role in the job campaign.

Although we've stressed throughout this text the importance of communication skills for success on the job, one of your first professional applications of what you've learned will be in actually securing a job. Think for a moment about some of the important communication skills you've developed thus far—for example, how to analyze your audience, write effective letters, research and analyze data, speak persuasively, and use nonverbal communication to achieve your objectives.

All these communication skills will serve you well when you apply for an internship or begin your job-getting campaign—from researching career, industry, and company information to writing effective résumés and application letters to conducting yourself effectively during the job interview. To refine these skills further, in this chapter you will learn how to plan your career, develop a résumé, and write application letters. Chapter 15 covers interviewing and writing post-interview letters.

You must put considerable time, effort, and thought into getting a job if you want to have a rewarding and fulfilling work life. The process is the same whether you're applying for an internship, beginning your first job, changing careers, or returning to the workplace after an extended absence; and it begins with a self-analysis.

Self-Analysis

Your job campaign begins with a self-analysis.

If you are typical of many students, you have changed your major at least once during your college career. Thus, you've already made many important decisions about your life and career. When it is time to decide how to use your college education, you must do some soul-searching to decide exactly how you wish to spend the working hours of your life. Recognize that during the typical week you will probably spend as many of your waking hours at the workplace as at home.

Think about your life, your interests, things you're good at (and those you're not), and the experiences that have given you the most satisfaction. Such introspection will help you make sound career decisions. Take a few moments now to answer these questions:

1. Which courses have you enjoyed most and least in school?
2. Recalling projects on which you've worked in class, in organizations, or at work, which kinds have you been most successful at and enjoyed the most? Which have you disliked?
3. Do you enjoy working most with records (reports, correspondence, and forms), people, ideas, or things? Do you enjoy working more with your mind or with your body?
4. Do you prefer working independently on a project or with a team?
5. How important to you is being your own boss?
6. In what type of work setting do you function best: a quiet office, an environment with lots of activity and people, or an outside location? Would you most enjoy working in the organization's home office, a branch, while traveling, or at home?
7. What type of work schedule would you prefer: fixed or flexible? days, nights, or weekends? How willing or eager are you to work overtime?
8. What is important about the geographical location of your job in terms of climate, size of metropolitan area, and location (downtown, suburban, or

rural)? Do you prefer a particular city, state, region of the country, or international setting (see Spotlight 23—Across Cultures on p. 460)? How willing or eager are you to relocate?

9. For what kind of organization would you like to work: large or small? established or new? commercial, government, or nonprofit?
10. What is important about the personalities of the people with whom you will work? Describe your ideal boss, subordinates, and colleagues.
11. How would you like to dress for work?
12. What types of material rewards are important for you in terms of salary, commissions, fringe benefits, job security, and the like?
13. How willing or eager are you to participate in an extensive on-the-job training program?
14. What are your career goals five years after graduating from college?

Your answers to these questions will help you identify the type of career that would offer you the most satisfaction and success. Remember that for any particular college major, many jobs are available. One of them will likely meet your needs and desires.

Research

Armed with your self-assessment, you are now ready to secure additional information—about possible occupations, demographic trends, and industries and companies in which you're interested. Many job seekers begin their search for occupational information by interviewing one or more people currently employed in the career or industry that interests them. Such sources can provide the current and detailed information you seek, and they're likely to be more objective than a recruiter. Locate such sources by reading the business section of the local newspaper, asking family and friends, or consulting with your college placement office or your professors.

Research possible professions, demographic trends, industries, and prospective employers.

Although the major purpose of such interviews is data gathering, these sessions also advertise your availability for and interest in a position. The interviewee may volunteer information about possible job leads. Avoid, however, turning the informational interview into an employment interview.

Occupational Information   One of the most comprehensive sources of up-to-date information about jobs is the *Occupational Outlook Handbook,* published by the U.S. Department of Labor. The handbook is available both in print and online (http://stats.bls.gov/ocohome.htm).

This handbook describes in detail the 250 occupations that account for seven out of every eight jobs in the U.S. economy. For each occupation, the volume gives detailed and accurate information regarding (1) the nature of the work; (2) working conditions; (3) employment levels; (4) training, qualifications, and advancement; (5) job outlook (that is, projected employment levels and factors influencing the future of the occupation); (6) earnings; (7) related occupations; and (8) sources of additional information.

Learn as much as you can about the occupations in which you're interested.

Other sources of job information are your college placement office, professional associations (see the *Encyclopedia of Associations,* published by Gale Research Company of Detroit, Michigan, for a list of professional associations in your area of interest), and business periodicals, such as the *Wall Street Journal, Business Week,* and *Forbes.* The latter two publications are especially helpful because each issue contains an index of those companies mentioned in that issue.

Working in the International Arena

Many recent graduates elect to work temporarily overseas before "settling down" to a career stateside. Fortunately, many countries allow students or recent graduates to receive a temporary work permit with little hassle. For example, the United Kingdom issues $100 permits, enabling Americans to work in England, Scotland, Wales, or Northern Ireland for up to six months. Many of these temporary employees work as servers, bartenders, hotel staff, secretaries, or retail clerks and then return to the United States to attend graduate school or begin their careers with an international experience added to their résumés.

SPOTLIGHT 23

ACROSS CULTURES

Working for a Japanese Firm

Suppose, however, you wish to secure a more or less permanent position at an American subsidiary of a Japanese firm. You may wonder how to conduct yourself during the intensive interviewing that precedes a job offer. The best advice is just to be yourself. When you meet your interviewers, for example, you do not need to bow; neither, however, should you appear to be too effervescent—wildly shaking hands and talking in a loud voice, with exaggerated body language.

If you're the type of person who needs an immediate decision and who dislikes meetings, you will quickly decide that you should look for a job elsewhere. The Japanese style of consensus management means that you will attend lots of meetings in which every nuance of every decision is discussed. The advantage of such a strategy is that all issues are raised and debated, everyone has his or her say, and everyone thus feels a part of the final decision. Therefore, although decision making may take longer than in an American firm, implementation is likely to be faster and easier.

Job interviews are often very involved and time-consuming. The Japanese view the organization as an extended family and are quite interested in how the applicants as well as their families would fit into the organizational family. Look for an opportunity to show that you are a team member, are eager to work with others, and get along well with your colleagues.

You will likely rise faster and higher in a Japanese-owned firm if you're in the sales or human resources area, which is often headed by an American. Finance, however, which requires close coordination with the headquarters in Japan, is typically headed by a Japanese. And the chief executive officer is invariably Japanese.

Speaking the Language

Although it is not absolutely necessary in all cases, competence in the native language is a very strong qualification—and one that will set you apart from most of your competitors. Only through learning the native language is a person truly able to appreciate a culture, understand how its members think, and become accepted by them. Even if the native businesspeople speak English, as many of them surely will, the fact that you've taken the trouble to learn their language, albeit haltingly and with a pronounced accent, will demonstrate vividly your interest in and respect for them.

Tapping into a Trend

The opportunities for important and satisfying careers in the international arena are enormous and growing rapidly each year. In addition to large international firms, small and medium-sized companies are finding a ready market for their products and services on both sides of both oceans—as well as in Mexico and Canada. Also don't overlook U.S. government positions, including positions in the foreign service and in such organizations as the U.S. Agency for International Development.

If you are adventuresome, self-confident, independent, flexible, curious, and open-minded, perhaps the *world,* rather than any particular country or city, will become your new home.

Demographic Information   Smart career choices are dictated not only by personal interest but also by demographic characteristics, with which you should become familiar. For example, no matter how much you enjoy handwriting and no matter how clear and lovely your lettering is, it is unlikely that you would be able to make a good living today as a scribe (a copier of manuscripts) because technology has preempted that occupation. Some of the demographic trends that the U.S. Department of Labor believes will affect employment through the year 2005 are as follows:[1]

- Over the 1994–2005 period, employment is projected to increase by 18 million or 14%, most of it in the services (especially health and education) and retail trade industries. Manufacturing employment will decline by 7%.

- The fastest-growing occupations reflect growth in computer technology and health services.

- Jobs requiring the most education and training will grow faster than jobs with lower education and training requirements.

- The three occupations having the largest numerical increase in employment for new college graduates are teaching, systems analysis, and social work.

- Women will represent 48% of the labor force in 2005, up from 46% in 1994.

- The number of Hispanics, Asians, and other races in the labor force will increase much faster than the number of blacks and white non-Hispanics; blacks will increase faster than white non-Hispanics.

Study the environment in which you will be working.

Industry and Company Information   Now that you have analyzed yourself in relation to a career, investigated possible professions, and studied demographic trends, you probably have a good idea of the career you want to pursue. You're ready to research industry and company information. No organization exists in a vacuum. Each is affected by the economic, political, and social environment in which it operates.

Start with the Standard Industry Classification (SIC) code for the industry in which you're interested. Also helpful are the *U.S. Industrial Outlook,* published by the U.S. Department of Commerce, and *Standard and Poor's Industry Surveys.*

After learning about the industry, pick out a few companies to explore further. Be guided by your interests—large versus small firms, geographical constraints, and so forth. This research will give you a better framework for evaluating the specific companies with whom you will be interviewing.

It's often helpful to go online and visit the home page of a prospective employer. Don't consider these Web sites sources of objective information because companies use them to market themselves, but they can reveal how a firm likes to see itself and provide key details about the company. Look especially for current company news, its mission statement, most recent annual report, and advertised career opportunities.

Audience Analysis   As noted throughout this text, the task of audience analysis is pivotal to every type of communication skill. Learn as much as you can about the specific employment environment so that you can customize your employment communications to the needs of the employer.

For example, an effective résumé is tailored to the needs of the prospective employer. Analyzing the audience—your potential employer—will show you how to emphasize what you have gained from your education or work experience that

Analyzing the specific organization enables you to tailor your credentials in terms of the organization's needs.

will benefit the company. Employers do not hire you as a reward for what you've accomplished in the past but rather for the promise of what you can do for them in the future. So treat your résumé as an advertisement of good things to come rather than as an obituary of what has already happened.

Currently an organization spends $10,043 just to hire one employee earning more than $20,000 annually,[2] so the cost of making a wrong decision is great. And if you multiply your likely salary times three or four years in a job, you'll see that the organization is making a very expensive purchase when it hires you. If you were making that large an investment, wouldn't you go to great lengths to make the right choice?

To convince the employer that you're worth the investment, learn as much about the organization as possible so that you can then present your credentials in terms of specific reader benefits.

Networking   In the job-getting process, "networking" refers to developing a group of acquaintances who might provide job leads and career guidance. The term has been used so much recently that it has perhaps become a buzzword, but it is still an important job-getting tool. Everyone searching for a job—from the most recent college graduate to the president of a Fortune 500 firm—has a network on which to draw.

Seek the help of professional and personal acquaintances in your job campaign.

Your initial network might include friends, family, professors, former employers, social acquaintances, college alumni, your dentist, family doctor, insurance agent, local businesspeople, your minister or rabbi—in short, anyone you know who might be able to help. Ideally, your network will combine both personal and professional connections. That's one benefit of belonging to professional associations, and college isn't too early to start. Most professional organizations either have student chapters of their associations or provide reduced-rate student memberships in the parent organization.

Certainly, you don't develop a network of acquaintances purely for personal gain; the friendships gained through such contacts can last a lifetime. But don't

Never underestimate the power of networking. Ivy Ang, a human resources pro, got a dream Silicon Valley job by networking relentlessly. Three nights a week she arranged to have dinner with a professional contact. She kept a "call list" in her datebook to help her stay in touch with members of her network, and she was constantly identifying companies she was interested in, often in far-flung industries. As a result, Ang landed a job running the human resources department of a company with 2,000 employees worldwide.

forget to seek the advice and help of everyone who can be of assistance in this important endeavor.

And don't forget to expand your networking efforts into cyberspace. Sign up for online mailing lists, bulletin boards, and newsgroups targeted to your particular interests. You can gain new contacts from around the globe. And log on to one of the many employment sites on the World Wide Web for leads about job vacancies, résumé preparation, interview techniques, career guidance, and the like. Three good places to start are these:

word**wise**

Get the Message?

- "Sure, I can climb cliffs," he bluffed.
- "I love hot dogs," she said frankly.
- "I'm cramming for an exam," he muttered testily.
- "Our field is arthritis research," they explained jointly.
- "I must have that large diamond," she cried Hopefully.

- *What Color Is Your Parachute: The Net Guide* (http://www.washingtonpost.com/wp-adv/classifieds/careerpost/parachute/), which is maintained by the author of the best-selling job-hunting book in the world.

- *JobTrak* (http://www.jobtrak.com/), which works with more than 600 college and university career centers nationwide.

- *The Riley Guide* (http://www.jobtrak.com/jobguide/), which provides an extremely wide range of useful resources for the job seeker.

Preparing Your Résumé

A **résumé** is a brief record of one's personal history and qualifications that is typically prepared by an applicant for a job. Although recruiters sometimes refer to the résumé as a *wilawid* ("What I've learned and what I've done"), the emphasis in the résumé should be on the future rather than on the past: you must show how your education and work experience have prepared you for future jobs—specifically, the job for which you are applying.

Right from the start, be realistic about the purpose of your résumé. Few people are actually hired on the basis of their résumés alone. (However, many people are *not hired* because of their poorly written or poorly presented résumés.) Instead, applicants are generally hired on the basis of their performance during a job interview.

Thus, the purpose of the résumé is to get you an interview, and the purpose of the interview is to get you a job. Remember, however, that the résumé and accompanying application letter (cover letter) are crucial in advancing you beyond the mass of initial applicants and into the much smaller group of potential candidates invited to an interview.

The purpose of a résumé is to get you a job interview— not to get you a job.

Résumé Length

Decisions about résumé length become much easier when you consider what happens on the receiving end: recruiters typically spend no more than 35 seconds looking at each résumé during their initial screening to pare down the perhaps hundreds of applications for a position into a manageable number to study in more detail.[3] How much information can the recruiter be expected to read in less than a minute? It won't matter how well qualified you are if no one ever reviews those qualifications.

Most recruiters prefer a one-page résumé for entry-level positions.

As one recruiter for a larger corporation has noted, the perfect résumé is "like a Henny Youngman two-liner. No fat. Get to the point and then say goodbye. . . . Remember: You're trying to get us to hire you, not to marry you."[4]

How much is too much? Surveys of employment and human resource executives consistently show that most managers prefer a one-page résumé for the entry-level positions typically sought by recent college graduates, with a two-page résumé being reserved for unusual circumstances or for higher-level positions.[5] True or not, take note of the old placement-office adage, "The thicker the résumé, the thicker the applicant."

According to one survey of 200 executives from major U.S. firms, the most serious mistake job candidates make is including too much information in their résumés. Their ranking (in percentages of the whole) of the most serious résumé errors is as follows:[6]

Too long	32%
Typographical or grammatical errors	25%
No descriptions of job functions	18%
Unprofessional appearance	15%
Achievements omitted	10%
	100%

A one-page résumé is *not* the same as a two-page résumé crammed onto one page by means of small type and narrow margins. Your résumé must be attractive and easy to read. Shorten your résumé by making judicious decisions about what to include and then by using concise language to communicate what is important.

Do not, on the other hand, make your résumé *too* short. A résumé that does not fill one page may tell the prospective employer that you have little to offer. It has been estimated that one page is ideal for 85% of all résumés, and that is the length you should target.[7]

Résumé Format

Although the content of your résumé is obviously more important than the format, remember that first impressions are lasting. As pointed out earlier, those first impressions are formed during the half-minute that is typically devoted to the initial screening of each résumé. Therefore, even before you begin writing your résumé, think about the format, because some format decisions will affect the amount of space available to discuss your qualifications and background.

If you prepare your résumé and application letter on a computer, you can easily customize them for each employment opportunity. In addition, you'll be sending the employer a nonverbal message that you know how to use a computer and word processing software.

If you print your résumé on a laser printer, it will be nearly indistinguishable from a typeset one. With laser printers, you have the option of using different typefaces (such as Times Roman or Helvetica) and different sizes and styles (such as boldface and italics) to make different parts stand out. Consider, for example, the two versions of the same résumé shown in Spotlight 24—On Technology. Both contain identical information; which one makes the better first impression?

Use a clear, simple design, with plenty of white space.

Choose a simple, easy-to-read typeface, and avoid the temptation to use a lot of "special effects" just because they're available on your computer. One or two typefaces in one or two different sizes should be enough. Use a simple format, with lots of white space, short paragraphs, and a logical organization. Through the use of

First Impressions Count!

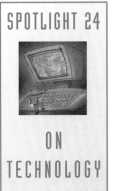

PATRICIA L. BAILEY

(Address until May 10, 1998)   (Address after May 10, 1998)
112 Campus Drive, Apt. B   915 North Jay Street
Bloomington, IN 47401   Indianapolis, IN 46204
Phone: 812-555-9331   Phone: 317-555-0328

JOB OBJECTIVE
Professional position in hotel management in the Chicago metropo-
    litan area

EDUCATION
Bachelor of Science in Business Administration
    Indiana University: May 1998
    Major: Hospitality Services Administration
    Minor: Marketing
        Achieved overall grade-point average of 3.4 (on a 4.0 scale).
        Received Board of Regents' tuition scholarship.
        Financed 75% of college expenses through savings and part-
        time work.

WORK EXPERIENCE
Assistant Manager, McDonald's Restaurant
    Bloomington, Indiana: 1994-Present
    part-time during school year)
        Advanced to this position after
        clerk and cook; developed work
        ployees; designed and administe
        incentive projects; gained cons
        in supervising employees and ha

Student Intern, Valley Hideaway
    South Bend, Indiana: September-Dece
    ship sponsored by Indiana Universit
        Worked as the assistant to the
        resort; gained experience in op
        ment system; was responsible fo
        occupancy reports; wrote two a
        newsletter.

PERSONAL
Active member of Sigma Iota Epsilon (b
Treasurer of Hospitality Services Asso
Special Olympics volunteer--Summer 199

REFERENCES AVAILABLE

Patricia L. Bailey

(Address until May 10, 1998)   *(Address after May 10, 1998)*
112 Campus Drive, Apt. B   915 North Jay Street
Bloomington, IN 47401   Indianapolis, IN 46204
Phone: 812-555-9331   Phone: 317-555-0328

Job Objective
Professional position in hotel management in the Chicago metropolitan area

Education
Bachelor of Science in Business Administration   Indiana University, May 1998
Major: Hospitality Services Administration
Minor: Marketing
- Achieved overall grade-point average of 3.4 (on a 4.0 scale).
- Received Board of Regents' tuition scholarship.
- Financed 75% of college expenses through savings and part-time work.

Work Experience
Assistant Manager, McDonald's Restaurant   Bloomington, Indiana
1994-Present (full-time during summers; part-time during school year)
- Advanced to this position after only six months as a counter clerk and cook.
- Developed work schedules for 23 part-time employees.
- Designed and administered several successful employee incentive projects.
- Gained considerable practical experience in supervising employees and handling
  human-relations problems.

Student Intern, Valley Hideaway   South Bend, Indiana
September-December 1997 (full-time internship sponsored by Indiana University)
- Worked as the assistant to the night manager of a 200-room resort.
- Gained experience in operating the GuestServ management system.
- Was responsible for producing daily and weekly occupancy reports.
- Wrote two articles for the employee newsletter.

Personal
Active member of Sigma Iota Epsilon (business honor society)
Treasurer of Hospitality Services Association
Special Olympics volunteer—Summer 1997

References Available Upon Request

The above version of the résumé was typed on an electronic typewriter and arranged in an attractive, easy-to-read format. However, the absence of different type styles and sizes limits design flexibility.

The version to the right was typed on a microcomputer using word processing software and printed on a laser printer. It contains the same information as the typewritten version, but it is much more attractive and readable.

type size and style, indentation, bullets, and the like, make clear which parts are subordinate to main features.

Format your résumé on standard-sized paper (8½ by 11 inches) so that it can be filed easily. Also, avoid brightly colored papers: they'll get attention but perhaps the wrong kind. Dark colors do not photocopy well, and you want photocopies of your résumé (whether made by you or by the potential employer) to look professional. Choose white or an off-white (cream or ivory) paper of good quality—at least 20-pound bond.

Unless you're applying for a creative position (such as a copywriter of advertising material) and know your intended audience well, avoid being too artistic and original in formatting your résumé. If you are applying for the typical business position, the overall appearance of your résumé should present a professional, conservative appearance—one that adds to your credibility. Don't scare off your readers before they have a chance to meet you.

Finally, your résumé and application letter must be 100% free from error—in content, spelling, grammar, and format. Ninety-nine percent accuracy is simply not good enough when seeking a job. One recent survey of large-company executives showed that fully 80% of them had decided against interviewing a job seeker simply because of poor grammar, spelling, or punctuation in his or her résumé.[8] Don't write, as one job applicant did, "Education: Advanced Curses in Accounting," or as another did, "I have an obsession for detail; I make sure that I cross my i's and dot my t's." Show right from the start that you're the type of person who takes pride in his or her work.

Résumé Content

Fortunately, perhaps, there is no such thing as a standard résumé; each is as individual as the person it represents. There are, however, standard parts of the résumé—those parts recruiters expect and need to see to make valid judgments. For example, one survey of 152 Fortune 500 company personnel indicated that 90% or more wanted the following information on a résumé:[9]

- Name, address, and telephone number

- Job objective

Include the information employers want; exclude the information they do not want.

- College major, degree, name of college, and date of graduation

- Jobs held, employing company or companies (but not complete mailing address or the names of your supervisors), dates of employment, and job duties

- Special aptitudes and skills

Similarly, items *not* wanted on the résumé (items rated unimportant by over 90% of those surveyed) related primarily to bases for discrimination: religion, ethnicity, age, gender, photograph, and marital status. Additionally, most of the employers questioned thought high school activities should not be included on the résumés of college graduates.

The standard and optional parts of the résumé are discussed here in the order in which they typically appear on the résumé of a recent (or soon-to-be) college graduate.

LYING ON YOUR RÉSUMÉ

NOBODY EVER GOT A JOB BY BEING COMPLETELY HONEST ON THEIR RÉSUMÉ. MAKE YOUR LIES BOLD, CREATIVE, AND ABOVE ALL: UNVERIFIABLE.

YOUR RÉSUMÉ SHOWS TWENTY YEARS AS A SENIOR EXECUTIVE AT THE CIA...

YES, AND THEY ARE INSTRUCTED TO KILL ANYBODY WHO TRIES TO CHECK ON IT.

Identifying Information   It doesn't do any good to impress a recruiter if he or she cannot locate you easily to schedule an interview; therefore, your name and complete address (including phone number) are crucial.

Your name should be the very first item on the résumé, arranged attractively at the top. Use whatever form you typically use for signing your name (for example, with or without initials). Give your complete name, avoiding nicknames, and do not use a personal title such as *Mr.* or *Ms.*

It is not necessary to include the heading "Résumé" at the top (any more than it is necessary to use the heading "Letter" at the top of a business letter). The purpose of the document will be evident to the recruiter. Besides, you want your name to be the main heading—where it will stand out in the recruiter's mind.

If you will soon be changing your address (as from a college address to a home address), include both, along with the relevant dates for each. If you are away from your telephone most of the day and no one is at home to answer it and take a message, you would be wise to secure phone company voice mail, invest in an answering machine, or get permission to use the telephone number where you work as an alternate phone listing. The important point is to be available for contact.

Display your name, address, and phone number in a prominent position.

Increasingly, employers are also expecting an e-mail address to be listed. An e-mail address not only provides another means of contact but also sends a nonverbal message that you are computer savvy.

Job Objective   The job objective is a short summary of your area of expertise and career interest. As indicated, most recruiters want the objective stated so that they will know where you might fit into their organization. Don't force the employer to guess about your career goals.

Furthermore, don't waste the objective's prominent spot at the top of your résumé by giving a weak, over-general goal like these:

> **NOT:**   "A position that offers both a challenge and an opportunity for growth."
> "Challenging position in a progressive organization."
> "A responsible position that lets me use my education and experience and that provides opportunities for increased responsibilities."

The problem with such goals is not that they're unworthy objectives; they are *very* worthwhile. That is why everyone—including the recruiter presumably—wants such positions. The problem is that such vague, high-flown goals don't help the recruiter find a suitable position for *you*. They waste valuable space on your résumé.

Include a job objective if you have specific requirements.

For your objective to help you, it must be personalized—both for you and for the position you're seeking. Also, it must be specific enough to be useful to the prospective employer but not so specific as to exclude you from many types of similar positions. The following job objectives meet these criteria:

> **BUT:**   "A paid, one-semester internship in marketing or advertising."
> **BUT:**   "Position in personal sales in a medium-sized manufacturing firm."
> **BUT:**   "Opportunity to apply my accounting education and Spanish-language skills in a corporation overseas."
> **BUT:**   "A public relations position requiring well-developed communication, administrative, and computer skills."

Note that after reading these objectives, you feel you know a little about each candidate, a feeling you did not get from reading the earlier general objectives. If your goals are so broad that you have difficulty specifying a job objective, consider either eliminating this section of your résumé or developing several résumés, each with a different job objective and emphasis.

You should be aware that an increasing number of large corporations have begun scanning the résumés they receive into their computer systems and then searching this computerized database by key word. Be certain, therefore, that the title of the actual position you desire and other relevant terms are included somewhere in your résumé. (Later in this chapter, see the section on electronic résumés.)

Education   Unless your work experience has been extensive, fairly high level, and directly related to your job objective, your education is probably a stronger job qualification than your work experience and should therefore come first on the résumé.

List the title of your degree, the name of your college and its location if needed, your major and (if applicable) minor, and your expected date of graduation (month and year).

List your grade-point average if it will set you apart from the competition (generally, at least a 3.0 on a 4.0 scale). If you've made the dean's list or have financed any substantial portion of your college expenses through part-time work, savings, or scholarships, mention that. Unless your course of study provided distinctive experiences that uniquely qualify you for the job, avoid including a lengthy list of college courses.

Work Experience   Today, almost half of all full-time college students are employed, most of them working between 15 and 29 hours a week.[10] And most other students have had at least some work experience in the past—for example, summer jobs. Thus, most students will have some work experience to bring to their future jobs.

Work experience—*any* work experience—is a definite plus. It shows the employer that you've had experience in satisfying a superior, following directions, accomplishing objectives through group effort, and being rewarded for your labors. If your work experience has been directly related to your job objectives, consider putting it ahead of the education section, where it will receive more emphasis.

In relating your work experience, use either a chronological or a functional organizational pattern.

Regardless of which type of organizational pattern you use, provide complete information about your work history.

- *Chronological:* In a chronological arrangement, you organize your experience by date, describing your most recent job first and working backward. This format is most appropriate when you have had a strong continuing work history and much of your work has been related to your job objective (see Model 29, p. 470). About 95% of all résumés are chronological, beginning with the most recent information and working backward.[11]

- *Functional:* In a functional arrangement, you organize your experience by type of function performed (such as *supervision* or *budgeting*) or by type of skill developed (such as *human relations* or *communication skills*). Then, under each, are specific examples (evidence) as illustrated in Model 30 on page 471. Functional résumés are most appropriate when you're changing industries, moving into an entirely different line of work, or reentering the work force after a long period of unemployment, because they emphasize your skills rather than your employment history and let you show how these skills have broad applicability to other jobs.

In actual practice, the two patterns are not mutually exclusive; you can use a combination. And regardless of which arrangement you ultimately decide on, remember that more than 90% of the employers in the survey cited earlier indicated they want to see on a résumé the jobs held, employing company or companies, dates of employment, and job duties.

Remember that the purpose of describing your work history is to show the prospective employer what you've learned *that will benefit the organization.* No matter what your previous work, you've developed certain traits or had certain experiences that can be transferred to the new position. On the basis of your research into the duties of the job you are seeking, highlight those transferable skills.

If you can honestly do so, show in your résumé that you have developed as many of the following characteristics as possible:

- Ability to work well with others

- Communication skills

MODEL 29 **Résumé in Chronological Format**

This résumé presents the most recent job experience and education first and works backward.

Provides specific enough objective to be useful.

Places work experience before education because applicant considers it to be her stronger qualification.

Uses action words like *assisted* and *developed;* uses incomplete sentences to emphasize the action words and to conserve space.

Provides degree, institution, major, and graduation date.

Provides additional data to enhance her credentials.

Does not include actual names and addresses of references.

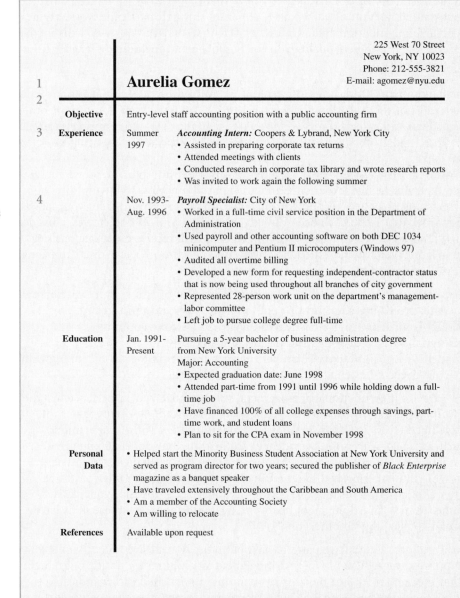

225 West 70 Street
New York, NY 10023
Phone: 212-555-3821
E-mail: agomez@nyu.edu

1

Aurelia Gomez

2

Objective		Entry-level staff accounting position with a public accounting firm
3 **Experience**	Summer 1997	***Accounting Intern:*** Coopers & Lybrand, New York City • Assisted in preparing corporate tax returns • Attended meetings with clients • Conducted research in corporate tax library and wrote research reports • Was invited to work again the following summer
4	Nov. 1993-Aug. 1996	***Payroll Specialist:*** City of New York • Worked in a full-time civil service position in the Department of Administration • Used payroll and other accounting software on both DEC 1034 minicomputer and Pentium II microcomputers (Windows 97) • Audited all overtime billing • Developed a new form for requesting independent-contractor status that is now being used throughout all branches of city government • Represented 28-person work unit on the department's management-labor committee • Left job to pursue college degree full-time
Education	Jan. 1991-Present	Pursuing a 5-year bachelor of business administration degree from New York University Major: Accounting • Expected graduation date: June 1998 • Attended part-time from 1991 until 1996 while holding down a full-time job • Have financed 100% of all college expenses through savings, part-time work, and student loans • Plan to sit for the CPA exam in November 1998
Personal Data		• Helped start the Minority Business Student Association at New York University and served as program director for two years; secured the publisher of *Black Enterprise* magazine as a banquet speaker • Have traveled extensively throughout the Caribbean and South America • Am a member of the Accounting Society • Am willing to relocate
References		Available upon request

Grammar and Mechanics Notes

1 The name is formatted in larger type for emphasis.   2 Horizontal and vertical rules separate the heading information from the body of the résumé.   3 The major section headings are parallel in format and in wording.   4 The side headings for the dates are formatted in a column for ease of reading. Note that abbreviations may be used.

MODEL 30 Résumé in Functional Format

RAYMOND J. ARNOLD

1 **OBJECTIVE**

Labor relations position in a large multinational firm that requires
well-developed labor relations, management, and communication skills

SKILLS

LABOR RELATIONS
- Majored in labor relations; minored in psychology
- Belong to Local 463 of International Office Workers Union
- Was crew chief for the second-shift work team at Wainwright Bank

2

MANAGEMENT
- Learned time-management skills by working 30 hours per week while attending school full-time
- Was promoted twice in three years at Wainwright Bank
- Practiced discretion while dealing with the financial affairs of others; treated all transactions confidentially

COMMUNICATION
- Was the newsletter editor for Alpha Kappa Psi, professional business fraternity
- Ran for senior class vice president, making frequent campaign speeches and impromptu remarks

3
- Took elective classes in report writing and business research
- Know how to use Windows word processing, spreadsheet, and desktop-publishing software

4

EDUCATION

B.S. Degree from Boston University
- Major: Labor Relations; Minor: Psychology
- Degree to be awarded June 1998

EXPERIENCE

Bank teller, Wainwright Bank, Boston, Massachusetts: 1995-Present
Salesperson, JC Penney, Norfolk, Nebraska: Summer 1993

REFERENCES

Available from the Career Information Center, Boston
University, Boston, MA 02215; phone: 617-555-2000

15 TURNER HALL, BOSTON UNIVERSITY, BOSTON, MA 02215-8134 • PHONE: 617-555-9833 • E-MAIL: RJARNOLD@BU.EDU

Sidebar annotations:

Introduces three skill areas and expands on each with bulleted examples.

Relates each listed item directly to the desired job.

Provides specific evidence to support each skill.

Weaves work experiences, education, and extra-curricular activities into the skill statements.

Avoids repeating the duties given earlier.

Grammar and Mechanics Notes

1 Putting the headings along the side and indenting the copy opens up the résumé, providing more white space. (This document was formatted using the "Elegant" résumé template in Microsoft® Word.)   2 Bullets are used to highlight the individual skills; asterisks would have worked just as well.   3 All items are in parallel format.   4 More space is left *between* the different sections than *within* sections (to clearly separate each section).

Show how your work experience qualifies you for the type of job for which you are applying.

- Competence and good judgment
- Innovation
- High-level computer proficiency
- Reliability and trustworthiness
- Enthusiasm
- Honest and moral character
- Increasing responsibility

Complete sentences are not necessary. Instead, start your descriptions with action verbs, using present tense for current duties and past tense for previous job duties or accomplishments. Concrete words such as the following make your work experience come alive:

Use concrete, achievement-oriented words to describe your experience.

accomplished	designed	operated
achieved	determined	ordered
administered	developed	organized
analyzed	diagnosed	oversaw
applied	directed	planned
approved	edited	prepared
arranged	established	presented
assisted	evaluated	presided
authorized	forecast	produced
balanced	generated	purchased
budgeted	guided	recommended
built	handled	reported
changed	hired	researched
collected	implemented	revised
communicated	increased	scheduled
completed	instituted	screened
conceived	interviewed	secured
concluded	introduced	simplified
conducted	investigated	sold
consolidated	led	studied
constructed	maintained	supervised
contracted	managed	taught
controlled	marketed	trained
coordinated	modified	transformed
created	motivated	updated
delegated	negotiated	wrote

Avoid weak verbs such as *attempted, endeavored, hoped,* and *tried,* and avoid sexist language such as *manpower* or *chairman.* When possible, ensure credibility by listing specific accomplishments, giving numbers or dollar amounts. Highlight especially those accomplishments that have direct relevance to the desired job. Here are some examples:

NOT: I was responsible for a large sales territory.

BUT: Managed a six-county sales territory; increased sales 13% during first full year.

NOT: I worked as a clerk in the cashier's office.

BUT: Balanced the cash register every day; was the only part-time employee entrusted to make nightly cash deposits.

NOT: Worked as a bouncer at a local bar.

BUT: Maintained order at Nick's Side-Door Saloon; learned firsthand the importance of compromise and negotiation in solving problems.

NOT: Worked as a volunteer for Art Reach.

BUT: Personally sold more than $1,000 worth of tickets to annual benefit dance; introduced an "Each one, reach one" membership drive that increased membership every year during my three-year term as membership chairperson.

As illustrated in the last example, if you have little or no actual work experience, show how your involvement with professional, social, or civic organizations has helped you develop skills that are transferable to the workplace. Volunteer work, for example, can help develop valuable skills in time management, working with groups, handling money, speaking, accepting responsibility, and the like. In addition, many schools offer internships in which a student receives course credit and close supervision while holding down a temporary job.

Work experience need not be restricted to paid positions.

It has been said that the closest any of us comes to perfection is when we develop our résumé, which has also been called "a balance sheet without any liabilities." Employers recognize your right to put your best foot forward in your résumé—that is, to highlight your strengths and minimize your weaknesses. However, you must never lie about anything and must never take credit for anything you did not do. A simple telephone call can verify any statement on your résumé.

The *Wall Street Journal* calls the background checking of job applicants a growth industry.[12] Screening firms can electronically tap into public records and purchase the computerized files of credit-reporting firms, often producing résumé verifications within 24 hours at a cost of a few dollars per search. Don't risk destroying your credibility before being hired, and don't risk the possibility of being dismissed later for misrepresenting your qualifications.

Be ethical in all aspects of your résumé.

Other Relevant Information   If you have special skills that might give you an edge over the competition (such as knowledge of a foreign language), list them. Although competence in common software programs such as spreadsheets, word processing, and databases was considered a special skill in the past, today employers assume that most business graduates will have such skills; therefore, listing them will not be of special benefit to you. However, nonbusiness majors should list these and any other specific business skills on their résumés.

Include any honors or recognitions that have relevance to the job you're seeking. Memberships in business-related organizations demonstrate your commitment to your profession, and you should list them if space permits. Likewise, involvement in volunteer, civic, and other extracurricular activities gives evidence of a well-rounded individual and reflects your values and commitment.

Avoid including any data that can become grounds for a discrimination suit—such as information about age, gender, race, religion, handicaps, marital status, and the like. Do not include a photograph with your application papers. Some employers like to have the applicant's Social Security number included as an aid in verifying college or military information. If you have military experience, include it. If your name stereotypes you as a possible noncitizen and citizenship is important for the job you want, you may want to explicitly state your citizenship.

Other optional information includes hobbies and special interests, travel experiences, willingness to travel, and health status. (However, because it is unlikely that anyone has ever written "Health—Poor" on a résumé, a health statement may be meaningless.) Such information may be included if it has direct relevance to your desired job and if you have room for it, but it may be safely omitted if you need space for more important information.

As space permits, include other information that uniquely qualifies you for the type of position for which you're applying.

References   A **reference** is a person who has agreed to provide information to a prospective employer regarding a job applicant's fitness for a job. As a general rule, the names and addresses of references should not be included on the résumé itself. Instead, give a general statement that references are available. This policy ensures that you will be contacted before your references are called. The exception to this practice is if your references are likely to be known by the person reading the résumé; in this case, list their names.

The names of references are generally not included on the résumé.

Your references should be professional references rather than character references. The best ones are employers, especially your present employer. University professors with whom you have had a close and successful relationship are also valuable references. When asking for references, be prepared to sign a waiver stating that you forgo your right to see the recommendation or that you won't claim that a reference prevented you from getting a job. Many firms are becoming reluctant to authorize their managers to provide reference letters because of the possibility of being sued.

Study the résumé presented earlier in Spotlight 24 (p. 465) and the two résumés shown in Models 29 and 30. Note the different formats that can be used to present the data. As stated earlier, there is no standard résumé format. Use these résumés or others to which you have access (available from your college career-center office or from job-hunting books) to glean ideas for formatting your own.

Note also the different organizational patterns used to convey work experience. The résumé in Model 29 is arranged in a chronological pattern (with the most recent work experience listed first), whereas the one in Model 30 is arranged in a functional pattern that stresses the skills learned rather than the jobs held. Note how job descriptions and skills are all geared to support the applicant's qualifications for the desired job. Note also the concise, concrete language used and the overall tone of quiet confidence.

Electronic Résumés

An **electronic résumé** is a résumé that is stored in a computer database designed to help manage and initially screen job applicants. These résumés come from a variety of sources; applicants may simply mail or fax a paper copy of their standard résumé, which is then scanned into a database; they may fill out (type in) an online résumé form and submit it; they may send the résumé as an e-mail message; or they may post their résumé on the Internet, using a bulletin board system, a newsgroup, or a personal home page on the World Wide Web.

Electronic résumés provide many benefits—both to the recruiter and to the job seeker:

- The job seeker's résumé is potentially available to a large number of employers.

- The job seeker may be considered for positions he or she wasn't even aware of.

- The initial screening is done by a bias-free computer.

- Employers are relieved of the drudgery of having to manually screen and acknowledge résumés.

- A focused search can be conducted quickly.

- Information is always available until the individual résumé is purged from the system (often in six months).

Two types of systems are in use. An applicant-tracking system (ATS) is a computerized database that companies purchase and maintain to help them track incoming résumés—no small task for many companies. According to Karen Cross, a Nike employment specialist, "Nobody at Nike ever looked at the résumé files because they were just too huge"; at Stratus, a computer manufacturer that receives 15,000 résumés a year, "Recruiters lugged hundreds of résumés home to cull while watching *Monday Night Football,*" according to Elliot Wells, human resources manager.[13]

The second type of system in use is a commercial résumé databank. Commercial software firms solicit and store thousands of electronic résumés submitted by job applicants nationwide. Hiring companies then use key words to do an electronic search for applicants meeting their qualifications. Fees may be paid by either the applicant or the employer.

In either system, when jobs need to be filled, a computer is fed a list of keywords and phrases. The computer looks through the database and prints out a list of candidates with the most keyword matches. A person picks it up from there, manually studying each selected résumé to determine whom to invite for an interview. (So far, electronic tools alter only the screening, not the selection, process. People are still hired by people.)

Building appropriate keywords into your résumé is essential to successfully using automated résumé systems. Keywords are the descriptive terms that employers search for when trying to fill a position. They are the words and phrases employers believe best summarize the characteristics that they are seeking in candidates for particular jobs, such as college degree, foreign language skills, job titles, specific job skills, software packages, or the names of competitors for whom applicants may have worked. Examples of key terms include *human resources manager, Hughes Aircraft, Windows 97, teamwork,* or *ISO 9000.*

Electronic résumés must be picked up by a computer search before they are even seen by human eyes. OCR software creates an ASCII (text) file of your résumé, and artificial intelligence software then "reads" the text and extracts important information about you. Thus, your first hurdle is *to be selected by the computer.*

Because you can never be sure how your résumé will be treated, you should prepare two résumés—one for the computer to read and one for people to read. When mailing a résumé, you may wish to include both versions, making note of that fact in your cover letter. Differences between the two versions concern both content and format.

Content Guidelines for Electronic Résumés   Using your standard résumé as a starting point, make these modifications to ensure that your résumé is "computer-friendly" and to maximize the chance that your résumé will be picked by the computer for further review by humans:

1. Think "nouns" instead of "verbs" (users rarely search for verbs). Use concrete words rather than vague descriptions. Include industry-specific descriptive nouns that characterize your skills accurately and that people in your field use and commonly look for. (Browse other online résumés, newspaper ads, and industry publications to see what terms are currently being used.)
2. Put keywords in proper context, weaving them throughout your résumé. (This is considered a more polished and sophisticated approach than listing them in a block at the beginning of the résumé.)
3. Use a variety of different words to describe your skills, and don't overuse important words. In most searches, each word counts once, no matter how many times it is used.
4. Because your résumé is going to look very bland in plain ASCII text, stripped of all formatting, consider adding a sentence such as this to the end of your posted résumé: "An attractive and fully formatted hard-copy version of this résumé is available upon request."

Format Guidelines for Electronic Résumés   The following guidelines will ensure that your résumé is in a format that can be scanned accurately and transmitted accurately as an e-mail message.

1. First, create a traditionally formatted résumé following the guidelines discussed earlier in this chapter, and save it as you normally would (so that you will always have the formatted version available).
2. Then save the résumé as a text-only file; most word processors allow you to save a file as an ASCII or DOS file, which has a file name with a .txt extension. Special formatting, fonts, tabs, margin changes, and the like are lost in a text file. Only the following ASCII characters are allowed:

   . , ; : ? ! - / | \ " ( ) [ ] { } < > ^ ' ~ @ # $ % & * + - =
   0 1 2 3 4 5 6 7 8 9
   A B C D E F G H I J K L M N O P Q R S T U V W X Y Z
   a b c d e f g h i j k l m n o p q r s t u v w x y z

   By saving your scannable résumé as a text file, you can view a printout of your résumé pretty much as it will look after it has been scanned by the prospective employer.
3. Now reopen the text file and make any needed changes to your résumé (see the remaining guidelines). Make sure you always save the document as a text file—not as a word processing document.
4. To ensure accurate reading by computer software, make the format as plain as possible. Do not change typefaces, justification, margins, tabs, font sizes, and the like; do not insert underlines, bold, or italic; and do not use horizontal or

Aliza Sherman, founder of Webgrrls, has seen the future, and it is wired. Webgrrls is a group of female professionals in lower Manhattan who meet regularly to network, explore job opportunities via the Internet, and provide support and savvy inside advice to one another. No matter whether you submit your résumé on the Web, via mail, or in person, it must be persuasive, specific, ethical, and error-free.

vertical rules, graphics, boxes, tables, or columns. None of these will show up in a printout or scan of a text file. (If necessary for clarity, you can insert a row of hyphens to simulate a horizontal rule.)

5. Use a line length of no more than 70 characters per line. Because you can't change margins in a text file, press Enter at the ends of lines if necessary.

6. Do not divide (hyphenate) words at the end of a line.

7. Change bullets to * or + signs at the beginning of the line; then insert spaces at the beginning of runover lines to make all lines of a bulleted paragraph begin at the same point.

8. Press the space bar (instead of the tab) to show any needed indentions.

9. Type your name on the first line by itself, use a standard address format below your name, and type each phone number on its own line. Include an e-mail address if possible.

10. Make the résumé as long as necessary (most database résumés average 2–3 pages).

11. After making all needed changes, as a test, mail your text file in the body of an e-mail message to yourself or to a friend to see how it looks after being mailed. This will help you identify any more formatting problems before you send it out to possible employers.

12. Use white 8½-by-11-inch paper, printed on one side only. Do not use textured paper.

13. Submit a clean, laser-printed original copy; do not fold or staple.

14. If responding via e-mail, use the job title or noted reference number as the subject of your message. Always send the résumé in the body of the e-mail message. Don't assume that you can attach a word-processed document to an e-mail message; it may or may not be readable.

15. Whenever you update your résumé, remember to update both versions.

These guidelines are illustrated in Model 31—an electronic version of the standard résumé shown in Model 29. The savvy job seeker would probably send both versions to a prospective employer.

As illustrated in Figure 14.1, when formatted in plain ASCII text, an electronic résumé can be sent as an e-mail message with the assurance that it will arrive in readable format.

Because your résumé is about you, it is perhaps the most personal business document you'll ever write. Use everything you know about successful communication techniques to ensure that you tell your story in the most effective manner possible. After you're satisfied with the content and arrangement of your résumé, proofread your document carefully and have several others proofread it also. Then have it printed on high-quality white or off-white 8½-by-11-inch paper, and turn your attention to your cover letters.

The guidelines for developing a résumé are summarized in Checklist 16 (p. 480).

Writing Job-Application Letters

A résumé itself is all that is generally needed to secure an interview with an on-campus recruiter. However, you will likely not want to limit your job search to those

FIGURE 14.1 An electronic résumé in an e-mail message

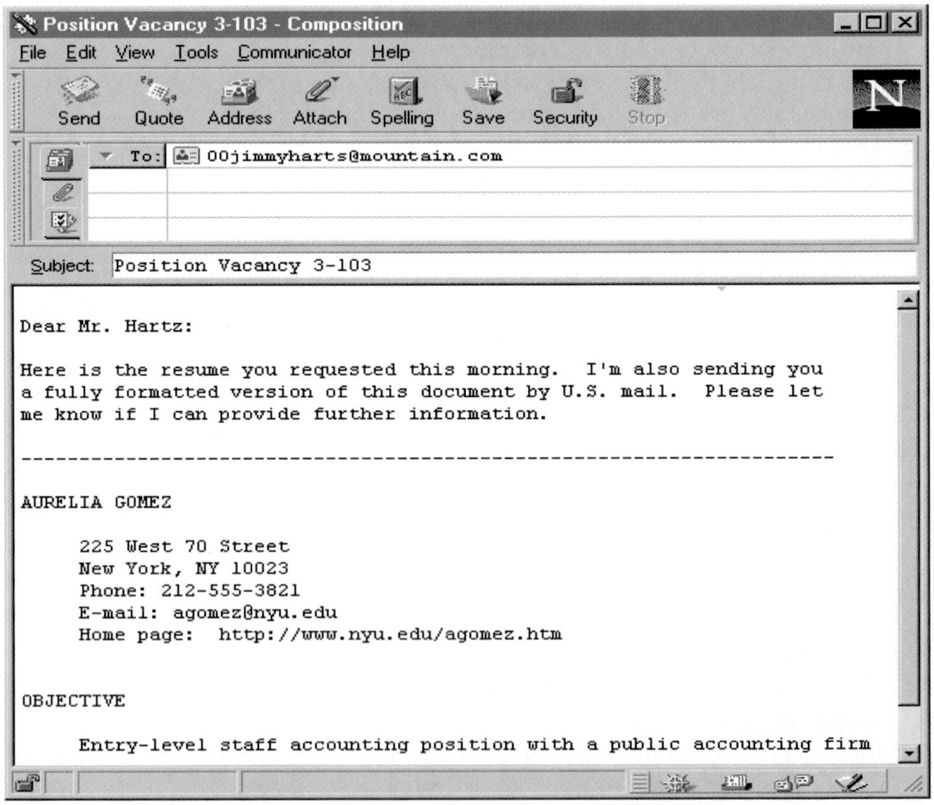

MODEL 31   Electronic Résumé

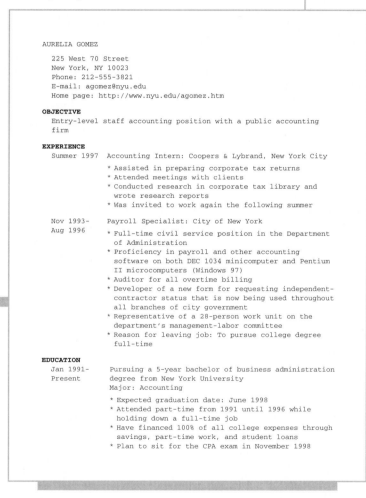

PERSONAL DATA
 * Helped start the Minority Business Student Association at New
   York University and served as program director for two years;
   secured the publisher of BLACK ENTERPRISE magazine as a banquet
   speaker
 * Have traveled extensively throughout the Caribbean and South
   America
 * Am a member of the Accounting Society
 * Am willing to relocate

REFERENCES
 Available upon request

NOTE
 An attractive and fully formatted hard-copy version of this resume
 is available upon request.

AURELIA GOMEZ

 225 West 70 Street
 New York, NY 10023
 Phone: 212-555-3821
 E-mail: agomez@nyu.edu
 Home page: http://www.nyu.edu/agomez.htm

OBJECTIVE
 Entry-level staff accounting position with a public accounting
 firm

EXPERIENCE
 Summer 1997   Accounting Intern: Coopers & Lybrand, New York City

               * Assisted in preparing corporate tax returns
               * Attended meetings with clients
               * Conducted research in corporate tax library and
                 wrote research reports
               * Was invited to work again the following summer

 Nov 1993-   Payroll Specialist: City of New York
 Aug 1996   * Full-time civil service position in the Department
                 of Administration
               * Proficiency in payroll and other accounting
                 software on both DEC 1034 minicomputer and Pentium
                 II microcomputers (Windows 97)
               * Auditor for all overtime billing
               * Developer of a new form for requesting independent-
                 contractor status that is now being used throughout
                 all branches of city government
               * Representative of a 28-person work unit on the
                 department's management-labor committee
               * Reason for leaving job: To pursue college degree
                 full-time

EDUCATION
 Jan 1991-   Pursuing a 5-year bachelor of business administration
 Present   degree from New York University
               Major: Accounting

               * Expected graduation date: June 1998
               * Attended part-time from 1991 until 1996 while
                 holding down a full-time job
               * Have financed 100% of all college expenses through
                 savings, part-time work, and student loans
               * Plan to sit for the CPA exam in November 1998

Runs longer than one page (acceptable with electronic résumés).

Includes notice of availability of a fully formatted version.

Begins with name at the top, followed immediately by addresses (both an e-mail address and a home page address).

Emphasizes, where possible, nouns as keywords.

Grammar and Mechanics Notes

Only ASCII characters are used; all text is one size with no special formatting; no rules, graphics, columns, tables, and the like are used. Vertical line spaces (Enter key) and horizontal spacing (space bar) show relationship of parts. Lists are formatted with asterisks instead of bullets.

✔ CHECKLIST 16 Résumés

Length and Format

☑ Use a one-page résumé (neither longer nor shorter) when applying for most entry-level positions.

☑ For maximum impact and flexibility, format your résumé on a computer with word processing software and print it on a laser printer.

☑ Use a simple format, with lots of white space and short blocks of text. By means of type size, indenting, bullets, boldface, and the like, show which parts are subordinate to other parts.

☑ Print your résumé on standard-sized ($8\frac{1}{2} \times 11$ inches), good-quality, white or off-white (cream or ivory) paper.

☑ Make sure the finished document looks professional, attractive, and conservative and that it is 100% error-free.

Content

☑ Type your complete name without a personal title at the top of the document (omit the word *résumé*), followed by an address (or by temporary and permanent addresses if needed) and a daytime phone number.

☑ Include a one-sentence job objective that is specific enough to be useful to the employer but not so specific as to preclude consideration for similar jobs.

☑ Decide whether your education or work experience is your stronger qualification, and list it first. For education, list the title of your degree, the name of your college and its location, your major and minor, and your expected date of graduation (month and year). List your grade-point average if it is impressive and any academic honors. Avoid listing college courses that are part of the normal preparation for your desired position.

☑ For work experience, determine whether to use a chronological (most recent job first) or a functional (list of competencies and skills

developed) organizational pattern. For either, stress those duties or skills that are transferable to the new position. Use short phrases and action verbs, and provide specific evidence of the results you achieved.

☑ Include any additional information (such as special skills, professional affiliations, and willingness to travel or relocate) that will help to distinguish you from the competition. Avoid including such personal information as age, gender, ethnicity, religion, disabilities, or marital status.

☑ Provide a statement that references are available on request.

☑ Throughout, highlight your strengths and minimize any weaknesses, but always tell the truth.

Electronic Résumés

☑ In general, describe your qualifications and experiences in terms of nouns rather than verbs. Weave these keywords throughout your résumé—do not list them in a block at the beginning of the résumé.

☑ Save the electronic résumé in plain ASCII text. Do not include any special formatting such as font size and face changes; margin or justification changes; bold, italic, or underlining; or special features such as horizontal or vertical rules, bullets, graphics, boxes, tables, or columns.

☑ Use a line length of no more than 70 characters—manually inserting a carriage return if necessary.

☑ Include a note at the end of your text résumé that a fully formatted version is available upon request.

☑ Print your résumé on plain $8\frac{1}{2}$-by-11-inch smooth white paper (print on one side only) and mail unfolded and unstapled.

employers that interview on campus. Campus recruiters typically represent large organizations or regional employers. Thus, if you want to work in a smaller organization or in a distant location, you will need to contact those organizations by writing application letters.

An **application letter** communicates to the prospective employer your interest in and qualifications for a position within the organization. The letter is also called a *cover letter,* because it introduces (or "covers") the major points in your résumé, which you should include with the application letter. A **solicited application letter** is written in response to an advertised vacancy, whereas an **unsolicited application letter** (also called a *prospecting letter*) is written to an organization that has not advertised a vacancy.

Most job applicants use the same résumé when applying for numerous positions and then use their application letter to personalize their qualification for the specific job for which they are applying.

Because the application letter is the first thing the employer will read about you, it is of crucial importance. Make sure the letter is formatted appropriately, looks attractive, and is free from typographical, spelling, and grammatical errors. Don't forget to sign the letter and don't forget to enclose a copy of your résumé (or perhaps both versions—formatted and plain-text).

Your cover letter is a sales letter—you're selling your qualifications to the prospective employer. You should use the same persuasive techniques you learned earlier; for example, provide specific evidence, stress reader benefits, avoid exaggeration, and show confidence in the quality of your product.

An application letter should be no longer than one page. Let's examine each part of a typical letter. Model 32 (on p. 482) shows a solicited application letter, written to accompany the résumé presented in Model 29. (An unsolicited application letter appears in the 3Ps microwriting model on p. 488.)

Use the application letter, which is often your first contact with the potential employer, to personalize your qualifications for one specific job.

Address and Salutation

Your letter should be addressed to an individual rather than to an organization or department. Remember, the more hands your letter must go through before it reaches the right person, the more chance for something to go wrong. Ideally, your letter should be addressed to the person who will actually interview you and who will likely be your supervisor if you get the job.

If you do not know enough about the prospective employer to know the name of the appropriate person (the decision maker), you have probably not gathered enough data. If necessary, call the organization to make sure you have the right name—including the correct spelling—and position title. In your salutation, use a courtesy title (such as *Mr.* or *Ms.*) along with the person's last name.

Some job-vacancy ads are blind ads; they do not identify the hiring company by name and provide only a box number address, often in care of the newspaper or magazine that contains the ad. In such a situation, you (and all others responding to that ad) have no choice but to address your letter to the newspaper and to use a generic salutation, such as "Dear Human Resources Manager." Consider inserting a subject line to identify immediately the purpose of this important message.

Opening

The opening paragraph of a solicited application letter is fairly straightforward. Because the organization has advertised an opening, it is eager to receive quality

Use the direct organizational plan for writing a solicited application letter.

MODEL 32 Job-Application Letter

This is an example of a solicited application letter; it accompanies the résumé in Model 29.

March 13, 1998

Mr. David Norman, Partner
Ross, Russell & Weston
452 Fifth Avenue
New York, NY 10018

1   Dear Mr. Norman:

Subject: EDP Specialist Position (Reference No. 103-G)

My varied work experience in accounting and payroll services, coupled with my accounting degree, has prepared me for the position of EDP specialist that you adver-
2   tised in the March 9 *New York Times.*

3   In addition to taking required courses in accounting and management information systems as part of my accounting major at New York University, I also took an elective course in EDP auditing and control. The training I received in this course in applications, software, systems, and service-center records would enable me to immediately become a productive member of your EDP consulting staff.

My college training has been supplemented by an internship in a large accounting firm. In addition, my two and a half years of experience as a payroll specialist for the city of New York have given me firsthand knowledge of the operation and needs of nonprofit agencies. This experience should help me to contribute to your large consulting practice with governmental agencies.

4   After you have reviewed my enclosed résumé, I would appreciate having the opportunity to discuss with you in person why I believe I have the right qualifications and personality to serve you and your clients. I can be reached by phone after 3 p.m. daily.

Sincerely,

Aurelia Gomez

Aurelia Gomez
5   225 West 70 Street
New York, NY 10023
Phone: 212-555-3821

Enclosure

Begins by identifying the job position and the source of advertising.

Emphasizes a qualification that might distinguish her from other applicants.

Relates her work experience to the specific needs of the employer.

Provides a telephone number (may be done either in the body of the letter or in the last line of the address block).

Grammar and Mechanics Notes

1 This letter is formatted in modified-block style with standard punctuation (colon after the salutation and comma after the complimentary closing).   2 *New York Times:* Italicize (or underline) the names of newspapers.   3 *accounting and management information systems:* Do not capitalize the names of college courses unless they include a proper noun. 4 *résumé:* This word may also properly be written without the accent marks: *resume.* 5 Putting the writer's name and address together at the bottom of the letter makes it convenient for the reader to respond.

applications, so use a direct organization: state (or imply) the reason for your letter, identify the particular position for which you're applying, and indicate how you learned about the opening.

Gear your opening to the job and to the specific organization. For positions that are widely perceived to be somewhat conservative (such as in finance, accounting, and banking), use a restrained opening. For more creative work (like sales, advertising, and public relations), you might start out on a more imaginative note. Here are two examples:

Conservative:

Mr. Adam Storkel, manager of your Fleet Street branch, has suggested that I submit my qualifications for the position of assistant loan officer that was advertised in last week's *Indianapolis Business.*

Creative:

If quality is Job 1 at Ford, then Job 2 must surely be communicating that message effectively to the public. My degree in journalism and work experience at the Kintzell agency will enable me to help you achieve that objective. The enclosed résumé further describes my qualifications for the position of advertising copywriter posted in the June issue of *Automotive Age.*

For unsolicited application letters, you must first get the reader's attention. You can gain that attention most easily by talking about the company rather than about yourself. One effective strategy is to show that you know something about the organization—its recent projects, awards, changes in personnel, and the like—and then show how you can contribute to the corporate effort.

Now that Russell Industries has expanded operations to Central America, can you use a marketing graduate who speaks fluent Spanish and who knows the culture of the region?

Your opening should be short, interesting, and reader-oriented. Avoid tired openings such as "This is to apply for . . ." or "Please consider this letter my application for. . . ." Maintain an air of formality. Don't address the reader by a first name and don't try to be cute. Avoid such attention-grabbing stunts as sending a worn, once-white running shoe with the note "Now that I have one foot in the door, I hope you'll let me get the other one in" or writing the application letter beginning at the bottom of the page and working upward (to indicate a willingness to start at the bottom and work one's way up). Such gimmicks send a nonverbal message to the reader that the applicant may be trying to deflect attention from a weak résumé.

Body

In a paragraph or two, highlight your strongest qualifications and show how they can benefit the employer. Show—don't tell; that is, provide specific, credible evidence to support your statements, using wording different from that used in the résumé. Tell an anecdote about yourself ("For example, recently I . . ."). Your discussion should reflect modest confidence rather than a hard-sell approach. Avoid starting too many sentences with *I.*

Don't repeat all the information from the résumé.

NOT: I am an effective supervisor.

BUT: Supervising a staff of five counter clerks taught me. . . .

NOT: I am an accurate person.

BUT: In my two years of experience as a student secretary, none of the letters, memorandums, and reports I typed was ever returned with a typographical error marked.

NOT: I took a course in business communication.

BUT: The communication strategies I learned in my business communication course will enable me to solve customer problems as a customer-service representative at Allegheny Industries.

Refer the reader to the enclosed résumé. Subordinate the reference to the résumé, and emphasize instead what the résumé contains.

NOT: I am enclosing a copy of my résumé for your review.

BUT: As detailed in the enclosed résumé, my extensive work experience in records management has prepared me to help you "take charge of this paperwork jungle," as headlined in your classified ad.

Closing

Politely ask for an interview.

You are not likely to get what you do not ask for, so close by asking for a personal interview. Indicate flexibility regarding scheduling and location. Provide your phone number, either in the last paragraph or immediately below your name and address in the closing lines.

> After you have reviewed my qualifications, I would appreciate your calling or writing to let me know when we can meet to discuss further my employment with Connecticut Power and Light. I will be in the Hartford area from December 16 through January 4 and could come to your office at any time that is convenient for you.

Or:

> I will call your office next week to see if we can arrange a meeting at your convenience to discuss my qualifications for working as a financial analyst with your organization.

Use a standard complimentary closing (such as "Sincerely"), leave enough space to sign the letter, and then type your name, address, and phone number. Even though you may be sending out many application letters at the same time, take care with each individual letter. You never know which one will be the one that actually gets you an interview. Sign your name neatly in blue or black ink, fold each letter and accompanying résumé neatly, and mail.

The guidelines for writing an application letter are summarized in Checklist 17.

✔ CHECKLIST 17   **Job-Application Letters**

☑ Use your job-application letter to show how the qualifications listed in your résumé have prepared you for the specific job for which you're applying.

☑ If possible, address your letter to the individual in the organization who will interview you if you're successful.

☑ When applying for an advertised opening, begin by stating (or implying) the reason for the letter, identify the position for which you're applying, and tell how you learned about the opening.

☑ When writing an unsolicited application letter, first gain the reader's attention by showing that you are familiar with the company and can make a unique contribution to its efforts.

☑ In one or two paragraphs, highlight your strongest qualifications and relate them directly to the needs of the specific position for which you're applying. Refer the reader to the enclosed résumé.

☑ Treat your letter as a persuasive sales letter: provide specific evidence, stress reader benefits, avoid exaggeration, and show confidence in the quality of your product.

☑ Close by tactfully asking for an interview.

☑ Maintain an air of formality throughout the letter. Avoid cuteness.

☑ Make sure the finished document presents a professional, attractive, and conservative appearance and that it is 100% error-free.

PROBLEM

Y ou are Ray Arnold, a senior labor relations major at Boston University. You have analyzed your interests, strengths and weaknesses, and preferred lifestyle and have decided you would like to work in some area of labor relations for a large multinational firm in Southern California. Because you attend a school in the East, you decide not to limit your job search to on-campus interviewing.

In your research you learned that Precision Systems, Inc. (PSI), has recently been awarded a $23 million contract by the U.S. Department of State to develop a high-level computerized message system to provide fast and secure communications among U.S. government installations throughout Europe. PSI, which is headquartered in Los Angeles, will build a new automated factory in Cuidad Juárez, Mexico, to assemble the electronic components for the new system.

You decide to write to PSI to see whether they might have an opening for someone with your qualifications. You will, of course, include a copy of your résumé with your letter. (See Model 30 for the résumé.) Send your letter to Ms. Phyllis Morrison, Assistant Director of Personnel, Precision Systems, Inc., P.O. Box 18734, Los Angeles, CA 90018.

PROCESS

1. Will this be a solicited or unsolicited (prospecting) letter?

   Unsolicited—I don't know whether or not PSI has an opening.

2. Write an opening paragraph for your letter that gets attention and that relates your skills to PSI's needs. Make sure the purpose of your letter is made clear in your opening paragraph.

   PSI's recently accepted proposal to the State Department estimated that you would be adding up to 3,000 new staff for the Cuidad Juárez project. With this dramatic increase in personnel, do you have an opening in your human resources department for a college graduate with a major in labor relations and a minor in psychology?

3. Compare your education with PSI's likely requirements. What will help you stand out from the competition?

   ■ It's somewhat unusual for a labor relations major to have a psychology minor.

   ■ My course work in my major and minor were pretty standard, so there's no need to list individual courses.

4. Compare your work experiences with PSI's likely requirements. What qualifications from your résumé should you highlight in your letter?

   ■ The interpersonal and human relations skills developed as a teller will be an important asset in labor management.

- Written and oral communications skills developed through work and extracurricular activities will enable me to communicate effectively with a widely dispersed work force.

5. What other qualifications should you mention?

My degree in labor relations, combined with my union membership, will help me look at each issue from the perspective of both management and labor.

6. Write the sentence in which you request the interview.

I would welcome the opportunity to come to Los Angeles to discuss with you the role I might play in helping PSI manage its human resources in an efficient and humane manner.

PRODUCT

This prospecting letter accompanies the résumé in Model 30.

Begins with an attention-getting opening that relates the writer's skills to the needs of the company.

Shows how the writer's unique qualifications will benefit the company.

Provides specific evidence to support his claims: *shows* rather than *tells*.

Gives the reader the option of phoning the applicant or having him phone her.

---

15 Turner Hall
Boston University
Boston, MA 02215-8134
February 7, 1998

1

Ms. Phyllis Morrison
Assistant Director of Personnel
Precision Systems, Inc.
P.O. Box 18734
Los Angeles, CA 90018

Dear Ms. Morrison

2

PSI's recent proposal to the State Department estimated that you would be adding up to 3,000 new positions for the Ciudad Juárez project. With this increase in personnel, will you have an opening in your human resources department for a recent college graduate with a major in labor relations and a minor in psychology?

3

My combination of course work in business and liberal arts will enable me to approach each issue from both a management and a behavioral point of view. Further, my degree in labor relations along with my experience as a union member will help me consider each issue from the perspective of both management and labor.

During my term as editor of a student newsletter, the Scholastic Press Association recognized our publication for its "original, balanced, and refreshingly candid writing style." On the job, dealing successfully with customers' overdrawn accounts, bank computer errors, and delayed-deposit recording has taught me the value of active listening and has provided me experience in explaining and justifying the company's position. As detailed on the enclosed résumé, these communication and human relations skills will help me to interact and communicate effectively with PSI employees at all levels and at widely dispersed locations.

4

I would welcome the opportunity to come to Los Angeles at your convenience to discuss with you the role I might play in helping PSI manage its human resources in an efficient and humane manner. I will call your office on February 15, or you may call me at any time after 2 p.m. daily at 617-555-9833.

Sincerely

Raymond J. Arnold

Raymond J. Arnold

Enclosure

Grammar and Mechanics Notes

1 In a personal business letter, the writer's return address may be typed above the date (as shown here) or below the sender's name in the closing.   2 This letter is formatted in block style, with all lines beginning at the left margin, and in open punctuation style, with no punctuation after the salutation and complimentary closing.   3 *major in labor relations:* Do not capitalize the names of college majors and minors.   4 *writing style.":* A period goes inside the closing quotation marks.

SUMMARY

One of the most important communication tasks you will ever face is securing a rewarding and worthwhile job. The job-seeking campaign thus requires considerable time, effort, and thought.

The planning phase begins with a self-analysis of your interests, strengths, weaknesses, and needs. Then you should gather data about possible jobs, demographic trends, and industries and companies that interest you.

The purpose of your résumé is to get you a job interview. Strive for a one-page document, preferably typed in a simple, readable format on a computer and output on a laser printer. Include your name, address, phone number, job objective, information about your education and work experience, and special aptitudes and skills. Include other information only if it will help distinguish you favorably from the other applicants. Use either a chronological or functional organization for your work experience, and stress those skills and experiences that can be transferred to the job you want. Consider formatting an electronic version of your résumé for e-mailing or computer scanning. This version should be in plain text, with no special formatting, printed on standard white paper (one side only) and mailed unfolded and unstapled.

You will typically use the same résumé when applying for numerous positions and then construct an application letter that discusses how your education and work experience qualify you specifically for the job at hand. If possible, address your letter to the person who will interview you for the job. When writing a solicited application letter, begin by stating the reason for your letter, identify the position for which you're applying, and tell how you learned about the position. When writing an unsolicited letter, first gain the reader's attention. Then use the body of your letter to highlight one or two of your strongest qualifications, relating them to the needs of the position for which you're applying. Close by politely asking for an interview.

If your application efforts are successful, you will be invited to come for an interview. Successful interviewing strategies are covered in the next chapter.

KEY TERMS

application letter	résumé
electronic résumé	solicited application letter
reference	unsolicited application letter

REVIEW AND DISCUSSION

1. **Communication at Computer Sciences Corporation Revisited**   Electronic résumés are required at Computer Sciences Corporation, where Paul Orvos and his colleagues use descriptive nouns to search the company's résumé data to find candidates for open positions.
   a. If you were an experienced programmer applying for a job with CSC, what key words could you include in your résumé to describe your skills and background?
   b. What job objective might you state on your résumé when you apply for the job?
   c. If no job opening for a computer programmer has been advertised, write the first sentence of the unsolicited application letter you would send with your résumé.
2. Think of two different occupations. How might the answers to the 14 self-assessment questions on pages 458–459 differ for someone interested in each of these occupations?

3. What types of career information are contained in the *Occupational Outlook Handbook?*
4. What services does the placement office or career-information center at your institution provide?
5. What is the purpose of a résumé?
6. How long should a résumé be?
7. Under what conditions should the education section of a résumé precede the work experience section?
8. What kinds of information should *always* go into a résumé?
9. What kinds of information should *never* go into a résumé?
10. What is the difference between a chronological and a functional organizational pattern?
11. How should references be treated in a résumé?
12. How do standard and electronic résumés differ in terms of format? content?
13. What is the difference between a solicited and an unsolicited application letter?
14. When might it be necessary *not* to address the application letter to the specific person who will be interviewing you?
15. Should the focus of an application letter be on the past or the future? Explain.

Help Wanted

Casey Justin drafted this résumé in preparation for applying for an internship position. Revise it to make it more effective, taking into consideration the editor's marginal comments.

Casey Justin

5001 Northlake Avenue, Muncie, Ind. 47304

Phone: 765-555-4490; E-mail: 0cojustin@bsu.edu

Use the 2-letter USPS state abbreviation.

Job Objective

A full-time one-semester accounting internship in the Indianapolis metropolitan area.

Special Skills

Is this the best position for this section?

Speak and write Spanish flouently.
Experienced in using Microsoft Word, Excel, and PowerPoint for Windows and in locating electronic data sources on the Internet.

Education

Bachelor of Science, Ball State University, Muncie, IN

- Major in Accounting (expected date of graduation: May 1998).
- *Do you really want to include?* Grade point average of 2.7 in 18 semester hours of accounting courses, including Principles of Accounting 1-2, Intermediate Accounting 1-2, Cost Acounting, and Income Tax.
- Secretary of the BSU Accounting Club.

There's a misspelled word somewhere in your résumé; find and correct it!

Work Experience

Trainer, Special Olympics of Delaware County, Muncie, IN
Summers, 1996, 1997
- Volunteered for the United Way-sponsored program.
- Developed individualized training programs.
- Taught 12 nonswimmers how to swim well enough to pass Red Cross swimming certification.
- Used interpersonal skills to motivate youngsters and solve human-relations problems.

disc

Salesman, CarSmart, Carmel, IN

Delete the "I's"

Summers, 1993-1996
- I helped customers select automotive supplies.
- I assisted in ordering mechandise, stocking the department, and resolving customer problems.
- I served as interim department manager for two months while permanent manager was on sick leave.
- I was chosen Employee of the Month twice.

What about references?

EXERCISES

1. The 3Ps Microwriting Model: Communication Applications at Computer Sciences Corporation When Paul Orvos and his colleagues get ready to fill an open position at CSC, they no longer have to read through thousands of résumés on file. Instead, they use keywords to search the company's database of electronic résumés for candidates with the appropriate experience and background. Although content is his top priority, Orvos still expects to see good grammar, spelling, and punctuation on every résumé he reviews.

Problem

Imagine that you are getting ready to apply to CSC for a full-time job in finance, sales, human resources, information technology, or another functional area. In preparation, you need to find out more about CSC and its industry. This research will help you understand the company's direction and its employment needs, both immediate and long-term, so you can tailor your résumé accordingly and ask relevant questions about CSC during an interview.

Process

a. What kinds of job opportunities are you interested in researching at CSC?
b. Visit CSC's Web site (http://www.csc.com) and/or look through a copy of its annual report. What industry is CSC in? What does the company do? What types of customers does it serve? Where are its offices?
c. How do your skills and personal interests match up with CSC's industry, operations, and locations?

d. Browse through CSC's online job listings. What types of positions does CSC recruit for? Are your education and work experience appropriate for the positions that sound interesting? What other qualifications do you need to apply for the jobs that interest you?

e. Look up two or three jobs that CSC is offering in the *Occupational Outlook Handbook*. What can you learn about training, qualifications, and advancement in each field? What is the outlook for each job?

Product

Using your knowledge of employment communication, write a brief analysis of CSC and a job that you find interesting, including details that will help you customize your résumé and be prepared for a personal interview with Paul Orvos.

2. The 3Ps Microwriting Model: A Résumé—Getting to Know You

Problem

Assume that you are beginning your last term of college before graduating. Using factual data from your own education, work experience, and so on (include any data that you expect to be true at the time of your graduation), prepare a résumé in an effective format. (*Note:* You will probably want to complete Exercises 3–7 on the following pages before composing your résumé.)

Process

a. How will you word your name at the top of your résumé—for example, with or without any initials? (Remember *not* to include a personal title before your name.)

b. What is your mailing address? If you will be changing addresses during the job search, include both addresses, along with the effective dates of each.

c. What is your daytime phone number? When can you typically be reached at this number?

d. For what type of position are you searching? Prepare an effective one-sentence job objective—one that is neither too general nor too specific.

e. What is the title of your degree? the name of your college? the location of the college? your major and minor? your expected date of graduation (month and year)?

f. What is your grade-point average overall and in your major? Is either one high enough to be considered a personal selling point?

g. Have you received any academic honors throughout your collegiate years, such as scholarships or being named to the dean's list? If so, list them.

h. Did you take any elective courses (courses that most applicants for this position probably did *not* take) that might be especially helpful in this position? If so, list them.

i. List in reverse chronological order (most recent job first) the following information for each job you've held during your college years: job title, organizational name, location (city and state), inclusive dates of employment, and full- or part-time status. Describe your specific duties in each position, stressing those duties that helped prepare you for your job objective. Use short phrases, beginning each duty or responsibility with one of the action verbs on page 472 and showing, where possible, specific evidence of the results you achieved.

j. Will your education or your work experience be more likely to impress the recruiter?

   k. What additional information might you include, such as special skills, professional affiliations, offices held, or willingness to relocate or travel?

   l. Are your reference letters on file at your school's placement office? If so, provide the office name, address, and phone number. (If not, you should include a statement such as "References available on request" at the bottom of your résumé.)

Product

Using the above information, draft, revise, format, and then proofread your résumé. Then prepare an electronic version of this résumé for computer scanning. Submit both of your résumés and your responses to the process questions to your instructor.

3. **Self-Assessment**   As a first step in your job campaign, answer the 14 questions given on pages 458–459. Type each question and then your answer. Although the content of the answer is certainly more important than mechanics and format, use this exercise as a measure of your basic writing skills as well, taking care to use complete sentences, correct grammar, and competent writing style.

4. **Tell Me About Yourself**   One of the most common strategies an interviewer uses to start an interview is to ask you to tell something about yourself. Of course, you need to think about this question much earlier than the interview; the start of your job campaign is the time for this self-disclosure. In approximately 250 words (about a one-page double-spaced report), respond to the interviewer's request to "tell me about yourself." Keep in mind your job objective.

5. **Audience Analysis—International**   Assume that you wish to work in another country upon graduation from college. Select a company headquartered abroad and research that organization. Learn about its products, economic outlook, employment needs, politics, organizational climate, and the like. Considering what you know about the company, what points about your own background might you stress, in your application letter and résumé, that would be of particular interest to this employer? Write a two-page memo report to your instructor detailing what you've learned about the organization (and about yourself).

6. **Career Planning**   Select a career in which you might be interested. Using at least four references (one of which should be the latest edition of the *Occupational Outlook Handbook),* write a two- or three-page memo report to your instructor with the following sections:

   a. *Job description:* Include in this section a description of the job, including perhaps a definition of the job, typical duties, working conditions, and the kinds of knowledge, skills, and education needed.

   b. *Employment levels:* Nationally, how many people are employed in this type of job? Are employment levels increasing or decreasing? Why? What industries or what parts of the country are experiencing the greatest and the least demand for this job? What are the projected employment levels in the future?

   c. *Salary:* Discuss the latest salary statistics for this job—actual salaries, changes, trends, and projections.

   d. *Expected changes:* What changes are expected in this career within the next ten years or so? Discuss both the expected changes and the factors causing such changes. For example, will technology have any impact on this job? will international business competition? federal or state regulations?

Provide a concluding paragraph, for your memo report, that summarizes the career information you've discussed; then indicate whether your initial opinion about the job has changed as a result of your research.

7. **Work-Team Communication—Job-Getting Techniques**   Working in a group of four to five students, complete the following tasks:
   a. Select an occupation (perhaps to be fair to everyone, you might select one that none of you plans to pursue as a career).
   b. Compose a list of five people any of you know who might provide information about this career or possible job leads. Tell why each person in your network of contacts was chosen.
   c. Interview (either in person or by telephone) a counselor at a nearby private employment service to determine what help the service could provide in securing a job in this occupation.
   d. Review the help-wanted ads in your local newspaper to determine what types of jobs are available in this occupation.

   Write a memo report to your instructor presenting the results of your research.

8. **Résumé Feedback**   Make five photocopies of the standard résumé you created in Exercise 2 on appropriate paper—the kind you would use for your job campaign. Meet with three professionals who have expertise in your career area—the type of people who might be interviewing you for a job. Ask them to critique your résumé for you, commenting both on positive aspects and on any areas that should be strengthened. Revise your résumé on the basis of this feedback. Submit a copy of both your original résumé and your revised version to your instructor, along with a memo explaining what you revised and why.

9. **Résumé Project—Format**   Review the final résumé you developed in Exercise 8. Using the same information, prepare another version in a different format; that is, include the same content but arrange it on the page differently. Which format do you think works better? Why? Submit both résumés, along with a short memo to your instructor evaluating the format of each document.

10. **Application Letter Project**   This project consists of writing both a solicited and an unsolicited application letter. Prepare each letter in an appropriate format and on appropriate paper. Include a copy of your résumé with each letter. Submit each letter to your instructor folded and inserted into a correctly addressed envelope (don't forget to sign your letter).
   a. Identify a large prospective employer—one that has not advertised for an opening in your field. Using one of the résumés you developed earlier, write an unsolicited application letter.
   b. For various reasons, you might not secure a position directly related to your college major. In such a situation, it is especially important to be able to show how your qualifications (no matter what they are) match the needs of the employer. Using your own background, apply for the following position, which was advertised in last Sunday's *New York Times:*

   MANAGER-TRAINEE POSITION. Philip Morris is looking for recent college graduates to enter its management-trainee program in preparation for an exciting career in one of the diversified companies that make up Philip Morris. Excellent beginning salary and benefits, good working conditions, and a company that cares about you. (Reply to Box 385-G in care of this newspaper.)

"Help Wanted"

When Neelima Shrikhande accepted the position of vice president of administration at Urban Systems, she knew she would have to work closely with Marc Kaplan, vice president of marketing. However, she resented Marc's condescending attitude toward her and his chauvinistic remarks toward female employees in general.

Despite her best efforts, their relationship has now deteriorated to the point where Neelima believes it is adversely affecting her ability to perform her job effectively. Knowing that Marc (one of the two founders of the company) has no plans to leave, Neelima has decided to explore other career opportunities.

Neelima is savvy enough to recognize that she is highly marketable and that many organizations would be eager to create a position for her even if they had no advertised openings. She is interested in finding a position in information management at a large organization located in a metropolitan area. She is free to relocate anywhere in the country. Hoping to avoid the kind of situation she presently faces, she would like to become associated with a progressive organization, preferably one whose top-level officers are active in social and political causes. An organization with other females in prominent executive positions who could serve as her mentors would be especially attractive.

Note: Although you already know quite a bit about Neelima, you may assume any additional, reasonable information you need to complete this project.

Critical Thinking

1. Is Neelima making the right decision in leaving? Why or why not?

2. Review what you know about Neelima—both from the background information contained in the Appendix to Chapter 1 and from the case studies in previous chapters. Develop a list of short phrases that describe her. What implication might each of these characteristics have for choosing a suitable new work environment?

Writing Project

3. Locate three organizations that would be top prospects for Neelima to explore for a career move. Identify the organizations for Neelima in terms of the criteria just discussed. Present a balanced view of the organizations, incorporating both positive and negative information. Finally, provide the name, address, and phone number of an appropriate person for Neelima to contact. Organize your information in a logical manner, and present it as a letter report to Neelima.

15 The Job Interview and Follow-Up

An Insider's Perspective

Whether you're in front of the camera or behind the scenes, every second counts. Split-second timing is just one aspect of working for CNN and CNNfn that Elizabeth Semple stresses to job candidates. As Manager of Human Resources in the New York headquarters, Semple interviews and hires for a variety of positions that support the television network's award-winning news and business reporting. One day, she may be doing preliminary screening of candidates for supervising producer, the manager who oversees planning, writing, and scheduling for a particular show. The next day, she may be talking with college students who want to join the company's internship program to get a taste of broadcast journalism by helping anchors with research or working the booking desk to gather background information.

During interviews, Semple rarely asks the standard questions because she knows that savvy job-seekers have already polished their responses. Instead, she asks questions designed to reveal what candidates are really like and how they might act on the job, where timing is critical. "CNN shows are scheduled in one-minute slots, so we think in terms of seconds," she explains. "We want to hire people who can react well under pressure and keep a cool head to get a show on the air."

Because CNN and CNNfn cover the globe, employees must be able to communicate with people from other countries and be open to new concepts. To get a sense of how comfortable applicants are with different groups of people and different ideas, Semple asks how they spend their spare time, what books they read, and where they want to travel. She also looks for clues that interviewees can process information and act independently. For example, she wants candidates to speak up if they don't understand a question. "Don't just give me an answer," she says. "If you ask me to repeat or rephrase a question, that shows you are more likely to take the initiative on the job by thinking about what you've been asked to do rather than simply reacting."

COMMUNICATION OBJECTIVES

After you have finished this chapter, you should be able to

- Prepare for an employment interview.

- Conduct yourself appropriately during an employment interview.

- Complete the communication tasks needed after the employment interview.

Although Semple welcomes questions at any point in the interview, she always reserves some time at the end for applicants to ask about the job, the company, and the future. "The questions that candidates ask show me how they see themselves fitting into CNN," she says. "When people ask about the station's growth, they seem to be setting the stage for their progression through a series of jobs they might hold in the next five or ten years." She also listens for probing questions about the company's practices, which reveal a deeper level of interest.

Technology is at the heart of CNN's operations, which is why Semple prefers that candidates e-mail a thank-you message after an interview rather than sending an ordinary thank-you letter. No flowers or other gimmicks, please; she wants only a straightforward thank-you message reiterating the person's qualifications and interest. Semple suggests that applicants use thank-you notes to make a good impression and to make themselves stand out. "I meet a lot of people," she observes.

Elizabeth Semple

Manager, Human Resources, New York CNN and CNNfn (New York City, New York)

"To jog my memory, candidates should mention the specific position they are seeking and include one or two things we discussed during the interview."

Whether you're just starting your career or you're looking for a more challenging job, Elizabeth Semple offers this advice for successful interviewing: "Be yourself all the way—don't change your personality for an interview. And if you don't get a particular job, don't leave a bad impression; down the line, the interviewer may consider you for another job if you have behaved professionally."

Preparing for a Job Interview

Ninety-five percent of all employers require one or more employment interviews before extending a job offer, resulting in up to 150 million employment interviews being conducted annually.[1] The employer's purpose in these interviews is to verify information on the résumé, explore any issues raised by the résumé, and get some indication of the probable chemistry between the applicant and the organization. (It is estimated that 90% of all job failures result from personality clashes or conflicts—not incompetence.[2]) The job applicant will use the interview to glean important information about the organization and to decide whether the culture of the organization meshes with his or her personality (see Spotlight 25—On Law and Ethics for some ethical dimensions of the job campaign).

Consider the employment interview as a sales presentation. Just as any good sales representative would never attempt to walk into a potential customer's office without having a thorough knowledge of the product, neither should you. You are both the product and the product promoter, so do your homework—both on yourself and on the potential customer.

Researching the Organization

Learn as much as you can about the organization—your possible future employer.

As a result of having developed your résumé and written your application letters, you have probably done enough general homework on yourself. You are likely to have a reasonably accurate picture of who you are and what you want out of your career. Now is the time to zero in on the organization.

It is no exaggeration to say that you should learn everything you possibly can about the organization. Research the specific organization in depth, using the research techniques you developed in Chapter 11. Search the current business periodical indexes and go online to learn what has been happening recently with the company. Many libraries maintain copies of the annual reports from large companies, either in hard copy or on microfiche. Study these or other sources for current product information, profitability, plans for the future, and the like. Learn about the company's products and services, its history, the names of its officers, what the business press has to say about the organization, its recent stock activity, financial health, corporate structure, and the like.

Relate what you discover about the individual company to what you've learned about competing companies and about the industry in general. By trying to fit what you've learned into the broader perspective of the industry, you will be able to discuss matters more intelligently during your interview instead of just having a bunch of jumbled facts at your disposal.

If you're interviewing at a governmental agency, determine its role, recent funding levels, recent activities, spending legislation affecting the agency, and the extent to which being on the "right" side (that is, the official side) of a political question matters. If you're interviewing for a teaching position at an educational institution, determine the range of course offerings, types of students, conditions of the facilities and equipment, professionalism of the staff, and funding levels. In short, every tidbit of information you can learn about your prospective employer will help you make the most appropriate career decision.

Avoid "showing off" your knowledge of the organization.

You will use this information as a resource to help you understand and discuss topics with some familiarity during the interview. No one is impressed by the interviewee who, out of the blue, spouts, "I see your stock went up $5\frac{1}{2}$ points last week." However, in response to the interviewer's comment about the company's recent

The Ethical Dimensions of the Job Campaign

SPOTLIGHT 25

ON LAW AND ETHICS

Most recruiters have heard the story about the job applicant who, when told that he was overqualified for a position, pleaded in vain, "But I lied about my credentials." When constructing your résumé and application letter, when completing an application form, and when answering questions during an interview, you will constantly have to make judgments about what to divulge and what to omit. Everyone would agree that outright lying is unethical (and clearly illegal as well). But when is hedging or omitting negative information about yourself simply being smart, and when is it unethical?

The Ethics of Constructing a Résumé

Recruiters believe that the problem they call "résumé inflation" has increased in recent years, and plenty of research backs them up. One survey of executives found that 26% of them reported hiring employees during the previous year who had misrepresented their qualifications, education, or salary history. By far, the most frequent transgression is misrepresenting one's qualifications.

Acting ethically does not, of course, require that you emphasize every little problem that has occurred in your past. Indeed, one study showed that the majority of Fortune 500 human resource directors agree with the statement "Interviewees should stress their strengths and not mention their weaknesses unless the interviewer asks for information in an area of weakness."

Recognize, however, that many employers have a standard policy of terminating all employees who are found to have falsely represented their qualifications on their résumés. Generally, the employer must show evidence that the employee intentionally misrepre-

sented his or her qualifications so as to fraudulently secure a job. Claiming to have a college degree when, in fact, one does not would likely be grounds for termination, whereas an unintentional mistake in the dates of previous employment would probably not be.

The Ethics of Accepting a Position

For some applicants, another ethical dilemma occurs when they receive a second, perhaps more attractive, job offer after having already accepted a prior offer. Most professionals believe that such a situation should not present a dilemma. A job acceptance is a promise that the applicant is expected to keep. The hiring organization has made many decisions based on the applicant's acceptance, not least of which was to notify all other candidates that the job had been filled. Reneging on the commitment to the employer not only puts the applicant in a bad light (and don't underestimate the power of the network in spreading such information) but also puts the applicant's school in a bad light.

If you're unsure about whether to accept a job offer, ask for a time extension. Once you've made your decision, however, stick to it and have no regrets. If you decide to accept the job, immediately notify all other employers that you are withdrawing from further consideration. If you decide to decline the job, move on to your next interviews without looking back. Learn to live with your decisions.

Sources: "Creative Résumés," *Dun's Business Month,* June 1985, p. 20; Nelda Spinks and Barron Wells, "Employment Interviews: Trends in the Fortune 500 Companies—1980–1988," *ABC Bulletin,* December 1988, p. 17; "Will Ethical Conflicts Undo Your Career?" *Mt. Pleasant (MI) Morning Sun,* May 12, 1988, p. 9.

---

announcement of a new product line, it would be quite appropriate to respond, "That must have been the reason your stock jumped 5½ points last week."

In short, bring up such information only if it flows naturally into the conversation. Even if you're never able to discuss some of the information you've gathered, the knowledge itself will still provide perspective in helping you to make a reasonable decision if a job offer is extended.

Practicing Interview Questions

Practice your responses to typical interview questions.

Following is a sample of typical questions that are often asked during an employment interview. Questions such as these provide the interviewer important clues to the applicant's qualifications, personality, poise, and communication skills. The interviewer is interested not only in the content of your responses but also in your reaction to the questions themselves and *how* you communicate your thoughts and ideas.

Before going for your interview, practice dictating a response to each of these questions into a cassette recorder. Then assume the role of the interviewer and play back your responses. How acceptable and appropriate was each response?

- Tell me about yourself.

- How would you describe yourself?

- Tell me something about yourself that I won't find on your résumé.

- What do you take real pride in?

- Why would you like to work for our organization?

- Why should we hire you?

- What are your long-range career objectives?

- What types of work do you enjoy doing most? least?

- What accomplishment has given you the greatest satisfaction?

- What would you like to change in your past?

- What courses did you like best and least in college?

- Specifically, how does your education or experience relate to this job?

These questions are fairly straightforward and not especially difficult to answer if you have practiced them. Not infrequently, however, interviewers may pose more difficult questions—ones that seemingly have no "right" answer. Sometimes they even try to create a stressful situation by asking pointed questions, interrupting, or feigning disbelief in an attempt to gauge your behavior under stress.

Answer each question honestly, but in a way that highlights your qualifications.

The strategy to use in such a circumstance is to keep the desired job firmly in mind and to formulate each answer—no matter what the question—so as to highlight your ability to perform the desired job competently. You don't have to accept each question as asked. You can ask the interviewer to be more specific or to rephrase the question. Doing so not only will provide guidance for answering the question but will give you a few additional moments to prepare your response.

Here are examples of some challenging questions you might be asked, along with possible strategies for answering these and similar questions. Again, you should recognize that the interviewers may be more interested in your reaction and poise under stress than in your actual words, so be aware of the nonverbal signals you are communicating.

- *Tell me about your strengths and weaknesses.* When asked about a strength, mention one of your qualifications that is directly related to the specific job. If asked about a weakness, you might identify a relatively harmless matter or even a strength that you sometimes carry to excess, such as "I tend to work too hard"; "I'm very tenacious; once I've started a project, I won't relax until I've

Just as you would practice for a sales presentation, it makes sense to practice for your job interview because you are, in fact, trying to sell yourself to the organizaation. You are both the product and the product promoter. Here, Jim Borland of Goodrich & Sherwood, an executive search and outplacement firm, helps a job applicant hone her interview skills by videotaping a mock interview.

finished it"; or "I tend to ask a lot of questions." Answer the weakness part of the question first, ending with a discussion of some job-related strength. Relate an anecdote or give some examples when possible.

- *Suppose you had to pick between two equally qualified subordinates for promotion. One was a black male and the other a handicapped female. Whom would you select?* Whenever you're asked a question that has no right answer, avoid answering the question directly. Instead, talk about related issues—in this case, your respect for affirmative action and equal opportunity efforts, your interest in working for an organization that had such a wonderful "problem," or some other issue that relates to the question but does not force an unreasonable choice. If you're asked for the "most important" something, you're generally safer instead to list several items as being very important, without assigning any one of them the top position.

- *What position do you expect to hold in five years?* Avoid telling the interviewer, "your job." He or she won't appreciate it, even if that is an accurate answer. Instead, talk about what you hope to have accomplished by then, the types of increasing responsibility you hope to be given, or the opportunities to make a greater contribution to the organization's efforts.

- *Tell me about your personal interests.* Your investigation of the organization should have revealed its attitudes and "personality." Rightly or wrongly, most organizations reflect upper-middle-class attitudes and mores. If you wish to fit in at such organizations, you should provide honest, middle-of-the-road responses. This would not be the time then to discuss your preoccupation with the occult. Also avoid appearing *too* interested in any outside pursuit. Organizations are looking for well-rounded individuals who enjoy outside interests but who do not have such a consuming interest that it might interfere with their jobs.

How you respond to difficult questions may be as important as what you say.

■ *What do you like most or least about your present job?* For the most-liked part of this question, select an aspect of your present job that you both enjoy and that is directly related to the new position. For the least-liked part of the question, select an aspect of your present job that you dislike and that the new position does not involve.

■ *Can you work effectively in an environment that emphasizes diversity?* The ability to fit in and function productively around people of widely varying backgrounds is becoming increasingly important. Emphasize whatever experiences you have had in working with people of different cultures, ages, economic backgrounds, religions, and the like. Provide evidence that you value diversity if, in fact, that is the case.

Preparing Your Own Questions

Ensure that any relevant questions you may have are answered during the interview.

During the course of the interview, many of the questions you may have about the organization or the job will probably be answered. However, an interview is a two-way conversation, so it is legitimate for you to pose relevant questions at appropriate moments, and you should prepare those questions beforehand.

Questions such as the following will provide useful information on which to base a decision if a job is offered:

■ How would you describe a typical day on the job?

■ How is an employee evaluated and promoted?

■ What types of training are available?

■ What are your expectations of new employees?

■ What are the organization's plans for the future?

■ To whom would I report? Would anyone report to me?

■ What are the advancement opportunities for this position?

Each of these questions not only secures needed information to help you make a decision but also sends a positive nonverbal message to the interviewer that you are interested in this position as a long-term commitment. Do not, however, ask so many questions that the roles of the interviewer and the interviewee become blurred, and avoid putting the interviewer on the spot.

Avoid appearing to be overly concerned about salary.

Finally, avoid asking about salary and fringe benefits during the initial interview. There will be plenty of time for such questions later, after you've convinced the organization that you're the person they want. In terms of planning, however, you should know ahead of time the market value of the position for which you're applying. Check the classified ads, reports collected by your college career service, and library and Internet sources to learn what a reasonable salary figure for your position would be.

Dressing for Success

Prefer well-tailored, clean, conservative outfits for the interview.

The importance of making a good first impression during the interview can hardly be overstated. One study has shown that 75% of the interviewees who made a good impression during the first five minutes of the interview received a job offer, whereas only 10% of the interviewees who made a bad impression during the first five minutes received a job offer.[3]

The most effective strategy for making a good impression is to pay careful attention to your dress, grooming, and posture. Dress in a manner that flatters your appearance while conforming to the office norm. The employment interview is not the place for a fashion statement. You want the interviewer to remember what you had to say and not what you wore. Although different positions, different companies, different industries, and different parts of the country and world have different norms, in general prefer well-tailored, clean, conservative clothing for the interview.

For most business interviews, men should dress in a blue or gray suit and a white or pale blue shirt with a subtle tie, dark socks, and black shoes. Women should dress in a blue or gray tailored suit with a light-colored blouse and medium-height heels. Avoid excessive or distracting jewelry, heavy perfumes or after-shave lotions, and elaborate hairstyles. Impeccable grooming is a must, including clothing clean and free of wrinkles, shoes shined, teeth brushed, and hair neatly styled and combed. Blend in; you will have plenty of opportunity to express your individual style once you've been hired.

> ## word**wise**
>
> ### Which Proverb Do You Believe?
>
> - "The pen is mightier than the sword," or "Actions speak louder than words"?
> - "Silence is golden," or "The squeaky wheel gets the grease"?
> - "He who hesitates is lost," or "Look before you leap"?
> - "Birds of a feather flock together," or "Opposites attract"?
> - "You're never too old to learn," or "You can't teach an old dog new tricks"?

Controlling Nervousness

Control nervousness during the interview the same way you control it when making an oral presentation; that is, practice until you're confident you can face whatever the interviewer throws your way. The career centers at many colleges conduct mock interviews to prepare prospective interviewees. If yours does not, ask a professor or even another student to interview you. Practice answering lists of common questions.

Become so thoroughly familiar with your résumé, application letter, and (if used) application blank that you won't have to search for some particular item or try to remember exactly how you responded to a particular question.

Interviewers know you may be nervous so they will probably begin the interview with some fairly innocuous, easy-to-answer questions to break the ice. It is to their advantage to put you at ease so that the real you can shine through, and they will try to do so. Recognize also that some nervousness is helpful; a bit of nervous energy will keep you alert and give sharper focus to the verbal exchange.

Overpreparation is the best way to control nervousness.

One way to avoid excessive nervousness is to arrive properly equipped—with a pen and notebook, a list of questions you want to ask, two copies of your résumé (including, if appropriate, two copies each of both the formatted version and plain-text, scannable version), any past correspondence with the organization, a list of references (including addresses and phone numbers), and, if applicable, work samples.

Map out the route you will take to the interview site, and avoid the stress of having to rush to arrive on time. Plan to arrive 10 to 15 minutes early, but no more than that. Arriving too early makes you appear too eager and may disrupt the interviewer's prior plans. If you're a bit nervous, plan to arrive a half-hour early, find your way to the correct office, and then go for a walk. It will release some of the pent-up energy you may have stored on the drive over.

Conducting Yourself During the Interview

Observe the organizational environment very carefully and treat everyone you meet, including the receptionist and the interviewer's assistant or secretary, with scrupulous courtesy. Maintain an air of formality. When shown into the interview room, greet the interviewer by name, with a firm handshake, direct eye contact, and a smile.

At the beginning, address the interviewer as "Mr." or "Ms.," switching to a first-name basis only if specifically requested to do so. If you're not asked to be seated immediately, wait until the interviewer is seated and then take your seat. Sit with your feet planted firmly on the floor, lean forward a bit in your seat, and maintain comfortable eye contact with the interviewer. Avoid taking notes, except perhaps for a specific name, date, or telephone number.

Assume a confident, courteous, and conservative attitude during the interview.

Recognize that certain parts of the office are off-limits—especially the interviewer's desk and any area behind the desk. Do not rest your hands, purse, or notes on the desk and never wander around the office. Show interest in everything the interviewer is saying; don't concentrate so hard on formulating your response that you miss the last part of any question. Answer each question in a positive, confident, forthright manner. Recognize that more than yes-or-no answers are expected.

Throughout the interview, your attitude should be one of confidence and courtesy. Assume a role that is appropriate for you. Don't go in with the attitude that "You're lucky to have me here." The interviewer might not agree. Likewise, you needn't fawn or grovel. You're *applying*—not begging—for a job. If the match works, both you and the employer will benefit. Finally, don't try to take charge of the interview. Follow the interviewer's lead, letting him or her determine which questions to ask, when to move to a new area of discussion, and when to end the interview.

Answer each question put to you as honestly as you can (see Spotlight 26—On Law and Ethics). Keep your mind on the desired job and how you can show that you are qualified for that job. Don't try to oversell yourself, or you may end up in a job for which you're unprepared. However, if the interviewer doesn't address an area in which you believe you have strong qualifications, be on the alert to volunteer such information at the appropriate time, working it into your answer to one of the interviewer's questions.

If asked about your salary expectations, try to avoid giving a salary figure, indicating that you would expect to be paid in line with other employees at your level of expertise and experience. If pressed, however, be prepared to reveal your salary expectations, preferably using a broad range.

When discussing salary, talk in terms of what you think the position and responsibilities are worth rather than what you think *you* are worth. If salary is not discussed, be patient. Few people have ever been offered a job in industry without first being told what they would be paid.

It is possible that you may perceive an immediate rapport problem with the interviewer—either that the interviewer dislikes you or that you dislike the interviewer. In the former situation, take stock immediately of yourself and the verbal and nonverbal signals you're sending out, and try to adjust them to send a more appropriate message.

If your first impression of the interviewer is unfavorable, recognize that first impressions are not always valid. Also, remember that the interviewer may not be your superior or may not be your superior for long. Evaluate the long-term situa-

The Legal Dimensions of the Job Campaign

I applied for a job and was told I will be hired if I take a lie-detector test. Must I take this test? In most states, yes, if you want the job. A few states, however, prohibit employers from requiring a lie-detector test as a condition of employment.

The computer firm where I want to work requires all job applicants to take a psychological test as part of the application process. Is this legal?
Yes. Aptitude, personality, and psychological tests are legal as long as the results are accurate, are related to success on the job, and do not tend to eliminate anyone on the basis of gender, age, race, religion, or national origin.

SPOTLIGHT 26

ON LAW AND ETHICS

I work full-time and have been offered a dream job by another employer—if I can start the new job immediately. Do I have to give my current employer a certain number of days' notice?
No. You are not legally required to do so unless the contract you signed specifies how far in advance you must notify the company.

I'm an older student who will be applying for positions along with much younger ones. Can the interviewer ask my age?
No, not unless the employer can show that most people beyond a certain age cannot perform the job competently or safely. If you're worried about the possible impact of your age, you might wish to volunteer certain information to allay the interviewer's concerns—for example, mentioning some vigorous physical activity you regularly engage in.

What types of information may not be asked for on an application form or during a job interview?

- Race or national origin (including origin of a surname or place of birth; however, you may be asked to prove that you have legal authorization to work in the United States)
- Family information (including marital status, plans for marriage or children, number of children or their ages, child-care arrangements, spouse's occupation, roommate arrangements, and home ownership)
- Disabilities (unless they relate directly to the job)
- Arrests (you may, however, be asked about convictions for serious offenses)

How should I respond to an illegal question during a job interview?
The best response, assuming you want to continue to be considered for the position, may be to deflect the question by focusing on how you can contribute to the job. For example, if you were asked about your plans to have children in the immediate future, you might respond, "I assure you that I'm fully committed to my career and to making a real contribution to the organization for which I work." Or you may respond by saying you don't believe such questions are relevant to your ability to do the job, or by asking the interviewer to explain the relevance of the question. You could also, of course, file a complaint with the Equal Employment Opportunity Commission.

tion before making any immediate decision. At any rate, conduct yourself as professionally and as effectively as possible throughout the interview. You can make a final decision later, after you've had more time to evaluate the situation more clearly.

You might participate in a group interview, in which several people interview you at once. If possible, find out about this ahead of time so that you can learn the name, position, and rank of each interviewer. Address your responses to everyone, not just to the person who asked the question or to the most senior person present.

It is also likely that you will be interviewed more than once—having either multiple interviews the same day or, if you survive the initial interview, a more intense set of interviews to be scheduled for some later date. Be on the alert for clues you can pick up from your early interviews that might be of use to you in later interviews and be sure to provide consistent responses to the same questions asked by different interviewers. The different interviewers will typically get together later to discuss their reactions to you and your responses.

When the interview ends, if you've not been told, you have a right to ask the interviewer when you might expect to hear from him or her. You will likely be evaluated on these four criteria:

You will likely be evaluated on education and experience, mental qualities, manner and personal traits, and appearance.

- *Education and experience:* Your accomplishments as they relate to the job requirements, evidence of growth, breadth and depth of your experiences, leadership qualities, and evidence of your willingness to assume responsibility.

- *Mental qualities:* Intelligence, alertness, judgment, logic, perception, creativity, organization, and depth.

- *Manner and personal traits:* Social poise, sense of humor, mannerisms, warmth, confidence, courtesy, aggressiveness, listening ability, manner of oral expression, emotional balance, enthusiasm, initiative, energy, ambition, maturity, stability, and interests.

- *Appearance:* Grooming, dress, posture, cleanliness, and apparent health.

Communicating After the Interview

Although you may be exhausted (mentally and physically) from your interview sessions, there are several tasks that remain to be done. Some must be completed immediately after the interview; others must wait until you receive notice of the hiring decision.

Following Up the Interview

After the interview, critique your performance, your résumé, and your application letter.

Immediately after the interview, conduct a self-appraisal of your performance. Try to recall each question that was asked and evaluate your response. If you're not satisfied with one of your responses, take the time to formulate a more effective answer. Chances are that you will be asked a similar question in the future.

Also reevaluate your résumé. Were any questions asked during the interview that indicated some confusion about your qualifications? Does some section need to be revised or some information added or deleted? If you have composed your résumé on a computer, making the needed changes will be easy.

Determine too whether you can improve your application letter on the basis of your interview experience. Were the qualifications you discussed in your letter the ones that seemed to impress the interviewers the most? Were these qualifications discussed in terms of how they would benefit the organization? Did you provide specific evidence to support your claims?

Send a short thank-you note immediately after the interview.

You should also take the time to send the interviewer (or interviewers) a short thank-you note or e-mail message as a gesture of courtesy and to reaffirm your interest in the job. The interviewer, who probably devoted quite a bit of time to you before, during, and after the interview session, deserves to have his or her efforts on your behalf acknowledged.

Recognize, however, that your thank-you note may or may not have any effect on the hiring decision. Most decisions to offer the candidate a job or to invite him or her back for another round of interviewing are made the day of the interview, often during the interview itself. Thus, your thank-you note may arrive after the decision, good or bad, has been made.

The real purpose of a thank-you note is to express genuine appreciation for some courtesy extended to you; you do not write to earn points. Also, avoid trying to resell yourself. You've already made your case through your résumé, cover letter, and interview.

Your thank-you note should be short and may be either typed or handwritten. Consider it a routine message that should be written in a direct organizational pattern. Begin by expressing appreciation for the interview; then achieve credibility by mentioning some specific incident or insight gained from the interview. Close on a hopeful, forward-looking note. The thank-you note in Model 33 (p. 508) corresponds to the résumé and application letter presented in Chapter 14 (Models 29, p. 470, and 32, p. 482).

If you have not heard from the interviewer by the deadline date he or she gave you for making a decision, telephone or e-mail the interviewer for a status report. If no decision has been made, your inquiry will keep your name and your interest in the position in the interviewer's mind. If someone else has been selected, you need to know so that you can continue your job search.

Handling Rejection

Some job applicants become discouraged at the long wait between mailing out their initial résumés and being invited for an interview. You should recognize, however, that the first responses you will get are the rejections because it takes less time to eliminate those who are obviously unsuited for a specific position than to evaluate those who might qualify. Each of us is unsuitable for *some* position, but that doesn't mean we're unsuitable for *all* positions.

Similarly, don't spend your time after a job interview sitting by the phone waiting for word on the hiring decision. You may have to go on several employment interviews at different organizations before being offered a job, so don't waste valuable time. Immediately schedule additional interviews; you can always cancel them if necessary, but they will give you something to fall back on if you're passed over for one position. In addition, the perspective that comes from having interviewed at numerous organizations will help you make an informed decision when a job offer is made.

The job applicant who presents a well-groomed and confident appearance, who is well qualified, and who is well prepared for the interview has an excellent chance of being offered a position. You should know, however, that despite the employer's best efforts, job selection is as much an art as a science. Personal likes and dislikes and the right personal chemistry also play a role.

Although feelings of hurt and disappointment are natural in such circumstances, there is no reason to feel anger at the organization that rejects your application. If there are 200 applicants for the position, 199 of them are going to receive the same letter you did. Instead of getting mad, write a gracious note to the interviewer, such as the following:

> Although I'm naturally disappointed that I was not selected for the position, I do appreciate the professionalism and courtesy you showed me and hope you

Here's a technique definitely not appropriate for all situations: When author and *New York Times* columnist Anna Quindlen applied for a job at the *New York Post,* she sent this mock kidnapping note as a follow-up to her interview. Quindlen had judged her audience correctly; she got the job. You should use unusual techniques only when you know enough about the person you're dealing with to know that they'll appreciate the gesture.

The smart applicant sends a gracious note following a rejection.

Model 33   **Interview Follow-Up Letter**

The interview follow-up letter should be written within a day or two of the job interview.

Addresses the person in the salutation as he or she was addressed during the interview.

Begins directly, with a sincere expression of appreciation.

Mentions a specific incident that occurred and relates it to the writer's background.

Closes on a confident, forward-looking note.

April 15, 1998

1   Mr. David Norman, Partner
Ross, Russell & Weston
452 Fifth Avenue
New York, NY 10018

2   Dear Mr. Norman:

Thank you for the opportunity to interview for the position of EDP specialist yesterday. I very much enjoyed meeting you and Arlene Worthington and learning more about the position and about Ross, Russell & Weston.

3   I especially appreciated the opportunity to observe the long-range planning meeting yesterday afternoon and to learn of your firm's plans for increasing your consulting practice with nonprofit agencies. My experience working in city government leads me to believe that nonprofit agencies can benefit greatly from your expertise.

4   Again, thank you for taking the time to visit with me yesterday. I look forward to hearing from you.

Sincerely,

Aurelia Gomez

Aurelia Gomez
225 West 70 Street
New York, NY 10023

Grammar and Mechanics Notes

1 Use the ampersand (&) in a firm name only if it is used by the firm itself.   2 Use a colon (not a comma) even if the salutation uses the reader's first name.   3 *nonprofit:* Write most words beginning with *non* solid—without a hyphen.   4 *Again,:* Use a comma after an introductory expression.

will keep me in mind if a position for which I might qualify opens in the future.

Such a note speaks volumes about the maturity of the applicant and might open the door for future employment. Besides, it is not unusual for any successful job applicant to receive several offers, all but one of which must be declined. Your gracious note might just put you at the top of the list for a second interview if the chosen applicant declines the job.

Remember that the job campaign is a job itself—perhaps one of the most important jobs you'll ever undertake and maybe even one of the most difficult. Depersonalize any early rejections. Look at them objectively, determine what went wrong (if anything), and learn from the experience. As with most endeavors, perseverance, preparation, and a positive attitude will pay off in ultimate success.

Accepting, Delaying, and Refusing a Job Offer

Remember that a job offer is never "official" until it is in writing, so avoid making permanent plans until the confirming letter arrives. Accepting a job offer is easy. An acceptance letter is, of course, a good-news letter and should be written in the direct organizational pattern. Give the good news first; follow it with any necessary details, including salary, starting date, and other contractual items. Close with a positive look to the future. Always accept in writing, so that you and the organization have a permanent record of your decision (see Model 34, p. 510, for an acceptance letter that corresponds to the résumé in Model 30 and application letter in Chapter 14 Microwriting).

Use the direct organizational style when writing an acceptance letter.

Suppose you receive a job offer from one organization while you still have other job interviews pending. In such a case, you may be unsure whether to accept and need more time to make a decision. Recruiters are certainly aware that you are interviewing at more than one organization; on the other hand, they may be facing deadlines or putting other qualified candidates on hold until you respond, so your request for a time extension must be diplomatic. Your best strategy is to express appreciation for the job offer, tactfully ask for an extension, and close by reaffirming your interest in the job (see Model 35, p. 511).

Once you've accepted one job offer, you should immediately inform all other organizations at which you're being seriously considered for a position to withdraw your name from further consideration. Similarly, if you receive any subsequent job offers, you should immediately decline them. When withdrawing your name from further consideration for a job or declining a job, you may communicate either by letter or by telephone. Phone calls are faster, but you run the risk of being asked for more details than you care to divulge about either your reasons for declining or the job you've accepted. You have more control of what you communicate in a letter; in addition, letters provide a permanent record—both for you and for the employer.

Consider your acceptance of a job as a binding commitment.

Refusal letters are best written in the indirect organizational pattern, beginning on a neutral but relevant note, stating the refusal in neutral or positive terms, and closing on a pleasant, supportive note. Such letters may be brief and need not go into great detail. The important point is to convey in a professional manner the news that the organization needs to continue its search process. Model 36 (p. 512) shows a rejection letter.

Your refusal letter should be brief and written in the indirect organizational pattern.

If you accept a job while employed elsewhere, you must resign immediately from your present job. Your resignation may or may not come as a surprise to your

Model 34   **Job-Acceptance Letter**

This acceptance letter concludes a process begun with the résumé and application letter in Model 30 and Chapter 14 3Ps microwriting activity.

1

15 Turner Hall
Boston University
Boston, MA 02215-8134
March 17, 1998

Ms. Phyllis Morrison
Assistant Director of Personnel
Precision Systems, Inc.
P.O. Box 18734
Los Angeles, CA 90018

Dear Ms. Morrison:

Gives the good news (that you accept the job offer) first, where it will receive the most attention.

2   I am delighted to accept your offer of a position as EEOC coordinator for PSI at an annual salary of $28,600. I look forward to beginning my new position July 5.

Provides the needed additional details.

3   Enclosed are the completed medical examination and the insurance forms. I plan to be in the Los Angeles area on May 13 through 15 to secure an apartment and would be happy to meet with you then if any further matters related to my employment need to be resolved.

Closes on a friendly, forward-looking note.

4   Thanks, Ms. Morrison, for giving me this opportunity to make a contribution to the Human Resources Division and to Precision Systems, Inc.

Cordially,

Raymond J. Arnold

Raymond J. Arnold

Enclosures

Grammar and Mechanics Notes

1 Using a nine-digit zip code is optional.   2 You may indent paragraphs (as shown here) or block paragraphs in a letter.   3 *an apartment and:* Do not use a comma here because the second part of the sentence lacks a subject.   4 *Thanks, Ms. Morrison,:* Use commas to set off nouns of address.

Model 35 **Request to Delay a Job-Offer Decision**

8 Mullane Avenue
Hollbrook, MA 02343
June 3, 1998

Ms. Julia Marcos
Human Resources Department
Ohio Land Development Company
353 West 17 Avenue
Columbus, OH 43212

1 Dear Julia:

2 Thank you for your letter of May 30 offering me the position of manager-trainee at a salary of $27,500. This position represents a wonderful professional opportunity for me, and I'm giving it careful consideration.

3 I had previously scheduled another job interview on June 14, the day before you asked me for my acceptance decision. I feel obligated to keep this appointment and would
4 appreciate being able to give you my decision June 21—one week after this final interview.

The position you have offered is an exciting one, especially since you indicated the strong possibility of an overseas assignment after my one-year training program. But because my decision is so important to both of us, I'd be grateful to have one additional week to consider it.

Yours truly,

Matthew W. Mitchell

Matthew W. Mitchell

Expresses appreciation for the job offer.

Tactfully asks for an extension.

Closes on a confident note by reaffirming interest in the position.

Grammar and Mechanics Notes

1 Address the person in the salutation the same way you addressed him or her during the actual interview.   2 *May 30 offering:* Do not insert a comma after an incomplete date.   3 *June 14, the:* The comma here is to set off the nonrestrictive phrase following the date—not to set off the date.   4 *June 21—one:* It would also have been correct to use a comma instead of a dash here.

Model 36 **Job-Rejection Letter**

When Arnold accepted one job in Model 34, he had to decline all other offers.

1

15 Turner Hall
Boston University
Boston, MA 02215-8134
March 17, 1998

Mr. Stanley Scukanec, Director
Human Resources
Occidental Life, Inc.
1901 Avenue of the Stars
Los Angeles, CA 90067

Dear Mr. Scukanec:

Begins with a supportive, relevant, and neutral opening.

2   I certainly enjoyed meeting with you and your colleagues on March 3 and was pleased to receive an invitation to join your firm as wage and salary administrator.

Gives a simple statement of the facts (providing a reason for the refusal is optional).

After careful consideration of the offers I've received, I've decided to accept a position as EEOC coordinator at an electronics firm. This position will require substantially less travel time than would have been necessary with the Occidental position.

Closes with a sincere, gracious statement about the company.

3   I want to thank you and your colleagues for the time you spent with me. As I stated in my letter of March 5, I've always been impressed with the professionalism of your insurance agents and look forward to continuing my relationship with Occidental as a satisfied customer.

Cordially,

Raymond J. Arnold

Raymond J. Arnold

Grammar and Mechanics Notes

1 You may type the writer's return address above the date (as shown here) or as part of the closing lines, immediately below the writer's name.   2 Do not capitalize job titles in the body of a letter unless they are used in place of a personal title (for example *Vice President Smith*).   3 *March 5:* Use cardinal (rather than ordinal) numbers for dates unless the day precedes the month (for example, *the 5th of March*).

✓ CHECKLIST 18   **Employment Interviews**

Preparing for an Employment Interview

☑ Before going on an employment interview, learn everything you can about the organization.

☑ Practice answering common interview questions and prepare questions of your own to ask.

☑ Select appropriate clothing to wear.

☑ Control your nervousness by being well-prepared, well-equipped, and on time.

Conducting Yourself During the Interview

☑ Throughout the interview, be aware of the non-verbal signals you are communicating through your body language.

☑ Answer each question completely and accurately, always trying to relate your qualifications to the specific needs of the desired job.

☑ Whether you are interviewed by one person or a group of people, you will be evaluated on your education and experience, mental qualities, manner and personal traits, and general appearance.

Communicating After the Interview

☑ Immediately following the interview, critique your performance and also send a thank-you note or e-mail message to the interviewer.

☑ Recognize that several interviews at different organizations may be needed before you are offered a worthwhile job, so continue scheduling interviews.

☑ When you receive a job offer you want to accept, write the organization an acceptance letter and telephone or write all other employers, withdrawing your name from further consideration.

☑ If you need additional time to consider a job offer, write a tactful letter expressing appreciation for the offer, justifying your request, and assuring the organization of your continuing interest in the position.

☑ If you receive additional offers, reject them immediately.

☑ If you are presently employed, write a letter or memo of resignation as soon as you have accepted a job offer.

employer; either way, it should be in writing. Because you're writing to someone within the organization, an interoffice memorandum is the appropriate type of communication.

Because you're writing to your superior, you may decide to use a direct organizational pattern. Surely, however, your resignation will be bad news to the reader and so should be buffered somewhat. Regardless of your reason for leaving, now is not the time to bring up past injustices or to tell your superior how he or she should manage the organization's affairs. Dwell on the positive—what you've learned on the job and the satisfaction that came from making a contribution to the organization's welfare. Provide any additional details needed and close on a positive note (see Model 37, p. 514). Specific steps for succeeding at the interview phase of the job campaign are summarized in Checklist 18.

Model 37 **Job-Resignation Memo**

This resignation memo follows the indirect pattern and focuses on the positive aspects of the job.

1   **MEMO TO:** Austin Gibson

    FROM: Ray Arnold *R. J. a.*

    DATE: May 1, 1998

Begins directly by acknowledging what has been learned from the present job.

2   My position as a teller at the Franklin Street branch of Wainwright Bank has certainly been a rewarding experience—both in terms of providing funds for my college education and, just as important, in terms of the experience I gained in dealing with the public, learning time-management skills, and handling the confidential affairs of our customers.

Explains in a positive manner the reason for the resignation before actually communicating the bad news.

These skills will surely be of help to me in my chosen field of labor relations. Although you indicated to me earlier that a managment-trainee position would be available for me at Wainwright when I graduate in June, I think you know of my desire to live on the

3   West Coast. Therefore, I've accepted a position as EEOC coordinator for Precision Systems, Inc., in Los Angeles.

Provides needed details and offers to help.

My first day of work at PSI will be July 5, and I would like to end my present position on Friday, June 7. The intervening five weeks should allow sufficient time for you to hire a replacement and for me to provide whatever on-the-job training you might desire.

Closes on a positive note.

I will always be grateful for the opportunities you provided me, Mr. Gibson, and will

4   remember my two and one-half years here with great fondness.

5   c: Personnel Department

Grammar and Mechanics Notes

1 Use the memo format when writing to another employee within the same organization. Memos do not contain a salutation or closing lines.   2 *experience—both:* If your keyboard does not contain a dash, type two hyphens with no space before, between, or after. 3 *West Coast:* Capitalize a direction only when it is part of a proper name representing a part of the country.   4 *one-half:* Hyphenate fractions.   5 Use a copy notation to let the recipient know that a copy of the document is being sent to another party.

The 3Ps

A Job-Rejection Letter

You are Aurelia Gomez, whose résumé is shown in Model 29, page 470. As a result of your application letter to David Norman, partner at Ross, Russell & Weston (see Model 32, p. 482), you participated in two job interviews at the accounting firm and just received the following letter:

Dear Aurelia:

I am pleased to offer you the position of EDP specialist with our firm, effective July 1, at an annual salary of $34,400. Your duties are outlined in the enclosed job description.

This offer is conditional upon your passing a comprehensive medical examination (see enclosed). In addition, your probationary period, during which time you may be released with two weeks' notice, will extend until you receive a passing score on all parts of the New York State CPA examination.

I look forward to having you join our firm, Aurelia, and would appreciate receiving a written acceptance of this offer by May 30.

Sincerely,

Your excitement at receiving this letter is tempered by the fact that last week you orally accepted an offer of $30,200 from Modlin and Associates, another accounting firm, and their confirming letter arrived yesterday. Although you've not yet answered Modlin's letter, you planned to do so this weekend. You had also planned to write Ross, Russell & Weston this weekend, asking them to withdraw your name from further consideration.

1. Which job offer is more appealing to you?

   In addition to their offering a larger salary, another factor I like about Ross, Russell is that they are more active in city politics than Modlin. If their offer had arrived first, I would definitely have taken it.

2. Because you haven't responded in writing to the Modlin offer, are you still free to accept the Ross, Russell offer?

   No; I definitely did accept the Modlin offer over the phone. In addition to the ethical dimension, public accounting firms are a very "clubby" group. Partners in different firms tend to have frequent contacts with one another, and it is likely that my action would become known to both firms.

3. Should your rejection letter be written in the direct or indirect organizational pattern?

   Indirect. Presumably, they will consider my rejection of their job offer as bad news because they will have to reopen their search process.

4. Can you leave open the possibility of future employment with Ross, Russell?

Considering the fact that one in four entry-level employees fails to make it through the first year, there is always that possibility. However, any direct reference to future employment would be inappropriate.

5. Should you express regret that you cannot accept their offer?

No. It might invite additional job negotiations from Ross, Russell, which would not be in my best interests. I accepted the Modlin offer because I thought it would be a good career move. Despite the new offer, I still feel I will be happy and productive at Modlin.

April 20, 1998

Mr. David Norman, Partner
Ross, Russell & Weston
452 Fifth Avenue
New York, NY 10018

Dear Mr. Norman:

The opportunity to join a progressive accounting firm in New York City, especially one that is active in the political life of our city, is certainly attractive.

I am sure, therefore, that you can appreciate the mixed feelings with which I inform you that I accepted another job offer last week. Your letter arrived before I had a chance to inform you of my decision.

I thank you sincerely for the opportunity I had to learn about your firm, its employees, and its management philosophy. I found the entire process very educational and rewarding, and I look forward to continuing to get to know you and your firm better as my career in public accounting progresses.

Sincerely,

Aurelia Gomez

Aurelia Gomez
225 West 70 Street
New York, NY 10023

SUMMARY

To succeed at the interview phase of the job campaign, prepare for the interview, conduct yourself appropriately during the interview, and complete the communication tasks needed after the interview. The specific steps are summarized in Checklist 18.

REVIEW AND DISCUSSION

1. **Communication at CNN and CNNfn Revisited**

   When Elizabeth Semple interviews applicants for jobs at CNN and CNNfn, she looks for people who can stick to tight schedules, communicate with people of all backgrounds, and use the latest technology.

   a. On Friday, you will be interviewing for a college internship with CNN. If Friday is CNN's casual-dress day, what should you wear to the interview?

   b. What specific company information would you want to research in advance of your interview?

   c. What might you do during your interview with Semple to show that you are aware of the importance of sticking to strict schedules?

2. What types of information should you research about the organization with which you will be interviewing?

3. What overall strategy should you use when answering questions during the interview?

4. Describe item by item what articles of clothing and accessories from your own wardrobe you might wear to a job interview.

5. What should you do if an interviewer does not ask about an area in which you feel you are uniquely qualified for the position?

6. What criteria does an organization generally use to assess the interviewee?

7. Should you ask about salary during the interview? Why or why not?

8. Why should a thank-you note follow the interview?

9. What are the disadvantages of declining a job offer by phone?

10. If you accept one job offer and then receive a better offer a few days later from another firm, what are the ethical implications of accepting the second job offer?

11. What organizational pattern should be used for writing job-rejection letters?

Help Wanted

Directions: This thank-you note is from Anna Douglas to a potential employer. Revise the letter to make it more effective, taking into consideration the editor's marginal comments.

October 5, 19—

Use personal title and last name only.

Dear Mr. Roger Ellis:

org—dir

What do you and I have in common?

A strong desire to contribute to the profitability of Tristar Electronics, that's what. I tried to show you during my interview yesterday how my education and work experience can contribute directly to Tristar's bottom line.

Remember: The main purpose of this note is to express thanks for the interview — not to resell yourself!

conf

Thanks for taking the time to interview me. I hope you will agree that I'm the best candidate for this job.

Sincerely,

EXERCISES

1. The 3Ps Microwriting Model: Communication Applications at CNN and CNNfn   After an interview, Elizabeth Semple appreciates receiving a thank-you message reiterating the candidate's interest in the company. A follow-up message is also a good opportunity for an applicant to ask additional questions about the job or provide some information requested by the interviewer.

Problem

Earlier today, you interviewed with Elizabeth Semple for one of CNN's college intern positions. When she asked about your career goals, you were unsure of whether you wanted to specialize in production or writing. However, now that you know more about CNN, you have a better idea of the direction you'd like to take. Write a follow-up message to Ms. Semple in which you express appreciation for the interview and briefly explain your career goals.

Process

a. Who is the audience for this thank-you message?

b. Should you use the direct or indirect organizational pattern? Explain.

c. Write a descriptive subject line for your e-mail message.

d. Draft the first paragraph of your e-mail, in which you express appreciation for the interview.

e. Draft the second paragraph, in which you explain your career goals.

f. Draft the third paragraph, in which you reiterate your interest in the internship position at CNN.

Product

Using your knowledge of employment communication, write, revise, and proofread an e-mail thank-you message to Elizabeth Semple. Submit the e-mail and the answers to the process questions to your instructor.

2. **The 3Ps Microwriting Model: A Letter Asking to Delay a Job-Offer Decision**

Problem

Assume that you were offered the position of manager-trainee at Philip Morris (see Exercise 10b in Chapter 14) at a salary of $27,500, starting June 15. However, you've interviewed at two other firms and expect to learn their decisions by May 5 (10 days after Ms. Trimmer from Philip Morris asked you to respond to her job offer). Write to Ms. Trimmer, tactfully asking for a delay.

Process

a. Describe your audience.

b. Should your letter be written in the direct or indirect organizational pattern? Why?

c. Compose the first paragraph of your letter, in which you express appreciation for the job offer.

d. Compose the middle paragraph of your letter, in which you tactfully ask for a time extension, explaining the reason for the request.

e. Compose the last paragraph of your letter, in which you reaffirm your interest in the job.

Product

Revise, format, and proofread your letter (addressed to Ms. Janice Trimmer, Personnel Manager, Kraft Food Division, Philip Morris Companies, 120 Park Avenue, New York, NY 10017). Be careful to maintain a tone of sincerity throughout. Submit both your letter and your responses to the process questions to your instructor.

3. **Preparing for the Interview**   Page 500 contains a list of commonly asked interview questions. Prepare a written answer for each of these questions based on your own qualifications and experience. Then select two of the stress questions on pages 500–502 and answer them in terms of your own situation. Type each question and then your answer.

4. **Researching the Employer**   Refer to Exercise 10b in Chapter 14. Assume that Philip Morris has invited you to interview for the manager-trainee position. Research this company prior to your interview. Prepare a two-page, double-spaced report on your findings. You will, of course, concentrate on that information most likely to help you during the interview. As you're conducting your research, some questions are likely to occur to you that you'll want to get answered during the interview. Prepare a list of these questions and attach it as an appendix to your report.

5. **Work-Team Communication—Mock Interviews**   This project uses information collected as part of Exercise 4. Divide into groups of six students. Draw straws to determine which three members will be interviewers and which three will be job applicants. Both groups now have homework to do. The interviewers must get

together to plan their interview strategy (10 to 12 minutes for each candidate); and the applicants, working individually, must prepare for this interview.

The interviews will be conducted in front of the entire class, with each participant dressed appropriately. On the designated day, the three interviewers as a group will interview each of the three job applicants in turn (while the other two are out of the room). Given the short length of each interview, the applicant should refrain from asking any questions of his or her own, except to clarify the meaning of an interviewer's question.

After each round of interviews, the class as a whole will vote for the most effective interviewer and interviewee.

6. **Accepting a Job Offer**   Neither of the other two jobs panned out (see Exercise 2 on p. 520). Write your acceptance letter to Ms. Trimmer.

7. **Rejecting a Job Offer**   Assume that you were offered the job in Exercise 2 above. Even though the position is with the Kraft Food Division of Philip Morris, you've had second thoughts about working for an organization so closely associated with tobacco products. You prefer to take your chances on getting another job offer, one with which you will be more comfortable. Write your letter of rejection to Ms. Trimmer.

Neelima Takes a Walk

CONTINUING
CASE 15

Neelima Shrikhande has been on two job interviews and is scheduled to go on a third next week. Yesterday in the mail she received a job offer from Applied Biosystems (James R. Douglas, Vice President, 850 Lincoln Centre Drive, Foster City, CA 94404) to begin work on September 1 as director of management information systems at an annual salary of $81,500. Today, she received a phone call from Anne McKenzie, president of Stride Rite (5 Cambridge Center, Cambridge, MA 02142), offering her the newly created position of director of corporate communications at an annual salary of $72,500, effective at her convenience but not later than 60 days from acceptance of the job offer.

Despite the lower salary, Neelima immediately decides to accept the position at Stride Rite. She will report directly to Anne McKenzie, and she feels she will enjoy living in the Boston metropolitan area. She will cancel her interview next week with Victor DeJorgé at Southeast Banking in Miami.

Critical Thinking

1. How should Neelima inform Victor DeJorgé of her decision?

2. One week later, Neelima received an overnight express letter from Jim Douglas proposing a counteroffer: Neelima's salary will be increased to $84,500, and she will be named to head a corporate-wide task force to coordinate Applied Biosystems' efforts to increase the role of women in technical and engineering positions within the organization. What should Neelima do?

Writing Projects

3. Assume the role of Neelima Shrikhande. Write letters to Anne McKenzie and James R. Douglas giving your decision.

Reference Manual

Language Arts Basics

LAB 1: Punctuation—Commas

Punctuation serves as a roadmap to help guide the reader through the twists and turns of your message—pointing out what is important (italics or underscores), subordinate (commas), copied from another source (quotation marks), explained further (colon), considered as a unit (hyphens), and the like. Sometimes correct punctuation is absolutely essential for comprehension. Consider, for example, the different meanings of the following sentences, depending upon the punctuation:

What's the latest, Dope?
What's the latest dope?

The social secretary called the guests names as they arrived.
The social secretary called the guests' names as they arrived.

Our new model comes in red, green and brown, and white.
Our new model comes in red, green, and brown and white.

The play ended, happily.
The play ended happily.

A clever dog knows it's master.
A clever dog knows its master.

We must still play Michigan, which tied Ohio State, and Minnesota.
We must still play Michigan, which tied Ohio State and Minnesota.

"Medics Help Dog Bite Victim"
"Medics Help Dog-Bite Victim"

The comma rules presented in LAB 1 and the other punctuation rules presented in LAB 2 do not cover every possible situation; comprehensive style manuals, for example, routinely present more than 100 rules just for using the comma rather than just the 12 rules presented here. These rules cover the most frequent uses of punctuation in business writing. Learn them—because you will be using them frequently.

Commas are used to connect ideas and to set off elements within a sentence. When typing, leave one space after a comma. Many writers use commas inappropriately. No matter how long the sentence, make sure you have a legitimate reason before inserting a comma.

1.1   Adjectives   Use a comma to separate two or more adjectives that modify the same noun if the adjectives are *not* joined by a coordinate conjunction.

, adj

He was an aggressive, unpleasant manager.

But: He was an aggressive_and unpleasant manager.

Note: The major coordinate conjunctions are *and, but, or,* and *nor;* they join elements of equal rank. Do not use a comma if the first adjective modifies the combined idea of the second adjective plus the noun: *Please order a new* **bulletin board** *for the conference room.* Do not use a comma between the last adjective and the noun: *Wednesday was a long, hot, humid_day.*

1.2   Complimentary Closing   Use a comma after the complimentary closing of a business letter formatted in the standard punctuation style.

, clos

Yours truly,

Sincerely yours,

Note: With standard punctuation, a colon follows the salutation and a comma follows the complimentary closing. With open punctuation, no punctuation follows the salutation or complimentary closing.

1.3   Date   Use commas before and after the year in a complete date.

, date

The note is due on May 31, 1998, at 5 p.m.

Note: Do not forget the comma *after* the year. A comma should not be used after a partial date: *The note is due on May 31_at 5 p.m.*

1.4   Direct Address   Use commas before and after a name used in direct address.

, dir ad

Thank you, Ms. Cross, for bringing the matter to our attention.

Ladies and gentlemen, we appreciate your attending our session today.

1.5   Independent Clauses   Use a comma to connect independent clauses joined by a coordinate conjunction (unless both clauses are short and closely related).

, ind

Mr. Karas discussed last month's performance, and Ms. Daniels presented the sales projections.

The meeting was running late, but Mr. Mears was in no hurry to adjourn.

But: The firm hadn't paid_and John was angry.

Note: An independent clause is a subject-verb combination that can stand alone as a complete sentence. Do not confuse two independent clauses joined by a coordinate conjunction and a comma with a compound predicate, whose verbs are not to be separated by a comma:

Mrs. Ames had read the merger report, but she had not discussed it with her colleagues.

But: Mrs. Ames had read the merger report_but had not discussed it with her colleagues.

1.6   Interrupting Expression   Use commas before and after an interrupting expression.

, inter

I believe it was John, not Nancy, who raised the question.

It is still not too late to make the change, is it?

, intro

1.7 Introductory Expression   Use a comma after an introductory expression (unless it is a short prepositional phrase).

No, the status report is not ready.

When the status report is ready, I shall call you.

But: I shall call you_when the status report is ready.

To finish the task on time, Frank hired temporary help.

But: In 1990 we expanded into South America.

Note: An introductory expression is a word, phrase, or clause that comes before the subject and verb of the independent clause. Do not use a comma between the subject and verb: *To finish that boring and time-consuming task in time_for the monthly sales meeting_was a major challenge.*

, nonr

1.8 Nonrestrictive Expression   Use commas before and after a nonrestrictive expression.

Nonrestrictive:	Ann Cosgrave, who has had some experience, should apply for the position.
Restrictive:	Anyone_who has had some experience_should apply for the position.
Nonrestrictive:	Those papers, which we had left on the conference table, are missing.
Restrictive:	Only those papers_that we had left on the conference table are missing.
Nonrestrictive:	Wagner's latest book, *Merger Mania*, was the topic of the session.
Restrictive:	The book_Merger Mania_was the topic of the session.

Note: A nonrestrictive expression is a word, phrase, or clause that may be omitted without changing the basic meaning of the sentence. A restrictive expression, on the other hand, limits (restricts) the meaning of the noun or pronoun that it follows; because it is essential to the meaning of the sentence, it is *not* set off by commas. Always examine the noun or pronoun that comes before the expression to determine whether the noun or pronoun needs that expression to complete its meaning; if it does, do *not* use a comma.

In the last pair of sentences, note that an appositive (a noun that renames the preceding noun) is set off by commas only if it is nonrestrictive.

, place

1.9 Place   Use commas before and after a state or country that follows a city.

The sales conference will be held in Phoenix, Arizona, on May 13–15.

Our business agent is located in Brussels, Belgium, in the P.O.M. Building.

Note: Do not forget to insert the comma *after* the state or country.

, quot

1.10 Quotation   Use commas before and after a direct quotation in narrative material.

The president said, "You have nothing to fear," and I believed him.

"I assure you," the vice president said, "that no positions will be terminated."

Note: If a quotation at the beginning of a sentence is a question, use a question mark instead of a comma: *"How many have applied?" she asked.*

1.11   Series   Use commas to separate three or more items in a series.   *, ser*

The committee may meet on Wednesday, Thursday, or Friday.

Carl wrote the questionnaire, Anna distributed it, and Tim tabulated the results.

Note: Some style manuals indicate that the last comma (before the conjunction) is optional. However, to avoid ambiguity in business writing, you should insert this comma. Do not use a comma after the last item in a series: *Planning the agenda, preparing the handouts, and recording the minutes_are the three jobs left to complete.*

1.12   Transitional Expression   Use commas before and after a transitional expres-   *, tran*
sion or independent comment.

You may, of course, cancel your subscription at any time.

One suggestion, for example, was to undertake a leveraged buyout.

Note: Examples of transitional expressions and independent comments are *in addition, as a result, therefore, in summary, on the other hand, however, unfortunately,* and *as a matter of fact.*

APPLICATION

DIRECTIONS   Insert any needed commas in the following sentences. In the blank at the left, write the abbreviation for the comma rule (or rules) being applied. If a sentence is correctly punctuated as shown, write a *C* in the blank.

Examples: ___*, tran*___ We cannot, therefore, accept your offer.

___*C*___ I hoped to receive permission but was disappointed.

_____   **1.** The contracts to be signed were left on the supervisor's desk.

_____   **2.** Portland Oregon is a lovely city.

_____   **3.** Leonard has prepared numerous reports news releases and sales presentations.

_____   **4.** At the sales manager's specific direction we are extending store hours until 7 p.m.

_____   **5.** I will attend the conference in August and let you know what happens.

_____   **6.** You may make the slides yourself or you may request assistance from audiovisual services.

_____   **7.** I assumed as a matter of fact that the project was finished.

_____   **8.** We signed the original lease on January 1 1995.

_____   **9.** I hope you will purchase Excel and will make use of it in budgeting.

_____   **10.** They must have your answer by June 15 before the board meeting.

_____   **11.** The group of co-op students from Los Angeles visited our offices today.

A

_____ **12.** Ross hopes to get the figures to you soon but cannot promise delivery by a certain date.

_____ **13.** The consultant was pressed for time to complete the analysis before closing time.

_____ **14.** Their software-support department for example handles more than a thousand calls daily.

_____ **15.** To end the quarter with a small surplus is the major goal for the division.

_____ **16.** Richardson gave a concise reasoned explanation of the process.

_____ **17.** You will note Bonnie that your signature appears on the document.

_____ **18.** It is not too early I suspect to begin planning our tenth-anniversary sale.

_____ **19.** Their catalog states "All merchandise is guaranteed for 90 days."

_____ **20.** To end the quarter with a small surplus we must reduce costs by at least 8%.

_____ **21.** Everyone please be seated so that President Mary Webler can tell us about her short conversation.

_____ **22.** His attempt to conceal his role in the cover-up of the savings-and-loan scandal was not successful.

_____ **23.** Identifying prospects qualifying them and determining their preferences will consume most of the afternoon of June 13 1998 for Anne's group.

_____ **24.** I agree with you but do not feel that such drastic action is necessary.

_____ **25.** To do your job well you will require some assistance from another department.

_____ **26.** To do your job well will require a major time commitment.

_____ **27.** A noun that comes before a nonrestrictive expression is followed by a comma but one that comes before a restrictive expression is not.

_____ **28.** By working hard we gained approval to hold our conference in Phoenix not in Springfield.

_____ **29.** John drove and I navigated.

_____ **30.** The fact that Pete Johnson and I both came from San Francisco and had been with the company for a total of 32 years did not persuade the human resources director to approve our request that the retirement plan be modified to permit early retirements.

LAB 2:   Punctuation—Other Marks

Apostrophes

Apostrophes are used to show that letters have been omitted (as in contractions) and to show possession. When typing, do not space before or after an apostrophe (unless a space after is needed before another word).

A

2.1   Gerund   Use the possessive form for a noun (or pronoun) that comes before a gerund. *'ger*

> Garth questioned Karen**'s** leaving so soon.
>
> Stockholders**'** raising so many questions delayed the adjournment.
>
> Mr. Matsumoto knew Karl and objected to **his** going to the meeting.

Note: A gerund is the *-ing* form of a verb used as a noun.

2.2   Pronoun   Use an apostrophe plus the letter *s* to form the possessive of indefinite pronouns; do not use an apostrophe to form the possessive of personal pronouns. *'pro*

> It is someone**'s** responsibility.   The responsibility is theirs**.**
>
> I will review everybody**'s** figures.   The company used its**s** credit.

Note: Examples of indefinite possessive pronouns are *anybody's, everyone's, no one's, nobody's, one's,* and *somebody's.* Examples of personal possessive pronouns are *hers, his, its, ours, theirs,* and *yours.* Do not confuse the possessive pronouns *its, theirs,* and *whose* with the contractions *it's, there's,* and *who's:* **It's** *time to put litter in* **its** *place.* **There's** *no reason to take* **theirs.** **Who's** *determining* **whose** *jobs will be eliminated?*

2.3   Singular Nouns   Use an apostrophe plus *s* to form the possessive of a singular noun. *'sing*

> Al Brown**'s** office   Gil Hodges**'s** record
>
> brother-in-law**'s** problem   a year**'s** time
>
> Mr. and Mrs. Smith**'s** home   the CPA**'s** opinion
>
> Michigan National Bank**'s** assets   the boss**'s** contract
>
> the buyer's and the seller**'s**   Clinton and Gore**'s**
> signatures   administration

Note: To indicate joint ownership, make only the last noun possessive: *John and Mary's report.* To indicate separate ownership, make both nouns possessive: *John's and Mary's reports.* Add the apostrophe plus *s* to the last word in a compound possessive (*attorney general's opinion*).

2.4   Plural Nouns   Use only an apostrophe, without an *s*, to form the possessive of plural nouns that end in *s*.

> the two companies**'** agreement   *But:* the children**'s** books
>
> both girls**'** statements   the men**'s** dressing room
>
> the Smiths**'** home
>
> all the doctors**'** offices
>
> two years**'** worth

Note: Make sure that what comes before the apostrophe is a complete word, for example, *juries' verdicts* and not *jurie's verdicts.* To avoid problems with plural possessives, first make the noun plural; then form the possessive of the plural noun: *child, children, children's shoes; city, cities, the two cities' boundaries.* Do not confuse plural nouns with possessive nouns (singular or plural). Whenever a noun ending in *s* is followed by another noun, the first noun is probably a possessive, requiring an apostrophe; for example, write *company's policies* or *companies' policies*, but not *companies_policies.*

Colons

Colons are used (1) after an independent clause that introduces explanatory material and (2) after the salutation of a business letter that uses the standard punctuation style. When typing, leave two spaces after a colon; do not begin the following word with a capital letter unless it begins a quoted sentence.

: exp

2.5   Explanation   Use a colon to introduce explanatory material that is preceded by an independent clause.

> Just remember this: you may need a reference from her in the future.

> The fall trade show offers the following advantages: inexpensive show space, abundant traffic, and free press publicity.

Note: An independent clause is a subject-verb combination that can stand alone as a complete sentence. Expressions commonly used to introduce explanatory material are *the following, as follows,* and *these.* The explanatory material may be a listing, a restatement, an example, or a quotation.

Make sure the clause preceding the explanatory material can stand alone as a complete sentence. Otherwise, no punctuation is needed: *The fall trade show offers_inexpensive show space, abundant traffic, and free press publicity.*

: salut

2.6   Salutation   Use a colon after the salutation of a business letter that uses the standard punctuation style.

> Dear Mr. Jones:

> Dear Alice:

Note: Never use a comma after the salutation in a business letter. (A comma is appropriate only in a personal letter.) With standard punctuation, a colon follows the salutation and a comma follows the complimentary closing. With open punctuation, no punctuation follows the salutation or complimentary closing.

Ellipsis

An ellipsis is an omission. Three periods, with one space before and after each, are used to show that something has been left out of a quotation. Four periods (the sentence period plus the three ellipsis periods) indicate the omission of the last part of a quoted sentence, the first part of the next sentence, or a whole sentence or paragraph. Here is an example:

Complete Quotation:

> The average age of homebuyers has risen to 31.5 years from 29.6 years in 1995. This increase is partly due to the rising cost of new home mortgages. Adjustable-rate mortgages now account for 60% of all new mortgages.

Shortened Quotation:

> The average age of homebuyers has risen to 31.5 years. . . . Adjustable-rate mortgages now account for 60% of all new mortgages. (The typing sequence is *years.*(space).(space).(space).(2 spaces)*Adjustable-rate.*)

2.7 Omission Use ellipsis periods to indicate that one or more words have been omitted from quoted material.

. . . omi

> According to *Business Week,* "A continuing protest could shut down . . . Pemex, which brought in 34% of Mexico's dollar income last year."

Hyphens

Hyphens are used to form some compound adjectives, to link some prefixes to root words (such as *quasi-public*), and to divide words at the ends of lines. When typing, do not leave a space before or after a regular hyphen. Likewise, do not use a hyphen with a space before and after to substitute for a dash. (If your keyboard does not have a dash character, make a dash by typing two hyphens with no space before, between, or after.)

2.8 Compound Adjective Hyphenate a compound adjective that comes *before* a noun (unless the adjective is a proper noun or unless the first word is an adverb ending in *-ly*). Leave one space after a "suspended" hyphen unless it is followed by a punctuation mark.

- adj

> We hired a first-class management team.
>
> *But:* Our new management team is first_class.
>
> The long-term outlook for our investments is excellent.
>
> *But:* We intend to hold our investments for the long_term.
>
> *But:* The General_Motors warranty received high ratings.
>
> *But:* Alice presented a poorly_conceived proposal.
>
> Only first- and second-class mail will arrive on time.

Note: Don't confuse compound adjectives (which are generally temporary combinations) with compound nouns (which are generally well-established concepts). Compound nouns (such as *social security, life insurance, word processing,* and *high school*) are not hyphenated when used as adjectives that come before a noun; thus, use *income_tax form, real_estate agent, public_relations firm,* and *data_processing center.* In the last sentence above, note that when two hyphenated adjectives have a common base, you may use a "suspended" hyphen rather than repeating the base word (*class* is the base word in this example).

2.9 Numbers Hyphenate fractions and compound numbers 21 through 99 when they are spelled out.

- num

> Nearly three-fourths of our new applicants were unqualified.
>
> Last week seventy-two orders were processed incorrectly.

Periods

Periods are used at the ends of declarative sentences and polite requests and in abbreviations. When typing, leave two spaces after a period (or any other punctuation mark) that ends a sentence.

2.10 Request Use a period to end a sentence that is a polite request.

. req

Would you please sign the form on page 2.

May I please have the report by Friday.

Note: Consider the statement a polite request if you expect the reader to respond by *acting* rather than by giving a yes-or-no answer. *Would you be willing to take this assignment?* is a real question, requiring a question mark, whereas *Would you let me know your answer by Friday.* is a polite request, requiring a period.

Quotation Marks

Quotation marks are used around direct quotations, titles of some publications and conferences, and special terms. When typing, do not space after the opening quotation mark or before the closing quotation mark. Type the closing quotation mark after a period or comma but before a colon or semicolon. Type the closing quotation mark after a question mark or exclamation point if the quoted material itself is a question or an exclamation; otherwise, type it before the question mark or exclamation point. Capitalize the first word of a quotation that begins a sentence.

"quot

2.11   Quotation   Use quotation marks around a direct quotation.

"When we return on Thursday," Luis said, "we would like to meet with you."

Did Helen say, "He will represent us"?

Note: Do not confuse a direct quotation with an indirect quotation, which is not enclosed in quotation marks: *Warren said_that he wanted to meet with me on Thursday.*

"term

2.12   Term   Use quotation marks around a term to clarify its meaning or to show that it is being used in a special way.

Net income after taxes is known as "the bottom line."

The job title was changed from "chairman" to "chief executive officer."

The president misused the word "effect" in last night's press conference.

"title

2.13   Title   Use quotation marks around the title of a newspaper or magazine article, chapter in a book, report, conference, and similar items.

Read the article entitled "Wall Street Recovery."

Chapter 4, "Market Segmentation," of *Industrial Marketing* is of special interest.

The theme of this year's sales conference is "Quality Sells."

The report "Common Carriers" shows the extent of the transportation problems.

Note: The titles of *complete* published works are underscored or shown in italics. The titles of *parts* of published works and most other titles are enclosed in quotation marks.

Semicolons

Semicolons are used to show where elements in a sentence are separated. The separation is stronger than a comma but not as strong as a period. When typing, leave one space after a semicolon and begin the following word with a lowercase letter.

2.14 **Comma**   If a misreading might otherwise occur, use a semicolon (instead of a comma) to separate independent clauses that contain internal commas.   *; comma*

Confusing: I ordered juice, toast, and bacon, and eggs, toast, and sausage were sent instead.

Clear: I ordered juice, toast, and bacon; and eggs, toast, and sausage were sent instead.

But: Although high-quality paper was used, the photocopy machine still jammed, and neither of us knew how to repair it. (*no misreading likely to occur*)

Note: Make sure the semicolon is inserted *between* the independent clauses—not *within* one of the clauses.

2.15 **Independent Clauses**   Use a semicolon to separate independent clauses that are not connected by a coordinate conjunction.   *; no conj*

The president was eager to proceed with the plans; the board still had some reservations.

I slept through my alarm; consequently, I was late for the meeting.

Note: If a coordinate conjunction (such as *and, but, or,* or *nor*) connects the two clauses, use a comma: *The president was eager to proceed with the plans, but the board still had some reservations.* Do not use a comma to separate two independent clauses that are not joined by a coordinate conjunction (such an error is called a *comma splice*).

2.16 **Series**   Use semicolons to separate items in a series if any of the items already contain commas.   *; ser*

The personnel department will be interviewing in Dallas, Texas; Stillwater, Oklahoma; and Little Rock, Arkansas, for the new position.

Among the guests were Henry Halston, our attorney; his wife, Edith; and Lisa Hart-Wilder, our new controller.

Note: Make sure the semicolon is inserted between (not within) the items in the series. Even if only one of the items contains an internal comma, separate all of them with semicolons.

Underscores (or Italics)

An underscore (or underline) is a line typed under an expression to show emphasis or to substitute for italic type. When typing a title, underscore the spaces between the words, but do not underscore any punctuation after the title. When underscoring individual words, do not underscore the spaces between the words: *Does the author of <u>The Last Almighty Dollar</u> spell her name <u>Joanne</u>, <u>Joann</u>, or <u>Jo Ann</u>?*

2.17 **Title**   Underscore or italicize the title of a book, magazine, newspaper, and other complete published works.   *title*

Roger's newest book, <u>All That Glitters</u>, was reviewed in <u>The New York Times</u>.

The Alaco oil spill was the cover story in last week's *Time*.

APPLICATION

DIRECTIONS   Insert any needed punctuation (including commas) in the following sentences. In the blank at the left, write abbreviations for the punctuation rules being applied; some sentences will apply more than one rule. If a sentence is correctly punctuated as shown, write a *C* in the blank. Each numbered item is one sentence.

Examples: _'sing_   We received our money's worth.

_C_   Your presentation to the president was first class.

_____   **1.** I plan to attend Judys session Gretchen does not.

_____   **2.** Doris finished the newsletter on time but in the meantime her other duties were left undone.

_____   **3.** Please consult with Mr. McGlynn training director Ms. Little forms analyst and me before taking any action.

_____   **4.** You must read the article in Business Week entitled Japanese Carmakers Flash Their Cash.

_____   **5.** Chris Overmans updating of the lobbies furnishings was widely appreciated.

_____   **6.** Will your remarks be off the record?

_____   **7.** If Agnes intends to go she should notify Mark he will make all the arrangements.

_____   **8.** They will first paint my office then after five minutes rest they will paint yours.

_____   **9.** These are the new requirements three years experience and union membership.

_____   **10.** Those peoples computers are privately owned.

_____   **11.** They were careful workers nevertheless two errors slipped by them.

_____   **12.** Its about time your division was given its due share of resources.

_____   **13.** Dayle is certainly a highly valued employee of ours.

_____   **14.** Betty wanted to attend the APICS meeting but she was out of town.

_____   **15.** Mens wallets and womens handbags are featured in this weeks sale.

_____   **16.** The award ceremony was a never to be forgotten experience for that workers family.

_____   **17.** You may test up to three fourths of the workers said Mr. Palmer if you notify them ten days prior to the testing.

_____   **18.** The two dates to remember are March 15 1997 and April 15 1998.

_____   **19.** It took Mavis only two hours to do the five hour job.

_____   **20.** The Browns automobile is two years newer than the Wilsons.

_____   **21.** Bills leaving delayed our new product introduction by two weeks.

_____   **22.** My superiors wife used the term nonboring to describe their new family life.

_____   **23.** Twenty one of the reports were prepared on the secretaries computers.

_____   **24.** The inns guests complained about the geeses honking.

_____ **25.** Here is the latest development Business Week will feature the company in its next issue.

_____ **26.** The mayors voted to coordinate their efforts in attracting the new firm we should be receiving their joint plan soon.

_____ **27.** Would you please photocopy the article entitled Green Is the Color of Money that appeared in last weeks Money magazine.

_____ **28.** The commerce official said We will trim imports by two thirds by the end of the quarter.

_____ **29.** You will be meeting our Milan agent next week but do not forget to visit Rudolpho Angeletti our Rome distributor on your way home.

_____ **30.** Casey nominated Maria Tony and Ken and Barbie Andy and Jo seconded the nomination.

LAB 3: Grammar

Suppose the vice president of your organization asked you, a systems analyst, to try to locate a troublesome problem in a computer spreadsheet. After some sharp detective work, you finally resolved the problem and wrote a memo to the vice president saying, "John and myself discovered that one of the formulas were incorrect, so I asked he to revise it."

Instantly, you've turned what should have been a "good-news" opportunity for you into, at best, a "mixed-news" situation. The vice president will be pleased that you've uncovered the bug in the program but will probably focus entirely too much attention on your poor grammar skills.

Grammar refers to the rules for combining words into sentences. The most frequent grammar problems faced by business writers are discussed below. Learn these common rules well so that your use of grammar will not present a communication barrier to the message you're trying to convey.

Complete Sentences

3.1   Fragment   Avoid sentence fragments.

NOT: He had always wanted to be a marketing representative. Because he liked to interact with people.

BUT: He had always wanted to be a marketing representative because he liked to interact with people.

Note: A fragment is a part of a sentence that is incorrectly punctuated as a complete sentence. Each sentence must contain a complete thought.

3.2   Run-on Sentences   Avoid run-on sentences.

NOT: Karen Raines is a hard worker she even frequently works through lunch.

NOT: Karen Raines is a hard worker, she even frequently works through lunch.

BUT: Karen Raines is a hard worker; she even frequently works through lunch.

OR: Karen Raines is a hard worker. She even frequently works through lunch.

Note: A run-on sentence is two independent clauses run together without any punctuation between them or with only a comma between them (the latter error is called a *comma splice*).

Modifiers (Adjectives and Adverbs)

An adjective modifies a noun or pronoun; an adverb modifies a verb, an adjective, or another adverb.

3.3   Modifiers   Use a comparative adjective or adverb (*-er, more,* or *less*) to refer to two persons, places, or things and a superlative adjective or adverb (*-est, most,* or *least*) to refer to more than two.

> The Datascan is the fast**er** of the two machines.
> The XR-75 is the slow**est** of all the machines.
>
> Rose Marie is the **less** qualified of the two applicants.
> Rose Marie is the **least** qualified of the three applicants.

Note: Do not use double comparisons, such as "more faster."

Agreement (Subject/Verb/Pronoun)

Agreement is correspondence in number between related subjects, verbs, and pronouns. All must be singular if they refer to one, plural if they refer to more than one.

3.4   Agreement   Use a singular verb or pronoun with a singular subject and a plural verb or pronoun with a plural subject.

> The four **workers have** a photocopy of **their** assignments.
>
> Roger's **wife was** quite late for **her** appointment.
>
> **Mr. Tibbetts and Mrs. Downs plan** to forgo **their** bonuses.
>
> Included in this envelope **are a contract and an affidavit.**

Note: This is the general rule; variations are discussed below. In the first sentence, the plural subject (*workers*) requires a plural verb (*have*) and a plural pronoun (*their*). In the second sentence, the singular subject (*wife*) requires a singular verb (*was*) and a singular pronoun (*her*). In the third sentence, the plural subject (*Mr. Tibbetts and Ms. Downs*) requires a plural verb (*plan*) and a plural pronoun (*their*). In the last sentence, the subject is *a contract and an affidavit*—not *envelope.*

3.5   Company Names   Company names may be singular or plural so long as consistency is maintained.

> **NOT:** Bickley and Bates **has** paid for **its** last order. **They** are ready to reorder.
>
> **BUT:** Bickley and Bates **has** paid for **its** last order. **It** is now ready to reorder.
>
> **OR:** Bickley and Bates **have** paid for **their** last order. **They** are now ready to reorder.

3.6   Expletives   In sentences that begin with an expletive, the true subject follows the verb. Use *is* or *are,* as appropriate.

There **is** no **reason** for his behavior.

There **are** many **reasons** for his behavior.

Note: An expletive is an expression such as *there is, there are, here is,* and *here are* that comes at the beginning of a clause or sentence. Because the topic of a sentence that begins with an expletive is not immediately apparent, such sentences should be used sparingly in business writing.

3.7   Intervening Words   Disregard any words that come between the subject and verb when establishing agreement.

Only **one** of the mechanics **guarantees his** work. (not *their work*)

The **appearance** of the workers, not their competence, **was** being questioned.

The **secretary,** as well as the clerks, **was** late filing **her** form. (not *their forms*)

Note: First determine the subject; then make the verb agree. Other intervening words that do not affect the number of the verb are *together with, rather than, accompanied by, in addition to,* and *except.*

3.8   Pronouns   Some pronouns (*anybody, each, either, everybody, everyone, much, neither, no one, nobody,* and *one*) are always singular. Other pronouns (*all, any, more, most, none,* and *some*) may be singular or plural, depending on the noun to which they refer.

Each of the laborers **has** a different view of **his or her** job.

Neither of the models **is** doing **her** job well.

Everybody is required to take **his or her** turn at the booth. (not *their turn*)

All the **pie has** been eaten.   **None** of the **work is** finished.

All the **cookies have** been eaten.   **None** of the **workers are** finished.

3.9   Subject Nearer to Verb   If two subjects are joined by correlative conjunctions (*or, either/or, nor, neither/nor,* or *not only/but also*), the verb and any pronoun should agree with the subject that is nearer to the verb.

Either Robert or **Harold is** at **his** desk.

Neither the receptionist nor the **operators were** able to finish **their** tasks.

Not only the actress but also the **dancer has** to practice **her** routine.

The tellers or the **clerks have** to balance **their** cash drawers before leaving.

Note: The first noun in this type of construction may be disregarded when determining whether the verb should be singular or plural. Pay special attention to using the correct pronoun; do not use the plural pronoun *their* unless the subject and verb are plural. Note that subjects joined by *and* or *both/and* are always plural: *Both **the actress and the dancer have** to practice **their** routines.*

3.10   Subjunctive Mood   Verbs in the subjunctive mood require the plural form, even when the subject is singular.

I wish the situation **were** reversed.

If I **were** you, I would not mention the matter.

Note: Verbs in the subjunctive mood refer to conditions that are impossible or improbable.

Case

Case refers to the form of a pronoun and indicates its use in a sentence. There are three cases: nominative, objective, and possessive. (Possessive-case pronouns are covered under "Apostrophes" in the section on punctuation in LAB 2.) Reflexive pronouns, which end in *-self* or *-selves,* refer to nouns or other pronouns.

3.11   Nominative Case   Use nominative pronouns (*I, he, she, we, they, who, whoever*) as subjects of a sentence or clause and with the verb *to be.*

> The customer representative and **he** are furnishing the figures. (***he** is furnishing*)
>
> Mrs. Quigley asked if Oscar and **I** were ready to begin. (***I** was ready to begin*)
>
> **We** old-timers can provide some background. (***we** can provide*)
>
> It was **she** who agreed to the proposal. (***she** agreed*)
>
> **Who** is chairing the meeting? (***he** is chairing*)
>
> Mr. Lentzner wanted to know **who** was responsible. (***she** was responsible*)
>
> Anna is the type of person **who** can be depended upon. (***she** can be depended upon*)

Note: If you have trouble determining which pronoun to use, ignore the plural subject or substitute another pronoun. See the reworded clauses in parentheses above.

3.12   Objective Case   Use objective pronouns (*me, him, her, us, them, whom, whomever*) as objects in a sentence, clause, or phrase.

> Thomas sent a fax to Mr. Baird and **me.** (*sent a fax to **me***)
>
> This policy applies to Eric and **her.** (*applies to **her***)
>
> Joe asked **us** old-timers to provide some background. (*Joe asked **us** to provide*)
>
> The work was assigned to **her** and **me.** (*the work was assigned to **me***)
>
> To **whom** shall we mail the specifications? (*mail them to **him***)
>
> Anna is the type of person **whom** we can depend upon. (*we can depend upon **her***)

Note: For *who/whom* constructions, if *he/she* can be substituted, *who* is the correct choice; if *him/her* can be substituted, *whom* is the correct choice. Remember: *who-he, whom-him.* The difference is apparent in the final examples shown here and under "Nominative Case," Rule 3.11: **who** *can be depended upon* versus **whom** *we can depend upon.*

3.13   Reflexive Pronouns   Use reflexive pronouns (*myself, yourself, himself, herself, itself, ourselves, yourselves,* or *themselves*) to refer to or emphasize a noun or pronoun that has already been named. Do not use reflexive pronouns to *substitute for* nominative or objective pronouns.

> I **myself** have some doubts about the proposal.
>
> You should see the exhibit **yourself.**

> **NOT:** Virginia and **myself** will take care of the details.
>
> **BUT:** Virginia and **I** will take care of the details.

NOT: Mary Louise administered the test to Thomas and **myself.**

BUT: Mary Louise administered the test to Thomas and **me.**

APPLICATION

DIRECTIONS   Select the correct word or words in parentheses.

1. Sherrie Marshall, in addition to James M. Smith, (are/is) in line for an appointment to the Federal Trade Commission. (Who/Whom) do you know on the FTC staff? None of the people I contacted (has/have) heard of them. Smith, I believe, is the (younger/youngest) of the two.

2. Tower and Associates is moving (it's/its/their) headquarters. (It/They) (are/is) selling (its/their) old furniture and equipment at auction. Not only a conference table but also a high-speed collator (are/is) for sale. The facilities manager asked that all inquiries be directed to (her/she).

3. If he (was/were) honest about his intentions, Carl Ichan would talk directly to Ivan and (me/myself). After all, he knows that it was (I/me) (who/whom) made the offer originally. Between the two of us, Ivan is the (more/most) supportive of Ichan's position.

4. Here (are/is) the reports on Hugo's bankruptcy. It seems that (us/we) investors were a little overconfident, but it is generally the early investors (who/whom) make the most money.

5. Neither our savings account nor our long-term securities (are/is) earning adequate interest. Everybody in finance (are/is) trying to improve the performance of (his or her/their) portfolio. Each of the analysts (are/is) trying to maintain quarterly investment goals.

6. There (was/were) several people in the audience (who/whom) questioned whether each of our divisions (was/were) operating efficiently. The CEO asked (us/we) division managers to respond to their questions.

7. Neither Lan Yang nor the two programmers (was/were) able to resolve the problem. In fact, neither of the two programmers (was/were) successful in locating the source of the problem. However, Lan Yang, as well as the programmers, (are/is) continuing (her/their) efforts.

8. John is the (more slower/most slower/slower/slowest) of the two welders. Only one of his jobs (has/have) been finished, so I asked (he/him) to work overtime this weekend.

9. (Who/Whom) will you ask to assist (I/me/myself)? Alex is the (more accurate/most accurate) typist on our entire staff; however, Jill is the type of worker (who/whom) can coordinate the entire project.

10. I wish it (was/were) possible for Ella and (I/me) to ask both Roger and David about (his/their) experience in using temporary help. Getting their answers to our questions (are/is) going to require some real detective work, and it is (I/me) (who/whom) will have to do it.

DIRECTIONS   Revise the following paragraph to eliminate any fragments and run-on sentences.

The Zippo Manufacturing Company is the largest producer of refillable lighters in the world. Since the company's founding in 1932 by George G.

Blaisdell. Zippo has managed to corner 40% of this market in the United States and is growing larger every year. Both in the United States and abroad. Zippo has used its excellent consumer relations and its recent innovative marketing and sales techniques to make the company a common household name, also, Zippo has made use of changing product lines and expanding markets to achieve unprecedented growth in sales. Zippo is one of the most successful privately owned companies in America it would make an excellent take-over target.

LAB 4:   Mechanics

Writing mechanics include those elements in communication that are evident only in written form: abbreviations, capitalization, number expression, spelling, and word division. (Punctuation, also a form of writing mechanics, was covered in LABS 1 and 2.) While creating a first draft, you need not be too concerned about the mechanics of your writing. However, you should be especially alert during the editing and proofreading stages to follow these common rules.

Abbreviations

Use abbreviations sparingly in narrative writing; many abbreviations are appropriate only in technical writing, statistical material, and tables. Consult a dictionary for the correct form for abbreviations, and follow the rule "When in doubt, write it out." When typing, do not space within abbreviations except to separate each initial of a person's name. Leave one space after an abbreviation unless another mark of punctuation follows immediately.

4.1   Not Abbreviated   In narrative writing, do not abbreviate common nouns (such as *acct., assoc., bldg., co., dept., misc.,* and *pkg.*) or the names of cities, states (except in addresses), months, and days of the week.

4.2   With Periods   Use periods to indicate many abbreviations.

No.	8 a.m.	4 ft.
Dr. M. L. Peterson	P.O. Box 45	e.g.

4.3   Without Periods   Write some abbreviations in all capitals, with no periods—including all two-letter state abbreviations used in addresses with zip codes.

CPA	IRS	CT
TWA	UNESCO	OK

Note: Use two-letter state abbreviations in bibliographic citations.

Capitalization

The function of capitalization is to emphasize words or to show their importance. For example, the first word of a sentence is capitalized to emphasize that a new sentence has begun.

4.4   Compass Point   Capitalize a compass point that designates a definite region or that is part of an official name. (Do not capitalize compass points used as directions.)

Margot lives in the **S**outh.

Our display window faces **w**est.

Is **E**ast Orange in **W**est Virginia?

4.5   Letter Part   Capitalize the first word and any proper nouns in the salutation and complimentary closing of a business letter.

Dear **M**r. Smith:	**S**incerely **y**ours,
Dear **M**r. and **M**rs. Ames:	**Y**ours **t**ruly,

4.6   Noun Plus Number   Capitalize a noun followed by a number or letter (except for page and size numbers).

Table 3	**p**age 79
Flight 1062	**s**ize 8D

4.7   Position Title   Capitalize an official position title that comes before a personal name, unless the personal name is an appositive set off by commas. Do not capitalize a position title used alone.

Vice **P**resident Alfredo Tenegco	Shirley Wilhite, **d**ean,
our **p**resident, Joanne Rathburn,	The **c**hief **e**xecutive **o**fficer retired.

4.8   Proper Noun   Capitalize proper nouns and adjectives derived from proper nouns. Do not capitalize articles, conjunctions, and prepositions of four or fewer letters (for example, *a, an, the, and, of,* and *with*). The names of the seasons and the names of generic school courses are not proper nouns and are not capitalized.

Xerox copier	**A**mherst **C**ollege (*but:* the **c**ollege)
New **Y**ork **C**ity (*but:* the **c**ity)	the **M**exican border
the **F**ourth of **J**uly	**F**riday, **M**arch 3,
Chrysler **B**uilding	**B**ank of **A**merica
First-**C**lass **S**torage **C**ompany	**M**argaret **A**dams-**W**hite
business **c**ommunication	the **w**inter holidays

4.9   Quotation   Capitalize the first word of a quoted sentence. (Do not capitalize the first word of an indirect quotation.)

According to Hall, "**T**he goal of quality control is specified uniform quality."

Hall thinks we should work toward "**s**pecified uniform quality."

Hall said that **u**niform quality is the goal.

4.10   Title   In a published title, capitalize the first and last words, the first word after a colon or dash, and all other words except articles, conjunctions, and prepositions of four or fewer letters.

"**A W**ord to the **W**ise"

Pricing Strategies: The Link with Reality

Numbers

Authorities do not agree on a single style for expressing numbers—whether to spell out a number in words or to write it in figures. The following guidelines apply to typical business writing. (The alternative is to use a *formal* style, in which all numbers that can be expressed in one or two words are spelled out.) When typing numbers in figures, separate thousands, millions, and billions with commas; and leave a space between a whole-number figure and its fraction unless the fraction is a character on the keyboard.

4.11   General   Spell out numbers for zero through ten and use figures for 11 and over.

the first three pages	ten complaints
18 photocopies	5,376 stockholders

Note: Follow this rule only when none of the following special rules apply.

4.12   Figures   Use figures for

- dates. (Use the endings *-st, -d, -rd,* or *-th* only when the day precedes the month.)

- all numbers if two or more *related* numbers both above and below ten are used in the same sentence.

- measurements—such as time, money, distance, weight, and percentage. Be consistent in using either the word *percent* or (more typically) the symbol %.

- mixed numbers.

May 9 (or the 9th of May)	10 miles
4 men and 18 women	*But:* The **18** women had **four** cars.
$6	5 p.m. (or 5 o'clock)
5% (or 5 percent)	$6\frac{1}{2}$
	But: 6 3/18

4.13   Words   Spell out

- a number used as the first word of a sentence.

- the smaller number when two numbers come together.

- fractions.

- the words *million* and *billion* in even numbers.

Thirty-two people attended.	nearly two-thirds of them
three 34-cent stamps	150 two-page brochures
37 million	$4.8 billion

Note: When fractions and the numbers 21 through 99 are spelled out, they should be hyphenated.

Spelling

Correct spelling is essential to effective communication. A misspelled word can distract the reader, cause misunderstanding, and send a negative message about the writer's competence. Because of the many variations in the spelling of English words, no spelling guidelines are foolproof; there are exceptions to every spelling rule. The five rules that follow, however, may be safely applied in most business writing situations. Learning them will save you the time of looking up many words in a dictionary.

4.14   Doubling a Final Consonant   If the last syllable of a root word is stressed, double the final consonant when adding a suffix.

Last Syllable Stressed		Last Syllable Not Stressed	
prefer	preferring	happen	happening
control	controlling	total	totaling
occur	occurrence	differ	differed

4.15   One-Syllable Words   If a one-syllable word ends in a consonant preceded by a single vowel, double the final consonant before a suffix starting with a vowel.

Suffix Starting with Vowel		Suffix Starting with Consonant	
ship	shipper	ship	shipment
drop	dropped	glad	gladness
bag	baggage	bad	badly

4.16   Final E   If a final e is preceded by a consonant, drop the e before a suffix starting with a vowel.

Suffix Starting with Vowel		Suffix Starting with Consonant	
come	coming	hope	hopeful
use	usable	manage	management
nerve	nervous	sincere	sincerely

Note: Words ending in *ce* or *ge* usually retain the *e* before a suffix starting with a vowel: *noticeable, advantageous.*

4.17   Final Y   If a final y is preceded by a consonant, change y to i before any suffix except one starting with i.

Most Suffixes		Suffix Starting with i	
company	companies	try	trying
ordinary	ordinarily	forty	fortyish
hurry	hurried		

4.18   EI and IE Words   Remember the rhyme:

Use *i* before *e*	believe	yield
Except after *c*	receive	deceit
Or when sounded like *a*	freight	their
As in *neighbor* and *weigh*.		

Word Division

When possible, avoid dividing words at the end of a line, because word divisions tend to slow down or even confuse a reader (for example, *rear- range* for *rearrange* or *read- just* for *readjust*). However, when necessary to avoid grossly uneven right margins, use the following rules. Most word processing software programs have a hyphenation feature that automatically divides words to make a more even right margin; you can change these word divisions manually if necessary. When you are typing, do not space before a hyphen.

4.19 Compound Word Divide a compound word either after the hyphen or where the two words join to make a solid compound.

> self- service   free- way   battle- field

4.20 Division Point Leave at least two letters on the upper line and carry at least three letters to the next line.

> ex- treme   typ- ing

4.21 Not Divided Do not divide a one-syllable word, contraction, or abbreviation.

> straight   shouldn't
> UNESCO   approx.

4.22 Syllables Divide words only between syllables.

> per- sonnel   knowl- edge

Note: When in doubt about where a syllable ends, consult a dictionary.

APPLICATION

DIRECTIONS   Rewrite the following paragraphs so that all words and numbers are expressed correctly. Do not change the wording in any sentences.

1. 5,000 of our employees will receive their bonus checks at 4 o'clock tomorrow. According to dorothy k. needles, human resources director, employees in every dept. will receive a bonus of at least 4% of their annual salary.

2. As of june 30th, nearly ¾ of our inventory consisted of overpriced computer chips. The vice president for finance, o. jay christensen, presented this and other information in figure 14 of our quarterly status report.

3. The public relations director of our firm gave 14 1-hour briefings during the 3-day swing. Then he drove west to columbus, oh, for a talk-show interview.

4. In response to the $4 drop in price that was reported on page 45 of yesterday's newspaper, president ronald bradley said that next quarter's earnings are expected to be 1⅔ times higher than this quarter's earnings.

5. Today's los angeles herald-examiner quoted jason fowler as saying, "we're proud of the fact that 4 of our regional managers and 13 of our representatives donated a total of 173 hours to the hospice project."

DIRECTIONS   Correct the one misspelling in each line.

1. phenomenon	hypocricy	assistance
2. liaison	precedant	miniature
3. surprise	harrass	nickel
4. similiar	occasionally	embarrassing

5.	concensus	innovate	irresistible
6.	benefited	exhaustible	parallell
7.	seperately	inadvertent	exhilarated
8.	efficiency	insistance	disapproval
9.	accidentally	camouflage	alloted
10.	criticize	innocence	indispensible
11.	accommodate	perserverance	plausible
12.	apparent	deterrant	license
13.	category	occurrence	wierd
14.	recommend	changeable	hairbrained
15.	argument	boundry	deceive

DIRECTIONS   Write the following words, inserting a hyphen at the first correct division point. If a word cannot be divided, write it without a hyphen.

Examples: mis-spelled
            thought

1.	desktop	released	safety
2.	abundant	rhythm	masterpiece
3.	ILGWU	loudly	planned
4.	importance	couldn't	senator-elect
5.	ahead	extremely	going

LAB 5: Word Usage

The following words and phrases are often used incorrectly in everyday speech and in business writing. Learn to use them correctly to help yourself achieve your communication goals.

In some cases in the following list, one word is often confused with another similar word; in other cases, the structure of our language requires that certain words be used only in certain ways. Because of space, only brief and incomplete definitions are given here. Consult a dictionary for more complete or additional meanings.

5.1 Accept/Except   *Accept* means "to agree to"; *except* means "with the exclusion of."

I will **accept** all the recommendations **except** the last one.

5.2 Advice/Advise   *Advice* is a noun meaning "counsel"; *advise* is a verb meaning "to recommend."

If I ask for her **advice,** she may **advise** me to quit.

5.3 Affect/Effect   *Affect* is most often used as a verb meaning "to influence" or "to change"; *effect* is most often used as a noun meaning "result" or "impression."

The legislation may **affect** sales but should have no **effect** on gross margin.

5.4   All Right/Alright   Use *all right*. (*Alright* is considered substandard.)

The arrangement is **all right** (not *alright*) with me.

5.5   A Lot/Alot   Use *a lot*. (*Alot* is considered substandard.)

We used **a lot** (not *alot*) of overtime on the project.

5.6   Among/Between   Use *among* when referring to three or more; use *between* when referring to two.

Among the three candidates was one manager who divided his time **between** London and New York.

5.7   Amount/Number   Use *amount* to refer to money or to things that cannot be counted; use *number* to refer to things that can be counted.

The **amount** of consumer interest was measured by the **number** of coupons returned.

5.8   Anxious/Eager   Use *anxious* only if great concern or worry is involved.

Jon was **eager** to get the new car although he was **anxious** about making such high payments.

5.9   Any One/Anyone   Spell as two words when followed by *of*; spell as one word when the accent is on *any*.

Anyone is allowed to attend **any one** of the sessions.

Between   See *Among/Between*.

5.10   Can/May   *Can* indicates ability; *may* indicates permission.

I **can** finish the project on time if I **may** hire an additional secretary.

5.11   Cite/Sight/Site   *Cite* means "to quote" or "to mention"; *sight* is either a verb meaning "to look at" or a noun meaning "something seen"; *site* is most often a noun meaning "location."

The **sight** of the high-rise building on the **site** of the old battlefield reminded Monica to **cite** several other examples to the commission members.

5.12   Complement/Compliment   *Complement* means "to complete" or "something that completes"; *compliment* means "to praise" or "words of praise."

I must **compliment** you on the new model, which will **complement** our line.

5.13   Could of/Could've   Use *could've* (or *could have*). (*Could of* is incorrect.)

We **could've** (not *could of*) prevented that loss had we been more alert.

5.14   Different from/Different than   Use *different from*. (*Different than* is considered substandard.)

Your computer is **different from** (not *different than*) mine.

5.15   Each Other/One Another   Use *each other* when referring to two; use *one another* when referring to three or more.

The two workers helped **each other,** but their three visitors would not even look at **one another.**

> **Eager**   See *Anxious/Eager.*

> **Effect**   See *Affect/Effect.*

5.16   e.g./i.e.   The abbreviation *e.g.* means "for example"; *i.e.* means "that is." Use *i.e.* to introduce a restatement or explanation of a preceding expression. Both abbreviations, like the expressions for which they stand, are followed by commas. (Many writers prefer the full English wordings to the abbreviations because they are clearer.)

The proposal has merit; **e.g.,** it is economical, forward-looking, and timely. Unfortunately, it is also a hot potato; **i.e.,** it will generate unfavorable publicity.

5.17   Eminent/Imminent   *Eminent* means "well-known"; *imminent* means "about to happen."

The arrival of the **eminent** scientist from Russia is **imminent.**

5.18   Enthused/Enthusiastic   Use *enthusiastic.* (*Enthused* is considered substandard.)

I have become quite **enthusiastic** (not *enthused*) about the possibilities.

> **Except**   See *Accept/Except.*

5.19   Farther/Further   *Farther* refers to distance; *further* refers to extent or degree.

We drove 10 miles **farther** while we discussed the matter **further.**

5.20   Fewer/Less   Use *fewer* to refer to things that can be counted; use *less* to refer to money or to things that cannot be counted.

Alvin worked **fewer** hours at the exhibit and therefore generated **less** interest.

> **Further**   See *Farther/Further.*

5.21   Good/Well   *Good* is an adjective; *well* is an adverb or (with reference to health) an adjective.

Joe does a **good** job and performs **well** on tests, even when he does not feel **well.**

> **i.e.**   See *e.g./i.e.*

> **Imminent**   See *Eminent/Imminent.*

5.22   Imply/Infer   *Imply* means "to hint" or "to suggest"; *infer* means "to draw a conclusion." Speakers and writers *imply;* readers and listeners *infer.*

The president **implied** that changes will be forthcoming; I **inferred** from his tone of voice that these changes will not be pleasant.

5.23   Irregardless/Regardless   Use *regardless.* (*Irregardless* is considered substandard.)

He wants to proceed, **regardless** (not *irregardless*) of the costs.

5.24   Its/It's   *Its* is a possessive pronoun; *it's* is a contraction for "it is."

It's time to let the department increase **its** budget.

5.25   Lay/Lie   *Lay* (principal forms: *lay, laid, laid, laying*) means "to put" and requires an object to complete its meaning; *lie* (principal forms: *lie, lay, lain, lying*) means "to rest."

Please **lay** the supplies on the shelf.	I **lie** on the couch after lunch each day.
I **laid** the folders in the drawer.	The report **lay** on his desk yesterday.
She had **laid** the notes on her desk.	The job has **lain** untouched for a week.

Less   See *Fewer/Less.*

Lie   See *Lay/Lie.*

5.26   Loose/Lose   *Loose* means "not fastened"; *lose* means "to be unable to find."

Do not **lose** the **loose** change in your pocket.

May   See *Can/May.*

Number   See *Amount/Number.*

One Another   See *Each Other/One Another.*

5.27   Passed/Past   *Passed* is a verb (the past tense or past participle of *pass,* meaning "to move on or by"); *past* is an adjective, adverb, or preposition meaning "earlier" or "bygone."

The committee **passed** the no-confidence motion at a **past** meeting.

5.28   Percent/Percentage   With figures, use *percent;* without figures, use *percentage.*

We took a commission of 6 **percent** (or 6%), which was a lower **percentage** than last year.

5.29   Personal/Personnel   *Personal* means "private" or "belonging to one individual"; *personnel* means "employees."

I used my **personal** time to draft a memo to all **personnel.**

5.30   Principal/Principle   *Principal* means "primary" (adjective) or "sum of money" (noun); *principle* means "rule" or "law."

The guiding **principle** is fair play, and the **principal** means of achieving it is a code of ethics.

5.31   Real/Really   *Real* is an adjective; *really* is an adverb. Do not use *real* to modify another adjective.

She was **really** (not *real*) proud that her necklace contained **real** pearls.

5.32   Reason Is Because/Reason Is That   Use *reason is that.* (*Reason is because* is considered substandard.)

The **reason** for such low attendance **is that** (not *is because*) the weather was stormy.

Regardless   See *Irregardless/Regardless*.

5.33   Same   Do not use *same* to refer to a previously mentioned item. Use *it* or some other wording instead.

We have received your order and will ship **it** (not *same*) in three days.

5.34   Set/Sit   *Set* (principal forms: *set, set, set, setting*) means "to place"; *sit* (principal forms: *sit, sat, sat, sitting*) means "to be seated."

Please **set** your papers on the table.	Please **sit** in the chair.
She **set** the computer on the desk.	I **sat** in the first-class section.
I have **set** the computer there before.	I had not **sat** there before.

5.35   Should of/Should've   Use *should've* (or *should have*). (*Should of* is incorrect.)

We **should've** (not *should of*) been more careful.

Sight   See *Cite/Sight/Site*.

Sit   See *Set/Sit*.

Site   See *Cite/Sight/Site*.

5.36   Stationary/Stationery   *Stationary* means "remaining in one place"; *stationery* is writing paper.

I used my personal **stationery** to write them to ask whether the minicomputer should remain **stationary.**

5.37   Sure/Surely   *Sure* is an adjective; *surely* is an adverb. Do not use *sure* to modify another adjective.

I'm **surely** (not *sure*) glad that she is running and feel **sure** that she will be nominated.

5.38   Sure and/Sure to   Use *sure to*. (*Sure and* is considered substandard.)

Be **sure to** (not *sure and*) attend the meeting.

5.39   Their/There/They're   *Their* means "belonging to them"; *there* means "in that place"; and *they're* is a contraction for "they are."

They're too busy with **their** reports to be **there** for the hearing.

5.40   Theirs/There's   *Theirs* is a possessive pronoun; *there's* is a contraction for "there is."

We finished our meal but **there's** no time for them to finish **theirs.**

They're   See *their/there/they're.*

5.41   Try and/Try to   Use *try to*. (*Try and* is considered substandard.)

Please **try to** (not *try and*) attend the meeting.

A

Well   See *Good/Well.*

5.42   Whose/Who's   *Whose* is a possessive pronoun; *who's* is a contraction for "who is."

Who's going to let us know **whose** turn it is to make coffee?

5.43   Your/You're   *Your* means "belonging to you"; *you're* is a contraction for "you are."

You're going to present **your** report first.

APPLICATION

DIRECTIONS   Select the correct words in parentheses.

1. Please (advice/advise) the (eminent/imminent) educator of the (real/really) interest we have in his lecture.

2. The three workers on the (stationary/stationery) platform (can/may) help (each other/one another) if they are running late.

3. The writer (implied/inferred) that she and her colleagues divided (their/there/they're) time about evenly (among/between) the two projects.

4. (Whose/Who's) convinced that (fewer/less) of our employees (can/may) pass the exam?

5. If you (loose/lose) seniority, (your/you're) work schedule might be (affected/effected).

6. Mary Ellen (cited/sighted/sited) several examples showing that our lab employees are (real/really) (good/well) protected from danger.

7. In comparing performance (among/between) the two companies, Brenda noted that our company earned 7 (percent/percentage) more than (theirs/there's).

8. Try (and/to) (complement/compliment) the advertising group for (its/it's) stunning new brochure.

9. When Susan (laid/lay) the models on the table, I was surprised at the (amount/number) of moving parts; (e.g./i.e.), I had expected simpler designs.

10. The reason the (personal/personnel) department (could of/could've) been mistaken is (that/because) we failed to keep them informed.

11. Sherry refused to (accept/except) the continuous-form (stationary/stationery) because it had (fewer/less) absorbency than expected.

12. (Your/You're) being paid by the (amount/number) of defective finished products you (cite/sight/site) while observing on the assembly line.

13. The (principal/principle) reason we're (anxious/eager) to solve this problem is that (a lot/alot) of workers have complained of dizziness.

14. All our customers are (enthused/enthusiastic) about the new pricing (accept/except) for Highland's, which asked for a quantity discount and expected (it/same) to be granted.

A

15. Be sure (and/to) point out to her that the (percent/percentage) of commission we pay new agents is no different (from/than) that which we pay experienced agents.

16. I am (anxious/eager) to see if (its/it's) going to be Arlene (whose/who's) design will be selected.

17. I (implied/inferred) from Martin's remarks that Austin is a (sure/surely) bet as the (cite/sight/site) for our new plant.

18. The (principal/principle) (advice/advise) that Michelle gave was to (set/sit) long-term goals and stick to them.

19. Although (their/there/they're) located (farther/further) from our office than I would like, I believe their expertise will (complement/compliment) our own.

20. (Any one/Anyone) who can (farther/further) refine the (loose/lose) ends of our proposal should come back this afternoon.

21. In the previous shot, Joyce and Kathy (should of/should've) been (laying/lying) next to (each other/one another) on the beach, discussing their plans for the evening.

22. Please (set/sit) awhile and tell them about your (passed, past) adventures in the Foreign Service, (e.g./i.e.), the time you were arrested in Buenos Aires for doing a (good/well) deed for a local shopkeeper.

23. (Theirs/There's) no reason to pry into an applicant's (personal/personnel) life; however, it is (all right/alright) to ask about the applicant's general state of health.

24. (Any one/Anyone) of the stockbrokers, (irregardless/regardless) of his or her philosophy, would (sure/surely) question such a strategy.

25. (Their/There/They're) will be little (affect/effect) on operations from the (eminent/imminent) change in ownership of the firm.

Formatting Business Documents

Formatting Letters and Memos

The most common features of business letters and memos are discussed in the following sections and illustrated in Figures B.1, B.2 and B.3.

Letter and Punctuation Styles

The *block style* is the simplest letter style to type because all lines begin at the left margin. In the *modified block style,* the date and closing lines begin at the center point. Offsetting these parts from the left margin enables the reader to locate them quickly. In the *simplified style,* which is actually seldom used, all lines begin at the left margin, the salutation and complimentary closing are omitted, and the subject line and writer's identification are typed in all-capital letters.

The *standard punctuation style*—the most common format—contains a colon (never a comma) after the salutation and a comma after the complimentary closing. The *open punctuation style,* on the other hand, uses no punctuation after these two lines. Figure B.4 shows how these styles differ.

Stationery and Margins

Most letters are typed on standard-sized stationery, $8^1/_2$ by 11 inches. The first page of a business letter is typed on letterhead stationery, which shows company information printed at the top. Subsequent pages of a business letter and all pages of a personal business letter (a letter written to transact one's personal business) are typed on good-quality plain paper.

Side, top, and bottom margins should be 1 to $1^1/_2$ inches (most word processing programs have default margins of 1 inch, which works just fine). Vertically center one-page letters and memos. Set a tab at the center point if you're formatting a modified block style letter.

Required Letter Parts

The required letter parts are as follows:

Date Line   Type the current month (spelled out), day, and year on the first line. Begin either at the center point for modified block style or at the left margin for all other styles.

Inside Address   The inside address gives the name and location of the person to whom you're writing. Include a personal title (such as *Mr., Mrs., Miss,* or *Ms.*). If you use the addressee's job title, type it either on the same line as the name (separated from the name by a comma) or on the following line by itself. In the address, use the two-letter U.S. Postal Service abbreviation, typed in all capitals with no period (see Figure B.5), and leave one to two spaces between the state and the zip code. Type the inside address at the left margin four lines below the date; that is, press Enter four times. For international letters, type the name of the country in all-capital letters on the last line by itself.

Salutation   Use the same name in both the inside address and the salutation. If the letter is addressed to a job position rather than to a person, use a generic but non-sexist greeting, such as "Dear Personnel Manager." If you typically address the reader in person by first name, use the first name in the salutation (for example, "Dear Lois:"); otherwise, use a personal title and the surname only (for example, "Dear Ms. Lane:"). Leave one blank line before and after the salutation.

Body   Single-space the lines of each paragraph and leave one blank line between paragraphs. Follow correct word-division rules (see LAB 4 on p. 540) when hyphenating a word at the end of a line.

Page 2 Heading   Type the addressee's name, the page number, and the date beginning 1 inch from the top of the page, blocked at the left margin. Leave one or two blank lines (that is, press Enter two or three times) before continuing with the text. You should carry forward to a second page at least two lines of the body of the message.

Complimentary Closing   Begin the complimentary closing at the same horizontal point as the date line, capitalize the first word only, and leave one blank line before and three blank lines after, to allow room for the signature. If a colon follows the salutation, use a comma after the complimentary closing; otherwise, no punctuation follows.

Signature   Some women insert the personal title they prefer (*Ms., Miss,* or *Mrs.*) in parentheses before their signature. Men never include a personal title.

Writer's Identification   The writer's identification (name or job title or both) begins on the fourth line immediately below the complimentary closing. Do not use a personal title. The job title may go either on the same line as the typed name, separated from the name by a comma, or on the following line by itself.

Reference Initials   When used, reference initials (the initials of the typist) are typed at the left margin in lowercase letters without periods, with one blank line before. Do not include reference initials if you type your own letter.

Envelopes   Business envelopes have a printed return address. You may type your name above this address, if you wish. Use plain envelopes for personal business letters; you should type the return address (your home address) at the upper left corner. Envelopes may be typed either in standard upper- and lowercase style or in all-capital letters without any punctuation. On large (No. 10) envelopes, begin typing the mailing address 2 inches from the top edge and 4 inches from the left edge. On small (No. 6¾) envelopes, begin typing the mailing address 2 inches from the top edge and 2½ inches from the left edge. Fold letters as shown in Figure B.5.

FIGURE B.1   Standard Business Letter

This letter is shown in block style with standard punctuation.

Date Line: Date the letter is typed.

Inside Address: Name and address of the person to whom you're writing.

Salutation: Greeting.

Subject Line: Topic of the letter.

Body: Text of the letter.

Complimentary Closing: Parting farewell.

Writer's Identification: Name and/or title of the writer.

Reference Initials: Initials of the person who typed the letter (if other than the signer).

Notations: Indications of items being enclosed with the letter, copies of the letter being sent to another person, special delivery instructions, and the like.

THE BOOK MARK   *18615 Silver Center, Bozeman, MT 59715*

Phone: 406-555-3856 • Fax 406-555-3893 • E-Mail: jdye@bookmark.com

November 1, 19-- ↓ 4

Center page vertically; use default margins.

Ms. Ella Shore, Professor
Department of Journalism
Mountainside College
Paseo Canyon Drive
Great Falls, MT 59404 ↓ 2

Dear Ms. Shore: ↓ 2

Subject: Newspaper Advertising ↓ 2

Thank you for thinking of The Book Mark when you were planning the advertising for the back-to-school edition of your campus newspaper at Mountainside College. We appreciate the wide acceptance your students and faculty give our merchandise, and we are proud to be represented in the *Mountain Lark*. Although budget restrictions prevent us from taking a full-page ad, we are happy to purchase a quarter-page ad, as follows:

• The ad should include our standard trademark and the words "Welcome to The Book Mark." Please note that the word "The" is part of our name and should begin with a capital letter.

• We would prefer that our ad appear in the top right corner of a right-facing page, if possible.

Our logo is enclosed for you to duplicate. I am also enclosing a check for $375 to cover the cost of the ad. Best wishes as you publish this special edition of your newspaper. ↓ 2

Sincerely, ↓ 4

Joseph W. Dye
Sales Manager ↓ 2

rmt
Enclosures
c: Advertising Supervisor

Grammar and Mechanics Notes

The arrows indicate how many lines or inches to space down before typing the next part. For example, ↓ *4* after the complimentary closing means to press Enter four times before typing the writer's name.

FIGURE B.2 Standard Memorandum

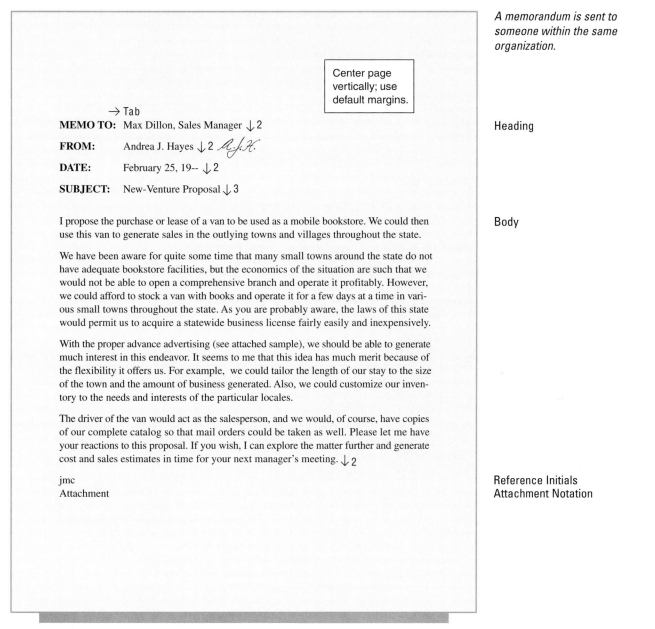

A memorandum is sent to someone within the same organization.

Center page vertically; use default margins.

→ Tab

MEMO TO: Max Dillon, Sales Manager ↓ 2

FROM: Andrea J. Hayes ↓ 2 *A.J.H.*

DATE: February 25, 19-- ↓ 2

SUBJECT: New-Venture Proposal ↓ 3

I propose the purchase or lease of a van to be used as a mobile bookstore. We could then use this van to generate sales in the outlying towns and villages throughout the state.

We have been aware for quite some time that many small towns around the state do not have adequate bookstore facilities, but the economics of the situation are such that we would not be able to open a comprehensive branch and operate it profitably. However, we could afford to stock a van with books and operate it for a few days at a time in various small towns throughout the state. As you are probably aware, the laws of this state would permit us to acquire a statewide business license fairly easily and inexpensively.

With the proper advance advertising (see attached sample), we should be able to generate much interest in this endeavor. It seems to me that this idea has much merit because of the flexibility it offers us. For example, we could tailor the length of our stay to the size of the town and the amount of business generated. Also, we could customize our inventory to the needs and interests of the particular locales.

The driver of the van would act as the salesperson, and we would, of course, have copies of our complete catalog so that mail orders could be taken as well. Please let me have your reactions to this proposal. If you wish, I can explore the matter further and generate cost and sales estimates in time for your next manager's meeting. ↓ 2

jmc
Attachment

Heading

Body

Reference Initials
Attachment Notation

B

Grammar and Mechanics Notes

Type the standard heading entries (*MEMO TO:*, *FROM:*, *DATE:*, and *SUBJECT:*) in bold and all-capital letters. Then turn off bold and press Tab (tabs are preset at $^1/_2$-inch intervals) to get to the position for typing the variable information. Memos may be typed on plain paper or on letterhead stationery.

FIGURE B.3 E-mail Message

Heading

Salutation

Body

Closing

Writer's Identification

Attachment Icon:
Automatically inserted when
writer uses the Attachment
command.

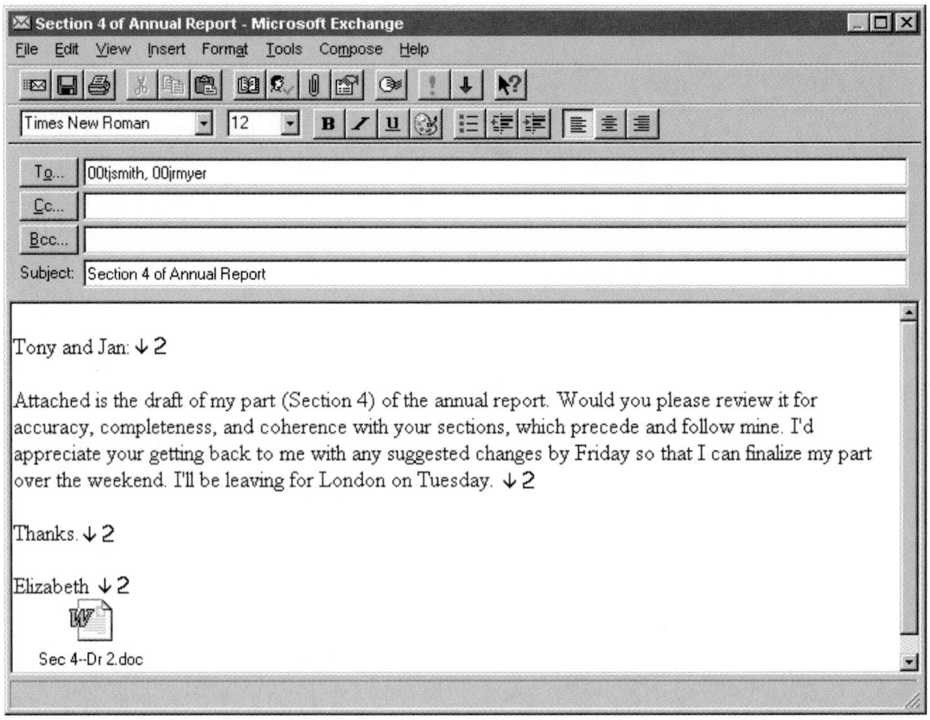

B

[Screen capture of e-mail window]

Section 4 of Annual Report - Microsoft Exchange

File   Edit   View   Insert   Format   Tools   Compose   Help

Times New Roman   12   **B** *I* u

To...   00tjsmith, 00jrmyer

Cc...

Bcc...

Subject: Section 4 of Annual Report

Tony and Jan: ↓ 2

Attached is the draft of my part (Section 4) of the annual report. Would you please review it for accuracy, completeness, and coherence with your sections, which precede and follow mine. I'd appreciate your getting back to me with any suggested changes by Friday so that I can finalize my part over the weekend. I'll be leaving for London on Tuesday. ↓ 2

Thanks. ↓ 2

Elizabeth ↓ 2

Sec 4--Dr 2.doc

Grammar and Mechanics Notes

Pay special attention when typing the e-mail addresses in the *To:* and *Cc:* boxes; a single typo will cause the message not to be delivered. Use fairly short lines (even if you have to press Enter at the end of each line) and double-space between parts. Include identifying information (such as your e-mail address) in the closing lines.

FIGURE B.4 **Letter and Punctuation Styles**

THE BOOK MARK   18615 Silver Center, Bozeman, MT 59715

Phone: 406-555-3856 • Fax 406-555-3893 • E-Mail: jdye@bookmark.com

Center point → November 1, 19-- ↓4

Ms. Ella Shore, Professor
Department of Journalism
Mountainside College
Paseo Canyon Drive
Great Falls, MT 59404 ↓2

Dear Ms. Shore ↓2

Subject: Newspaper Advertising ↓2

Thank you for thinking of The Book Mark when you were planning the advertising for the back-to-school edition of your campus newspaper at Mountainside College. We appreciate the wide acceptance your students and faculty give our merchandise, and we are proud to be represented in the *Mountain Lark*. Although budget restrictions prevent us from taking a full-page ad, we are happy to purchase a quarter-page ad. The ad should include our standard trademark and the words "Welcome to The Book Mark." Please note that the word "The" is part of our name and should begin with a capital letter. We would prefer that our ad appear in the top right corner of a right-facing page, if possible. Our logo is enclosed for you to duplicate. I am also enclosing a check for $375 to cover the cost of the ad.

You also asked about the possibility of our expanding our line of hypergraphics books. I am pleased that Mountainside College has recently implemented a diploma program in hypergraphics and want to assure you that your students will be able to find a wide variety of textbooks and manuals on this topic in our store. In addition to carrying how-to books for many different hypergraphics software programs, we also carry general design books. In addition, in our periodicals section we carry the latest issues of numerous magazines devoted to this topic.

As you are no doubt aware, The Book Mark publishes its quarterly catalog online at our Web site (http://www.bookmark.com). Although my assistant has been doing most of the design work for our home page, we would be quite interested in discussing the possibility of hiring one of your students as an intern for this task.

Modified block style letter with open punctuation

↓ Default top margin of 1"
Ms. Ella Shore
Page 2
November 1, 19-- ↓2

Specifically we are looking for someone who is proficient in using Microsoft FrontPage software and in writing html markup language. We would expect to need this person full-time for the 12-week summer period and are prepared to pay a competitive wage. Please call me if you have someone we might interview.

In the meantime, best wishes to you and your staff as you prepare this special issue of the *Mountain Lark*. I look forward to receiving my copy and to hearing from you regarding a prospective internship candidate. ↓2

Center point → Sincerely ↓4

Joseph W. Dye

Joseph W. Dye
Sales Manager ↓2

rmt
Enclosures
By Federal Express
c: Advertising Supervisor ↓2

PS: Because The Book Mark is such an important part of the lives of many Mountainside College students, we would be happy to have your photographer take some candid shots of students in our store. Just have him or her call to arrange an appointment.

Page 2 of modified block style letter with open punctuation

Center point → January 6, 19-- ↓4

Mutual Fund Manager
MDC Asset Investors, Inc.
2801 East Bancroft Street
Toledo, OH 43606-4728 ↓2

> Center page vertically; use default margins.

Dear Mutual Fund Manager: ↓2

Would you please send me information regarding your mutual fund as a vehicle for long-term investment and retirement income.

For the past five years I have contributed $7,500 annually to a Simplified Employee Pension (SEP) plan, based on my Schedule C income derived from a small carpet-cleaning business I operate part-time from my home. Thus far, I've invested this amount, which now totals approximately $40,700, in a time-savings account at my local bank. I am interested in transferring half of this amount into a conservative mutual fund. I would plan to begin making withdrawals in 16 years, at the age of 63.

Please send me any available information you have on your Columbus Fund. I am especially interested in (a) the fund's ten-year history, (b) any annual fees, and (c) the type of periodic reports that are furnished to investors. Would you also please send me the forms I would need to complete in case I decide to invest in the Columbus Fund.

I appreciate your supplying this information to help me evaluate this investment opportunity. ↓2

Center point → Sincerely, ↓4

Marilyn J. Aoyama
Marilyn J. Aoyama
750 Madison Avenue
York, PA 17404

Personal business letter in modified block style

THE BOOK MARK   18615 Silver Center, Bozeman, MT 59715

Phone: 406-555-3856 • Fax 406-555-3893 • E-Mail: jdye@bookmark.com

November 1, 19-- ↓6

Ms. Ella Shore, Professor
Department of Journalism
Mountainside College
Paseo Canyon Drive
Great Falls, MT 59404 ↓3

NEWSPAPER ADVERTISING ↓3

Thank you for thinking of The Book Mark when you were planning the advertising for the back-to-school edition of your campus newspaper at Mountainside College. We appreciate the wide acceptance your students and faculty give our merchandise, and we are proud to be represented in the *Mountain Lark*.

Although budget restrictions prevent us from taking a full-page ad, we are happy to purchase a quarter-page ad. The ad should include our standard trademark and the words "Welcome to The Book Mark." Please note that the word "The" is part of our name and should begin with a capital letter. Also, we would prefer that our ad appear in the top right corner of a right-facing page, if possible.

Our logo is enclosed for you to duplicate. I am also enclosing a check for $375 to cover the cost of the ad. Best wishes as you publish this special edition of your newspaper. ↓4

Joseph W. Dye
JOSEPH W. DYE, SALES MANAGER ↓2

rmt
Enclosures
c: Advertising Supervisor

Simplified style letter

FIGURE B.5 **Correspondence Formats**

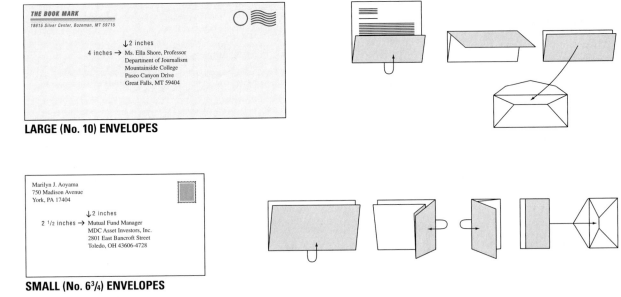

LARGE (No. 10) ENVELOPES

SMALL (No. 6¾) ENVELOPES

POSTAL SERVICE ABBREVIATIONS

U.S. POSTAL SERVICE ABBREVIATIONS
FOR STATES, TERRITORIES, AND CANADIAN PROVINCES

States and Territories

Alabama . . . . AL	Kansas . . . . KS	North Dakota . . . . ND	Wyoming . . . . WY
Alaska . . . . AK	Kentucky . . . . KY	Ohio . . . . OH	
Arizona . . . . AZ	Louisiana . . . . LA	Oklahoma . . . . OK	
Arkansas . . . . AR	Maine . . . . ME	Oregon . . . . OR	*Canadian Provinces*
California . . . . CA	Maryland . . . . MD	Pennsylvania . . . . PA	Alberta . . . . AB
Colorado . . . . CO	Massachusetts . . . . . . MA	Puerto Rico . . . . PR	British Columbia . . . . BC
Connecticut . . . . CT	Michigan . . . . MI	Rhode Island . . . . RI	Labrador . . . . LB
Delaware . . . . DE	Minnesota . . . . MN	South Carolina . . . . . . SC	Manitoba . . . . MB
District of Columbia . DC	Mississippi . . . . MS	South Dakota . . . . SD	New Brunswick . . . . . NB
Florida . . . . FL	Missouri . . . . MO	Tennessee . . . . TN	Newfoundland . . . . . . NF
Georgia . . . . GA	Montana . . . . MT	Texas . . . . TX	Northwest Territories NT
Guam . . . . GU	Nebraska . . . . NE	Utah . . . . UT	Nova Scotia . . . . NS
Hawaii . . . . HI	Nevada . . . . NV	Vermont . . . . VT	Ontario . . . . ON
Idaho . . . . ID	New Hampshire . . . . . NH	Virgin Islands VI	Prince Edward Island . PE
Illinois IL	New Jersey . . . . NJ	Virginia . . . . VA	Quebec . . . . PQ
Indiana . . . . IN	New Mexico . . . . NM	Washington . . . . WA	Saskatchewan . . . . SK
Iowa . . . . IA	New York . . . . NY	West Virginia . . . . WV	Yukon Territory . . . . . YT
	North Carolina . . . . . NC	Wisconsin . . . . WI	

Optional Letter Parts

Optional letter parts are as follows:

Subject Line   You may include a subject line (identified by the words *Subject, Re,* or *In Re* followed by a colon) to identify the topic of the letter. Type it below the salutation, with one blank line before and one after.

Enumerations in the Body   Begin an enumeration (a numbered list) at the left margin and leave two spaces between the period after the number and the following text. Indent runover lines four spaces (typically 0.4 inch). If every item takes up only a single line, single-space the items; otherwise, single-space the lines within each item and double-space between items. Either way, leave one blank line before and after the list.

Enclosure Notation   Use an enclosure notation if any additional items are to be included in the envelope. Type "Enclosure" on the line immediately below the reference initials, and as an option, add the description of what is enclosed. (*Note:* For memos, the appropriate term is "Attachment" instead of "Enclosure" if the items are to be physically attached to the memo instead of being enclosed in an envelope.)

Copy Notation   If someone other than the addressee is to receive a copy of the letter, type a copy notation ("c:") immediately below the enclosure notation or reference initials, whichever comes last. Then follow the copy notation with the names of the people who will receive copies.

Postscript   If you add a postscript to a letter, type it as the last item, preceded by one blank line. The heading "PS:" is optional. Postscripts are used most often in sales letters.

Formatting Reports and Documenting Sources

If the reader or organization has a preferred format style, use it. Otherwise, follow these generally accepted guidelines for formatting business reports. Make use of your computer's automatic or formatting features to enhance the appearance and readability of your report and to increase the efficiency of the process.

Margins

Memo and letter reports use regular correspondence margins as discussed earlier in this manual. For reports typed in manuscript (formal report) format, use a 2-inch top margin for the first page of each special part (for example, the table of contents, the executive summary, the first page of the body of the report, and the first page of the reference list). Leave a 1-inch top margin for all other pages and at least a 1-inch bottom margin on all pages. If the report is to be bound at the left, set a $1\frac{1}{2}$-inch left margin and a 1-inch right margin. If the report is to be unbound, set 1-inch side margins on both the left and right.

Spacing

Memo and letter reports are typed single-spaced. Manuscript reports may be either single- or double-spaced. Double spacing is preferred if the reader will likely make many comments on the pages. Note that double spacing leaves one blank line between each line of type; do not confuse double spacing with $1\frac{1}{2}$ spacing, which leaves only *half* a blank line between lines of type.

Regardless of the spacing used for the body of the report, single spacing is typically used for the table of contents, the executive summary, long quotations, tables, and the reference list. Use a $1/2$-inch paragraph indention for double-spaced paragraphs. Do not indent single-spaced paragraphs; instead, double-space between them.

Report Headings

The number of levels of headings used will vary from report to report. Memo reports may have only first-level subheadings, with no part titles or other headings. Long reports may have as many as four levels of headings. One standard format for the various levels is given here. Recognize, however, that the format presented here is only one of several that might be used. Again, consistency and readability should be your major goals. Regardless of the format used, make sure that the reader can instantly tell which are major headings and which are subordinate headings.

Part Title   Using a slightly larger font size than used for the body of the report, center a part title (for example, "Contents" or "References") in all capitals and in bold on a new page, leaving a 2-inch top margin. Double-space titles of two or more lines, using an inverted pyramid style (the first line longer). Triple-space after the part title.

First-Level Subheading   Using the same font size as that used in the body of the report, center and bold the first-level subheading in all-capital letters. Double-space before and after the heading.

Second-Level Subheading   Begin the second-level subheading at the left margin. Use bold type and all-capital letters as in first-level headings. Double-space before and after the heading.

Third-Level Subheading   Double-space before the third-level subheading, indent, and bold. Capitalize the first letter of the first and last words and all other words except articles, prepositions with four or fewer letters, and conjunctions. Leave a period and two spaces after the subheading, and begin typing the text on the same line.

Pagination

Number the preliminary pages, such as the table of contents, with lowercase roman numerals centered on the bottom margin. The title page is counted as page i, but no page number is shown. Page numbers appear on all other preliminary pages, centered at the bottom margin. For example, the executive summary might be page ii and the table of contents page iii.

Number all pages beginning with the first page of the body of the report with Arabic numerals. The first page of the body is counted as page 1, but no page number is typed (in word processing terminology, the page number is *suppressed*). Beginning with page 2 of the body and continuing through the reference pages, number all pages consecutively at the top right of the page.

FIGURE B.6   Sample Report

Center each line; type the title in all capitals and in bold, perhaps in a larger font than normal. Double-space and use inverted pyramid style for multiline titles.

Use upper- and lowercase letters for all other lines.

Leave the same amount of blank space between each of the sections.

Vertically center the title page.

STAFF EMPLOYEES' EVALUATION OF THE BENEFIT PROGRAM AT ATLANTIC STATE UNIVERSITY

Prepared for

David Riggins
Director of Human Resources
Atlantic State University

Prepared by

Loretta J. Santorini
Assistant Director of Human Resources
Atlantic State University

December 8, 19—

Title Page

A title page is typically used for manuscript reports but not for memo or letter reports. The report title, reader's name, writer's name, and submission date are required; other information is optional. An academic report might also contain a section immediately after the title, with this wording (diagonals indicate line breaks and are not to be typed): "A Research Report / Submitted in Partial Fulfillment / of the Requirements for the Course / *Course Number and Title.*"

FIGURE B.6 Sample Report (*Continued*)

Use a memo format for an internal reader and a letter format for an external reader. Ensure that the memo date agrees with the date on the title page.

Triple-space after the subject line.

Use standard correspondence margins and format.

MEMO TO: David Riggins, Director of Human Resources

FROM: Loretta J. Santorini, Assistant Director of Human Resources

DATE: December 8, 19--

SUBJECT: Staff Employees' Evaluation of the Benefit Program at Atlantic State University

Here is the report evaluating our staff benefit program that you requested on October 15.

The report shows that overall the staff is familiar with and values most of the benefits we offer. At the end of the report, I've made several recommendations regarding issuing individualized benefit statements annually and determining the usefulness of the automobile insurance benefit, the feasibility of offering compensation for unused sick leave, and the competitiveness of our retirement program.

I enjoyed working on this assignment, Dave, and learned quite a bit from my analysis of the situation that will help me during the upcoming labor negotiations. Please let me know if you have any questions about the report.

emc
Attachment

Type the report page number in lowercase roman numerals at the bottom margin (the title page is considered page i).

ii

Transmittal Document

The transmittal document—either a letter or a memo—is an optional part of a report. Use a direct organizational pattern and conversational language, even if the report itself uses formal language. Give a brief overview of the major conclusions and recommendations unless you expect the reader to react negatively to such information. Close with goodwill comments.

FIGURE B.6 **Sample Report (*Continued*)**

EXECUTIVE SUMMARY

STAFF EMPLOYEES' EVALUATION OF THE BENEFIT PROGRAM

AT ATLANTIC STATE UNIVERSITY

Loretta J. Santorini

December 8, 19—

Nationwide, employee benefits now account for more than a third of all payroll costs. Thus, on the basis of cost alone, an organization's benefit program must be carefully monitored and evaluated.

The problem in this study was to determine the opinions of the nearly 2,500 staff employees at Atlantic State University regarding the employee benefit program. Specifically, the investigation included determining the employees' present level of knowledge about the program, their opinions of the benefits presently offered, and their preferences for additional benefits. A survey of 206 staff employees and interviews with three managers familiar with the ASU employee benefits program provided the primary data for this study.

Overall, nearly 70% of the employees feel the benefit program has been explained adequately to them. However, a majority of the employees would prefer to have an individualized benefit statement instead of the brochures now used to explain the benefit program.

Employees are most familiar with the benefits having to do with paid time off; more than 90% are familiar with ASU policies concerning vacation, holidays, and sick leave. Similarly, more than 95% of the employees rank these three benefits as most important to them; they rank auto insurance and bookstore discounts as least important. Employees are most satisfied with the ASU vacation policy (90% satisfied) and least satisfied with the retirement policy (20% dissatisfied). The only benefit that a majority of the staff employees would like to see added is compensation for unused sick leave.

The university should study further the offering of individualized benefit statements, automobile insurance, compensation for unused sick leave, and retirement benefits. In the meantime, this employee assessment of ASU's benefit program should help the administration ensure that the program operates as effectively as possible.

iii

Use an inverted pyramid style for multiline titles.

Triple-space after the date.

Single-space the body of the summary, with double spacing between paragraphs.

Margins:
   2-inch top
   1-inch left and right
      (1½-inch left for bound reports)
   1-inch bottom

Type the report page number in lowercase roman numerals at the bottom margin.

Executive Summary

The executive summary, also called an *abstract* or *synopsis,* is an optional part of a report. If used, it goes immediately before the table of contents. If a transmittal document is not included, the summary page would be numbered ii.

FIGURE B.6 Sample Report (*Continued*)

Triple-space after the *CONTENTS* heading.

Triple-space before each part title and double-space after.

Align page numbers at the right.

Indent each lower-level heading ½ inch.

Use either leaders or spaced leaders (period, space, period) between the headings and page numbers.

Margins:
   2-inch top
   1-inch left and right
   (1½-inch left for
   bound reports)
   1-inch bottom

Table of Contents

Use a table of contents for long reports with numerous headings. The wording in the headings on the contents page must be identical with that used in the report itself. Identify only the page on which each heading is located, even though the section may comprise several pages. Generic headings (noun phrases) are used in this sample.

FIGURE B.6   Sample Report (*Continued*)

**STAFF EMPLOYEES' EVALUATION OF THE BENEFIT PROGRAM
AT ATLANTIC STATE UNIVERSITY**

INTRODUCTION

Employee benefits are a rapidly growing and increasingly important form of employee compensation for both profit and nonprofit organizations. According to a recent U.S. Chamber of Commerce survey, benefits now constitute 37% of all payroll costs, costing an average of $9,857 a year for each full-time employee (Berelson, Lazarsfield, & Connell, 1996, p. 183). Thus, on the basis of cost alone, an organization's employee benefit program must be carefully monitored and evaluated.

Atlantic State University employs nearly 2,500 staff personnel, and they have not received a cost-of-living increase in two years. As a result, staff salaries may not have kept pace with private industry, and the university's employee benefit program may become more important in attracting and retaining good workers. In addition, the contracts of three of the four staff unions expire next year, and the benefit program is typically a major area of bargaining.

PURPOSE AND SCOPE OF THE STUDY

As has been noted by one management consultant, "The success of employee benefit programs depends directly on whether employees need, understand, and appreciate the value of the benefits provided" (Egan, 1996, p. 220). Thus, to help ensure that the benefit program is operating as effectively as possible, David Riggins, director of personnel, authorized this report on October 15, 199—.

Triple-space after the title; double-space after the first-level subheading (*INTRODUCTION*). Format all headings in bold.

Begin the introduction by providing background information and establishing a need for the study.

Cite references appropriately; the author-date method is used here.

Count the first page of the body of the report as page 1, even though the page number is not typed on the page.

B

Body of the Report

This recommendation report is written in manuscript format and in formal style (note the absence of first- and second-person pronouns). An indirect organizational pattern is used.

FIGURE B.6   **Sample Report (*Continued*)**

2

Use your word processing program's pagination feature to number pages at the top right.

Use your word processing program's enumeration feature to format enumerated lines (numbered lists).

Early in the report, discuss the parameters of your study (the scope) to avoid questions by the reader.

Use a double-spaced format (as shown here) for reports if you expect the reader to insert numerous comments or if your reader prefers. In a single-spaced format, leave a blank line between paragraphs but do not indent.

Specifically, the following problem was addressed in this study: What are the opinions of staff employees at Atlantic State University regarding their employee benefits? To answer this question, the following subproblems were addressed:

1.   How knowledgeable are the employees about the benefit program?

2.   What are the employees' opinions of the value of the benefits that are presently available to them?

3.   What benefits, if any, would the employees like to have added to the program?

This study explored the attitudes of the staff employees at Atlantic State University. Although staff employees at all three state universities receive the same benefits, no attempt has been made to generalize the findings beyond Atlantic State University because the communication of the benefits may be different, geographical differences may make some benefits of more use at one institution than at another, and similar considerations. In addition, this study attempted to determine employee preferences only. The question of whether employee preferences are economically feasible is not within the scope of this study.

PROCEDURES

A list of the 2,489 staff employees who are eligible for benefits (that is, those who are employed at least 20 hours a week) was generated from the October 15 payroll run. Using a 10% systematic sample, 250 employees were selected for the survey. On November 3, each of the selected employees was sent the cover letter and questionnaire shown in Appendixes A and B via campus mail. A total of 206 employees completed usable questionnaires, for a response rate of 82%.

In addition to the questionnaire data, personal interviews were held with Lois White, compensation specialist at ASU; Roger Ray, chair of the Staff Personnel Committee at

FIGURE B.6   **Sample Report (*Continued*)**

3

ASU; and Lewis Rigby; director of the State Personnel Board. The primary data provided by the survey and personal interviews was then analyzed and compared with findings from secondary sources to determine the staff employees' opinions of the benefit program at ASU.

FINDINGS

For a benefit program to achieve its goals, employees must be aware of the benefits provided. Thus, the first section that follows discusses the effectiveness of the university's present method of communicating benefits as well as those methods that employees would prefer. An effective benefit package must also include benefits that are relevant to employee needs. Thus, the employees' opinions of the importance of and their satisfaction with each benefit offered are discussed next. The section concludes with a discussion of those benefits employees would like to see added to the benefit program at ASU.

KNOWLEDGE OF BENEFITS

Several studies (Egan, 1996; Ignatio, 1997; Meany, 1993) have shown that employees' satisfaction with benefits is directly correlated with their knowledge of such benefits. Thus, an indication of the staff employees' level of familiarity with their benefits and suggestions for improving communication were solicited.

Familiarity with Benefits. The staff employees were asked to rate their level of familiarity with each benefit. As shown in Table 1, most staff employees believe that most benefits have been adequately communicated to them. At least three-fourths of the employees are familiar with all major benefits except for long-term disability insurance, which is familiar to only a slight majority, and auto insurance, which is familiar to only a third of the respondents. The low level of knowledge about auto insurance is probably attributable to the fact that this benefit started only six weeks before the survey was taken.

Provide an appropriate closing statement for the Introduction section.

First-level subheadings: Center, bold, and type in all capitals; leave one blank line before and after.

Second-level subheadings: Begin at the left margin, bold, and type in all capitals; leave one blank line before and after.

Third-level subheadings: Indent, use initial capitals, bold, and end with a period; leave one blank line before and begin the first word of the paragraph two spaces following the period.

The Findings (also called *Results*) begins by providing an overview of the organization of this section. Each of the subsections that follow discusses one of the subproblems; thus, the organizational basis used in this report is the criteria identified earlier for solving this problem.

FIGURE B.6 **Sample Report (*Continued*)**

4

TABLE 1. LEVEL OF FAMILIARITY WITH THE BENEFIT PROGRAM

Employee Benefit	Level of Familiarity				
	Familiar	Unfamiliar	Undecided	No Resp.	Total
Sick leave	94%	4%	1%	1%	100%
Vacation	93%	4%	2%	1%	100%
Paid holidays	92%	3%	4%	1%	100%
Hospital/medical ins.	90%	7%	3%	0%	100%
Life insurance	84%	10%	5%	1%	100%
Retirement	76%	14%	8%	2%	100%
Long-term disability ins.	53%	33%	14%	0%	100%
Auto insurance*	34%	58%	7%	1%	100%

* This benefit started six weeks before the survey was taken.

In general, benefit familiarity is not related to length of employment at ASU. Most employees are familiar with most benefits regardless of their length of employment. However, as shown in Figure 1, the only benefit for which this is not true is life insurance. The longer a person has been employed at ASU, the more likely he or she is to know about this benefit.

FIGURE 1. KNOWLEDGE OF LIFE INSURANCE BENEFITS

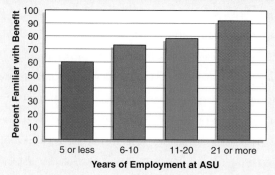

Present Methods of Communication. A variety of methods is presently being used to communicate the fringe benefits to employees. According to Lewis Rigby, director of the State Personnel Board, every new state employee views a 30-minute video entitled

---

Leave two or three blank lines before and after each table or figure.

Keep charts simple and of an appropriate size.

If you must divide a paragraph between pages, leave at least two lines of the paragraph at the bottom of the previous page and bring at least two lines forward to the next page.

Tables and Charts

Introduce each table before showing it. Always refer to tables by table number instead of by their location (that is, avoid phrases like "as shown below"). Discuss only the most important data from the table in the narrative. Tables may be presented in any standard table format, but be consistent throughout the report. If necessary, create the chart in another program, leave space for the chart on your report page, tape the chart onto the page, and then submit a good-quality photocopy of the entire report (never photocopy just one page).

FIGURE B.6 **Sample Report (*Continued*)**

14

that showed that such compensation has been cost-effective over the long run for companies in the manufacturing and service industries.

CONCLUSIONS AND RECOMMENDATIONS

These findings show that staff employees at Atlantic State University are extremely knowledgeable about all benefits except long-term disability and automobile insurance. However, a majority would prefer to have an individualized benefit statement instead of the brochures now used to explain the benefit program. They consider paid time off as the most important benefit and automobile insurance as the least important. A majority are satisfied with all benefits, although retirement benefits generated substantial dissatifaction. The only additional benefit desired by a majority of the employees is compensation for unused sick leave.

The following recommendations are based on these conclusions:

1. Determine the feasibility of generating for each staff employee an annual individualized benefit statement.

2. Reevaluate the attractiveness of the automobile insurance benefit in one year to determine staff employees' knowledge about, use of, and desire for this benefit. Consider the feasibility of substituting compensation for unused sick leave for the automobile insurance benefit.

3. Conduct a follow-up study of the retirement benefits at ASU to determine how competitive they are with comparable public and private institutions.

These recommendations, as well as the findings of this study, should help the university ensure that its benefit program is accomplishing its stated objectives of attracting and retaining high-quality employees and meeting their needs once employed.

If your Conclusions and Recommendations section is short, omit second-level subheadings.

Double-space the lines within an enumeration in a report.

Provide an appropriate concluding paragraph that gives a sense of completion to the report.

B

Conclusions and Recommendations

This is the last page of the report. Ensure that the conclusions and recommendations stem directly from the findings and that you have presented ample supporting evidence. Avoid extreme or exaggerated language.

FIGURE B.6   **Sample Report (*Continued*)**

18

REFERENCES

Book—one author	Adams, J. B. (1997). *Compensation systems.* Boston: Benson, Inc.
Book—two authors	Adams, J. M., & Stearns, G.R. (1994). *Personnel administration.* Cambridge, MA: All-State Press.
Book—three or more authors	Berelson, B. R., Paul Lazarsfield, P. F., & Connell, W., Jr. (1996). *Managing your benefit program (*2nd ed.). Chicago: Novak-Siebold.
Book—organization as author	*Directory of business and financial services.* (1998). New York: Corporate Libraries Association.
Book—edited volume	Egan, J. D. (Ed.). (1996). *Human resources.* London: Varsity Press.
Book—component part	Gowens, J. A. (1998). Cafeteria-style benefits. In R. Anshen (Ed.), *Personnel management* (pp. 661-672). New York: Gump Bros.
Journal article—paged continuously throughout the year	Ignatio, E. (1997). Flexible benefits are the key to compensation. *Personnel Quarterly, 61,* 113-125.
Second work by same author —in chronological order	Ignatio, E. (1998). Employee benefits in transition: Managers look to the past to move employee benefits into the future. *Supervisory Management Today, 28,* 36-39.
Magazine article	Kean, T. J., III. (1996, November). Employee benefits: Then and now. *Business Monthly, 14,* pp. 39-41.
Newspaper article— unsigned	Letting employees determine their own benefits. (1998, January 12). *New York City Times,* pp. E21, E26.
Dissertation or thesis	Meany, G. (1993). Employee benefits at American universities. *Dissertation Abstracts International, 52,* Z5455. (University Mircofilms No. 92-60181)
Government document	National Institute of Mental Health. (1995) *Who pays the piper? Ten years of passing the buck* (DHHS Publication No. ADM 82-1195). Washington, DC: U.S. Government Printing Office.
Paper presented at a meeting	Potts, R. (1996, August). Tuition reimbursement. Paper presented at the meeting of the National Mayors' Conference, Trenton, NJ.
Television broadcast	Preminger, L. (Executive Producer). (1993, August 5). *The WKVX-TV Evening News.* Los Angeles: Valhalla Broadcasting Company.

References

This reference list is shown in APA format. For all formats, arrange all entries in one alphabetical listing according to the author's last name. Include only those sources actually cited in the report, not every source read. Begin each entry at the left margin and indent runover lines $^1/_2$ inch. Single-space each entry and double-space between entries.

FIGURE B.6   Sample Report (*Continued*)

19

Quincy, D. C. (1996, February 14). Welcome to MarxCorp. [Online]. MarxCorp. Available: http://www.marxcorp/ [1997, November 14].

Reskow, R. J. (1995, March). Is the WWW a fringe benefit or workplace necessity? *Journal of Electronic Marketing* [Online], n. pag. Available: telnet://.aui.edu.jem. benefit [1996, January 23].

Salary Survey of Service Industries. (1997, May) [Online database]. Washington, DC: U.S. Census Bureau. Available: http://www.census.gov/ind.lib/ms0315.html [1998, March 23].

Snipes, J. (1997, February 23). I beg to differ. *Personnel Postings.* [Online]. Available E-mail: PERPOST@cob.vstu.edu [1996, December 13].

Training doesn't always last. (1996, June 3). International employment trends. Available: news:clari.biz.economy.world [1997, April 20].

United States: Employment trends and statistics. (1996). In *Hoover's Encyclopedia* [Online]. Available: http://www.hoover.com [1997, October 13].

Wage administration. (1996). In *Martindale's Interactive Business Encyclopedia.* Available: [CD-ROM] Pompton Lakes, NJ: Martindale, Inc.

Wrege, W. T. (wtwrege@allied.com). (1997, June 18). *Your Request for May Sales Figures.* E-mail to J. T. Olivas (jtolivas@allied.com).

Margin annotations:

WWW home page—with [access date]

Online journal article—with [access date]

Online database material—with [access date]

Discussion-list message—with [access date]

Newsgroup article—with [access date]

Online encyclopedia article—with [access date]

CD-ROM encyclopedia article

Personal electronic communication—e-mail

B

If necessary, break an online address after a punctuation mark; do not divide a word and do not insert a hyphen. Type magazine, journal, and newspaper titles in upper- and lowercase letters. Type book and article titles in sentence style: capitalize the first word, proper nouns, and the first word after a colon. Do not enclose article titles in quotation marks. Italicized titles may be typed underlined instead.

FIGURE B.7 Three Documentation Formats

Number the endnotes consecutively throughout the report, using superior numbers (or your word processing program's endnote feature). The actual citations are given on a separate Notes page at the end of the report.

Number the footnotes consecutively, starting with 1 on each page, using superior numbers (or your word processing program's footnote feature). Position the actual citations at the bottom of the same page as the text references.

The author-date method refers readers to the References section of the report. Put the author's name and the publication date in parentheses. If the author's name is given in the narrative, put only the year in parentheses. Include page numbers for direct quotations and for cited statistics.

Endnotes

One out of ten adults nationwide inquires about moving or storage every year, and a slight majority of these people turn to the Yellow Pages for guidance.[1] Consumers in general do not have a specific company in mind when they begin searching the Yellow Pages for a particular product or service.[2] Size appears to be the single most important factor in a Yellow Pages display ad because "the eye focuses first on a large ad and later on the smaller ads."[3]

1

Footnotes

One out of ten adults nationwide inquires about moving or storage every year, and a slight majority of these people turn to the Yellow Pages for guidance.[1] Consumers in general do not have a specific company in mind when they begin searching the Yellow Pages for a particular product or service.[2] Size appears to be the single most important factor in a Yellow Pages display ad because "the eye focuses first on a large ad and later on the smaller ads."[3]

2   ⎯⎯⎯⎯⎯⎯⎯

3   [1]Max Voight, *Marketing Techniques for the Moving and Storage Industry,* Midwest Publishing Co., Chicago, 1994, p. 54.

[2]Lisa Poston, "Eye-Perception Research: A Marketing Tool," *Journal of Telecommunications,* Vol. 15, No. 4, May 1996, pp. 75-76.

[3]Larry R. Chilton and Harry M. Raines, "Who Really Reads the Yellow Pages?" *Business Monthly,* October 1997, p. 13.

Author-Date Method

One out of ten adults nationwide inquires about moving or storage every year, and a slight majority of these people turn to the Yellow Pages for guidance (Voight, 1994, p. 54). Consumers in general do not have a specific company in mind when they begin searching the Yellow Pages for a particular product or service (Poston, 1996). Size appears to be the single most important factor in a Yellow Pages display ad because "the eye focuses first on a large ad and later on the smaller ads"(Chilton & Raines, 1997, p. 13).

4

Mechanics Notes

1 Insert the superior numbers immediately after punctuation and after closing quotation marks.   2 Single-space before and double-space after a 2-inch divider line.   3 Single-space the lines within a citation; double-space between citations.   4 Type the parenthetical reference before any punctuation but after the closing quotation mark.

FIGURE B.8 **Three Bibliographic Formats**

1

For Endnotes

1. Max Voight, *Marketing Techniques for the Moving and Storage Industry,* Midwest Publishing Co., Chicago, 1994, p. 54.

2

2. Lisa Poston, "Eye-Perception Research: A Marketing Tool," *Journal of Telecommunications,* Vol. 15, No. 4, May 1996, pp. 75-76.

3. Larry R. Chilton and Harry M. Raines, "Who Really Reads the Yellow Pages?" *Business Monthly,* October 1997, p. 13.

For Footnotes

3

Chilton, Larry R., and Harry M. Raines, "Who Really Reads the Yellow Pages?" *Business Monthly,* October 1997, pp. 12-17.

Poston, Lisa, "Eye-Perception Research: A Marketing Tool," *Journal of Telecommunications,* Vol. 15, No. 4, May 1996, pp. 75-79.

Voight, Max, *Marketing Techniques for the Moving and Storage Industry,* Midwest Publishing Co., Chicago, 1994.

For Author-Date Method

Chilton, L. R., & Raines, H. M. (1997, October). Who really reads the Yellow Pages? *Business Monthly, 37,* 12-17.

Poston, L. (1996, May). Eye-perception research: A marketing tool. *Journal of Telecommunications, 15,* (4), 75-79.

Voight, M. (1994). *Marketing techniques for the moving and storage industry,* Chicago: Midwest Publishing.

Use the same basic format for the notes as for the footnote citations, except that numbers should be followed by periods instead of formatted as superior numbers. Arrange the entries in the order in which they appear in the body of the report.

Arrange the entries in alphabetical order according to the first author's last name. List the first author's name in reverse order (last name first), but type the other author names in normal order. Use capital and lowercase letters for publication titles.

Arrange the entries in alphabetical order according to the first author's last name. List all authors' names in reverse order, and use initials only for the given names. Capitalize only the first word, proper nouns, and the first word following a colon or dash in the titles of journal and magazine articles and of books. Do not use quotation marks around article titles. (The format shown here follows APA style.)

B

Mechanics Notes

1 No matter which format you use, begin the list on a separate page, leaving a 2-inch top margin. 2 Indent the first line of each endnote citation ½ inch. Single-space the lines of each citation, but double-space between citations. 3 Begin the first line at the left margin, and indent runover lines ½ inch.

FIGURE B.9 **Report Page in MLA Style**

Type the author's name and the page number at the right margin ½ inch from the top.

Type the heading information as shown on the first page of the report.

Leave 1-inch margins on all four sides (other than for the page number).

Double-space every single line of the report—including enumerated lists, tables, and the reference list (entitled "Works Cited").

Include the author's last name and page number (if citing a part of a source)—but not the date—in the parenthetical reference.

Santorini 1

Loretta J. Santorini

Professor Riggins

Management 348

8 December 19--

Staff Employees' Evaluation of the Benefit Program

at Atlantic State University

Employee benefits are a rapidly growing and an increasingly important form of employee compensation for both profit and nonprofit organizations. According to a recent U.S. Chamber of Commerce survey, benefits now constitute 37 percent of all payroll costs, costing an average of $9,857 a year for each full-time employee (Berelson, Lazarsfield, and Connell 183). Thus, on the basis of its cost alone, an organization's employee benefit program must be carefully monitored and evaluated.

Atlantic State University employs nearly 2,500 staff personnel, and they have not received a cost-of-living increase in two years. As a result, staff salaries may not have kept pace with private industry, and the university's employee benefit program may become more important in attracting and retaining good workers. In addition, the contracts of three of the four staff unions expire next year, and the benefit program is typically a major area of bargaining.

As has been noted by one management consultant, "The success of employee benefit programs depends directly on whether employees need, understand, and appreciate the value of the benefits provided" (Egan 220). Thus, to help ensure that the benefit program is operating as effectively as possible, David Riggins, director of personnel, authorized this report on October 15, 19--. Specifically, the following problem was addressed in this study: What are the opinions of staff employees at Atlantic State

---

MLA Style

For further information, see Joseph Gibaldi, *MLA Handbook for Writers of Research Papers,* 4th ed. New York: Modern Language Association, 1995.

FIGURE B.10 Works-Cited Page

Santorini 18

Works Cited

Adams, John B. *Compensation Systems.* Boston: Benson, 1997.

Adams, J. Marlene, and George R. Stearns. *Personnel Administration.* Cambridge: All-State, 1994.

Berelson, Bret R., Paul Lazarsfield, and Will Connell, Jr. *Managing Your Benefit Program.* 2nd ed. Chicago: Novak-Siebold, 1996.

Corporate Libraries Association. *Directory of Business and Financial Services.* New York: Corporate Libraries Association, 1998.

Egan, Jean, ed. *Human Resources.* London: Varsity, 1996.

Gowens, Joanne. "Cafeteria-Style Benefits." *Personnel Management.* Ed. Rose Anshen. New York: Gump, 1998. 661-672.

Ignatio, Earl. "Flexible Benefits Are the Key to Compensation." *Personnel Quarterly* 61 (1997): 113-125.

---. "Employee Benefits in Transition: Managers Look to the Past to Move Employee Benefits into the Future." *Supervisory Management Today* 28 (1998): 36-39.

Kean, T. J., III. "Employee Benefits: Then and Now." *Business Monthly* Nov. 1993: 39-41.

"Letting Employees Determine Their Own Benefits." *New York City Times* 12 Jan. 1998: E21, E26.

Quincy, Donald C. "Welcome to MarxCorp." 14 Feb. 1996. Online. MarxCorp. Available: http://www.marxcorp/ 14 Nov. 1997.

"Salary Survey of Service Industries." May 1997. Online. Available: http://www.census.gov/ind.lib/ms0315.html 23 Mar. 1998.

United States. Department of Health and Human Services. National Institute of Mental Health. *Who Pays the Piper? Ten Years of Passing the Buck.* Washington: GPO, 1995.

Book—one author

Book—two authors

Book—three or more authors

Book—organization as author

Book—editor as author

Book—component part

Journal article

Second work by same author—in chronological order

Magazine article

Newspaper article (unsigned)

WWW home page—with access date

Online database material—with access date

Government document

B

Works-Cited Page, MLA Style

Center the heading "Works Cited" 1 inch from the top in upper- and lowercase letters. Double-space the lines within and between each citation. Compare the format of this listing with the References list shown in APA format on Reference Manual pages 570 and 571.

Glossary

Abstract word   A word that identifies an idea or feeling as opposed to a concrete object.

Active voice   The sentence form in which the subject performs the action expressed by the verb.

Adjustment letter   A letter written to inform a customer of the action taken in response to the customer's claim letter.

Agenda   An ordered list of topics to be considered at a meeting, along with the name of the person responsible for each topic.

Application letter   A letter from a job applicant to a prospective employer explaining the applicant's interest in and qualifications for a position within the organization; also called a *cover letter*.

Audience   The person or persons with whom you're communicating.

Audience analysis   Identification of the needs, interests, and personality of the receiver of a communication.

Bar chart   A graph with horizontal or vertical bars representing values.

Brainstorming   Jotting down ideas, facts, possible leads, and anything else that might be helpful in constructing a message.

Buffer   A neutral and supportive opening statement designed to lessen the impact of negative news.

Business etiquette   The practice of polite and appropriate behavior in a business setting.

Buzz word   An important-sounding term used mainly to impress people.

CD-ROM database   A collection of information stored on a high-capacity disk that is accessible by a microcomputer with a CD drive.

Central selling theme   The major reader benefit that is introduced early and emphasized throughout a sales letter.

Claim letter   A letter from the buyer to the seller, seeking some type of action to correct a problem with the seller's product or service.

Cliché   An expression that has become monotonous through overuse.

Communication   The process of sending and receiving messages.

Complex sentence   A sentence that has one independent clause and at least one dependent clause.

Compound sentence   A sentence that has two or more independent clauses.

Conclusions   The answers to the research questions raised in the introduction.

Concrete word   A word that identifies something the senses can perceive.

Connotation   The subjective or emotional feeling associated with a word.

Cross-tabulation   A process by which two or more pieces of data are analyzed together.

Dangling expression   Any part of a sentence that does not logically connect to the rest of the sentence.

Database   A computer-searchable collection of information on a general subject area, such as business, education, or psychology.

Defamation   Any false and malicious statement that is communicated to others and that injures a person's good name or reputation.

Denotation   The literal, dictionary meaning of a word.

Derived benefit   The benefit a potential customer would receive from using a product or service.

Desktop publishing   The writing, assembling, and designing of such publications as company newsletters, brochures, catalogs, and reports on a microcomputer.

Direct organizational plan   A plan in which the major purpose of the message is communicated first, followed by any needed explanation.

Direct quotation   The exact words of another.

Documentation   Giving credit to another person for his or her words or ideas that you have used.

Drafting   Composing a preliminary version of a message.

Editing   The stage of revision which ensures that writing conforms to standard English.

Electronic résumé   A résumé that is stored in a computer database designed to help manage and initially screen job applicants.

E-mail   A message trasmitted electronically over a computer network most often connected by cable, telephone lines, or satellites.

Empathy   The ability to project oneself into another person's position and to understand that person's situation, feelings, motives, and needs.

Ethics   Rules of conduct.

Ethnocentrism   The belief that one's own cultural group is superior.

Euphemism   An inoffensive expression used in place of an expression that may offend or suggest something unpleasant.

Executive summary   A condensed version of the report body; also called an *abstract* or *synopsis.*

Expletive   An expression such as *there is* or *it is* that begins a clause and for which the pronoun has no antecedent.

Factoring   Breaking a problem down into its component parts so that data-collection needs are known.

Feedback   The receiver's reaction or response to a message.

Filter   The mental process of perceiving stimuli based on one's knowledge, experience, and viewpoints.

Form letter   A letter with standardized wording that is sent to different people.

Formal communication network   The transmission of prescribed information through downward, upward, horizontal, and cross-channel routes.

Fraud   A deliberate misrepresentation of the truth that is made to induce someone to give up something of value.

Free writing   Writing continuously for 5 to 10 minutes without stopping as a means of generating a large quantity of material that will be revised later.

Generic heading   A report heading that identifies only the topic of a section without giving the conclusion.

Goodwill message   A message that is sent strictly out of a sense of kindness and friendliness.

Gopher   An Internet software program that provides access to text-only documents typically stored at sites maintained by government agencies or educational institutions.

Groupthink   A barrier to communication that results from an overemphasis on group cohesiveness, which stifles opposing ideas and the free flow of information.

Groupware   A broad category of business software that automates information sharing and enables work teams to communicate electronically and to coordinate their efforts.

Indirect organizational plan   A plan in which the reasons or rationale are presented first, followed by the major idea.

Informal communication network   The transmission of information through nonofficial channels within the organization; also called the *grapevine*.

Internet   A worldwide collection of interconnected computers housed in university labs, business offices, and government centers—all filled with massive amounts of information that is accessible to anyone with an Internet account.

Interview guide   A list of questions to ask, with suggested wording and possible follow-up questions.

Invasion of privacy   Any unreasonable intrusion into the private life of another person or denial of a person's right to be left alone.

Jargon   The technical terminology used within specialized groups.

Letter   A written message sent to someone outside the organization.

Libel   Defamation in a permanent form such as in writing or on videotape.

Line chart   A graph based on a grid, with the vertical axis representing values and the horizontal axis representing time.

Mailing list   An Internet discussion group in which messages are sent directly to members via e-mail; also called a *listserv*.

Mechanics   Those elements in communication that show up only in written form, including spelling, punctuation, abbreviations, capitalization, number expression, and word division.

Medium   The form of a message—for example, a memo or telephone call.

Memorandum   A written message sent to someone within the organization.

Message   The information (either verbal or nonverbal) that is communicated.

Mind mapping   Generating ideas for message content by first writing the purpose of the message in the center of a page and circling it and then writing possible points to include, linking each one to either the purpose or to another point; also called *clustering*.

Minutes   An official record of the proceedings of a meeting that summarizes what was discussed and what decisions were made.

Misrepresentation   A false statement made innocently with no intent to deceive the other party.

Newsgroup   An Internet discussion group in which messages (called *articles*) are posted at the newsgroup site, rather than being sent directly to the members as e-mail.

Noise   Environmental or competing elements that distract one's attention during communication.

Nondiscriminatory language   Language that treats everyone equally, making no unwarranted assumptions about any group of people.

Nonverbal message   A nonwritten and nonspoken signal consisting of facial expressions, gestures, voice qualities, and the like.

Online database   A collection of information stored in a mainframe computer that is accessible by microcomputer or terminal and a telephone hookup.

Organization   The sequence in which topics are presented in a message.

Parallelism   Using similar grammatical structure to express similar ideas.

Paraphrase   A summary or restatement of a passage in one's own words.

Parliamentary procedure   Written rules of order that permit the efficient transaction of business in meetings.

Passive voice   The sentence form in which the subject receives the action expressed by the verb.

Persuasion   The process of motivating someone to take a specific action or to support a particular idea.

Pie chart   A circle graph whose area is divided into component wedges.

Plagiarism   Using another person's words or ideas without giving proper credit.

Platitude   A trite, obvious statement.

Policy   A broad operating guideline that governs the general direction or activities of an organization.

Presentation software   Computer software (similar to word processing and desktop publishing software) that is used to produce audiovisual aids for oral presentations.

Primary data   Data collected by the researcher to solve the specific problem at hand.

Primary audience   The reader of a message whose cooperation is most crucial if the message is to achieve its objective.

Procedure   The recommended methods or sequential steps to be followed when performing a specific activity.

Proposal   A written report that seeks to persuade a reader outside the organization to do as the writer wants.

Questionnaire   A written instrument containing questions designed to obtain information from the individual being surveyed.

Readability   The ease with which a passage can be understood, based on its style of writing.

Reader benefits   The advantages a reader would derive from granting the writer's request or from accepting the writer's decision.

Redundancy   The unnecessary repetition of an idea that has already been expressed or intimated.

Reference   A person who has agreed to provide information to a prospective employer regarding a job applicant's fitness for a job.

Report   An orderly and objective presentation of information that assists in decision making and problem solving.

Resale   Information that reestablishes a customer's confidence in the product purchased or in the company that sold the product.

Résumé   A brief record of one's personal history and qualifications that is typically
prepared by a job applicant.

Revising   The process of modifying the content and style of a draft to increase its
effectiveness.

Rhetorical question   A question asked strictly to get the reader thinking about the
topic; a literal answer is not expected.

Secondary data   Data collected by someone else for some other purpose; it may be
published or unpublished.

Secondary audience   Any reader other than the primary audience who will be
affected by the message.

Simple sentence   A sentence that has one independent clause.

Slander   Defamation in a temporary form such as in oral communication.

Slang   An expression, often short-lived, that is identified with a specific group of
people.

Solicited sales letter   A reply to a request for product information from a potential customer.

Solicited application letter   An application letter written in response to an advertised job vacancy.

Stimulus   An event that creates within an individual the need to communicate.

Style   The manner in which an idea is expressed (rather than the *substance* of the
idea).

Survey   A data-collection method that gathers information through questionnaires, telephone inquires, or interviews.

Table   An orderly arrangement of data into columns and rows.

Talking heading   A report heading that identifies not only the topic of the report
section but also the major conclusion.

Team   A group of individuals who depend on one another to accomplish a common objective.

Teleconference   A meeting in which members in different locations are linked by
simultaneous electronic communications, using camera, projection screens,
microphones, and computer equipment.

Tone   The writer's attitude toward the reader and the subject of the message.

Transmittal document   A letter or memorandum that conveys the finished report to
the reader.

Unsolicited application letter   An application letter written to an organization that
has not advertised a vacancy; also called a *prospecting letter*.

Unsolicited sales letter   A letter promoting a firm's products mailed to a potential
customer who has not expressed any prior interest in the product; also called a
prospecting letter.

Verbal message   A message comprising spoken or written words.

Visual aids   Tables, charts, photographs, and other graphic materials used in communication to aid comprehension and add interest.

Word processing   The production of letters, memorandums, reports, and other documents through the use of automated electronic equipment.

World Wide Web   The newest and fastest-growing segment of the Internet, which comprises documents (called *pages*) that contain text, graphics, sounds, and video, as well as electronic links (called *hypertext*) that let the user move quickly from one document to another.

Writer's block   The inability to focus one's attention on the writing process and to draft a message.

"You" attitude   A viewpoint that emphasizes what the reader wants to know and how the reader will be affected by the message.

C

References

Chapter 1

1. Leland V. Gustafson, Jack E. Johnson, and David H. Hovey, "Preparing Business Students—Can We Market Them Successfully?" *Business Education Forum,* Vol. 47, April 1993, pp. 23–26; "It's All Just Bossiness," *Indianapolis Star,* April 4, 1992, p. C3; "Mediocre Memos," *Detroit Free Press,* May 26, 1990, p. 9A; "Speak the Language," *Indianapolis Star,* January 30, 1991, p. A9; "Workplace Literacy," *USA Today,* September 21, 1992, p. B1.
2. Robert L. Montgomery, *Listening Made Easy: How to Improve Listening on the Job, at Home, and in the Community,* American Management Association, New York, 1981, p. 6.
3. John Gerstner, "Executives Evaluate the Importance of Grapevine Communication," *Communication World,* March 1994, p. 17.
4. Donald B. Simmons, "The Nature of the Organizational Grapevine," *Supervisory Management,* Vol. 30, November 1985, p. 40; Alan Zaremba, "Working with the Organizational Grapevine," *Personnel Journal,* Vol. 67, July 1988, p. 40; Carol Hymowitz, "Spread the Word: Gossip Is Good," *The Wall Street Journal,* October 4, 1988, p. B1.
5. Stephen Karel, "Learning Culture the Hard Way," *Consumer Markets Abroad,* Vol. 7, May 1988, pp. 1, 15.
6. Ruth Mullen, "Sounding Chill," *Indianapolis Star,* October 18, 1996, pp. D1–D2.
7. Donald Harris, "A Matter of Privacy: Managing Personal Data in Company Computers," *Personnel,* Vol. 65, June 1988, p. 52.

Chapter 2

1. John R. Pierce, "Communication," *Scientific American,* Vol. 227, September 1972, p.36.
2. Irving R. Janis, *Victims of Groupthink,* Houghton Mifflin, Boston, 1972.
3. These guidelines are based on principles contained in Peter R. Scholtes, *The Team Handbook: How to Use Teams to Improve Quality,* Madison, WI: Joiner Associates, 1988, pp. 6.23–6.28.
4. Peter F. Drucker, quoted by Bill Boyers in *A World of Ideas,* Doubleday, Garden City, NY, 1990.
5. Albert Mehrabian, "Communicating Without Words," *Psychology Today,* September 1968, pp. 53–55.
6. Judee K. Burgoon and Thomas Saine, *The Unspoken Dialogue: An Introduction to Nonverbal Communication,* Houghton Mifflin, Boston, 1978, p. 123.
7. See, for example, Mark L. Knapp, *Essentials of Nonverbal Communication,* Holt, Rinehart & Winston, New York, 1980, pp. 21–26; "Study: Good Looks Bring Bigger Bucks in Business World," *USA Today,* August 8, 1989, p. 2B.
8. Edward T. Hall, *The Hidden Dimension,* Doubleday, Garden City, NY, 1966, pp. 107–122.
9. *The Universal Almanac: 1992,* Andrews and McMeel, Kansas City, MO, p. 316.
10. *World Almanac and Book of Facts: 1992,* Pharos Books, New York, p. 573.
11. Margaret L. Usdansky, "Minority Majorities in One in Six Cities," *USA Today,* June 9, 1993, p. 10A.
12. Sondra Thiederman, "The Diverse Workplace: Strategies for Getting 'Culture Smart'," *The Secretary,* March 1996, p. 8.
13. Ralph G. Nichols, "Listening Is a Ten-Part Skill," *Nation's Business,* September 1987, p. 40; "Listen Up!" *American Salesman,* July 1987, p. 29.
14. Michael Doyle and David Straus, *How to Make Meetings Work,* Wyden Books, New York, 1976, p. 4; Marcy E. Mullins, "Are Meetings Worthwhile?" *USA Today,* August 28, 1989, p. B1; "Profile of the Typical Meeting," *Presentation Products Magazine,* February 1990, p. 8; E. F. Wells, "Rules for a Better Meeting," *Mainliner,* May 1978, p. 56; E. J. McGarry, "Presentations Can be Economical and Effective," *Office Dealer 92,* March/April 1992, p. 18.
15. "Managing Meetings: A Critical Role," *The Office,* November 1989, p. 20.
16. "Managing Meetings," p. 20.
17. Henry M. Robert, *The Scott, Foresman Robert's Rules of Order, Newly Revised,* Scott, Foresman, Glenview, IL, 1981.
18. Robert, p. xiii.
19. T. Brown, "The Dress-Down Debate," *Industry Week,* June 20, 1994, p. 43.

20. *Casual Clothing in the Workplace,* Levi Strauss & Co., San Francisco, 1995.

Chapter 3

1. Timothy J. O'Leary and Linda I. O'Leary, *Internet,* New York: McGraw-Hill, 1996, p. IN3.
2. Byron J. Finch, *The Management Guide to Internet Resources,* New York: McGraw-Hill, 1997, pp. 6–7.
3. "Internet Search Engines." 3 Dec. 1996. Online. *PC Magazine.* http://www.pcmag.com/edchoice/1521/ ed1521i1.htm 5 Jan. 1997.
4. Amarendra Singh and David Lidsky, "All-Out Search," *PC Magazine,* December 3, 1996, p. 229.
5. Alan Russell and Norris McWhirter (eds.), *1988 Guiness Book of World Records,* Bantam Books, New York, 1987, p. 418; Tom Heymann, *On an Average Day,* Fawcett Columbine, New York, 1989, p. 185.
6. John T. Molloy, "Dress for Success," *Detroit Free Press,* December 19, 1989, p. 3C.

Chapter 4

1. Richard Lederer, "Strength of a Single Syllable," *Reader's Digest,* June 1991, p. 157.
2. Richard A. Lanham, *Revising Business Prose,* Scribner's, New York, 1981, p. 2.
3. Eve Nagler, "A Macaroni Company with Homespun Appeal," *The New York Times,* December 12, 1993, section 13, p. 22.

Chapter 6

1. Marshall Cook, "Seven Steps to Better Manuscripts," *Writer's Digest,* September 1987, p. 30.
2. Julie Schmit, "Continental's $4 Million Typo," *USA Today,* May 25, 1993, p. B1.

Chapter 7

1. Marj Jackson Levin, "Don't Get Mad: Get Busy," *Detroit Free Press,* March 10, 1989, p. B1.

Chapter 8

1. Herschell Gordon Lewis, *Direct Mail Copy That Sells!* Prentice-Hall, Englewood Cliffs, NJ, 1984, p. iii.
2. Ed Cerny, "Listening for Effect," *American Salesman,* May 1986, p. 28.
3. Linda Lynton, "The Fine Art of Writing a Sales Letter," *Sales & Marketing Management,* August 1988, p. 55.

Chapter 9

1. For a discussion of the empirical rationale for using an indirect versus a direct approach, see Marsha Bayless, "Business and Education: Perceptions of Written Communication," *NABTE Review,* 1991, pp. 32–35; D. Brent, "Indirect Structure and Reader Response," *Journal of Business Communication,* Spring 1985, pp. 5–7; Mohan Limaye, "Buffers in Bad News Messages and Recipient Perceptions," *Management Communication Quarterly,* August 1988, pp. 90–101; Kitty O. Locker, "The Rhetoric of Negative Messages," *English for Specific Purposes,* July 1984, pp. 1–2; and Douglas Salerno, "An Interpersonal Approach to Writing Negative Messages," *Journal of Advanced Composition,* 1985–86, pp. 139–149.

Chapter 10

1. Scot Ober, "The Physical Format of Memorandums and Business Reports," *Business Education World,* November–December 1981, pp. 9–10, 24.
2. John Naisbitt, *Megatrends: Ten New Directions Shaping Our Lives,* Warner Books, New York, 1984, p. 17.

Chapter 11

1. Robert Rosenthal and Ralph L. Rosnow, *The Volunteer Subject,* John Wiley, New York, 1975, pp. 195–196.
2. See, for example, "Tabling the Move to Computer Graphics," *Wall Street Journal,* January 30, 1991, p. B1; Jerimiah J. Sullivan, "Financial Presentation Format and Managerial Decision Making: Tables Versus Graphs," *Management Communication Quarterly,* Vol. 2, November 1988, pp. 194–216.
3. Edward Tufte, *The Visual Display of Quantitative Information,* Graphics Press, Cheshire, Ct, 1983.

Chapter 13

1. Adapted from Leonard F. Meuse, Jr. *Mastering the Business and Technical Presentation,* CBI Publishing, Boston, 1980, pp. 2–7.
2. Kerry L. Johnson, "You Were Saying," *Managers Magazine,* February 1989, p. 19.
3. Wharton Applied Research Center, "A Study of the Effects of the Use of Overhead Transparencies on Business Meetings, Final Report," Philadelphia: University of Pennsylvania, September 14, 1981; "Why Presentations?" *MacWorld,* April 1988, p. 143.
4. Albert Mehrabian, "Communicating Without Words," *Psychology Today,* September 1968, pp. 53–55.
5. David Wallechinsky, Irving Wallace, and Amy Wallace, *The Book of Lists,* William Morrow, New York, 1977, pp. 469–470.
6. Jolie Solomon, "Executives Who Dread Public Speaking Learn to Keep Their Cool in the Spotlight," *Wall Street Journal,* May 4, 1990, p. B1.

Chapter 14

1. U.S. Department of Labor, *Occupational Outlook Handbook,* 1996–97 ed. Online. Bureau of Labor Statistics. Available: *http://stats.bls.gov/ocohome.htm.* April 3, 1997.
2. Elizabeth Sheley, "Hi-Tech Recruiting Methods," *Human Resource Management,* September 1995, p. 61.
3. Sandra L. Latimer, "First Impressions," *Mt. Pleasant (MI) Morning Sun,* May 8, 1989, p. 6.
4. Larry McCoy, "Tell Me About Yourself . . . That's Enough!" *Wall Street Journal,* April 5, 1989, p. A10.
5. See, for example, Jules Harcourt and A. C. "Buddy" Krizan, "A Comparison of Résumé Content Preferences of Fortune 500 Personnel Administrators and Business Communication Instructors," *Journal of Business Communication,* Spring 1989, pp. 177–190; Rod Little, "Keep Your Résumé Short," *USA Today,* July 28, 1989, p. B1; Darlene C. Pibal, "Criteria for Effective Résumés as Perceived by Personnel Directors," *Personnel Administrator,* May 1985, pp. 119–123.
6. "Most Serious Résumé Gaffes," *Communication Briefings,* March 1991, p. 6.
7. "To Be or Not To Be," *The Secretary,* April 1991, p. 6.
8. Albert P. Karr, "Labor Letter," *Wall Street Journal,* September 1, 1992, p. A1.
9. Harcourt and Krizan, pp. 177–190.
10. "Flashcard," *Education Life* (Supplement to the *New York Times*), November 5, 1989, p. 21.
11. Therese Droste, "Executive Résumés: The Ultimate Calling Card," *Hospitals,* March 5, 1989, p. 72.
12. Eugene Carlson, "Business of Background Checking Comes to the Fore," *Wall Street Journal,* August 31, 1993, p. B2.
13. Del Jones, "Résumé Advice: It's as Simple as Black and White," *USA Today,* January 24, 1996, p. 4B.

Chapter 15

1. Lynn Ulrich and Don Trumbo, "The Selection Interview Since 1949," *Psychological Bulletin,* Vol. 43, 1956, p. 100.
2. Shelley Liles, "Wrong Hire Might Prove Costly," *USA Today,* June 6, 1989, p. 6B.
3. Mary Bakeman et al., *Job-Seeking Skills Reference Manual,* 3d ed., Minnesota Rehabilitation Center, Minneapolis, MN, 1971, p. 57.

Acknowledgments

Grateful acknowledgment is made to the following companies and individuals for allowing their interviews to be included in this book:

Chapter 2: Hilliard-Jones Marketing Group/Amy Hilliard-Jones; *Chapter 3:* 3M/James Radford; *Chapter 4:* Bank of Montreal/Martha Durdin; *Chapter 5:* Wrangler V.F. Corporation/Michael Penn; *Chapter 6:* Coopers & Lybrand Consulting/Michael Hanley; *Chapter 7:* PaineWebber/Gwen Salley; *Chapter 8:* The Wilderness Society/Jim Waltman; *Chapter 9:* Intel Corporation/Howard High; *Chapter 10:* Experian/Janis Lamar; *Chapter 11:* Domino's Pizza/Chris Wall; *Chapter 12:* Congressional Research Service/Donna Porter; *Chapter 13:* Royal Caribbean Cruises/David Hancock; *Chapter 14:* Computer Sciences Corporation/Paul Orvos; *Chapter 15:* New York CNN and CNNfn/Elizabeth Semple

Grateful acknowledgment is made to the following companies for allowing their letterhead to be included in this book:

Page 125: Barnes & Noble Inc.; *page 194:* Hewlett-Packard Company; *page 199:* Rubbermaid Inc.; *page 210:* The Home Depot; *page 279:* General Mills; *page 514:* Wainwright Bank.

TEXT CREDITS

Chapter 1

Spotlight 2—On Law and Ethics, The Hanson Group, Los Altos, CA. Used with permission of the author.

Chapter 4

Excerpt on pages 111–112: Richard Lederer, excerpted with permission from June 1991 *Reader's Digest.* Copyright © 1991 by Richard Lederer. Reprinted by permission of Pocket Books, a division of Simon & Schuster, Inc.

Spotlight 7—Across Cultures, Ge-Lin Zhu, Chief Editor, *Practical Commercial English Handbook,* Commercial Publishing Company, Beijing, China, 1981, p. 49.

Chapter 6

Spotlight 10—On Technology, "Writing Analysis Software" is reprinted by permission of RightSoft, Inc. Copyright © RightSoft, Inc.

Chapter 7

The 3Ps microwriting activity: A Routine Adjustment Letter, information from The Sharper Image advertising brochure.

Chapter 10

Figure 10.3, "Policy," is reprinted with the permission of Central Michigan University.

Figure 10.4, "Procedure for Hiring a Temporary Employee," is adapted by permission from Leslie H. Matthies, "Writing Your First Procedure—How to Go About It," *Journal of Systems Management,* November 1987, pp. 25–29.

Chapter 13

Spotlight 22—On Technology, © Aldus Corporation. Used with the express permission of Aldus Corporation. Aldus®, Pagemaker®, Persuasion®, and Aldus FreeHand® are registered trademarks of Aldus Corporation. All rights reserved.

Figure 14.5, used with permission by Robert W. Pike, President, Creative Training Techniques International, Inc., Eden Prairie, MN.

PHOTO CREDITS

Chapter 1

Page 3: Andy Freeberg; *page 4:* John Abbott; *page 10:* John Abbott; *page 16:* Andy Freeberg; *page 21:* Bill Nation/Sygma; *page 29:* Bill Varie/The Image Bank; *page 32:* (Neelima Shirkhande): Jim Whitmer.

Chapter 2

Page 35: Courtesy of Hilliard-Jones Marketing Group Incorporated; *page 38:* Andy Freeberg; *page 40:* Andy Freeberg; *page 42:* Andy Freeberg; *page 43:* DILBERT reprinted by permission of United Feature Syndicate, Inc.; *page 48:* John Abbott; *page 50:* Copyright 1996, USA TODAY. Reprinted with permission.

Chapter 3

Page 73: Courtesy of 3M Corporate Marketing and Public Affairs; *page 75:* John Abbott; *page 76:* John Abbott; *page 92:* Andy Freeberg.

Chapter 4

Page 105: Courtesy of Bank of Montreal; *page 106:* Andy Freeberg; *page 109:* DILBERT reprinted by permission of United Feature Syndicate, Inc.; *page 123:* Brian Smale.

Chapter 5

Page 133: Courtesy of Wrangler; *page 139:* John Abbott; *page 144:* John Abbott.

Chapter 6

Page 153: Courtesy of Coopers & Lybrand Consulting; *page 158:* John Abbott; *page 163:* Kevin Horan/Stock Boston; *page 165:* Smithsonian Institution photo by Michael Anderson.

Chapter 7

Page 185: Courtesy Gwen Salley; *page 187:* John Abbott; *page 188:* DILBERT reprinted by permission of United Feature Syndicate, Inc.; *page 197:* Richard Pasley/Stock Boston; *page 202:* J. Greenberg/The Image Works.

Chapter 8

Page 221: Courtesy of the Wilderness Society; *page 223:* Lee Snider/Image Works; *page 238:* J. Sohm/The Image Works.

Chapter 9

Page 255: Media Relations Manager/Intel Corporation; *page 257:* John Abbott; *page 263:* Tony O'Brien/The Image Works.

Chapter 10

Page 291: Courtesy of Janis Lamar; *page 296:* Courtesy of Motorola; *page 300:* Quinn/SABA; *page 313:* David Parker/Science Photo Library.

Chapter 11

Page 327: Courtesy of Domino's Pizza; *page 336:* Bob Kalman/The Image Works; *page 339:* Per Breiehagen; *page 347:* Andy Freeberg; *page 353:* Texastock.

Chapter 12

Page 367: Courtesy Michael M. Simpson; *page 378:* Daniel Peebles; *page 389:* Bob Daemmrich/The Image Works; *page 393:* DILBERT reprinted by permission of United Feature Syndicate, Inc.

Chapter 13

Page 417: Courtesy of Royal Caribbean; *page 422:* John Coletti/Stock Boston; *page 424:* Mark Peterson/SABA; *page 434:* David Weintraub/Stock Boston.

Chapter 14

Page 457 (margin): Courtesy Paul Orvos, Computer Sciences Corporation; *page 457* (bottom): Photo by Dennis Brack/Black Star; *page 462:* Andrew Brusso; *page 467:* DILBERT reprinted by permission of United Feature Syndicate, Inc.; *page 477:* Erica Lansner/Black Star.

Chapter 15

Page 497 (margin): Vanessa Vick; *page 497* (bottom): William Johnson/Stock Boston; *page 501:* John Abbott; *page 507:* Lars Klove.

Index

abb   Do not abbreviate this word. *(page 540)*

acc   Verify the accuracy of this statement or figure. *(pages 108–109, 294–295)*

act   Prefer active voice. *(pages 107, 120–121, 139, 146)*

agr   Make sure subjects, verbs, and pronouns agree; use plural verbs and pronouns with plural subjects and singular verbs and pronouns with singular subjects. *(pages 298, 303, 536–538)*

apol   Do not apologize in this instance. *(page 200)*

app   Make sure that the appearance of your document does not detract from its effectiveness. *(pages 166–168, 394–395)*

aud   Make sure the content and tone of your message are appropriate for your specific audience. *(pages 156–161, 308–309, 421–423)*

conc   Be more concise; use fewer words to express this idea. *(pages 117–118)*

conf   Use a more confident style of writing; avoid doubtful expressions. *(pages 134–135)*

cons   Be consistent; do not contradict yourself.

dang   Avoid dangling expressions; place modifiers close to the words they modify. *(page 110)*

disc   Avoid discriminatory language. *(pages 140–143)*

emp   Emphasize this point. *(pages 137–140)*

end   Make the ending of your message more effective—more interesting, more positive, or more original. *(pages 190, 193, 198, 201–202, 229, 263–264, 429–430, 484)*

evid   Give more evidence to support this point. *(pages 226–227, 237–239)*

expl   Use expletive beginnings (such as *there are* or *it is*) sparingly. *(page 116)*

for   Use correct format. *(pages 552–574)*

frag   Avoid sentence fragments. Each sentence must contain a complete thought. *(page 535)*

head   Use report headings effectively—descriptive, concise, parallel, and not too many or too few. *(pages 374–377, 560, 567)*

info   Use all the relevant information in the problem; make only reasonable assumptions.

int   Interpret this point. Don't simply state facts or repeat data from tables and figures; give more information so that the reader understands the importance and implications. *(pages 349–352)*

list   Consider putting these ideas in a numbered (sequence important) or bulleted (sequence not so important) list. *(pages 393, 559)*

mean   Reword to make your meaning clearer or to be more precise. *(pages 108–111)*

mod   Use modifiers (adjectives and adverbs) correctly. *(page 536)*

num   Express numbers correctly (either in words or in figures). *(pages 542–543)*

obv   Avoid obvious statements. *(page 135)*

org-dir   Use a direct organizational pattern here—main idea before the supporting data. *(pages 186, 224–226, 256–258)*

org-ind   Use an indirect organizational pattern here—supporting data before the main idea. *(pages 186–187, 225–226, 258–260)*

orig   Use more original wording; avoid clichés and avoid copying the wording from the problem or text examples. *(pages 112–114)*

par   Use parallel structure; express similar ideas in similar grammatical form. *(pages 124–125, 302, 375)*

para   Do not make paragraphs so long that they appear uninviting to read. *(page 125)*

plur   Do not confuse plurals and possessives. *(pages 528–530)*

pos   Use positive language to express this idea. *(pages 117–118)*

pro   Use pronouns and antecedents correctly. *(pages 536–538)*

punc   Use appropriate punctuation to help your reader understand your message. *(pages 524–533)*

quot   Use direct quotations sparingly; paraphrasing is usually more effective. *(page 385)*

read   Put the reader in the action; state this idea in terms of reader response or reader benefits; use the "you" attitude. *(pages 143–144)*